T5-ARV-972

THE CIVIL WAR IN THE NORTH

WARS OF THE UNITED STATES
(Editor: Richard L. Blanco)
Vol. 9

GARLAND REFERENCE LIBRARY
OF SOCIAL SCIENCE
Vol. 254

WARS OF THE UNITED STATES
(Richard L. Blanco, General Editor)

1. *The War of the American Revolution: A Selected, Annotated Bibliography of Published Sources*
   by Richard L. Blanco

2. *World War II: The European and Mediterranean Theaters: An Annotated Bibliography*
   by Myron J. Smith, Jr.

3. *The War of 1812: An Annotated Bibliography*
   by Dwight L. Smith

4. *The United States in the Vietnam War, 1954–1975: A Selected, Annotated Bibliography*
   by Louis A. Peake

5. *Intervention and Counterinsurgency: An Annotated Bibliography of the Small Wars of the United States, 1898–1984*
   by Benjamin R. Beede

6. *America and World War I: A Selected Annotated Bibliography of English-Language Sources*
   by David R. Woodward and Robert Franklin Maddox

7. *Struggle for Empire: A Bibliography of the French and Indian War*
   by James G. Lydon

8. *The Korean War: An Annotated Bibliography*
   by Keith D. McFarland

9. *The Civil War in the North: A Selective Annotated Bibliography*
   by Eugene C. Murdock

THE CIVIL WAR IN THE NORTH
A Selective Annotated Bibliography

Eugene C. Murdock

GARLAND PUBLISHING, INC. • NEW YORK & LONDON
1987

Library of Congress Cataloging-in-Publication Data

Murdock, Eugene Converse.
The Civil War in the north.

(Wars of the United States ; v. 9) (Garland reference library of social science ; v. 254)
Includes indexes.
1. United States—History—Civil War, 1861–1865—Bibliography. I. Title. II. Series. III. Series: Garland reference library of social science ; v. 254.
Z1242.M87 1987 [E468] 016.9737 86-19582
ISBN 0-8240-8941-3

Printed on acid-free, 250-year-life paper
Manufactured in the United States of America

To Gordon and Kathy,
who began learning about
these things at an early age.

CONTENTS

GENERAL EDITOR'S PREFACE

In his THE CIVIL WAR IN THE NORTH, Dr. Eugene C. Murdock has compiled a unique bibliographic study of a major era in American history. The Civil War was a bloody, protracted struggle which nearly wrecked the nation. More than any other military conflict of the United States--with the possible exception of current interest in World War II--it is the Civil War which continues to fascinate us. The scope of the military campaigning between the forces of the Union and the Confederacy was vast, and the seafighting and riverine operations were crucial to the conduct of the struggle. The issues that provoked the war, and that were debated during the course of the fighting, invariably caused intense controversy by class level, sectional interest, and political persuasion. The influence of the Civil War, in fact, is still pervasive in modern America, well over a century later.

To provide an audience with the most reliable material in the English language about this American epic, Professor Murdock, now retired after being Chairman of the History Department of Marietta College, Ohio, offers concise, colorful summaries in over 5,600 entries of the rich and abundant literature of the Civil War fought by the northern states. Whatever the reader's preference--fierce skirmishes, dramatic battles, the triumph and tragedies of generals, the fascinating raids and expeditions in the west, or the polemical debate about the conduct of the war--the researcher will find here innumerable items that are conveniently and professionally annotated. By organizing his subject matter into eleven broad topics with ample subdivisions, the author covers the origins and historiography of the war, the complexities of military and naval campaigns, the diplomacy employed with European powers, and the social-economic-cultural ramifications of the war experience. Mr. Murdock's coverage is comprehensive indeed, for he cites books, essays, articles, diaries, memoirs, speeches, music, novels, poetry, drama, biographies, newspapers, official documents, and unpublished Ph.D. dissertations. Thus, with such an array of works to select, along with a convenient author-subject index, a reader can readily locate the most reliable sources on a particular subject. In his work, the author has not only incorporated the traditional themes of military history as reflected by recent research--a titanic task in itself--but he has astutely blended into the broad military and political themes many major topics from social history as well. Subjects such as draft resistance, prisoners of war, medical services, the role of blacks and other minorities, the daily life of a typical soldier, the importance of journalism, an invaluable summary of works about President Abraham Lincoln, along with many related areas, all enhance the utility of this work and attest to Dr. Murdock's scholarship. This study is indeed the most comprehensive current bibliography about the Civil War, fought by the Union.

The Civil War was a crucial factor in the consolidation of a growing national consensus in the north about the slavery issue and about the future of the Republic. This study, the ninth volume in the series of the Wars of the United States, is an essential tool written by an eminent scholar (not only on the Civil War but in sports history and the history of Ohio), who is the author of innumerable books, articles, and book reviews and who is the recipient of many academic honors. Students in high school, college, and graduate school, genealogists, history "buffs," researchers in the social sciences, as well as general readers, can learn much about their heritage and the formation of American society from this very readable and highly informative work.

Richard L. Blanco
General Editor

PREFACE

I doubt whether anyone has ever counted the number of books, articles, dissertations, and miscellaneous monographs that have been written on the American Civil War. It must add up to a goodly amount. Mercifully, the editor of this series of bibliographies of American wars has divided the Civil War into two volumes. Still, in this work on THE CIVIL WAR IN THE NORTH, the amount of material that had to be sifted through was formidable. Perhaps a few items are not listed that should be, but, I hope, nothing of significance has been omitted.

Thousands of items were rejected for different reasons. Maybe the subject matter was not of sufficient importance. Or perhaps so much had been written about the subject that it was necessary to include only a representative sampling of entries pertaining to it. Possibly the item appeared in an obscure journal not likely to be found in most public or small college libraries. Also, it would serve no purpose to list long out-of-print books not available anywhere except from rare book dealers. Thus the initial weeding process was ruthless. Other rules of selectivity which were adopted quite early led to the exclusion of manuscript collections, most government documents and other primary source materials, most Ph.D. dissertations, and most wartime publications. But it is not true that any card which fell to the floor accidentally was automatically excluded.

Much more difficult than choosing the final 5,600 entries cited in this book was the problem of organization. No existing Civil War bibliography seemed quite suited to serve as a model for the material at hand. From the time work commenced in 1983, no less than eight outlines were used, although each new one was built on its predecessor. Categories have been divided, reunited, and redivided or merged with other categories countless times. Similarly sub-categories have been shifted about frequently, like a football defense trying to present its strongest front. At length, what seemed a sensible framework emerged. Common subjects were brought together and overlappings were, I hope, reduced to a minimum. Everyone may not agree with the plan of organization, but it was the best of the several with which I experimented.

Early in the process of gathering materials for this volume, yeoman service was performed by Richard Hall. I am indebted to him for his important contributions. Douglas Full also helped greatly with annotations. Several sections and sub-sections have been compiled by others. A list of these contributors and a short sketch of each may be found in the back of the book. Many thanks to them. In addition, I would like to express my appreciation to the Marietta College librarians Bernice Barry, Barbara Geisey, and Phyllis Zoerkler, who have been as helpful as they could be in responding to my many demands. Finally, as is generally the case in matters of this kind, the brunt of the work fell on my wife Peg. While a bad accident on Friday, April 13, 1984, kept her housebound for well over a year and forced her to stay home and work on this project, I expect she would have done as much had she been able to get around. At any rate, the value of her contributions to diverse aspects of this book has been incalculable and I am grateful for her help.

Eugene C. Murdock
Williamstown, West Virginia
July 1986

LIST OF PERIODICALS CITED

A BAR ASSN J	American Bar Association Journal
A BOOK COLL	American Book Collector
A ECON R	American Economic Review
A F A J	American Forensic Association Journal
A GER R	American-German Review
AGRIC HIS	Agricultural History
A HIS ILL	American History Illustrated
AHR	American Historical Review
A J ECON SOC	American Journal of Economics and Sociology
A JEW ARCH	American Jewish Archives
A JEW HIS Q	American Jewish Historical Quarterly
A JEW HIS SOC PUB	American Jewish Historical Society Publications
A JEW Q	American Jewish Quarterly
A J INT LAW	American Journal of International Law
A J LEG HIS	American Journal of Legal History
ALA HIS Q	Alabama Historical Quarterly
ALA LAW	Alabama Lawyer
ALA R	Alabama Review
A LIB ASSN BULL	American Library Association Bulletin
A LIT	American Literature
A LIT REAL	American Literary Realism
ALQ	Abraham Lincoln Quarterly
	Americana
	American Notes and Queries
	Americas, The
A MIL INST J	American Military Institute Journal
AM NEP	American Neptune
ANN IOWA	Annals of Iowa
A PHIL SOC PROC	American Philosophical Society, Proceedings
A PHIL SOC TRAN	American Philosophical Society, Transactions
AQ	American Quarterly
ARIZ Q	Arizona Quarterly
ARIZ W	Arizona and the West
ARK HIS Q	Arkansas Historical Quarterly
	Army
ARMY INFO DIG	Army Information Digest
ARMY QDJ	Army Quarterly and Defense Journal
ARR	American Review of Reviews
AS	American Scholar
ATLAN MON	Atlantic Monthly
ATL HIS BULL	Atlanta Historical Bulletin
AW	American West
BALL ST UNIV F	Ball State University Forum
BERKS CTY HIS R	Berks County Historical Review

BG MAG	Blue and Gray Magazine
	Blackwood's Magazine
	Books at Brown
BUS HIS GR BR	Business History of Great Britain
BUS HIS R	Business History Review
CAL HIS Q	California Historical Quarterly
CAL HIS SOC Q	California Historical Society Quarterly
	Canada
CAN HIS R	Canadian Historical Review
CAN J HIS SPORT	Canadian Journal of the History of Sport and Physical Education
CAN LAW TIMES	Canadian Law Times
CAP STUD	Capitol Studies
CATH DIG	Catholic Digest
CATH HIS R	Catholic Historical Review
CEDAR CTY HIS R	Cedar County [Iowa] Historical Review
CEN R	Centennial Review
CEN ST SPEECH J	Central States Speech Journal
CHEM ENG NEWS	Chemical and Engineering News
CH HIS	Church History
CHI HIS	Chicago History
CH OK	Chronicles of Oklahoma
CHRIS ADV	Christian Advocate
CIN HIS SOC BULL	Cincinnati Historical Society Bulletin
	Clinical Anesthesia
COLL COMP COM	College Composition and Communication
COL MAG	Colorado Magazine
	Commentary
COMP STUD SOC HIS	Comparative Studies in Society and History
	Conflict
CONT R	Contemporary Review
	Crisis
CUR HIS	Current History
CWH	Civil War History
CWTI	Civil War Times Illustrated
	Daedalus
DAR MAG	Daughters of the American Revolution Magazine
DAUPHIN CTY HIS R	Dauphin County Historical Review
DEL HIS	Delaware History
DEL NOTES	Delaware Notes
	Denver Westerners' Monthly Roundup
DET HIS SOC BULL	Detroit Historical Society Bulletin
DUQ R	Duquesne Review
	Ebony
ED THEA J	Education Theater Journal
EMER SOC Q	Emerson Society Quarterly
ENG HIS R	English Historical Review
ESSEX INST HIS COLL	Essex Institute Historical Collections
E TENN HIS SOC PROC	East Tennessee Historical Society Proceedings
E TENN HIS SOC PUB	East Tennessee Historical Society Publications

EXPLO ECON HIS	Explorations in Economic History
EXPLO ENTRE HIS	Explorations in Entrepreneurial History
FCHQ	Filson Club Historical Quarterly
FLA HIS Q	Florida Historical Quarterly
	Foundations
FRIENDS HIS ASSN BULL	Friends Historical Association Bulletin
GA HIS Q	Georgia Historical Quarterly
GA R	Georgia Review
HARP MAG	Harper's Magazine
HARP MON	Harper's Monthly
HARV LIB BULL	Harvard Library Bulletin
HEARST'S MAG	Hearst's Magazine
HIS ED J	History of Education Journal
HIS J W MASS	Historical Journal of Western Massachusetts
HIS MAG PROT EPI CH	Historical Magazine of the Protestant Episcopal Church
HIS MED BULL	History of Medicine Bulletin
HIS NH	Historical New Hampshire
HISP A HIS R	Hispanic American Historical Review
HIS PHIL SOC OH BULL	Historical and Philosophical Society of Ohio Bulletin
HIS PHIL SOC OH PUB	Historical and Philosophical Society of Ohio Publications
HIS TOD	History Today
	Historian
	History
	History and Theory
HIS WYO	Historical Wyoming
HUNT LIB BULL	Huntington Library Bulletin
HUNT LIB Q	Huntington Library Quarterly
ILL Q	Illinois Quarterly
ILL ST HIS LIB PUB	Illinois State Historical Library Publications
ILL ST HIS LIB TRAN	Illinois State Historical Library Transactions
IND HIS BULL	Indiana History Bulletin
IND MAG HIS	Indiana Magazine of History
INFO J	Information Journal
	Instructor
INT R SOC HIS	International Review of Social History
IOWA J HIS	Iowa Journal of History
IOWA J HIS POL	Iowa Journal of History and Politics
	Irish Sword
J AB SOC PSYCH	Journal of Abnormal and Social Psychology
JAH	Journal of American History [Before 1967, Mississippi Valley Historical Review]
J AM STUD	Journal of American Studies
J ARIZ HIS	Journal of Arizona History
J ECON HIS	Journal of Economic History
J FRIENDS HIS SOC	Journal of the Friends' Historical Society
J HIS IDEAS	Journal of the History of Ideas

J HIS MED ALL SCI	Journal of the History of Medicine and Allied Sciences
J HU REL	Journal of Human Relations
JISHS	Journal of the Illinois State Historical Society
J INTER HIS	Journal of Interdisciplinary History
JMH	Journal of Modern History
J MISS HIS	Journal of Mississippi History
J NEG ED	Journal of Negro Education
JNH	Journal of Negro History
JOUR Q	Journalism Quarterly
J PRES HIS	Journal of Presbyterian History
J PRES HIS SOC	Journal of the Presbyterian Historical Society
JSH	Journal of Southern History
J SPORT HIS	Journal of Sport History
JUDGE ADVO GEN BULL	Judge Advocate General, Bulletin
JUSCA	Journal of the United States Cavalry Association
JW	Journal of the West
J W VA HIS ASSN	Journal of the West Virginia Historical Association
KAN HIS	Kansas History
KAN HIS Q	Kansas Historical Quarterly
KAN HIS SOC TRAN	Kansas Historical Society, Transactions
KY HIS SOC REG	Kentucky Historical Social Register
LAB HIS	Labor History
LA HIS	Louisiana History
LA HIS Q	Louisiana Historical Quarterly
LA STUD	Louisiana Studies
LIB J	Library Journal
LIN HER	Lincoln Herald
LIN LORE	Lincoln Lore
	Long Island Forum
MAG A HIS	Magazine of American History
	Mankind
MANU	Manuscripts
	Marine Corps Gazette
MASS HIS SOC PROC	Massachusetts Historical Society Proceedings
MASS R	Massachusetts Review
MASS REG	Massachusetts Register
McCLURE'S MAG	McClure's Magazine
McNEESE R	McNeese Review
MD HIS	Maryland Historian
MD HIS MAG	Maryland Historical Magazine
MED HIS	Medical History
MED TIMES	Medical Times
MEN HIS BULL	Mennonite Historical Bulletin
MENNON LIFE	Mennonite Life
METH HIS	Methodist History
MICH ACAD	Michigan Academician
MICH HIS	Michigan History

MICH HIS COLL	Michigan Historical Collections
MICH HIS MAG	Michigan History Magazine
MICH LAW R	Michigan Law Review
MID AM	Mid-America
MIDWEST FOLK	Midwest Folklore
MIDWEST Q	Midwest Quarterly
MIDWESTERN Q	Midwestern Quarterly
MIL AFF	Military Affairs
MIL COL HIS	Military Collector and Historian
MIL ENG	Military Engineer
MIL HIS ECON	Military Historian and Economist
MIL HIS SOC BULL	Military History Society Bulletin
MIL HIS TEXAS SW	Military History of Texas and the Southwest
MIL LAW R	Military Law Review
MIL MED	Military Medicine
MIL R	Military Review
MINN HIS	Minnesota History
MINN HIS BULL	Minnesota History Bulletin
MISS HIS SOC PUB	Mississippi Historical Society Publications
MISS Q	Mississippi Quarterly
	Modern Age
	Modern Maturity
MO HIS R	Missouri Historical Review
MO HIS SOC BULL	Missouri Historical Society Bulletin
MON	Montana
MON MAG HIS	Montana Magazine of History
MON MAG W HIS	Montana Magazine of Western History
MOR HIS SOC TRAN	Moravian Historical Society Transactions
MUSIC J	Music Journal
MVHR	Mississippi Valley Historical Society
NAV WAR COLL R	Naval War College Review
NC HIS R	North Carolina Historical Review
N DEF TRANS J	National Defense Transportation Journal
ND HIS	North Dakota History
ND HIS Q	North Dakota History Quarterly
NEB HIS	Nebraska History
NEB HIS MAG	Nebraska History Magazine
NEB HIS SOC Q	Nebraska Historical Society Quarterly
NEG HIS BULL	Negro History Bulletin
NE MAG	New England Magazine
NEQ	New England Quarterly
NEV HIS SOC Q	Nevada Historical Society Quarterly
NEW ENG GAL	New England Galaxy
NEW ENG HIS SOC Q	New England Historical Society Quarterly
NEW ENG SOC STUD BULL	New England Social Studies Bulletin
	New Letters
NG	National Geographic
NIAG FRON	Niagara Frontier
NJ HIS	New Jersey History
NJ HIS SOC PROC	New Jersey Historical Society Proceedings
NM HIS R	New Mexico Historical Review
NOVA SCOTIA HIS Q	Nova Scotia Historical Quarterly
	Now and Then
NW OHIO Q	Northwest Ohio Quarterly

NY FOLK Q	New York Folklore Quarterly
NY HIS	New York History
NY HIS Q	New York Historical Quarterly
NY HIS SOC Q	New-York Historical Society Quarterly
NY HIS SOC QTLY BULL	New-York Historical Society Quarterly Bulletin
OHIO HIS	Ohio History
OHIO HIS Q	Ohio Historical Quarterly
OKLA ST MED ASSN J	Oklahoma State Medical Association Journal
	Old Santa Fe
ONT HIS	Ontario History
ORD	Ordnance
ORE HIS Q	Oregon Historical Quarterly
ORE HIS SOC Q	Oregon Historical Society Quarterly
OSAHQ	Ohio State Archaeological and Historical Society Quarterly
	Outlook, The
PAC HIS	Pacific Historian
PAC HIS R	Pacific Historical Review
PAC HISTORY	Pacific History
PAC NW Q	Pacific Northwest Quarterly
	Palacio, El
PALIMP	Palimpsest
PA MHB	Pennsylvania Magazine of History and Biography
PAN PLAINS H R	Pangandle Plains Historical Review
PART R	Partisan Review
PENN HIS	Pennsylvania History
PERS A HIS	Perspectives in American History
	Personalist
	Phylon
PHYS ED	Physical Education
PLAINS HIS R	Plains Historical Review
	Plays
PMHSM	Papers of the Military History Society of Massachusetts
POL AM STUD	Polish-American Studies
POL R	Polish Review
PROC BRIT ACAD	Proceedings of the British Academy
	Prologue
Q J LIB CONGRESS	Quarterly Journal of the Library of Congress
Q J SPEECH	Quarterly Journal of Speech
QUAKER HIS	Quaker History
QUAR R	Quarterly Review
R A HIS	Reviews in American History
READERS DIG	Readers Digest
RED RIVER VALL HIS R	Red River Valley Historical Review
	Reporter, The
RES Q	Research Quarterly
ROCH HIS SOC PUB	Rochester Historical Society Publications

ROCH UNIV LIB BULL	Rochester University Library Bulletin
ROYAL SOC MED PROC	Royal Society of Medicine Proceedings
RR LOCO HIS SOC BULL	Railway and Locomotive Historical Society Bulletin
RUSS R	Russian Review
RUTGERS UNIV LIB J	Rutgers University Library Journal
SAN DIEGO HIS SOC Q	San Diego Historical Society Quarterly
SAN JOSE STUD	San Jose Studies
S ATL BULL	South Atlantic Bulletin
S ATL Q	South Atlantic Quarterly
SAT R	Saturday Review
SAT R LIT	Saturday Review of Literature
S CAL Q	Southern California Quarterly
SC HIS MAG	South Carolina Historical Magazine
SCI SOC	Science and Society
SD HIS	South Dakota History
SD HIS Q	South Dakota Historical Quarterly
SD HIS SOC Q	South Dakota Historical Society Quarterly
SD LAW R	South Dakota Law Review
SEWANEE R	Sewanee Review
SHSP	Southern Historical Society Papers
	Signal
SMITH J HIS	Smithsonian Journal of History
SOC CASE	Social Casework
SOC SCI	Social Science
SOC SCI R	Social Science Review
SOC STUD	Social Studies
SOUTH CAL HIS SOC Q	Southern California Historical Society Quarterly
SOUTH Q	Southern Quarterly
SOUTH SPEECH J	Southern Speech Journal
SOUTH STUD	Southern Studies
STATEN ISLAND HIS	Staten Island Historian
ST JOHNS LAW R	St. Johns Law Review
STRAT TAC	Strategy and tactics
STUD PHIL	Studies in Philology
SWED PION HIS Q	Swedish Pioneer Historical Quarterly
SW HIS Q	Southwestern Historical Quarterly
SWR	Southwest Review
SW SOC SCI Q	Southwestern Social Science Quarterly
TENN HIS MAG	Tennessee Historical Magazine
TENN HIS Q	Tennessee Historical Quarterly
TENN VALL HIS R	Tennessee Valley Historical Review
	Texana
TEXAS MED	Texas Medicine
TEXAS STUD LIT LANG	Texas Studies in Literature and Language
TEX MIL HIS	Texas Military History
	Timeline
	Topic
TULANE STUD ENG	Tulane Studies in English
UNIV COLL Q	University College Quarterly
UNIV DET LAW J	University of Detroit Law Journal
UNIV MICH MED BULL	University of Michigan Medical Bulletin
UNIV R [Kansas City]	University Review [Kansas City]

UNIV TEXAS STUD ENG	University of Texas Studies in English
US GRANT ASSN NEWS	U.S. Grant Association Newsletter
US INF J	U.S. Infantry Journal
US LIB CONG Q J	U.S. Library of Congress Quarterly Journal
US NAV INST PROC	United States Naval Institute Proceedings
US SERV MAG	United States Service Magazine
UTAH HIS Q	Utah Historical Quarterly
VA CAV	Virginia Cavalcade
VA MED MON	Virginia Medical Monthly
VA MHB	Virginia Magazine of History and Biography
VA Q R	Virginia Quarterly Review
VINE HIS MAG	Vineland Historical Magazine
VT HIS	Vermont History
VT Q	Vermont Quarterly
WALT WHITMAN R	Walt Whitman Review
WASH ST UNIV RES STUD	Washington State University Research Studies
WEST HIS Q	Westport Historical Quarterly
WEST RES MAG	Western Reserve Magazine
W FOLK	Western Folklore
W HIS Q	Western Historical Quarterly
WIS ACAD SCI ARTS LET TRAN	Wisconsin Academy of Science, Arts, and Letters of Transactions
WIS MAG HIS	Wisconsin Magazine of History
WIS THEN NOW	Wisconsin Then and Now
W PA HIS MAG	Western Pennsylvania History Magazine
W TENN HIS SOC PAPERS	Western Tennessee Historical Society Papers
W VA HIS	West Virginia History
W VA R	West Virginia Review
YALE R	Yale Review
YALE UNIV LIB GAZ	Yale University Library Gazette
	York State Tradition

The Civil War in the North

I

INTRODUCTION

A. REFERENCE WORKS

By Linda L. Geary

This unit focuses on reference materials pertaining to the North during the Civil War. The types of material here include dictionaries, encyclopedias, guides, handbooks, indexes, almanacs, chronologies, compendiums, and bibliographies. By no means comprehensive, the list is a selection of basic reference materials dealing with a wide variety of Civil War topics.

The items annotated below are mainly twentieth-century publications, many from the Centennial and post-Centennial years. A few classic nineteenth-century titles are also included because they remain unsurpassed. Also listed are special topic bibliographies of a unique character, such as the list of Braille books. Included, too, are articles that are valuable as guides to further study. For example, Aimone's article is quite helpful as an introductory guide to the OFFICIAL RECORDS.

Additional reference materials, especially pre-Centennial and minor works can be found in many of the bibliographies listed below. Readers should be sure to consult the very important CIVIL WAR BOOKS: A CRITICAL BIBLIOGRAPHY, edited by Allan Nevins, James Robertson, and Bell Wiley, and the invaluable three-volume MILITARY BIBLIOGRAPHY OF THE CIVIL WAR by Charles E. Dornbusch.

Among the types of sources excluded from this unit are quasi-reference books that belong more appropriately in one of the subject area units or under general works. Also bibliographies of individual states or western territories will be found under the unit of state or local government. Specialized bibliographies, such as those dealing with Lincoln, Grant, Gettysburg, or The Arts, will be found in those units. Also books of maps and pictures can be found in another unit, although guides to, or bibliographies of, maps and pictures are listed here.

The principal focus of this unit, however, is on reference titles. It includes neither works pertaining solely to the South such as the DICTIONARY OF THE CONFEDERACY, nor general reference sources of American history such as the HARVARD GUIDE, ENCYCLOPEDIA OF AMERICAN HISTORY, or DICTIONARY OF AMERICAN BIOGRAPHY. Readers who are interested in conducting an in-depth analysis should be sure to examine the above works, as well as other reference tools, including WRITINGS IN AMERICAN HISTORY, AMERICA: HISTORY AND LIFE, and DISSERTATION ABSTRACTS.

1. Abbot, George M. CONTRIBUTIONS TOWARDS A BIBLIOGRAPHY ON THE CIVIL WAR IN THE UNITED STATES. Philadelphia, 1886.

   A compilation of regimental histories, which has since been superceded by Dornbusch.

2. Amann, William F., editor. PERSONNEL OF THE CIVIL WAR. Volume 2: THE UNION ARMIES. New York: Yoseloff, 1961.

   The first part of this standard reference work is a list of general officers and their commands, identical to that found in Phisterer [number 56], but with no index. The second part consists of two lists of synonyms of volunteer organizations.

3. AMERICAN HERITAGE CIVIL WAR CHRONOLOGY, WITH NOTES ON THE LEADING PARTICIPANTS. New York: American Heritage, 1960.

   This 39-page pamphlet contains a general chronology, an index to military events, and a list of leading participants with summaries of their activities. Useful for quick reference.

4. Anderson, Charles C. FIGHTING BY SOUTHERN FEDERALS. New York, 1911.

   The author describes the activities of over 430,000 men, both black and white, living in the South who fought for the Union. He also points out that over 200,000 southern-born men living in the North fought for the Union.

5. APPLETON'S AMERICAN ANNUAL CYCLOPEDIA. 1861-1865. New York, 1862-1866.

   Published annually, these massive tomes present a wealth of facts and statistics which are both valuable and interesting.

6. Baggett, James A. THE CIVIL WAR AND RECONSTRUCTION: A DISSERTATION BIBLIOGRAPHY. Ann Arbor, Michigan: University Microfilms International, 1979.

   A 17-page listing of dissertations from the 1940s to the 1970s, which are available from University Microfilms International. For more recent dissertations see DISSERTATIONS AND HISTORY and DISSERTATION ABSTRACTS.

7. Barton, Michael. "A Selected Bibliography of Civil War Soldier's Diaries." BULLETIN OF BIBLIOGRAPHY AND MAGAZINE NOTES, 85 [1978]: 19-29.

   An excellent list of 232 published diaries of Union and Confederate officers and enlisted men. Author includes only those diaries which have been determined to be authentic.

8. BATTLES AND LEADERS OF THE CIVIL WAR. 4 v. New York: Yoseloff, 1956.

This outstanding supplement to the OFFICIAL RECORDS was first published in ten volumes in the 1880s. It contains detailed memoirs of high-ranking officers on both sides and is profusely illustrated.

9. Boatner, Mark M. THE CIVIL WAR DICTIONARY. New York: David McKay, 1959.

This work is a standard and classic reference source for Civil War studies. Major personalities and events are treated with brief articles. It also includes maps, diagrams, and a basic chronology.

10. Bowman, John S., editor. THE CIVIL WAR ALMANAC. New York: Facts On File, 1982.

Although not as detailed as Long's ALMANAC, this is a reliable source for day-to-day chronology, descriptions of equipment and weapons and brief biographies.

11. Brubaker, Robert L. "Recent Aquisitions to the Historical Library." JISHS, 58 [1965]: 200-204.

A discussion of Civil War source materials at the Illinois State Historical Library.

12. CATALOGUE OF BOOKS RELATING TO THE AMERICAN CIVIL WAR. Cleveland: Arthur H. Clark Co., 1917.

A listing of 1,849 titles in this work, although it has been superceded by a number of more recent volumes.

13. Cromie, Alice H. A TOUR GUIDE TO THE CIVIL WAR. New York: Dutton, 1975.

A skillfully compiled, state-by-state guide for Civil War site tourists. It includes summaries of each state's status on the eve of the war, descriptions, location, special features and significance of each site, as well as maps.

14. Cullom, George W. BIOGRAPHICAL REGISTER OF THE OFFICERS AND GRADUATES OF THE UNITED STATES MILITARY ACADEMY. 2 v. New York, 1868.

Gives a full record of all Academy graduates from 1802 and provides good introductory data on the men who led the Union and Confederate armies.

15. Donald, David. THE NATION IN CRISIS, 1861-1877. New York: Appleton-Century-Crofts,1969.

Although not annotated, the items in this classified bibliography are included on the basis of their significance and usefulness. It is a useful selection tool for students, teachers, and librarians.

16. Dornbusch, Charles E. MILITARY BIBLIOGRAPHY OF THE CIVIL WAR. 3 v. New York: New York Public Library, 1961-1972.

Volume 1: REGIMENTAL PUBLICATIONS AND PERSONAL NARRATIVES OF THE CIVIL WAR: NORTHERN STATES. This volume is an essential starting point for northern unit studies. It lists books, articles, and documents pertaining to over 2,000 units and provides summaries of unit histories, as well as an extensive list of personal narratives.

Volume 2: REGIMENTAL PUBLICATIONS AND PERSONAL NARRATIVES: SOUTHERN, BORDER AND WESTERN STATES AND TERRITORIES: FEDERAL TROOPS AND THE UNION AND CONFEDERATE BIOGRAPHIES. This is similar to the first volume, but deals with units whose main activities occurred in non-northern states.

Volume 3: GENERAL REFERENCES, ARMED FORCES AND CAMPAIGNS AND BATTLES. This ranks among the best bibliographies in terms of its coverage of pertinent material through 1962. It also offers a section "Poetry and Song" which, among its nearly 50 entries, includes several 19th-century anthologies of Civil War verse.

17. Dyer, Frederick H. A COMPENDIUM OF THE WAR OF THE REBELLION. 3 v. Des Moines, Iowa: 1908.

In terms of scope and detail, this compilation of facts and statistics is an indispensable tool to Civil War scholars. In three parts, the work covers numbers and organization, treats 10,455 military engagements and 3,550 unit histories. It is a monumental contribution to Civil War literature. Several reprints are available.

18. Eisenschiml, Otto. "Too Many Civil War Books?" CWH, 6 [1960]: 250-257.

Author discusses the quality and value of the flood of literature on the Civil War recently published.

19. FODOR'S CIVIL WAR SITES. New York: David McKay, 1979.

One of Fodor's well-known travel guides, but for historical background, it is not as comprehensive as Cromie's work.

20. Fox, William F. REGIMENTAL LOSSES IN THE AMERICAN CIVIL WAR, 1861-1865. Albany, New York: 1889. Reprint 1974.

The forerunner to Livermore's classic NUMBERS AND LOSSES, this long-standing reference work is full of detailed and exhaustive statistics. It also includes short histories of army units.

21. Fry, James B. MILITARY MISCELLANIES. New York, 1889.

An evaluation of numerous writings, books, and articles on the war by the Civil War Provost Marshal General. The main focus is on military matters.

22. Gould, Benjamin A. INVESTIGATIONS IN THE MILITARY AND ANTHROPOLOGICAL STATISTICS OF AMERICAN SOLDIERS. New York, 1869.

A huge compilation of statistical data on the physical dimensions of northern soldiers in the Civil War, prepared by the actuary to the United States Sanitary Commission.

23. Groene, Bertram H. TRACING YOUR CIVIL WAR ANCESTOR. Winston-Salem, North Carolina: John F. Blair, 1973.

A well-written guidebook to genealogical research using published and archival sources.

24. Hamersly, Thomas H.S., compiler. COMPLETE REGULAR ARMY REGISTER OF THE UNITED STATES: FOR ONE HUNDRED YEARS [1779-1879].... Washington, D.C.: 1880.

A huge book containing tables, histories of the War Department and staff departments of the army, and official records of officers.

25. Hardesty, Jesse. KILLED AND DIED OF WOUNDS IN THE UNION ARMY DURING THE CIVIL WAR. San Jose, California: 1915.

This 34-page pamphlet lists each regiment's losses.

26. HARPER'S WEEKLY. New York: Harper and Brothers, 1857-1916.

This was the most popular periodical of its day, and the issues for the war years are excellent, with extraordinary illustrations. A facsimile reprint was issued weekly during the Civil War Centennial by Living History, Inc. of Shenandoah, Iowa.

27. Heaps, Willard A. "The Civil War, Fifty of the Best Books Published, 1958-1961." LIB J, 86 [1961]: 3432-3426.

An annotated, informed bibliography, intended as a guide to selecting the "best" among the magnitude of material published before the Centennial.

28. ———. "The Civil War in Children's Books: Selected Titles Published, 1958-1961." LIB J, 86 [1961]: 3612-3613.

A companion source to the above article. The author identifies gaps in Civil War children's literature during the period under consideration and notes basic collection titles.

29. Heitman, Francis B. HISTORICAL REGISTER AND DICTIONARY OF THE UNITED STATES ARMY, FROM ITS ORGANIZATION, SEPTEMBER 29, 1789, TO MARCH 2, 1903. 2 v. Washington, D.C.: 1903. Reprint 1965.

A well-known and valuable tool for Civil War as well as other military researchers. It contains hundreds of capsule biographies of army officers, chronological rosters of field and staff officers, statistical tables of strength and losses in ten wars, as well as a list of all campaigns, battles, and skirmishes.

30. Hetrich, George and Julius Guttag. CIVIL WAR TOKENS AND TRADESMEN'S STORE CARDS. Stow, Massachusetts: Alfred D. Hoch, 1968.

First published in 1924, this is a well-known title among American numismatists and Civil War collectors. It characterizes over 7,000 varieties of tokens and store cards, many of which are pictured.

31. Joyce, Donald F., compiler. THE CIVIL WAR: A LIST OF ONE HUNDRED BOOKS IN BRAILLE AND ON TALKING BOOK RECORDS. Washington: Library of Congress, 1961.

This useful bibliography was compiled from the Books for the Blind Department, Chicago Public Library. The non-annotated selections are arranged by fiction, non-fiction, adult and juvenile categories.

32. Kibby, Leo P. BOOK REVIEW REFERENCE FOR A DECADE OF CIVIL WAR BOOKS, 1950-1960. San Jose, California: Spartan Bookstore, 1961.

Over 400 books and book reviews are included in this useful guide.

33. Kremer, Wesley P. 100 GREAT BATTLES OF THE REBELLION: A DETAILED ACCOUNT OF REGIMENTS AND BATTERIES ENGAGED--CASUALTIES, KILLED, WOUNDED AND MISSING, AND THE NUMBER OF MEN IN ACTION IN EACH REGIMENT.... Hoboken, New Jersey: 1906.

Drawn largely from public records, this book appears to live up to its lengthy title.

34. Lambert, William H. LIBRARY OF THE LATE MAJOR WILLIAM H. LAMBERT OF PHILADELPHIA. 5 v. New York, 1914.

A catalog of items--books, pamphlets, and manuscripts--from this exceptional collection offered for sale at the Anderson Galleries in 1914.

35. Lane, Jack C. AMERICA'S MILITARY PAST: GUIDE TO INFORMATION SOURCES. Detroit: Gale, 1980.

Pages 111-136 of this military bibliography are devoted to Civil War sources. The entries include short, critical annotations.

36. Lawrence, Samuel C. CATALOGUE OF THE MASONIC LIBRARY. MASONIC MEDALS, WASHINGTONIANA, ANCIENT AND HONORABLE ARTILLERY COMPANY'S SERMONS, REGIMENTAL HISTORIES, AND OTHER LITERATURE RELATING TO THE LATE CIVIL WAR, BELONGING TO SAMUEL C. LAWRENCE, MEDFORD, MASSACHUSETTS. Boston, 1891.

Another private collection catalogue.

37. LESLIE'S ILLUSTRATED NEWSPAPER. New York: Frank Leslie, 1855-1922.

An illustrated weekly newspaper in which the 1861-1865 issues rank close to those in HARPER'S WEEKLY. A facsimile reprint was issued by Living History, Inc. of Shenandoah, Iowa during the Centennial.

38. Livermore, Thomas L. NUMBERS AND LOSSES IN THE CIVIL WAR IN AMERICA, 1861-1865. Boston, 1900. Reprint 1957.

A classic analysis and detailed account of troop numbers. It includes narrative, tables and index, and covers the subject matter on a large scale as well as battle-by-battle.

39. Long, E.B. THE CIVIL WAR DAY BY DAY: AN ALMANAC, 1861-1865. Garden City, New York: Doubleday, 1971.

This work is fast-becoming a modern reference classic. In addition to the detailed and thoroughly researched day by day narrative, it includes maps, special studies, bibliography, and index by dates. In all, it is a fascinating and very readable collection of facts.

40. Lord, Francis A. "Army and Navy Textbooks Used by the North During the Civil War." MIL COLL HIST, 9 [1957]: 61-67,95-102.

Divided into two parts, the first section of this intriguing study concerns the historical background, development, and use of various manuals. The second portion consists of an extensive classified bibliography of the most widely used manuals and texts.

41. ———. CIVIL WAR COLLECTOR'S ENCYCLOPEDIA: ARMS, UNIFORMS, AND EQUIPMENT OF THE UNION AND CONFEDERACY. Harrisburg: Stackpole, 1963.

This work is filled with over 400 outstanding illustrations and researched descriptions of all types of collector's artifacts. The bibliography lists manuals, regulations, textbooks, and more specialized secondary sources on particular types of equipage, for both the armies and the navies.

42. ——— and Arthur Wise. UNIFORMS OF THE CIVIL WAR. Cranbury, New Jersey: Yoseloff, 1970.

In this illustrated history of Civil War uniforms, North and South, the authors have assembled over 100 photographs, sketches, and paintings--some fresh, some familiar. None in color. Useful for the specialist, perhaps not quite so for the casual peruser.

43. McPherson, Edward, editor. THE POLITICAL HISTORY OF THE UNITED STATES OF AMERICA DURING THE GREAT REBELLION. Washington, D.C., 1865. Reprint 1984.

A collection of official reports, congressional enactments, and state papers available at that time.

44. Mebane, John, compiler. BOOKS RELATING TO THE CIVIL WAR: A PRICED CHECK LIST, INCLUDING REGIMENTAL HISTORIES, LINCOLNIANA, AND CONFEDERATE REPRINTS. New York: Yoseloff, 1963.

Lists 4,600 items offered for sale by dealers from 1959-1962. It is useful now as a price check for booksellers and collectors to find out what a title cost during the Centennial.

45. Moore, Frank, editor. THE REBELLION RECORD: A DIARY OF AMERICAN EVENTS, WITH DOCUMENTS, NARRATIVES, ILLUSTRATIVE INCIDENTS, POETRY, ETC. 12 v. New York, 1862-1868. Reprint 1977.

A classic record of the events of the war as it proceeded. The chronology consists mainly of newspaper accounts with interpolated documents, speeches, and maps. The first nine volumes include hundreds of poems by well-known and obscure writers who chronicle a massive array of Civil War leaders, events, conditions, and issues.

46. Munden, Kenneth W. and Henry P. Beers. GUIDE TO FEDERAL ARCHIVES RELATING TO THE CIVIL WAR. Washington: National Archives, 1962.

This excellent guide provides informative background narrative and descriptions of Record Groups, as well as a lengthy subject index. It is a convenient starting point for researchers who plan to visit the National Archives.

47. Nevins, Allan, James I. Robertson, Jr., and Bell I. Wiley, editors. CIVIL WAR BOOKS: A CRITICAL BIBLIOGRAPHY. 2 v. Baton Rouge: Louisiana State University Press, 1967-1969.

Spearheaded by the United States Civil War Centennial Commission, this much needed bibliography lists over 5,000 books pertaining to both the Union and the Confederacy. Entries include major, as well as minor works and public documents. Unfortunately, the brief annotations are not always helpful.

48. Newman, Ralph G. and E.B. Long. CIVIL WAR DIGEST. New York: Grosset and Dunlap, 1960.

A handy, one-volume reference work with month-to-month chronology, photographs, biographies, maps, and bibliographies.

49. ———. A BASIC CIVIL WAR LIBRARY. Springfield, Illinois: Civil War Centennial Commission of Illinois, 1964.

From the estimated 40,000 titles that had been published on the Civil War by the time of the Centennial, these well-known compilers list approximately 400 works that they consider to be "essential to a basic Civil War library."

50. Nicholson, John P. CATALOGUE OF LIBRARY OF BREVET LIEUTENANT-COLONEL JOHN PAGE NICHOLSON . . . RELATING TO THE WAR OF THE REBELLION, 1861-1866. Philadelphia, 1914.

A veteran of the 28th Pennsylvania, Nicholson amassed approximately 20,000 items in his Civil War library. The catalog is an alphabetical listing of this impressive collection, now located in the Huntington Library in San Marino, California.

51. Niven, Alexander C., compiler. CIVIL WAR DAY BY DAY: A CHRONOLOGY OF THE PRINCIPAL EVENTS OF THE WAR'S FIRST YEAR. Cambridge, Massachusetts: Berkshire Publishing, 1961.

A useful, daily record of the first months of the war.

52. OFFICIAL RECORDS OF THE UNION AND CONFEDERATE NAVIES IN THE WAR OF THE REBELLION. 30 v. Washington: Navy Department, 1894-1922.

The nuts and bolts of the naval aspects of the Civil War. There are omissions and errors, but it is still indispensable. Bound copies are not plentiful but microfilm copies of each volume are available from the National Archives.

53. Pakula, Marvin H. CENTENNIAL ALBUM OF THE CIVIL WAR. William J. Ryan and David K. Rothstein, collaborators. New York: Yoseloff, 1960.

A good introductory book containing information on uniforms, equipment, and generals.

54. Parish, Peter J. THE AMERICAN CIVIL WAR. New York: Holmes and Meier, 1975.

The bibliographic essay in this volume is exceptionally readable and well-organized.

55. Phisterer, Frederick. STATISTICAL RECORD OF THE ARMIES OF THE UNITED STATES. New York, 1883.

As Volume 13 of CAMPAIGNS OF THE CIVIL WAR [see III, G, 3], this account is a long-standing source of facts and figures. Its three parts cover numbers and organizations, chronology and records of officers. Also included is a name index to the record of officers, not found in Amann's PERSONNEL OF THE CIVIL WAR, Volume Two.

56. Powell, William H., editor. OFFICERS OF THE ARMY AND NAVY [VOLUNTEER] WHO SERVED IN THE CIVIL WAR. Philadelphia, 1893.

Short biographies of volunteer officers.

57. ——— and Edward Shippen, editors. OFFICERS OF THE ARMY AND NAVY [REGULAR] WHO SERVED IN THE CIVIL WAR. Philadelphia, 1892.

Intended as a companion volume to the previous entry.

58. Robertson, James I., Jr. "Graduate Writings on the Civil War: A Bibliography." CWH, 5 [1959]: 145-155.

Author lists 212 unpublished Ph.D and M.A. theses, originating from 54 institutions for the years 1956 to 1959. He points out the value and scholarship of these often neglected contributions to Civil War literature. Broader access to this body of material can be obtained by consulting DISSERTATION ABSTRACTS [1938-] and MASTERS ABSTRACTS [1962-].

59. ———. "With Pen in Hand...." CWH, 8 [1962]: 64-75.

A survey of 20 books dealing with a variety of wartime experiences.

60. Schweitzer, George K. CIVIL WAR GENEALOGY. Knoxville, Tennessee: By the author, 1981.

A step-by-step guide to digging into the records. Included are brief bibliographies of basic research tools. A storehouse of information that should be used in conjunction with Groene's guide [number 24].

61. Simmons, Henry E., compiler. A CONCISE ENCYCLOPEDIA OF THE CIVIL WAR. New York: Barnes, 1965.

A basic, dictionary-type guide for students and general readers. Brief narratives cover important events, issues, and figures. But the volume does contain a number of errors.

62. STATISTICAL POCKET MANUAL OF THE ARMY, NAVY AND CENSUS OF THE UNITED STATES OF AMERICA. 2 v. Boston, 1862.

Ancient and not easily available, but a gold mine of miscellaneous information.

63. Strait, Newton A., compiler. AN ALPHABETICAL LIST OF THE BATTLES OF THE WAR OF THE REBELLION WITH DATES.... Washington, D.C.: 1883.

A list of Civil War battles as well as battles of other wars.

64. Strickler, Theodore, D., compiler. WHEN AND WHERE WE MET EACH OTHER ON SHORE AND AFLOAT.... Washington, D.C.: 1899.

A listing of land and sea engagements and other matter.

65. Thruston, Gates P. THE NUMBER AND ROSTERS OF THE TWO ARMIES IN THE CIVIL WAR. Nashville, Tennessee: 1911.

A brief but useful discussion of troop numbers.

66. Tredwell, Daniel M. A CATALOGUE OF BOOKS AND PAMPHLETS.... Brooklyn, 1874.

A list of 1,268 items in the collection of Daniel M. Tredwell.

67. UNION ARMY, THE: A HISTORY OF MILITARY AFFAIRS IN THE LOYAL STATES, 1861-1865--RECORDS OF THE REGIMENTS IN THE UNION ARMY--CYCLOPEDIA OF BATTLES--MEMOIRS OF COMMANDERS AND SOLDIERS.... 8 v. Madison, Wisconsin, 1908.

The series consists of four volumes on military affairs and regimental histories, two volumes on battles, one on the navy and one deals with biographies.

68. U.S. Adjutant-General's Office. OFFICIAL ARMY REGISTER FOR 1861-1865.... 7 v. Washington, D.C.: 1861-1865.

69. ———. MEDALS OF HONOR AWARDED FOR DISTINGUISHED SERVICE DURING THE WAR OF THE REBELLION. Washington, D.C.: 1886.

A 32-page pamphlet which lists the who, when, where, and why of medals awarded.

70. U.S. Air Force Academy. Library. MILITARY ASPECTS OF THE CIVIL WAR. N.P.: n.p., 1961.

An unannotated bibliography of books, articles, newspapers, and recordings available at the Academy. As a list of basic sources it is still useful to beginning readers interested in the military side of the war.

71. U.S. Census Office. 8th Census, 1860. THE UNITED STATES ON THE EVE OF THE CIVIL WAR, AS DESCRIBED IN THE 1860 CENSUS. Washington, D.C.: U.S. Civil War Centennial Commission, 1963.

This slim book provides a statistical overview of the country's social makeup on the eve of war. Topics include population, slavery, immigration, education, agriculture, banks, and railroads. Valuable information in a convenient readable format.

72. U.S. Civil War Centennial Commission. THE CIVIL WAR CENTENNIAL: A REPORT TO THE CONGRESS. Washington, D.C.: U.S. Civil War Centennial Commission, 1968.

The report summarized the activities of the commission, other federal agencies, and state groups from 1961 to 1965. Of notable reference value is its bibliography of the many commemorative works on the Centennial that were issued by various federal, state, and local agencies.

73. U.S. Congress. JOINT COMMITTEE ON THE CONDUCT OF THE WAR, REPORT OF. 8 v. Washington, D.C.: 1863-1865.

Investigations of several of the war's battles and controversies by the Radical Republican-controlled committee.

74. U.S. Department of the Army. Army Library. THE CIVIL WAR.... Prepared by the Catalog Unit. Washington, D.C.: 1961.

A catalog of material available in the Army Library.

75. ———. Military History Institute. THE EAR OF THE CIVIL WAR, 1820-1876. Louise Arnold, compiler. Carlisle Barracks, Pennsylvania: U.S. Army Military History Institute, 1982.

Lists the extensive Civil War holdings of the Institute. Although not indexed or annotated, the catalog is of great help to researchers at this repository since the entries give the call numbers of the books.

76. U.S. Department of Commerce. National Oceanic and Atmospheric Administration. National Ocean Survey. NATIONAL OCEAN SURVEY CARTOBIBLIOGRAPHY, CIVIL WAR COLLECTION. Rockville, Maryland: National Ocean Survey, 1980.

This bibliography provides access to a sizeable collection of Civil War cartographic materials in National Ocean Survey archival holdings. Entries include title, description, author, scale, type of print, date and size. Researchers are invited to send for reproductions from the National Ocean Survey Map Library.

77. U.S. Department of the Interior. Geological Survey. Circular 462. A BIBLIOGRAPHY OF MAPS OF CIVIL WAR BATTLEFIELD AREAS. Irwin Gottschall, compiler. Washington: U.S. Geological Survey, 1962.

A list of maps and charts covering 68 major battlefield areas that are available from the Geological Survey Office. Information includes pertinent topographic quadrangle maps, scale, contour, year of publications, as well as special maps and charts of the area. Hydrographic charts are helpful for the study of certain naval battles.

78. U.S. Department of the Navy. Marine Corps. AN ANNOTATED BIBLIOGRAPHY OF THE UNITED STATES MARINES IN THE CIVIL WAR. Michael O'Quinlivan and Rowland P. Gill, compilers. Washington: Government Printing Office, 1968.

A basic list of 78 books and articles pertaining to both Union and Confederate marines.

79. ———. Naval History Division. CIVIL WAR CHRONOLOGY. 6 v. Washington: Government Printing Office, 1961-1966. Reprint in one volume, 1971.

Volumes One through Five cover the events from 1861 to 1865. Each of these volumes gives a summary of the year, table of significant events, followed by a detailed chronology. Volume Six is devoted to special studies. Particularly fascinating are the captioned illustrations which include pictures, maps, photographs, and drawings.

80. U.S. Department of War. Library. BIBLIOGRAPHY OF STATE PARTICIPATION IN THE CIVIL WAR, 1861-1866.... Washington, D.C.: 1913. Reprint 1961.

Although updated by Dornbusch's volumes, this is still a useful tool.

81. U.S. Library of Congress. General Reference and Bibliography Division. THE AMERICAN CIVIL WAR: A SELECTED READING LIST. Donald H. Mugridge, compiler. Washington, D.C.: Library of Congress, 1960.

A categorized list of 256 books, many of which were regarded as standard on the eve of the Centennial. No annotations, but full citations include the page numbers of bibliographies in the books.

82. ———. General Reference and Bibliography Division. THE CIVIL WAR IN PICTURES, 1861-1961: A CHRONOLOGICAL LIST OF SELECTED PICTORIAL WORKS. Donald H. Mugridge, compiler. Washington: Library of Congress, 1961.

Lists 85 outstanding pictorial works in their order of publication from the collections of Leslie, Gardner, and Brady to the various works arising from Centennial exhibitions. Each entry is annotated with a description of the contents, origin, and significance of the item.

83. ———. Map Division. CIVIL WAR MAPS: AN ANNOTATED LIST OF MAPS AND ATLASES IN MAP COLLECTIONS OF THE LIBRARY OF CONGRESS. Richard W. Stephenson, compiler. Washington, D.C.: Library of Congress, 1961.

A list of some 700 maps indicating troop movements, battles, fortifications, and theaters of war. Divided by large portions of the country and by state. Map features are fully identified and indexed. The Hotchkiss maps are not included in this source.

84. ———. Map Division. THE HOTCHKISS MAP COLLECTION. Clara Egli LeGear, compiler. Washington: Library of Congress, 1951.

The booklet describes 341 manuscript maps of this famous southern cartographer. It includes general maps, field sketches, campaigns and battles, and an index.

85. ———. Prints and Photographs Division. CIVIL WAR PHOTOGRAPHS, 1861-1865: A CATALOG OF COPY NEGATIVES MADE FROM ORIGINALS SELECTED FROM THE MATHEW B. BRADY COLLECTIONS.... Hirst D. Milhollen and Donald H. Mugridge, compilers. Washington: Library of Congress, 1961.

This is a catalog of the "best" and "most interesting" negatives in the library's Brady collection. Its five parts include battles, naval expeditions, the West, Washington, and portraits of officers.

86. ———. Stack and Reader Division. THE CIVIL WAR IN MOTION PICTURES: A BIBLIOGRAPHY OF FILMS PRODUCED IN THE UNITED STATES SINCE 1897. Paul C. Spehr, compiler. Washington, D.C.: Library of Congress, 1961.

A list of 868 motion pictures and newsreels pertaining, in fact or fiction, to events that occurred from 1855 to 1870. Entries include title, producer, date, length, color, format, summary, cast, and credits.

87. U.S. Military Secretary's Department. ... MEMORANDUM RELATIVE TO THE GENERAL OFFICERS IN THE ARMIES OF THE UNITED STATES DURING THE CIVIL WAR--1861-1865. Washington, D.C.: 1908.

A list of general officers.

88. U.S. National Archives. CIVIL WAR MAPS IN THE NATIONAL ARCHIVES. Charlotte M. Ashby et. al., compilers. Washington: National Archives, 1964.

The National Archives has the largest collection of cartographic material relating to the war. This is a descriptive guide to 8,000 maps, most pertaining to operations, installations, and surrounding areas. For a guide to still other maps, researchers should consult Munden's and Beer's GUIDE. [number 46]

89. U.S. National Museum. UNIFORM REGULATIONS FOR THE ARMY OF THE UNITED STATES, 1861. Washington: Smithsonian, 1961.

A re-issue of a 61-page 1862 manual of dress for Union soldiers. Thirty-six full page photographs reveal every kind of uniform the Yanks were supposed to wear.

90. U.S. Quartermaster's Department. MILITARY COMMANDERS AND DESIGNATING FLAGS OF THE UNITED STATES ARMY, 1861-1865. Philadelphia, 1888.

Lists units and commanders and contains many colored pictures of unit flags.

91. ———. ROLL OF HONOR.... Washington, D.C.: 1865.

Arranged by cemetery (National), lists all those interred therein during the Civil War.

92. ———. STATEMENT OF THE DISPOSITION OF SOME OF THE BODIES OF DECEASED UNION SOLDIERS AND PRISONERS OF WAR WHOSE REMAINS HAVE BEEN REMOVED TO NATIONAL CEMETERIES IN THE SOUTHERN AND WESTERN STATES. 4 v. Washington, D.C.: 1868-1869.

A listing of names of soldiers who had been re-interred after the war.

93. WAR OF THE REBELLION, THE: A COMPILATION OF THE OFFICIAL RECORDS OF THE UNION AND CONFEDERATE ARMIES. Washington: 1881-1901. 70 volumes in 128 parts.

The OFFICIAL RECORDS are the basic source, the "must," for any serious student of the Civil War. His work begins here. The massive collection contains major reports and correspondence from the leading figures on both sides. Very little of significance has been left out. Several articles have been written and a multi-volume work has been compiled to provide the history behind the OFFICIAL RECORDS and to facilitate their usage. They are:

94. Aimone, Alan C. "Official Data Gold Mine: The Official Records of the Civil War." LIN HER, 74 [1972]: 192-202.

Excellent background reading for those who want to delve into the 128 volumes and do not know where to begin.

95. Eisendrath, Joseph L., Jr. "The Official Records--Sixty-three Years in the Making." CWH, 1 [1955]: 89-94.

A useful history of the steps which led to the decision to collect and publish the vast accumulation of documents pertaining to the war.

96. Irvine, Dallas D. "The Genesis of the Official Records." MVHR, 24 [1937]: 221-229.

While written eighteen years before the previous entry, this is also a very good review of the history of the OFFICIAL RECORDS. General Henry W. Halleck was the principal originator of the project.

97. ———. MILITARY OPERATIONS OF THE CIVIL WAR: A GUIDE-INDEX TO THE OFFICIAL RECORDS OF THE UNION AND CONFEDERATE ARMIES, 1861-1865. 5 v. Washington: National Archives, 1968-1980.

This reference set is a welcome step-saver for anyone using, or planning to use, the OFFICIAL RECORDS. Volume One gives an overview of the records and their arrangement. Volumes Two to Five index the records of theaters of operation, broken down by state. Irvine's work makes the very important OFFICIAL RECORDS more accessible and their arrangement more understandable.

B. GENERAL WORKS

By Harry F. Lupold

98. Adams, James T. AMERICA'S TRAGEDY. New York: Scribners, 1934.

Adams wrestles with the cause of the war and emphasizes slavery as the primary factor.

99. Angle, Paul and Earl Schenck Miers. TRAGIC YEARS, 1860-1865: A DOCUMENTARY HISTORY OF THE AMERICAN CIVIL WAR. 2 v. New York: Simon and Schuster, 1960.

An excellent chronological history of the war written with the general reader in mind. The focus is chiefly on military events.

100. ANNALS OF THE WAR WRITTEN BY LEADING PARTICIPANTS NORTH AND SOUTH. Philadelphia, 1879.

Originally published in the PHILADELPHIA WEEKLY TIMES, these are very good essays composed by a number of military commanders.

101. "Athos." "Some Aspects of the American Civil War 1861-1865." JOURNAL ROYAL UNITED SERVICE INSTITUTE, 101 [1956]: 387-385.

A summary of land operations in which a number of logistical and military matters are analyzed.

102. Barker, Alan. THE CIVIL WAR IN AMERICA. Garden City, New York: Doubleday, 1961.

Barker originally designed this brief introduction for British readers. It is not a complete history of the war.

103. Barnes, Eric. W. THE WAR BETWEEN THE STATES. New York: Whittlesey House, 1959.

A brief, well-balanced volume for young readers, in which the author discusses the causes and progress of the war against the contemporary social and economic background.

104. Barstow, Charles L., editor. THE CIVIL WAR. New York, 1912.

An anthology of readings dealing with the military aspects of the war taken from BATTLES AND LEADERS OF THE CIVIL WAR.

105. Basler, Roy P. A SHORT HISTORY OF THE AMERICAN CIVIL WAR. New York: Basic Books, 1967.

The beginning student might find this 140-page, readable, non-chronological book useful on certain specific topics.

106. Blythe, Vernon. A HISTORY OF THE CIVIL WAR IN THE UNITED STATES. New York, 1914.

This is strictly a military survey by an author who had a southern background.

107. Carpenter, John and others. CIVIL WAR. Washington, Pennsylvania: Washington and Jefferson College, 1961.

A collection of papers dealing with numerous topics in both the military and political spheres.

108. Churchill, Winston S. THE AMERICAN CIVIL WAR. New York: Dodd, Mead, 1961.

This short work might appeal to the popular audience primarily for Churchill's interpretation. The material is not original, being drawn from the author's HISTORY OF THE ENGLISH SPEAKING PEOPLES.

109. CIVIL WAR, THE. 2 v. New York: Grosset and Dunlap, 1956.

A collection of eyewitness accounts, this book of readings also includes a chronology and brief biographies.

110. Cole, Arthur C. THE IRREPRESSIBLE CONFLICT. New York: Macmillan, 1934.

A good social and cultural history of the United States from the Compromise of 1850 through Appomattox. The author adheres to the "conflicting civilizations" theory of causation. This is not a military account.

111. Commager, Henry S., editor. THE BLUE AND THE GRAY: THE STORY OF THE CIVIL WAR AS TOLD BY PARTICIPANTS. 2 v. Indianapolis: Bobbs-Merrill, 1950. Reprint, in one volume, 1960.

Probably the best of all the readers, this massive collection of materials is drawn from many sources and divided into 31 convenient, chronological topics. The editor uses statements from high-ranking civil and military people, as well as letters and diaries from the enlisted men. This good mix makes for an effective anthology.

112. Congdon, Don, editor. COMBAT: THE CIVIL WAR. New York: Delacorte Press, 1967.

A useful reader, but not as comprehensive as some of the others. The war is reported through the words of eyewitnesses, both North and South.

113. Cruden, Robert. THE WAR THAT NEVER ENDED: THE AMERICAN CIVIL WAR. Englewood Cliffs: Prentice-Hall, 1973.

A well-written, well-researched, substantive account, although not a lengthy survey of the war.

114. Davis, Burke. OUR INCREDIBLE CIVIL WAR. New York : Holt, Rinehart, Winston, 1960.

The unusual event is the focus of this book rather than the continuing story of the war. Yet, an absorbing study.

115. Davis, William C. DEEP WATERS OF THE PROUD. Garden City, New York: Doubleday, 1982.

The first of a projected three-volume history of the Civil War, this work takes the story through the Preliminary Emancipation Proclamation.

116. Dodge, Theodore A. A BIRD'S-EYE VIEW OF OUR CIVIL WAR. Boston, 1883.

Though very old, this remains a good military history of the war. The author was a respected military historian.

117. Dodwell, H.B. "American Civil War." CONT R, 206 [1965]: 192-204.

A generalized, undocumented account of the war's origins as well as a brief survey of the war. Slavery caused the trouble.

118. Donald, David H. LIBERTY AND UNION. Lexington, Massachusetts: Heath, 1956.

Author deals with majority rule and minority rights during the ante- and post-bellum years. A well-written, conservative, nationalist view, covering the years from 1845 to 1890.

119. Draper, John W. HISTORY OF THE AMERICAN CIVIL WAR. 3 v. New York, 1896-1898.

One of the good, early, detailed histories of the war, but long since replaced by various other works.

120. Dupuy, R. Ernest and Trevor N. Dupuy. THE COMPACT HISTORY OF THE CIVIL WAR. New York: Hawthorn Books, 1960.

The Dupuys, both military men, present a brief and readable introduction to the battles and issues of the Civil War. The description of Civil War tactics is of particular interest.

121. ———. MILITARY HERITAGE OF AMERICA. New York: McGraw-Hill, 1956.

A short, analytical work, but very well done.

122. Eisenschiml, Otto and Ralph Newman, editors. THE AMERICAN ILIAD: THE EPIC STORY OF THE CIVIL WAR. Indianapolis: Bobbs-Merrill, 1947.

Another good anthology of writings by over 200 participants. Yet it is not as comprehensive as Commager's THE BLUE AND THE GRAY and is restricted largely to military matters.

123. ———. THE CIVIL WAR. 2 v. New York: Grosset and Dunlap, 1956.

Volume One is a reprint of THE AMERICAN ILIAD, while Volume Two, subtitled "The Picture Chronicle," is a fine book of pictures and battle scenes. It also includes a chronicle of events of the war and an 11-page bibliography.

124. Fiebeger, Gustave J. CAMPAIGNS OF THE CIVIL WAR. West Point, New York: 1914.

A good, solid military record written by a West Point professor and military specialist.

125. Fish, Carl R. THE AMERICAN CIVIL WAR. William E. Smith, editor. New York: Longmans, Green, 1937.

This work was incomplete at the time of the author's death and was finished by another. Good in its time, it has become increasingly out of date.

126. Foote, Shelby. THE CIVIL WAR: A NARRATIVE. 3 v. New York: Random House, 1958-1974.

A lengthy, military study written from a southern point of view, although not necessarily biased. A massive project, reflecting careful research and the able utilization of secondary sources. Well-written, it is a pleasure to read.

127. Fromby, John. THE AMERICAN CIVIL WAR: A CONCISE HISTORY OF ITS CAUSES, PROGRESS, AND RESULTS. New York, 1910.

Written by an Englishman, this is a straightforward history of the war.

128. Fuller, J.F.C. DECISIVE BATTLES OF THE USA. New York: Harper, 1942.

A survey of the major American battles from the Revolutionary through the First World War. The engagements are set in the larger economic and political context.

129. Greeley, Horace. THE AMERICAN CONFLICT. 2 v. Hartford, Connecticut: 1864-1866.

While very old and written by a celebrated journalist with strong feelings, this work can still be read with profit.

130. Greer, Walter. CAMPAIGNS OF THE CIVIL WAR. New York: Brentano's, 1926.

A good reliable account of the major battles with numerous maps and illustrations.

131. Hale, Edward E. STORIES OF WAR TOLD BY SOLDIERS. Boston, 1879.

An early anthology of soldiers' stories compiled by one of the most famous literary figures of the day.

132. Hansen, Harry. THE CIVIL WAR. New York: New American Library, 1961.

Ideally suited for non-specialists, this is a direct account of the war. Yet the fact-filled review of the battles and leaders falls short of being the definitive one-volume history.

133. Hart, Albert B., editor. THE ROMANCE OF THE CIVIL WAR. Elizabeth Stevens, collaborator. New York, 1903.

An anthology of readings drawn from fictional as well as non-fictional sources. It was designed as a book of supplementary sources.

134. Harwell, Richard B., editor. THE UNION READER. New York: Longmans, Green, 1958.

Civilian and military subjects are covered in excerpts from diverse contemporary sources.

135. Hattaway, Herman and Archer Jones. HOW THE NORTH WON: A MILITARY HISTORY OF THE CIVIL WAR. Urbana: University of Illinois Press, 1983.

Deals almost exclusively with tactical, strategic and logistical problems of the armies. The serious student of the war will find this a scholarly, comprehensive study. It is not recommended for the casual reader.

136. Henderson, George F.R. THE CIVIL WAR: A SOLDIER'S VIEW, A COLLECTION OF CIVIL WAR WRITINGS. Jay Luvaas, editor. Chicago: University of Chicago Press, 1958.

Selected writings by the famous British military historian and biographer of "Stonewall" Jackson. The work includes essays on Fredericksburg and Jackson and material from the author's SCIENCE OF WAR.

137. Hesseltine, William B., editor. THE TRAGIC CONFLICT: THE CIVIL WAR AND RECONSTRUCTION. New York: George Braziller, 1962.

A volume of absorbing contemporary accounts from lesser known eyewitnesses.

138. Holmes, Prescott. THE BATTLES OF THE WAR FOR THE UNION.... Philadelphia, 1897.

This old volume discusses the main military operations of the war.

139. Hosmer, James K. THE AMERICAN CIVIL WAR. 2 v. New York, 1913.

A general text that adequately covers the military events of the war. It is a good starting point, but must be supplemented by more recent works that allow for new interpretations.

140. Humphrey, Willis C. THE GREAT CONTEST.... Detroit, 1886.

Another old, popular account of military and naval operations.

141. Jacobs, Donald M. and Raymond H. Robinson. AMERICA'S TESTING TIME, 1848-1877. Boston: Allyn and Bacon, 1973.

A useful enough work for general purposes although it contains nothing original and lacks interpretive qualities.

142. Johannsen, Robert. THE UNION IN CRISIS, 1850-1877. New York: Free Press, 1965.

A good, although not necessarily an inspired collection of readings. One of the best pieces is an extract from Walt Whitman's diary.

143. Johnson, Ludwell H. DIVISION AND REUNION: AMERICA, 1848-1877. New York: Wiley, 1978.

A provocative textbook with a strong pro-southern flavor.

144. Johnson, Rossiter. THE FIGHT FOR THE REPUBLIC: A NARRATIVE OF THE MORE NOTEWORTHY EVENTS IN THE WAR OF SECESSION.... New York: Putnam, 1917.

An old, readable history by one of the more prolific writers and editors of his day.

145. Jones, Robert H. DISRUPTED DECADES: THE CIVIL WAR AND RECONSTRUCTION YEARS. New York: Scribners, 1913.

This is a well-written, easy-to-read survey that covers both North and South, the events leading to the war, the war itself and Reconstruction. While the war may have been avoidable at one time, it soon became unavoidable.

146. Jordan, Robert P. THE CIVIL WAR. Washington: National Geographic Society, 1969.

Although the narrative is a very condensed version of history, the abundance of illustrations, both in color and black and white, makes this an interesting book for the general reader.

147. Lewis, Lloyd. IT TAKES ALL KINDS. New York: Harcourt, Brace, 1947.

A number of the essays in this compilation of newspaper and magazine articles by the influential Chicago journalist deal with the Civil War.

148. Lindsey, David. AMERICANS IN CONFLICT: THE CIVIL WAR AND RECONSTRUCTION. Boston: Houghton Mifflin, 1974.

An excellent, short survey of the pre-war, war, and Reconstruction years, 1830-1877. The book is well-organized, well-written, has useful maps and a good bibliography.

149. Luvaas, Jay. THE MILITARY LEGACY OF THE CIVIL WAR. Chicago: University of Chicago Press, 1959.

A study in which the author shows how English, French, and German observers strongly objected to American battlefield tactics, which emphasized Jomini's strategy.

150. Macartney, Clarence E.N. HIGHWAYS AND BYWAYS OF THE CIVIL WAR. Pittsburgh: Gibson Press, 1938.

A volume devoted to descriptions of the battlefields and campaigns of the war.

151. Mahan, Asa. A CRITICAL HISTORY OF THE LATE AMERICAN WAR. New York, 1877.

A dependable, yet opinionated survey of the major campaigns in both theaters.

152. McCann, Thomas H. THE CAMPAIGNS OF THE CIVIL WAR IN THE UNITED STATES OF AMERICA, 1861-1865. Hoboken, New Jersey: 1915.

A very brief military survey written by a former member of the 90th New York.

153. McJimsey, George T. THE DIVIDING AND REUNITING OF AMERICA: 1848-1877. Arlington Heights, Illinois: Forum Press, 1982.

A comprehensive survey of events focusing on the political differences of Republicans and Democrats.

154. McMaster, John B. A HISTORY OF THE PEOPLE OF THE UNITED STATES DURING LINCOLN'S ADMINISTRATION. New York: Appleton, 1927.

The pioneer among American "social historians" has condensed material from his eight volume history into a single volume on the Civil War.

155. McPherson, James M. ORDEAL BY FIRE: THE CIVIL WAR AND RECONSTRUCTION. New York: Knopf, 1982.

The author deals with every aspect of the Civil War with scholarly depth, in this fresh, imaginative interpretation. The classified bibliography in this text is extensive and consists of a judicious selection of important sources.

156. Miers, Earl S. THE GREAT REBELLION: THE EMERGENCE OF THE AMERICAN CONSCIENCE. Cleveland: World, 1958.

A close look at three episodes in the story of the war: South Carolina's secession, Ft. Sumter, and Appomattox. In this carefully planned and well-told story, the author argues that the American conscience emerged between the second and third episodes.

157. Milton, George F. CONFLICT: THE AMERICAN CIVIL WAR. New York: Coward-McCann, 1941.

Although economic and social consequences are discussed, this volume is primarily a military history. For the general reader.

158. Mitchell, Joseph B. DECISIVE BATTLES OF THE CIVIL WAR. New York: Putnam, 1955.

Author uses road maps and well known landmarks with operational maps overdrawn to serve as a guide for the battlefield tourist.

159. Morris, Richard B. and James Woodress, editors. A HOUSE DIVIDED: THE CIVIL WAR, 1850-1865. St. Louis: Webster Publishing, 1961.

A brief 51-page book of readings to be used in a college course.

160. Nevins, Allan. ORDEAL OF THE UNION. 1847-1857. 2 v.; THE EMERGENCE OF LINCOLN. 1857-1861. 2 v.; THE WAR FOR THE UNION. 1861-1865. 4 v. New York: Scribners, 1947-1971.

This eight-volume masterpiece supercedes anything that has gone before or come after. An outstanding Civil War scholar poured his all into this epic. The work excels both as an account of the fighting and as an interpretation of social, economic, and political developments. A must for the true student of the Civil War.

161. Nichols, Roy F. THE STAKES OF POWER, 1847-1877. New York: Hill and Wang, 1961.

A scholarly interpretation of the first order, which might be too demanding for the beginning student. Almost one-third of the book is devoted to pre-war years.

162. O'Conner, Thomas H. THE DISUNITED STATES: THE ERA OF CIVIL WAR AND RECONSTRUCTION. New York: Dodd, Mead, 1972.

A brief military and political account of the war designed to supplement college texts. It does not quite achieve its purpose.

163. Paris, L.P.A. d'Orleans, Comte de. HISTORY OF THE CIVIL WAR IN IN AMERICA. 4 v. H. Coupee, editor. Philadelphia, 1875-1888.

An excellent study of the war through 1863 by a French nobleman who served on McClellan's staff. Describes military operations and analyzes organizational and logistical matters.

164. Parish, Peter J. THE AMERICAN CIVIL WAR. New York: Holmes and Meier, 1975.

Comparable to the work by Hansen but not as scholarly as McPherson, Parish presents another one-volume compendium of the war.

165. Pratt, Fletcher. ORDEAL BY FIRE. New York: Sloane Associates, 1948.

An informal, readable military history. It was reissued in paperback form in 1951 under the title A SHORT HISTORY OF THE CIVIL WAR.

166. Randall, James G. and David Donald. THE CIVIL WAR AND RECONSTRUCTION. Boston: Heath, 1969.

Originally published in 1937 by Randall, this work became the standard textbook on the Civil War. It was an excellent study for its day, but became outmoded with a newer generation of scholarship. Following Randall's death in 1953, David Donald revised the book in 1961 and again in 1969. It remains one of the best one volume texts.

167. Reeder, Russell P. THE STORY OF THE CIVIL WAR. New York: Duell, Sloan and Pearce, 1958.

Another military account that young readers should enjoy.

168. Rhodes, James F. HISTORY OF THE UNITED STATES FROM THE COMPROMISE OF 1850 ... TO 1877. 8 v. New York, 1893-1906. Reprint 1967.

The first comprehensive study of the Civil War era was a landmark in historical writing. However, Rhodes' focus was narrow as he emphasized principally the military and military matters. Nevins' eight volume history has replaced Rhodes, but the latter can still be read with profit. Rhodes argued that slavery was the central cause of the war, while Nevins broadened this to include the issue of race adjustment.

169. ———. HISTORY OF THE CIVIL WAR, 1861-1865. New York: Macmillan, 1917.

Volumes Three, Four, and Five of the above dealt with the war years. This one volume abridgement is drawn from those three volumes.

170. Robertson, James I. THE CIVIL WAR. Washington: United States Civil War Centennial Commission, 1963.

High school students and beginning readers on the war will find this a fascinating, easily read pamphlet.

171. Ropes, John C. and W. R. Livermore. THE STORY OF THE CIVIL WAR. 4 v. New York: Putnam, 1933.

Almost exclusively, this is a military history with the

emphasis on two of the war's turning points, Vicksburg and Gettysburg. The account does not go very much beyond those two campaigns.

172. Sandburg, Carl. STORM OVER THE LAND. New York: Harcourt, Brace, 1942.

This is a one-volume abridgment of Sandburg's four-volume THE WAR YEARS, which constituted the last part of the author's six-volume study of Lincoln. It is good, but suffers from the difficulties of any abridgment.

173. Steele, Matthew F. AMERICAN CAMPAIGNS. 2 v. Washington, D.C.: United States Infantry Association, 1922. Reprint 1953.

Although somewhat dated, this work is still valuable for its accounts of the campaigns of the war and its battle maps. It was reissued in 1953 by the United States Military Academy, Vincent J. Esposito, editor.

174. Stern, Philip V.D., editor. THE CIVIL WAR CHRISTMAS ALBUM. New York: Hawthorn, 1961.

Written primarily for popular consumption, the essays recount wartime holidays.

175. Street, James H. THE CIVIL WAR. New York: Dial Press, 1953.

Street subtitled his book, AN UNVARNISHED ACCOUNT OF THE LATE BUT STILL LIVELY HOSTILITIES. It is too hurriedly written and does not do justice to its theme.

176. Thomas, Emory M. THE AMERICAN WAR AND PEACE, 1860-1877. Englewood Cliffs, New Jersey: Prentice-Hall, 1973.

A brief, competent, entertaining account evidently written for the undergraduate student and casual reader. It is organized in outline fashion.

177. Thompson, Charles W. THE FIERY EPOCH, 1830-1877. Indianapolis: Bobbs-Merrill, 1931.

Thompson saw the rebellion as an attack on the nation itself, against a government that wished to uphold law and order against the threat of anarchy. This is not a very objective account.

178. Unger, Irwin, editor. ESSAYS ON THE CIVIL WAR AND RECONSTRUCTION. New York: Holt, Rinehart and Winston, 1970.

A useful book of readings.

179. Vineyard, Thomas E. BATTLES OF THE CIVIL WAR. Spencer, West Virginia: 1914.

A readable, but short military history.

180. Werner, Edgar A., compiler and editor. HISTORICAL SKETCH OF THE WAR OF THE REBELLION, FROM 1861 to 1865. Albany, New York: 1890.

A selective military history with good statistical tables.

181. Wheeler, Richard, editor. VOICES OF THE CIVIL WAR. New York: Crowell, 1976.

Narration and quotations of eyewitnesses are joined together to tell the story of the war. Includes maps, chronologies, and sketches by war artists.

182. Wood, Walter B., and J.E. Edmonds. A HISTORY OF THE CIVIL WAR IN THE UNITED STATES, 1861-1865. New York, 1905.

An excellent military account. It was reprinted in 1960.

183. Wood, William. CAPTAINS OF THE CIVIL WAR. New Haven: Yale University Press, 1921.

A brief account well suited for the beginning student.

184. ———. IN DEFENSE OF LIBERTY. New Haven: Yale University Press, 1928.

Another illustrated text that will appeal to the young or beginning student of the war.

185. Woodward, William E. YEARS OF MADNESS. New York: Putnam, 1951.

The author propounds the "needless war" theory strongly urged by revisionists.

* * * *

BRUCE CATTON

Because of the vast number of books and articles written by Bruce Catton, perhaps the most prolific and readable of all Civil War historians, his works are brought together in one place for the convenience of Catton "fans" everywhere. His unnumbered introductions to other peoples' volumes are not included here. The writings are grouped under three headings: [1] trilogies, [2] individual books, and [3] articles.

Trilogies

Army of the Potomac

186. MR. LINCOLN'S ARMY. Garden City, New York: Doubleday, 1951.

Catton's first Civil War book describes the Union army in the East from the outbreak of war through McClellan's dismissal in November, 1862. This exciting, readable narrative was a preview of the many fine books yet to come from the author's pen.

187. GLORY ROAD. Garden City, New York: Doubleday, 1952.

Volume Two in this series carries the story from Fredericksburg through Chancellorsville and Gettysburg.

188. A STILLNESS AT APPOMATTOX. Garden City, New York: Doubleday, 1953.

The third volume in three years completes the trilogy with an account of the remainder of the fighting in the East. As one reviewer wrote, "It is a dramatic narrative, capturing the sounds of battle and the emotions of the soldiers."

<u>The Centennial History of the Civil War</u>

189. THE COMING FURY. Garden City, New York: Doubleday, 1961.

In Volume One Catton dramatically describes the early months of the war. He deals with both the North and the South as he sets the stage for "the coming fury."

190. TERRIBLE SWIFT SWORD. Garden City, New York: Doubleday, 1963.

Volume Two covers the period from First Bull Run through McClellan's dismissal. The Union forces appeared on the verge of victory in the summer and fall of 1862, but through McClellan's failure the opportunity was lost. The vivid battle and personality descriptions are maintained at the same high level of the earlier volumes.

191. NEVER CALL RETREAT. Garden City, New York: Doubleday, 1965.

Volume Three surveys the last two and one-half years of war. The scholarship, comprehensiveness, and graceful style, characteristic of all of Catton's writings, mark this concluding work of the Centennial History.

<u>Grant</u>

The trilogy on General U.S. Grant was not all of Catton's own work. Lloyd Lewis brought out CAPTAIN SAM GRANT [see number 3844] in 1950, but died before he was able to publish a second volume. Catton was given access to Lewis' notes and wrote the other two books in the series. He sought to perpetuate Lewis' own thinking about Grant while writing the material in his own way.

192. GRANT MOVES SOUTH. Boston: Little, Brown, 1960.

Lewis' CAPTAIN SAM GRANT covered Grant's life up to the onset of the Civil War. This book continues the story from the time Grant took command of the 21st Illinois in June 1861, through the fall of Vicksburg two years later. An excellent, well-written work, in which the reader sees the development of a great military leader.

193. GRANT TAKES COMMAND. Boston: Little, Brown, 1969.

After taking a few years off to write the Centennial History, Catton got back to Grant and completed the trilogy with this work. It is another superb book, narrating Grant's progress from the siege of Vicksburg to the end of the war.

Individual Books

194. AMERICA GOES TO WAR. Middletown, Connecticut: Wesleyan University Press, 1958.

A series of carefully written, thought-provoking lectures by the master of the topic. Catton attempts to relate the Civil War to our lives today.

195. GETTYSBURG: THE FINAL FURY. Garden City, New York: Doubleday, 1974.

A detailed and richly personal account of the great battle, illustrated with maps and Brady photographs.

196. THIS HALLOWED GROUND. Garden City, New York: Doubleday, 1956.

In a brilliantly written narrative history, Catton presents the story of the Civil War as seen from the Union side. This is history at its best; it delights and entertains with its dramatic and skillful prose.

197. REFLECTIONS ON THE CIVIL WAR. John Leckley, editor. Garden City, New York: Doubleday, 1981.

Catton's final work, published posthumously. Based on hundreds of hours of taped commentary, it draws a poignant picture of the war experience.

198. U.S. GRANT AND THE AMERICAN MILITARY TRADITION. Boston: Little, Brown, 1954.

A good, concise biography of Grant, including a useful analysis of Grant's failure in the political realm.

199. TWO ROADS TO SUMTER. With William Catton. New York: McGraw-Hill, 1963.

A valuable study of Lincoln and Davis and the policies they pursued which led them to Fort Sumter and the outbreak of war.

Articles

200. "Asa Smith Leaves the War." AM HER, 22 [2] [1971]: 54-59, 103-105.

An incredible tale of the survival of a foot soldier in the 16th Massachusetts, who later became a successful doctor. He had been wounded at Glendale [Frayser's Farm] on June 30, 1862, during the Seven Days' Battle.

201. "Billy Yank and the Army of the Potomac." MIL AFF, 18 [1954]: 169-176.

A good article on the life of the common soldier in the Army of the Potomac.

202. "Crisis at Antietam." AM HER, 9 [5] [1958]: 54-57, 93-96.

An account of the battle and its consequences, with a note on the favorable public response to the issuing of the Preliminary Emancipation Proclamation.

203. "The Day the Civil War Ended: Gettysburg, Fifty Years After." AM HER, 29 [4] [1978]: 56-61.

A look back at the reenactment of Pickett's Charge by survivors of the original cast, at the fiftieth reunion of the Battle of Gettysburg in July 1913.

204. "Glory Road Began in the West." CWH, 6 [1960]: 229-237.

A tribute to the part played by troops in the western theater in determining the outcome of the war.

205. "Grant and the Politicians." AM HER, 19 [6] [1968]: 32-35, 81-87.

Catton analyzes Grant's political acumen in the summer of 1864, when Union fortunes were sagging and Lincoln's reelection prospects waning. He recognized that military success would lead to political success and was instrumental in bringing about the victories of Sheridan in the Shenandoah Valley that fall.

206. "Grant Writes Home." AM HER, 24 [6] [1973]: 16-19, 92-93.

Reprints of some of Grant's letters to his wife during the war.

207. "Hayfoot, Strawfoot!" AM HER, 8 [3] [1957]: 30-37.

Author comments on the training and discipline of the troops. The weapons, the food, the foraging, and the soldiers' attitude toward slavery are all surveyed.

208. "Lincoln's Difficult Decisions." CWH, 2 [1956]: 5-12.

Based on a speech delivered at the 125th anniversary of Lincoln's arrival in New Salem, Illinois, Catton traces Lincoln's most important decisions from Fort Sumter to the Emancipation Proclamation.

209. "Lincoln's Mastery in the Use of Volunteer Soldiers and Political Generals." LIN HER, 57 [1955]: 3-11.

210. "On Writing About the Civil War." AM HER, 17 [3] [1966]: 104-105.

The author reviews his own experience in writing about the Civil War and offers his opinion as to the meaning of the war for modern America.

211. "Prison Camps of the Civil War." AM HER, 10 [5] [1959]: 4-13, 96-97.

A review of the life of prisoners in both Union and Confederate prison camps.

212. "Sheridan at Five Forks." JSH, 21 [1955]: 305-315.

In concluding that General Gouverneur Warren was unjustly dismissed by Sheridan after Five Forks, author urges that on a number of occasions the tough, inflexible demands of a Sheridan might have served the Union well and shortened the war.

213. "Union Discipline and Leadership in the Civil War." MARINE CORPS GAZETTE, 40 [1956]: 18-25.

A discussion of the "loose-jointed, informal, almost slapdash" drill and discipline system which prevailed during the war. Nevertheless, it proved effective.

214. "U.S. Grant: Man of Letters." AM HER, 19 [4] [1968]: 97-100.

Grant was an able writer and craftsman, in the author's view, and proof of this was most apparent in the last days of his life as he completed his memoirs. Rejecting the demands of Adam Badeau for more money to edit the work, Grant said flatly that he would permit no book bearing his imprint to go before the public for which he was not fully responsible in the literary sense.

* * * *

TIME-LIFE SERIES

215. THE CIVIL WAR.

THE CIVIL WAR is a multi-volume, original set of over-sized, leather bound books published by Time-Life Books. As of November 1, 1985, 17 volumes were in print and nine more were in the planning stage. No authors are identified for any of the works.

216. COLLECTOR'S LIBRARY OF THE CIVIL WAR.

The COLLECTOR'S LIBRARY is a reprint series of 30 important Civil War volumes published by Time-Life Books in the late 1970s and early 1980s. Exact reproductions of the originals, the books are bound in dark blue leather with gilt stamping. The subject matter is evenly divided between the North and the South.

* * * *

C. CAUSATION, HISTORIOGRAPHY, INTERPRETATION

217. Aptheker, Herbert. THE AMERICAN CIVIL WAR. New York: International Publishers, 1961.

A very brief survey of the Civil War with "strong Marxist overtones."

218. Barney, William L. FLAWED VICTORY: A NEW PERSPECTIVE ON THE CIVIL WAR. New York: Praeger, 1975. Reprint 1980.

Concentrating on the social aspects of the war, this volume presents the idea that a new re-interpretation of the powers of the federal government was necessary to allow for mobilization as well as a reorganization of the American economy. The social implications of this as well as the involvement of blacks is considered.

219. Beale, Howard K. "What Historians Have Said About the Causes of the Civil War." In THEORY AND PRACTICE IN HISTORICAL STUDY: A REPORT OF THE COMMITTEE ON HISTORIOGRAPHY. New York: Social Science Research Council, 1946. Pages 55-102.

The first effort to examine and bring together all of the different theories on causation, Beale's monograph was a landmark in Civil War historiography. An excellent text and a valuable in-depth study of all the works dealing with the causes of the war.

220. Beard, Charles A. and Mary R. Beard. "The Clash of Rival Economies." In THE RISE OF AMERICAN CIVILIZATION. Volume 2. New York: Macmillan, 1927. Pages 3-10.

In one of the most famous challenges to the traditional interpretation [Rhodes] that slavery was the main cause of the war, the Beards argue that the conflict was brought about by the emerging differences in economic systems: the agrarian South versus the industrial North. Slavery is dismissed as a cause of the war.

221. Benson, Lee and Cushing Strout. "Causation and the American Civil War: Two Appraisals." HISTORY AND THEORY, 1 [1960/1961]: 163-185.

Authors consider various problems in dealing with Civil War causation and suggest several methodological tools which might be used to meet the problems.

222. Bonner, Thomas N. "Civil War Historians and the 'Needless War' Doctrine." J HIST IDEAS, 17 [1956]: 193-216.

A discussion of how historians who support this theory--that the war could have been avoided--have affected historiography and how their weaknesses are being exposed.

223. Britton, Bruce. "The Civil War Need Not Have Taken Place." CWTI, 3 [10] [1965]: 12-15.

It is contended that the war was the result of the failure to make use of the democratic machinery.

224. Brogan, Denis. "The Debate on the American Civil War." PROC BRIT ACAD, 49 [1963]: 203-232.

Because of its cost and consequences, the Civil War may have been the central event of the American experience, in the view of this eminent British historian.

225. ———. "A Fresh Appraisal of the Civil War." In author's AMERICAN ASPECTS. New York: Harper and Row, 1964. Pages 22-51.

A fair and sympathetic treatment of both sides from the perspective of one who thoroughly understands American history.

226. Campbell, A.E. "An Excess of Isolation: Isolation and the American Civil War." JSH, 29 [1963]: 161-174.

Disputing David Donald's contention that "An excess of democracy" explains the coming of the Civil War, the author proposes as an alternative that it was "an excess of isolationism" which allowed an unimportant social discourse to grow into a civil war.

227. Churchill, Winston. "If Lee Had Not Won the Battle of Gettysburg." WIS MAG HIS, 44 [1960/1961]: 243-251.

A strange exercise in fantasy, wherein the celebrated British statesman, after concluding that Lee had won at Gettysburg, traces what might have been the course of western history had Lee not won. This is a reprint of a 1930 Scribners' article.

228. Clebsch, William A. "Christian Interpretations of the American Civil War." CH HIS, 30 [1961]: 212-222.

A study of a neglected area of Civil War historiography, in which theories on the role of divine intervention in bringing about the war are discussed.

229. Collins, Bruce. THE ORIGINS OF AMERICA'S CIVIL WAR. New York: Holmes and Meier, 1984.

Author summarizes the differences between the North and South, abolitionism, proslavery sentiments, and the reasons for the rise of the Republican party.

230. Commager, Henry S., editor. THE DEFEAT OF THE CONFEDERACY. Malabar, Florida: Krieger, 1984.

Originally published in the "Anvil" series in 1964, this is a collection of documents and readings which reflect the different theories on why the North won the war.

231. Connelly, T.L. "The Cycle of Military and Economical Interest: A Theory of Confederate Defeat." ALA HIS Q, 30 [1968]: 111-125.

Connelly suggests that a poor economic policy doomed the Confederates. By withholding cotton from the market, the South caused a shortage of credit for themselves.

232. Craven, Avery. AN HISTORIAN AND THE CIVIL WAR. Chicago: University of Chicago Press, 1964.

A major revisionist scholar, Craven has brought together 14 of his most important essays written between 1928 and 1964. His views have changed somewhat over the years as he grapples honestly with the problem of Civil War causation.

233. ———. THE CIVIL WAR IN THE MAKING. 1815-1860. Baton Rouge: Louisiana State University Press, 1959.

This slim volume reflects Craven's thinking on the forces which led to war, as presented in the Walter L. Fleming Lectures at Louisiana State University. Earlier he had spoken of a "repressible conflict." Here he leans more toward the "inevitability" position.

234. ———. THE COMING OF THE CIVIL WAR. Chicago: University of Chicago Press, 1957.

When this volume first appeared in 1942 it provoked a storm of controversy because of its advocacy of the "needless war" doctrine. In the preface to the new edition, Craven remarks that he had "no intention of saying [in 1942] that the war was a 'needless war'." Nor, he adds, did he have any "desire to defend slavery." In this revision he concedes that the war may have been inevitable and that slavery played a more central role in bringing it about.

235. ———. "The 1840's and the Democratic Process." JSH, 16 [1950]: 161-176.

An adherent of the "repressible conflict" school revisionists, Craven argues that it was the breakdown of democratic processes which prevented the Civil War generation from resolving problems which they should have resolved.

236. Crowe, Charles, editor. THE AGE OF CIVIL WAR AND RECONSTRUCTION, 1830-1900: A BOOK OF INTERPRETIVE ESSAYS. Homewood, Illinois: Dorsey Press, 1966.

A solid collection of 42 essays which present differing views on ten subjects, emphasizing the most recent scholarship since

1960. Each subject is accompanied by an introductory note and a list of readings. The Civil War years do not receive their expected stress, while the issue of race is a major theme in most of the articles.

237. Cunliffe, Marcus. "The Causes of the American Civil War." HIS TOD, 3 [1953]: 753-761.

After considering a number of revisionist theories on Civil War causation, it is argued that Negro slavery was the fundamental reason for the conflict.

238. ———. "Recent Writing on the American Civil War." HISTORY, 50 [1965]: 26-35.

A review of the voluminous recent Civil War scholarship--a little bit of which is good, but the great proportion of which is mediocre.

239. Curry, Richard O. "The Civil War and Reconstruction, 1861-1877: A Critical Overview of Recent Trends and Interpretations." CWH, 20 [1974]: 215-238.

Author deals with party rivalries in the North, Lincoln as a war leader, and aspects of the revisionist evaluation of Reconstruction.

240. Degler, Carl N. "One Among Many." VA Q R, 39 [1963]: 289-306.

A discussion of the similarities and parallels between the Civil War and several nationalist uprisings elsewhere, 1845-1870, thus putting the war in a world perspective.

241. De Voto, Bernard. "The Easy Chair." HARP MAG, [February 1946]: 123-126.

An attack on the revisionists for their failure to understand the moral crisis generated by slavery. Slavery would not have "just ended," as revisionists argue; rather, it was the rock upon which the Union was rent.

242. Donald, David H. "American Historians and the Causes of the Civil War." S ATL Q, 59 [1960]: 351-355.

A brief note trying to explain why so little had been written on the Civil War since 1950.

243. ———. "An Excess of Democracy: The American Civil War and the Social Process." CEN R, 5 [1961]: 21-39.

Originally presented as a lecture at Oxford University the year before, Donald asserts that the war might have been the result of too much freedom in our democratic society.

244. ———, editor. WHY THE NORTH WON THE CIVIL WAR. Baton Rouge: Louisiana State University Press, 1960.

An outgrowth of a conference held at Gettysburg College on the eve of the Civil War Centennial, the book contains the thinking of Richard Current, T. Harry Williams, Norman A. Graebner, David M. Potter, and the editor as they debate the economic, military, diplomatic, social, and political reasons for the South's failure. Excellent examples of what Donald calls "the complexity of historical causation and the dangers of oversimplification."

245. Dray, William. "Some Causal Accounts of the American Civil War." DAEDALUS, 91 [1962]: 578-598.

A consideration of the problem of Civil War causation by an examination of the "conspiracy," "conflict," and "revisionist" theories. A comment on the article is supplied by Newton Garver, pages 592-598.

246. Dunning, William A. ESSAYS ON THE CIVIL WAR AND RECONSTRUCTION AND RELATED TOPICS. New York, 1898.

A collection of essays dealing with constitutional problems by a distinguished Columbia University professor. The essays originally appeared in different journals.

247. Eisenschiml, Otto. THE HIDDEN FACE OF THE CIVIL WAR. Indianapolis: Bobbs-Merrill, 1961.

A collection of a number of unconventional opinions and interpretations on the Civil War, including an analysis of the military leadership North and South. The latter is based on a rating system, the results of which are interesting, to say the least.

248. ———. O.E.: HISTORIAN WITHOUT AN ARMCHAIR. Indianapolis: Bobbs-Merrill, 1963.

An entertaining, retrospective memoir of a generation's worth of Civil War research. The author includes some new material pertaining to his study of Lincoln's assassination.

249. ——— and E.B. Long. AS LUCK WOULD HAVE IT: CHANCE AND COINCIDENCE IN THE CIVIL WAR. Indianapolis: Bobbs-Merrill, 1948.

An entertaining volume, not to be taken too seriously, in which the authors discuss some of the major events which were the result of "accidents."

250. Fischer, LeRoy H. "Another Look at the Civil War." LIN HER 67 [1956]: 174-183.

Argues that American history reached a turning point with the war.

251. Foner, Eric. "The Causes of the American Civil War: Recent Interpretations and New Directions." CWH, 20 [1974]: 197-214.

Despite a flood of writings on abolitionism and slavery in the last 15 years, historians are no more agreed on what caused the Civil War than they were before 1960.

252. ———. POLITICS AND IDEOLOGY IN THE AGE OF THE CIVIL WAR. New York: Oxford University Press, 1981.

The causes and consequences of the Civil War are covered in this collection of essays. The author hopes for "a more cohesive interpretation of the Civil War era."

253. Franklin, John H. "A Century of Civil War Observance." JNH, 47 [1962]: 97-107.

The author laments the vast outpouring of funds and the patriotic speeches glorifying the Civil War during the Centennial observance, when in fact, the war was a failure, if measured by the quality of freedom granted the former slaves.

254. Froehling, William F. "The Editorial Revolution, Virginia, and the Coming of the Civil War: A Review Essay." CWH, 16 [1970]: 64-72.

An analysis of the four-volume edition of the Virginia Secession Convention proceedings of 1861, which sheds new light on the question of Civil War causation.

255. Gara, Larry. "Slavery and the Slave Power: A Crucial Distinction." CWH, 15 [1969]: 5-18.

Author points out the important distinction between moral objections to slavery and political objections to the "slave power." Understanding this distinction is essential to an analysis of Civil War causation.

256. Garfinkle, Norton, editor. LINCOLN AND THE COMING OF THE CIVIL WAR. Boston: Heath, 1959.

A series of 13 essays are included in this "problems book," dealing with Lincoln's role during the secession crisis. Several of the selections are from the speeches of Lincoln and Stephen A. Douglas, while the balance of the book contains interpretations by leading historians, who explain why, in their opinion, war broke out.

257. Geyl, Pieter. "The American Civil War and the Problem of Inevitability." NEQ, 24 [1951]: 147-168.

The Dutch historian takes to task supporters of the economic and "needless war" theories for oversimplifying the critical issue facing the Civil War generation and exercising an easy "20-20 hindsight."

258. Greene, Marc. "The War Between the States." QUAR R, 301 [1963]: 89-101.

Reflections upon the causes and military conduct of the Civil War, which was the bitterest in human history, but which also "forged the bonds that welded the American nation into one unbreakable unit."

259. Gunderson, Gerald, "The Origin of the American Civil War." J ECON HIS, 34 [1974]: 915-950.

Based on recent economic studies, author concludes that by 1860 slavery represented such a large and profitable institution for southerners that the only way anti-slavery interests could end it was by war. It was not a "blundering generation," but the economic circumstances of the time over which politicians had no control, that brought on war.

260. Halsey, Ashley. WHO FIRED THE FIRST SHOT? AND OTHER UNTOLD STORIES OF THE CIVIL WAR. New York: Hawthorn Books, 1963.

A collection of previously untold stories which reflect the emotional atmosphere of the war years.

261. Johnson, Ludwell H. "Civil War Military History: A Few Revisions in Need of Revising." CWH, 17 [1971]: 115-130.

Recent revisionist writings on Civil War military history reveal that the four traditional weaknesses of the Confederate war effort have been exaggerated, as have been the four traditional strengths of the Union war effort.

262. Lindsey, David. LINCOLN/DAVIS: THE HOUSE DIVIDED. Cleveland: Howard Allen, 1960.

An excellent "problems" book, in which the author sets the stage and then allows the presidents to express their own views on such issues as slavery, the tariff, individual liberties, Reconstruction, and other matters.

263. Lodgson, Joseph A. "The Civil War--Russian Version II: The Soviet Historians." CWH, 8 [1962]: 365-372.

A discussion of Russian historians and their Marxist interpretations of the Civil War.

264. Luvaas, Jay. "G.F.R. Henderson and the American Civil War." MIL AFF, 20 [1956]: 139-153.

An analysis of the writings of the British military historian Henderson, who intended to draw on the Civil War to illustrate principles of war for a British audience. He did not quite succeed because of an undue emphasis on the eastern theater.

265. Marx, Karl and Friedrich Engels. THE CIVIL WAR IN THE UNITED STATES. Richard Enmale, editor. London: Lawrence and Wiehart, 1938.

The volume includes the correspondence between Marx and Engels pertaining to the Civil War.

266. McWhiney, Grady. "Who Whipped Whom? Confederate Defeat Re-Examined." CWH, 11 [1965]: 5-26.

Author observes that the South lost the war because, under pressure from many civilian and political leaders, it abandoned a sound defensive strategy and adopted a debilitating offensive strategy.

267. Moffat, Charles H. "Conflicting Interpretations as to the Causes of the Civil War." W VA HIS, 23 [1961]: 5-14.

A survey of a number of differing interpretations on Civil War causation. Among the historians whose ideas are examined are the Beards, Schlesinger, Randall, Craven, Nevins, Nichols, and Owsley.

268. Nevins, Allan. "A Major Result of the Civil War." CWH, 5 [1959]: 237-250.

A discussion of the effects of the war on the character of the American people. The war transformed the United States into a well-organized nation brimming with a new spirit of nationalism.

269. ———. THE STATESMANSHIP OF THE CIVIL WAR. New York: Macmillan, 1953.

Based on the Page-Barbour Lectures delivered at the University of Virginia in 1951, the author has produced in brief compass an excellent study of leadership. In comparing Lincoln with Davis, the northern president emerges triumphant, being "more than a statesman."

270. Nichols, Roy F. "A Hundred Years Later: Perspectives on the Civil War." JSH, 33 [1967]: 153-162.

Drawn from a speech delivered before the Southern Historical Association in 1966, Nichols offers six perspectives which he believes came out of the many round-tables, meetings, and conferences held during the Centennial celebration.

271. ———. "The Operation of American Democracy, 1861-1865: Some Questions." JSH, 25 [1959]: 31-52.

The author raises several questions about the functioning of the democratic system, North and South, during the war years. He feels that these questions have not as yet been properly addressed and suggests tentative answers as the basis for further research on the subject.

272. ———. "The Problem of Civil War Historiography." A PHIL SOC PROC, 106 [1962]: 36-40.

An analysis of the causes and results of the Civil War based on a paper read at a "Symposium on European Perspectives on the American Civil War," April 21, 1961.

273. Owsley, Frank L. "The Fundamental Cause of the Civil War: Egocentric Sectionalism." JSH, 7 [1941]: 3-18.

Owsley blames the "egocentric sectionalism" of the plutocratic North for causing the war by trying to impose its will on the South. He is very hard on abolitionists.

274. Padover, Saul K., editor. KARL MARX ON AMERICA AND THE CIVIL WAR. New York: McGraw-Hill, 1972.

Includes much of his correspondence with various economists and journalists throughout Europe. Covers many subjects and has the text of two articles which Marx wrote for the New York TRIBUNE.

275. Paludan, Phillip S. "The American Civil War Considered as a Crisis in Law and Order." AHR, 77 [1972]: 1013-1034.

The author's thesis is that secession and the firing on Fort Sumter led to widespread northern involvement because supporters of the Union wished to uphold law and order against anarchy.

276. ———. "The American Civil War: Triumph Through Tragedy." CWH, 20 [1974]: 239-250.

A criticism of John S. Rosenberg's 1969 essay "Toward a New Civil War Revisionism," which argued that from the perspective of the 1960s, the Civil War was a mistake. Paludan insists that the war was definitely worth the cost and objects to the "presentist" approach to historical data.

277. Parrish, William E. THE CIVIL WAR: A SECOND AMERICAN REVOLUTION. Malabar, Florida: Krieger, 1978.

Originally published in 1970, this book of readings contains varying viewpoints on the question, "Did the Civil War bring about a second American revolution?"

278. Potter, David M. "The Background of the Civil War." In INTERPRETING AND TEACHING AMERICAN HISTORY. William H. Cartwright and Richard Watson, Jr., editors. Washington, D.C.: National Council for the Social Studies, 1961. Pages 87-119.

A major American historian examines the historiography of Civil War causation.

279. ———. THE SOUTH AND THE SECTIONAL CONFLICT. Baton Rouge: Louisiana State University Press, 1968.

A collection of ten very thoughtful and provocative essays

published over a thirty year period by the author. They are grouped in three categories, John Brown and the problem of black leadership, southernism, and the Civil War. Some of the earlier articles have been revised for this edition.

280. Prescott, Brainard E. "The Meaning of Appomattox." NIAG FRON, 9 [1962]: 3-6.

In a speech by a retired army general at Appomattox on April 8, 1962, Lee's surrender is recounted.

281. Pressly, Thomas J. AMERICANS INTERPRET THEIR CIVIL WAR. Princeton: Princeton University Press, 1954. Reprint 1962.

Although there has been some controversy over the author's evaluations of various historians, this volume is a classic in its survey of interpretive writings on the Civil War. An absolute must for anyone studying the historiography of the war.

282. "Raminov." "American Civil War." US INF J, 89 [2959]: 177-183.

A broad general survey of the causes of the Civil War, in which a sympathy for the "Lost Cause" is apparent.

283. Ramsdell, Charles W. "The Changing Interpretation of the Civil War." JSH, 3 [1937]: 3-27.

In his 1936 presidential address before the Southern Historical Association, Charles Ramsdell provides one of the earliest surveys of interpretative writings on Civil War causation. He views with favor the more recent "revisionist" works.

284. Randall, James G. "The Blundering Generation." MVHR, 27 [1940]: 3-28.

Perhaps the most celebrated revisionist attack on the slavery-causation theory. Randall argues that the war was repressible and had it not been for numerous avoidable errors committed by people in power it would have been repressed.

285. ———. The Civil War Re-studied." JSH, 6 [1940]: 439-457.

After reviewing some of the recent revisionist writings which challenge "old myths," the author points out areas in which much more research needs to be done.

286. Rawley, James A. LINCOLN AND CIVIL WAR POLITICS. Malabar, Florida: Krieger, 1977.

Originally published in 1969, this is a slim, but useful volume of articles reflecting different and controversial interpretations of Lincoln's leadership.

287. ———. TURNING POINT OF THE CIVIL WAR. Lincoln, Nebraska: University of Nebraska Press, 1966.

A nice synthesis of secondary materials focusing on seven pivotal situations during the war: Kentucky in 1861, the TRENT affair, Antietam, emancipation, Gettysburg, Vicksburg, and the 1864 election.

288. Rhodes, James F. LECTURES ON THE AMERICAN CIVIL WAR. New York, 1913.

Rhodes set the pattern for a generation of historians in insisting that slavery was the cause of the war. His thinking appeared first in his multi-volume history and is restated in these lectures.

289. Rosenberg, John S. "The American Civil War and the Problem of 'Presentism': A Reply to Phillip S. Paludan." CWH, 21 [1975]: 242-253.

In reply to Paludan's criticism of his "New Civil War Revisionism" theory [number 276], author still argues that the Civil War was a mistake. While the war generation could not perhaps stop the drift toward war, it should not be praised for what the war did--preserve the Union and free the slaves.

290. ———. Towards a New Civil War Revisionism." AS, 38 [1968/1969]: 250-272.

Rosenberg argues that from the present day vantage point, in contrast to orthodox opinion, the loss of life and the devastation caused by the war was too big a price to pay for the results achieved, preservation of the Union and termination of slavery. This was the essay which induced Pauldan's rebuttal, which in turn prompted Roseberg's rebuttal to Paludan's rebuttal.

291. Rozwenc, Edwin C., editor. THE CAUSES OF THE AMERICAN CIVIL WAR. Boston: Heath, 1961.

A much broader problems book than the following entry, containing 23 essays, divided into six categories. The categories are grouped into chronological time periods, reflecting changing interpretations.

292. ———. SLAVERY AS A CAUSE OF THE CIVIL WAR. Boston: Heath, 1949.

A good early problems book for students. It includes eight important essays which interpret, from different perspectives, the question of slavery as a cause of the war.

293. Runkle, Gerald. "Karl Marx and the American Civil War." COMP STUDIES SOC HIS, 6 [1963]: 117-141.

Both Marx and Engels agreed that the Civil War was a revolt by northern capitalists against slaveholding aristocrats.

294. Schlesinger, Arthur M., Jr. "The Causes of the Civil War: A Note on Historical Sentimentalism." PART R, 16 [1949]: 969-981.

One of the sharpest attacks on revisionists, wherein the author charges the latter with a "sentimental optimism" in thinking that a moral issue as profound as slavery could have been resolved by means other than force.

295. Silbey, Joel H. "The Civil War Synthesis in American Political History." CWH, 10 [1964]: 130-140.

Using recent revisionist studies, the author challenges the popular view that sectional strife was the major political factor leading to the Civil War. The theories upon which the "sectional strife" idea is founded turn out to be highly questionable.

296. Stampp, Kenneth M., editor. THE CAUSES OF THE AMERICAN CIVIL WAR. Englewood Cliffs, New Jersey: Prentice-Hall, 1959.

A valuable collection of 91 essays from both primary and secondary sources. These essays are divided into seven broad categories of "causes" of the war. Stampp observes that the "historians will never know objectively ... what caused the war."

297. Stoflet, Ada M., translator and editor. "Russian Version of the American Civil War." CWH, 8 [1962]: 357-364.

The Soviet historians see the war as a political and economic struggle, slavery versus free labor. This is the first of a two part series. See Joseph A. Lodgson [number 263] for part two.

298. Swierenga, Robert P. BEYOND THE CIVIL WAR SYSTHESIS: POLITICAL ESSAYS OF THE CIVIL WAR. Westport, Connecticut: Greenwood, 1975.

A collection of 20 articles which first appeared in CIVIL WAR HISTORY, 1964-1975, which is divided into five topics: politics, historiography, roll call votes in Congress, "the Ethno-religious Dimension," and anti-slavery ideology.

299. Trefousse, Hans L., editor. THE CAUSES OF THE CIVIL WAR: INSTITUTIONAL FAILURE OR HUMAN BLUNDER. Malabar, Florida: Krieger, 1982.

A readings book which was first published in 1971. The causes of the war are examined from different perspectives, both contemporary and modern.

300. Vandiver, Frank E. "The Civil War as an Institutionalizing Force." In ESSAYS ON THE AMERICAN CIVIL WAR. Frank E. Vandiver, editor. Austin: University of Texas Press, 1968. Pages 73-87.

Out of the crucible of war came new techniques of governmental administration and business management, the emergence of the city, the expansion of the Industrial Revolution, and a new nation "tested and toughened for the challenge of world leadership."

301. Warren, Robert P. THE LEGACY OF THE CIVIL WAR: MEDITATIONS ON THE CENTENNIAL. New York: Random House, 1961.

This thought-provoking volume presents the author's opinions on how the Civil War shaped America. Warren also expresses the hope that the lessons learned from this traumatic experience will help the country to prepare for the future.

302. Waters, William R. "The Economic Basis of the Civil War: A Reappraisal." TOPIC, 2 [1961]: 30-39.

Discusses the unfavorable balance of payments in the South, especially with regard to the Northeast, as a factor of causation.

303. Whitridge, Arnold. NO COMPROMISE! THE STORY OF THE FANATICS WHO PAVED THE WAY TO THE CIVIL WAR. New York: Farrar, Straus, and Cudahy, 1960.

Drawing on secondary accounts, the author blames both sides for causing the war and expresses the opinion that too much freedom of speech in a democratic society can be dangerous.

304. Wilson, Major L. "The Repressible Conflict: Seward's Concept of Progress and the Free Soil Movement." JSH, 37 [1971]: 533-574.

The article examines Seward's approach to slavery in the years prior to the war. Author argues that Seward felt the war was avoidable because slavery was doomed anyway.

305. Woodward, C. Vann. "Reflections on a Centennial: The American Civil War." THE YALE REVIEW, 50 [1961]: 481-490.

Drawing on Robert Penn Warren's recent essay THE LEGACY OF THE CIVIL WAR, the author speculates on the deeper meaning of the war on the eve of the Centennial.

II

GOVERNMENT

A. 1860-1861

By Eric Cardinal

306. Abbot, Martin. "The First Shot at Fort Sumter." CWH, 3 [1957]: 41-45.

The claim that Edmund Ruffin fired the first shot at Fort Sumter is refuted.

307. Adams, Henry. "The Great Secession Winter of 1860-1861." MASS HIS SOC PROC, 43 [1910]: 660-687.

A still classic account by a literate, urbane, and reliable eyewitness.

308. Auchampaugh, Philip G. JAMES BUCHANAN AND HIS CABINET ON THE EVE OF SECESSION. Lancaster, Pennsylvania: n.p., 1926.

A thorough look at Buchanan and the machinations within his cabinet in 1860-1861. The author is sympathetic to the much maligned president.

309. Baringer, William E. "Campaign Techniques in Illinois in 1860." ILL ST HIS SOC TRAN, [1932]: 202-281.

A very thorough account of the campaign in the home state of both Lincoln and Douglas.

310. ———. A HOUSE DIVIDING: LINCOLN AS PRESIDENT ELECT. Springfield, Illinois: Abraham Lincoln Association, 1945.

A lively account of Lincoln as president-elect, with special focus on his role during the interregnum.

311. Bearss, Edwin C. "The Seizure of the Forts and Public Property in Louisiana." LA HIS, 2 [1961]: 401-409.

Following the secession of Louisiana from the Union in January 1861, the state authorities seized all federal installations and property within the state boundaries.

312. Bonner, Thomas N. "Horace Greeley and the Secession Movement." MVHR, 38 [1951]: 425-444.

The crux of Greeley's secession policy was a willingness to accept a peaceable division of the Union. A United States based on order, stability, and control of the West could flourish without the South.

313. Boritt, Gabor S. "Was Lincoln a Vulnerable Candidate in 1860?" CWH, 27 [1981]: 32-48.

A discussion of ways in which "Honest Abe" Lincoln might have been a more vulnerable candidate had his honesty been successfully impugned in a good government campaign.

314. Brown, George W. BALTIMORE AND THE NINETEENTH OF APRIL 1861: A STUDY OF THE WAR. Baltimore, 1887.

A documented, defensive account of the Baltimore riot written by the mayor of the city.

315. Buchanan, James. MR. BUCHANAN'S ADMINISTRATION ON THE EVE OF THE REBELLION. New York, 1866.

The "lame-duck" president defends his policies during the winter of secession.

316. Campbell, Mary E.R. THE ATTITUDE OF TENNESSEANS TOWARD THE UNION, 1847-1861. New York: Vantage, 1961.

During the 14 years before the war Tennesseans were willing to accept any compromise which would insure preservation of the Union and guarantee their "rights." Following the secession of the states of the Deep South, public opinion gradually swung over to support of secession by a two-to-one margin.

317. Cardinal, Eric J. "The Ohio Democracy and the Crisis of Dis-Union, 1860-1861." OHIO HIS, 86 [1977]: 19-40.

A discussion of Unionism and party revival as themes during the secession crisis and the early weeks of the war.

318. Castel, Albert. "Fort Sumter: 1861." CWTI, 15 [6] [1976]: 3-50.

An excellent issue of CIVIL WAR TIMES ILLUSTRATED, in which the entire contents are devoted to the Sumter crisis. The author provides a short history of the establishment of the fort and discusses personnel, battles, and strategy.

319. Chittenden, Lucius E. A REPORT OF THE DEBATES AND PROCEEDINGS IN THE SECRET SESSION OF THE CONFERENCE CONVENTION, FOR PROPOSING AMENDMENTS TO THE CONSTITUTION OF THE UNITED STATES.... New York, 1864.

A full report of the proceedings of the late, but doomed Washington "peace convention," held in February 1861.

320. Clark, Charles B. "Baltimore and the Attack on the Sixth Massachusetts Regiment, April 19, 1861." MD HIS MAG, 56 [1961]: 39-71.

An account of the assault on the Sixth Massachusetts as it passed through Baltimore and its aftermath. For about ten days the city and state vacillated between Union and secession, but finally loyal interests triumphed.

321. Cole, Arthur C. "Lincoln's Election an Immediate Menace to Slavery in the States?" AHR, 36 [1931]: 740-767.

Concludes that Lincoln's election was not such a menace.

322. Crawford, Samuel W. THE GENESIS OF THE CIVIL WAR: THE STORY OF SUMTER, 1860-1861. New York, 1887.

An old but still useful study of the fort's history until it surrendered. The author was a federal worker at the site. See also Crawford's HISTORY OF THE FALL OF FORT SUMTER. New York, 1898.

323. Crofts, Daniel W. "A Reluctant Unionist: John A. Gilmer and Lincoln's Cabinet." CWH, 24 [1978]: 225-249.

Although dealing primarily with Gilmer, a North Carolinian, the article details the machinations associated with Lincoln's cabinet-making process during the winter of secession.

324. ———. "The Union Party of 1861 and the Secession Crisis." PERS A HIS, 11 [1977/1978]: 325-376.

Members of the Constitutional Union party did not want to secede, a view shared by most residents of the Upper South. It is suggested that had Lincoln not forced their hand by his decision to reprovision Sumter, war might have been averted.

325. Crook, D.P. "Portents of War: English Opinion on Secession." J AM STUD, 4 [1971]: 163-179.

A useful survey of British opinion during the secession crisis. The heterogeneity of British interests made the English response exceedingly complex.

326. Cuthbert, Norma B., editor. LINCOLN AND THE BALTIMORE PLOT, 1861: FROM PINKERTON RECORDS AND RELATED PAPERS. San Marino, California: Huntington Library, 1949.

A useful documentary work which includes all the evidence of importance relating to the alleged plot to assassinate Lincoln on his way through Baltimore in February, 1861.

327. Curl, Donald W. "The Baltimore Convention of the Constitutional Union Party." MD HIS MAG, 67 [1972]: 254-277.

The Constitutional Union party needed strong and vigorous leaders as it prepared for the 1860 presidential campaign. But the choice of John Bell to head the ticket was a poor one, even though he was the unanimous choice of the party.

328. Current, Richard N. LINCOLN AND THE FIRST SHOT. Philadelphia: Lippincott, 1963.

An excellent discussion of the two major theories on the chief responsibility for the firing on Fort Sumter. Charles Ramsdell argues that Lincoln provoked the firing, while James Randall and David Potter deny this. Current occupies a middle position.

329. Daniels, George H. "The Immigrant Vote in the 1860 Election." MID AM, 44 [1962]: 146-162.

Iowa German voters went Democratic because they perceived the Republicans as both prohibitionists and nativists.

330. Dibble, Ernest F. "War Averters: Seward, Mallory and Fort Pickens." FLA HIS Q, 49 [1971]: 232-244.

The efforts of Secretary of State William Seward to bring about a peaceful resolution of the Sumter crisis are the focus of this article.

331. DiNunzio, Mario R. "Secession Winter: Lyman Trumbull and the Crisis of Congress." CAP STUD, 1 [1972]: 29-39.

A study of the problems confronting Congress during the winter of secession, focusing on the actions of this important senator from Illinois.

332. Dodd, William E. "The Fight For the Northwest, 1860." AHR, 16 [1911]: 774-788.

A dated, but still useful account of the 1860 campaign. Lincoln's popular margin over Douglas in the region was slight. Dodd attributes it to foreign-born voters whom, he believes, voted overwhelmingly Republican.

333. Doubleday, Abner. REMINISCENCES OF FORTS SUMTER AND MOULTRIE IN 1860-1861. New York, 1876.

A valuable account of events at both Moultrie and Sumter by a captain of artillery in the 60-man federal force. Incidentally, Doubleday did not invent baseball.

334. Dumond, Dwight. THE SECESSION MOVEMENT, 1860-1861. New York: Macmillan, 1931.

Although dealing primarily with the secession movement itself [and thus focusing largely on the South], this work contains useful material on northern attitudes.

335. DuPont, Henry A. "A Crisis of Conscience: West Point Letters of Henry A. DuPont, October, 1860-June, 1861." Virginia Lake, editor. CWH, 25 [1979]: 55-65.

This interesting collection details the indecision of a Border state West Point cadet who was torn between his own southern sympathies and the firm Unionism of his father. Choosing the Union, DuPont's letters reveal the wrenching crisis of decision faced by so many during the secession winter.

336. Edwards, Thomas. "Holding the Far West For the Union: The Army in 1861." CWH, 14 [1968]: 307-324.

Despite the subtitle, the article discusses chiefly the political means by which California was held in the Union.

337. Eisenschiml, Otto. WHY THE CIVIL WAR? Indianapolis: Bobbs-Merrill, 1958.

Author accuses Lincoln of provoking war by sending "bread" to Anderson at Fort Sumter and thus prompting the Confederates to fire the first shot.

338. Elbert, E. Duane. "Southern Indiana in the Election of 1860: The Leadership and the Electorate." IND MAG HIS, 68 [1972]: 1-24.

Both the leadership and the electorate of all parties in this region had a strong southern orientation making the section a southern enclave in the North.

339. Emory, Charles W. "The Iowa Germans in the Election of 1860." ANN IOWA, 22 [1940]: 421-453.

The Iowa Germans were found to be vocally Republican.

340. Everett, Edward G. "The Baltimore Riots, April 1861." PENN HIS, 24 [1957]: 331-342.

An account of the Baltimore riots and the response of the state of Pennsylvania to them.

341. Fischer, Roger A. "The Republican Campaigns of 1856 and 1860: Analysis Through Artifacts." CWH, 27 [1981]: 123-137.

An interesting discussion of the evolution of the Republican party from a single-issue party to a multi-issue party through the analysis of campaign ephemera.

342. Fite, Emerson D. THE PRESIDENTIAL CAMPAIGN OF 1860. New York, 1911.

While this volume is somewhat aged, it remains one of the best accounts of the election.

343. Graebner, Norman L., editor. POLITICS AND THE CRISIS OF 1860. Urbana: University of Illinois Press, 1961.

An anthology of five essays by William Baringer, Avery Craven, Don Fehrenbacher, Robert Johannsen, and the editor, in which it becomes clear that the national consensus had splintered into fragments by 1860 and that war was unavoidable.

344. ———. "Thomas Corwin and the Sectional Crisis." OHIO HIS, 86 [1977]: 229-247.

A discussion of the role of this important conservative who sought to secure a compromise to the sectional crisis in the winter of 1860-1861.

345. Greeman, Betty D. "The Democratic Convention of 1860: Prelude to Secession." MD HIS MAG, 67 [1972]: 225-253.

Focusing on the Baltimore convention, the theme is apparent from the subtitle. The formal dismemberment of the Democratic party placed the survival of the Union in imminent peril.

346. Gunderson, Robert G. OLD GENTLEMEN'S CONVENTION: THE WASHINGTON PEACE CONFERENCE, 1861. Madison, Wisconsin: University of Wisconsin Press, 1961.

An able monograph dealing with the unsuccessful attempt of the peace convention to forestall disunion.

347. ———. "The Washington Peace Conference of 1861: Selection of Delegates." JSH, 24 [1958]: 347-359.

In this discussion of the selection process, radicals from both North and South, fearful that a peace conference might succeed, sought to prevent the sending of any delegates. In the event they were overruled, they pressed for the selection of people opposed to compromise.

348. Halstead, Murat. THREE AGAINST LINCOLN: MURAT HALSTEAD REPORTS THE CAUCUSES OF 1860. William B. Hesseltine, editor. Baton Rouge: Louisiana State University Press, 1960.

An excellent account of the 1860 conventions by an acute eyewitness. The work is a valuable resource for sensing the political flavor of the conventions.

349. Hamilton, J.G. de Roulhac. "Lincoln's Election an Immediate Menace to Slavery in the States?" AHR, 37 [1932]: 700-711.

The author concludes that Lincoln's election did pose such a threat.

350. Harrison, Lowell H. "Governor Magoffin and the Secession Crisis." KY HIS SOC REG, 72 [1974]: 91-110.

The Kentucky governor tried to resolve the secession crisis while keeping the state in the Union. He failed and was compelled to resign.

351. Hemmer, Joseph J. "The Charleston Platform Debate in Rhetorical-Historical Perspective." Q J SPEECH, 56 [1970]: 406-416.

Rhetorical tactics, as well as sharp sectional sentiments, functioned against party unity at the first Democratic convention in 1860.

352. Hoogenboom, Ari. "Gustavus Fox and the Relief of Fort Sumter." CWH, 9 [1963]: 383-398.

Author rejects the theory that Lincoln "maneuvered" the South into firing the first shot.

353. Hubbell, John T. "The Douglas Democrats and the Election of 1860." MID AM, 54 [1973]: 108-133.

A discussion of the strategies and tactics of the Northern Democracy in the 1860 election.

354. ———. "Jeremiah Sullivan Black and the Great Secession Winter." W PENN HIS MAG, 57 [1974]: 255-274.

An account of the role played by this one strong bulwark--secretary of state--of the Buchanan administration.

355. ———. "Politics as Usual: The Northern Democracy and Party Survival, 1860-1861." ILL Q, 36 [1973]: 22-35.

The resurgence of the Democratic party after the divisive 1860 campaign is noted.

356. Johannsen, Robert W. "The Douglas Democrats and the Crisis of Disunion." CWH, 9 [1963]: 229-247.

Author details the actions of the Douglas Democrats during the secession crisis and contends that with Douglas's death in June 1861 the Northern Democracy was leaderless and doomed to an erratic, confused, and disorganized course during the war.

357. ———. "The Sectional Crisis and the Frontier: Washington Territory, 1860-1861." MVHR, 39 [1952]: 415-440.

Although the entire spectrum of public opinion regarding secession was present in Washington, the territory's strong dependence on the national government was in itself sufficient to bind it so the Union.

358. ———. STEPHEN A. DOUGLAS. New York: Oxford University Press, 1973.

A good biography of the Democratic leader, in which the last few chapters provide a wealth of detail on Douglas's course throughout the election year of 1860, the secession crisis, and the first weeks of conflict.

359. ———. "Stephen A. Douglas's New England Campaign, 1860." NEQ, 35 [1962]: 162-186.

A discussion of Douglas's campaign strategy in his native land of New England.

360. Johnson, Hildegard B. "The Election of 1860 and the Germans of Minnesota." MINN HIS, 28 [1947]: 20-36.

Germans in Minnesota supported Lincoln over Douglas by a two-to-one margin.

361. Keene, Jesse L. THE PEACE CONVENTION OF 1861. Tuscaloosa, Alabama: Confederate Publishing, 1961.

A short but well-done account of the ill-fated Washington Peace Convention held on the eve of war.

362. Kleppner, Paul J. "Lincoln and the Immigrant Vote: A Case Study of Religious Polarization." MID AM, 48 [1966]: 176-195.

A study of foreign-born voters in Pittsburgh in 1860, in which it was found that cultural and religious issues influenced the choice of party. Immigrants, especially Catholic immigrants, voted overwhelmingly Democratic.

363. Klingberg, Frank W. "James Buchanan and the Crisis of the Union." JSH, 9 [1943]: 453-474.

Essentially, the article defends Buchanan's cautious policy.

364. Knoles, George H., editor. THE CRISIS OF THE UNION, 1860-1861. Baton Rouge: Louisiana State University Press, 1965.

Volume contains a stimulating discussion of various aspects of the secession crisis written by different historians.

365. Kremm, Thomas W. "Cleveland and the First Lincoln Election: The Ethnic Response to Nativism." J INTER HIS, 8 [1977]: 69-86.

It is shown that Cleveland immigrants, especially Catholics, voted Democratic in 1860.

366. Krummel, Carl F. "Henry J. Raymond and the NEW YORK TIMES in the Secession Crisis, 1860-1861." NY HIS, 32 [1951]: 377-398.

The attitudes and influence of this important newspaperman are explored. Raymond was counting upon a resurgence of southern Unionism which never truly occurred.

367. Lanis, Edward S. "Allen Pinkerton and the Baltimore 'Assassination' Plot Against Lincoln." MD HIS MAG, 45 [1950]: 1-13.

A look at the role of the famous detective during the nocturnal journey of the president-elect through Baltimore in February 1861.

368. Lee, R. Alton. "The Corwin Amendment in the Secession Crisis." OHIO HIS Q, 70 [1961]: 1-26.

A detailed study of the life of this abortive 13th amendment, which would have forever protected slavery where it existed at that time.

369. Long, John S. "The Gosport Affair, 1861." JSH, 23 [1957]: 155-172.

An examination of the events leading to the attempted destruction of the Gosport Naval Yard prior to its abandonment by Union forces in April 1861.

370. Lorenz, Alfred L. "Lincoln, Medill and the Republican Nomination of 1860." LIN HER, 69 [1966]: 199-205.

Discusses the role played by Joseph Medill and the CHICAGO TRIBUNE in Lincoln's nomination in 1860.

371. Luebke, Frederick C., editor. ETHNIC VOTERS AND THE ELECTION OF LINCOLN. Lincoln: University of Nebraska Press, 1971.

A provocative collection of essays which, by the use of quantitative techniques, analyze the ethnic influences of Lincoln's election.

372. Luthin, Reinhard H. THE FIRST LINCOLN CAMPAIGN. Cambridge: Harvard University Press, 1944.

An excellent monograph on Lincoln's own role in the 1860 election, solidly grounded in manuscripts and newspaper sources.

373. ———. "Organizing the Republican Party in the 'Border Slave' Regions: Edward Bates' Presidential Candidacy in 1860." MO HIS R, 38 [1944]: 138-161.

Focuses on the conservatism of the Republicans in the Border states. Bates was consistent in his attempts to preserve the Union and avoid sectionalism of any type, but failed to secure the party's support of this policy. He served as Lincoln's attorney general until November 1864.

374. ———. "Pennsylvania and Lincoln's Rise to the Presidency." PA MHB, 67 [1943]: 61-82.

A discussion of the crucial importance of the Keystone state in the election of Lincoln.

375. McDonald, Archie P. "Washington in February, 1861." W VA HIS, 27 [1965/1966]: 201-210.

A quick look at Washington in the last days of Buchanan's administration, in which is noted the social life, peace conference, and preparations for Lincoln's inauguration.

376. McGraw, Robert F. "Minutemen of '61: The Pre-Civil War Massachusetts Militia." CWH, 15 [1969]: 101-115.

The quick and effective response of the Massachusetts militia was due to the unit's long and distinguished record and the leadership of General Ebenezer W. Stone.

377. McWhiney, Grady. "The Confederacy's First Shot." CWH, 14 [1968]: 5-14.

An overlooked letter suggests that Jefferson Davis tried to "provoke" war at Fort Pickens before Lincoln had a chance to "provoke" war at Fort Sumter.

378. Meerse, Donald E. "Buchanan, Corruption, and the Election of 1860." CWH, 12 [1966]: 116-131.

Suggests that "corruption" in the Buchanan administration was a useful tool for the Republicans. The latter, to safeguard themselves, chose "Honest Abe" whose honesty appears to have been of more importance than his stand on slavery.

379. Meredith, Roy. STORM OVER SUMTER: THE OPENING ENGAGEMENT OF THE CIVIL WAR. New York: Simon and Schuster, 1957.

A fairly readable survey of the period between the election and the firing on Fort Sumter.

380. Nichols, Roy F. THE DISRUPTION OF AMERICAN DEMOCRACY. New York: Macmillan, 1948.

The last portion of this excellent account of the breakup of the Democratic party is valuable on the 1860 election and the last days of the Buchanan administration.

381. Odle, Thomas D. "The Commercial Interests of the Great Lakes and the Campaign Issues of 1860." MICH HIS, 40 [1956]: 1-23.

The failure of the Buchanan administration to consider the interests of the commerce of the Great Lakes region was one of the factors which led to that area's strong support for the Republican ticket in the 1860 election.

382. Perkins, Howard C. "The Defense of Slavery in the Northern Press on the Eve of the Civil War." JSH, 9 [1943]: 501-531.

Draws the distinction between pro-slavery northern newspapers and those that were opposed to abolition. He asserts that less than two per cent was actually in favor of slavery.

383. ———. NORTHERN EDITORIALS ON SECESSION. New York: Appleton-Century, 1942.

A valuable and interesting compilation of northern editorial opinion on secession.

384. Pitkin, Thomas M. "Western Republicans and the Tariff in 1860." MVHR, 27 [1940]: 401-420.

Western Republicans were unhappy with the high tariff stand of eastern Republicans in the 1860 campaign. Had not the outbreak of war muffled their differences, there was a good chance a split over the tariff might have weakened the party at this early stage of its history.

385. Porter, David. "The Southern Press and the Presidential Election of 1860." W VA HIS, 33 [1971/1972]: 1-13.

A statistical study of the attitudes of newspapers of the 11 Confederate states toward the candidates and issues of the 1860 election.

386. Potter, David M. "Horace Greeley and Peaceable Secession." JSH, 7 [1941]: 145-159.

Greeley had no real desire to divide the Union, and he coupled his dictum to "go in peace" with a firm belief that southern Unionism would maintain national unity. When it did not, he quickly retreated from secession.

387. ———. THE IMPENDING CRISIS, 1848-1861. Don E. Fehrenbacher, editor. New York: Harper and Row, 1976.

David Potter's final work, published posthumously, was edited by Don Fehrenbacher, who also wrote the last two chapters. The editor maintained the author's high standard in this penetrating study of politics in the decade before the war.

388. ———. LINCOLN AND HIS PARTY IN THE SECESSION CRISIS. New Haven: Yale University Press, 1942.

An excellent, closely argued and extremely readable study of Lincoln and other Republican leaders throughout the secession crisis. It has not been superceded.

389. Pratt, Jabez D. and John C. Pratt. "Brother Against Brother." Bruce Catton, editor. AM HER, 12 [3] [1961]: 4-7, 89-93.

A severe exchange of letters between two brothers, one in Boston and one in Baltimore, over the Baltimore riot in April 1861.

390. Preston, James R. "Political Pageantry in the Campaign of 1860 in Illinois." ALQ, 4 [1947]: 313-347.

Article captures the excitement of the "Wide-Awake" campaign.

391. Price, Robert. "Young Howells Drafts a 'Life' For Lincoln." OHIO HIS, 76 [1967]: 232-246.

An account of the writing of one of Lincoln's campaign biographies, this one by a young William Dean Howells.

392. Prucha, F. Paul. "Minnesota's Attitude Toward the Southern Case for Secession." MINN HIS, 24 [1943]: 307-317.

In this survey of Minnesota editorial opinion little sympathy is found for the southern position on secession, even among those willing to compromise to avoid disunion.

393. Ramsdell, Charles W. "Lincoln and Fort Sumter." JSH, 3 [1937] 259-288.

The classic view that Lincoln "maneuvered" the South into firing the first shot.

394. Randall, James G. "When War Came in 1861." ALQ 1 [1940]: 3-42.

The classic view, opposed to Ramsdell, that Lincoln did not "maneuver" the South into firing the first shot.

395. Reilly, Tom. "Early Coverage of a President-Elect: Lincoln at Springfield, 1860." JOUR Q, 50 [1972]: 469-479.

A discussion of the quantity and character of the coverage of the president-elect.

396. Robinson, Edward A. "Some Recollection of April 19, 1861." MD HIS MAG, 27 [1932]: 274-279.

A short eyewitness account of the Baltimore riot, April 19-22, 1861 by Edward Ayrault Robinson, a member of the 5th Regular Maryland Guard, a volunteer unit.

397. Schafer, Joseph. "Who Elected Lincoln?" AHR, 47 [1941]: 51-63.

An early but still useful analysis of which voters made up Lincoln's 1860 constituency. Schafer correctly believed that the accepted assumption of an overwhelming foreign-born vote in Lincoln's favor was "100 percent wrong."

398. Scrugham, Mary. THE PEACEABLE AMERICANS OF 1860-1861. New York: Columbia University Press, 1921.

A narrative of the unsuccessful peace negotiations during the winter of secession.

399. Simon, Donald E. "Brooklyn in the Election of 1860." NY HIS Q, 51 [1967]: 249-262.

A good local study of the campaign. Anti-black prejudice,

commercial interests, and opposition to interference with private property combined to create a large Democratic majority in Brooklyn.

400. Simms, Henry R. OHIO POLITICS ON THE EVE OF THE CIVIL WAR. Columbus: The Ohio State University Press, 1961.

Published as an Ohio Civil War Centennial pamphlet, this account provides a readable, brief overview of the Ohio political scene from the election of Lincoln to the firing on Fort Sumter.

401. Smith, Donald V. "The Influence of the Foreign Born of the Northwest in the Election of 1860." MVHR, 19 [1932]: 192-204.

Author stresses the importance of the foreign-born vote in this region and concludes that the vast majority of such voters went Republican.

402. Sowle, Patrick. "A Reappraisal of Seward's Memorandum of April 1, 1861 to Lincoln." JSH, 33 [1967]: 234-239.

A letter from James B. Swain to John Hay in 1888 suggests that Seward's famous "Some Thoughts For the President's Consideration," was the collective effort of Seward, Thurlow Weed, and Henry Raymond. The purpose was to cause Lincoln to hand over the conduct of foreign policy to his secretary of state.

403. Stampp, Kenneth M. AND THE WAR CAME: THE NORTH AND THE SECESSION CRISIS. Baton Rouge: Louisiana State University Press, 1950.

An excellent study of the changing course of northern sentiment during the secession crisis.

404. ———. "Lincoln and the Strategy of Defense in the Crisis of 1861." JSH, 11 [1945]: 297-323.

A discussion, somewhat critical of Lincoln, of the strategies surrounding the reprovisioning of Fort Sumter in March and April 1861.

405. Staudenraus, P.J., editor. THE SECESSION CRISIS, 1860-1861. Chicago: Rand-McNally, 1963.

A good documentary work, containing primary materials essential to the study of the secession crisis.

406. Suppiger, Joseph E. "In Defense of Washington." CWTI, 15 [5] [1976]: 38-45.

An interesting article that discusses Cassius Marcellus Clay and his "Clay Battalion" that defended Washington in the first few weeks after the fall of Sumter. Much to the chagrin of President Lincoln and other officials, Clay was insistent on maintaining and commanding his motley group of office-seekers and bureaucrats until the first volunteer regiments arrived in Washington.

407. Swanberg, W.A. FIRST BLOOD. New York: Scribners, 1957.

An excellent account not only of the firing on Sumter, but of the political issues leading to it.

408. Swierenga, Robert P. "The Ethnic Voter and the First Lincoln Election." CWH, 11 [1965]: 27-43.

Focusing on the Dutch of Marion County, Iowa, author shows that these voters overwhelmingly supported the Democratic party at the polls for cultural reasons, in spite of the pro-Republican stance of many of their leaders.

409. Talmadge, John E. "A Peace Movement in Civil War Connecticut." NEQ, 37 [1964]: 306-331.

Connecticut's peace movement was the expression of a resolute minority, largely anti-abolitionist, which grew bolder after the Union defeat at First Bull Run. As a whole, the state stood for war.

410. Thayer, William S. "Politicians in Crisis: The Washington Letters of William S. Thayer, December 1860-March 1861." Martin Crawford, editor. CWH 27 [1981]: 231-247.

The letters of Thayer, Washington correspondent of the New York EVENING POST, to John Chandler Bancroft Davis, the New York correspondent of THE TIMES of London, form a detailed political record from a Washington insider. Because of the positions of the correspondents, Thayer's views were reflected in THE TIMES and thus were influential in Britain.

411. Tilley, John S. LINCOLN TAKES COMMAND. Chapel Hill, N.C.: University of North Carolina Press, 1941.

A hostile study of Lincoln and the secession crisis.

412. Wallace, Doris D. "The Political Campaign of 1860 in Missouri." MO HIS R, 70 [1976]: 162-183.

A description of the political campaign of 1860 in this crucial Border state. A process of radicalization of the electorate took place during the course of the campaign.

413. Weed, Thurlow. "Thurlow Weed's Analysis of William H. Seward's Defeat in the Republican Convention of 1860." Glyndon G. Van Deusen, editor. MVHR, 34 [1947]: 101-104.

In a communication to Seward shortly after the convention, Weed observed that treachery by Horace Greeley and other New Yorkers helped seal Seward's fate.

414. Weisberger, Bernard A. "Horace Greeley: Reformer as Republican." CWH, 23 [1977]: 5-25.

This is a detailed discussion of Greeley's initial advocacy of a peaceful separation early in the secession winter and his swing away from that view.

415. Woodward, Isaiah A. "Lincoln and the Crittenden Compromise." NEG HIS BULL, 22 [1959]: 153-154.

A brief discussion of Lincoln's refusal to accept the Crittenden Compromise since it would open new territory to slavery. Because of this the compromise failed.

416. Worley, Ted R. "The Arkansas Peace Society of 1861: A Study in Mountain Unionism." JSH, 24 [1958]: 445-456.

Although Arkansas seceded, Unionism was strong in the upland counties of northwestern and north central Arkansas. A secret society was uncovered. Its members were arrested for disloyalty to the South and pressed into the Confederate army.

417. Wright, Quincy. "Stephen A. Douglas and the Campaign of 1860." VT HIS, 28 [1960]: 250-255.

A view of the native Vermonter's election campaign.

418. Zorn, Roman J. "Minnesota Public Opinion and the Secession Controversy, December 1860-April 1861." MVHR, 36 [1949]: 435-456.

A thorough examination of public opinion in Minnesota during the secession crisis. People in the state buried their political differences to stand loyally behind the national government in its moment of need.

B. NATIONAL GOVERNMENT AND POLITICS

419. Allen, Richard. LINCOLN v. DOUGLAS: THE GREAT DEBATES CAMPAIGN. Washington, D.C.: Public Affairs Press, 1967.

Author believes the importance of the debates has been exaggerated.

420. Ames, Susie M. "Federal Policy Toward the Eastern Shore of Virginia in 1861." VA MHB, 69 [1961]: 432-459.

Federal forces occupied the strongly secessionist Eastern Shore in November 1861 without incident.

421. Amundson, R.J. "Sanford and Garibaldi." CWH, 14 [1968]: 40-45.

An account of the unsuccessful attempt to secure the services of Garibaldi, the Italian hero, as commander of federal forces around Washington in August 1861.

422. Avilo, Philip J., Jr. "Ballots for the Faithful: The Oath and the Emergence of Slave State Republican Congressmen, 1861-1867." CWH, 22 [1976]: 164-174.

A survey of loyalty oath legislation in the Border states during the war.

423. Baylen, Joseph O. "Dr. John McClintock: Union Propagandist, 1860-1864." CWH, 5 [1959]: 133-144.

The Reverend Dr. John McClintock, a strong Unionist, was pastor of the non-sectarian American Chapel in Paris during the war. He used this strategic post to advise Americans about European opinion and to correct any misconceptions Europeans had about the Union cause.

424. Belz, Herman. EMANCIPATION AND EQUAL RIGHTS: POLITICS AND CONSTITUTIONALISM DURING THE WAR. New York: Norton, 1978.

A well-researched and well-written study of a somewhat complex subject.

425. ———. "The Etheridge Conspiracy of 1863: A Projected Conservative Coup." JSH, 36 [1970]: 548-567.

An account of the unsuccessful attempt, led by a southern Unionist, Emerson Etheridge of Tennessee, to block organization by Republicans of the House of Representatives of the 38th Congress in December 1863. If the plot had worked, control of the House would have been in the hands of a coalition of Democrats and Border state Unionists.

426. ———. "The Freedmen's Bureau Act of 1865 and the Principle of No Discrimination According to Color." CWH, 21 [1975]: 197-217.

The Freedmen's Bureau Act would not have passed had not a provision for white refugees been included in it.

427. ———. "Henry Winter Davis and the Origins of Congressional Reconstruction." MD HIS MAG, 67 [1972]: 129-143.

A discussion of the origins of the Wade-Davis Bill of 1864. A growing number of Republicans believed that intervention in the seceding states by the national government would be necessary before those states could be readmitted to the Union.

428. ———. "Protection of Personal Liberty in Republican Emancipation Legislation of 1862." JSH, 42 [1976]: 385-400.

The measures of 1862 indicate a lack of concern about Negro liberty. By depriving the South of labor, the Union would have a military advantage.

429. ———. A NEW BIRTH OF FREEDOM: THE REPUBLICAN PARTY AND FREEDMEN'S RIGHTS 1861 TO 1866. Westport, Connecticut: Greenwood, 1976.

This volume concentrates on congressional politics and the development of a federal policy for handling freed slaves. Focus is on the question of protection of the "civil liberties" of the freed slaves.

430. ———. RECONSTRUCTING THE UNION: THEORY AND POLICY DURING THE CIVIL WAR. Ithaca: Cornell University Press, 1969.

Examines the Reconstruction ideas of the wartime Congress and Lincoln in great detail. In particular, this is a probing study of how the legislature grappled with the many complex issues which lay ahead.

431. Benton, Josiah H. VOTING IN THE FIELD.... Boston, 1915.

An in-depth study of a neglected aspect of the war, the soldier vote.

432. Bogue, Allan G. "Bloc and Party in the United States Senate: 1861-1863." CWH, 13 [1967]: 221-241.

A roll call analysis of Republican voting in the 37th Congress.

433. ———. THE EARNEST MEN: REPUBLICANS OF THE CIVIL WAR SENATE. Ithaca: Cornell University Press, 1961.

Examines and classifies Republicans into Radicals and Moderates through the use of statistical analysis.

434. Boykin, Edward C. CONGRESS AND THE CIVIL WAR. New York: McBride, 1955.

Only deals briefly with Congress during the war although the title indicates otherwise. Emphasis is on pre- and post-war periods.

435. Bradley, Erwin S. THE TRIUMPH OF MILITANT REPUBLICANISM.... Philadelphia: University of Pennsylvania Press, 1964.

An examination of Pennsylvania politics from the election of 1860 through the election of 1872.

436. Brichford, Maynard J. "Congress at the Outbreak of War." CWH, 3 [1957]: 153-162.

Discusses the speeches, recommendations, enlistments, and other activities of different congressmen prior to the convening of Congress in July 1861.

437. Brumgardt, John R. "'Overwhelmingly for "Old Abe"': Sherman's Soldiers and the Election of 1864." LIN HER, 78 [1976]: 153-160.

Soldiers in Sherman's forces during the Atlanta Campaign strongly supported Lincoln's re-election bid in 1864. It was their feeling that if McClellan won, the war--in one way or another--would be lost.

438. Cardoso, J.J. "Lincoln, Abolitionism, and Patronage: The Case of Hinton Rowan Helper." JNH, 53 [1968]: 144-160.

Hinton Rowan Helper, the anti-slavery writer, helped Lincoln and the Republicans in the 1860 campaign and expected a job as a reward. He was put off, however, until November 1861 when he was given the consulate at Buenos Aires.

439. Carman, Harry J. and Reinhard H. Luthin. LINCOLN AND THE PATRONAGE. New York: Columbia University Press, 1943.

A detailed and well researched examination of how Lincoln went about filling government positions--from cabinet member down to postmaster.

440. "Chicago's Second National Convention." CHI HIS, 7 [1964]: 104-115.

Describes the Democratic convention of 1864.

441. Chittenden, Lucius E. RECOLLECTIONS OF PRESIDENT LINCOLN AND HIS ADMINISTRATION. New York, 1901.

Lincoln and political Washington are remembered fondly.

442. Cole, Arthur C. "President Lincoln and the Illinois Radical Republicans." MVHR, 4 [1918]: 417-436.

Radical criticism of Lincoln concentrated in three areas: 1) Lincoln's slavery policy, 2) direction of military operations, 3) conduct of diplomatic relations.

443. Cooney, Charles F. "Treason or Tyranny? The Great Senate Purge of '62." CWTI, 18 [4] [1979]: 30-31.

An account of the expulsion of Jesse D. Bright of Indiana from the Senate for treason.

444. Cullen, Joseph P. "The McClellan-Lincoln Controversy." CWTI, 5 [7] [1966]: 34-43.

Examines the relationship between the two men with regard to the Peninsular Campaign.

445. Curry, Earl R. "Pennsylvania and the Republican Convention of 1860...." PA MHB 97 [1973]: 183-198.

A discussion of the reasons why most Pennsylvania Republicans opposed Seward's nomination in 1860.

446. Curry, Leonard P. "Congressional Democrats, 1861-1863." CWH, 12 [1966]: 213-229.

A statistical study of key votes in the 37th Congress, designed to show the relative unity of the Democratic membership and its loyal support of the Union.

447. ———. BLUEPRINT FOR MODERN AMERICA: NON-MILITARY LEGISLATION OF THE FIRST CIVIL WAR CONGRESS. Nashville: Vanderbilt University Press, 1968.

A good solid work dealing with non-military legislation of the 37th Congress. Divided into eleven segments, it covers such topics as transportation, currency, confiscation, and taxation. A well written, organized account of the vast amount of legislation passed by the 37th Congress.

448. Donald, David, editor. INSIDE LINCOLN'S CABINET: THE CIVIL WAR DIARIES OF SALMON P. CHASE. New York: Longmans, Green, 1954.

Details the workings of Lincoln's Cabinet from Chase's viewpoint.

449. ———. THE POLITICS OF RECONSTRUCTION, 1863-1867. Baton Rouge: Louisiana State University Press, 1967.

The author suggests use of the quantitative approach toward congressional behavior to provide fresh understanding of Reconstruction politics.

450. Dorris, Jonathan. PARDON AND AMNESTY UNDER LINCOLN AND JOHNSON. Chapel Hill: University of North Carolina Press, 1953.

Lincoln was granted wide discretionary power by the Confiscation Acts of 1861 and 1862. The controversies which arose as a result of this legislation are the subjects of this valuable study.

451. ———. "The Treatment of Confederates." LIN HER, 61 [1959]: 142-152; 62 [1960]: 18-23, 70-77.

This three part series considers the pardon and amnesty policies of Lincoln and Johnson and reviews congressional action on the 14th Amendment.

452. Doster, William E. LINCOLN AND EPISODES OF THE CIVIL WAR. New York: Putnam, 1915.

A collection of essays dealing with Lincoln and various war topics.

453. Doyle, Elizabeth J. "Rottenness in Every Direction: The Stokes Investigation in Civil War New Orleans." CWH, 18 [1972]: 24-41.

An account of the Stokes investigation of alleged corruption in the Quartermaster's Department at New Orleans in 1864. The charges appear to have been substantiated, although none of the accused were brought to trial.

454. Dudley, Harold M., "The Election of 1864." MVHR, 18 [193]: 500-518.

The chief issue of the 1864 election was the continuation of the war. Lincoln, the Republican candidate, maintained his position of fighting to the bitter end. The Democrats nominated General George B. McClellan and adopted the platform of "immediate cessation of hostilities."

455. Edwards, G. Thomas. "Benjamin Stark, the U.S. Senate and 1862 Membership Issues." ORE HIS Q, 72 [1971]: 315-338; 73 [1972]: 31-59.

Describes the fight in the Senate over the seating of this pro-southern senator from Oregon and the difficulties he faced after he was confirmed.

456. Ellis, Richard N. "Political Pressure and Army Policies on the Northern Plains 1862-1865." MINN HIS, 42 [1970]: 43-53.

Two Minnesota senators--Republican Senator Morton S. Wilkinson and Democratic Senator Henry M. Rice--continually meddled in war department decisions. This was especially true with regard to the Sioux uprisings.

457. Farnham, Wallace D. "The Pacific Railroad Act of 1862." NEB HIS, 43 [1962]: 141-167.

An examination of the origins of the Railroad Act, plus an analysis of the several controversies about its value, Congress's purpose in passing the law, and the government's role in its operations.

458. Fischer, LeRoy H. "Adam Gurowski Discovers a Cabinet Secretary." LIN HER, 66 [1964]: 3-13.

Only one of Lincoln's cabinet met Gurowski's standards.

459. ———. "Adam Gurowski Views Lincoln's Re-election." LIN HER, 66 [1964]: 83-86.

When Lincoln was re-elected, Gurowski believed it was a Republican victory rather than a Lincoln victory. He had opposed Lincoln's renomination.

460. Foner, Eric. FREE SOIL, FREE LABOR, FREE MEN: THE IDEOLOGY OF THE REPUBLICAN PARTY BEFORE THE CIVIL WAR. New York: Oxford University Press, 1970.

A solid study of the roots of Lincoln Republicanism, whose main principle was the sanctity of free labor.

461. Harbison, Winifred A. "Zachariah Chandler's Part in the Reelection of Abraham Lincoln." MVHR, 21 [1935]: 267-276.

The Radicals had nominated Fremont on an independent ticket. Chandler persuaded Lincoln to dismiss Postmaster Blair (a conservative) in return for Fremont's withdrawal from the election. This united the Republican party and gave Lincoln the victory.

462. Harrington, Fred. "A Peace Mission of 1862." AHR, 46 [1940/1941]: 76-86.

A documentary account of an abortive peace mission to Richmond by one Dr. Issachak Zacharie, a Jewish chiropodist and spy in late July 1863. Despite its failure, the mission revealed the state of mind of both northern and southern government officers after Gettysburg.

463. Hendrick, Burton J. LINCOLN'S WAR CABINET. Boston: Little, Brown, 1946.

A readable account of Lincoln's relations with the various members of his cabinet.

464. Hendrickson, James E. JOE LANE OF OREGON: MACHINE POLITICS AND THE SECTIONAL CRISIS, 1849-1861. New Haven: Yale University Press, 1967.

An analysis of the complex politics of the Pacific Northwest on the eve of war, neatly interwoven with the national scene. Lane's career--he was a southern sympathizer--was ended with Lincoln's election in 1860.

465. Hesseltine, William B. "Abraham Lincoln and the Politicians." CWH, 5 [1960]: 43-55.

A good introduction to an understanding of Lincoln's political skill as president.

466. ———. LINCOLN AND THE WAR GOVERNORS. New York: Knopf, 1948.

Useful analysis of the various conflicts between the states and the federal government and Lincoln's relations with the governors.

467. ———. LINCOLN'S PLAN OF RECONSTRUCTION. Tuscaloosa, Alabama: Confederate Publishing, 1960.

Advances the theory that even if Lincoln had lived the events of Reconstruction would not have changed.

468. ———. "Lincoln's Problems in Wisconsin." WIS MAG HIS, 48 [1965]: 187-195.

Discusses the problems involved in strengthening the Union with regard to the various states--particularly Wisconsin.

469. Hood, James L. "For the Union: Kentucky's Unconditional Unionist Congressmen and the Development of the Republican Party in Kentucky, 1863-1865." KY HIS SOC REG, 76 [1978]: 197-215.

The dissident Union Democrats, Lucien Anderson, Green Clay Smith, and William Harrison Randall, supported Lincoln and formed the basis for a permanent Republican party in Kentucky. They voted with the Republicans to organize Congress.

470. Hyman, Harold M. "Lincoln and Congress: Why Not Congress and Lincoln." JISHS, 68 [1975]: 57-73.

The Civil War Congress has not been studied in depth. Given the present state of sources, methods, and literature, the author believes a means must be found to recreate the history of Congress and Lincoln. Hyman suggests a nation-wide computerized locator.

471. Johannsen, Robert W. "Stephen A. Douglas and the South." JSH, 33 [1967]: 26-50.

Examines the relationship between Douglas and the Southern Democrats.

472. Johnson, Ludwell H. "Lincoln's Solution to the Problem of Peace Terms, 1864-1865." JSH, 34 [1968]: 576-586.

To prevent a takeover of the party by the Radicals, Lincoln hoped for a conservative coalition which would include southerners. To accomplish this a negotiated peace was necessary.

473. Jones, James P., editor. "'Your Left Arm'; James H. Wilson's Letters to Adam Badeau." CWH, 12 [1966]: 230-245.

Six letters from the Union general to Grant's military secretary in the spring of 1865.

474. Kelley, Brooks M. "Fossildom, Old Fogeyism, and Red Tape." PA MHB, 90 [1966]: 93-114.

Author argues that circumstances rather than ineptitude or corruption were the cause of Cameron's problems as Lincoln's first secretary of war.

475. Kirkland, Edward C. THE PEACEMAKERS OF 1864. New York: Macmillan, 1927.

An old but good volume, particularly in its analysis of personalities.

476. Klein, Frederic S. "The War Election of 1864." A HIS ILL, 3 [1968]: 4-9, 45-48.

An analysis of the 1864 election which Lincoln believed he would lose. Eight days before the election Nevada entered the Union, "just in time to provide a Republican majority...." The president did carry 22 of the 25 states.

477. Klement, Frank L. "The Soldier Vote in Wisconsin During the Civil War." WIS MAG HIS, 28 [1944]: 37-47.

The Republicans visualized a controlled soldiers' vote as a medium through which they could win the 1862 election. Soldiers were allowed to vote in the field, under the supervision of their Republican regimental officers.

478. Klingberg, Frank W. THE SOUTHERN CLAIMS COMMISSION. Berkeley: University of California Press, 1955.

An exhaustive study of the federal commission which examined claims of southern Unionists who demanded restitution for the destruction/confiscation of their property by federal forces.

479. Linden, Glenn M. "'Radicals' and Economic Policies: The House of Representatives, 1861-1873." CWH, 13 [1967]: 51-65.

A statistical analysis of congressional voting to determine who the real "Radicals" were.

480. ———. POLITICS OR PRINCIPLE: CONGRESSIONAL VOTING ON THE CIVIL WAR AMENDMENTS AND PRO-NEGRO MEASURES. 1838-1869. Seattle: University of Washington Press, 1976.

Useful tables showing voting patterns on the three wartime amendments and other issues.

481. Longacre, Edward G. "Mr. Lincoln's Policeman...." CWTI, 9 [7] [1970]: 22-31.

A brief look at Brigadier General Marsena Rudolph Patrick.

482. Luthin, Reinhard H. "A Discordant Chapter in Lincoln's Administration: The Davis-Blair Controversy." MD HIS MAG, 39 [1944]: 25-48.

A story of the bitter rivalry between Lincoln's two most influential supporters in Maryland--Radical Henry Winter Davis and Conservative Montgomery Blair.

483. Macartney, Clarence E. LINCOLN AND HIS CABINET. New York: Scribners, 1931.

In this study of eight members of Lincoln's cabinet and their relationship with the President, the author has adopted a new approach to a tricky problem. However, there is not a great deal that is new and one comes away from the book without feeling a sense of the conflict that often prevailed between the President and the cabinet.

484. Mallam, William D. "Lincoln and the Conservatives." JSH, 28 [1962]: 31-45.

This article provides a brief review of Lincoln's relations with various "blocs" in the 37th and 38th Congresses. Focuses on the attitude toward emancipation and confiscation.

485. Marszalek, John F., Jr. "Lincoln's Special Session 1861." CWTI, 10 [3] [1971]: 22-27.

An interesting account of the activities of the Special Session of the 37th Congress which convened July 4, 1861. In 29 days,

76 bills were passed. On the last day of the session a bill was rather reluctantly passed validating the many strong measures taken by Lincoln (blockade, etc.) before Congress had met.

486. Maslowski, Peter. TREASON MUST BE MADE ODIUS:.... Millwood, New York: Kraus International, 1979.

Details the military occupation of Nashville during the war.

487. McCarthy, Charles H. LINCOLN'S PLAN OF RECONSTRUCTION. New York, 1901.

Although somewhat outdated, this is an excellent discussion of the give-and-take between the White House and Capitol Hill in planning for post-war reconstruction.

488. McClure, Alexander K. ABRAHAM LINCOLN AND MEN OF WAR-TIMES. Philadelphia, 1892.

Personal recollections of the people in Lincoln's administration and the president's relationships with them.

489. McKitrick, Eric L. "Party Politics and the Union and Confederate War Efforts." In THE AMERICAN PARTY SYSTEMS.... William N. Chambers and Walter D. Barnham, editors. New York: Oxford University Press, 1967.

An exceptional study of the differences between the political systems of the Union and the Confederacy.

490. McMurtry, R. Gerald. "Chase's Abortive Effort to Win the Presidential Nomination in 1864. LIN LORE, 1612 [1972]: 3.

The "Pomeroy Circular" of February 1864 which launched Chase's bid for the Republican presidential nomination is reprinted.

491. McWhiney, Grady, editor. GRANT, LEE, LINCOLN, AND THE RADICALS. Evanston, Illinois: Northwestern University Press, 1964.

Two essays compare Grant with Lee, while the other two deal with Lincoln and the Radicals.

492. Merrill, George D. "Jonathan Turner or Justin Morrill: A New Look at the Authorship of the Land Grant Act of 1862." VT HIS, 36 [1968]: 204-209.

Discusses the authorship of this act which had such a wide ranging effect on higher education. Author concludes Morrill, having collected many reports and much information, sponsored the bill.

493. Mitgang, Herbert. "Garibaldi and Lincoln." AM HER, 26 [6] [1975]: 34-39, 98-101.

Describes Lincoln's attempt to engage Giuseppe Garibaldi for service in the United States army after the Union disaster at Bull Run. Garibaldi's terms were too high, so the plan failed.

494. Monteiro, George, editor. "John Hay and the Union Generals." JISHS, 69 [1976]: 46-66.

John Hay's attitude toward various Union generals. Among those considered are McClellan, Hooker, Meade, Grant, Rosecrans. and Thomas.

495. Moore, J. Preston. "Lincoln and the Escape of the Confederate Commissioner...." JISHS, 51 [1964]: 23-29.

Ambrose Dudley Mann was a Confederate diplomat. He claimed to have taken a copy of the new Confederate Constitution to Washington. Lincoln failed to take advantage of this easy opportunity to arrest him.

496. Morris, Robert L. "The Lincoln-Johnson Plan for Reconstruction and the Republican Convention of 1864." LIN HER, 71 [1969]: 33-40.

An examination of Lincoln's motives with respect to the 1864 Republican convention suggests he favored Andrew Johnson as his running mate because Johnson was supportive of the president's moderate Reconstruction plan.

497. Nelson, Larry E. "Independence or Fight." CWTI, 15 [3] [1976]: 10-14.

A discussion of the Jacques and Gilmore diplomatic mission to Jefferson Davis in an attempt to end the war in 1864.

498. Nichols, Roy F. "The Operation of American Democracy, 1861-1865; Some Questions." JSH, 25 [1959]: 31-52.

Despite the Civil War, elections were held on schedule in both North and South. The Confederate political organization was, however, unorganized (like their army) as opposed to the strong political organization of the Union. Many think this had an effect on the outcome of the war.

499. Nicklason, Fred. "The Civil War Contracts Committee." CWH, 17 [1971]: 232-244.

An account of the efforts of Henry Dawes of the War Contracts Committee to expose fraud in the first year of the war.

500. Niven, John. "Gideon Welles and Naval Administration During the Civil War." A NEP, 35 [1975]: 53-66.

Although he may have blundered at first, Welles kept a close watch on the navy department. Contrary to popular opinion he ran his own department.

501. Northrup, Jack. "Richard Yates and President Lincoln." LIN HER, 70 [1968]: 193-206.

Reviews the relationship between the Illinois governor and Lincoln. Emphasizes the governor's policies on the state's participation in the war.

502. Oates, Stephen B. "Lincoln and Stanton: An Uncommon Friendship." TIMELINE, 1 [1984]: 2-11.

In this new publication by the Ohio Historical Society can be found an excellent account of the relations between Lincoln and Stanton before and during the war.

503. Oliver, David L. "The Contribution of Kentucky to Lincoln's Fourth of July Session of Congress, 1861." KY HIS SOC REG, 60 [1962]: 134-142.

Kentucky's representatives and senators at the special session of Congress, while the state still professed its neutrality, expressed both Unionist and anti-Unionist views. Once the state became firmly attached to the Union, such differences ended and those supporting the anti-Union position were forced to resign.

504. Pedersen, Gilbert J. "A Yankee in Arizona: The Misfortunes of William S. Grant, 1860-1861." J ARIZ HIS, 16 [1975]: 127-144.

Traces the "ups and downs" of this business man who held many government supply contracts at the beginning of the war. He finally filed claims for losses due to the capture of his supplies by the Confederates.

505. Pierson, William W., Jr. "The Committee on the Conduct of the Civil War." AHR, 23 [1918]: 550-576.

A joint committee of Congress was established to follow the conduct of the war. They were critical of McClellan, condemned Meade, and were loyal to Hooker. They tried to suggest and even to control various campaigns but did not have the expertise to perform such duties.

506. Pomeroy, Earl S. "Lincoln, the Thirteenth Amendment and the Admission of Nevada." PAC HIS R, 12 [1943]: 362-368.

The President's advocacy of the admission of Nevada to the Union in 1864 was not based solely on his desire to assure passage of the 13th Amendment, but on broader political issues as well.

507. Potter, Henry A. "Lincoln's Policies as Seen by a Michigan Soldier." Donald W. Disbrow, editor. MICH HIS, 45 [1961]: 360-364.

A captain in the 4th Michigan Cavalry, Potter wrote knowledgeably about political matters, reflecting the doubts of many soldiers from the North over Lincoln's emancipation policy and discussing the issues of the 1864 campaign.

508. Pratt, Harry E. "The Repudiation of Lincoln's War Policy in 1862--the Stuart-Swett Congressional Campaign." JISHS, 24 [1931]: 129-140.

Illinois Republicans sought to gerrymander the 8th congressional district in 1862 so as to bring about the election of Republican Leonard Swett over Democrat John T. Stuart. They succeeded in the gerrymander, but the Democrats carried the state in the fall elections, including the 8th district.

509. Rawley, James E., editor. LINCOLN AND CIVIL WAR POLITICS. Magnolia, Massachusetts: Peter Smith, 1969.

A good collection of writings with a number of differing points of view represented.

510. Republican Party. PROCEEDINGS OF THE FIRST THREE REPUBLICAN NATIONAL CONVENTIONS OF 1856, 1860, AND 1864.... Minneapolis, 1893.

An account of Republican strategy in the early days as seen through the pen of Horace Greeley.

511. Rosenberg, Norman L. "Personal Liberty Laws and Sectional Crises: 1850-1861. CWH, 17 [1971]: 24-44.

A survey of "personal liberty" legislation from 1842 through the winter of 1860-1861.

512. Shaffer, Dallas S. "Lincoln and the 'Vast Question' of West Virginia." W VA HIS, 32 [1971]: 86-100.

Lincoln approved West Virginia statehood for one basic reason. To him it depended upon whether the admission or rejection of a new state would contribute more strongly to the restoration of national authority.

513. Shover, Kenneth B. "Maverick at Bay: Ben Wade's Senate Re-election Campaign, 1862-1863. CWH, 12 [1966]: 23-42.

An analysis of the attitude of Ohio's Union Party in Ben Wade's re-election bid in 1863. While War Democrats in the party opposed Wade's radicalism, he refused to make concessions to their viewpoint.

514. Shutes, Milton H. LINCOLN AND CALIFORNIA. Stanford: Stanford University Press, 1943.

Author attempts to show Lincoln's relationship to the state of California, although not in a very thoroughgoing way.

515. Silbey, Joel H. A RESPECTABLE MINORITY: THE DEMOCRATIC PARTY IN THE CIVIL WAR ERA, 1860-1868. New York: Norton, 1977.

A quantitative study focusing on the Democrats, in which the author shows how the Democrats rebounded from early embarrassments.

516. Smith, Donnal V. CHASE AND CIVIL WAR POLITICS. Columbus, Ohio: Heer, 1931.

A detailed study of Secretary of Treasury Salmon P. Chase's close alliance with the Radicals in Congress during the war and his unsuccessful maneuvering to win the Republican presidential nomination in 1864.

517. Spencer, Ivor D. "Chicago Helps to Reelect Lincoln." JISHS, 63 [1970]: 167-179.

Lincoln won Chicago by a large majority in the 1864 election due in part to the discovery of a plot two days before the election. Copperhead Democrats planned to free the Confederate prisoners at Camp Douglas, but the plot was foiled at the last moment.

518. Stampp, Kenneth M. "The Milligan Case and the Election of 1864 in Indiana." MVHR, 31 [1944]: 41-58.

The arrest of Milligan and his fellows for conspiracy gave the Republicans a victory in the 1864 election in Indiana. Prior to the publicity pertaining to the Milligan case the Republicans had not been optimistic about their chances of winning.

519. Stebbins, Phillip E. "Lincoln's Dictatorship." A HIS ILL, 6 [1971]: 32-37.

In the first weeks of the war, after the firing on Fort Sumter in April and before Congress met in July, Lincoln acted on his own in a number of matters. This "eleven-week dictatorship" raised some perplexing questions not fully resolved today.

520. Swift, Lester L. "Jaquess' Second Peace Mission." LIN HER, 71 [1969]: 3-13.

Emissaries from President Lincoln had an interview with President Davis in 1864, and the author believes this was instrumental in cooling Radical opposition to Lincoln.

521. Tegeder, Vincent G. "Lincoln and the Territorial Patronage...." MVHR, 35 [1948]: 77-90.

The 1860 victory gave the Republicans the opportunity to make territorial appointments. The final disposition of the job question in the territories by the Lincoln administration found numerous Radicals in important positions.

522. Thomas, Richard J. "Lisping Caleb Smith: Whig Orator on the Stump." CIN HIS SOC BULL, 30 [1972]: 21-49.

An intimate glimpse of Caleb Smith of Indiana, Lincoln's secretary of the interior.

523. Trefousse, Hans L. "A Radical Reconsidered: Ben Wade, Lincoln, and the Civil War." TOPIC, 2 [1961]: 16-29.

Author concludes that Wade's eagerness and firm convictions plus Lincoln's political know-how did a great deal of good for the country. Wade certainly was not as "bad" as he has been portrayed.

524. ———. THE RADICAL REPUBLICANS: LINCOLN'S VANGUARD FOR RACIAL JUSTICE. New York: Knopf, 1969.

Author stresses the cooperation between Lincoln and the Radicals rather than the conflict between the two. He suggests that Lincoln used the Radicals to move the Republican party forward to a more enlightened position on the race question.

525. ———. "The Joint Committee on the Conduct of the War: A Reassessment." CWH, 10 [1964]: 5-19.

Trefousse challenges the traditional view that the committee was an inquisitorial, trouble-making body.

526. ———. "Lincoln and Johnson." TOPIC, 5 [1965]: 63-75.

Author points out the differences between Lincoln and Johnson. The former was flexible, sensitive to political necessity, and masterful with people. Johnson was just plain stubborn, sticking to his preconceived notions in spite of everything and everyone.

527. ———. "Zachariah Chandler and the Withdrawal of Fremont in 1864: New Answer to an Old Riddle." LIN HER, 70 [1968]: 181-188.

A new letter found in the S.F. DuPont Papers, indicates that Fremont withdrew from the 1864 presidential race independently, rather than as a result of negotiations conducted by Senator Zachariah Chandler.

528. Van Riper, Paul P. and Keith A. Sutherland. "The Northern Civil Service, 1861-1866." CWH, 11 [1965]: 351-369.

It is argued that the number of persons employed in the federal civil service during the war was far greater than had been previously thought.

529. Wagandt, Charles L. "Election by Sword and Ballot: The Emancipationist Victory of 1863." MD HIS MAG, 59 [1964]: 143-164.

An analysis of the critical Maryland state election of 1863, where, not without a little assistance from the federal government, the emancipationists emerged victorious.

530. Weeden, William B. WAR GOVERNMENT, FEDERAL AND STATE.... Boston, 1906. Reprint 1972.

A useful introduction to the adjustments made between the federal government and the state governments of Massachusetts, New York, Pennsylvania, and Indiana.

531. Werstein, Irving. ABRAHAM LINCOLN VERSUS JEFFERSON DAVIS. New York: Crowell, 1959.

While the author is not too adept at handling certain matters of controversy, this is still a useful book for the general reader.

532. Whalon, Michael W. "Israel Washburn and the War Department." SOC SCI, 46 [1971]: 79-85.

Author examines how state governors contributed to the war effort, with special emphasis on the Republican Washburn of Maine.

533. Wieczerzak, Joseph W. "Some Friendly Swipes at 'Lincoln's Gadfly.'" POL R, 10 [1965]: 90-98.

While reviewing LeRoy Fischer's book, LINCOLN'S GADFLY, ADAM GUROWSKI, the author cites various instances where the role of Gurowski may have been exaggerated.

534. Williams, T. Harry. "Benjamin F. Wade and the Atrocity Propaganda of the Civil War." OSAHQ, 48 [1939]: 33-43.

Although many individuals and agencies turned out propaganda leaflets, the chief and most successful architect of the new war psychology was Senator Ben Wade of Ohio, chairman of the Joint Committee on the Conduct of the War.

535. ———. LINCOLN AND THE RADICALS. Madison: University of Wisconsin Press, 1941.

A study of the intense struggle between Lincoln and the Radical Republicans in Congress and the cabinet with the Radicals pressing for a more vigorous prosecution of the war. In this pioneering work the author appears to feel that they succeeded.

536. ———. "Voters in Blue, the Citizen Soldiers of the Civil War." MVHR, 31 [1944]: 187-204.

The federal army was composed overwhelmingly of men drawn from civilian life. They did not shed their political ideas or ambitions when they donned uniforms. But political ideas, however sincerely they might be held, interfered with military efficiency and upset the needed unity.

537. Wilson, Charles R. "McClellan's Changing Views on the Peace Plank of 1864." AHR, 38 [1932/1933]: 498-505.

The traditional view that McClellan backed the Union cause unflinchingly at the time of the 1864 Democratic convention, is questioned. At one time, between his nomination and his acceptance speech, he appeared to support the position of the "peace men" in the party.

538. ———. "New Light on the Lincoln-Blair-Fremont 'Bargain' of 1864." AHR, 42 [1936/1937]: 71-78.

The circumstances surrounding Fremont's withdrawal from the presidential campaign of 1864 and Blair's dismissal from Lincoln's cabinet the following day have long puzzled historians. Most believe Fremont accepted Blair's dismissal as sufficient reward for his withdrawal. New evidence seems to indicate no bargain existed between Fremont and Lincoln. Rather they intimate that Fremont came close to withdrawing in favor of McClellan and the Democrats.

539. Wilson, Henry. MILITARY MEASURES OF THE UNITED STATES CONGRESS, 1861-1865. New York, 1866.

A summary of congressional action during the war.

540. Winston, Sheldon. "Statehood for West Virginia: An Illegal Act?" W VA HIS, 30 [1969]: 530-534.

Author notes the fragility of the "restored" state of Virginia and doubts that the creation of West Virginia was carried out in a legal fashion.

541. ———. "West Virginia's First Delegation to Congress." W VA HIS, 29 [1968]: 274-277.

West Virginia's first elected representatives to Congress practiced moderation and conciliation. They urged loyalty to the Union but not hatred of the South.

542. Winther, Oscar O. "The Soldier Vote in the Election of 1864." NY HIS, 25 [1944]: 440-458.

A review of the wartime state laws permitting soldiers in the field to vote in elections. An analysis of the 1864 presidential election reveals that although the soldiers favored Lincoln over McClellan by a 78-22 margin, their vote was not decisive in the outcome.

543. Zettl, Herbert, editor. "Garibaldi and the American Civil War." CWH, 22 [1976]: 70-76.

A short letter describing the federal government's unsuccessful efforts to secure the services of the Italian patriot, Garibaldi, for the Union army at the outset of the war.

544. Zingg, Paul J. "John Archibald Campbell and the Hampton Roads Conference: Quixotic Diplomat, 1865." ALA HIS Q, 36 [1974]: 21-34.

A good description of peace efforts during the Civil War.

545. Zornow, William. "California Sidelights on the Presidential Election of 1864." CAL HIS SOC Q, 34 [1955]: 49-64.

An interesting article on Lincoln and California.

546. ———. "The Democratic Convention at Chicago in 1864." LIN HER, 54 [1952]: 2-12.

The problem facing the convention was how to create harmony among the many divergent groups, and Vallandigham's return did little to help solve the problem.

547. ———. "The Kansas Senators and the Re-election of Lincoln." KAN HIS Q, 19 [1961]: 133-144.

Kansas Senators James H. Lane and Samuel C. Pomeroy were both Radical Republicans but split over the choice of candidates in the 1864 election. Lane supported Lincoln, while Pomeroy opted for Chase.

548. ———. LINCOLN AND THE PARTY DIVIDED. Norman: University of Oklahoma Press, 1954.

A thorough, carefully researched study of the 1864 election. Although the author does not reach any new conclusions, he does present a very readable and worthwhile volume.

549. ———. "McClellan and Seymour in the Chicago Convention of 1864." JISHS, 43 [1950]: 282-295.

An account of the political in-fighting over Horatio Seymour as a possible nominee prior to the 1864 Democratic national convention.

C. FOREIGN AFFAIRS AND OPINION

By John Kesler

General

550. Albion, Robert G. and Jennie B. Pope. SEA LANES IN WARTIME: THE AMERICAN EXPERIENCE, 1775-1942. New York: Norton, 1942.

While a general survey of vast dimensions, the work offers a solid introduction to some of the complexities of international law and the Civil War.

551. Brauer, Kinley J. "Seward's 'Foreign War Panacea': An Interpretation." NY HIS, 55 [1974]: 133-157.

An effort to refute the war panacea theory by claiming that Seward's efforts were designed to minimize foreign influences on American affairs.

552. ———. "The Slavery Problem in the Diplomacy of the American Civil War." PAC HIS R, 46 [1977]: 439-469.

Brauer argues that the issue of slavery in the arena of international relations played a role far larger than most historians have believed.

553. Crook, David P. DIPLOMACY DURING THE CIVIL WAR. New York: Wiley, 1975.

A good general introduction to the subject, in which the author brings together 15 years' material from his articles and books.

554. ———. THE NORTH, THE SOUTH, AND THE POWERS, 1861-1865. New York: Wiley, 1974.

A synthetic work that provides a useful introduction to the topic. Author deals with the interplay of forces among Great Britain, France, Russia, and the United States.

555. Ferris, Norman B. DESPERATE DIPLOMACY: WILLIAM H. SEWARD'S FOREIGN POLICY, 1861. Knoxville: University of Tennesse Press, 1976.

A study which focuses to a large extent on Great Britain more than other powers and which praises Seward's diplomatic skills, while noting some of his weaknesses.

556. Graebner, Norman A. "European Interventionism and the Crisis of 1862." JISHS, 69 [1976]: 35-45.

A wide-ranging analysis of the factors involved in the crisis of 1862, including the questions of slavery, the lack of military success on the part of the North and European views on Lincoln's administration.

557. ———. "Northern Diplomacy and European Neutrality." In WHY THE NORTH WON THE CIVIL WAR. David Donald, editor. Baton Rouge: Louisiana State University Press, 1960, pages 49-75.

A provocative essay which provides a sound basis for an examination of this rather complex topic.

558. Hyman, Harold, editor. HEARD ROUND THE WORLD: THE IMPACT OF THE CIVIL WAR. New York: Knopf, 1969.

A good collection of six essays dealing with the impact of the Civil War on different areas of the world.

559. Jordan, Donaldson and Edwin J. Pratt. EUROPE AND THE AMERICAN CIVIL WAR. Boston: Houghton Mifflin, 1931.

An early and still useful work dealing with European views on the war, although it has been challenged in recent scholarship.

560. Monaghan, Jay. DIPLOMAT IN CARPET SLIPPERS: ABRAHAM LINCOLN DEALS WITH EUROPEAN AFFAIRS. Indianapolis: Bobbs-Merrill, 1945.

An easy-to-read, perhaps overly friendly, account of Lincoln's role in foreign affairs.

561. Moore, John B. A DIGEST OF INTERNATIONAL LAW AS EMBODIED IN

DIPLOMATIC DISCUSSIONS, TREATIES, AND OTHER INTERNATIONAL AGREEMENTS.... 8 v. Washington, 1906.

Included in this massive work are useful descriptions of many Anglo-American controversies that erupted during the war.

562. Nevins, Allan. "Britain, France and the War Issues." In author's THE WAR FOR THE UNION: WAR BECOMES REVOLUTION, 1862-1863. New York: Scribners, 1960. pp. 242-274.

A brilliant summary of the issues involved in the diplomacy of the Civil War.

563. Owsley, Harriet C. "Henry Shelton Sanford and Federal Surveillance Abroad, 1861-1865." MVHR, 48 [1961]: 211-228.

Author argues that the surveillance overseas by northern agents provided valuable intelligence for the North during the war.

564. Paolino, Ernest N. THE FOUNDATIONS OF THE AMERICAN EMPIRE: WILLIAM HENRY SEWARD AND UNITED STATES FOREIGN POLICY. Ithaca: Cornell University Press, 1973.

An excellent work. It is well researched, well documented, and filled with provocative insights.

565. Peyton, Thomas J., Jr. "Charles Sumner and United States Foreign Relations During the American Civil War." Ph.D. dissertation. Georgetown University, 1972.

An analysis of Sumner's role in the implementation of northern wartime foreign policy.

566. Rawley, James A. "The American Civil War and the Atlantic Community." GA R, 21 [1967]: 185-194.

A discussion of the importance of the American Civil War to the Old World, which itself was confronted with a number of developing cultural and political problems.

567. Rhodes, James F. LECTURES ON THE AMERICAN CIVIL WAR DELIVERED BEFORE THE UNIVERSITY OF OXFORD.... New York, 1913.

The third lecture by the first and one of the most celebrated historians of the Civil War deals with foreign affairs. It has, however, been superceded by more recent works.

568. Sharrow, Walter G. "William Henry Seward and the Basis for American Empire, 1850-1860." PAC HIS R, 36 [1967]: 325-342.

An examination of Seward's pre-war thinking as background for an understanding of his wartime diplomacy.

569. Sideman, Belle B. and Lillian Friedman, editors. EUROPE LOOKS AT THE CIVIL WAR. New York: Orion, 1960.

A collection of essays that covers a wide range of topics; a good, general introductory work. Some of the articles are translated from many foreign sources.

570. Stern, Philip Van Doren. WHEN THE GUNS ROARED: WORLD ASPECTS OF THE AMERICAN CIVIL WAR. Garden City, New York: Doubleday, 1965.

A popular history in which the author discusses both Union and Confederate attempts to get sympathy and support from abroad, as well as foreign attitudes on that subject. The focus is chiefly on Great Britain and France.

571. Warren, Gordon H. "Imperial Dreamer: William Henry Seward and American Destiny." In MAKERS OF AMERICAN DIPLOMACY FROM BENJAMIN FRANKLIN TO HENRY KISSINGER. Frank J. Merli and Theodore A. Wilson, editors. 2 v. New York: Scribners, 1974.

This article should be a starting point for any student wishing to study the complexities of Seward's foreign policy.

Great Britain

572. Adams, Charles F., Jr. "A Crisis in Downing Street." MASS HIS SOC PROC, 47 [1914]: 372-424.

A participant's view that may overemphasize the role played by the Emancipation Proclamation in Europe's diplomatic decisions during the war.

573. Adams, Ephraim D. GREAT BRITAIN AND THE AMERICAN CIVIL WAR. 2 v. New York: Longmans, Green, 1925. Reprint 1957.

An older, lengthy work, but still a good place for students to commence a study of Anglo-American relations during the war.

574. Allen, H.C. GREAT BRITAIN AND THE UNITED STATES: A HISTORY OF ANGLO-AMERICAN RELATIONS [1783-1952]. New York: St. Martin's 1955.

Although a broad survey of the subject matter, the work contains a sound analysis of the Civil War period.

575. Argyll, George D.C., 8th Duke of. ... AUTOBIOGRAPHY AND MEMOIRS. 2 v. Duchess of Argyll, editor. London, 1906.

A member of the British cabinet the Duke strongly supported the federal government, as revealed in his correspondence.

576. Atkins, John B. THE LIFE OF SIR WILLIAM HOWARD RUSSELL.... 2 v. London, 1911.

The pro-southern views of THE TIMES of London's ace correspondent affected Anglo-American diplomacy and public opinion. Russell was in the United States in the early months of the war.

577. Baxter, James P., III. "The British Government and Neutral Rights, 1861-1865." AHR, 34 [1928]: 9-29.

Still a pioneer work on a critical aspect of the Civil War and northern diplomacy.

578. ———. "Some British Opinions as to Neutral Rights, 1861 to 1865." A J INT LAW, 23 [1929]: 517-537.

The recent opening of the Admiralty Papers for the Civil War years makes possible a more accurate study of Britain's neutral rights policy toward the United States.

579. Beloff, Max. "Historical Revisions No. CXVIII: Great Britain and the American Civil War." HISTORY, 37 [1952]: 40-48

A provocative article examining Anglo-American relations.

580. Bernath, Stuart L. "British Neutrality and the Civil War Prize Cases." CWH, 15 [1969]: 320-331.

A careful and detailed examination of British reaction to the rulings, in the press and in Parliament, and the development of British policy toward the North.

581. ———. SQUALL ACROSS THE ATLANTIC: AMERICAN CIVIL WAR PRIZE CASES AND DIPLOMACY. Berkeley: University of California Press, 1970.

Bernath provides both a detailed analysis of a very complex and often confusing subject and includes an excellent bibliography.

582. Bourne, Kenneth. BRITAIN AND THE BALANCE OF POWER IN NORTH AMERICA, 1815-1908. Berkeley: University of California Press, 1967.

Although containing only two chapters relevant to the Civil War, this work provides solid evaluations of the impact of British military and strategic considerations on Anglo-American relations.

583. Brauer, Kinley J. "British Mediation and the American Civil War: A Reconsideration." JSH, 38 [1972]: 49-64.

A reevaluation of Britain's offer to mediate the American war during the fall of 1862, interweaving political and diplomatic factors. Author rejects the familiar thesis that Britain chose not to intervene because of the northern victory at Antietam.

584. Colp, Ralph, Jr. "Charles Darwin: Slavery and the American Civil War." HARV LIB BULL, 26 [1978]: 471-489.

A look at Darwin's opposition to slavery and his wavering support of the Union.

585. Courtemanche, Regis A. NO NEED FOR GLORY: THE BRITISH NAVY IN AMERICAN WATERS, 1860-1864. Annapolis: Naval Institute Press, 1977.

A study of Britain's concern with events in North America during the war, especially the federal government's implementation of its blockade of the South.

586. Crook, David P. "Portents of War: English Opinion of Secession." J AM STUD, 4 [1971]: 163-179.

An essay arguing that the British response to the American Civil War is far more complex than most historians had thought before.

587. Doyle, Elisabeth J. "Report on Civil War America: Sir James Ferguson's Five-Week Visit." CWH, 12 [1966]: 347-362.

A perceptive early account of the war in the fall of 1861 by a young member of the British Parliament.

588. Dyer, Brainerd. "Thomas H. Dudley." CWH, 1 [1955]: 401-413.

An interesting study of the little-known American consul at Liverpool, who played a central role in frustrating Confederate efforts to build ships in England.

589. Ellison, Mary. SUPPORT FOR SECESSION: LANCASHIRE AND THE AMERICAN CIVIL WAR. Chicago: University of Chicago Press, 1972.

A case study refuting the belief that British textile workers supported the North. Author demonstrates that in Lancashire, at least, the workers were united in their support of the South.

590. Ellsworth, Edward W. "Lord John Russell and British Consuls in America in 1861." LIN HER, 66 [1964]: 34-40.

A survey of consular reports to the British foreign secretary in the early months of the war, which helped shape Russell's opinion that federal troops were not capable of achieving total victory.

591. ———. "Anglo-American Affairs in October of 1862." LIN HER, 66 [1964]: 80-96.

An account of the efforts of Lord Russell to bring about the intervention of Britain and other powers in the Civil War and to mediate the conflict.

592. Foner, Philip S. BRITISH LABOR AND THE AMERICAN CIVIL WAR. New York: Holmes and Meier, 1984.

An accomplished student of labor history examines the attitude of the British workingmen toward the Civil War. Not a lengthy work, but an important one.

593. Forbes, John M. LETTERS AND RECOLLECTIONS OF JOHN MURRAY FORBES. Sarah Forbes Hughes, editor. 2 v. Boston, 1889.

A wealthy American businessman, Forbes went to England in 1863 and his letters reflect his reactions to what he saw and heard.

594. Green, Thomas W. and Frank J. Merli. "Could the Laird Rams Have Lifted the Union Blockade?" CWTI, 2 [1] [1963]: 14-17.

After a discussion of the potential threat to the Union navy which the Laird rams represented, the authors conclude that they would not have broken the blockade.

595. Harrison, Royden. "British Labor and American Slavery." In author's BEFORE THE SOCIALISTS: STUDIES IN LABOUR AND POLITICS, 1861-1881. London: Routledge and Kegan Paul, 1965. Pages 40-65.

Author contends that most of British labor supported the North because most of the trade union leaders and the British press supported the South.

596. ———. "British Labour and the Confederacy." INT R SOC HIS, 2 [1957]: 78-105.

A solid piece of social history which provides insight into labor's role in the British government's handling of the American war.

597. Heckman, Richard A. "The British Press Reacts to Lincoln's Election." JISHS, 63 [1970]: 257-269.

A survey of the major English newspapers at the time of the 1860 election reveals general approval of Lincoln's triumph. Within two years, however, much of the British press would turn against Lincoln.

598. Henderson, Conway W. "The Anglo-American Treaty of 1862 in Civil War Diplomacy." CWH, 15 [1969]: 308-319.

This pact which tightened control over the trans-Atlantic slave trade was impossible to negotiate prior to the withdrawal of the southern states from the Union.

599. Hernon, Joseph M., Jr. "British Sympathies in the American Civil War: A Reconsideration." JSH, 33 [1967]: 356-367.

Author contends that it was a hatred of democracy rather than an affinity for the southern aristocracy which motivated upper class British support for the South.

600. ———. CELTS, CATHOLICS, AND COPPERHEADS: IRELAND VIEWS THE AMERICAN CIVIL WAR. Columbus: Ohio State University Press, 1968.

In a book that plows new ground, Hernon examines the dual questions of southern independence and Irish home rule. Irish public opinion sided with the Confederacy. An able analysis of a tricky subject.

601. Higginbotham, Don. "A Raider Refuels: Diplomatic Repercussions." CWH, 4 [1958]: 129-142.

A British Foreign Office decision in January 1862 allowed belligerent vessels to refuel at British overseas possessions once every three months. When the FLORIDA exceeded the maximum number, a diplomatic crisis arose almost as serious as that at the time of the TRENT affair.

602. Jenkins, Brian. BRITAIN AND THE WAR FOR THE UNION. Montreal: McGill-Queen's University Press, 1974.

In Volume One of a two-volume work, covering 1860-1862, the author attempts a fresh treatment of Anglo-American relations. While he does not fully succeed in his effort, the work still is a useful one.

603. Jones, Robert H. "Anglo-American Relations, 1861-1865: Reconsidered." MID AM, 45 [1963]: 36-49.

An article that will be worthwhile for those interested in studying primary sources for themselves.

604. Jones, Robert O. BRITISH PSEUDO-NEUTRALITY DURING THE AMERICAN CIVIL WAR. Washington, D.C.: n.p., 1952.

Author draws heavily on the dispatches of Thomas Dudley, the American consul at Liverpool in developing this account.

605. Jones, Wilbur D. THE AMERICAN PROBLEM IN BRITISH DIPLOMACY, 1841-1861. Athens: University of Georgia Press, 1974.

Jones examines the "American Problem" in the context of British decision-making and supplies a thoughtful perspective.

606. ———. "The British Conservatives and the American Civil War." AHR, 58 [1953]: 527-543.

In an article that argues that the Conservatives were far less favorably disposed to the South than most have believed, the author makes an excellent contribution to scholarship in the field.

607. ———. THE CONFEDERATE RAMS AT BIRKENHEAD: A CHAPTER IN ANGLO-AMERICAN RELATIONS. Tuscaloosa, Alabama: Confederate Publishing, 1961.

The best account of the Laird ram crisis and the decision by the British to seize the rams prior to their sailing in the fall of 1863. This decision removed an important source of friction between the federal government and Great Britain.

608. Kaplan, Lawrence S. "The Brahmin as Diplomat in Nineteenth Century America: Everett, Bancroft, Motley, Lowell." CWH, 19 [1973]: 5-28.

An analysis of four American diplomats who, while talented, exerted very little influence on American diplomacy during the middle years of the century. Some astute observations on Anglo-American relations are included in the article.

609. Krein, David F. "Russell's Decision to Detain the Laird Rams." CWH, 22 [1976]: 158-163.

Based on a careful examination of the papers of Austin H. Layard, the British undersecretary of state, the author analyzes the British decision to prohibit the rams from sailing.

610. Large, David. "An Irish Friend and the Civil War." FRIENDS HIS ASSN BULL, 47 [1958]: 20-29.

A discussion of the opinions of Joshua E. Todhunter, an Irish Quaker, on the South and slavery.

611. Logan, Kevin J. "The Bee-Hive Newspaper and British Working Class Attitudes Toward the American Civil War." CWH, 22 [1976]: 337-348.

An examination of the Lancashire workers suggest that the attitudes held by this segment of British labor may be unique, shaped by circumstances peculiar to Lancashire.

612. Mathieson, W.L. GREAT BRITAIN AND THE SLAVE TRADE, 1839-1865. London: Longmans, Green, 1929.

A sound and still valuable analysis of Britain's role in attempting to end the slave trade. It is helpful for a full understanding of Anglo-American wartime relations.

613. Maynard, Douglas H. "The Forbes-Aspinwall Mission." MVHR, 45 [1958]: 67-89.

The purpose of the Forbes-Aspinwall mission to England in 1863 was to purchase for the Union, ships being built there for the Confederacy. It failed to achieve that goal, but it did sharpen the American presence in England and helped maintain peaceful relations between the two countries.

614. ———. "Plotting the Escape of the ALABAMA." JSH, 20 [1954]: 197-209.

This is the story of the race against time to complete the construction of the Confederate raider ALABAMA. The ship sailed from Liverpool on July 31, 1862, just before Her Majesty's officers received instructions to seize it.

615. ———. "Union Efforts to Prevent the Escape of the ALABAMA." MVHR, 41 [1954]: 41-60.

An account of the unsuccessful northern efforts to block the sailing of the ALABAMA from the Laird shipyards in Liverpool in June and July 1862.

616. Merli, Frank J. GREAT BRITAIN AND THE CONFEDERATE NAVY, 1861-1865. Bloomington: Indiana University Press, 1970.

A thorough examination of a small but significant issue in the general context of Anglo-Americans relations.

617. ——— and Theodore A. Wilson. "The British Cabinet and the Confederacy, Autumn, 1862." MD HIS MAG, 65 [1970]: 239-262.

A study of the question of possible British intervention in the war in the fall of 1862. Author concludes that such a course of action was barely averted.

618. Milne, A. Taylor. "The Lyons-Seward Treaty of 1862." AHR, 38 [1932]: 511-525.

An early study of the treaty which provided for greater control of the Trans-Atlantic slave trade, but one which has been superceded by more recent scholarship.

619. Moran, Benjamin. THE JOURNAL OF BENJAMIN MORAN, 1857-1865. 2 v. Sarah A. Wallace and Frances E. Gillespie, editors. Chicago: University of Chicago Press, 1948.

The interesting journal of an astute commentator, who happened to be in the American legation in London.

620. Newton. A.P. "Anglo-American Relations During the Civil War, 1860-1865." In THE CAMBRIDGE HISTORY OF BRITISH FOREIGN POLICY, 1783-1919. 3 v. A.W. Ward and G.P. Gooch, editors. New York: Macmillan, 1922-1923. Volume 2, pages 488-521.

A concise survey of British-American relations from Lincoln's election through the Laird ram crisis. Written by a British historian, the account is somewhat critical of the federal government's policies.

621. Newton, [T.W.L.] Lord. LORD LYONS: A RECORD OF BRITISH DIPLOMACY. 2 v. New York, 1913.

The private and public papers of Lord Lyons, the British minister in Washington, are important for a study of diplomatic relations between the two countries.

622. Pole, J.R. ABRAHAM LINCOLN AND THE WORKING CLASSES OF BRITAIN. London: Commonwealth-American Current Affairs Unit of the English Speaking Union, 1959.

A concise account of the British workers and their thoughts on the war. They were, traditionally, hostile to the South and friendly to the North.

623. Reid, Robert L., editor. "William E. Gladstone's 'Insincere Neutrality' During the Civil War." CWH, 15 [1969]: 293-307.

An 1872 letter by Gladstone in which the chancellor of the exchequer during the Civil War sought to explain his alleged pro-southern attitudes.

624. Robinton, Madeline R. AN INTRODUCTION TO THE PAPERS OF THE NEW YORK PRIZE COURT, 1861-1865. New York: n.p., 1945.

An important study of the legal difficulties which the blockade posed for the two countries.

625. Sanders, Neil F. "Freeman Harlow Morse and the Forbes-Aspinwall Mission: An Aberration in Union Foreign Policy." LIN HER, 80 [1978]: 15-25.

The Forbes-Aspinwall mission, inspired by Morse, American consul in London, would have had the federal government purchase ships under construction in Britain for Confederate use. Lincoln killed the plan.

626. Smith, Goldwin. ENGLAND AND AMERICA: A LECTURE READ BEFORE THE BOSTON FRATERNITY.... Boston, 1865.

In a discussion of the issues dividing the two countries, the well-known British historian urges closer cooperation between Britain and the United States.

627. ———. A LETTER TO A WHIG MEMBER OF THE SOUTHERN INDEPENDENCE ASSOCIATION. Boston, 1864.

Smith argues strongly and eloquently against British support of the South.

628. Stansky, Peter. GLADSTONE: A PROGRESS IN POLITICS. Boston: Little, Brown, 1979.

A biography which enables students of the Civil War to understand Gladstone's views on both slavery and moral principles in the field of foreign relations.

629. Thomas, Mary E. "The C.S.S. TALLAHASSEE: A Factor in Anglo-American Relations, 1864-1866." CWH, 21 [1975]: 148-159.

A record of the depredations of the Confederate raider TALLAHASSEE, which destroyed a large amount of Union shipping in 1864-1865.

630. Wade, William W. "The Man Who Stopped the Rams." AM HER, 14 [3] [1963]:18-23, 78-81.

An account of the activities of Thomas H. Dudley, the American consul at Liverpool, who played an important role in preventing the Laird rams from sailing.

631. Weinberg, Adelaide. JOHN ELLIOT CAIRNES AND THE AMERICAN CIVIL WAR: A STUDY IN ANGLO-AMERICAN RELATIONS. London: Kingswood, 1968.

The work of Cairnes, an Irish economist-publicist, who aroused British public opinion in favor of the North on the issue of slavery, is examined in the context of the overall British response to the Civil War.

632. Whitridge, Arnold. "British Liberals and the American Civil War." HIS TOD, 12 [1962]: 688-695.

The author examines the attitudes of leading British political leaders and intellectuals toward the war.

633. ———. "The Peaceable Ambassadors." AM HER, 8 [3] [1957]: 40-43, 89-103.

A discussion of the efforts of the American ambassador to Great Britain and the British minister to Washington in maintaining peace between the two countries during the war.

634. Wolseley, Garnet J., Viscount. THE AMERICAN CIVIL WAR: AN ENGLISH VIEW. James A. Rawley, editor. Charlottesville: University of Virginia Press, 1964.

A well-edited collection of pro-southern writings on the war by one of England's most distinguished soldiers of the Victorian age.

635. Wright, D.E. "English Opinion of Secession: A Note." J AM STUD, 5 [1971]: 151-154.

A separatist solution to the American dilemma was favored for a variety of reasons.

The TRENT Affair

636. Adams, Charles F., Jr. "The TRENT Affair." AHR, 17 [1912]: 540-562.

A criticism of the handling of the TRENT affair by the son of the American minister in London. While Wilkes' act was wrong, the opportunity for a great propaganda victory was missed.

637. Bourne, Kenneth. "British Preparations for War With the North, 1861-1862." ENG HIS R, 76 [1961]: 600-632.

A section on the TRENT affair puts the incident in the context of military and diplomatic matters.

638. Cohen, V.H. "Charles Sumner and the TRENT Affair." JSH, 22 [1956]: 205-219.

A look at the influential senator's role in the resolution of the crisis. He opposed keeping Mason and Slidell from the outset.

639. Drake, F.C. "The Cuban Background of the TRENT Affair." CWH, 19 [1973]: 29-49.

Robert W. Shufeldt, the American consul in Havana, worked closely with Captain Charles Wilkes in planning the seizure of the TRENT.

640. Ferris, Norman B. "The Prince Consort, 'The Times,' and the TRENT Affair." CWH, 6 [1960]: 152-156.

It is suggested that the Prince Consort derived his idea of softening the TRENT dispatch to Lord Lyons from editorials in THE TIMES.

641. ———. THE TRENT AFFAIR: A DIPLOMATIC CRISIS. Knoxville: University of Tennessee Press, 1977.

A comprehensive and detailed study that attempts to explain how the incident escalated into a major crisis for Lincoln's administration.

642. ———. "Abraham Lincoln and the 'TRENT' Affair." LIN HER, 69 [1967]: 131-135.

Lincoln himself prepared a reply to England based on ideas of John Bright expressed to Charles Sumner. However, he urged that Seward draft his own response.

643. Hancock, Harold B. and Norman B. Wilkinson. "'The Devil to Pay': Saltpeter and the TRENT Affair." CWH, 10 [1964]: 20-32.

It is suggested that the need for British saltpeter was an important consideration in the decision to release Mason and Slidell.

644. John, Evan. ATLANTIC IMPACT. New York: Putnam, 1952.

A fairly good, readable study of the subject, although there are no footnotes and a list of sources is also missing.

645. Large, David. "Friends and the American Civil War: The TRENT Affair." J FRIENDS HIS SOC, 48 [1957]: 163-167.

A discussion of the efforts of the Society of Friends to try to convince the British to find a peaceful solution to the TRENT affair.

646. Long, John S. "Glory-Hunting Off Havana: Wilkes and the TRENT Affair." CWH, 9 [1963]: 133-144.

An examination of Wilkes' motives in initiating the TRENT episode. Long concludes that Wilkes marched to his own drumbeat.

647. O'Rourke, Alice. "The Law Officers of the Crown and the TRENT Affair." MID AM, 54 [1972]: 157-171.

O'Rourke argues that Seward's stand on the TRENT affair, from a legal viewpoint, had already been foreshadowed by the development of similar views among the crown's legal advisors.

648. Smith, Geoffrey S. "Charles Wilkes and the Growth of American Naval Diplomacy." In MAKERS OF AMERICAN DIPLOMACY FROM BENJAMIN FRANKLIN TO HENRY KISSINGER. Frank J. Merli and Theodore A. Wilson, editors. 2 v. New York: Scribners, 1974.

An argument that places Wilkes, along with many naval officers of the time, in the driver's seat in terms of the development of American foreign policy.

649. Warren, Gordon H. FOUNTAIN OF DISCONTENT: THE TRENT AFFAIR AND FREEDOM OF THE SEAS. Boston: Northeastern University Press, 1981.

A well-written, day-by-day study that provides a good examination of the legal aspects of the TRENT affair.

650. Wheeler-Bennett, J. "The TRENT Affair: How the Prince Consort Saved the United States." HIS TOD, 11 [12] [1961]: 805-816.

A popular account which contains some rare documentary materials.

651. Whitridge, Arnold. "The TRENT Affair, 1861." HIS TOD, 4 [6] [1954]: 394-402.

A short review of the famous episode which nearly brought about war between the United States and the United Kingdom.

France

652. Bandy, William T., translator and editor. "Civil War Notes of a French Volunteer." WIS MAG HIS, 43 [1962]: 239-245.

A collection of four letters by an unknown Frenchman who served in the Army of the Potomac in 1862-1863. The letters were originally published in France in 1864.

653. Barker, Nancy N. DISTAFF DIPLOMACY: THE EMPRESS EUGENIE AND THE FOREIGN POLICY OF THE SECOND EMPIRE. Austin: University of Texas Press, 1967.

An interesting examination of the role played by a woman in the diplomacy of France with respect to the Civil War.

654. Bigelow, John. FRANCE AND THE CONFEDERATE NAVY, 1862-1865. New York, 1888. Reprint 1968.

An interesting appraisal, by the American consul in Paris, of the confusion behind France's response to Confederate requests for the construction of ironclads.

655. ———. RETROSPECTIONS OF AN ACTIVE LIFE. 5 v. New York, 1909-1913.

Useful primary material concerning Bigelow's wartime activities in France may be found in this voluminous memoir.

656. Blumenthal, Henry. FRANCE AND THE UNITED STATES: THEIR DIPLOMATIC RELATIONS, 1789-1914. Chapel Hill: University of North Carolina Press, 1970.

A general survey in which the author has included several excellent chapters on Franco-American relations during the war.

657. Carroll, Daniel B. "America in 1861: A French View." JISHS, 67 [1974]: 133-153.

A survey of American life through the eyes of a group of French aristocrats who traveled throughout the North for two months in the summer of 1861.

658. ———. HENRI MERCIER AND THE AMERICAN CIVIL WAR. Princeton: Princeton University Press, 1971.

A substantial work dealing with the relationship between Seward and Henri Mercier the French ambassador. An excellent glimpse of wartime Washington and the problems the war created for France.

659. Case, Lynn M., compiler and editor. ... FRENCH OPINION ON THE UNITED STATES AND MEXICO, 1860-1867.... New York: Appleton-Century, 1936.

A valuable collection of materials, reports of the procureurs generaux, which reflect the impact of the Civil War on France.

660. ——— and Warren F. Spencer. THE UNITED STATES AND FRANCE: CIVIL WAR DIPLOMACY. Philadelphia: University of Pennsylvania Press, 1970.

A scholarly study, presented more from a European view than an American, which should stand the test of time. A must for anyone concerned with this facet of Civil War diplomacy.

661. Gavronsky, Serge. THE FRENCH LIBERAL OPPOSITION AND THE AMERICAN CIVIL WAR. New York: Humanities Press, 1968.

A good readable analysis of the impact of the American Civil War on French liberalism. French liberals supported the North.

662. ———. "American Slavery and the French Liberals: An Interpretation of the Role of Slavery in French Politics During the Second Empire." JNH, 51 [1966]: 36-38.

While French opinion was anti-slavery, Louis Napoleon viewed a southern victory or a mediated settlement as a possible aid to his Mexican policy.

663. Hanna, Alfred J. and Kathryn A.Hanna. NAPOLEON III AND MEXICO:

AMERICAN TRIUMPH OVER MONARCHY. Chapel Hill: University of North Carolina Press, 1971.

A traditional study that examines the policies of both Seward and the French government.

664. Johnston, William E. MEMOIRS OF "MALAKOFF" [pseud.]. BEING EXTRACTS FROM THE CORRESPONDENCE AND PAPERS OF.... R.M. Johnston, editor. 2 v. London, 1907.

Johnston was the Paris correspondent of the NEW YORK TIMES during the war.

665. Nasatir, A.P. "The French Attitude in California During the Civil War Decade." CAL HIS SOC Q, 43 [1964]: 19-35.

Twenty-five thousand French nationals were in California when the war broke out. The attitude of the French government toward the war and its advice to the French nationals is told through the dispatches of the French consuls at Los Angeles and San Francisco.

666. Spencer, Warren. "The Jewett-Greeley Affair: A Private Scheme for French Mediation in the American Civil War." NY HIS, 51 [1970]: 238-268.

A look at a case of personal diplomacy which failed to bring about French mediation in the war.

667. West, Warren. ...CONTEMPORARY FRENCH OPINION ON THE AMERICAN CIVIL WAR. Baltimore: Johns Hopkins Press, 1924.

A brief but good survey of the subject, drawing largely on published materials here and in France.

Other Powers

668. Adamov, E.A. "Russia and the United States at the Time of the Civil War." J MOD HIS, 2 [1930]: 586-602.

Adamov, a Russian historian, unaware of Golder's original work [number 681], repeats the story that the Russian fleet came to the United States to better position it for war with Britain.

669. Bailey, Thomas A. "The Russian Fleet Myth Re-Examined." MVHR, 38 [1951]: 81-90.

The author examines and rejects William E. Nagengast's theory [number 692] that Americans in general knew of the real purpose of the visit of the Russian fleet to the United States in the fall of 1863. The real purpose was to remove the fleet from the icebound waters of the Baltic Sea in the event of war with England and France over the Polish insurrection. The traditional belief was that the fleet's visit was a friendly act, perhaps intended to lead to a United States-Russian alliance in the event of

British-French intervention in the Civil War. Bailey argues that most Americans believed in the friendship-alliance theory and were unaware of the real purpose of the fleet's visit.

670. Blegen, Theodore C. ABRAHAM LINCOLN AND EUROPEAN OPINION. Minneapolis: n.p., 1934.

Relying on the writings of Europeans, the author seeks to show how Lincoln rose to the stature of an international hero.

671. Blinn, Harold E. "Seward and the Polish Rebellion of 1864." AHR, 45 [1940]: 828-833.

Seward is praised for adroitly avoiding involvement with other European powers on behalf of Poland at the time of the rebellion.

672. Blumberg, Arnold. "The Diplomacy of the Mexican Empire, 1863-1867." A PHIL SOC TRAN, 61 [1971]: 1-152.

While more oriented to European diplomatic questions, this lengthy essay does contain a small section that deals with Seward's policies.

673. Bondestead, Kjell. "The American Civil War and Swedish Public Opinion." SWED PION HIS Q, 19 [1968]: 95-115.

The Swedish conservative view was that American society was a bad example of rule by the people, while the liberals held that the country was a model for other societies to emulate.

674. Brauer, Kinley J. "The Appointment of Carl Schurz as Minister to Spain." MID AM, 56 [1974]: 75-84.

Schurz's appointment created a problem for the federal government inasmuch as he was viewed as a radical by Spain. The author's study examines the efforts made to prevent the problem from provoking a crisis between the two countries.

675. ———. "Gabriel Garcia y Tassara and the American Civil War: A Spanish Perspective." CWH, 21 [1975]: 5-27.

An examination of American-Spanish relations during the war, based to a large extent on Spanish primary sources, through the eyes of the Spanish minister in Washington.

676. Callahan, James M. ... RUSSO-AMERICAN RELATIONS DURING THE AMERICAN CIVIL WAR. Morgantown, West Virginia: 1908.

A brief seminal study, but one which has long since been superceded.

677. Cortada, James W. SPAIN AND THE AMERICAN CIVIL WAR: RELATIONS AT MID-CENTURY, 1855-1868. Philadelphia: American Philosophical Society, 1980.

While surveying American-Spanish relations during this larger period, the work has some excellent insights into that relationship in the war years.

678. Egan, Clifford L. "Friction in New Orleans: General Butler Versus the Spanish Consul." LA HIS, 9 [1968]: 43-52.

General Ben Butler's dealings with the Spanish Consul in New Orleans in 1862 were about as tempestuous as they were with everyone else with whom he had relations. He reacted heavy-handedly when Spanish ships gave sanctuary to Confederates, or when Spanish merchants in New Orleans handled goods brought in through the blockade.

679. Ferris, Nathan L. "The Relations of the United States With South America During the American Civil War." HISP A HIS R, 21 [1941]: 51-78.

Until the Civil War, the United States had almost ignored South America. The war, however, brought changes. The chief goal was to prevent recognition of the Confederacy. A side effect was the tremendous goodwill built up under Seward's policies.

680. Golder, Frank A. "The American Civil War Through the Eyes of a Russian Diplomat." AHR, 26 [1921]: 454-463.

Author observes that Edoard de Stoeckl, the Russian minister in Washington during the Civil War, failed to grasp the deeper meaning of the conflict.

681. ———. "The Russian Fleet and the Civil War." AHR, 20 [1915]: 801-812.

Basing his research on documents in the Russian archives, Golder was the first historian to establish the real motives behind the visit of the Russian fleet to the United States in 1863. Namely, the purpose was to prevent the fleet's being "bottled up" in the Baltic if war broke out between Russia, on the one hand, and France and England on the other. Russia needed neutral, warm water ports to attack French and British commerce, if necessary. Author refutes the friendship-alliance theory.

682. Hill, Lawrence F. DIPLOMATIC RELATIONS BETWEEN THE UNITED STATES AND BRAZIL. Durham, North Carolina: Duke University Press, 1932.

An authoritative work on the subject.

683. Johnson, Ludwell H. "Beverley Tucker's Canadian Mission, 1864-1865." JSH, 29 [1963]: 88-99.

An account of the trade mission to Canada of the Confederate agent, Beverley Tucker. His purpose was to arrange with officials of the federal government for the transfer of southern cotton for northern meat, but he failed to attain his objective.

684. Kaufman, Martin. "1863: Poland, Russia and the United States." POL AM STUD, 21 [1964]: 10-15.

The Polish insurrection against Czarist rule won much sympathy in the American press. However, the northern government, anxious to maintain good relations with Russia, gave little support to the rebels.

685. Kendall, John C. "The New York City Press and Anti-Canadianism: A New Perspective on the Civil War Years." JOUR Q, 52 [1975]: 522-530.

Author questions the belief that the hostility of the New York city newspapers was largely responsible for whatever anti-northern sentiment existed in Canada.

686. Kennedy, Philip W. "Union and Confederate Relations with Mexico." DUQ R, 11 [1966]: 47-64.

A discussion of the problems both the North and the South encountered in their dealings with Mexico.

687. Koerner, Gustave P. MEMOIRS OF GUSTAVE KOERNER, 1809-1896.... 2 v. Thomas J. McCormack, editor. Cedar Rapids, Iowa: 1909.

Koerner was the American minister in Madrid during the war.

688. Kushner, Howard I. "The Russian Fleet and the American Civil War: Another View." HISTORIAN, 34 [1972]: 633-649.

Author argues that Lincoln and Seward were aware of the real reason for the arrival of the Russian fleet in New York in 1863, but made excellent use of the opportunity to secure diplomatic benefits for the government.

689. Kutolowski, John. "The Effect of the Polish Insurrection of 1863 on American Civil War Diplomacy." HISTORIAN, 27 [1965]: 560-577.

The Polish uprising diminished the prospects of foreign recognition of the Confederacy.

690. Lowenthal, David. GEORGE PERKINS MARSH: VERSATILE VERMONTER. New York: Columbia University Press, 1958.

An excellent biography of the man who served as the United States minister to Italy during the war.

691. MacDonald, Helen G. CANADIAN PUBLIC OPINION ON THE AMERICAN CIVIL WAR. New York: Columbia University Press, 1926.

An early effort to examine an often overlooked aspect of Civil War diplomacy, but one now superceded by the writings of Robin Winks.

692. Nagengast, William E. "The Visit of the Russian Fleet to the United States: Were Americans Deceived?" RUSS R, 8 [1949]: 560-577.

This is the first attempt to demonstrate that Americans knew the true purpose of the visit of the Russian fleet in 1863. However, Bailey [number 669] attacks the theory, arguing that Nagengast's samplings of editorial opinion in contemporary newspapers and magazines was too limited to be representative.

693. Orzell, Laurence J. "A Favorable Interval: The Polish Insurrection in Civil War Diplomacy, 1863." CWH, 24 [1978]: 332-350.

The 1863 outbreak of revolution in Poland against Russian rule diverted European attention--and possible intervention--in the Civil War. France and Britain, in particular, were partial to the South, but their interest in the American struggle waned because of their concern about events in Poland.

694. Pattock, Florence B. "Cassius M. Clay's Mission to Russia: 1861-1862; 1863-1869." FCHQ, 43 [1969]: 325-344.

Cassius M. Clay, in the author's view, has never received the recognition he deserves for his wartime diplomatic service in Russia. His mission was to keep the Czar on the Union side and he succeeded admirably.

695. Pomeroy, Earl S. "The Myth After the Russian Fleet, 1863." NY HIS, 31 [1950]: 169-176.

The author follows the Nagengast theory, arguing that many Americans understood the real purpose of the visit of the Russian fleet. He concedes that some people followed the friendship-alliance school of thought but thinks they were a minority.

696. Robertson, James R. A KENTUCKIAN AT THE COURT OF THE TSARS: THE MINISTRY OF CASSIUS MARCELLUS CLAY TO RUSSIA.... Berea, Kentucky: Berea College Press, 1935.

The best study of the service of the American minister to Russia.

697. Shippee, Lester B. CANADIAN-AMERICAN RELATIONS, 1848-1874. New Haven: Yale University Press, 1939.

A thorough examination of the subject drawn largely from primary source materials.

698. Stevenson, Charles S. "Abraham Lincoln and the Russian Fleet Myth." MIL R, 50 [1970]: 35-37.

A brief review of the subject, wherein the author believes that the real purpose of the fleet's visit was not revealed until Golder's 1915 article.

699. Thomas, Benjamin P. RUSSO-AMERICAN RELATIONS, 1815-1867. Baltimore: Johns Hopkins Press, 1930.

An excellent general survey of the subject with a good discussion of the war period.

700. Tyrner-Tyrnauer, A.R. LINCOLN AND THE EMPERORS. New York: Harcourt, Brace, World, 1962.

Drawn from Austrian archives, the material does not quite sustain the author's thesis that Lincoln devoted a great amount of time in personal diplomacy with Europe's emperors.

701. Winks, Robin W. CANADA AND THE UNITED STATES: THE CIVIL WAR YEARS. Baltimore: Johns Hopkins Press, 1960.

A heavily researched volume, the author's Ph.D. dissertation does a fairly good job in covering the subject matter. While some reviewers have been rather critical of it, the book contributes to an understanding of our wartime relations with our neighbor to the north.

702. Woldman, Albert A. LINCOLN AND THE RUSSIANS. Cleveland, Ohio: World, 1952.

A readable useful study which relies considerably on the correspondence of the Russian minister in Washington to his home office.

D. STATE AND LOCAL GOVERNMENT, TERRITORIES, AND OCCUPIED AREAS

General

703. Hubbart, Henry C. THE OLDER MIDDLE WEST, 1840-1880.... New York: Appleton-Century, 1936.

A good introduction to the economic, social, and political life of the region.

704. Jones, Robert H. THE CIVIL WAR IN THE NORTHWEST: NEBRASKA, WISCONSIN, IOWA, MINNESOTA, AND THE DAKOTAS. Norman: University of Oklahoma Press, 1960.

An able and well-written study of the military administration of the Department of the Northwest. General John Pope, who commanded the department from 1862-1865, comes through as a respected figure who did a difficult job in a capable fashion.

705. Smith, Edward C. THE BORDERLAND IN THE CIVIL WAR. New York: Macmillan, 1927.

Focuses on the complicated problems of the Border states during the war. Numerous difficult situations confronted the people of the region and this major study contributes substantially to a better grasp of the matter, for both scholars and laymen alike.

Connecticut

706. Croffut, William and John Morris. THE MILITARY AND CIVIL HISTORY OF CONNECTICUT DURING THE WAR OF 1861-1865. New York, 1868.

A potpourri of events on the home front, regimental histories, and biographical sketches of soldiers.

707. Eliot, Ellsworth, Jr. YALE IN THE CIVIL WAR. New Haven: Yale University Press, 1932.

Lists Yale men serving in the armed forces and discusses briefly the various aspects of college life in 1861.

708. Lane, Jarlath R. ... A POLITICAL HISTORY OF CONNECTICUT DURING THE CIVIL WAR.... Washington: Catholic University of America Press, 1941.

An excellent study of the state during the pre-war and war years. A useful bibliographic essay is also included.

709. Niven, John. CONNECTICUT FOR THE UNION: THE ROLE OF THE STATE IN THE CIVIL WAR. New Haven: Yale University Press, 1965.

A good study of all aspects of life in Civil War Connecticut. The author particularly emphasizes the vital role played by the young men of the state in developing a war-like spirit before Sumter and in bringing distinction to the state on the battlefield.

Delaware

710. Hancock, Harold. "Civil War Comes to Delaware." CWH, 2 [1956]: 29-46.

A few sections of this study discuss the activities of this Border state in raising local and federal troops during the first weeks of the war.

711. ———. DELAWARE DURING THE CIVIL WAR: A POLITICAL HISTORY. Wilmington: Historical Society of Delaware, 1961.

Although loyal to the Union, Delaware was split in sentiment with most of its leaders being pro-South.

712. ———. "The Income and Manufacturers' Tax of 1862-1872 As Historical Source Material." DEL HIS, 14 [1971]: 255-261.

The war helped Delaware's economy, and Wilmington became a boom town.

713. Wilkinson, Norman B. THE BRANDYWINE HOME FRONT DURING THE CIVIL WAR, 1861-1865. Wilmington: Kaumagraph, 1966.

An excellent record of the DuPont family of Wilmington during the war, as well as a wartime social history of Delaware. The

DuPonts were active Unionists, but Delaware itself could not make up its mind on the matter.

714. Wilson, W. Emerson, editor. DELAWARE IN THE CIVIL WAR. Dover: Civil War Centennial Commission, 1962.

A very brief history of Delaware and its contributions to the Union war effort.

District of Columbia

715. Ames, Mary. TEN YEARS IN WASHINGTON.... Hartford, Connecticut: 1873.

An early account of wartime Washington.

716. Barber, Edward H. "Men and Events in Washington During and After the Civil War." MICH HIS COLL, 30 [1906]: 212-243.

A Michigan newspaperman who was reading clerk in the House of Representatives from 1863 to 1869 remembers his experiences in the war.

717. Benjamin, Marcus, editor. WASHINGTON DURING WAR TIME.... Washington, D.C.: 1902.

A collection of essays on wartime Washington assembled and published as a souvenir of the 36th encampment of the Grand Army of the Republic.

718. Cooling, Benjamin F. SYMBOL, SWORD, AND SHIELD: DEFENDING WASHINGTON DURING THE CIVIL WAR. Hamden, Connecticut: Archon, 1975.

An excellent study of the military defenses around the national capital. By 1862 Washington was a well-protected fortress. The defense system was the shield while the Army of the Potomac was the sword to attack the foe.

719. Gobright, Lawrence A. RECOLLECTIONS OF MEN AND THINGS AT WASHINGTON.... Philadelphia, 1869.

A longtime observer of the scene in the capital, the author comments on his experiences both before and during the war.

720. Green, Constance M. WASHINGTON: VILLAGE AND CAPITAL, 1800-1878. Princeton: Princeton University Press, 1962.

First of a multi-volume history of the nation's capital, this book takes the story to 1878. Three chapters deal with the war years. The book is not on the same scale as REVEILLE IN WASHINGTON by Margaret Leech, but it nevertheless provides a good glimpse of the time and the place.

721. Jordan, Philip D. "The Capital of Crime." CWTI, 13 [10] [1975]: 4-9, 44-47.

Crime and police activity in Washington while the war was in progress are the focus of this article.

722. Kimmel, Stanley P. MR. LINCOLN'S WASHINGTON. New York: Coward-McCann, 1957.

A pleasant, pictorial history of the Washington that Lincoln knew.

723. Leech, Margaret. REVEILLE IN WASHINGTON, 1860-1865. New York: Harper, 1941. Reprint 1962.

This Pulitzer Prize volume vividly describes the social and political life of Washington during the war. A classic.

724. SYMBOL AND THE SWORD, THE. Washington: Civil War Centennial Commission, 1962.

A good study of wartime Washington, emphasizing the importance of the national capital as the psychological as well as the geographical center for the Union government.

725. Wilson, Rufus H. WASHINGTON, THE CAPITAL CITY.... 2 v. Philadelphia, 1901.

An old social history, which has since been superceded by a number of other works.

Illinois

726. Adams, David W. "Illinois Soldiers and the Emancipation Proclamation." JISHS, 68 [1974]: 407-421.

Illinois volunteers supported the Republican party and the Emancipation Proclamation. This did not necessarily imply an acceptance of the idea of racial equality. It was not unusual for a soldier to favor emancipation and express anti-Negro sentiments.

727. Barnet, James, editor. THE MARTYRS AND HEROES OF ILLINOIS IN THE GREAT REBELLION. Chicago, 1865.

Biographical sketches of and tributes to some residents of Illinois.

728. Burton, William L. DESCRIPTIVE BIBLIOGRAPHY OF CIVIL WAR MANUSCRIPTS IN ILLINOIS. Evanston: Northwestern University Press, 1966.

A product of the Illinois Civil War Centennial Commission, this volume brings together material which had previously been widely scattered. It is well done and should be a valuable tool for researchers.

729. Cole, Arthur C. THE ERA OF THE CIVIL WAR, 1848-1870. Springfield, Illinois: Illinois Centennial Commission, 1919.

An excellent non-military history.

730. Cook, Frederick F. BYGONE DAYS IN CHICAGO; RECOLLECTIONS OF THE "GARDEN CITY" OF THE SIXTIES. Chicago, 1911.

A beautifully illustrated history of life in Chicago during the war.

731. Cross, Jasper W., Jr. "The Civil War Comes to Egypt." JISHS, 44 [1951]: 160-169.

The hostile reaction of southern Illinois to the outbreak of war produced resolutions highly critical of Lincoln's anticipated policy toward the South, opposition to the expected use of troops against the South, and a declaration that it would be the duty of Egypt to leave the Union if such actions were taken.

732. Dick, David B. "Resurgence of the Chicago Democracy, April-November, 1861. JISHS, 56 [1963]: 139-149.

In May 1861 Senator Stephen Douglas made his last speech in his home city. In it he gave Chicago Democrats a much-needed platform by urging support for the war to preserve both the Union and the Constitution.

733. Hamand, Lavern M. COLES COUNTY IN THE CIVIL WAR, 1861-1865. Charleston, Illinois: Eastern Illinois University, 1961.

A brief discussion of Coles County during the war.

734. Hartman, Linda. "The Issue of Freedom Under Governor Yates, 1861-1865." JISHS, 57 [1964]: 293-297.

This former Democrat, the first Republican governor of the state, was the object of much abuse during his term of office, especially at the hands of the Democrats who had been so long in power.

735. Hicken, Victor. ILLINOIS IN THE CIVIL WAR. Urbana, Illinois: University of Illinois Press, 1966.

A well-documented state history which deals with prominent individuals as well as Illinois regiments. Primarily military in scope, it tells the story of the "fighting Illini."

736. Johns, Jane M. PERSONAL RECOLLECTIONS OF EARLY DECATUR, ABRAHAM LINCOLN, RICHARD J. OGLESBY AND THE CIVIL WAR. Howard C. Schaub, editor. Decatur, Illinois: 1912.

Sentimental reminiscences.

737. Northrup, Jack. "Yates, The Prorogued Legislature, and the Constitutional Convention." JISHS, 62 [1969]: 5-34.

Because of his war efforts, Yates' evaluation of the state's 1862 constitutional convention as a seditious gathering has been accepted and his dismissal of the legislature in 1863 condoned.

738. Owens, Kenneth N. GALENA, GRANT, AND THE FORTUNES OF WAR.... DeKalb, Illinois: Northern Illinois University, 1963.

A social history of wartime Galena which gave to the Union nine generals, among them Ulysses S. Grant.

739. Pye, Carol B., editor. "Letters from an Illinois Farm, 1864-1865." JISHS, 66 [1973]: 387-403.

Nine letters from Louisa Jane Phifer to her husband, who served in the army from October 1864 to September 1865. The letters reflect the everyday life of a farm family in wartime, where a woman managed affairs.

740. Raum, Green B. HISTORY OF ILLINOIS REPUBLICANISM.... Chicago, 1900.

A history of the Republican party in Illinois with some good material on the Civil War era.

741. Smith, George W. A HISTORY OF SOUTHERN ILLINOIS.... 3 v. Chicago, 1912.

A comprehensive history of the area commonly called "Little Egypt."

742. Staudenraus, P.J., editor. "'The Empire City of the West'--A View of Chicago in 1864." JISHS, 56 [1963]: 340-349.

Staudenraus has edited an excellent description of Chicago in 1864, written by the noted reporter, Noah Brooks.

743. Walton, Clyde C. ILLINOIS IN THE CIVIL WAR. Springfield: Civil War Centennial Commission of Illinois, 1962.

A reprint of an article originally appearing in a Union League Club of Chicago publication.

Indiana

744. Baker, Ward N. "Mishawaka and its Volunteers through the Shiloh Campaign." IND MAG HIS, 58 [1962]: 117-140.

The citizens of Mishawaka regarded the problems caused by the war as troublesome but temporary. The bloody fighting at Shiloh abruptly changed their thinking.

745. Barnhart, John D. "The Impact of the Civil War on Indiana." IND MAG HIS, 57 [1961]: 185-224.

The Civil War was the greatest challenge Indiana's government had ever faced. The war affected all citizens of the state, disrupted their social relations, and threatened their necessary and cherished organizations.

746. Calhoun, Charles W. "'Incessant Noise and Tumult': Walter Q. Gresham and the Indiana Legislature During the Secessionist Crisis." IND MAG HIS, 74 [1978]: 223-251.

This ambitious Indiana assemblyman was determined to keep the Union intact even though he disliked slavery.

747. Harbison, Winifred A. "Lincoln and the Indiana Republicans 1861-1862." IND MAG HIS, 33 [1937]: 277-303.

A review of the attitude of Indiana Republicans toward Lincoln's policies in 1861-1862: disappointment over First Bull Run, anger at Fremont's removal, hope with McClellan on the Peninsula, and frustration when he failed. Emancipation earned the president a mixed response.

748. ———. "Indiana Republicans and the Re-Election of President Lincoln." IND MAG HIS, 34 [1938]: 42-64.

Author observes that Lincoln's re-election prospects were not good as far as Indiana Republicans were concerned. After the fall of Atlanta, McClellan's nomination, and the collapse of Fremont's candidacy, the president's re-election was assured.

749. Holliday, John H. INDIANAPOLIS AND THE CIVIL WAR. Indianapolis, 1911.

A good account of the city's response to the challenge of war.

750. Merrill, Catharine. THE SOLDIER OF INDIANA IN THE WAR FOR THE UNION.... 2 v. Indianapolis, 1866-1869.

A big group of articles, sketches, and memoirs about Indiana soldiers hurriedly put together without much plan.

751. Stampp, Kenneth M. INDIANA POLITICS DURING THE CIVIL WAR. Indianapolis: Indiana Historical Bureau, 1949.

An interpretive study emphasizing the economic differences within the state. Contains much on Democratic dissent.

752. Stevenson, David. INDIANA'S ROLL OF HONOR. 2 v. Indianapolis: 1864-1866.

Histories of Indiana regiments with biographical sketches of some major personalities.

753. Thornbrough, Emma L. INDIANA IN THE CIVIL WAR ERA 1850-1880. Indianapolis: Indiana Historical Bureau, 1965.

A good study of the state's transition from a Democratic to a Republican stronghold and its role in the Civil War. Covers such diverse subjects as education, agriculture, religion, and social life. One-third of the book covers the Civil War period. Includes various Indiana regiments and the battles in which they served.

754. ———. "Judge Perkins, the Indiana Supreme Court, and the Civil War." IND MAG HIS, 60 [1964]: 79-96.

Perkins had Copperhead leanings, and his position helped him "hedge in" Republican power in the state.

Iowa

755. Byers, Samuel H.M. IOWA IN WAR TIMES. Des Moines, 1888.

Iowa's regiments are chronicled as well as the state's war efforts.

756. Clark, Olynthus B. THE POLITICS OF IOWA DURING THE CIVIL WAR AND RECONSTRUCTION. Iowa City, Iowa: 1911.

A basic work for any study of politics in Iowa.

757. Curtis, Samuel R. "Frontier War Problems, Letters of Samuel Ryan Curtis Pioneer--Congressman--Engineer--Soldier." ANN IOWA, 24 [1943]: 298-315.

Curtis was an early settler in Iowa who became a Republican congressman and rose to the rank of major general during the war. The dozen letters printed here cover the period December 9, 1861 to January 4, 1862, while Curtis was stationed in Missouri.

758. Ellis, Richard N. "The Civil War Letters of an Iowa Family." ANN IOWA, 39 [1969]: 561-586.

Contains a selection of 17 letters from various members of the Simeon Stevens family of Oskaloosa, Iowa. The eldest son, Benjamin, author of 12 of the letters, enlisted in 1861 and fought with the 15th Iowa at Vicksburg.

759. Gue, Benjamin F. HISTORY OF IOWA FROM THE EARLIEST TIMES TO THE BEGINNING OF THE TWENTIETH CENTURY. 4 v. New York, 1903.

Although this is a broad survey of Iowa history, considerable space is devoted to the war years. Such matters as regimental histories, politics, and the home front are covered.

760. Ingersoll, Lurton D. IOWA AND THE REBELLION.... Philadelphia, 1867.

History of Iowa's regiments and the battles in which they fought.

761. Lendt, David L. "Iowa's Civil War Marshal: A Lesson in Expedience." ANN IOWA, 43 [1975]: 132-139.

Herbert M. Hoxie, federal marshal for Iowa during the Civil War, may have served "faithfully and well" as his Republican contemporaries claimed, but he did a disservice to Iowa in his ruthless persecution of Copperheads.

762. Petersen, William J. "Congressional Medal of Honor...." PALIMP, 53 [1972]: 185-197.

Stories of the Iowans who won the Medal of Honor.

763. ———. IOWA HISTORY REFERENCE GUIDE. Iowa City: State Historical Society of Iowa, 1952.

"Iowa and the Civil War" is found on pages 95-104.

764. Pollock, Ivan L. "State Finances in the Civil War." IOWA J HIS, 16 [1918]: 53-107.

An excellent account of this sometimes complicated subject.

765. Robertson, James I., Jr., compiler. "Iowa in the Civil War: A Reference Guide." IOWA J HIS, 59 [1961]: 129-172.

An unannotated listing of over 600 items dealing with Iowa's participation in the Civil War, grouped in eleven categories.

766. Stevenson, Nancy. "Iowa Volunteers Become Generals." JW, 14 [1975]: 60-82.

A survey of Civil War Iowa, which covers the economy, politics, and military matters, including campaigns in which Iowans participated.

767. Stuart, Addison A. IOWA COLONELS AND REGIMENTS, BEING A HISTORY OF IOWA REGIMENTS.... Des Moines, 1865.

The author, a captain in the 17th Iowa, includes accounts of all the battles in which Iowans participated.

768. Throne, Mildred. "Iowans and the Civil War." PALIMP, 40 [1959]: 369-448; 50 [1969]: 65-144.

Between 72,000 and 76,000 Iowans served in the Union army. Iowa regiments fought primarily in the West. From the first battle at Wilson's Creek, to Fort Donelson, Pea Ridge, Shiloh, Iuka and Corinth, Vicksburg, Chattanooga, Atlanta to the sea, Nashville, and final victory with the surrender of Confederate General Johnston, Iowa troops were there.

769. Wubben, H.H. "The Maintenance of Internal Security in Iowa, 1861-1865." CWH, 10 [1964]: 401-415.

Iowa's wartime governors Samuel Kirkwood and William F. Stone were able to maintain firm control of affairs within the state despite border raids from Missouri and anti-war activities of Copperheads.

Kansas

770. Burch, Paul W. "Kansas: Bushwhackers vs. Jayhawkers." JW, 14 [1975]: 83-104.

Deals with the contributions of Kansas to the Union during the Civil War.

771. Castel, Albert. A FRONTIER STATE AT WAR: KANSAS, 1861-1865. Ithaca, New York: Cornell University Press, 1958.

In this well-written, carefully researched volume the political problems and rivalries which beset a new state are thoroughly examined.

772. ———. "The Jayhawkers and the Copperheads of Kansas." CWH, 5 [1959]: 283-293.

The outnumbered Copperheads were not much of a problem for strongly Unionist Kansas, but the irresponsible Unionist Jayhawkers caused difficulties with their "free-booting" raids into Missouri.

773. Crawford, Samuel J. KANSAS IN THE SIXTIES. Chicago, 1911.

Crawford, governor of Kansas [1865-1868] recalls his service in the 2nd Kansas Cavalry and as commander of the 83rd U.S. Colored Infantry.

774. Decker, Eugene D. A SELECTED, ANNOTATED BIBLIOGRAPHY OF SOURCES IN THE KANSAS STATE HISTORICAL SOCIETY PERTAINING TO KANSAS IN THE CIVIL WAR. Emporia: Kansas State Teachers College, 1961.

A useful 95-page bibliography on Kansas in the war.

775. Gambone, Joseph G. "Samuel C. Pomeroy and the Senatorial Election of 1861, Reconsidered." KAN HIS Q, 37 [1971]: 15-32.

Pomeroy came to Kansas in 1854 as an agent for the Emigrant Aid Society, helped found the Republican party in that state, and was chosen to the U.S. Senate in 1861 in a very controversial election.

Kentucky

776. Barnett, James. "Munfordville in the Civil War." KY HIS SOC REG, 69 [1971]: 339-361.

Two battles were fought at Munfordville and each side won one. The town was important because of the railroad bridge which linked the Great Lakes with the Gulf of Mexico.

777. Calbert, Jack. "The Jackson Purchase and the End of the Neutrality Policy in Kentucky." FCHQ, 38 [1964]: 206-223.

The "Jackson Purchase," the western part of Kentucky, was more strongly secessionist than the rest of the state. This sentiment plus the strategic importance of Columbus and Paducah dictated Polk's decision to invade the state and end Kentucky's neutrality.

778. Chenault, John C. OLD CANE SPRINGS: A STORY OF THE WAR BETWEEN THE STATES IN MADISON COUNTY, KENTUCKY. Revised by Jonathan T. Dorris. Louisville, Kentucky: Standard Printing, 1936.

Memoirs which were written by Chennault many years later.

779. Coleman, John W. LEXINGTON DURING THE CIVIL WAR. Lexington, Kentucky: Commercial Printing, 1938.

Deals primarily with the 1862 military campaign in Kentucky.

780. Collins, Richard H. "Civil War Annals of Kentucky." Hambleton Tapp, editor. FCHQ, 35 [1961]: 205-322.

A detailed, almost daily record of events in Kentucky during the war. Richard H. Collins [1824-1888], a celebrated editor, lawyer, judge, and historian compiled this valuable guide to the study of wartime Kentucky.

781. Coulter, Ellis M. THE CIVIL WAR AND READJUSTMENT IN KENTUCKY. Chapel Hill: University of North Carolina Press, 1926.

A fairly comprehensive survey of Kentucky life during wartime.

782. Crocker, Helen B. "A War Divides Green River Country." KY HIS SOC REG, 70 [1972]: 295-311.

A good study of the disruption caused by the war. It destroyed the river trade, the government, families, and homes.

783. Harrison, Lowell. THE CIVIL WAR IN KENTUCKY. Lexington: University Press of Kentucky, 1975.

An able, scholarly study of the military campaigns and political battles in Kentucky during the war. This is not purely a state history.

784. McDowell, Robert E. CITY OF CONFLICT: LOUISVILLE IN THE CIVIL WAR, 1861-1865. Louisville: Louisville Civil War Round-Table, 1962.

This well-written book is based mostly on secondary sources and may not entirely satisfy those with more than a surface interest in the subject. Still, the author scores a few points.

785. Quisenberry, Anderson C. "Kentucky Union Troops in the Civil War." KY HIS SOC REG, 18 [1920]: 13-18.

Article includes a list of units with their commanding officers.

786. Speed, Thomas. THE UNION CAUSE IN KENTUCKY, 1860-1865. New York, 1907.

Written by an adjutant in the 12th Kentucky infantry, this work relates the contributions of Kentucky forces in an effort to hold the state for the Union.

787. ———, R.M. Kelly, and Alfred Pirtle. THE UNION REGIMENTS OF KENTUCKY. Louisville, Kentucky: 1897.

This large book, sponsored by the Union Soldiers and Sailors Monument Association of Louisville, includes regimental histories, battle accounts, biographical sketches, and a description of political conditions during the war.

788. Townsend, William H. LINCOLN AND THE BLUEGRASS: SLAVERY AND THE CIVIL WAR IN KENTUCKY. Lexington: University of Kentucky Press, 1955.

A labored and not too successful attempt to trace Lincoln's understanding of slavery to his life in Kentucky and his Kentucky relationships. While a readable work, it is marred by a number of errors.

789. Williams, Gary L. "Lincoln's Neutral Allies: The Case of the Kentucky Unionists." S ATL Q, 73 [1974]: 70-84.

Before Fort Sumter, neutrality meant a desire to act as a peacemaker. After it, neutrality was seen by the Union as a means to keep the state in the Union.

Maine

790. Hutchinson, Vernal. A MAINE TOWN IN THE CIVIL WAR.... Freeport, Maine: Bond Wheelwright, 1967.

Concentrates on the town of Deer Isle, Maine, in wartime. Mention is also made of her sons who served in the Union army.

791. Jordan, William R., compiler. MAINE IN THE CIVIL WAR: A BIBLIOGRAPHICAL GUIDE. Portland, Maine: Maine Historical Society, 1976.

A compilation of biographies, monographs, unit histories, and specialized works. This slim volume provies an excellent "starting place for a study of Maine in the Civil War."

792. Stanley, Ruel H. EASTERN MAINE AND THE REBELLION: BEING AN ACCOUNT OF THE PRINCIPAL LOCAL EVENTS IN EASTERN MAINE DURING THE WAR. Bangor, Maine: 1887.

Gives a general account of the various events which took place in eastern Maine as well as brief histories of the regiments from the area. "An excellent regional study; fascinating reading."

793. Whitman, William E.S. and Charles H. True. MAINE IN THE WAR FOR THE UNION.... Lewiston, Maine: 1865.

A large work detailing the role of Maine troops in the war.

Maryland

794. Ashcraft, Allan C. "Fort McHenry and the Civil War." MD HIS MAG, 59 [1964]: 297-299.

The story of Fort McHenry which served principally as a prison.

795. Baker, Jean R. THE POLITICS OF CONTINUITY: MARYLAND POLITICAL PARTIES FROM 1858-1870. Baltimore: Johns Hopkins University Press, 1973.

An excellent study of mid-century Maryland.

796. Clark, Charles B. POLITICS IN MARYLAND DURING THE CIVIL WAR. Chestertown, Maryland: n.p., 1952.

A good study of the subject. Originally appeared as a series of articles in MARYLAND HISTORY MAGAZINE 1941-1946.

797. ———. "Suppression and Control of Maryland, 1861-1865...." MD HIS MAG, 54 [1959]: 241-271.

A valuable study of the problems in this Border state.

798. Duncan, Richard R. "The Impact of the Civil War on Education in Maryland." MD HIS MAG, 61 [1966]: 37-52.

The loss of southern patronage and adverse economic conditions compounded problems for private schools. Those which could not adjust suspended their operations during the war period.

799. ———. "Marylanders and the Invasion of 1862." CWH, 11 [1965]: 370-383.

Although pro-southern manifestations continued to persist, the occupation affirmed Maryland's adherence to the Union and dispelled some northern suspicions concerning the state's loyalty.

800. ———. "The College of St. James and the Civil War: A Casualty of War." HIS MAG PROT EPI CH, 39 [1970]: 265-286.

Enrollment dropped sharply with the outbreak of war as most of the students came from the South. The "perils of war" eventually caused the school to close.

801. Harvey, Katherine A. "The Civil War and the Maryland Coal Trade." MD HIS MAG, 62 [1967]: 361-380.

Traces the problems of coal production and transportation in Maryland during the Civil War.

802. Klein, Frederic S., editor. JUST SOUTH OF GETTYSBURG: CARROLL COUNTY, MARYLAND IN THE CIVIL WAR. Westminster, Maryland: Newman Press, 1963.

Drawing on over 100 wartime memoirs, the author has pieced together an excellent portrait of life in wartime in a troubled border area. Carroll County lay across the road leading to Gettysburg and that campaign occupies much, but by no means all, of the space in the book.

803. Manakee, Harold R. MARYLAND IN THE CIVIL WAR. Baltimore: Maryland Historical Society, 1961.

A good, though undocumented look at wartime Maryland. In addition to a description of events taking place within the state, unit synopses, and biographical sketches of prominent persons make the book a helpful one for those with a general interest in the subject.

804. Scharf, John T. HISTORY OF BALTIMORE CITY AND COUNTY.... Philadelphia, 1881.

Although this huge book covers the subject from its earliest period, it remains a good source for background material on this Border city and county during the war.

805. Seabrook, William L.W. MARYLAND'S GREAT PART IN SAVING THE UNION.... Westminster, Maryland: 1913.

Written by the commissioner of the Land Office in Maryland who was a friend of Governor Thomas Hicks, this brief book gives personal glimpses of the governor and other political figures of this Border state.

806. Wagandt, Charles L. "The Army Versus Maryland Slavery." CWH, 10 [1964]: 141-148.

Discusses the continual harassment of Maryland slaveowners by Union military officers.

Massachusetts

807. Bowen, James L. MASSACHUSETTS IN THE WAR, 1861-1865. Springfield, Massachusetts, 1889.

A massive work which includes sketches of general officers.

808. Brown, Francis H. HARVARD UNIVERSITY IN THE WAR OF 1861-1865. Boston, 1886.

A list of the graduates and students of both the college and professional schools who took part in the Civil War.

809. Burr, Fearing and George Lincoln. THE TOWN OF HINGHAM IN THE LATE CIVIL WAR.... Boston, 1876.

Rosters, recollections, and tributes delivered at the dedication of the Solders' and Sailors' monument in Hingham.

810. Creasey, George W. THE CITY OF NEWBURYPORT IN THE CIVIL WAR.... Boston, 1903.

Another city wartime history with emphasis on genealogical data.

811. Headley, Phineas C. MASSACHUSETTS IN THE REBELLION. Boston, 1866.

A very good record of Massachusetts' role in the Civil War. Deals with statesmen, colleges, and the people, but the emphasis is primarily military.

812. Higginson, Thomas W., editor. HARVARD MEMORIAL BIOGRAPHIES. 2 v. Cambridge, Massachusetts: 1866.

Biographies of Harvard men who were killed in the Civil War.

813. ———. MASSACHUSETTS IN THE ARMY AND NAVY DURING THE WAR OF 1861-1865. 2 v. Boston, 1895-1896.

Authorized by the state, this is the basic work for an understanding of Massachusetts during the war.

814. Kirkland, Edward C. "Boston During the Civil War." MASS HIS SOC PROC, 71 [1953-1957]: 194-203.

Describes the impact of the war on young Bostonians as well as the Negro residents.

815. Marvin, Abijah P. HISTORY OF WORCESTER IN THE WAR OF THE REBELLION. Worcester, Massachusetts, 1870.

An old but good history of the city.

816. MASSACHUSETTS IN THE CIVIL WAR. Boston: Civil War Centennial Commission, 1960-1965.

A series of essays with emphasis on the military side of the war.

817. Morin, Edward M. "Springfield During the Civil War Years...." HIS J W MASS, 3 [1974]: 25-28.

Battles and losses of the 10th, 27th, 37th and 46th Massachusetts' regiments, composed primarily of Springfield residents. The arsenal at Springfield is also discussed.

818. Norton, John F. THE RECORD OF ATHOL, MASSACHUSETTS, IN SUPPRESSING THE GREAT REBELLION. Boston, 1866.

A local history prepared "by a committee of the town."

819. Raymond, Samuel, compiler. THE RECORD OF ANDOVER DURING THE REBELLION. Andover, 1875.

A good local history.

820. Schouler, William. A HISTORY OF MASSACHUSETTS IN THE CIVIL WAR. 2 v. Boston, 1868-1871.

The first volume is largely political in nature. The various activities and contributions of counties and cities are detailed in Volume 2.

821. Ware, Edith E. POLITICAL OPINION IN MASSACHUSETTS DURING THE CIVIL WAR AND RECONSTRUCTION. New York: n.p., 1916.

Evaluates the press in the state and details changes in public opinion throughout the course of the war.

822. Warner, Madeline. "The Westfield Home Front During the Civil War." HIS J W MAG, 3 [1974]: 24-41.

Election campaigns, recruiting, taxation, and the effects of war on local industry are among the subjects covered in this article.

823. Willis, Henry A. FITCHBURG IN THE WAR OF THE REBELLION. Fitchburg, Massachusetts: 1866.

Rosters, biographies, and prison accounts make up the main part of this volume.

Michigan

824. Brinks, Herbert. "The Effect of the Civil War in 1861 on Michigan Lumber and Mining Industries." MICH HIS, 44 [1960]: 101-107.

Discusses the production of copper, iron ore, and lumber and the impact the war had on these industries during the first year.

825. Brown, Ida C. MICHIGAN MEN IN THE CIVIL WAR. Ann Arbor: University of Michigan Press, 1959.

This is an informative guide to 113 collections of soldiers' letters as well as other papers in the Michigan Historical Collection at the University of Michigan. A supplement was issued in 1960 with an additional 126 collections listed.

826. Dunbar, Willis F., editor. MICHIGAN INSTITUTIONS OF HIGHER EDUCATION IN THE CIVIL WAR. Lansing: Michigan Civil War Centennial Commission, 1964.

A comprehensive survey of Michigan colleges during the war.

827. Freitag, Alfred J. DETROIT IN THE CIVIL WAR. Joe L. Norris, editor. Detroit: Wayne State University Press, 1951.

A very brief account of activities during the war, including non-military as well as military events.

828. Havran, Martin, Jr. "Windsor and Detroit Relations During the Civil War." MICH HIS, 38 [1954]: 371-389.

Covers among other things recruitment in Windsor, the Johnson's Island plot, and desertion from the United States to Canada.

829. Mason, Philip P. and Paul J. Pentecost. FROM BULL RUN TO APPOMATTOX.... Detroit: Wayne State University Press, 1961.

Michigan's role in the Civil War is depicted in a number of brief sketches.

830. May, George S. MICHIGAN AND THE CIVIL WAR YEARS.... Lansing, Michigan: Michigan Civil War Centennial Commission, 1964.

Political as well as military events are covered in a concise manner.

831. ———, editor. MICHIGAN CIVIL WAR HISTORY; AN ANNOTATED BIBLIOGRAPHY. Detroit: Wayne State University Press, 1961.

This excellent reference book is extremely useful for any study of Michigan's role in the war. Over 700 books and pamphlets are listed.

832. Milbrook, Minnie D., editor. TWICE TOLD TALES OF MICHIGAN AND HER SOLDIERS IN THE CIVIL WAR. Lansing, Michigan: Michigan Civil War Centennial Observance Commission, 1966.

A book of colorful anecdotes pertaining to the war and the Michigan men who served in it.

833. Petersen, Eugene T. "The Civil War Comes to Detroit." DET HIS SOC BULL, 18 [summer 1961]: 4-11.

This illustrated study discusses the state of unpreparedness in Michigan on the eve of Fort Sumter and traces the raising of the 1st Michigan regiment in the early days of the war.

834. Pritchett, John P. "Michigan Democracy in the Civil War." MICH HIS, 11 [1927]: 92-109.

A discussion of the paper written by William V. Morrison, one of the most conspicuous Copperheads in Michigan. Written in February 1863 at the request of the Democratic State Central Committee to set "forth the attitude of the Democratic party toward the Lincoln administration."

835. Robertson, John, compiler. MICHIGAN IN THE WAR. Lansing, 1882.

This stout book of regimental histories was compiled by the adjutant general and is a revision of an earlier edition.

836. Robinson, Orrin W. "Recollections of Civil War Conditions in the Copper Country." MICH HIS, 3 [1919]: 598-609.

Robinson was employed at the Quincy mine in Houghton County in 1862 and recalls the conditions prevailing at that time.

837. Woodford, Frank B. FATHER ABRAHAM'S CHILDREN: MICHIGAN EPISODES IN THE CIVIL WAR. Detroit: Wayne State University Press, 1961.

A collection of interesting war "episodes" written in a popular manner by the chief editorial writer for the DETROIT FREE PRESS. The main focus is on people.

Minnesota

838. Carley, Kenneth. MINNESOTA IN THE CIVIL WAR. Minneapolis: Rose & Haines, 1961.

Appearing originally in newspapers, these articles highlight events in Minnesota's Civil War history.

839. Downs, Lynwood G. "The Soldier Vote and Minnesota Politics, 1862-1865." MINN HIS, 26 [1945]: 187-210.

Minnesota has reason to be proud of its record in granting suffrage to its soldier volunteers. Any disfranchisement was due to the exigencies of war rather than the law or its administration.

840. Fridley, Russell W. "April, 1861: Minnesota Goes to War." MINN HIS, 37 [1961]: 212-215.

On April 14, 1861, Minnesota became the first state to offer troops for the Union cause. Within two weeks ten companies had been formed.

841. Heilbron, Bertha L. "Manifest Destiny in Minnesota's Republican Campaign of 1860." MINN HIS, 37 [1960]: 52-57.

An account of the meeting between Seward and the Right Reverend David Anderson in St. Paul, where they touched upon Canadian annexation and "Continental Union"--the "Manifest Destiny."

842. MINNESOTA IN THE CIVIL AND INDIAN WARS 1861-1865. 2 v. St. Paul, 1890-1893.

Contains interesting material on the Sioux uprisings, as well as pertinent information on various military affairs in the state.

843. MINNESOTANS IN THE CIVIL AND INDIAN WARS.... Saint Paul: The Minnesota Historical Society, 1936.

A good index to the rosters of those who served in the Civil and Indian wars, 1861-1865. This was a W.P.A. project for the Minnesota Historical Society.

844. Trenerry, Walter N. "Votes for Minnesota's Civil War Soldiers." MINN HIS, 36 [1959]: 167-172.

The Soldiers' Vote law applied to the congressional election of November 4, 1862 and to all subsequent elections during the war. If a man was not a qualified voter before entering the service, the act did not help him.

845. ———. "The Minnesota Rebellion Act of 1862: A Legal Dilemma of the Civil War." MINN HIS, 35 [1956]: 1-10.

The dilemma was that, on one hand, the North held that the Union was one and inseparable and that no state could secede. On the other hand, by treating some citizens as "foreign foes," it implied that the South had been successful in withdrawing from the Union and in establishing a new government.

Missouri

846. Anderson, Galusha. THE STORY OF A BORDER CITY DURING THE CIVIL WAR. Boston, 1908.

Written by a Baptist clergyman, this volume deals with local conditions and gives good insight into the various political factions in St. Louis.

847. Edom, Clifton C. MISSOURI SKETCH BOOK; A COLLECTION OF WORDS AND PICTURES OF THE CIVIL WAR. n.p.: Lucas, 1963.

A pictorial history of Missouri in the Civil War, with a not quite satisfactory narrative.

848. Frizzell, Robert W. "'Killed by Rebels': A Civil War Massacre and its Aftermath." MO HIS R, 71 [1977]: 369-395.

This October 1864 massacre at Concordia, Missouri had a long-lasting effect on the Germans who had settled there. The violence drove them further into isolation with their different values, culture, and religious beliefs.

849. Kirkpatrick, Arthur R. "Missouri in the Early Months of the Civil War." MO HIS R, 55 [1961]: 235-266.

Missouri's position and influence in the Confederacy was jeopardized from the beginning of the war. A series of unfortunate events, personality clashes among her leaders, and disagreements between her leaders and the Confederate government caused the problems.

850. ———. "Missouri on the Eve of the Civil War." MO HIS R, 55 [1961]: 99-108.

On the eve of the Civil War, Missouri desired preservation of the Union, compromise on the issues of the day, and above all, peace.

851. ———. "Missouri's Secessionist Government, 1861-1865." MO HIS R, 45 [1951]: 124-137.

Missouri's pro-South government was outlawed by the state convention in July 1861. It was admitted to the Confederacy on November 28, 1861.

852. Laughlin, Sceva B. MISSOURI POLITICS DURING THE CIVIL WAR. Salem, Oregon: n.p., 1930.

A useful work in its time, but it has since been superceded by other studies.

853. Lee, Bill R. "Missouri's Fight Over Emancipation in 1863." MO HIS R, 45 [1951]: 256-274.

The point of contention was gradual emancipation or immediate emancipation. Ultimately the Radical Republicans and immediate emancipation prevailed.

854. McElroy, John. THE STRUGGLE FOR MISSOURI. Washington, D.C.: 1909.

A readable account of the struggle for control of the state, dealing with events through the Battle of Pea Ridge in March 1862.

855. Murphy, Bonnie. "Missouri: A State Asunder." JW, 14 [1975]: 105-129.

Discusses the several conflicting factions in this badly divided state.

856. Ness, George T. "Missouri at West Point: Her Graduates Through the Civil War." MO HIS R, 38 [1942/1943]: 162-169.

Brief biographies of Missouri's 23 West Pointers, 13 of whom were still living when the war broke out.

857. Parrish, William E. A HISTORY OF MISSOURI, VOLUME III, 1860 TO 1875. Columbia, Missouri: University of Missouri Press, 1973.

In the third volume in the Missouri sesquicentennial history, the author reviews the Civil War and Reconstruction years in scholarly fashion. Missouri gradually became more of a northern than southern state in the 1850s, which paved the way for the bitter internecine battling during the war.

858. ———. TURBULENT PARTNERSHIP: MISSOURI AND THE UNION, 1861-1865. Columbia, Missouri: University of Missouri Press, 1963.

A well-balanced account of Missouri's relationship with the national government during the war. It was the only state to oppose Lincoln's renomination and was one of the president's worst headaches.

859. Rombauer, Robert J. THE UNION CAUSE IN ST. LOUIS IN 1861: AN HISTORICAL SKETCH. St. Louis, 1909.

A good discussion of Union activities and operations in St. Louis. The book also contains rosters of Missouri units.

860. Ryle, Walter H. MISSOURI: UNION OR SECESSION. Nashville, Tennessee: George Peabody College of Teachers, 1931.

Details events leading up to and through the secession convention of March 1861.

861. Schrantz, Ward L. JASPER COUNTY, MISSOURI, IN THE CIVIL WAR. Carthage, Missouri: Carthage Press, 1923.

This southwestern county was beset by violence and guerrilla warfare.

862. Shoemaker, Floyd C. "The Story of the Civil War in Northwest Missouri." MO HIS R, 7 [1913]: 63-75, 113-131.

A survey of military campaigns and political events.

863. Smith, W. Wayne. "An Experiment in Counterinsurgency: The Assessment of Confederate Sympathizers in Missouri." JSH, 35 [1969]: 361-366.

Describes the Union efforts to control secessionists and undermine guerrilla insurgency in Missouri during the war.

864. Webb, William L. BATTLES AND BIOGRAPHIES OF MISSOURIANS: OR THE CIVIL WAR PERIOD OF OUR STATE. Kansas City, Missouri: 1900.

Contains brief biographies of both pro- and anti-Union civilians and military men as well as short descriptions of the military actions in the state.

New Hampshire

865. Cleveland, Mather. NEW HAMPSHIRE FIGHTS THE CIVIL WAR. Hanover, New Hampshire: University Press of New England, 1969.

A good illustrated state history based on soldiers' letters and diaries.

866. Gilmore, George C. MANCHESTER MEN. Concord, New Hampshire: 1898.

A list of soldiers and sailors from Manchester and environs, who served in the war.

867. NEW HAMPSHIRE AND THE CIVIL WAR. Concord: New Hampshire Civil War Centennial Commission, 1962-1965.

Consists of a series of booklets published by the state's centennial commission.

868. Robinson, H.L. HISTORY OF PITTSFIELD, N.H. IN THE GREAT RE-BELLION. Concord, New Hampshire: 1893.

Another useful roster list with brief biographical sketches of Pittsfield men.

869. Waite, Otis F.R. CLAREMONT WAR HISTORY ... WITH SKETCHES OF NEW HAMPSHIRE REGIMENTS.... Concord, New Hampshire: 1868.

Brief sketches of the regiments in which Claremont men served.

870. ———. NEW HAMPSHIRE IN THE GREAT REBELLION. Claremont, New Hampshire: 1870.

Contains information on regiments and battle sketches and also includes civilian biographies.

New Jersey

871. Foster, John Y. NEW JERSEY AND THE REBELLION.... Newark, 1868.

This 800 page volume gives sketches of New Jersey regiments. It also covers, although not in as much detail, the people, the church, their attitudes, and some political considerations.

872. Greene, Larry A. "The Emancipation Proclamation in New Jersey and the Paranoid Style." NJ HIS, 91 [1973]: 108-124.

Discusses the "peace resolution" passed by the New Jersey legislature denying Lincoln's power to free the slaves and advocating a peaceful settlement with the Confederacy.

873. Knapp, Charles M. NEW JERSEY POLITICS DURING THE PERIOD OF THE CIVIL WAR AND RECONSTRUCTION. Geneva, New York: Humphrey, 1924.

Drawn from newspapers, this is an interesting introduction to the politics in the state during the war.

874. Miers, Earl S., editor. NEW JERSEY AND THE CIVIL WAR: AN ALBUM OF CONTEMPORARY ACCOUNTS. Princeton: Van Nostrand, 1964.

A small book with 31 sets of recollections about social, political, and military life during the war by New Jerseyites. It provides a good taste of the mood of the people during the tragic years.

875. Sinclair, Donald A. A BIBLIOGRAPHY: THE CIVIL WAR AND NEW JERSEY. New Brunswick, New Jersey: Friends of the Rutgers Library, 1968.

An excellent annotated reference work containing over 1,350 entries. Lists pamphlets, books, articles, reminiscences, sermons, and political tracts covering almost every aspect of New Jersey's participation in the war.

876. Tandler, Maurice. "The Political Front in Civil War New Jersey." NJ HIS SOC PROC, 83 [1965]: 223-233.

Describes successful opposition by the Democratic party to the Lincoln administration. Not until 1865 were the Republicans finally victorious in the state.

New York

877. Brummer, Sidney D. ... POLITICAL HISTORY OF NEW YORK STATE DURING THE PERIOD OF THE CIVIL WAR. New York, 1911.

This work deals with all aspects of politics--leaders, political conventions, speeches, and platforms.

878. Burt, Silas W. MY MEMOIRS OF THE MILITARY HISTORY OF THE STATE OF NEW YORK DURING THE WAR FOR THE UNION.... Albany, 1902.

Issued as one volume in a series, this sound work covers the state's military endeavors in the first two years of the war.

879. Frost, James A. "The Home Front in New York During the Civil War." NY HIS, 42 [1961]: 273-397.

A good survey of newspapers, journals, diaries, and letters. The article also includes material on Democratic dissidence.

880. McKelvey, Blake, editor. ROCHESTER IN THE CIVIL WAR. Rochester: The Society, 1944.

A very readable account of life in Rochester drawn from many newspapers, as well as letters and diaries of service men.

881. Naylor, Colin T. CIVIL WAR DAYS IN A COUNTRY VILLAGE. Peekskill, New York: Highland Press, 1961.

A small book devoted to life in wartime Peekskill, New York. A mild anti-Republican party prevailed in the village of 4,000, which seemed to experience many of the difficulties which faced larger cities.

882. NEW YORK STATE AND THE CIVIL WAR. Albany: New York State Civil War Centennial Commission, 1961-1963.

An excellent series which dealt with all phases of the war in New York. This was a monthly publication.

883. Phisterer, Frederick, compiler. NEW YORK IN THE WAR OF THE REBELLION, 1861-1865. 6 v. Albany, 1912.

A massive compilation dealing largely with regimental histories. There is very little discussion of political or civil matters.

884. Plank, Will. BANNERS AND BUGLES.... Marlborough, New York: Centennial Press, 1963. Reprint 1972.

An interesting potpourri of regimental information, soldiers' diaries, and anecdotes about life, both at the front and at home in Ulster County, New York. A model for wartime local history.

885. Rayback, Robert J. "New York State in the Civil War." NY HIS, 42 [1961]: 56-70.

The author suggests that the traditional view of New York in the Civil War be revised.

886. Townsend, Thomas S. THE HONORS OF THE EMPIRE STATE IN THE WAR OF THE REBELLION. New York, 1889.

A diversified volume covering many subjects on the civilian side of the war.

Ohio

887. Abbott, Richard H. OHIO'S WAR GOVERNORS. Columbus, Ohio: Ohio State University Press, 1962.

Introduces the reader to the war governors of Ohio: William Dennison, David Tod, and John Brough.

888. Becker, Carl M. "Entrepreneurial Invention and Innovation in the Miami Valley During the Civil War." CIN HIS SOC BULL, 22 [1964]: 5-28.

A useful article about regional wartime economic growth and wartime industry.

889. Harper, Robert S. OHIO HANDBOOK OF THE CIVIL WAR. Columbus, Ohio: Ohio Historical Society, 1961.

This 78-page book, which contains everything a handbook should have, was sponsored by the state Civil War Centennial Commission.

890. Lottick, Kenneth V. "The Connecticut Reserve and the Civil War." HIS ED J, 8 [1957]: 92-104.

Describes the Connecticut Reserve of Ohio as an important force of Puritanism, New England type democracy, and abolitionism. Needless to say these ideas were in direct conflict with those of the South.

891. MARIETTA COLLEGE IN THE WAR OF SECESSION, 1861-1865. Cincinnati, Ohio: 1878.

A record of the faculty and students who served in the war and the impact of the war on this small liberal arts college.

892. Porter, George H. OHIO POLITICS DURING THE CIVIL WAR PERIOD.... New York, 1911.

An all-inclusive, objective description of Ohio's three wartime administrations.

893. Reid, Whitelaw. OHIO IN THE WAR: HER STATESMEN, HER GENERALS, AND SOLDIERS. 2 v. Cincinnati, Ohio: 1868.

An excellent two volume work covering military matters as well as politics.

894. Roseboom, Eugene H. THE CIVIL WAR ERA, 1850-1873. Columbus: Ohio State Archaeological and Historical Society, 1944.

An excellent social and cultural history of Ohio from the Campaign of 1850 until 1873, although only 80 out of the 485 pages deal with the war years. Subjects are organized in topical fashion.

895. Ryan, Daniel J. THE CIVIL WAR LITERATURE OF OHIO.... Cleveland, Ohio: 1911.

A useful bibliography which includes the majority of the books published in the previous 45 years.

896. Schaefer, James A. "Governor William Dennison and Military Preparations in Ohio, 1861." LIN HER, 78 [1976]: 52-61.

Describes Dennison's efforts to raise troops and organize the logistical problems. The organization he established managed to purchase superior arms and also managed to establish two laboratories to supply the needed ammunition.

897. Simms, Henry R. OHIO POLITICS ON THE EVE OF CONFLICT. Columbus: Ohio State University Press, 1961.

Although Ohioans hoped for a compromise solution to avert war, they did not believe in compromise on the tariff and other issues adversely affecting their interests.

898. Turner, Justin G. "The Squirrel Hunters." A BOOK COLL, 14 [1964]: 7-11.

When Confederate armies threatened Cincinnati, Governor Tod of Ohio issued a call for men to come to its defense. The result was that 15,766 men responded; they were called the "Squirrel Hunters."

899. Weisenburger, Francis P. COLUMBUS DURING THE CIVIL WAR. Columbus: Ohio State University Press, 1963.

Social and economic aspects of life in Columbus during the war are dealt with in this booklet.

900. Wheeler, Kenneth W., editor. FOR THE UNION: OHIO LEADERS IN THE CIVIL WAR. Columbus: Ohio State University Press, 1968.

A collection of ten essays on prominent Ohioans in the Civil War.

Pennsylvania

901. Bates, Samuel P. HISTORY OF PENNSYLVANIA VOLUNTEERS, 1861-1865. 5 v. Harrisburg, 1869-1871.

A roster of state volunteers.

902. ———. MARTIAL DEEDS OF PENNSYLVANIA. Philadelphia, 1875.

Over 1,000 pages long, this volume is divided into two sections --biographical and historical. The coverage is comprehensive.

903. Book, Janet M. NORTHERN RENDEZVOUS; HARRISBURG DURING THE CIVIL WAR. Harrisburg: Telegraph Press, 1951.

A good account of Pennsylvania's capital during the war.

904. Bradley, Erwin S. THE TRIUMPH OF MILITANT REPUBLICANISM: A STUDY OF PENNSYLVANIA AND PRESIDENTIAL POLITICS, 1860-1872. Philadelphia: University of Pennsylvania Press, 1964.

Author discusses the ultimate success of Radical Republicans in Pennsylvania, commencing with the 1860 election.

905. Burgess, Milton V. MINUTE MEN OF PENNSYLVANIA.... Martinsburg, Pennsylvania: MORRISON'S COVE HERALD, 1962.

The people of Blair, Bedford, and Cambria counties prepare to defend themselves from the Confederate invasion of 1863.

906. Burkhart, William H. and others. SHIPPENSBURG IN THE CIVIL WAR. Shippensburg, Pennsylvania: Shippensburg Historical Society, 1964.

Includes a number of diversified items such as soldiers' memoirs, muster rolls, newspaper accounts, and some modern material.

907. Davis, Stanton L. PENNSYLVANIA POLITICS, 1860-1863. Cleveland, Ohio: Western Reserve University, 1955.

Describes the political intrigues and struggles involved in Pennsylvania's conversion to a Republican state.

908. Dusinberre, William. CIVIL WAR ISSUES IN PHILADELPHIA, 1856-1865. Philadelphia: University of Pennsylvania Press, 1965.

Discusses Democratic responses to Republican policies. It also examines the efforts to raise troops in the city in 1862 and 1863 and focuses on the difficulties encountered in June 1863. As Confederate forces threatened the state, good Union men showed a reluctance to defend their home land.

909. Hammond, William W. "The Military Occupation of Columbia County: A Re-examination." PA MHB, 80 [1956]: 320-329.

Union army occupation in 1864 was supposedly the result of efforts to impose a Republican party dictatorship. The real purpose was to round up deserters.

910. Hoke, Jacob. ... REMINISCENCES OF THE WAR ... INCIDENTS WHICH TRANSPIRED IN AND ABOUT CHAMBERSBURG.... Chambersburg, Pennsylvania: 1884.

Life in wartime Chambersburg and the burning of the city are described in this volume.

911. MacKay, Winnifred. "Philadelphia During the Civil War, 1861-1865." PA MHB, 70 [1946]: 3-51.

A fairly good discussion of a major northern city in wartime.

912. McClure, Alexander K. OLD TIME NOTES OF PENNSYLVANIA.... 2 v. Philadelphia, 1905.

The first volume of this standard work about commerce, education, and industry deals with wartime matters.

913. Pleasonton, General A.J. REPORT OF ... PLEASONTON COMMANDING THE HOME GUARD OF THE CITY OF PHILADELPHIA.... 3 v. Philadelphia, 1862-1864.

The defense of Philadelphia is related in detail along with much statistical information covering the first three years of the war.

914. Rosenberger, Francis C., editor. THE CUMBERLAND VALLEY OF PENNSYLVANIA IN THE 1860'S.... Gettysburg: n.p., 1963.

The six essays deal with the various sections of Pennsylvania which saw military action, including the burning of Chambersburg.

915. Shankman, Arnold. "John P. Penny, Harry White and the 1864 Pennsylvania Senate Deadlock." W PA HIS MAG, 55 [1972]: 77-86.

Describes the political struggle for the speakership of the state Senate between the Democrats and Unionists.

916. Siebenback, Henry K. "Pittsburgh's Civil War Fortification Claims." W PA HIS MAG, 27 [1944]: 1-20.

In June 1863 the federal government thought an attack might be made on Pittsburgh. Many people and companies advanced money to pay for the new defenses. In 1866 the city's claim for compensation was rejected. The battle was still being fought in 1905.

917. Taylor, Frank H. PHILADELPHIA IN THE CIVIL WAR, 1861-1865. Philadelphia, 1913.

Another history of wartime Philadelphia, in which most subjects receive rather superficial treatment. Illustrated with prints, photographs, and drawings.

Rhode Island

918. Burrage, Henry S. BROWN UNIVERSITY IN THE CIVIL WAR. Providence, 1868.

A memorial to those students and graduates who died in the war plus a list of those who served, and the university's role in the war.

Tennessee

919. Wright, Marcus J. TENNESSEE IN THE WAR, 1861-1865. New York, 1908.

This work contains a list of military organizations and their officers from Tennessee. Quite comprehensive in that it includes those who served in both the southern and northern armies.

Vermont

920. Beers, Lorna. "The Sleeping Sentinel William Scott." NEW ENG GAL, 7 [1965]: 3-14.

An account of the war's impact on a little community located near St. Johnsbury, Vermont.

921. Benedict, George C. VERMONT IN THE CIVIL WAR.... 2 v. Burlington, Vermont: 1886-1888.

An account of the service of Vermont soldiers and sailors in the war.

922. Costello, Bartley, III. "Vermont in the Civil War." VT HIS, 29 [1961]: 220-226.

A capsule history of Vermont which deals with the troops and where they served. "One of the finer achievements our troops attained ... in four years of service, [they] did not surrender a single flag to the enemy."

923. Goulding, Joseph H. OFFICIAL MILITARY AND NAVAL RECORDS OF RUTLAND, VERMONT.... Rutland, 1891.

A listing of people from Rutland who served in the war and also those who moved to the town after the war.

924. Melville, Dorothy S. TYLER-BROWNS OF BRATTLEBORO. New York: Exposition, 1973.

The wartime story of two fiercely patriotic Vermont families, related by marriage, as told principally through their letters.

925. PERSONAL NARRATIVES OF THE CIVIL WAR IN THE COLLECTION OF THE VERMONT HISTORICAL SOCIETY. VT HIS, 31 [1963]: 117-121.

Includes samples of orders, drawings, letters, diaries, cash accounts, and records of service of common soldiers and officers.

926. Soule, Allen. "Vermont in 1861." VT HIS, 30 [1962]: 149-161.

Agriculture, transportation, industry, migration, religion, temperance, and the anti-slavery movement during the first year of the war are covered in this address delivered at the annual meeting of the Vermont Historical Society.

927. Waite, Otis F.R. VERMONT IN THE GREAT REBELLION. Claremont, New Hampshire: 1869.

Mainly regimental summaries with a few biographical sketches.

West Virginia

928. Ambler, Charles H. "The Cleavage Between Eastern and Western Virginia." AHR, 15 [1910]: 762-780.

A helpful aid to understanding the political and ideological differences in the state.

929. ———. "Disfranchisement in West Virginia." YALE R, 14 [1905]: 38-59, 155-180.

Disfranchisement through the Voters' Test Oath was largely a local problem. The western part of the state was the least concerned. In the counties bordering Virginia returning veterans from the Confederate army not only were not allowed to vote, but they also could not hold public office or teach without taking the oath.

930. ———. A HISTORY OF WEST VIRGINIA. New York: Prentice-Hall, 1933.

This is the standard work on wartime problems and the politics which led to the establishment of the new state.

931. Asher, Marguerite. "The Civil War in Border West Virginia." W VA R, 13 [1936]: 150-153.

Tells of the problems in the counties bordering Virginia, focusing on the imprisonment of Mary Louise Entler and a friend by federal troops at Martinsburg and Harper's Ferry in 1863.

932. Cook, Roy B. LEWIS COUNTY IN THE CIVIL WAR, 1861-1865. Charleston, West Virginia: Jarrett Printing, 1924.

Covers the militia system, the arrest and confinement of civilians at Camp Chase, and guerilla warfare in this county which saw frequent action during the war. A very good county history for these years.

933. Curry, Richard O. "A Reappraisal of Statehood Politics in West Virginia." JSH, 28 [1962]: 403-421.

The counties of Western Virginia were almost evenly divided in their sympathies between North and South. Author explains why the breakaway state was formed.

934. ———. "Documents: A Note on the Motives of Three Radical Republicans." JNH, 47 [1962]: 273-277.

West Virginia radicals were more interested in political advantage than the welfare of the blacks.

935. ———. A HOUSE DIVIDED; A STUDY OF STATEHOOD POLITICS AND THE COPPERHEAD MOVEMENT IN WEST VIRGINIA. Pittsburgh: University of Pittsburgh Press, 1964.

This solid work deals with the "why" as well as the "what" of the formation of the state. John Carble and other Copperheads, although critics of Lincoln's administration, are portrayed as conservatives. Bolsters the traditional view that in 1861 northwestern Virginia was pro-Union.

936. Forbes, Gerald. "The Civil War and the Beginning of the Oil Industry in West Virginia." W VA HIS, 8 [1947]: 382-391.

The non-combatants who remained to work the oil wells in the state lived a harried existence, constantly tormented by guerrilla raids.

937. Goodall, E.J. "The Virginia Debt Controversy and Settlement." W VA HIS, 24 [1962]: 42-74.

Prior to the war Western Virginia was responsible for part of Virginia's debt. This article details the conflict, disagreement, and financial difficulties concerning that debt after West Virginia's statehood.

938. Ham, F. Gerald. "The Mind of a Copperhead: Letters of John J. Davis on the Secession Crisis and Statehood Politics in Western Virginia 1860-1862." W VA HIS, 24 [1962]: 89-109.

John J. Davis, a young, obscure Clarksburg lawyer, was opposed to the secession of West Virginia from Virginia, but he was not opposed to Virginia's secession from the Union.

939. Hecht, Arthur. "Federal Postal History of Western Virginia 1861-1865." W VA HIS, 26 [1964/1965]: 67-79.

Discusses development of the postal service in the section of Virginia which broke away during the war.

940. Hornbeck, Betty. UPSHUR BROTHERS OF THE BLUE AND THE GRAY. Parsons, West Virginia: McClain, 1967.

A very readable account of this central West Virginia county during the war. Roster lists are included.

941. Kincaid, Mary E. "Fayetteville, West Virginia, During the Civil War." W VA HIS, 14 [1953]: 339-364.

Describes wartime military action in a small pro-Confederate West Virginia town.

942. Lang. Theodore F. LOYAL WEST VIRGINIA FROM 1861 TO 1865. Baltimore, 1895.

The reader of this book, which is primarily a military history, will also find the social and political background of the war.

943. Lewis, Virgil A. "How West Virginia Became a Member of the Federal Union, a Reprint." W VA HIS, 30 [1969]: 598-606.

As the title suggests, this is an account of how the state of West Virginia was created.

944. Moore, George E. A BANNER IN THE HILLS: WEST VIRGINIA'S STATEHOOD. New York: Appleton-Century-Crofts, 1963.

The military and political happenings relating to the formation of the new state are told in detail.

945. Reed, Louis. "Colonel Rathbone of Burning Springs." W VA HIS, 23 [1962]: 205-218.

A discussion of the controversy attending the dismissal of Colonel Rathbone of the 11th West Virginia in January 1863 and the suppression of the news of the destruction of the oil fields at Burning Springs in May 1863.

946. ———. "Conflict and Error in the History of Oil." W VA HIS, 25 [1963]: 21-26.

Rathbone struck oil in 1860 thus precipitating the legendary Burning Springs, West Virginia oil rush. In May 1863 the town and oil fields were destroyed by Confederate cavalry. This was the most important industrial complex in the state which was wrecked by the "Rebels."

947. Richardson, Hila A. "Raleigh County, West Virginia in the Civil War." W VA HIS, 10 [1949]: 213-298.

In the more accessible districts of the county the sympathies were pro-Confederate, while the isolated areas enlisted soldiers for the Union.

948. Sevy, Ronald L. "John Letcher and West Virginia." W VA HIS, 27 [1965]: 10-55.

Letcher, elected governor of Virginia by votes from the western counties, refused to heed Lincoln's call for 75,000 troops. The article analyzes this apparent change in attitude.

949. Shetler, Charles. WEST VIRGINIA CIVIL WAR LITERATURE: AN ANNOTATED BIBLIOGRAPHY. Morgantown, West Virginia: West Virginia University Library, 1963.

An excellent reference guide to nearly 900 books, pamphlets, articles, theses, and broadsides. Also included is a listing of all the state's newspapers pertaining to the Civil War to be found in the university library. Descriptive annotations follow each entry.

950. Squires, J. Duane. "Lincoln and the West Virginia Statehood." W VA HIS, 24 [1963]: 325-331.

Author agrees with the statement that "if there had been no Lincoln, there would be no state of West Virginia...."

951. Stutler, Boyd. "The Civil War in West Virginia." W VA HIS, 22 [1961]: 76-82.

Author notes the contributions of West Virginia to the Union cause and laments the fact that so little has been written about these contributions. He might have an argument with the compiler of this bibliography.

952. ———. "Mr. Lincoln and the Formation of West Virginia." LIN HER, 69 [1958]: 3-11.

Discusses the desire of the people beyond the Alleghenies to secede from Virginia as far back as before the Revolutionary War. They finally succeeded during the Civil War.

953. ———. WEST VIRGINIA IN THE CIVIL WAR. Charleston, West Virginia: Education Foundation, 1963.

The focus is primarily on the military action in this nice collection of 58 well-told stories. The anguish and divided loyalties which troubled the state are quite evident.

954. Wellman, Manly W. HARPERS FERRY, PRIZE OF WAR. Charlotte, North Carolina: McNally, 1960.

A popularly written account of this border town during the war.

Wisconsin

955. Balasubramanian, D. "Wisconsin's Foreign Trade in the Civil War Era." WIS MAG HIS, 46 [1963]: 257-262.

A study of the war's effect on trade between Wisconsin and Canada. In spite of strained United States-Canadian relations, Wisconsin maintained its economic ties with Canada.

956. Bradley, Isaac S. ... A BIBLIOGRAPHY OF WISCONSIN'S PARTICIPATION IN THE WAR BETWEEN THE STATES.... Madison, Wisconsin: 1911.

A list of materials pertaining to military matters such as rosters, regimental histories, and documents located in the Wisconsin Historical Library.

957. Current, Richard K. THE HISTORY OF WISCONSIN: THE CIVIL WAR ERA 1848-1873. Madison, Wisconsin: State Historical Society of Wisconsin, 1976.

Volume 2 of a projected six volume opus, the author has produced a large, excellent study of Wisconsin before, during, and after the war. Though a happy mix of political, economic, cultural, and other matters, probably only one-quarter of the work deals with the war years.

958. Estabrook, Charles E., editor. RECORDS AND SKETCHES OF MILITARY ORGANIZATIONS, POPULATION, LEGISLATION, ELECTIONS AND OTHER STATISTICS.... Madison, Wisconsin: 1914.

Includes sketches of regiments and a chronological list of engagements of Wisconsin's regiments.

959. ———. WISCONSIN LOSSES IN THE CIVIL WAR.... Madison, Wisconsin: 1915.

The official listing of all Wisconsin soldiers who died while in service.

960. Glazer, Walter E. "Wisconsin Goes to War: April 1861," WIS MAG HIS, 50 [1966]: 147-164.

A thorough examination of the level of public support for recruiting, as well as the nascent opposition to the war effort, in the first few weeks following the attack on Fort Sumter.

961. Klement, Frank L. WISCONSIN AND THE CIVIL WAR. Madison, Wisconsin: State Historical Society of Wisconsin. 1963.

Covers all aspects of Wisconsin in the Civil War--military contributions, politics, and industry.

962. Love, William D. WISCONSIN IN THE WAR OF THE REBELLION.... Chicago, 1866.

A huge book which contains a record of all military units which served in the field plus an account of political affairs on the home front.

963. Merk, Frederick. ECONOMIC HISTORY OF WISCONSIN DURING THE CIVIL WAR DECADE. Madison, Wisconsin: State Historical Society of Wisconsin, 1971.

A reissue of the 1916 classic, with a new introduction by the author. In this study of Wisconsin's wartime economy, Professor Merk demonstrates that the Union benefited from the state's economic growth.

964. Paul, William G. WISCONSIN'S CIVIL WAR ARCHIVES. Madison, Wisconsin: State Historical Society of Wisconsin, 1965.

A useful though slim [66 pages] booklet, which lists 171 manuscript collections, grouped into ten categories. Each collection is carefully annotated.

965. Quiner, Edwin B. THE MILITARY HISTORY OF WISCONSIN.... Chicago, Illinois: 1866.

Regimental histories, biographical sketches, and actions of state officials to support the war effort.

966. Sellers, James L. "Republicanism and States Rights in Wisconsin." MVHR, 17 [1930]: 213-229.

As the sectional crisis worsened, the states' rights spirit among the Republicans in Wisconsin gradually gave way to a sense of national consolidation.

967. Wells, Robert W. WISCONSIN IN THE CIVIL WAR. Milwaukee, Wisconsin: MILWAUKEE JOURNAL, 1962.

A series of thirty-nine vignettes which were published in the MILWAUKEE JOURNAL.

Western States and Territories

968. Atshuler, Constance W. "The Case of Sylvester Mowery: The Charge of Treason." ARIZ W, 15 [1973]: 63-82.

Mowery was prominent in the movement for territorial status. As the war progressed, he was accused of being involved in pro-Confederate activities, was arrested, and his mine was confiscated. His version of the story has become part of the folklore and legend of Arizona history.

969. Ashcraft, Allan C., editor. "The Union Occupation of the

Lower Rio Grande Valley in the Civil War." TEX MIL HIS, 8 [1970]: 13-26.

The story of the 38th Iowa and its role in the occupation.

970. Athearn, Robert G. "The Civil War and Montana Gold." MON, 12 [1962]: 62-73.

Discusses the effects of the Civil War on Montana. The war kept almost hidden from view one of the most significant gold rushes in the country. It also helped establish the Democratic party in Montana.

971. ———. "Civil War Days in Montana." PAC HIS R, 29 [1960]: 19-33.

The primacy of the Civil War obscured from general view developments in the Montana Territory in the 1860s. There were several gold rushes and the Democratic party became firmly established there.

972. ———. "West of Appomattox." MON, 12 [1962]: 2-11.

Maintains the West should not be ignored in any discussion of the Civil War.

973. Bullard, Frederick L. "Abraham Lincoln and the Statehood of Nevada." A BAR ASSN J, 34 [3,4] [1940]: 210-213, 236; 313-317.

Nevada's admission to the Union was a war measure in that votes from the new state were necessary to carry the 13th Amendment and the 1864 election for Lincoln.

974. Carson, James F. "California: Gold to Help Finance the War." JW, 14 [1975]: 25-41.

Author describes the contributions of California to the Union war effort, including manpower and economic resources. Most important among the latter was the $185,000,000 in gold which "was instrumental in keeping the North in the fight."

975. Carter, John D. "Abraham Lincoln and the California Patronage." AHR, 48 [1943]: 495-506.

A useful description of the relations between California and the president.

976. Dyer, Brainerd. "California's Civil War Claims." S CAL Q, 45 [1963]: 1-21.

Details California's attempt to gain reimbursement for raising troops at their own expense.

977. Elliott, Claude. "Union Sentiment in Texas." SW HIS Q, 50 [1946/1947]: 449-477.

One-third of the Texans actively or passively, supported the Union cause, but their plight was not an easy one.

978. Fischer, LeRoy H., editor. THE CIVIL WAR IN INDIAN TERRITORY. Los Angeles, California: Lorrin L. Morrison, 1974.

Written by graduate students at Oklahoma State University, this volume deals with the little recognized events in Indian Territory during the Civil War. "For the 60,000 Indians of the Five Civilized Tribes ... the years of the Civil War ... were likely more disruptive and destructive in Indian Territory than anywhere in the Southern States, the seat of the war."

979. ———, editor. "Western States in the Civil War." JW, 14 [1975]: 1-184.

The entire issue is devoted to essays written by Fischer's graduate students at Oklahoma State University. Covers Oregon, California, Minnesota, Iowa, Kansas, Missouri, Texas, Louisiana, and Arkansas. A good introduction to the subject.

980. ———, editor. THE WESTERN TERRITORIES IN THE CIVIL WAR. Manhattan, Kansas: JOURNAL OF THE WEST, 1977.

Eight articles written by the editor's graduate students. Fischer's introduction summarizes the war's effect on Western Territories, internal politics, relations with the Indians, and economic developments. Territories covered: Washington and Idaho, Nevada, Utah, Colorando, Nebraska, New Mexico and Arizona, and the Indian Territory.

981. Fisher, Margaret M., compiler. UTAH AND THE CIVIL WAR.... Salt Lake City, Utah: Deseret Book Co., 1929.

Relates the response of Brigham Young to Lincoln's request for troops to guard against Indian attacks on the mail routes and telegraph lines to California.

982. Frazier, J.L., compiler. "Civil War Bibliography." COL MAG, 38 [1961]: 65-69.

A representative listing of some of the materials available at the State Historical Society of Colorado. Periodicals, general and specialized histories, manuscripts, interviews, and newspapers are included.

983. Ganaway, Loomis M. NEW MEXICO AND THE SECTIONAL CONFLICT. Santa Fe, New Mexico: Historical Society of New Mexico, 1944.

A thorough study of public and official opinions. Editors and the politicians generally favored the Union.

984. Gilbert, Benjamin F. "California and the Civil War," CAL HIS SOC Q, 20 [1941]: 289-306.

An excellent bibliographic essay.

985. ———. "The Confederate Minority in California." CAL HIS SOC Q, 20 [1941]: 154-170.

The author contends that a very small minority of people in California favored the Confederacy.

986. ———. "The Mythical Johnston Conspiracy." CAL HIS SOC Q, 28 [1949]: 165-173.

Gilbert attempts to explode the myth that General Albert Sidney Johnston, Commander of the Department of the Pacific, was involved in a plot to induce California to join the Confederacy.

987. ———. "San Francisco Harbor Defences During the Civil War." CAL HIS SOC Q, 32 [1954]: 299-340.

Drawn mainly from the legislative journals of Oregon and California, this is one of the few articles dealing with the subject.

988. Goff, John S. "The Civil War Confiscation Cases in Arizona Territory." A J LEG HIS, 14 [1970]: 349-354.

Discusses the confiscation of property under the congressional acts of 1861 and 1862. The six men whose property was seized were regarded as "rebels."

989. Hanft, Marshall. "The Cape Forts: Guardians of the Columbia." ORE HIS Q, 45 [1964]: 325-361.

A detailed description of the fortifications along the Columbia River.

990. Hill, Gertrude. "The Civil War in the Southwest, 1861-1862: A List of Books Old and New." ARIZ Q, 18 [1962]: 166-170.

A critical survey of a number of recent books dealing with the Civil War in the southwest.

991. Johannsen, Robert W. FRONTIER POLITICS AND THE SECTIONAL CONFLICT: THE PACIFIC NORTHWEST ON THE EVE OF THE CIVIL WAR. Seattle: University of Washington Press, 1955.

A scholarly study of the complex inner workings of parties and politics, chiefly in Oregon, at the time war broke out.

992. ———. "A Political Picture of the Pacific Northwest in the Civil War." MON, 12 [1962]: 38-48.

An excellent introduction to the subject. The Pacific Northwest, conservative by nature and separated geographically from the rest of the country, wanted the Union preserved. Little success was enjoyed by the Copperheads in this region.

993. Kennedy, Elijah R. THE CONTEST FOR CALIFORNIA IN 1861: HOW COLONEL E.D. BAKER SAVED THE PACIFIC STATES TO THE UNION. Boston, 1912.

Although probably no one person saved California for the Union, this is a good presentation of the divisions within the state at the start of the war.

994. Kibby, Leo P. "California, the Civil War and the Indian Problem: An Account of California's Participation in the Great Conflict." JW, 4 [1965]: 183-209, 377-410.

A good analysis. After federal troops were withdrawn from western territories, volunteers were recruited to protect the region. The service of California Volunteers in Arizona, New Mexico, and Utah is covered.

995. ———. "Some Aspects of California's Military Problems During the Civil War." CWH, 5 [1959]: 251-262.

It certainly had a number of them.

996. ———. "Union Loyalty of California's Civil War Governors." CAL HIS SOC Q, 44 [1965]: 311-321.

Includes a refutation of the Russian charge d'affaires' claim that California made "only small financial contributions" and had not supplied a "single man during the entire war."

997. Lamar, Howard R. DAKOTA TERRITORY, 1861-1869: A STUDY OF FRONTIER POLITICS. New Haven: Yale University Press, 1956.

The outgrowth of a Ph.D. dissertation, this essay describes in meticulous detail the evolution of a political system in the Dakota Territory.

998. Larson, Gustave O. "Utah and the Civil War." UTAH HIS Q, 33 [1965]: 55-77.

Concentrates on the relatively good relationship which developed between the Mormons and the federal government.

999. Long, E.B. THE SAINTS AND THE UNION: UTAH TERRITORY DURING THE CIVIL WAR. Urbana: University of Illinois Press, 1981.

This work contributes to a greater understanding of the war of words waged between Brigham Young and the Mormons and General Patrick E. Connor. Author draws on Salt Lake City newspapers, sermons, Young's correspondence, and Connor's dispatches.

1000. Ostrander, George M. NEVADA: THE GREAT ROTTEN BOROUGH 1859-1964. New York: Knopf, 1966.

An account of Nevada's history, concentrating primarily on the post-Civil War years. The state was born of political expediency in 1864 and developed for the benefit of numerous self-interest groups.

1001. Ruhlen, George. "Early Nevada Forts." NEV HIS SOC Q, 7 [1964]: 1-62.

Brief concise accounts, both historical and descriptive, of the forts. Photographs and maps are included.

1002. ———. "San Diego and the Civil War." SAN DIEGO HIS SOC Q, 7 [1961]: 17-22.

The activities of the federal garrison in and around San Diego are covered in this article.

1003. Sacconaghi, Charles D., editor. "A Bibliographical Note on the Civil War in the West." AZ WEST, 8 [1966]: 349-364.

An annotated list of approximately 130 books and articles pertaining to the Trans-Mississippi military events. Most of the listings were published during the centennial years.

1004. Spaulding, Imogene. "The Attitude of California to the Civil War." ANNUAL PUBLICATION OF THE HISTORICAL SOCIETY OF SOUTHERN CALIFORNIA, 9 [1912]: 104-131.

This article focuses on the trends in public opinion.

1005. Thomas, James. "Nevada Territory." JW, 16 [1977]: 36-43.

The loyalty of Nevada to the Union was important because of the Overland Mail Route which linked East and West, as well as the bullion which was needed to help finance the war.

1006. Unrau, William E. "The Civil War Career of Jesse Henry Leavenworth." MON, 12 [1962]: 74-83.

Tells the story of Jesse Leavenworth, a federal officer who was sent west to raise troops but ran afoul of the military because of his opposition to army policies. Leaving the army he returned to the west as an Indian agent.

1007. Waldrip, William I. "New Mexico During the Civil War." NM HIS R, 28 [1953]: 163-182, 251-290.

A discussion of the politics of the territory, its loyalty to the Union, and the rivalry between Confederate and Union interests there.

1008. Wiel, Samuel C. LINCOLN'S CRISIS IN THE FAR WEST. San Francisco: Privately printed, 1949.

Author concentrates on California, discussing the disposition of public lands, Lincoln's problem with the New Almaden mine, and gold mining in general.

1009. Winther, Oscar O. and Richard A. Van Orman, editors. A CLASSIFIED BIBLIOGRAPHY OF THE PERIODICAL LITERATURE OF THE TRANS-MISSIPPI WEST [1811-1967]. Westport, Connecticut: Greenwood, 1972.

A good collection of Civil War articles may be found in this massive compilation of 9,244 entries, grouped in 65 major categories.

1010. Woodward, Walter C. THE RISE AND EARLY HISTORY OF POLITICAL PARTIES IN OREGON 1843-1868. Portland, Oregon, 1913.

Wartime politics in the Far West are discussed in depth.

1011. Wroten, William H., Jr. "Colorado and the Advent of Civil War." COL MAG, 36 [1959]: 174-186.

Author credits the Colorado newspapers with saving the territory for the Union even though one-third of the population was from the South and two regiments for the Confederate forces were raised there.

Occupied Southern States

1012. Bryann, Charles F., Jr. "Nashville Under Federal Occupation." CWTI, 13 [9] [1975]: 4-11, 40-47.

With the occupation of the city by federal forces in 1862, Nashville became crucially important to the North as a major supply, rail, and medical center for the western armies.

1013. Byrne, Frank L. "'A Terrible Machine': General Neal Dow's Military Government on the Gulf Coast." CWH, 12 [1966]: 5-22.

Discusses the harsh rule of Maine prohibitionist Neal Dow when he served as military commander on the Gulf Coast in 1862-1863.

1014. Capers, Gerald M., Jr. "Confederates and Yankees in Occupied New Orleans, 1862-1865." JSH, 30 [1964]: 405-426.

A discussion of the policies of the three federal commanders of occupied New Orleans: Generals Benjamin Butler, Nathaniel Banks, and Stephen Hurlbut.

1015. ———. OCCUPIED CITY: NEW ORLEANS UNDER THE FEDERALS, 1862-1865. Lexington: University of Kentucky Press, 1965.

An informative study of the federal occupation of New Orleans under the commands of Generals Butler, Banks, and Hurlbut, with the emphasis being on the response of the native inhabitants to an alien, military rule.

1016. Chambers, Lenoir. "Notes on Life in Occupied Norfolk." VA MHB, 72 [1965]: 131-144.

Norfolk "sank toward physical lethargy, economic misery, and spiritual dissolution" when Union troops occupied the city. The federals remained in possession of Norfolk throughout the war.

1017. Cowen, Ruth C. "Reorganization of Federal Arkansas, 1862-1865." ARK HIS Q, 18 [1959]: 32-57.

Union forces occupied the capital in 1863. A reorganization of the state, both politically and militarily, quickly ensued.

1018. Doyle, Elisabeth J. "Rottenness in Every Direction: The Stokes Investigation in Civil War New Orleans." CWH, 18 [1972]: 24-41.

An account of the alleged corruption in the Quartermaster's Department at New Orleans in 1864.

1019. Egan, Clifford L. "Friction in New Orleans: General Butler Versus the Spanish Consul." LA HIS, 9 [1968]: 43-52.

Author outlines the disputes between the flamboyant federal commander at New Orleans, General Butler, and the consul for Spain, Juan Callejon.

1020. James, Nola A. "The Civil War Years in Independence County." ARK HIS Q, 28 [1969]: 234-274.

A history of a north central Arkansas county during the war.

1021. Johnson, Howard P. "New Orleans Under Ben Butler." LA HIS Q, 24 [1941]: 434-536.

In this lengthy article, the author examines in detail all facets of Butler's command at New Orleans. He concludes that the general was "less the monster that a subject people thought him than an embodiment ... of the immemorial ways of the victor with the vanquished."

1022. Johnson, Ludwell H. "The Butler Expedition of 1861-1862: The Profitable Side of War." CWH, 11 [1965]: 229-236.

Describes the corrupt practices indulged in by General Butler as he outfitted his force in Massachusetts prior to his move to New Orleans in the winter of 1861-1862. Butler loaded his command with cousins and cronies and countenanced many frauds connected with the supplying, feeding, and transporting of his troops.

1023. Jones, Allen W. "Military Events in Louisiana During the Civil War, 1861-1865." LA HIS, 2 [1961]: 302-321.

A list of more than 500 military actions which took place in the state.

1024. Nellis, David M. "'The Damned Rascal': Benjamin Butler in New Orleans." CWTI, 12 [6] [1973]: 4-6, 8-10, 41-47.

Deals with Butler's tenure as governor of New Orleans.

1025. Parton, James. GENERAL BUTLER IN NEW ORLEANS. New York, 1864.

A detailed, heavily-documented record of General Benjamin O. Butler's command of the Department of the Gulf in 1862. His previous military and political career is traced. Despite its age, this is still a useful volume.

1026. Ripley, Peter C. SLAVES AND FREEDMEN IN CIVIL WAR LOUISIANA. Baton Rouge: Louisiana State University Press, 1976.

The volume deals almost exclusively with a study of federal policies in the Military Department of the Gulf. The title is misleading. Only two chapters consider the problems and expectations of the blacks.

1027. Robbins, Peggy. "Union Soldiers and Confederate Civilians Mingled Together ... When the Yankees Held Memphis." CWTI, 16 [9] [1978]: 26-37.

Discusses battle of Memphis and its aftermath. Comments on various generals and their influence plus social and economic conditions in the city.

1028. Robertson, James I., Jr. "Danville Under Military Occupation, 1865." VA MHB, 75 [1967]: 331-348.

After Danville surrendered, the city was beset by riots. Order was restored and the federal occupation was courteous, compassionate, and went far to heal the scars of war.

1029. Simms, L. Moody, Jr., editor. "The Occupation of Southeastern Louisiana: Impressions of a New York Volunteer, 1862-1863." LA STUD, 7 [1968]: 83-91.

The edited letters of a Union soldier, Amberto O. Remington of Ira Hill, New York, written between September 7, 1862 and January 30, 1863, while he was stationed in Louisiana.

1030. Somers, Dale A. "War and Play: The Civil War in New Orleans." MISS Q, 26 [1973]: 3-28.

Even though the city was occupied for almost three years, the people managed to enjoy the same social activities they had participated in during the pre-war years.

1031. Thomas, David Y. ARKANSAS IN WAR AND RECONSTRUCTION, 1861-1874. Little Rock: United Daughters of the Confederacy, Arkansas Division, 1926.

Facts and photographs not generally available elsewhere are contained herein. The 446-page work takes the story through the restoration of "home rule."

E. DISSENT

"Dissent" has been a difficult term to define. Where does one draw the line between the "loyal opposition" and opposition which borders on treason? Many of the entries which follow can be classed as "loyal opposition," but of a very extreme nature. For less radical forms of political opposition the reader is directed to NATIONAL GOVERNMENT AND POLITICS [II, B]. Entries dealing with draft resistance may be found under MANPOWER MOBILIZATION [III, C].

The term "Copperhead," the traditional epithet used to describe anti-war Democrats, has undergone substantial revision in the past 30 years. Whereas the earlier writers did not hesitate to label many of the Copperheads as traitors and spoke darkly of "treasonable plots" and "conspiracies," recent scholarship has modified that interpetation. To the revisionists Copperheads were largely loyal Americans who were strongly opposed to the war for political, economic, or ideological reasons, but who were not engaged in treasonable behavior. Whereas I was first skeptical of the revisionist argument, I have now been "converted." Probably the best overall view of the subject is the recent work of the foremost revisionist, Frank L. Klement: DARK LANTERNS: SECRET POLITICAL SOCIETIES, CONSPIRACIES, AND TREASON TRIALS IN THE CIVIL WAR.

1032. Abrams, Ray H. "The Copperhead Newspapers and the Negro." JNH, 20 [1935]: 131-152.

A useful, early study of the subject.

1033. ———. "THE JEFFERSONIAN: Copperhead Newspaper." PA MHB, 48 [1933]: 260-283.

Editor John Hodgson's anti-war editorials exceeded the bounds of propriety and the West Chester, Pennsylvania newspaper was suppressed in 1862.

1034. Abzug, Robert H. "The Copperheads: Historical Approaches to Civil War Dissent in the Midwest." IND MAG HIS, 66 [1970]: 40-55.

Author discusses several approaches to the study of Civil War dissent. He believes that the most profound questions still remain unexplored.

1035. Alotta, Robert I. STOP THE EVIL: A CIVIL WAR HISTORY OF DESERTION AND MURDER. San Rafael, California: Presidio Press, 1978.

A sympathetic examination of the conviction and execution by hanging for desertion and murder of William H. Howe, a "simple German farmer," of the 116th Pennsylvania.

1036. Arena, Frank C. "Southern Sympathizers in Iowa During the Civil War Period." ANN IOWA, 30 [1951]: 486-538.

Based on an examination of state documents and newspapers,

this is a study of the not inconsiderable southern, anti-war influences which prevailed in Iowa during the war.

1037. Baker, Jean H. AFFAIRS OF PARTY: THE POLITICAL CULTURE OF NORTHERN DEMOCRATS IN THE MID-NINETEENTH CENTURY. Ithaca, New York: Cornell University Press, 1983.

Author views the Civil War Democrats as the "loyal opposition."

1038. ———. "A Loyal Opposition: Northern Democrats in the Thirty-Seventh Congress." CWH, 25 [1979]: 139-155.

An incisive discussion of the subject which is developed more fully in the author's book, cited in the previous entry.

1039. Becker, Carl M. "The Death of J.F. Bollmeyer: Murder Most Foul?" CIN HIS SOC BULL, 24 [1966]: 249-269.

The account of the murder of a Copperhead newspaper editor, who was a protege of Clement L. Vallandigham.

1040. ———. "Disloyalty and the Dayton Public Schools." CWH, 11 [1965]: 58-68.

Author traces the events leading up to riots between Union Leaguers and Copperheads in the Dayton, Ohio, public schools in 1863. Children of Copperheads faced difficult problems.

1041. ———. "The Genesis of a Copperhead." HIS PHIL SOC OHIO BULL, 19 [1961]: 235-253.

A study of the formative years of Tom Lowe of Batavia, Ohio, in which his Copperhead thinking was shaped. The most important influence was a two-year residency in Nashville, Tennessee, 1855-1857, wherein he cultivated a sympathetic understanding of the South.

1042. ———. "Picture of a Young Copperhead." OHIO HIS, 71 [1962]: 3-23.

A description of the actions and attitudes of Thomas Owen Lowe, a young disciple of Vallandigham. Lowe blamed the abolitionists for the war and advocated peace and the recognition of southern independence.

1043. Beisel, Suzanne. "Henry Clay 'Dirty Dean.'" ANN IOWA, 36 [1963]: 502-524.

Relates incidents in the life of the celebrated Iowa Copperhead. Orator, writer, politician, lawyer, and minister, Clay delivered such venemous anti-war speeches that he was once almost hung on the spot. He earned his nickname because he was always dirty and shabby.

1044. Benton, Elbert J. THE MOVEMENT FOR PEACE WITHOUT A VICTORY DURING THE CIVIL WAR. New York: Da Capo, 1972.

This 80-page pamphlet, a reprint of a 1918 publication, was one of the first efforts by a scholar to pin the tag of treason on the Copperheads. It is badly outdated.

1045. Bernard, Kenneth H. "Lincoln and the Civil War As Viewed By A Dissenting Yankee of Connecticut." LIN HER, 76 [1974]: 208-214.

Richard Harvey Phelps opposed Lincoln, the war, and all its works.

1046. Britzinger, Alphonse J. "The Father of Copperheadism in Wisconsin." WIS MAG HIS, 39 [1955]: 17-25.

A look at Edward G. Ryan, a leading critic of Lincoln.

1047. Cardinal, Eric J. "Disloyalty or Dissent: The Case of the Copperhead." MIDWEST Q, 19 [1977]: 24-35.

Originally supportive of a war to preserve the Union, many Copperheads came to oppose it as they increasingly believed that the government was undermining the political and social institutions of the country.

1048. Carleton, William G. "Civil War Dissidence in the North: The Perspective of a Century." S ATL Q, 65 [1966]: 390-402.

A good overview, in which it is pointed out that the more diversified North had much more internal dissent than the South. While the War Democrats supported the administration without reservation, a majority of the Democrats supported the war while attacking the administration on other issues.

1049. Chandler, Robert J. "Crushing Dissent: The Pacific Coast Tests Lincoln Policy of Suppression." CWH, 30 [1984]: 235-254.

A well-done study of the problem as it arose on the west coast.

1050. ———. "The Press and Civil Liberties in California During the Civil War." Ph.D. Dissertation: University of California-Riverside, 1978.

A detailed, definitive study of this complex issue.

1051. Coleman, Charles H. "The Use of the Term 'Copperhead' During the Civil War." MVHR, 25 [1938/1939]: 263-264.

Author finds that the term "Copperhead" was first used in the Midwest in the CINCINNATI COMMERCIAL on August 17, 1861.

1052. ——— and Paul H. Spence. "Charleston [Illinois] Riot, March 28, 1864." JISHS, 33 [1940]: 7-56.

A detailed study of a riot in Charleston, Illinois. Trouble had been brewing for days between local Republicans and anti-war Democrats. Violence finally broke out when a Democratic meeting was disrupted by a group of Union soldiers passing through town.

1053. Cowden, Joanna D. "The Politics of Dissent: Civil War Democrats in Connecticut." NEQ, 56 [1983]: 538-554.

A survey of Democratic politics in Connecticut during the war, in which the beliefs of the peace faction are explained. It was a more numerous body than has been previously thought.

1054. Crenshaw, Ollinger. "The Knights of the Golden Circle: The Career of George Bickley." AHR, [1941/1942]: 23-50.

A sketch of George Bickley and an account of his founding of the Knights of the Golden Circle in the South before the outbreak of war.

1055. Curry, Richard O. "Copperheadism and Continuity: The Anatomy of a Stereotype." JNH, 57 [1972]: 29-36.

Author supports the "revisionist" view that rather than being traitors and subversives, Copperheads might better be described as "conservative Union Democrats."

1056. ———. "A Note on the Origins of the Term 'Butternut' During the Civil War." MID AM, 44 [1962]: 125-127.

A brief explanation of the origin of the use of the word "Butternut," which in some sections was another way of saying "Copperhead."

1057. ———. "The Union As It Was: A Critique of Recent Interpretations of the Copperheads." CWH, 13 [1967]: 25-39.

An important essay in which the author shows that recent works on the subject have destroyed the stereotype that painted the Copperheads as traitors.

1058. Dunning, William A. "Disloyalty in Two Wars." AHR, 24 [1919]: 625-630.

Dunning compares dissent in the Civil War with dissent in World War I.

1059. Ellis, L.E. "The CHICAGO TIMES During the Civil War." ILL ST HIS SOC TRAN, [1932]: 135-182.

In this study of the CHICAGO TIMES, the most bitter anti-administration newspaper in the North, dissent is equated with treason. The paper was suspended in June 1863 by General Burnside for publishing "incendiary sentiments," but the order was quickly revoked by Lincoln.

1060. Fesler, Mayo. "Secret Political Societies in the North During the Civil War." IND MAG HIS, 14 [1918]: 183-286.

An early work which charged the Copperheads and their organizations with treasonable purposes, a view rejected by recent scholarship. However, his ideas worked their way into textbooks and became widely accepted during the 1920s and 1930s.

1061. Geary, James W. "Clement L. Vallandigham Writes to John H. George, April 17, 1863: His Last Existing Letter Before the Arrest?" HIS NH, 30 [1975]: 12-19.

An examination of one of the few extant letters of Clement L. Vallandigham. It contains a succinct summary of events preceding and following the May 1863 arrest and trial of the Copperhead leader.

1062. George, Joseph, Jr. "'A Catholic Family Newspaper' Views the Lincoln Administration: John Mullaly's Copperhead Weekly." CWH, 24 [1978]: 112-132.

Mullaly distrusted abolitionists, but supported the Lincoln administration until the Emancipation Proclamation. At that point his paper joined the Copperhead ranks. A Democrat, Mullaly became bitterly anti-Lincoln and was arrested for resisting the draft.

1063. Gray, Wood. THE HIDDEN CIVIL WAR: THE STORY OF THE COPPERHEADS. New York: Viking Press, 1942.

One of the two classic works--George Fort Milton's EVE OF CONFLICT was the other--which viewed the Democratic oppositionists of the upper Midwest as traitors. The theory has been challenged and overturned by revisionists.

1064. Grayston, Florence L. "Lambdin P. Milligan--A Knight of the Golden Circle." IND MAG HIS, 43 [1947]: 379-391.

An unfriendly appraisal of the celebrated Indiana Copperhead, who was found guilty of treason, sentenced to be hanged, only to have his sentence reversed by the United States Supreme Court.

1065. Greenberg, Irvin F. "Charles Ingersoll: The Aristocrat as Copperhead." PA MHB, 93 [1969]: 190-217.

Ingersoll, a prominent Philadelphia lawyer, played an active role in Democratic politics and was an outspoken critic of the war policies of the Lincoln administration.

1066. Hubbart, Henry C. "Pro-Southern Influences in the Free West, 1840-1865." MVHR, 20 [1933]: 45-62.

An examination of the links, largely economic and cultural, which tied the old Southwest to the old Northwest before and during the war.

1067. Hubbell, John T. "Politics as Usual: The Northern Democracy and Party Survival." ILL Q, 36 [1973]: 22-35.

Douglas Democrats viewed themselves as the "conservative center" around which the North and Upper South could coalesce.

1068. Hummel, William. "The Military Occupation of Columbia County, Pennsylvania." PA MHB, 80 [1956]: 320-338.

Author argues that the military occupation of Columbia County, Pennslyvania, August-October 1864, was necessitated by the open opposition to the forthcoming draft rather than to insure a Republican election victory, as has been traditionally held.

1069. Hyman, Harold M. ERA OF THE OATH: NORTHERN LOYALTY TESTS DURING THE CIVIL WAR AND RECONSTRUCTION. Philadelphia: University of Pennsylvania Press, 1954.

This detailed and valuable survey of Union loyalty oaths from their inception in 1861 to their final repeal in 1884 demonstrates that they did not have much value in insuring loyalty. They were used for partisan purposes by Radicals and put beyond the pale of availability potentially useful public servants.

1070. Jones, Stanley L. "Agrarian Radicalism in the Illinois Constitutional Convention of 1862." JISHS, 48 [1955]: 271-282.

Anti-war Democrats dominated this convention.

1071. Kutcher, Phillip. "Treason in Illinois." MIL COLL HIS, 29 [1977]: 64-66.

Reprint of a short note written by a young boy in Illinois in 1863. He discusses his own and the public's view of Copperheads.

1072. Klein, Frederic S. "The Great Northwest Conspiracy." CWTI, 4 [3] [1965]: 21-26.

Author contends that there really was a "conspiracy" centering in Chicago at the time of the 1864 Democratic National Convention. Revisionists discount the seriousness of the Copperhead gathering.

1073. Klement, Frank L. "'Brick' Pomeroy and the Democratic Processes." WIS ACAD SCI ARTS LET TRAN, [1961]: 159-169.

Pomeroy was an influential Copperhead editor in Wisconsin and an angry critic of the president.

1074. ———. "'Brick' Pomeroy, Copperhead and Curmudgeon." WIS MAG HIS, 35 [1951]: 106-113, 156-157.

A sketch of Wisconsin's number one Democratic critic.

1075. ———. "Carrington and the Golden Circle Legend in Indiana During the Civil War." IND MAG HIS, 61 [1965]: 31-52.

One of several state studies in which the author debunks the idea of a strong Golden Circle organization. Carrington was a military adviser to Governor Morton who did much to promote the Golden Circle "legend."

1076. ———. "Civil War Politics, Nationalism and Postwar Myths." HISTORIAN, 38 [1976]: 419-438.

Author shows that false Republican charges linking Democrats with alleged treasonable plots have been perpetrated as "history" in the 20th century. Six myths, in particular, are still being repeated.

1077. ———. "Clement L. Vallandigham's Exile in the Confederacy, May 25--June 17, 1863." JSH, 31 [1965]: 149-163.

Based chiefly on newspaper sources, the article examines the almost hostile attitude toward Vallandigham during his 24-day exile.

1078. ———. "Copperheads and Copperheadism in Wisconsin: Democratic Opposition to the Lincoln Administration." WIS MAG HIS, 42 [1959]: 182-188.

Wisconsin Copperheads are viewed as conservatives.

1079. ———. THE COPPERHEADS IN THE MIDDLE WEST. Chicago: University of Chicago Press, 1960.

The first revisionist book on the Copperheads which directly challenges the conclusions of Gray, Milton, and others. Klement argues that anti-war Democrats were exercising the legitimate right of the loyal opposition. He emphasizes, among other things, the economic basis for the midwestern opposition to Lincoln.

1080. ———. "Copperhead Secret Societies in Illinois During the Civil War." JISHS, 48 [1955]: 152-180.

The secret societies, it is contended, were as much a myth in Illinois as they were in Indiana and elsewhere.

1081. ———. DARK LANTERNS: SECRET POLITICAL SOCIETIES, CONSPIRACIES, AND TREASON TRIALS IN THE CIVIL WAR. Baton Rouge: Louisiana State University Press, 1984.

Klement's most recent and most exhaustive study on the "myth" of the secret societies. The work is heavily documented. The "Epilogue," particularly pages 234-244, provides an excellent analysis of how the myth developed and prospered.

1082. ———. "Deuster as a Democratic Dissenter During the Civil War: A Case Study of a Copperhead." WIS ACAD SCI ARTS LET TRAN, [1957]: 21-38.

The forces motivating Peter V. Deuster, a prominent Copperhead editor in Milwaukee, are examined.

1083. ———. "Economic Aspects of Middle Western Copperheadism." HISTORIAN, 14 [1951]: 27-44.

An early discussion of a point more fully developed in THE COPPERHEADS IN THE MIDDLE WEST.

1084. ———. "Exile Across the Border: Clement L. Vallandigham at Niagara, Canada West." NIAG FRON, 10 [1964]: 69-91.

Vallandigham spent almost a year in Canadian exile but kept in communication with Copperheads south of the border.

1085. ———. "Franklin Pierce and the Treason Charges of 1861-1862." HISTORIAN, 23 [1961]: 438-448.

Republicans accused the former Democratic president of subversion. Pierce had made a visit to Michigan and was charged with being in on a conspiracy. [See next entry.]

1086. ———. "The Hopkins Hoax and Golden Circle Rumors in Michigan, 1861-1862." MICH HIS, 47 [1963]: 1-14.

Dr. Guy Hopkins, a friend of President Pierce, sent fabricated materials to Detroit newspapers alleging that Pierce was an agent for a conspiratorial group. The plan was to trap the Republicans into believing the story, which would be followed by their embarrassment when the hoax was revealed. The scheme backfired, however, and Hopkins was imprisoned.

1087. ———. LINCOLN'S CRITICS IN WISCONSIN. Madison: Lincoln Fellowship of Wisconsin, 1956. Historical bulletin 14.

In this 20-page pamphlet, author quotes frequently from both moderates and vicious critics of Lincoln and the war.

1088. ———. "Middle Western Copperheadism and the Genesis of the Granger Movement." MVHR, 38 [1952]: 679-694.

Another example of the economic forces behind Copperheadism in the Midwest was the Democrat's strong support for anti-railroad legislation.

1089. ———. "Ohio and the Knights of the Golden Circle: The Evolution of a Civil War Myth." CIN HIS SOC BULL, 32 [1974]: 7-27.

As in Indiana and Illinois, Ohio Republicans exaggerated the importance and influence of the Knights of the Golden Circle in their state.

1090. ———. "Phineas C. Wright, the Order of American Knights, and the Sanderson Expose." CWH, 18 [1972]: 5-23.

Author shows the falsity of Sanderson's 1864 report which was intended to indict the Order of American Knights as a treasonable organization. Wright was the head of the Knights.

1091. ———. "Rumors of Golden Circle Activity in Iowa During the Civil War Years." ANN IOWA, 37 [1965]: 523-536.

In Iowa, as well, rumors of Democratic subversion through the Golden Circle are found to be groundless.

1092. ———. "Sound and Fury: Civil War Dissent in the Cincinnati Area." CIN HIS SOC BULL, 35 [1977]: 99-114.

A discussion of the reasons for dissent in Cincinnati among the Irish and the Germans.

1093. ———. "Vallandigham as an Exile in Canada, 1863-1864." OHIO HIS, 74 [1965]: 151-168, 208-210.

Describes Vallandigham's friendly reception by several prominent Canadians upon his arrival there after his departure from the Confederacy. After his defeat in the Ohio gubernatorial election of 1863, he was largely ignored by Canadian newspapers.

1094. Koenig, Louis W. "The Most Unpopular Man in the North." AM HER, 15 [2] [1964]: 12-15, 81-88.

A look at Vallandigham's views. He wished to bring the South back into the Union without victory for the North. His activities are described as little short of treason.

1095. Lendt, David L. DEMISE OF THE DEMOCRACY: THE COPPERHEAD PRESS IN IOWA. Ames, Iowa: Iowa State University Press, 1973.

An examination of the editorial opposition to the Lincoln administration in the Copperhead press of Iowa. It led to the decline of the Democratic party.

1096. ———. "Iowa and the Copperhead Movement." ANN IOWA, 10 [1970]: 412-426.

Attacking Lincoln for his handling of the war, Iowa Copperheads thought of themselves as "exponents of loyal opposition, not as radical southern sympathizers."

1097. Mahoney, Dennis A. THE PRISONER OF STATE. New York, 1863.

Mahoney was a celebrated Iowa Copperhead editor who was arrested and confined for several months in a federal prison.

1098. Milton, George F. ABRAHAM LINCOLN AND THE FIFTH COLUMN. New York: Vanguard Press, 1942.

Along with Wood Gray's THE HIDDEN CIVIL WAR--although not as scholarly--this work seeks to confirm the secret society "myth" so eloquently advanced some years before by Mayo Fesler. Needless to say, it is rejected by revisionists.

1099. Morrow, Curtis. "Politico-Military Societies of the Northwest." SOC SCI, 4 [1928/1929]: 9-31, 222-242, 348-361, 463-476; 5 [1929/1930]: 73-84.

Author accepts the belief that the secret societies were well-established treasonable organizations.

1100. Mushkat, Jerome. "Ben Wood's FORT LAFAYETTE: A source For Studying the Peace Democrats." CWH, 21 [1975]: 160-171.

Unsuccessful in making his arguments heard through the press, Ben Wood, New York Peace Democratic journalist and brother of Fernando Wood, resorted to fiction to detail his opposition to war and emancipation and to express his belief that the war was destroying civil liberties. Wood's novel, FORT LAFAYETTE, though ignored by students of Civil War fiction, should be recognized as an important primary source for the study of the Peace Democratic movement, according to the author.

1101. Pomeroy, Marcus M. "Brick." JOURNEY OF LIFE: REMINISCENCES AND RECOLLECTIONS OF "BRICK" POMEROY. New York, 1890.

In his memoirs, the former editor of the LA CROSSE [Wisconsin] WEEKLY DEMOCRAT and perhaps Lincoln's most savage critic, attempts to justify his wartime behavior.

1102. Robinson, John W. "A California Copperhead: Henry Hamilton and the LOS ANGELES STAR." ARIZ W, 23 [1981]: 213-230.

This sketch of Henry Hamilton, rabid pro-southern editor of the LOS ANGELES STAR during the Civil War, reveals, among other things, how tolerant the federal authorities were in allowing the publication of dissenting views.

1103. Roseboom, Eugene. "The Mobbing of THE CRISIS." OSAHQ, 59 [1950]: 150-153.

A brief account of the mobbing of THE CRISIS in Columbus, Ohio, March 3, 1863. The paper was the most influential Copperhead journal in the land, and it was destroyed by this assault.

1104. ———. "Southern Ohio and the Union in 1863." MVHR, 39 [1952]: 29-44.

Author examines the widely-accepted theory that southern Ohio was a stronghold of Copperheadism in the state and finds that it does not hold up.

1105. Ross, Earle D. "Northern Sectionalism in the Civil War Era." IOWA J HIS POL, 30 [1932]: 455-512.

This study reveals a relationship between western sectionalism and western discontent.

1106. Russ, William, Jr. "Franklin Weirick: 'Copperhead' of Central Pennsylvania." PENN HIS, 5 [1938]: 245-256.

Weirick was the outspoken Copperhead editor of the SELINSGROVE TIMES in a Republican part of Pennsylvania. He hated abolitionism, the war, suppression of free speech, Lincoln, and much more. Although he was almost lynched on one occasion, he continued his attacks on the government and the Republicans to the end of the war.

1107. Rutland, Robert. "The Copperheads of Iowa: A Re-examination." IOWA J HIS, 52 [1954]: 1-30.

In this revisionist study, Democratic dissent in Iowa is found to be based on historic forces.

1108. Sanger, Donald B. "The CHICAGO TIMES and the Civil War." MVHR, 17 [1931]: 557-580.

An early study of the important anti-administration newspaper.

1109. Shankman, Arnold M. THE PENNSYLVANIA ANTIWAR MOVEMENT, 1861-1865. Rutherford, New Jersey: Fairleigh Dickinson Press, 1980.

A detailed, scholarly examination of the Copperhead movement in Pennsylvania, written from the revisionist standpoint.

1110. ———. "Soldier Votes and Clement L. Vallandigham in the 1863 Ohio Gubernatorial Election." OHIO HIS, 82 [1973]: 88-104.

Vallandigham was demolished by Brough in the 1863 Ohio election. The soldier vote helped the victor, favoring Brough by an 18-1 margin.

1111. ———. "William B. Reed and the Civil War." PENN HIS, 39 [1971]: 455-468.

The sketch of a prominent Pennsylvanian during the war.

1112. Skidmore, Joseph. "The Copperhead Press and the Civil War." JOUR Q, 16 [1939]: 345-355.

A small sketch of a large issue.

1113. Smith, Bethania M. "Civil War Subversives." JISHS, 55 [1951]: 220-240.

A flawed article, which accepts the "myth" of the secret societies.

1114. Smith, Thomas H. "Crawford County 'Ez Trooly Dimecratic." OHIO HIS, 76 [1967]: 33-53, 93-95.

Crawford County, located in the north central part of the state, remained staunchly Democratic throughout the war. These "hard shelled Democrats," motivated by neither race nor economics, believed it was their duty to oppose the Republicans.

1115. Smith, William J. and James L. Burke, editors. "The Destruction of 'The Crisis.'" CWTI, 9 [8] [1970]: 40-43.

Soldiers home on leave played a major part in the sacking of THE CRISIS. This is the account of one of the participants.

1116. Sprague, Dean. FREEDOM UNDER LINCOLN. Boston: Houghton Mifflin, 1965.

A somewhat thin survey of constitutional and political problems, such as arbitrary arrests, which the Lincoln administration dealt with in the first year of the war.

1117. Starr, Stephen Z. "Was There A Northwest Conspiracy?" FCHQ, 38 [1964]: 323-341.

Author accepts the traditional view that there was a conspiracy.

1118. Stidger, Felix G. TREASON HISTORY OF THE ORDER OF SONS OF LIBERTY.... Chicago, 1903.

Stidger, called the "spy compleat," was hired to infiltrate the Sons Liberty in Kentucky and Indiana, which he did. However, he gave an exaggerated importance to the things he heard and saw. His testimony at the Indianapolis "Treason Trials" has been largely discounted by revisionists.

1119. Stiles, C.C. "The Skunk River War [or Tally War], Keokuk County, August 1863." ANN IOWA, 19 [1935]: 614-631.

A documentary account of an outbreak of violence between antiwar Democrats and Republicans in July-August 1863 in southwestern Iowa which troops had to suppress. The institution of the draft, among other things, appeared to precipitate the incident.

1120. Talmadge, John E. "A Peace Movement in Civil War Connecticut." NEQ, 37 [1964]: 306-321.

A look at the Connecticut anti-war movement in 1861. While the majority of the state's people supported the war, Connecticut's Copperheads made their presence felt.

1121. Tenney, Craig D. "To Suppress or Not to Suppress: Abraham Lincoln and the CHICAGO TIMES." CWH, 27 [1981]: 248-259.

The TIMES was suppressed "on account of the repeated expression of disloyal and incendiary statements." Although Lincoln eventually rescinded the order, the author believes he did it for political reasons as the president had expressed tacit approval of press suppression early in the war.

1122. Thorp, Robert. "The Copperhead Days of Dennis Mahoney." JOUR Q, 43 [1966]: 680-686, 696.

A sketch of Mahoney and a critique of his editorials. Author suggests he was more misguided than disloyal; wrong on slavery but an honest critic of the Lincoln administration.

1123. Tredway, Gilbert R. DEMOCRATIC OPPOSITION TO THE LINCOLN ADMINISTRATION IN INDIANA. Indianapolis: Indiana Historical Bureau, 1973.

A solid work on the Democratic dissenters in Indiana from the revisionist position.

1124. Wainwright, Nicholas B. "The Loyal Opposition in Civil War Philadelphia." PA MHB, 88 [1964]: 294-315.

At the 1862 Democratic convention blame for the war was put on the shoulders of the abolitionists. It resolved that "the Union is the one condition of peace."

1125. Wilson, Buford. "Southern Illinois in the Civil War." ILL ST HIS SOC TRAN, [1911]: 93-103.

An early, traditional view that has long since been outdated.

1126. Wilson, Charles R. "Cincinnati as a Southern Outpost in 1860-1861?" MVHR, 24 [1938]: 473-482.

Author disputes the long-held opinion that Cincinnati was, in fact, a southern city in the North. He asserts that in politics, economics, and social and cultural preferences, the city's links were with the West and Northwest, not the South.

1127. ———. "Cincinnati's Reputation During the Civil War." JSH, 2 [1936]: 468-479.

A discussion of the pro-southern attitude of the Queen City.

1128. Wister, Fanny Kimbles. "Sarah Butler Wister's Civil War Diary." PA MHB, 102 [1979]: 271-327.

Sarah Wister was the daughter of a Pennsylvania Copperhead.

1129. Wubben, Hubert H. CIVIL WAR IOWA AND THE COPPERHEAD MOVEMENT. Ames: Iowa State University Press, 1980.

A thorough examination of the political and economic history of wartime Iowa with special attention devoted to Copperheadism. A revisionist view.

1130. ———. "Copperhead Charles Mason: A Question of Loyalty." CWH, 24 [1978]: 46-65.

A sketch of Charles Mason, an Iowa Democrat, who wanted Confederate armies to be successful on the field of battle, and the South to be restored to the Union on its own terms. Nevertheless, he considered himself a strong Unionist and loyalist.

1131. ———. "Dennis Mahoney and the DUBUQUE HERALD, 1860-1863." IOWA J HIS, 56 [1958]: 289-320.

A survey of the wartime career of editor Mahoney, Iowa'a best-known dissenter.

1132. ———. "The Maintenance of Internal Security in Iowa, 1861-1865." CWH, 10 [1964]: 401-415.

An interesting discussion of the successful efforts of Iowa's wartime governors to keep the state secure from raiders from Missouri and Copperheads at home.

III

THE ARMY

A. ADMINISTRATION AND ORGANIZATION

1133. Ambrose, Stephen E. "Upton's Military Reforms." CWTI, 2 [5] [1963]: 24-30.

Emory Upton, West Point class of 1861, rose rapidly in rank during the war, being breveted a major general at the age of 25. But after the war he strongly criticized what he thought were deficiencies in the army and endeavored to bring about the needed reforms. It was not until early in the 20th century, long after Upton's death, that significant changes were made.

1134. Bearss, Edwin C. "Federal Generals Squabble Over Fort Smith 1863-1864." ARK HIS Q, 29 [1970]: 119-151.

War Department orders detached Fort Smith and Indian Territory from the Department of Arkansas and assigned them to the Department of Kansas. The result was confusion.

1135. Ellet, Charles, Jr. THE ARMY OF THE POTOMAC, AND ITS MISMANAGEMENT.... Washington, D.C.: 1861.

A criticism of McClellan and his strategy in the early months of his tenure.

1136. Freidel, Frank B. "General Orders 100 and Military Government." MVHR, 32 [1946]: 541-556.

Issued in 1863, General Orders 100 standardized military government policies in occupied territories. They were based on international, rather than municipal law.

1137. Henry, Guy V. MILITARY RECORD OF CIVILIAN APPOINTMENTS IN THE UNITED STATES ARMY. 2 v. New York, 1870-1873.

Details the records of officers in the Union army who were not career men.

1138. Hyman, Harold M. "A Devil-Dog's Dogtag of the Civil War." LIN HER, 62 [1960]: 99-100.

The United States Christian Commission distributed identification tags to Union soldiers.

1139. Lord, Francis A. THEY FOUGHT FOR THE UNION. Harrisburg, Pennsylvania: Stackpole, 1960.

An excellent statistical and logistical account of the army and its organization. The book is profusely illustrated and covers every aspect of army life.

1140. Macartney, Clarence E. LINCOLN AND HIS GENERALS. Philadelphia: Dorrance, 1925.

The relations between Lincoln and ten of his generals are the subject of this book.

1141. Meneely, Alexander H. THE WAR DEPARTMENT, 1861: A STUDY IN MOBILIZATION AND ADMINISTRATION. New York: Columbia University Press, 1928.

A good discussion of the War Department during the change in administrations as well as the mobilization efforts under the department secretary, Simon Cameron. The contract frauds are also analyzed.

1142. Moore, Wilton P. "The Provost Marshal Goes to War." CWH, 5 [1959]: 62-71.

A description of the position of the army provost marshal in the Union army from the outbreak of war until it received full and permanent status.

1143. ———. "Union Army Provost Marshals in the Eastern Theater." MIL AFF, 26 [1962]: 120-126.

This study traces the general historical development of the provost marshal system. It focuses especially on those officers who had the responsibility for maintaining military discipline in the army, including the apprehension of deserters and the imposition of military law in occupied areas of the South.

1144. Murray, Robert B. "The Fremont-Adams Contracts." JW, 5 [1966]: 517-524.

An account of the litigation involved in contracts for the construction of mortar boats and tugboats negotiated between General John Fremont and Theodore Adams at St. Louis in 1861.

1145. Robertson, James I., Jr. "Military Executions." CWTI, 5 [2] [1966]: 34-39.

Author considers the use of executions as a means of maintaining discipline in the Union army. Although the policy was administered inconsistently throughout the army, its use increased as the war progressed.

1146. Shepard, James C. "'Miracles' and Leadership in Civil War Cavalry." MIL R, 55 [6] [1975]: 49-55.

Organization, skill, and the emergence of small unit leaders gave the federal cavalry superiority over the southern cavalry.

1147. Shirk, George H. "The Place of Indian Territory in the Command Structure of the Civil War." CH OK, 45 [1968]: 464-471.

The Indian Territory [now Oklahoma] was included in the regional organizational structure of both the Union and Confederate armies during the war.

1148. Sparks, David S. "General Patrick's Program: Intelligence and Security in the Army of the Potomac." CWH, 10 [1964]: 371-384.

Praises the work of General Marsena R. Patrick, provost marshal general of the Army of the Potomac.

1149. Swart, Stanley L. "The Military Examination Boards in the Civil War: A Case Study." CWH, 16 [1970]: 227-245.

Since many officers received their commissions because of political connections rather than military qualifications, the military examination board was established for evaluating and removing incompetent officers. The system was fair and worked well.

1150. Tarbell, Ida M. "How the Union Army Was Disbanded." CWTI, 6 [8] [1967]: 4-9, 44-47.

A description of the efficient manner in which the Union army was disbanded.

1151. Upton, Emory. ... THE MILITARY POLICY OF THE UNITED STATES. New York: Greenwood, 1968.

In this abridged version of the 1904 edition, Upton sharply criticizes the practice of permitting civilians to dictate army policies. He considers this one of the most important lessons learned in the Civil War.

1152. Wasson, Robert G. THE HALL CARBINE AFFAIR: A STUDY IN CONTEMPORY FOLKLORE. New York: Pandick Press, 1948.

J.P. Morgan's alleged participation in the sale of defective arms is discussed in detail in this revised version of an earlier work.

1153. Williams, T. Harry. AMERICANS AT WAR: THE DEVELOPMENT OF THE AMERICAN MILITARY SYSTEM. Baton Rouge: Louisiana State University Press, 1960.

Only one of these three J.P. Young Lectures, delivered at Memphis State University in 1956, discusses the Civil War, but it is a good one.

1154. ———. LINCOLN AND HIS GENERALS. New York: Knopf, 1952.

An excellent discussion of the relationship between Lincoln and his top generals. The work not only adds to an understanding of the American command system, but also introduces the reader to the birth of so-called "total" or "modern" warfare.

B. LEADERSHIP AND STRATEGY

1155. Adams, Michael C. OUR MASTERS THE REBELS: A SPECULATION ON UNION MILITARY FAILURE IN THE EAST, 1861-1865. Cambridge, Massachusetts: Harvard University Press, 1978.

A psychological explanation of why the Army of the Potomac did not accomplish more than it did. Northern soldiers believed that the Southern aristocracy provided better military leaders than the North and that rural-bred Johnny Rebs were more attuned to military matters than their federal fellows.

1156. Ambrose, Stephen E. "Dennis Hart Mahan." CWTI, 2 [7] [1963]: 30-34.

The theories of Mahan, the celebrated West Point instructor, found wide acceptance and greatly influenced the conduct of the war.

1157. ———. "The Union Command System and the Donelson Campaign." MIL AFF, 24 [1960]: 78-86.

Author analyzes the Union army's divided command system in the West at the time of Grant's victory at Fort Donelson early in 1862. From this experience it was recognized that the command must be unified.

1158. Burne, Alfred H. LEE, GRANT, AND SHERMAN: A STUDY IN LEADERSHIP IN THE 1864-65 CAMPAIGN. New York: Scribners, 1938.

This British scholar examines the qualities of the three men who played crucial roles in the final year of the war.

1159. Deadrick, Barron. STRATEGY IN THE CIVIL WAR. Harrisburg, Pennsylvania: Military Service Publishing Company, 1946.

A southern writer provides a somewhat biased account of the military action as he seeks to demonstrate how the maxims of war were followed by Civil War generals.

1160. DeForest, J.W. "First Time Under Fire." CWTI, 5 [5] [1966]: 4-11, 26-29.

This untried company commander, a captain of the 12th Connecticut, tells how it felt to lead green troops into battle for the first time.

1161. Dillon, John F. "The Role of Riverene Warfare in the Civil War." NAV WAR COLL R, 25 [4] [1973]: 46-57.

A new concept in warfare was introduced by a few far-sighted Union commanders. Riverene warfare involved cooperation between the infantry and an improvised river force.

1162. Dwight, Henry O. "Each Man His Own Engineer." CWTI, 4 [6] [1965]: 4-7, 30-31.

Describes battle tactics, assault formations, and the use of fortifications.

1163. Eckert, Edward K. "The McClellans and the Grants: Generalship and Strategy in the Civil War." MIL R, 55 [6] [1975]: 58-67.

Divides Union generals into two types. The "McClellans" were unwilling to fight unless the odds were in their favor. The "Grants" were daring, understood the political nature of war, and were the keys to a Union victory.

1164. Farley, Joseph P. WEST POINT IN THE EARLY SIXTIES, WITH INCIDENTS OF THE WAR. Troy, New York: 1902.

A glimpse of the academy in wartime.

1165. Fuller, J.F.C. THE GENERALSHIP OF ULYSSES S. GRANT. Bloomington, Indiana: Indiana University Press, 1958.

In this classic study, originally published in 1929, Fuller examines Grant's qualities and accomplishments in detail. He concludes that the general grasped the concept of "war's grand strategy" and is to be credited with transferring the strategy of mobility from the West to the East.

1166. ———. GRANT AND LEE, A STUDY IN PERSONALITY AND GENERALSHIP. London: Eyre and Spottiswoode, 1933. Reprint 1957.

In this comparative study of Grant and Lee, Grant is proven to be the superior.

1167. Grant, U.S., III. "Military Strategy of the Civil War." MIL AFF, 22 [1958]: 13-25.

A discussion of the development of strategy in the course of the war.

1168. Hagerman, Edward. "From Jomini to Dennis Hart Mahan: the Evolution of Trench Warfare in the American Civil War." CWH, 13 [1967]: 197-220.

Mahan's theory that the "entrenched tactical defensive" was the more suited to the United States than Jomini's massive assault tactics, caught on during the Civil War, as many of the commanders had studied under Mahan at West Point.

1169. ———. "The Tactical Thought of R.E. Lee and the Origins of Trench Warfare in the American Civil War, 1861-1862." HISTORIAN, 38 [1975]: 21-38.

After Fredericksburg Lee became committed to the "primacy of the entrenched tactical position over the frontal assault." The debate on the issue had been raging since before the war.

1170. Harsh, Joseph L. "Battlesword and Rapier: Clausewitz, Jomini, and The American Civil War." MIL AFF, 38 [1974]: 133-138.

A comparison of the ideas of Jomini and Clausewitz with regard to the Civil War.

1171. Hassler, Warren W. COMMANDERS OF THE ARMY OF THE POTOMAC. Baton Rouge: Louisiana State University Press, 1962.

A comparative study of seven Union commanders. Four held the title of Commander of the Federal Army of the Potomac. The other three, including Grant, merely commanded the forces in Virginia. Each chapter deals with one general's tour of duty. The final chapter analyzes their merits and weaknesses. Their relations with Washington are not covered in any detail.

1172. Hubbell, John T., editor. BATTLES LOST AND WON: ESSAYS FROM CIVIL WAR HISTORY. Westport, Connecticut: Greenwood, 1965.

An anthology of articles from CIVIL WAR HISTORY dealing with strategy, tactics, and leadership.

1173. Jones, Archer. "Jomini and the Strategy of the American Civil War, a Reinterpretation." MIL AFF, 36 [1970]: 127-131.

A review of Jomini's principles of war and how they were applied, modified, or abandoned during the Civil War.

1174. Luvaas, Jay. "Civil War Influences on Foreign Army Tactics and Strategy." ARMY INFO DIG, 16 [8] [1961]: 114-119.

Despite some interest in new weaponry and army organization in the American Civil War, European military specialists saw little that would be helpful to their own armies. Such innovations as volunteer troops, trench warfare, and a revolution in tactics went largely unnoticed.

1175. ———. THE MILITARY LEGACY OF THE CIVIL WAR: THE EUROPEAN INHERITANCE. Chicago: University of Chicago Press, 1959.

A well-researched, thorough review of the success and failures according to the European analysis of "the first modern war." They picked up the strategic importance of railroads but missed the tactical importance of mobility.

1176. Macartney, Clarence B. GRANT AND HIS GENERALS. New York: McBride, 1953.

A fresh look at standard interpretations of some major battles. Grant's relations with his commanders are also examined.

1177. Mahon, John K. "Civil War Infantry Assault Tactics." MIL AFF, 26 [1962]: 57-68.

An analysis of Civil War assault formations as they were

employed against changing weaponry. Assault tactics remained obsolete while weapons were steadily improving.

1178. Maul, David T. "A Man and His Book." KY HIS SOC REG, 65 [1967]: 212-229.

A sketch of the life of Major Theodore Talbot, to whom William Hardee dedicated his important book RIFLE AND LIGHT INFANTRY TACTICS.

1179. Maurice, Sir Frederick B. STATESMEN AND SOLDIERS OF THE CIVIL WAR; A STUDY OF THE CONDUCT OF THE WAR. Boston: Little, Brown, 1926.

A very useful study.

1180. McWhiney, Grady, editor. GRANT, LEE, LINCOLN AND THE RADICALS: ESSAYS ON CIVIL WAR LEADERSHIP. Evanston, Illinois: Northwestern University Press, 1964.

Contains four papers delivered at a Northwestern University symposium. It also includes a continuation of the debate between David Donald and T. Harry Williams on Lincoln's relations with the Radical Republicans.

1181. Miller, John, Jr. "The Execution of Union Strategy." ARMY INFO DIG, 16 [8] [1961]: 22-46.

A short history of the military and naval aspects of the war with a careful eye to the developing notions of grand strategy.

1182. Mitchell, Joseph B. MILITARY LEADERS IN THE CIVIL WAR. New York: Putnam, 1972.

A study of five Union and five Confederate generals who had "commanded armies for a considerable length of time." As a lieutenant colonel, the author views these men from a military standpoint. His conclusions are intriguing and interesting.

1183. Moore, John G, "Mobility and Strategy in the Civil War." MIL AFF, 24 [1960]: 68-77.

An analysis of the dubious wisdom of applying Napoleon's principles of war as set forth by Henry Jomini and studied by West Point cadets to the different conditions and technology of the American Civil War.

1184. Morrison, James L., Jr. "The Struggle Between Sectionalism and Nationalism at Ante-Bellum West Point, 1830-1861." CWH, 19 [1973]: 138-148.

A statistical refutation that West Point was a center for southern sedition in 1860-1861.

1185. Ropp, Theodore. "Anaconda Anyone?" MIL AFF, 27 [1963]: 71-76.

Discusses the conception and development of the "Anaconda Policy." The author suggests it was "considerably less fearsome at the time than in retrospect."

1186. Schaff, Morris. THE SPIRIT OF OLD WEST POINT, 1858-1862." Boston, 1909.

Describes the U.S. Military Academy on the eve of war and during the early stages of the war. This volume in conjunction with Farley's work [number 1164] present a complete picture of the Academy.

1187. Schalk, Emil. CAMPAIGNS OF 1862 and 1863, ILLUSTRATING THE PRINCIPLES OF STRATEGY. Philadelphia, 1863.

Schalk describes the geography of the areas and defines the "principles of strategy." He examines the military action with these in mind.

1188. Sergent, Mary E. "Classmates Divided." AM HER, 9 [2] [1958]: 86-87.

Describes the relationships between West Point classmates, some of whom served the North and others the South.

1189. Shepard, James C. "Gallant Debris." MIL R, 53 [9] [1973]: 73-85.

Examines the problems of small unit leadership. Lack of flexibility sometimes caused heavy losses.

1190. Simpson, Harold B. BRAWLING BRASS, NORTH AND SOUTH. Waco, Texas: Texian Press, 1960.

Some of the famous quarrels described involved Johnston and Hood, Lee and Longstreet, Meade and Sickles, and Jackson and Hill.

1191. Stackpole, E.J. "Generalship in the Civil War." MIL AFF, 24 [1960]: 57-67.

The author first sets forth nine "principles of war" and then measures the accomplishments of seven Civil War generals against the yardstick. Lee and Jackson pass the test easily, but Meade. Pope, McClellan, Burnside, and Hooker are found deficient.

1192. Trobriand, Phillippe de Keredern, Comte de. FOUR YEARS WITH THE ARMY OF THE POTOMAC. George K. Dauchy, translator. Boston, 1889.

The author rose to the rank of major general in the Second Corps. For an excellent insight into the workings of the high command of the Army of the Potomac, this book is a "must."

1193. Wade, Arthur P. "Civil War at West Point." CWH, [1957]: 5-15.

A description of the sub-course on the Civil War which is part of the course on the History of Military Art, a requirement for fourth year cadets at the Academy.

1194. Weigley, Russell. THE AMERICAN WAY OF WAR.... New York: Macmillan, 1973.

A valuable perspective on the Civil War in the context of American military history. Because it was an all-out war and a people's war, it changed military thinking--to crush the enemy as Grant and Sherman did.

———. HISTORY OF THE UNITED STATES ARMY. [Number 1316]

1195. ———. TOWARDS AN AMERICAN ARMY.... New York: Columbia University Press, 1962.

Presents the problems involved in having a professional army for security but citizen soldiers for a crisis. Concludes that although the solutions at any one point in time might be "good" they might not serve at another time.

1196. Williams, T. Harry. "The Attack Upon West Point During the Civil War." MVHR, 25 [1939]: 491-504.

An analysis of the criticism of the West Point program by Radical Republicans who argued that a number of the federal generals who graduated from the Academy were incompetent and pro-southern.

1197. ———. "Badger Colonels and The Civil War Officer." WIS MAG HIS, 47 [1964]: 35-46.

Although the top command posts were held by West Point graduates, it was a civilians' war. Cites the problems involved in having a civilian in the post of army colonel. Many of the problems which developed were the result of lack of military background and training.

1198. ———. McCLELLAN, SHERMAN AND GRANT. New Brunswick, New Jersey: Rutgers University Press, 1962.

These three essays cover the author's theories concerning northern military leadership. McClellan considered war a game and saw the military situations as he wished, not as they were. Sherman, a restless man, fought against enemy cities rather than armies. Grant, imaginative, grew steadily and was the "complete general."

1199. ———. THE MILITARY LEADERSHIP OF THE NORTH AND THE SOUTH. Colorado Springs, Colorado: U.S. Air Force Academy, 1960.

The second of the Harmon memorial lectures in military history delivered at the Academy is an analysis of the high commands of both armies.

1200. ———. "The Return of Jomini--Some Thoughts on Recent Civil War Writing." MIL AFF, 39 [1975]: 204-206.

Author defends his earlier downgrading of Jomini's theories with respect to the Civil War, in the face of more recent criticisms of his interpretations.

C. MANPOWER MOBILIZATION

By James W. Geary

MANPOWER MOBILIZATION focuses on northern efforts to raise men for the Union army and Union navy. In addition to the extant literature on recruiting, desertion, and conscription, it includes studies on overt physical resistance to the draft. It excludes all studies on the general anti-war movement as well as those on covert resistance. Individuals who were generally outspoken in their opposition to conscription and other war measures of President Lincoln's administration are also omitted. Such studies on Clement Lewis Vallandigham and Lambdin P. Milligan, or on Copperhead activities may be found in DISSENT [II, E]. Generally speaking, all biographical works, including those on Horatio Seymour, Edwin M. Stanton, and Henry Wilson can be found in BIOGRAPHIES AND PERSONAL ACCOUNTS [VI]. Lastly, this unit excludes works pertaining to mobilization for war in terms of logistics, armaments, railroads, and the like. They will be found in other sections of this topic on the ARMY.

This unit does encompass works dealing with the administration and operation of the conscription system in the North, resistance to the enforcement of the draft, desertion, and recruiting for the Union army and the Union navy. However, it was considered more convenient to locate entries pertaining to the 178,000 blacks, who served in the Union army and contributed to its success, in BLACKS AND EMANCIPATION [X. A]. As for other types of material, certain books and dissertations are included that devote at least a chapter, or a significant part of the study, to Civil War manpower mobilization broadly defined. For the convenience of the user who requires a briefer version of some aspect, both books and articles by the same author are included even though they may concern essentially the same subject.

As the reader peruses this section, certain trends should become apparent. There are, for example, comparatively few works on the subjects of desertion, the conscientious objector, and recruitment for the navy. However, a number of studies have appeared since the beginning of the Civil War centennial celebration in 1961 on the draft and recruiting. Many of these works are concerned with the actual operations of the draft as well as the variety of efforts used to recruit blacks, foreigners, and even former soldiers in order to keep as many northern males as possible from being drafted.

1201. Abbott, Richard H. "Massachusetts and the Recruitment of Southern Negroes, 1863-1865." CWH, 14 [1968]: 197-211.

This is an excellent account of one of the ways in which one Northern state sought to reduce white draft quotas through the use of black troops. On July 4, 1864, Congress authorized state executives to send agents into federally occupied areas of the South. Although 1,405 state agents went southward, only an additional 5,052 men were recruited. Approximately 25 per cent of these new recruits were credited to Massachusetts.

1202. Au Palladino, Grace. THE POOR MAN'S FIGHT: DRAFT RESISTANCE AND LABOR ORGANIZATION IN SCHUYLKILL COUNTY, PENNSYLVANIA, 1860-1865. Ph.D. dissertation, University of Pittsburgh, 1983.

One of many such studies pertaining to raising troops in the Keystone state. According to this study, Irish miners in Cass Township resisted the draft because they wanted more control over their work environment.

1203. Barnes, David M. THE DRAFT RIOTS IN NEW YORK, JULY, 1863. THE METROPOLITAN POLICE: THEIR HONORABLE RECORD. New York, 1863.

As a reporter for the NEW YORK TIMES, Barnes was an eyewitness to the 1863 disturbances. Although very laudatory of the role of the New York Metropolitan Police, it is a basic source for any examination of the New York draft riots.

1204. Barnett, James. "The Bounty Jumpers of Indiana." CWH, 4 [1958]: 429-436.

A good overview of the problems that bounty jumpers and brokers created in the Hoosier state. This article also contains an account of the execution of three bounty jumpers, one of whom was alleged to have enlisted in at least 30 different places, jumping his bounty in each case.

1205. Bernstein, J.L. "Conscription and the Constitution: The Amazing Case of Kneedler v. Lane." A BAR ASSN J, 53 [1967]: 708-712.

On November 9, 1863, the Pennsylvania Supreme Court found the Enrollment Act to be unconstitutional. With a change in its membership the following month, the court reversed itself.

1206. Berry, Mary F. MILITARY NECESSITY AND CIVIL RIGHTS POLICY: BLACK CITIZENSHIP AND THE CONSTITUTION, 1861-1868. Port Washington, New York: Kennikat, 1977.

Four of the eight chapters in this study pertain to blacks during the Civil War. The author concludes that the Enrollment Act was the "greatest single force" in encouraging the use of black soldiers.

1207. Billings, Elden E. "Civil War and the Conscription." CUR HIS, 54 [1968]: 333-338, 366.

A brief survey of recruiting and drafting policies, North and South, during the war.

1208. Bohigas, Nuria Sales de. "Some Opinions on Exemptions From Military Service in Nineteenth Century Europe." COMP STUD SOC HIS, 10 [1968]: 261-289.

Interesting study of the impact that commutation and substitution had in various European countries during the nineteenth century. Designed to protect wealthier classes from personal service, some of these systems underwent significant alteration by the 1870s. This work is useful for comparing European exemption practices with those in the Civil War North.

1209. Briggs, John E. "The Enlistment of Iowa Troops During the Civil War." IOWA J HIS POL, 15 [1917]: 323-392.

A very detailed account of the efforts that state officials in Iowa made in raising troops during the early days of war.

1210. Brock, Peter. PACIFISM IN THE UNITED STATES: FROM THE COLONIAL ERA TO THE FIRST WORLD WAR. Princeton: Princeton University Press, 1968.

One complete section of this work discusses how the North and South dealt with religious sects during the Civil War. For the most part, Union authorities were understanding and tolerant of those citizens whose religious beliefs prevented them from wholeheartedly supporting the war effort.

1211. Canup, Charles E. "Conscription and Draft in Indiana During the Civil War." IND MAG HIS, 10 [1914]: 70-83.

An early account of the operations of the draft in a typical midwestern state.

1212. Castel, Albert E. "Enlistment and Conscription in Civil War Kansas." KAN HIS Q, 27 [1961]: 313-319.

A succinct overview of Kansas' manpower contribution to the Union war effort. The author argues that, based on population, more men entered northern service from Kansas than from any other state.

1213. Clark, Charles B. "Recruitment of Union Troops in Maryland, 1861-1865." MD HIS MAG, 53 [1958]: 153-176.

Describes the problems of raising troops throughout the war in this Border state. Also reviews the efforts and reactions to recruiting black troops to help fill Maryland's quotas.

1214. Clark, J. Murray. "Lincoln and Conscription," CAN LAW TIMES, 37 [1917]: 737-739.

An outside view in which the author contends that President Lincoln pursued the proper course in enforcing the draft in the

North. Canada would be wise to follow the example of the United States by relying on a draft to meet its manpower needs for the World War.

1215. Coles, Harry L. OHIO FORMS AN ARMY. Columbus: Ohio State University Press, 1962.

Published under the auspices of the Ohio Civil War Centennial Commission, this study provides a good glimpse of the difficulties and problems in raising an army in the Buckeye state during the first year of the war.

1216. Cook, Adrian. THE ARMIES OF THE STREETS: THE NEW YORK CITY DRAFT RIOTS OF 1863. Lexington: University of Kentucky Press, 1974.

The best scholarly account of the New York draft riots of July 1863. Although the author holds to the traditional view that the draft law discriminated against the poor, one of the strengths of this work lies in its disspelling myths about the disturbances. He believes, for example, that "intense racial prejudice of white New Yorkers in the 1860s," not fear of economic competition, caused the riots.

1217. Cowdrey, Albert. "Slave Into Soldier: The Enlistment by the North of Runaway Slaves." HIS TOD, 20 [1970]: 704-715.

A popularized and illustrated account of the enlistment of contrabands into Union service.

1218. Cullop, Charles P. "An Unequal Duel: Union Recruiting in Ireland, 1863-1864." CWH, 13 [1967]: 101-113.

Author describes the relatively successful northern efforts to induce Irishmen to migrate to the United States to serve in the Union army.

1219. Dayton, Aretas A. RECRUITMENT AND CONSCRIPTION IN ILLINOIS DURING THE CIVIL WAR. Ph.D. dissertation, University of Illinois Press, 1940.

Among the numerous subjects covered in this study is the rapid decline in war fever that occurred in Illinois by the summer of 1861. The author examines the difficulties in recruiting men and describes the resistance that occurred to the enrollment process as well as other responses to the draft.

1220. Dupree, A. Hunter and Leslie H. Fishel, Jr., editors. "An Eyewitness Account of the New York Draft Riots, July, 1863." MVHR, 47 [1960]: 472-479.

The noted scientist Dr. John Torrey authored a letter to Asa Gray over the four day period, July 13-16, 1863. Although he lived in close proximity to where the riots occurred, his is nevertheless a very detached and objective account.

1221. Earnhart. Hugh G. "The Administrative Organization of the Provost Marshal General's Bureau in Ohio, 1863-1865." NW OHIO Q, 37 [1965]: 87-99.

This study describes the process of federal conscription in the Buckeye state and supports the view that citizens did not like the draft because they felt they were being placed under military jurisdiction.

1222. ———. "Commutation: 'Democratic or Undemocratic?'" CWH, 12 [1966]: 132-142.

In this study of four selected congressional districts in Ohio, Earnhart compares occupational groups before and after the repeal of commutation in July 1864. He concludes that the recall of the fee privilege "was unfair class legislation since it took from the poor man his only chance to escape service" while the wealthy could still furnish a substitute. [See also 1235, 1280.]

1223. Fernandez, Joseph R. CONSCRIPTION IN THE CIVIL WAR AND WORLD WAR I: THE REJECTION AND ACCEPTANCE OF AUTHORITY. Ph.D. dissertation, University of Connecticut, 1976.

In this sociological study, the author devotes some 20 pages to the Civil War draft in the North. He attributes the draft resistance to commutation, racism, the anti-war movement, and a feeling that the law was unconstitutional. By 1917, however, there was stronger support for "centralized political and military authority."

1224. Fish, Carl Russell. "Conscription in the Civil War." AHR, 12 [1915]: 100-103.

Author argues that the draft was not designed to replace volunteering but rather to encourage recruiting. He questions the importance of bounties attracting men because they would have enlisted anyway.

1225. Fitzpatrick, Edward A. CONSCRIPTION AND AMERICA: A STUDY OF CONSCRIPTION IN A DEMOCRACY. Milwaukee: Richard Publishing, 1940.

One of the six sections in this work, which appeared on the eve of America's entry into World War II, concerns "The Civil War Drafts--How Not to Conscript Men." The author reviews many of the lessons derived from that experience as well as those that were applied to the Selective Service System in World War I.

1226. ———. "The Volunteer and the Conscript in American Military History." CUR HIS [1960]: 205-213.

Based in part on the larger work above, this study consists of a concise review of conscription in the United States through the Cold War. Very critical of the Civil War draft, the author argues that the United States would not have its first true conscription system until World War I.

1227. Fletcher, Winona L. "Speech-making of the New York Draft Riots of 1863." Q J SPEECH, 54 [1968]: 134-139.

Based mainly on newspaper sources, this study explores the effect that rhetoric had on inciting and in quelling the New York disturbances.

1228. Foster, Ethan. THE CONSCRIPT QUAKERS, BEING A NARRATIVE OF THE DISTRESS AND RELIEF OF FOUR YOUNG MEN FROM THE DRAFT FOR THE WAR IN 1863. Cambridge, 1883.

Although published almost two decades after the Civil War ended, this account is useful for describing the general process through which four New England Quakers were released from military service after they were drafted.

1229. Fried, Joseph P. "The Story of the New York Draft Riots." CWTI, 4 [5] [1965]: 4-10, 28-31.

A well-illustrated popular version of this event. The author describes the role of various personalities including the Catholic archbishop of New York.

1230. Friedman, Leon. "Conscription and the Constitution: The Original Understanding." MICH LAW R, 67 [1969]: 1493-1552.

A critical examination of the SELECTIVE DRAFT LAW CASES [Arver v. United States] that emerged as a result of conscription in World War I. Among the various references that the Supreme Court pointed to in upholding "the constitutionality of congressional conscription" was the Civil War draft. The author reviews as well the actual and potential legal challenges to the Enrollment Act of 1863.

1231. Fry, James B. THE CONKLING AND BLAINE-FRY CONTROVERSY IN 1866. New York, 1893.

The former provost marshal general defends his administration of the Civil War draft in New York state against charges of favoritism and wrongdoing by Roscoe Conkling. It was from this dispute that the lifelong enmity between Conkling and James G. Blaine developed.

1232. ———. "Final Report to the Secretary of War by the Provost Marshal General." JOURNAL OF THE HOUSE OF REPRESENTATIVES, 39th Congress, 1st session, House Executive Document Number 1, volume 4, serials 1251-1252. Washington, 1866.

The basic source for the study of the Civil War draft. In addition to an extensive narrative, this work also includes numerous tables reflecting the operations of Provost Marshal General's Bureau from 1863 until it was disbanded in 1866.

1233. ———. NEW YORK AND THE CONSCRIPTION OF 1863: A CHAPTER IN THE HISTORY OF THE CIVIL WAR. New York, 1885.

Former Provost Marshal General Fry prepared this work two decades after the fact. This source contains numerous pieces of official correspondence both in the text and in eighteen appendices. Fry contends that Governor Horatio Seymour not only objected to the law but hindered its implementation.

1234. Geary, James W. "The Enrollment Act and the 37th Congress." HISTORIAN, 46 [1984]: 562-582.

This study traces the course of the Enrollment Act through Congress and analyzes the voting behavior on the measure. Among the author's findings is that the Democrats used parliamentary tactics effectively in order to modify the bill. Their goal was not to prevent its passage but to ensure that a federal draft did not intrude unnecessarily on states' rights and civil liberties.

1235. ———. A LESSON IN TRIAL AND ERROR: THE UNITED STATES CONGRESS AND THE CIVIL WAR DRAFT, 1862-1865. Ph.D dissertation, Kent State University, 1976.

This study focuses on the five major conscription laws enacted during the Civil War. Author concludes that although the draft was a failure, the legislation was perhaps the most democratic in American history. He goes beyond the findings of Hugh G. Earnhart and Eugene C. Murdock and argues that poor men not only paid commutation but furnished substitutes as well.

1236. ———. OHIO CONGRESSIONAL AND NEWSPAPER ATTITUDES TOWARD THE CONSCRIPTION LEGISLATION OF THE THIRTY-SEVENTH CONGRESS. M.A. thesis, Kent State University, 1971.

This study consists of chapters on historiography, Ohio newspaper and congressional views on the draft, and various appendices. In the segment on select Ohio newspapers, the author traces the shift in editorial opinion that occurred toward conscription between the summer of 1862 and early 1863.

1237. Gordon, Terry J. "Plattsburgh in the Civil War." YORK STATE TRADITION, 27 [1973]: 43-48.

Narrative account of early recruiting activities in upstate New York with emphasis on the 16th New York Volunteer Infantry, a unit that saw active service until May 1863.

1238. Hallock, Judith L. "The Role of the Community in Civil War Desertion." CWH, 29 [1983]: 123-134.

Although limited mainly to men who entered the military in 1862, this case-study definitely contributes to an understanding of desertion in the North. Based on a comparison between two townships in Suffolk County, New York, the author suggests that desertions were less likely to occur in a community that was more stable and more supportive of its men under arms. Also, she concludes that there existed a much greater tendency among the foreign-born to desert since they lacked strong ties to their respective communities.

1239. Hamer, Marguerite B. "Luring Canadian Soldiers into Union Lines During the War Between the States." CAN HIS R, 27 [1946]: 150-162.

Very interesting article on the methods used, on both sides of the border, to entice Canadians into the Union army.

1240. Hamilton, James A. "The Enrolled Missouri Militia: Its Creation and Controversial History." MO HIS R, 69 [1975]: 413-432.

An excellent study of the efforts to implement and sustain a special pro-Union force for home defense from 1862 to 1865 in this Border state. The author provides a cogent analysis of the program's effectiveness.

1241. Hanchett, William. "An Illinois Physician and the Civil War Draft, 1864-1865: Letters of Dr. Joshua Nichols Speed." JISHS, 59 [1966]: 143-160.

Speed, as examining surgeon for the local enrollment board, wrote these letters to his wife from Mount Sterling, Illinois. In these documents, he tells of the large number of exemptions for reasons of physical disability and the immense amount of paperwork that was required of his office.

1242. Harris, Emily J. "Sons and Soldiers: Deerfield, Massachusetts and the Civil War." CWH, 30 [1984]: 157-171.

This study examines one community's response to the numerous troop calls made during the Civil War. Prior to 1863, it was able to meet quotas from its native pool of manpower. In the last two years of the war not only did more foreign-born residents enter the military, but increasing reliance had to be placed on alternate sources.

1243. Harstad, Peter R., editor. "A Civil War Medical Examiner: The Report of Dr. Horace O. Crane." WIS MAG HIS, 48 [1965]: 222-231.

Crane served as surgeon in the 3rd Wisconsin Volunteer Infantry until April 1863 when he received an appointment as the examining surgeon for one of the state's local enrollment boards. This report, which he submitted shortly after the war ended, records his observations on the physical qualifications of drafted men and recruits for military service.

1244. ———. "Draft Dodgers and Bounty Jumpers." CWTI, 6 [2] [1967]: 28-36.

Author describes the evils of the bounty system and provides a number of examples of techniques used by prospective recruits to avoid passing the physical examination.

1245. Headley, Joel T. THE GREAT RIOTS OF NEW YORK, 1712 to 1873. New York, 1873.

Includes an early in-depth study of the 1863 New York Draft Riots.

1246. Hicks, John D. "The Organization of the Volunteer Army in 1861 With Special Reference to Minnesota." MINN HIS BULL, 2 [1918]: 324-368.

A detailed account of the difficulties encountered in faraway Minnesota in trying to raise an army.

1247. Hyman, Harold M. "Civil War Turncoats." MIL AFF, 22 [1958]: 134-138.

Author discusses Union efforts to recruit soldiers from among captured Confederate prisoners.

1248. ———, editor. "New Yorkers and the Civil War Draft." NY HIS, 36 [1955]: 164-171.

An interesting assemblage of letters written before and after the July 1863 disturbances. Based on experiences in the lower East Side of New York City, they nevertheless reveal some of the problems that a local provost marshal faced in enforcing the draft in the North.

1249. Imholte, John Q. "The Legality of Civil War Recruiting: U.S. Versus Gorman." CWH, 9 [1963]: 422-429.

Demoralization plagued the Union army particularly after its defeat at First Bull Run. This study examines the attempts of a soldier in the 1st Minnesota to be released from service on grounds that certain procedures had not been followed in his enlistment. Had the court ruled in his favor, the possible disintegration of the Union army could have resulted.

1250. Itter, William A. CONSCRIPTION IN PENNSYLVANIA DURING THE CIVIL WAR. Ph.D. dissertation, University of Southern California, 1941.

The author believes that military service during the Civil War was largely a personal choice because the draft failed. Consistent with American tradition, he contends that social class considerations influenced Civil War conscription legislation. Given the extent of draft resistance, he concludes that "a more efficient system might have resulted in bloody failure."

1251. "John M. Brenneman and the Civil War." MEN HIS BULL, 34 [1973]: 1-3.

Brenneman, a Mennonite bishop, prepared a petition to send to Abraham Lincoln after the president had ordered state drafts in the summer of 1862. An accompanying letter from Brenneman to a fellow Mennonite reveals that he was not optimistic that the president could or would respond favorably to a petition requesting special considerations for a religious sect.

1252. Johnson, Peter L. "Port Washington Draft Riot of 1862." MID AM, 1 [1930]: 212-222.

Johnson sees a religous basis for this riot.

1253. Jordan, Wayne. "The Hoskinville Rebellion." OSAHQ, 47 [1938]: 319-354.

Detailed account of the events that occurred when members of the Union army attempted to arrest a suspected deserter in Noble County, Ohio in March 1863.

1254. Kimmons, Neil C. "Federal Draft Exemptions, 1863-1865." MIL AFF, 15 [1951]: 25-33.

A succinct overview of exemptions under the Northern draft laws. Of particular use is the review of the seven major ways through which a person could escape service in 1863 without having to pay commutation or provide a substitute.

1255. Kreidberg, Marvin A. and Merton G. Henry. HISTORY OF MILITARY MOBILIZATION IN THE UNITED STATES ARMY, 1775-1945." Washington, D.C.: Department of the Army, 1955.

Chapter ten of this official history pertains to the Civil War. In addition to various tables and charts, it contains a list of ten areas where the Civil War provided lessons for the mobilization of future American armies.

1256. ———. "Raising the Armies." ARMY INFO DIG, 16 [8] [1961]: 52-59.

In this abridged version of the above work, the authors review some of the ten lessons learned from the Civil War. After discussing the mobilization of the Union army, they describe the replacement system, use of black troops, bounties and the draft.

1257. Lader, Lawrence. "New York's Bloodiest Week." AM HER, 10 [3] [1959]: 44-49, 95-98.

An amply illustrated, popular account of the 1863 draft riots. Although most of the rioters were Irish, the author discusses other Irishmen who attempted to quell the riots.

1258. Larsen, Lawrence H. "Draft Riot in Wisconsin, 1862." CWH, 7 [1961]: 421-427.

An account principally of the draft resistance that occurred at Port Washington, Wisconsin in November 1862. The resisters were largely Luxembourgers who were subsequently released due, for the most part, to President Lincoln's intervention.

1259. [Lea, Henry C.] "Volunteering and Conscription." US SERV MAG, 1 [1864]: 239-242.

In this generally overlooked work, the author argues that universal conscription is fair in theory but impractical in fact. Commutation and substitution are necessary so as to allow the contributors in a society to avoid personal service. Conscription falls unfairly on this group because the "shiftless classes" can elude service merely by moving from place to place. Among his recommendations, he believes that bounties should be denied to drafted men and that a "reserves" sysem should be instituted for the replenishing of the Union forces.

1260. Leach, Jack F. CONSCRIPTION IN THE UNITED STATES: HISTORICAL BACKGROUND. Tokyo, Japan: Tuttle, 1952.

In this essentially narrative account, the author suggests that partisan politics dominated the congressional debates and voting on federal draft legislation. He also argues that the Enrollment Act weakened states rights.

1261. Leonard, Ellen. "Three Days of Terror." HARP MAG, 34 [1867]: 225-233.

A somewhat detailed description of the New York draft riots written shortly after the war.

1262. Levine, Peter. "Draft Evasion in the North During the Civil War, 1863-1865." JAH, 67 [1981]: 816-834.

This study focuses on some 160,000 men who failed to report for the draft. In this interesting analysis, the author states that the draft not only "outlined class distinctions in terms of property but also ... in terms of culture and values."

1263. Levy, Virgil L. "Notre Dame and the Draft." LIN HER, 79 [1979]: 76-78.

Although the northern conscription laws neither authorized exemptions for a religious group nor empowered the president to grant a special dispensation, this study describes the preferential treatment that the Holy Cross brothers received from Lincoln and Secretary of War Stanton.

1264. Lonn, Ella. DESERTION DURING THE CIVIL WAR. New York: Century, 1928.

This is a standard work on the causes, nature, and results of desertion in both North and South. Among the various areas examined are the influence of practices such as bounty-jumping in depleting the ranks as well as the monthly rates of desertion from the Union army.

1265. Lord, Francis A. THE FEDERAL VOLUNTEER SOLDIER IN THE AMERICAN CIVIL WAR, 1861-1865. Ph.D. dissertation, University of Michigan, 1949.

This study examines certain patterns common to the experience of Union volunteers. Among the subjects covered are morale and the reasons behind enlistments.

1266. MacLochlainn, Alf. "Three Ballads of the American Civil War." IRISH SWORD (Ireland), 6 [1963]: 28-33.

One of these ballads, the originals of which are located in the National Library of Ireland, pertains to crimping. Although the piece is undated, the narrative accompanying suggests that the item may have been written in either 1863 or 1864.

1267. Man, Albon P., Jr. "Labor Competition and the New York Draft Riots of 1863." JNH, 36 [1951]: 375-405.

This study traces the cause of the New York riots to a fear of economic competition on the part of Irish longshoremen. They especially resented the use of blacks as strike-breakers.

1268. Marvel, William. "New Hampshire and the Draft, 1863." HIS NH, 36 [1981]: 58-72.

A good narrative account of the enrollment and draft resistance that occurred in this state during the first draft. The author attributes much of the trouble to the discriminatory nature of the commutation clause.

1269. Masterman, Frederick J. "Some Aspects of the Episcopate of William Heathcote Delancy, First Bishop of the Diocese of Western New York [1839-1865]." HIS MAG PROT EPI CH, 33 [1964]: 261-277.

This article includes some discussion of Bishop Delancy's position that his drafted clergy either be allowed to pay commutation or perform service as non-combatants.

1270. McCague, James. THE SECOND REBELLION: THE STORY OF THE NEW YORK CITY DRAFT RIOTS OF 1863. New York: Dial Press, 1968.

This book length study discusses earlier disturbances in New York City and the deplorable living conditions in the Five Points area, which in turn contributed to the July 1863 uprising. The author views this event as a "spontaneous eruption" and finds little evidence to support the theory that there was a Confederate conspiracy behind the 1863 disorders. For a briefer version of this work, see McCague's "Long Hot Summer: 1863," MANKIND, 1 [1968]: 10-17, 47-49.

1271. [McMurtry, R. Gerald, editor.] "Everybody is Afraid of Being Drafted...." LIN LORE, No. 1564 [1968]: 4.

This source consists of three published letters. Two of them provide a good contemporary view of local recruiting activities and the fear of being drafted during the summer of 1862 in East-hampton, Connecticut.

1272. Milani, Lois D. "Four Went to the Civil War." ONT HIS, 51 [1959]: 259-272.

This article contains excerpts of letters from four Canadian brothers who enlisted in the Union army in 1861. Assigned ultimately to the 50th New York. They enlisted of their own volition and not because of crimping or some other questionable reason.

1273. Murdock, Eugene C. "The Bounty System in Cincinnati." CIN HIS SOC BULL, 24 [1966]: 278-301.

A critical account of how the bounty system and the draft operated in Cincinnati during the latter half of 1864. Of particular interest is the author's discussion of the Cassett-Carberry episode that involved the hiring of a substitute who was subsequently arrested and jailed.

1274. ———. "Horatio Seymour and the 1863 Draft." CWH, 11 [1965]: 117-141.

This critical account of Horatio Seymour concurs with most contemporary assessments and departs from the revisionist interpretation of Stewart Mitchell's study. Rather than support the Lincoln administration, Murdock contends that the "politically-motivated" Seymour encouraged obstructionist activities such as non-compliance with the draft in New York.

1275. ———. "New York's Civil War Bounty Brokers." JAH, 53 [1966]: 259-278.

The brokerage system first emerged in the Empire state in the fall of 1862. The author describes the questionable activities of these agents and the problems they created especially in the last two years of the war.

1276. ———. OHIO'S BOUNTY SYSTEM IN THE CIVIL WAR. Columbus: Ohio State University Press, 1963.

Although part of the series sponsored under the auspices of the Ohio Civil War Centennial Commission, this work also represents the first of three monographs, in addition to numerous articles, that this author has published on the Civil War draft. In this work he surveys various areas such as recruiting efforts, evasion, and the problems that occurred with the bounty system in Ohio.

1277. ———. ONE MILLION MEN: THE CIVIL WAR DRAFT IN THE NORTH. Madison: The State Historical Society of Wisconsin, 1971.

This work is the departure point for any beginning study on Civil War conscription in the North. In this most comprehensive of Murdock's studies on the draft, he examines the difficulties involved in raising troops for the Union army especially through the utilization of bounties. Although he does not fully assess the influence that the draft laws had in determining the ultimate success of the conscription system, he concludes that it was nevertheless a success.

1278. ———. PATRIOTISM LIMITED, 1862-1865: THE CIVIL WAR DRAFT AND THE BOUNTY SYSTEM. Kent, Ohio: Kent State University Press, 1967.

The author lends credence to the view that pecuniary rather than patriotic motives dominated Civil War recruiting. His focus is principally on conscription and the abuses of the bounty system in New York State. Among the specific areas he examines is the trial of Major John A. Haddock and the subsequent controversy that ensued between Provost Marshal General James B. Fry and New York Congressman Roscoe Conkling.

1279. ———. "Pity the Poor Surgeon." CWH, 16 [1970]: 18-36.

This study, which also appears in large measure in Chapter Five of ONE MILLION MEN, provides the best overview of the numerous difficulties that surgeons faced in conducting medical examinations of draft liable men.

1280. ———. "Was it a 'Poor man's Fight?'" CWH, 10 [1964]: 241-245.

Although the methodology employed in this study has sometimes been criticized, it nevertheless represents the first scholarly examination that questions whether the Civil War draft discriminated against the poor. Using per capita valuation for districts in New York State, the author concludes that there "was just as much paying of commutation to avoid the draft in poor districts as there was in wealthy districts." [See also 1222, 1235.]

1281. Myton, T.W. and D.W. Woodring. "The Drafted Men and Substitute's Story." In THE STORY OF OUR REGIMENT.... Joseph Muffly, editor. Des Moines, Iowa: 1904.

The unhappy tale of a young Pennsylvanian who went as a substitute for his drafted brother only to find himself promptly lodged in jail.

1282. Oliver, John W. "Draft Riots in Wisconsin During the Civil War." WIS MAG HIS, 2 [1918/1919]: 334-336.

A brief account of riots in Wisconsin in November 1862 following enforcement of the Militia Draft.

1283. O'Sullivan, Hanora Marie. A RHETORICAL ANALYSIS OF THE STRUCTURE AND STRATEGIES OF THE CIVIL WAR ANTI-DRAFT MOVEMENT. Ph.D. Dissertation, University of Michigan, 1972.

Despite the potential influence that communication could have had in contributing to the success of the anti-draft forces, that movement nevertheless faltered. Through the use of various matrices, this study examines the causes of that failure.

1284. O'Sullivan, John and Alan M. Meckler, editors. THE DRAFT AND ITS ENEMIES: A DOCUMENTARY HISTORY. Urbana: University of Illinois Press, 1974.

This useful compilation of documents span almost three hundred years, from 1675 to 1973, of American history. The Civil War section has eight items including the complete text of the Enrollment Act as well as the critical post-war report by Brigadier General James Oakes, who served as the chief administrator of the Civil War draft in Illinois.

1285. Peterson, Robert L. and John A. Hudson. "Foreign Recruitment for Union Forces." CWH, 7 [1961]: 176-189.

Good overview of attempts by private agents to recruit men in Europe for the Union army. Although they operated without official sanction from the Lincoln administration, their activity prompted understandable concern from Confederate authorities as well as the British government.

1286. Raney, William F. "Recruiting and Crimping in Canada for the Northern Forces, 1861-1865." MVHR, 10 [1923]: 21-33.

Contrary to the intent of the British Foreign Enlistment Act of 1819, numerous Canadians entered the Union army. As the war progressed, the situation increasingly worsened and Canadian officials attempted to curb the problem through a variety of unsuccessful methods.

1287. Rappaport, Armin. "The Replacement System During the Civil War." MIL AFF, 15 [1951]: 95-106.

This study examines the ineffectiveness of the replacement system. Due in part to reluctant state governors, who did not want to lose this significant source of patronage, new recruits tended to enter new regiments rather than existing ones.

1288. Reekstin, William F. "The Draft Riots of July 1863, on Staten Island." STATEN ISLAND HIS, 19 [1958]: 27-30.

An account of the draft resistance on Staten Island from July 14 to 20, 1863. This disturbance was similar to that which had occurred a few days earlier in New York City. Not only did the rioters direct their anger toward blacks, but they also believed that the conscription law discriminated against the poor.

1289. Ripley, Peter C. "The Black Family in Transition: Louisana, 1860-1865." JSH, 42 [1975]: 369-380.

This study examines the harsh recruiting methods used in the occupied state of Louisiana to place blacks into military service. Even federal officials demonstrated a callous disregard for the adverse effect that a former slave's absence would have on his family.

1290. Robbins, Gerald. "Recruiting and Arming of Negroes in the South Carolina Sea Islands, 1862-1865." NEG HIS BULL, 28 [1965]: 150-151, 163-167.

This study primarily concerns the activities of Union generals David Hunter and Rufus Saxton in raising the first black regiments in 1862. The author discusses the various problems they encountered in their efforts to entice former slaves into service. Questionable recruiting tactics such as impressment were used and allegations of inhumane treatment became so serious by 1865 that Secretary of War Stanton finally had to investigate the matter personally.

1291. Sandburg, Carl. "Lincoln and Conscription." JISHS, 32 [1939]: 5-19.

This essay pertains to the part that President Lincoln played in the repeal of the commutation clause, July 4, 1864. Although the author believes that Lincoln did not receive what he wanted, he nevertheless went ahead and ordered a draft despite the effect it would have on his chances for reelection.

1292. Sanders, Neill F. "Consul, Commander and Minister: A New Perspective on the Queenstown Incident." LIN HER, 81 [1979]: 102-115.

This very detailed account describes the events that culminated in charges that United States naval officials had illegally recruited 16 British subjects aboard the USS KEARSEARGE, in the fall of 1863. British officials claimed that this incident violated the Foreign Enlistment Act of 1819.

1293. Schneider, John C. "Detroit and the Problem of Disorder: The Riot of 1863." MICH HIS, 58 [1974]: 4-24.

An account of a race riot in Detroit in February 1863, which was prompted by the racist DETROIT FREE PRESS and a trial over an alleged rape of a white girl by a black man. The fact that Detroit had no police force did not help the situation, while the Emancipation Proclamation and conscription added fuel to the fire.

1294. Schoonover, Thomas. "Manpower--North and South--in 1860." CWH, 6 [1960]: 170-173.

This study provides a good analysis of the manpower resources, including blacks, in both sections on the eve of war.

1295. Shankman, Arnold. "Draft Resistance in Civil War Pennsylvania." PA MHB, 101 [1977]: 190-204.

An excellent account of resistance to the enrollment and draft processes in the Keystone state, particularly in 1862 and 1863. The author concludes that the draft failed in Pennsylvania. A version of this article appears in Shankman's THE PENNSYLVANIA ANTIWAR MOVEMENT, 1861-1865 [number 1100].

1296. Shannon, Fred A. "The Mercenary Factor in the Creation of the Union Army." MVHR, 12 [1926]: 523-549.

The author contends that many northern men were interested less in patriotism and more in the money they could gain from bounties or as substitutes. Beginning with the 1862 militia drafts, these practices intensified and hurt poorer coomunities since they could not pay the high sums demanded.

1297. ———. THE ORGANIZATION AND ADMINISTRATION OF THE UNION ARMY, 1861-1865. 2 v. Cleveland: Clark, 1928.

In this benchmark study, Shannon examines a variety of subjects relating to conscription, including state recruiting, bounties, skedaddling, and the conscientious objector. The Enrollment Act was a weak measure, he argues, because congressmen were more interested in protecting states' rights and the well-to-do than they were in developing an effective conscription law.

1298. ———. "States Rights and the Union Army." MVHR, 12 [1925]: 51-71.

In this article Shannon contends that the individual states were primarily responsible for raising most of the 3,000,000 men who entered the Union army during the Civil War. He is very critical of the federal government for not taking the initiative in this important area in the early days of the conflict.

1299. Shaw, William L. "The Civil War Federal Conscription and Exemption System." JUDGE ADVO J, Bulletin 32 [1962]: 1-27.

This article reviews the stages through which the Union army increased its pre-war strength by over 60 times during the Civil War. The author examines the Militia Act of July 1862, legal challenges to the draft, the Enrollment Act, and the report of Brigadier General James Oakes.

1300. ———. "Conscription By the State Through the Time of the Civil War." JUDGE ADVO J, Bulletin 34 [1964]: 1-40.

A survey of conscription legislation from colonial times up through the Militia Act of 1862.

1301. Smith, John D. "The Health of Vermont's Civil War Recruits." VT HIS, 43 [1975]: 185-192.

This work describes the activities and certain recommendations of three surgeons who conducted physical examinations for Vermont's drafted men and recruits in the last two years of the war.

1302. ———. "Kentucky Civil War Recruits: A Medical Profile." MED HIS [Great Britain], 24 [1980]: 185-196.

To some extent this study resembles the author's earlier work on Vermont. However, this discussion of the examining surgeons in Kentucky's eight enrollment districts reveals that a relatively high percentage of blacks met the physical qualifications for military service in most parts of the state. Their generally healthy condition was attributed in part to their former status as slaves.

1303. Snyder, Charles M. "Oswego County's Response to the Civil War." NY HIS, 42 [1961]: 71-92.

Among one of the better synopses of one county's continuing response to the war. The author reviews the raising of the 24th, 81st, 110th, and 147th New York regiments.

1304. Steffen, Dorcas. "The Civil War and the Wayne County Mennonites." MEN HIS BULL, 26 [1965]: 1-3.

A cursory discussion of how Mennonites in Wayne County, Ohio, responded to the draft and how some fared while in service.

1305. Sterling, Robert E. "Civil War Draft Resistance in Illinois." JISHS, 64 [1971]: 244-266.

In this nicely illustrated study, the author discusses raising troops in the early days of the war and the later public reaction to the draft in Illinois. More resistance to the enrollment process occurred than to the actual draft, which had to be implemented through the use of military force in some areas.

1306. ———. CIVIL WAR RESISTANCE IN THE MIDDLE WEST. Ph.D. dissertation, Northern Illinois University, 1974.

A very detailed and extensively researched study that focuses on the states of Illinois, Indiana, Iowa, Michigan, Minnesota, Ohio, and Wisconsin. The author argues that midwestern draft resisters cannot be placed under the "umbrella of copperheadism." Aside from a distaste for mandatory military service, their reasons included racism, partisanship, and a rejection of the centralizing nature of the conscription laws.

1307. Suplick, Stanley M., Jr. THE UNITED STATES INVALID CORPS/VETERAN RESERVE CORPS. Ph.D. dissertation, University of Minnesota, 1969.

This frequently overlooked source of manpower for the Union army came into being in the spring of 1863. This study examines the purpose and success of this organization, which utilized the services of some 61,604 disabled officers and men who could not participate in active field service and were given tasks such as guard and clerical duties. They released the equivalent of over sixty infantry regiments for combat service.

1308. Taylor, John M. "Representative Recruit for Abraham Lincoln." CWTI, 17 [1978]: 34-35.

Designed to encourage the furnishing of able-bodied men for active military service by draft-exempt individuals, this recruiting method, which emerged in the summer of 1864, cannot be classified as overly successful. Only 1,291 individuals, including President Lincoln, took advantage of this scheme. This article describes the service of Lincoln's representative recruit, John Summerfield Staples.

1309. Theisen, Gerald, editor. "A Brief Memoir [Julian Aragon Y. Perea]." NM HIS R, 46 [1971]: 351-355.

Contains some comments about the organization of New Mexican troops into Company B, 4th Regiment of Mounted Volunteers.

1310. Thompson, Jerry D. "Mexican-Americans in the Civil War: The Battle of Valverde." TEXANA, 10 [1972]: 1-19.

This study gives an overview of raising troops in New Mexico in the early days of the war and provides a balanced assessment of the Union defeat at Valverde. This action effectively terminated any further recruitment of Mexican-American regiments.

1311. Trenerry, Walter N. "When the Boys Came Home." MINN HIS, 38 [1963]: 287-297.

One of few detailed accounts describing one community's response to returning veterans. It also discusses some of the problems they encountered as well as the opportunities that awaited them after their demobilization.

1312. U.S. Congress. PAPERS RELATING TO FOREIGN AFFAIRS. 1864. 3 v. Washington, D.C.: 1865.

Volume Three of this set [better known as DIPLOMATIC CORRESPONDENCE] carries extensive accounts of recruiting in Europe to raise troops for the Union army.

1313. Vance, J.R. "Holmes County Rebellion--Fort Fizzle." OSAHQ, 40 [1931]: 30-49.

A case study of violent resistance to the draft in a north central Ohio county.

1314. Wall, Alexander J. "The Administration of Governor Horatio Seymour During the War of the Rebellion and the Draft Riots in New York City, July 13-17, 1863, With the Events Leading Up to Them." NY HIS SOC QTLY BULL, [1928]: 79-115.

A defense of Seymour's actions during the Draft Riots.

1315. Warner, G.T. "From a Voluntary System to Compulsion: The Precedent of '63." BLACKWOOD'S MAGAZINE, 199 [1916]: 92-111.

As the feasibility of conscription was being discussed in Great Britain during World War I, this interesting account appeared with its distinct pro-draft viewpoint. The author contends that the Civil War draft succeeded because it revived volunteering, not because it conscripted men.

1316. Weigley, Russell F. HISTORY OF THE UNITED STATES ARMY. New York: Macmillan, 1967.

Chapter Ten in this work provides a succinct overview of the problems that hindered the mobilization of the Union army and its effectiveness in the field. Such matters as the organization of a regiment, casualties , the caliber of officers, and the supply system are also described.

1317. Werstein, Irving. JULY, 1863. New York: Messner, 1957.

A dramatized account of the New York City disturbances in the summer of 1863.

1318. Wilson, Keith. "Thomas Webster and the 'Free Military School for Applicants for Commands of Colored Troops.'" CWH, 29 [1983]: 101-122.

This article describes the Free Military School in Philadelphia, which was founded in late 1863 for the purpose of preparing individuals for appointments as officers in black regiments. Its graduates proved very successful in obtaining commissions.

1319. Winks, Robin W. "The Creation of a Myth: 'Canadian' Enlistments in the Northern Armies During the American Civil War." CAN HIS R, 39 [1958]: 24-40.

Consists of a detailed assessment on the validity of the commonly accepted figure that some 50,000 Canadians served in the Union forces.

1320. "A Workingman's Ideas of Conscription." MAGAZINE OF HISTORY, 16 [1917]: 103-107.

This is a reprint of an article which first appeared in FINCHER'S TRADE REVIEW: THE NATIONAL ORGAN OF THE PRODUCING CLASSES about 1863. This self-proclaimed "workingman" supports conscription but opposes the provision for substitutes. He also argues that "non-producers" should be taken before laborers whom he classifies as the "producers" in a society.

1321. Wright, Edward N. CONSCIENTIOUS OBJECTORS IN THE CIVIL WAR. Philadelphia: University of Pennsylvania Press, 1931.

This work focuses primarily on Quakers and their reactions to military service in both the North and the South. Although dated, this source contains useful information and should be consulted for any study involving religious groups and the draft.

1322. Wright, William C. "New Jersey's Role in the Civil War Reconsidered." NJ HIS, 92 [1974]: 197-210.

A very useful illustrated study that reassesses New Jersey's manpower contribution to the war effort. The author examines certain myths and concludes that this "Copperhead state" not only had to rely on conscription but failed to meet its quotas.

1323. Zornow, William F. "Lincoln and Private Lennan." IND MAG HIS, 49 [1953]: 267-272.

John Lennan, sentenced to be shot for desertion at Indianapolis in December 1864, is reprieved at the last moment by President Lincoln and disappears from the pages of history.

D. TOOLS OF WAR

1324. Adams, William G., Jr. "Spencers at Gettysburg: Fact or Fiction." MIL AFF, 29 [1965]: 41-42, 56.

If any Spencers were used at Gettysburg, then the "best kept secret of the war" was who provided them. Ordnance records show that the original contracts for these weapons were placed in July 1863 for delivery at the end of the year.

1325. Bruce, Robert V. LINCOLN AND THE TOOLS OF WAR. Indianapolis: Bobbs-Merrill, 1956.

Examines Lincoln's great interest in arms and armaments and discusses the technical and scientific work in the North. Lincoln receives some credit for the Union's use of breechloading rifles, improvements in cannons, and other innovations. His controversies with Brigadier General James W. Ripley, Chief of Ordnance, are also covered.

1326. Buckeridge, Justin O. LINCOLN'S CHOICE. Harrisburg, Pennsylvania: Stackpole, 1956.

Tells of Christopher Spencer's difficulties in trying to get the army to adopt his rifle. Lincoln made the final decision and they were adopted in 1863. The use of these rifles helped to shorten the war.

1327. Coggins, Jack. ARMS AND EQUIPMENT OF THE CIVIL WAR. Garden City, New York: Doubleday, 1962. Reprint 1983.

An excellent guide to weapons, equipment, and tools for all branches of the service--signal corps, medical department, quartermaster corps, and even railroads. Useful descriptions accompany the lavish illustrations.

1328. Colby, Carroll B. CIVIL WAR WEAPONS: SMALL ARMS AND ARTILLERY.... New York: Coward-McCann, 1962.

Illustrations and descriptions of small arms and artillery of the North and the South.

1329. Collins, Donald R. "How Bullets Were Made." CWTI, 4 [9] [1966]: 22-25.

Excerpts from a manuscript describing the production techniques used in manufacturing balls and cartridges.

1330. ———. "More on Bullets." CWTI, 5 [4] [1966]: 36-39.

Discusses the bullets, balls, and cartridges used in the war.

1331. Collins, Thomas. "Minie Balls--How To Find Them, What to Look For When You Do." CWTI, 4 [3] [1965]: 44-47.

A field trip guide for battlefield relic collectors. Includes descriptions of condition of various projectiles recovered from various sites.

1332. Davis, Carl L. ARMING THE UNION: SMALL ARMS IN THE CIVIL WAR. Port Washington, New York: Kennikat, 1973.

A fairly good, though not very exciting study of the Ordnance Department of the Union. The author seeks to restore the reputation of General James Wolfe Ripley, who as head of the department early in the war has suffered severely at the hands of historians. Ripley worked without sufficient staff and with little cooperation from Congress, which is blamed for many of the difficulties.

1333. Donnelly, Ralph W. "Rocket Batteries of the Civil War." MIL AFF, 26 [1962]: 69-93.

A survey of the development and use of rocket batteries from 1813 through the Civil War. While they were employed during the Civil War, neither the North nor South found them to be helpful for a number of reasons, including improvements in conventional artillery.

1334. Downey, Fairfax. "Arms and the Cavalryman." ORD, 43 [1958]: 412-413.

Describes the usual arms used by cavalrymen such as sabres, pistols, and carbines. The author also discusses pikes, lances, three-inch rifles, and smoothbore horse artillery.

1335. ———. "Field and Siege Pieces." CWH, 2 [1956]: 65-74.

A chapter from Downey's book SOUND OF GUNS. Relates the work done by the heavy artillery and describes those instances where the artillery was the deciding factor in the outcome of a battle.

1336. Edwards, William B. CIVIL WAR GUNS. Harrisburg, Pennsylvania: Stackpole, 1962.

A large book of over 300 illustrations, which include all the arms used in the Civil War.

1337. Evans, Ronald D. "Notes Concerning Wiard's System of Field Artillery." MIL COLL HIS, 19 [4] [1967]: 103-108.

Inventor Norman Wiard's study of field artillery revealed that the guns then in use suffered from a number of deficiencies.

1338. Falk, Stanley L. "How the Napoleon Came to America." CWH, 10 [1964]: 149-154.

Details the circumstances under which the "Napoleon," the most famous artillery piece of the Civil War came to be adopted by the U.S. Army.

1339. ———. "Maj. Alfred Mordecai." ORD, 44 [1959]: 395-397.

Mordecai was the "first ordnance officer to apply scientific methods to armaments." He resigned from the army in 1861 because he said he was a scientist rather than a soldier.

1340. Fuller, Claud E. THE RIFLED MUSKET. Harrisburg, Pennsylvania: Stackpole, 1958.

Author describes the "regulation rifled muskets, as well as breechloaders and repeating arms." The book contains data on ammunition and performance of these arms.

1341. Gavin, William G. ACCOUTREMENT PLATES, NORTH AND SOUTH, 1861-1865.... Philadelphia: Riling and Lentz, 1963.

Accoutrement plates are illustrated and detailed.

1342. Gross, Al. "Not Quite Flying Machines." CWTI, 13 [10] [1975]: 20-24.

Details several patents granted during the Civil War. The heavier-than-air craft never really "got off the ground." Most of the patents were granted for improvements in lighter-than-air balloons.

1343. Hackley, F.W. A REPORT ON CIVIL WAR EXPLOSIVE ORDNANCE. Indian Head, Maryland: U.S. Naval Propellant Plant, 1960.

A short account of the subject matter accompanied by diagrams and photographs.

1344. Hankee, William B. "Fire and Maneuver at the Battle of Booneville." MIL R, 53 [3] [1973]: 8-16.

Although the battle was of little importance, the victory of Union troops over a much larger Confederate force at Booneville, Mississippi, July 1, 1862, proved the interrelation of firepower, intelligence, flexibility, and the commander's influence on the outcome of the battle.

1345. Hardy, Robert R. "Explosive Bullets." CWTI, 5 [6] [1966]: 43-45.

The Gardiner explosive bullet and other types of explosive bullets are analyzed. The emphasis, however, is placed on the injuries inflicted by these bullets.

1346. Haselberger, Francis E. "The Ellsworth Guns." CWTI, 8 [1] [1969]: 33-35.

The Ellsworth Gun was the only breech-loading artillery piece manufactured [by military contract] in the United States for the Union army.

1347. Hassler, William W. "Professor T.S.C. Lowe." CWTI, 6 [5] [1967]: 12-21.

The achievements of Professor Lowe, the celebrated balloonist, are the subject of this article.

1348. Hazlett, James C. "The Federal Napoleon Gun." MIL COLL HIS, 15 [4] [1963]: 103-108.

A discussion of the manufacture of this famous gun in the United States and a list of the foundries which made it.

1349. ———. "The Napoleon Gun: Its Origins and Introduction Into American Service." MIL COLL HIS, 15 [1] [1963]: 1-5.

A discussion of the evolution of the "modified" Napoleons.

1350. ———. "The Napoleon Gun: Markings, Bore Diameters, Weights, and Costs." MIL COLL HIS, 18 [4] [1966]: 109-119.

Further details on the origins of the Napoleon and its use in war.

1351. ———. "The Parrott Rifles." CWTI, 5 [7] [1966]: 17-33.

Author describes these rifled, muzzle-loading cannons, which were designed by Robert Parker Parrott.

1352. ———. "The 3-inch Ordnance Rifle." CWTI, 7 [8] [1968]: 30-36.

This wrought-iron piece which could hit a target at any distance under a mile was the brain child of John Griffen.

1353. Huntington, R.T. HALL'S BREECHLOADERS.... York, Pennsylvania: Shumway, 1972.

The invention and development of a breech-loading rifle by John H. Hall is described. The gun had interchangeable parts.

1354. Jackson, Donald. "The Myth of the Fremont Howitzer." MO HIS SOC BULL, 23 [1967]: 205-214.

The author states that the howitzer itself was no myth, but that many of the stories regarding Fremont's howitzer were.

1355. Joyce, Marion D. "Tactical Lessons of the War." CWTI 2 [10] [1964]: 42-47.

The introduction of the rifled musket made all previous formations and tactics obsolete.

1356. Lederer, P.S. "Colonel Aspinwall and His Revolver." MIL COLL HIS, 21 [1] [1969]: 12-15.

A discussion of the Adams revolver [English] which was much like the Colt. Lloyd Aspinwall of New York City was the owner.

1357. Lewis, B.R. "Explosive Bullets." ORDNANCE, 38 [1954].

A brief examination of exploding small arms ammunition. The author notes that the war provided a great stimulus to inventors of arms and ammunition.

1358. ———. "Mystery Bullets." ORDNANCE, 40 [1956]: 616-618.

An illustrated look at several of the more unusual small arms projectiles used during the war.

1359. ———. NOTES ON AMMUNITION OF THE AMERICAN CIVIL WAR, 1861-1865. Washington, D.C.: American Ordnance Association, 1959.

Technical descriptions of ammunition for artillery and small arms, plus tables indicating the quantities used.

1360. Lewis, Emanuel R. "The Ambiguous Columbiads." MIL AFF, 28 [1964]: 111-122.

A discussion of Rodman's construction and modifications of this gun which was first used in the War of 1812. In 1860 it was adopted as a seacoast cannon but underwent many modifications by Rodman's system.

1361. Lobdell, Jared. "A Civil War Tank at Vicksburg." J MISS HIS, 25 [1963]: 279-283.

The "Saproller," an early day tank, was a wagon protected by cotton bales and hand-propelled by the use of wooden crowbars attached to the axles. It failed when used by Union troops in attacking Fort Hill at Vicksburg because its wheels squeaked, it was slow, and it was an easy target for Confederate "turpentine shells." Author discusses the conflicting testimony about what the saproller actually was and what it actually did.

1362. Lord, Francis A. "The Coehorn Mortar." CWTI, 5 [5] [1966]: 18-19.

An explanation of the characteristics and use of the Coehorn Mortar is the substance of the article. It was portable, used little powder, and was very effective in siege warfare.

1363. ———. "The Ketchum Hand Grenade." CWTI, 6 [3] [1967]: 18-19.

Author describes in detail the most commonly used grenade of the Civil War. Drawings accompany text.

1364. Marshall, Ronald. "Edged Weapons in the American Civil War." MIL HIS SOC BULL, 12 [48] [1962]: 83-85.

Although pikes and lances were issued to troops at the start of the war, they were soon rendered obsolete by rifles.

1365. Michigan Civil War Centennial Commission. SMALL ARMS USED BY MICHIGAN TROOPS IN THE CIVIL WAR. Lansing, Michigan: Michigan Civil War Centennial Commission, 1966.

A slim 133-page volume which covers the subject matter quite adequately.

1366. Naisawald, L. Van Loan. GRAPE AND CANISTER.... New York: Oxford University Press, 1960.

An expert study of the artillery branch of the Army of the Potomac, a branch whose role has been underestimated in studies of the Civil War. We are advised that the federals' eastern forces would have lost four important battles without skillful use of its cannons. Much is told here about the technical side of the arillery pieces as well as about the men who used them.

1367. Nye, Wilbur S. "The First Aeronaut of the War Was an Engineer." CWTI, 3 [6] [1964]: 19.

A description of the army's first balloon experiments, carried out in 1861 by Lieutenant Henry Larcom Abbot of the Engineers' Corps.

1368. ———. "Implements For Loading and Fuzing Civil War Artillery Were Many and Varied." CWTI, 3 [6] [1964]: 32-35.

A description of the projectiles, the implements for loading and fuzing the projectiles, and the implements for loading, unloading, and firing the cannons.

1369. Peterson, Harold L. NOTES ON ORDNANCE OF THE AMERICAN CIVIL WAR, 1861-1865. Washington, D.C.: American Ordnance Association, 1959.

A good introduction to the subject matter, accompanied by useful descriptions.

1370. Ripley, Warren. ARTILLERY AND AMMUNITION OF THE CIVIL WAR. New York: Van Nostrand Reinhold, 1970.

A complete book detailing all you want to know about Civil War cannons. In addition there is much information on various types of ammunition. Includes tables of data and over 600 illustrations. Even if one is not a cannon buff this makes fascinating reading.

1371. Sabine, David B. "Dr. Gatling and His Amazing Gun." AM HIS ILL, 1 [3] [1966]: 52-58.

Although not officially adopted by the U.S. Army until 1866, this rapid firing multiple-barreled weapon saw some use towards the end of the war.

1372. Salzer, Richard J. "Civil War Hand Grenades." MIL COLL HIS, 22 [1] [1970]: 14-18.

While not widely used during the Civil War, the conflict did stimulate interest in such devices.

1373. Starr, Stephen Z. "Cold Steel: the Saber and the Union Cavalry." CWH, 11 [1965]: 142-159.

Notes the declining effectiveness and use of the saber as the war progressed.

1374. Todd, Frederick P. AMERICAN MILITARY EQUIPAGE 1851-1872. Providence, Rhode Island: Company of Military Historians, 1974.

A catalog of military equipment--clothing, insignia, small arms, accoutrements, knapsacks, canteens and even bridles.

1375. Truby, J. David. "War in the Clouds: Balloons in the Civil War." MANKIND, 2 [11] [1971]: 64-71.

Discusses the work of Thaddeus Lowe, chief balloonist of the Union army and the use of balloons for gathering intelligence.

1376. Wegner, Dana. "Mr. Eads' Turret." CWTI, 12 [6] [1973]: 24-25, 28-31.

Descriptive article dealing with the gun turret designed by Eads for the Union navy's ironclads.

1377. Wilson, Spencer. "How Soldiers Rated Carbines." CWTI, 5 [2] [1966]: 40-44.

Reports how soldiers rated the performance of the different carbines. Three rating categories are used: [1] the worst weapons, [2] acceptable arms, and [3] the only carbine praised, the Spencer.

E. SUPPORT SERVICES

1378. Abdill, George B. CIVIL WAR RAILROADS. Seattle, Washington: Superior, 1961.

A good photographic history complete with narrative of the development of the railroads during the war. Over 200 photographs picture railroad officials, locomotives, railroad yards, railroad depots, and even railroad wrecks.

1379. Barton, John V. "The Procurement of Horses." CWTI, 6 [8] [1967]: 16-24.

The cavalry trooper supplied his own horse during the first year of the war. After July 1862 the government undertook to provide the mounts.

1380. Bates, David H. LINCOLN IN THE TELEGRAPH OFFICE.... New York, 1907.

Bates was manager of the war department telegraph office. His recollections include details on the operation, organization, and the part the telegraph played during the war.

1381. Brockman, Charles J., Jr., editor. "The John Van Duser Diary of Sherman's March From Atlanta to Hilton Head." GA HIS Q, 53 [1969]: 220-240.

A diary of the chief telegraph officer in the Military Division of Tennessee. It reveals the value of the telegraph officers who tapped into Confederate telegraph lines to get military information.

1382. Brown, Joseph W. THE SIGNAL CORPS.... Washington, D.C.: 1896.

The author served for four years in the Civil War and describes the role and activities of the Signal Corps. This voluminous work of 916 pages includes a roster of those who served in the corps.

1383. Chandler, Albert. "Lincoln and the Telegrapher." AM HER 12 [2] [1961]: 32-34.

A short memoir, recently rediscovered by E.B. Long, of one of three telegraph boys in the war department. Chandler relates a number of Lincoln stories.

1384. Clauss, Errol. "Sherman's Rail Support in the Atlanta Campaign." GA HIS Q, 50 [1966]: 413-420.

Realizing the importance of the railroad, Sherman created the District of the Etowah under Major General James B. Steedman to keep open the supply lines between Tennessee and the Georgia front. Some of the problems which arose and how they were solved are described.

1385. Coggins, Jack. "The Engineers Played A Key Role in Both Armies." CWTI, 3 [9] [1965]: 40-47.

The transportation of troops, artillery, food, and fodder required work on the part of the engineers. They constructed bridges, tunnels, and roads to help keep the army on the move.

1386. Colwell, Milton S. "The Keeper of the Key." AM HER, 20 [4] [1969]: 49-53.

Patrick "Granther" Sweeney, railroad switchman at Stuyvesant, New York, saved a Union troop train by his quick actions.

1387. Corliss, Carlton J. MAIN LINE OF MID-AMERICA: THE STORY OF THE ILLINOIS CENTRAL. New York: Creative Age, 1950.

An account of the role of the Illinois Central, one of the more important lines in the North.

1388. Crouch, Tom D. "Up, Up, and--Sometimes--Away." CIN HIS SOC BULL, 28 [1970]: 109-132.

A survey of balloon aviation in the mid-19th century with a passing reference to the Civil War accomplishments of Professor T.S.C. Lowe.

1389. East, Sherrod E. "Montgomery C. Meigs and the Quartermaster Department." MIL AFF, [Winter 1961/1962].

A West Point graduate of 1836, Meigs was appointed Quartermaster General in May 1861 and served in this very difficult and demanding position throughout the war.

1390. Fish. Carl R. "The Northern Railroads, April, 1861." AHR, 22 [1917]: 778-793.

A very useful article dealing with the state of the railroads in the North at the outbreak of the war.

1391. Fitzsimmons, Margaret L. "Missouri Railroads During the Civil War and Reconstruction." MO HIS R, 35 [1941]: 188-206.

Explains the importance of St. Louis, Missouri, as a railroad hub during the war. Battles and skirmishes are related to the particular railroad involved which makes for interesting reading, especially for railroad buffs.

1392. Funk, Arville L. "Military Installations in Indiana During the Civil War." IND HIS BULL, 39 [1962]: 10-17.

A brief description of the 100 military camps and other military facilities located in Indiana during the Civil War.

1393. Gray, Ralph D. "'The Key to the Whole Federal Situation'--The Chesapeake and Delaware Canal in the Civil War." MD HIS MAG, 60 [1965]: 1-14.

The Civil War period proved to be a prosperous one for the canal. After the Baltimore riots in April 1861 when Washington was cut off from the North, troops were shipped into the capital by the canal.

1394. Harlow, Alvin F. BRASS-POUNDERS: YOUNG TELEGRAPHERS OF THE CIVIL WAR. Denver: Colorado: Sage Books, 1962.

Colorful and highly romanticized tales about telegraphers and the important role they played during the war.

1395. Hart, Eugene F. "Revolution in Technology and Logistics." ARMY INFO DIG, 16 [8] [1961]: 100-114.

Innovations and advances in Civil War logistics, transportation, communications, weaponry, medical aid, and fortifications paved the way for the successes of the modern American army.

1396. Haydon, Frederick S. AERONAUTICS IN THE UNION AND CONFEDERATE ARMIES, WITH A SURVEY OF MILITARY AERONAUTICS PRIOR TO 1861. Baltimore: Johns Hopkins Press, 1941.

A history of balloons in the army and a detailed account of their use in the first year of the war.

1397. Hecht, Arthur. "Union Military Rail Service." FCHQ, 37 [1963]: 227-248.

An excellent account of the methods used--and problems faced--by the federal government in delivering mail to troops in the field during the war.

1398. Hoogenboom, Ari. "'Spy and Topog Duty Has Been ... Neglected.'" CWH, 10 [1964]: 368-370.

Little importance was attached to topographical analysis before and during the war.

1399. Huff, Lee E. "The Memphis and Little Rock Railroad During the Civil War." ARK HIS Q, 23 [1964]: 260-270.

This railway was important to both Union and Confederate forces for troop movements west of the Mississippi.

1400. Huston, James A. "Logistical Support of Federal Armies in the Field." CWH, 7 [1961]: 36-47.

A study of the able handling of logistical matters by the Union army, with particular focus on Sherman's campaigns in Georgia.

1401. Johnston, Angus J., II. VIRGINIA RAILROADS IN THE CIVIL WAR. Chapel Hill: University of North Carolina Press, 1961.

While this is a study of the inadequate southern railroad system during the war, comparisons are made with the better-run railroads of the North.

1402. Klein, Frederic S. "The Civil War Was a Pitchman's Paradise." CWTI, 2 [3] [1963]: 30-33.

An entertaining account of the successful salesmanship of Civil War hucksters. Soldiers would buy anything.

1403. Lord, Francis A. CIVIL WAR SUTLERS AND THEIR WARES. New York: Yoseloff, 1969.

A good glimpse of the sutler, the vendor who suppled the Civil War soldier with many necessaries not provided by the army, in those pre-post exchange days. A long-overlooked subject, the sutler has been brought to life in this book.

1404. ———. LINCOLN'S RAILROAD MAN: HERMAN HAUPT. Rutherford, New Jersey: Fairleigh Dickinson University Press, 1969.

A thorough examination of the federal government's railroad system and the man who managed it from April 1862 to September 1863. This is not a full-length biography of Haupt, who was a genius in the field of railroad engineering.

1405. ———. "The Military Telegraph Was Communications' Workhorse." CWTI, 3 [3] [1964]: 16-17.

A brief treatment of the important role played by the military telegraph.

1406. Meredith, Roy and Arthur Meredith. MR. LINCOLN'S MILITARY RAILROADS: A PICTORIAL HISTORY OF THE U.S. CIVIL WAR RAILROADS. New York: Norton, 1979.

A lavishly illustrated volume.

1407. Miles, Wyndham D. "The Civil War: A Discourse on How the Conflict Was Influenced by Chemistry and Chemists." CHEM ENG NEWS, 39 [14, 15] [1961]: 108-115, 116-123.

A good discussion of Union and Confederate scientists and what they achieved during the war. This rather unusual story of a relatively unknown aspect of the war is worth reading.

1408. Murphey, Hermon K. "The Northern Railroads and the Civil War." MVHR, 5 [1918]: 324-338.

Despite its age, this article remains a very useful introduction to the subject.

1409. Ness, George T., Jr. "Army Engineers of the Civil War." MIL ENG, 57 [375] [1965]: 38-40.

A table and summary of material found in the next entry.

1410. ———. "Engineers of the Civil War." MIL ENG, 44 [299] [1952]: 179-187.

A tabular study of the 93 men, who were regular army officers at the start of the war, and an account of their accomplishments during the war. Fifteen of the number were wartime casualties.

1411. Nye, Wilbur S. "The U.S. Military Telegraph Service." CWTI, 7 [7] [1968]: 28-34.

The use of telegraph nets was expanded during the war.

1412. O'Brien, John E. TELEGRAPHING IN BATTLE.... Scranton, Pennsylvania, 1910.

O'Brien, a cipher operator with the U.S. Military Telegraph Service, collected many short reminiscences from his fellow operators.

1413. Otis, George A. A REPORT ON A PLAN FOR TRANSPORTING WOUNDED SOLDIERS BY RAILWAY IN TIME OF WAR.... Washington, D.C., 1875.

A description of the methods by which wounded northern soldiers were transported during the war. The work also includes a good bibliography.

1414. Plum, William B. THE MILITARY TELEGRAPH DURING THE CIVIL WAR IN THE UNITED STATES.... Chicago, 1882.

Author relates a brief history of ancient and modern means of communication. Work also includes an account of the Union and Confederate systems with information on codes and the unique role of the telegraphers.

1415. Price, Charles L. "The United States Military Railroads in North Carolina, 1862-1865." NC HIS R, 53 [1976]: 243-264.

Author refutes the idea that the Union army "played a significant role in the reconstruction of Southern railroads."

1416. Rezneck, Samuel. "Horsford's 'Marching Ration' For the Civil War Army." MIL AFF, 33 [1969]: 249-255.

Eben N. Horsford, a scientist, proposed in 1864 that the army adopt a concentrated marching ration of his design. General Grant approved a trial use of this ration.

1417. Riegel, Robert E. "Federal Operators of Southern Railroads During the Civil War." MVHR, 9 [1922]: 126-138.

Operation of southern railroads on behalf of Union forces was ably managed by Daniel C. McCallum, "military director" of the system.

1418. Round, Harold F. "Federal Supply Bases on the Potomac." CWTI, 5 [7] [1966]: 20-26.

Union supply bases on Aquia Creek and Potomac Creek are the subject of this article.

1419. Sabine, David B. "Blue and Gray Chemistry." CWTI, 8 [6] [1969]: 22-29.

While Civil War chemistry produced better gunpowder, it also developed dehydrated vegetables, condensed milk, concentrated food, and new medicines.

1420. ———. "What the Soldier Ate." CWTI, 2 [6] [1963]: 22-27.

Soldiers rarely went without food for any length of time. A typical ration consisted of pork or fresh beef, hardtack, beans, and dessicated vegetables.

1421. Scheips, P.J. "Union Signal Communications: Innovation and Conflict." CWH, 9 [1963]: 399-421.

Traces origins and growth of the two communications organizations established by the federal government: the Military Telegraph and the Signal Corps.

1422. Smith, Raymond W. "Don't Cut! Signal Telegraph." CWTI, 15 [2] [1976]: 18-28.

The continuing conflict between the Signal Corps under Albert James Myer, "father" of the corps, and the U.S. Military Telegraph Service under Anson Stager, slowed the tactical use of the telegraph during the war.

1423. Smith, William P. B & O IN THE CIVIL WAR: FROM THE PAPERS OF WILLIAM PRESCOTT SMITH. William E. Bain, editor. Denver; Sage Books, 1966.

Smith, the Baltimore and Ohio's transportation chief, tells of the problems faced by the railroad during the war.

1424. Spear, Donald P. "The Sutler in the Union Army." CWH, 16 [1970]: 121-138.

An excellent study of the relationship between the army sutler and the enlisted man. Article presents many of the items which soldiers wanted and their prices.

1425. Summers, Festus P. "The Baltimore and Ohio, First in War." CWH, 7 [1961]: 239-254.

A useful introduction to the history and role of the Baltimore and Ohio railroad.

1426. ———. THE BALTIMORE AND OHIO IN THE CIVIL WAR. New York: Putnam, 1939.

A valuable work on this important railroad, with emphasis on West Virginia.

1427. Sutton, Robert M. "The Illinois Central, Thoroughfare For Freedom." CWH, 7 [1961]: 273-287.

Although the Illinois Central lost its profitable trade with the South when war broke out, it quickly became a major artery for troop movements in the West and was able to partly recoup its losses.

1428. Sylvester, Robert B. "The U.S. Military Railroad and the Siege of Petersburg." CWH, 10 [1964]: 309-316.

Describes the construction and importance of the railroad.

1429. Symonds, Henry C. REPORT OF A COMMISSARY OF SUBSISTENCE, 1861-1865. Sing Sing, New York: 1888.

Required reading for an understanding of the federal supply system and its administration.

1430. Taylor, George R. and Irene D. Neu. THE AMERICAN RAILROAD NETWORK, 1861-1890. Cambridge: Harvard University Press, 1956.

An important work which shows how the national railroad system developed in the course of the war.

1431. Thienel, Phillip M. "Engineers in the Union Army, 1861-1865." MIL ENG, 47 [1955]: 36-41, 110-115.

The three sections in this article examine the engineers with the Army of the Potomac, the engineers with the Department of the South and the Army of the James, and the engineers in the West.

1432. Todd, Frederick P. "Uniforms and Equipment of the Civil War." VT HIS, 31 [1963]: 85-93.

A look at the development of American military clothing and accoutrements.

1433. Turner, George B. VICTORY RODE THE RAILS: THE STRATEGIC PLACE OF THE RAILROADS IN THE CIVIL WAR. Indianapolis: Bobbs-Merrill, 1953.

Article shows the importance of railroads to both the North and South, by describing their use in specific campaigns.

1434. U.S. Military Railroad Department. ... REPORTS OF BVT. GEN. D.C. McCALLUM, DIRECTOR AND GENERAL MANAGER OF THE MILITARY RAILROADS OF THE UNITED STATES.... 2 v. Washington, D.C., 1866.

A basic source for an understanding of the problems and the role of the railroads during the war.

1435. ———. UNITED STATE MILITARY RAILROADS.... Washington, D.C., 1866.

A report on the military railroads, their operatons and their equipment.

1436. Weber, Thomas. THE NORTHERN RAILROADS IN THE CIVIL WAR, 1861-1865. New York, King's Crown, 1952.

A well-documented account of the railroads and their impact on the outcome of the war. Author states that the war helped improve the science of railroading.

1437. Wilson, Thomas. "Feeding a Great Army." CWTI, 4 [10] [1966]: 28-35.

Summarizes the logistical problems encountered during Grant's Virginia campaigns.

1438. Woodward, John H. "Herding Beef for the Union Army." CWTI, 9 [8] [1970]: 28-39.

Woodward was responsible for provisioning the Army of the Potomac.

F. REGIMENTS

The following list does not include all of the more than 800 northern regimental histories. It contains, however, a goodly representation of them. The works vary in length and quality. Some are brief, many are too long; some are objective, but most of them are told from the personal standpoint; some are well-written, while others are not distinguished by their style. The trickle of regimental histories became a flood after 1880, by which time the authors were beginning to look back on the Civil War nostalgically. Hence there is a tendency in these later works to minimize the evil and glorify the good in the war experience, even to the point of expressing greater understanding of the Confederate foe. A few scholarly regimental histories have appeared in recent times, which are somewhat superior to those of the 1880-1910 era. Also several journal articles of high quality have been published of late and they are included in this section. But because of the plethora of regimental histories and because of certain common characteristics among them, no annotations are included here. For an excellent introduction to a study of Civil War regiments see Stephen Z. Starr, "The Grand Old Regiment," WISCONSIN MAGAZINE OF HISTORY, 48 [1964]: 21-31. Entries on black military units will be found in BLACKS AND EMANCIPATION [X,A].

It should be added that, after the war, practically every state which provided troops for the Union, published a REPORT OF THE ADJUTANT GENERAL, consolidating material issued annually during the war. The dates of publication ranged from 1867 [Maine] to 1931-1935 [Massachusetts], with the bulk of them appearing between 1885 and 1905. The amount of material also varied greatly. Vermont and Maine published only one volume each, although very large ones; but the larger states issued many volumes. Rhode Island, New Jersey, and Maryland put out two, Iowa six, Indiana, Illinois, and Massachusetts nine each, Ohio 12, New York 43 and Michigan 46. These works generally contained regimental rosters [officers and men], sketches of units, historical memoranda, and other miscellaneous information. Readers interested in regimental statistical data should consult these reports.

States are listed alphabetically. Within each state, the artillery, cavalry, and infantry branches appear in that order. Within each branch, units are listed numerically.

Connecticut

1439. Tyler, Elnathan V. "WOODEN NUTMEGS" AT BULL RUN. A HUMOROUS ACCOUNT OF SOME OF THE EXPLOITS AND EXPERIENCES OF THE THREE MONTHS CONNECTICUT BRIDGADE, AND THE PART THEY BORE IN THE NATIONAL STAMPEDE. Hartford, Connecticut: 1872.

1440. HISTORY OF THE FIRST CONNECTICUT ARTILLERY AND OF THE SIEGE TRAINS OF THE ARMIES OPERATING AGAINST RICHMOND, 1862-1865. Hartford, Connecticut: 1893.

1441. Vaill, Dudley L. THE COUNTY REGIMENT; A SKETCH OF THE SECOND REGIMENT OF CONNECTICUT VOLUNTEER HEAVY ARTILLERY, ORIGINALLY THE NINETEENTH VOLUNTEER INFANTRY, IN THE CIVIL WAR. Winsted, Connecticut: 1908.

1442. Vaill, Theodore F. HISTORY OF THE SECOND CONNECTICUT VOLUNTEER HEAVY ARTILLERY.... Winsted, Connecticut: 1868.

1443. Beecher, Herbert W. HISTORY OF THE FIRST LIGHT BATTERY CONNECTICUT VOLUNTEERS, 1861-1865. PERSONAL RECORDS AND REMIniscences ... COMPILED FROM OFFICIAL RECORDS, PERSONAL INTERVIEWS, PRIVATE DIARIES, WAR HISTORIES.... 2 v. New York, 1901.

1444. Marvin, Edwin E. THE FIFTH REGIMENT, CONNECTICUT VOLUNTEERS. A HISTORY COMPILED FROM DIARIES AND OFFICIAL REPORTS. Hartford, Connecticut: 1889.

1445. Tourtellotte, Jerome. A HISTORY OF COMPANY K OF THE SEVENTH CONNECTICUT VOLUNTEER INFANTRY IN THE CIVIL WAR.... n.p., 1910.

1446. Walkley, Stephen W. HISTORY OF THE SEVENTH CONNECTICUT VOLUNTEER INFANTRY, HAWLEY'S BRIGADE, TERRY'S DIVISION, TENTH ARMY CORPS, 1861-1865. Hartford, Connecticut: 1905.

1447. Murray, Thomas H. HISTORY OF THE NINTH REGIMENT, CONNECTICUT VOLUNTEER INFANTRY, "THE IRISH REGIMENT," IN THE WAR OF THE REBELLION, 1861-1865. New Haven, Connecticut: 1903.

1448. DeForest, J.W. "First Time Under Fire." CWTI, 5 [5] [1966]: 4-11, 28-29. [12th Connecticut]

1449. Sprague, Homer B. HISTORY OF THE 13th INFANTRY REGIMENT OF CONNECTICUT VOLUNTEERS DURING THE GREAT REBELLION. Hartford, Connecticut: 1867.

1450. Page, Charles D. HISTORY OF THE FOURTEENTH REGIMENT, CONNECTICUT VOLUNTEER INFANTRY. Meriden, Connecticut: 1906.

1451. Thorpe, Sheldon B. THE HISTORY OF THE FIFTEENTH CONNECTICUT VOLUNTEERS IN THE WAR FOR THE DEFENSE OF THE UNION, 1861-1865. New Haven, Connecticut: 1893.

1452. Blakeslee, Bernard F. HISTORY OF THE SIXTEENTH CONNECTICUT VOLUNTEERS. Hartford, Connecticut: 1875.

1453. Walker, William C. HISTORY OF THE EIGHTEENTH REGIMENT CONNECTICUT VOLUNTEERS IN THE WAR FOR THE UNION. Norwich, Connecticut: 1885.

1454. Storrs, John Whiting. THE "TWENTIETH CONNECTICUT": A REGIMENTAL HISTORY. Ansonia, Connecticut: 1886.

1455. THE STORY OF THE TWENTY-FIRST REGIMENT, CONNECTICUT VOLUNTEER INFANTRY, DURING THE CIVIL WAR, 1861-1865. Middletown, Connecticut: 1900.

1456 Sheldon, Winthrop D. THE "TWENTY-SEVENTH." A REGIMENTAL HISTORY. New Haven, Connecticut: 1866.

Delaware

1457. Wild, Frederick W. MEMOIRS AND HISTORY OF CAPTAIN F.W. ALEXANDER'S BALTIMORE BATTERY OF LIGHT ARTILLERY.... Baltimore, Maryland: 1912.

1458. Murphey, Thomas G. FOUR YEARS IN THE WAR. THE HISTORY OF THE FIRST REGIMENT OF DELAWARE VETERAN VOLUNTEERS, CONTAINING AN ACCOUNT OF MARCHES, BATTLES, INCIDENTS, PROMOTIONS. Philadelphia, 1866.

1459. Seville, William P. HISTORY OF THE FIRST REGIMENT, DELAWARE VOLUNTEERS.... Wilmington, Delaware: 1884.

Illinois

1460. Kimbell, Charles B. HISTORY OF BATTERY "A" FIRST ILLINOIS LIGHT ARTILLERY VOLUNTEERS. Chicago, 1899.

1461. HISTORY OF THE ORGANIZATION, MARCHES, CAMPINGS, GENERAL SERVICES AND FINAL MUSTER OUT OF BATTERY M, FIRST REGIMENT ILLINOIS LIGHT ARTILLERY.... Princeton, Illinois: 1892.

1462. Shober, Charles. UNITED STATES MILITARY RECORD OF BATTERY G, 2nd ILLINOIS LIGHT ARTILLERY. Chicago, 1864.

1463. Brown, Thaddeus, Samuel J. Murphy, and William G. Putney. BEHIND THE GUNS: THE HISTORY OF BATTERY I, 2nd REGIMENT ILLINOIS LIGHT ARTILLERY. Clyde C. Walton, editor. Carbondale, Illinois: Southern Illinois University Press, 1965.

1464. Fletcher, Samuel H. THE HISTORY OF COMPANY A, SECOND CAVALRY. Chicago, 1912.

1465. Avery, Phineas O. HISTORY OF THE FOURTH ILLINOIS CAVALRY REGIMENT. Humboldt, Nebraska: 1903.

1466. Hard, Abner. HISTORY OF THE EIGHTH CAVALRY REGIMENT, ILLINOIS VOLUNTEERS, DURING THE GREAT REBELLION. Aurora, Illinois: 1868.

1467. Davenport, Edward A., editor. HISTORY OF THE NINTH REGIMENT ILLINOIS CAVALRY VOLUNTEERS. Chicago, 1888.

1468. Behlendorf, Frederick. THE HISTORY OF THE THIRTEENTH ILLINOIS CAVALRY REGIMENT OF VOLUNTEERS. Grand Rapids, Michigan: 1888.

1469. Sanford, Washington L. HISTORY OF THE FOURTEENTH ILLINOIS CAVALRY AND THE BRIGADES TO WHICH IT BELONGED. Chicago, 1898.

1470. Ambrose, Daniel L. HISTORY OF THE SEVENTH REGIMENT ILLINOIS VOLUNTEER INFANTRY.... Springfield, Illinois: 1868.

1471. Morrison, Marion. A HISTORY OF THE NINTH REGIMENT, ILLINOIS VOLUNTEER INFANTRY. Monmouth, Illinois: 1864.

1472. MILITARY HISTORY AND REMINISCENCES OF THE THIRTEENTH REGIMENT OF ILLINOIS VOLUNTEER INFANTRY IN THE CIVIL WAR IN THE UNITED STATES, 1861-1865. Prepared by the committee. Chicago, 1892.

1473. Dugan, James. HISTORY OF HURLBUT'S FIGHTING FOURTH DIVISION; AND ESPECIALLY THE MARCHES, TOILS, PRIVATIONS, ADVENTURES, SKIRMISHES AND BATTLES OF THE FOURTEENTH ILLINOIS INFANTRY. Cincinnati, 1863.

1474. Urban, William. "Monmouth College in the Civil War." JISHS, 71 [1978]: 13-21. [Company F, 17th Illinois]

1475. Pitkin, William A. "Michael K. Lawler's Ordeal With the 18th Illinois." JISHS, 58 [1965]: 357-377.

1476. Haynie, James H. THE NINETEENTH ILLINOIS: A MEMOIR OF A REGIMENT OF VOLUNTEER INFANTRY FAMOUS IN THE CIVIL WAR.... Chicago, 1912.

1477. Allendorfer, Frederick von. "The Western Irish Brigade [23rd Illinois Infantry Regiment]." IRISH SWORD, 2 [1955]: 177-183.

1478. Smith, Harold F. "Mulligan and the Irish Brigade." JISHS, 56 [1963]: 164-176. [23rd Illinois]

1479. Wagner, William. HISTORY OF THE 24TH ILLINOIS VOLUNTEER INFANTRY REGIMENT. Chicago, 1911.

1480. Schmitt, William A. HISTORY OF THE TWENTY-SEVENTH ILLINOIS VOLUNTEERS. Winchester, Illinois: 1892.

1481. McDonald, Granville B. A HISTORY OF THE 30TH ILLINOIS VOLUNTEER REGIMENT OF INFANTRY. Sparta, Illinois: 1916.

1482. Morris, William S. HISTORY OF THE 31ST REGIMENT OF VOLUNTEERS.... Evansville, Indiana: 1902.

1483. Ripley, Peter C. "A Period of Discontent: The 31st Illinois in Tennessee." TENN HIS Q, 29 [1970]: 49-61.

1484. Way, Virgil G. HISTORY OF THE THIRTY-THIRD REGIMENT ILLINOIS VETERAN VOLUNTEER INFANTRY IN THE CIVIL WAR, 22nd AUGUST, 1861, TO 7th DECEMBER, 1865. Gibson City, Illinois: 1902.

1485. Payne, Edwin W. HISTORY OF THE THIRTY-FOURTH REGIMENT OF ILLINOIS VOLUNTEER INFANTRY. Clinton, Iowa: 1903.

1486. Bennett, Lyman G. HISTORY OF THE THIRTY-SIXTH REGIMENT ILLINOIS VOLUNTEERS DURING THE WAR OF THE REBELLION. Aurora, Illinois: 1876.

1487. Clark, Charles M. THE HISTORY OF THE THIRTY-NINTH REGIMENT ILLINOIS VOLUNTEER VETERAN INFANTRY.... Chicago, 1889.

1488. Hart, Ephraim J. HISTORY OF THE FORTIETH ILLINOIS INFANTRY. Cincinnati, Ohio: 1864.

1489. COMPLETE HISTORY OF THE 46TH ILLINOIS VETERAN VOLUNTEER INFANTRY ... CONTAINING A FULL AND AUTHENTIC ACCOUNT OF THE PARTICIPATION OF THE REGIMENT IN THE BATTLES, SIEGES, SKIRMISHES, AND EXPEDITIONS.... Freeport, Illinois: 1866.

1490. Jones, Thomas B. COMPLETE HISTORY OF THE 46TH REGIMENT, ILLINOIS VOLUNTEER INFANTRY, A FULL AND AUTHENTIC ACCOUNT OF THE ... REGIMENT.... Freeport, Illinois: 1907.

1491. Bryner, Byron C. BUGLE ECHOES: THE STORY OF THE ILLINOIS 47th .... Springfield, Illinois: 1905.

1492. Burdette, Robert J. THE DRUMS OF THE 47th. Indianapolis, 1914.

1493. Hubert, Charles F. HISTORY OF THE FIFTIETH REGIMENT, ILLINOIS VOLUNTEER INFANTRY.... Kansas City, Missouri: 1894.

1494. Eisenschiml, Otto. "The 55th Illinois at Shiloh." JISHS, 56 [1963]: 193-211.

1495. THE STORY OF THE FIFTY-FIFTH ILLINOIS VOLUNTEER INFANTRY IN THE CIVIL WAR, 1861-1865. Written by a committee of veterans. Clinton, Massachusetts: 1887.

1496. Cluett, William W. HISTORY OF THE 57TH REGIMENT, ILLINOIS VOLUNTEER INFANTRY.... Princeton, Illinois: 1886.

1497. Lathrop, David. THE HISTORY OF THE FIFTY-NINTH REGIMENT ILLINOIS VOLUNTEERS, OR A THREE YEARS' CAMPAIGN THROUGH MISSOURI, ARKANSAS, MISSISSIPPI, TENNESSEE AND KENTUCKY.... Indianapolis, Indiana: 1865.

1498. Herr, George W. EPISODES OF THE CIVIL WAR, NINE CAMPAIGNS IN NINE STATES ... IN WHICH IS COMPRISED THE HISTORY OF THE FIFTY-NINTH REGIMENT ILLINOIS VETERAN VOLUNTEER INFANTRY.... San Francisco, California: 1890.

1499. Barker, Lorenzo A. MILITARY HISTORY OF COMPANY D, 66TH ILLINOIS, BIRGE's WESTERN SHARPSHOOTERS. Read City, Michigan: 1905.

1500. A HISTORY OF THE SEVENTY-THIRD REGIMENT OF ILLINOIS INFANTRY VOLUNTEERS, ITS SERVICES AND EXPERIENCES IN CAMP, ON THE MARCH.... Springfield, Illinois: 1890.

1501. Swift, Lester L. "The Preacher Regiment at Chickamauga and Missionary Ridge." LIN HER, 72 [1970]: 51-60. [73rd Illinois]

1502. ———."Tribulations of the Rev. Col. Jaquess and the Preacher Regiment: A New Lincoln Note Discovered." LIN HER, 69 [1967]: 165-177. [73rd Illinois]

1503. Dodge, William S. A WAIF OF THE WAR: OR, THE HISTORY OF THE SEVENTY-FIFTH ILLINOIS INFANTRY.... Chicago, 1866.

1504. Bentley, William H. HISTORY OF THE 77th ILLINOIS VOLUNTEER INFANTRY.... Peoria , Illinois: 1883.

1505. Simmons, Louis A. THE HISTORY OF THE 84TH REGIMENT ILLINOIS VOLUNTEERS. Macomb, Illinois: 1866.

1506. Aten, Henry J. HISTORY OF THE EIGHTY-FIFTH REGIMENT, ILLINOIS VOLUNTEER INFANTRY. Hiawatha, Kansas: 1901.

1507. Kinnear, John R. HISTORY OF THE EIGHTY-SIXTH REGIMENT, ILLINOIS VOLUNTEER INFANTRY.... Chicago, 1866.

1508. Beverly, James M. A HISTORY OF THE NINETY-FIRST REGIMENT, ILLINOIS VOLUNTEER INFANTRY.... White Hall, Illinois: 1913.

1509. NINETY-SECOND ILLINOIS VOLUNTEERS. Freeport, Illinois: 1875.

1510. Trimble, Harvey M. HISTORY OF THE NINETY-THIRD REGIMENT, ILLINOIS VOLUNTEER INFANTRY.... Chicago, 1898.

1511. Wood, Wales W. A HISTORY OF THE NINETY-FIFTH REGIMENT, ILLINOIS INFANTRY VOLUNTEERS.... Chicago, 1865.

1512. Partridge, Charles A. A HISTORY OF THE NINETY-SIXTH REGIMENT, ILLINOIS VOLUNTEER INFANTRY.... Chicago, 1887.

1513. Fleharty, Stephen F. OUR REGIMENT. A HISTORY OF THE 102ND ILLINOIS INFANTRY VOLUNTEERS, WITH SKETCHES OF THE ATLANTA CAMPAIGN, THE GEORGIA RAID, AND THE CAMPAIGN OF THE CAROLINAS. Chicago, 1865.

1514. REMINISCENCES OF THE CIVIL WAR FROM DIARIES OF MEMBERS OF THE 103RD ILLINOIS VOLUNTEER INFANTRY. Compiled by the committee. Chicago, 1904.

1515. Calkins, William W. THE HISTORY OF THE ONE HUNDRED AND FOURTH REGIMENT OF ILLINOIS VOLUNTEER INFANTRY. Chicago, 1896.

1516. Parks, George E. "One Story of the 109th Illinois Volunteer Infantry Regiment." JISHS, 56 [1963]: 282-297.

1517. Thompson, Bradford F. HISTORY OF THE 112TH REGIMENT OF ILLINOIS VOLUNTEER INFANTRY. Toulon, Illinois: 1885.

1518. Royse, Isaac H.C. HISTORY OF THE 115TH REGIMENT, ILLINOIS VOLUNTEER INFANTRY. Terre Haute, Indiana: 1900.

1519. Howard, Richard L. HISTORY OF THE 124TH REGIMENT ILLINOIS INFANTRY VOLUNTEERS, OTHERWISE KNOWN AS THE "HUNDRED AND TWO DOZEN,".... Springfield, Illinois: 1880.

1520. Rogers, Robert M. THE 125TH REGIMENT ILLINOIS VOLUNTEER INFANTRY.... Champaign, Illinois: 1882.

1521. Grunert, William. HISTORY OF THE ONE HUNDRED AND TWENTY-NINTH ILLINOIS VOLUNTEER INFANTRY. Winchester, Illinois: 1866.

Indiana

1522. Rowell, John. YANKEE ARTILLERYMEN THROUGH THE CIVIL WAR WITH ELI LILLY'S INDIANA BATTERY. Knoxville: University of Tennessee Press, 1975.

1523. Morgan, Otho H. HISTORY OF THE 7TH INDEPENDENT BATTERY OF INDIANA LIGHT ARTILLERY. Bedford, Indiana: 1898.

1524. Otto, John. HISTORY OF THE 11TH INDIANA BATTERY, CONNECTED WITH AN OUTLINE HISTORY OF THE ARMY OF THE CUMBERLAND.... Fort Wayne, 1894.

1525. Pickerill, William N. HISTORY OF THE THIRD INDIANA CAVALRY. Indianapolis, 1906.

1526. Cogley, Thomas W. HISTORY OF THE SEVENTH INDIANA CAVALRY VOLUNTEERS, AND THE EXPEDITIONS, CAMPAIGNS, RAIDS, MARCHES, AND BATTLES OF THE ARMIES WITH WHICH IT WAS CONNECTED.... LaPorte, Indiana: 1876.

1527. Briant, Charles C. HISTORY OF THE SIXTH REGIMENT INDIANA VOLUNTEER INFANTRY.... Indianapolis, 1891.

1528. Grayson, Andrew J. "THE SPIRIT OF 1861." HISTORY OF THE SIXTH INDIANA REGIMENT IN THE THREE MONTHS' CAMPAIGN IN WESTERN VIRGINIA.... Madison, Virginia: 1875.

1529. Kemper, William H. THE SEVENTH REGIMENT INDIANA VOLUNTEERS, THREE MONTHS ENLISTMENT. Muncie, Indiana: 1903.

1530. Shaw, James B. HISTORY OF THE TENTH REGIMENT INDIANA VOLUNTEER INFANTRY. Lafayette, Indiana: 1912.

1531. Gage, Moses D. FROM VICKSBURG TO RALEIGH, OR, A COMPLETE HISTORY OF THE TWELFTH REGIMENT INDIANA VOLUNTEER INFANTRY, AND THE CAMPAIGNS OF SHERMAN AND GRANT.... Chicago, 1865.

1532. Landon, William D. "Fourteenth Indiana Regiment: Letters to the VINCENNES WESTERN SUN." IND MAG HIS, 29 [1933]: 350-371; 30 [1934]: 275-298; 33 [1937]: 328-348; 34 [1938]: 71-98; 35 [1939]: 76-94.

1533. Fulfer, Richard J. A HISTORY OF THE TRIALS AND HARDSHIPS OF THE TWENTY-FOURTH INDIANA VOLUNTEER INFANTRY. Indianapolis, 1913.

1534. Brown, Edmund R. THE TWENTY-SEVENTH INDIANA VOLUNTEER INFANTRY IN THE WAR OF THE REBELLION.... Monticello, Indiana: 1899.

1535. Smith, John T. A HISTORY OF THE THIRTY-FIRST REGIMENT OF INDIANA VOLUNTEER INFANTRY IN THE WAR OF THE REBELLION. Cincinnati, 1900.

1536. Barnett, James. "Willich's Thirty-Second Indiana Volunteers." CIN HIS SOC BULL, 37 [1979]: 48-70.

1537. McBride, John R. HISTORY OF THIRTY-THIRD INDIANA VETERAN VOLUNTEER INFANTRY DURING THE FOUR YEARS OF CIVIL WAR ... AND INCIDENTALLY OF COL. JOHN COBURN'S SECOND BRIGADE, THIRD DIVISION, TWENTIETH ARMY CORPS.... Indianapolis, 1900.

1538. Fussell, J.L. HISTORY OF 34TH REGIMENT INDIANA VETERAN VOLUNTEER INFANTRY, "MORTON RIFLES." New Castle, Indiana: 1891.

1539. Grose, William. THE STORY OF THE MARCHES, BATTLES AND INCIDENTS OF THE 36TH REGIMENT INDIANA VOLUNTEER INFANTRY. New Castle, Indiana, 1891.

1540. Puntenney, George H. HISTORY OF THE THIRTY-SEVENTH REGIMENT OF INDIANA INFANTRY VOLUNTEERS. Rushville, Indiana, 1896.

1541. Funk, Arville L. "A Hoosier Regiment in Alabama." ALA HIS Q, 27 [1966]: 91-94. [38th Indiana]

1542. ———. "A Hoosier Regiment at Chattanooga." TENN HIS Q, 22 [1963]: 280-287. [38th Indiana]

1543. ———. "A Hoosier Regiment in Georgia, 1864." GA HIS Q, 48 [1964]: 104-109. [38th Indiana]

1544. Perry, Henry F. HISTORY OF THE THIRTY-EIGHTH REGIMENT INDIANA VOLUNTEER INFANTRY.... Palo Alto, California: 1906.

1545. Horrall, Spillard F. HISTORY OF THE FORTY-SECOND INDIANA VOLUNTEER INFANTRY. Chicago, 1892.

1546. Rerick, John H. THE FORTY-FOURTH INDIANA VOLUNTEER INFANTRY ... AND A PERSONAL RECORD OF ITS MEMBERS. Lagrange, Indiana: 1880.

1547. HISTORY OF THE FORTY-SIXTH REGIMENT INDIANA VOLUNTEER INFANTRY .... Compiled by the committee. Logansport, Indiana: 1888.

1548. Hartpence, William R. HISTORY OF THE FIFTY-FIRST INDIANA VETERAN VOLUNTEER INFANTRY. A NARRATIVE OF ITS ORGANIZATION, MARCHES, BATTLES AND OTHER EXPERIENCES.... Cincinnati, 1894.

1549. Kerwood, Asbury L. ANNALS OF THE FIFTY-SEVENTH REGIMENT INDIANA VOLUNTEERS. Dayton, Ohio: 1868.

1550. Hight, John J. HISTORY OF THE FIFTY-EIGHTH REGIMENT OF INDIANA VOLUNTEER INFANTRY ... FROM THE MANUSCRIPT PREPARED BY THE LATE CHAPLAIN JOHN J. HIGHT.... Princeton, Indiana: 1895.

1551. Scott, Reuben B. THE HISTORY OF THE 67TH REGIMENT INDIANA INFANTRY VOLUNTEERS. Bedford, Indiana: 1892.

1552. High, Edwin W. HISTORY OF THE SIXTY-EIGHTH REGIMENT, INDIANA VOLUNTEER INFANTRY.... Metamora, Indiana [?]: 1902.

1553. Mauzy, James H. HISTORICAL SKETCH OF THE SIXTY-EIGHTH REGIMENT INDIANA VOLUNTEERS, ITS COMMANDERS, OFFICERS, AND MEN.... Rushville, Indiana: 1887.

1554. Merrill, Samuel. THE SEVENTIETH INDIANA VOLUNTEER INFANTRY IN THE WAR OF THE REBELLION. Indianapolis, 1900.

1555. McGee, Benjamin F. HISTORY OF THE 72D INDIANA VOLUNTEER INFANTRY OF THE MOUNTED LIGHTNING BRIGADE.... Lafayette, Indiana: 1882.

1556. HISTORY OF THE SEVENTY-THIRD INDIANA VOLUNTEERS IN THE WAR OF 1861-1865. By the committee. Washington, D.C.: 1909.

1557. Floyd, David B. HISTORY OF THE SEVENTY-FIFTH REGIMENT OF INDIANA INFANTRY VOLUNTEERS, ITS ORGANIZATION, CAMPAIGNS, AND BATTLES. Philadelphia, 1893.

1558. HISTORY OF THE SEVENTY-NINTH REGIMENT INDIANA VOLUNTEER INFANTRY IN THE CIVIL WAR.... Indianapolis, 1899.

1559. Morris, George W. HISTORY OF THE EIGHTY-FIRST REGIMENT INDIANA VOLUNTEER INFANTRY IN THE GREAT WAR OF THE REBELLION.... Louisville, Kentucky: 1901.

1560. Hunter, Alfred G. HISTORY OF THE EIGHTY-SECOND INDIANA VOLUNTEER INFANTRY, ITS ORGANIZATION, CAMPAIGNS AND BATTLES.... Indianapolis, 1893.

1561. Grecian, Joseph. HISTORY OF THE EIGHTY-THIRD REGIMENT, INDIANA VOLUNTEER INFANTRY. FOR THREE YEARS WITH SHERMAN.... Cincinnati, 1865.

1562. Brant, Jefferson E. HISTORY OF THE EIGHTY-FIFTH INDIANA VOLUNTEER INFANTRY, ITS ORGANIZATION, CAMPAIGNS AND BATTLES. Bloomington, 1902.

1563. Barnes, James A. THE EIGHTY-SIXTH REGIMENT, INDIANA VOLUNTEER INFANTRY. A NARRATIVE OF ITS SERVICES IN THE CIVIL WAR OF 1861-1865. Written for the committee. Crawfordsville, Indiana: 1895.

1564. HISTORY OF THE EIGHTY-EIGHTH INDIANA VOLUNTEER INFANTRY. Fort Wayne, 1895.

1565. Craven, Hervey. A BRIEF HISTORY OF THE 89TH INDIANA VOLUNTEER INFANTRY. Wabash, Indiana: 1899.

1566. Lucas, Daniel R. HISTORY OF THE 99TH INDIANA INFANTRY, CONTAINING A DIARY OF MARCHES, INCIDENTS, BIOGRAPHY OF OFFICERS AND COMPLETE ROLLS. Lafayette, Indiana: 1865.

1567. Sherlock, Eli J. MEMORABILIA OF THE MARCHES AND BATTLES IN WHICH THE ONE HUNDREDTH REGIMENT OF INDIANA INFANTRY VOLUNTEERS TOOK AN ACTIVE PART.... Kansas City, Missouri: 1896.

Iowa

1568. Lord, Francis A. "Iowa Brigades in the Civil War." ANN IOWA, 39 [1968]: 275-281.

1569. Stuart, Addison A. IOWA COLONELS AND REGIMENTS: BEING A HISTORY OF IOWA REGIMENTS IN THE WAR OF THE REBELLION.... Des Moines, 1865. Reprint.

1570. Lothrop, Charles H. A HISTORY OF THE FIRST REGIMENT IOWA CAVALRY VETERAN VOLUNTEERS.... Lyons, Iowa: 1890.

1571. Pierce, Lyman B. HISTORY OF THE SECOND IOWA CAVALRY: CONTAINING A DETAILED ACCOUNT OF ITS ORGANIZATION, MARCHES, AND THE BATTLES IN WHICH IT HAS PARTICIPATED.... Burlington, Iowa: 1865.

1572. Scott, William F. THE STORY OF A CAVALRY REGIMENT. THE CAREER OF THE FOURTH IOWA VETERAN VOLUNTEER.... New York, 1893.

1573. Sloan, William D. "Iowa Cavalry-Sixth Regiment." CWH, 3 [1957]: 189-198.

1574. Mead, Homer. THE EIGHTH IOWA CAVALRY IN THE CIVIL WAR. Carthage, Illinois: n.p., 1925.

1575. Martin, Richard D. "First Regiment Iowa Volunteers." PALIMP, 46 [1965]: 1-59.

1576. Ware, Eugene F. THE LYON CAMPAIGN IN MISSOURI. BEING A HISTORY OF THE FIRST IOWA INFANTRY AND OF THE CAUSES WHICH LED UP TO ITS ORGANIZATION. Topeka, Kansas: 1907.

1577. Bell, John T. TRAMPS AND TRIUMPHS OF THE SECOND IOWA INFANTRY. Omaha, Nebraska, 1886.

1578. Thompson, Seymour D. RECOLLECTIONS WITH THE THIRD IOWA REGIMENT. Cincinnati, 1864.

1579. Wright, Henry H. A HISTORY OF THE SIXTH IOWA INFANTRY. Iowa City: State Historical Society of Iowa, 1923.

1580. Carpenter, C.C. and George W. Crissley. "Seventh Iowa Volunteers in the Civil War...." ANN IOWA, 34 [1957-1959]: 101-111.

1581. Smith, Henry I. HISTORY OF THE SEVENTH IOWA VETERAN VOLUNTEER INFANTRY DURING THE CIVIL WAR. Mason City, Iowa: 1903.

1582. Fultz, William S. "A History of Company D, Eleventh Iowa Infantry, 1861-1865." Mildred Throne, editor. IOWA J HIS, 55 [1957]: 35-90.

1583. Reed, David W. CAMPAIGNS AND BATTLES OF THE TWELFTH REGIMENT IOWA VETERAN VOLUNTEER INFANTRY.... Evanston, Illinois: 1903.

1584. Rood, L.H. HISTORY OF COMPANY "A" THIRTEENTH IOWA VETERAN INFANTRY FROM SEPTEMBER 12, 1861--JULY 21, 1865. Cedar Rapids, Iowa: 1889.

1585. Wieneke, Henry J. "Iowa Troops in Dakota Territory, 1861-1864." Mildred Throne, editor. IOWA J HIS, 57 [1959]: 97-190.

1586. Belknap, William W. HISTORY OF THE FIFTEENTH REGIMENT, IOWA VETERAN VOLUNTEER INFANTRY.... Keokuk, Iowa: 1887.

1587. Anderson, Donald M. "The Adventures of the Nineteenth Iowa." PALIMP, 58 [1977]: 162-173.

1588. Dungan, J. Irvine. HISTORY OF THE NINETEENTH IOWA VOLUNTEER INFANTRY. Davenport, Iowa: 1865.

1589. Crooke, George, compiler. THE TWENTY-FIRST REGIMENT OF IOWA VOLUNTEER INFANTRY: A NARRATIVE OF ITS EXPERIENCE IN ACTIVE SERVICE. Milwaukee, 1891.

1590. Jones, Samuel C. REMINISCENCES OF THE TWENTY-SECOND IOWA VOLUNTEER INFANTRY ... FROM THE DIARY OF LIEUTENANT S.C. JONES OF COMPANY A. Iowa City, 1907.

1591. Blake, Ephraim. A SUCCINCT HISTORY OF THE 28TH IOWA VOLUNTEER INFANTRY. Belle Plain, Iowa: 1896.

1592. Simmons, J.P. HISTORY OF THE TWENTY-EIGHTH IOWA VOLUNTEER INFANTRY. Washington, Iowa: 1865.

1593. Fowler, James A. HISTORY OF THE THIRTIETH IOWA VOLUNTEER INFANTRY. Mediapolis, Iowa: 1908.

1594. Scott, John. STORY OF THE THIRTY-SECOND IOWA INFANTRY VOLUNTEERS. Nevada, Iowa: 1896.

1595. Sperry, Andrew F. HISTORY OF THE 33RD IOWA INFANTRY VOLUNTEER REGIMENT, 1863-1866. Des Moines, 1866.

1596. Clark, James S. THE THIRTY-FOURTH IOWA REGIMENT, BRIEF HISTORY. Des Moines, 1892.

Kansas

1597. Gardner, Theodore. "The First Kansas Battery, An Historic Sketch ...." KAN HIS SOC TRAN, 14 [1918]: 235-282.

1598. Starr, Stephen Z. JENNISON'S JAYHAWKERS: A CIVIL WAR CAVALRY REGIMENT AND ITS COMMANDERS. Baton Rouge: Louisiana State University Press, 1973. [7th Kansas Cavalry]

1599. Greene, Albert R. "Campaigning in the Army of the Frontier." KAN HIS SOC TRAN, 14 [1918]: 283-310. [9th Kansas Cavalry]

1600. Palmer, Henry E. "Company A, Eleventh Kansas Regiment." KAN HIS SOC TRAN, 9 [1906]: 431-443. [11th Kansas Cavalry]

Kentucky

1601. Tarrant, Eastham. THE WILD RIDERS OF THE FIRST KENTUCKY CAVALRY. A HISTORY OF THE REGIMENT IN THE GREAT WAR OF THE REBELLION, 1861-1865. Louisville, 1895.

1602. Wright, Thomas J. HISTORY OF THE EIGHTH REGIMENT KENTUCKY VOLUNTEER INFANTRY DURING ITS THREE YEARS CAMPAIGNS ... WITH MUCH OF THE HISTORY OF THE OLD RELIABLE THIRD BRIGADE.... St. Joseph, Missouri: 1880.

Maine

1603. MAINE BUGLE. 5 v. Rockland, Maine: 1894-1898.

1604. Whitman, William E.S. and Charles H. True. MAINE IN THE WAR FOR THE UNION: A HISTORY OF THE PART BORNE BY MAINE TROOPS IN THE SUPPRESSION OF THE AMERICAN REBELLION. Lewiston, Maine: 1865.

1605. Coates, Earl J. "The Bloody First Maine." CWTI, 11 [4] [1972]: 36-42. [1st Maine Heavy Artillery]

1606. Shaw, Horace H. THE FIRST MAINE HEAVY ARTILLERY, 1862-1865: A HISTORY OF ITS PART AND PLACE IN THE WAR FOR THE UNION.... Portland, 1903.

1607. HISTORY OF THE FOURTH MAINE BATTERY, LIGHT ARTILLERY, IN THE CIVIL WAR ... FROM DIARIES OF ITS MEMBERS AND OTHER SOURCES .... Augusta, Maine: 1905.

1608. Twitchell, Albert S. HISTORY OF THE SEVENTH MAINE LIGHT BATTERY ... PERSONAL SKETCHES OF A LARGE NUMBER OF MEMBERS.... Boston, 1892.

1609. Merrill, Samuel H. THE CAMPAIGNS OF THE FIRST MAINE AND FIRST DISTRICT OF COLUMBIA CAVALRY. Portland, 1866.

1610. Tobie, Edward P. HISTORY OF THE FIRST MAINE CAVALRY, 1861-1865. Boston, 1887.

1611. Gould, John M. HISTORY OF THE FIRST, TENTH, TWENTY-NINTH MAINE REGIMENTS ... WITH THE HISTORY OF THE TENTH MAINE BATTALION. Portland, 1871.

1612. Bicknell, George W. HISTORY OF THE FIFTH REGIMENT MAINE VOLUNTEERS, COMPRISING BRIEF DESCRIPTIONS OF ITS MARCHES, ENGAGEMENTS, AND GENERAL SERVICES.... Portland, 1871.

1613. Brady, Robert, Jr. THE STORY OF ONE REGIMENT: THE ELEVENTH MAINE INFANTRY VOLUNTEERS IN THE WAR OF THE REBELLION. New York, 1896.

1614. Lufkin, Edwin B. HISTORY OF THE THIRTEENTH MAINE REGIMENT FROM ITS ORGANIZATION IN 1861 TO ITS MUSTER OUT IN 1865.... Bridgton, Maine: 1898.

1615. Shorey, Henry A. THE STORY OF THE MAINE FIFTEENTH: BEING A BRIEF NARRATIVE OF THE MORE IMPORTANT EVENTS IN THE HISTORY OF THE MORE IMPORTANT EVENTS IN THE HISTORY OF THE FIFTEENTH MAINE REGIMENT.... Bridgton, Maine: 1890.

1616. Houghton, Edwin B. THE CAMPAIGNS OF THE SEVENTEENTH MAINE. Portland, 1866.

1617. Smith, John D. THE HISTORY OF THE NINETEENTH MAINE REGIMENT OF MAINE VOLUNTEER INFANTRY, 1862-1865. Minneapolis, 1909.

1618. Pullen, John J. THE TWENTIETH MAINE: A VOLUNTEER REGIMENT IN THE CIVIL WAR. Philadelphia: Lippincott, 1957.

1619. Woodward, Joseph T. HISTORIC RECORD AND COMPLETE BIOGRAPHIC ROSTER, 21st MAINE VOLUNTEERS.... Augusta, Maine: 1907.

1620. Maddocks, Elden B. HISTORY OF THE TWENTY-SIXTH MAINE REGIMENT. Bangor, Maine: 1899.

1621. Pullen, John J. A SHOWER OF STARS: THE MEDAL OF HONOR AND THE 27th MAINE. Philadelphia: Lippincott, 1966.

1622. Stone, James M. THE HISTORY OF THE TWENTY-SEVENTH REGIMENT MAINE VOLUNTEER INFANTRY. n.p., 1895.

1623. Houston, Henry C. THE THIRTY-SECOND MAINE REGIMENT OF INFANTRY VOLUNTEERS: AN HISTORICAL SKETCH. Portland, 1903.

Maryland

1624. Camper, Charles. HISTORICAL RECORD OF THE FIRST REGIMENT MARYLAND INFANTRY, WITH AN APPENDIX CONTAINING A REGISTER OF OFFICERS AND ENLISTED MEN.... Washington, D.C.: 1871.

Massachusetts

1625. Bowen, James L. MASSACHUSETTS IN THE WAR, 1861-1865. Springfield, Massachusetts: 1889.

1626. Nason, George W. HISTORY AND COMPLETE ROSTER OF THE MASSACHUSETTS REGIMENTS, MINUTE MEN OF '61 WHO RESPONDED TO THE FIRST CALL OF PRESIDENT ABRAHAM LINCOLN, APRIL 15, 1861.... Boston, 1910.

1627. Morgan, William H. A NARRATIVE OF THE SERVICE OF COMPANY D, FIRST MASSACHUSETTS HEAVY ARTILLERY, IN THE WAR OF THE REBELLION, 1861 TO 1865.... Boston: 1907.

1628. Roe, Alfred S. HISTORY OF THE FIRST REGIMENT OF HEAVY ARTILLERY, MASSACHUSETTS VOLUNTEERS, FORMERLY THE FOURTEENTH REGIMENT OF INFANTRY.... Boston, 1917.

1629. Bennett, Andrew J. THE STORY OF THE FIRST MASSACHUSETTS LIGHT BATTERY, ATTACHED TO THE SIXTH ARMY CORPS.... Boston, 1886.

1630. Whitcomb, Caroline E. HISTORY OF THE SECOND MASSACHUSETTS BATTERY [NIMS' BATTERY] OF LIGHT ARTILLERY, 1861-1865.... Concord, New Hampshire: 1912.

1631. HISTORY OF THE FIFTH MASSACHUSETTS BATTERY.... Boston, 1902.

1632. Baker, Levi W. HISTORY OF THE NINTH MASSACHUSETTS BATTERY.... South Framingham, Massachusetts: 1888.

1633. Billings, John D. THE HISTORY OF THE TENTH MASSACHUSETTS BATTERY OF LIGHT ARTILLERY IN THE WAR OF THE REBELLION. FORMERLY OF THE THIRD CORPS, AND AFTERWARDS OF HANCOCK'S SECOND CORPS.... Boston, 1881.

1634. Crowninshield, Benjamin W. A HISTORY OF THE FIRST REGIMENT OF MASSACHUSETTS CAVALRY VOLUNTEERS. Boston, 1891.

1635. Starr, Stephen Z. "The First Massachusetts Volunteer Cavalry, 1861-1865: A Fresh Look." MASS HIS SOC PROC, 87 [1975]: 88-104.

1636. Ewer, James K. THE THIRD MASSACHUSETTS CAVALRY IN THE WAR FOR THE UNION. Maplewood, Massachusetts: 1903.

1637. Cudworth, Warren H. HISTORY OF THE FIRST REGIMENT [MASSACHUSETTS INFANTRY], FROM THE 25th OF MAY, 1861, TO THE 25th OF MAY, 1864.... Boston, 1866.

1638. Gordon, George H. BROOK FARM TO CEDAR MOUNTAIN, IN THE WAR OF THE GREAT REBELLION 1861-1862 ... A REVISION AND ENLARGEMENT ... OF PAPERS NUMBERED I, II, AND III, ENTITLED, "A HISTORY OF THE SECOND MASSACHUSETTS REGIMENT," AND THE "SECOND MASSACHUSETTS REGIMENT AND STONEWALL JACKSON." Boston, 1883.

1639. Quint, Alonzo H. THE RECORD OF THE SECOND MASSACHUSETTS INFANTRY, 1861-1865. Boston, 1867.

1640. Gammons, John G. THE THIRD MASSACHUSETTS REGIMENT VOLUNTEER MILITIA IN THE WAR OF THE REBELLION, 1861-1863. Providence, Rhode Island: 1906.

1641. Robinson, Frank T. HISTORY OF THE FIFTH REGIMENT, M.V.M. Boston, 1879.

1642. Roe, Alfred S. THE FIFTH REGIMENT MASSACHUSETTS VOLUNTEER INFANTRY IN ITS THREE TOURS OF DUTY, 1861, 1862-1863, 1864. Boston, 1911.

1643. Hanson, John W. HISTORICAL SKETCH OF THE OLD SIXTH REGIMENT OF MASSACHUSETTS VOLUNTEERS DURING ITS THREE CAMPAIGNS.... Boston, 1866.

1644. Watson, Benjamin F. ADDRESSES, REVIEWS AND EPISODES, CHIEFLY CONCERNING THE "OLD SIXTH" MASSACHUSETTS REGIMENT. New York, 1901.

1645. Hutchinson, Nelson V. HISTORY OF THE SEVENTH MASSACHUSETTS VOLUNTEER INFANTRY IN THE WAR OF THE REBELLION.... Taunton, Massachusetts: 1890.

1646. Macnamara, Daniel G. THE HISTORY OF THE NINTH REGIMENT, MASSACHUSETTS VOLUNTEER INFANTRY, SECOND BRIGADE, FIRST DIVISION, FIFTH ARMY CORPS, ARMY OF THE POTOMAC, JUNE, 1861-JUNE, 1864. Boston, 1899.

1647. Newell, Joseph K. "OURS." ANNALS OF THE 10TH REGIMENT, MASSACHUSETTS VOLUNTEERS.... Springfield, Massachusetts: 1875.

1648. Roe, Alfred S. THE TENTH REGIMENT, MASSACHUSETTS VOLUNTEER INFANTRY, 1861-1864, A WESTERN MASSACHUSETTS REGIMENT.... Springfield, Massachusetts: 1909.

1649. Hutchinson, Gustavus B. A NARRATIVE OF THE FORMATION AND SERVICES OF THE ELEVENTH MASSACHUSETTS VOLUNTEERS, FROM APRIL 15, 1861, TO JULY 14, 1865.... Boston, 1893.

1650. Cook, Benjamin F. HISTORY OF THE TWELFTH MASSACHUSETTS VOLUNTEERS [WEBSTER REGIMENT]. Boston, 1882.

1651. Davis, Charles E. THREE YEARS IN THE ARMY. THE STORY OF THE THIRTEENTH MASSACHUSETTS VOLUNTEERS FROM JULY 10, 1861 TO AUGUST 1, 1864. Boston, 1894.

1652. Ford, Andrew E. THE STORY OF THE FIFTEENTH REGIMENT MASSACHUSETTS VOLUNTEER INFANTRY IN THE CIVIL WAR, 1861-1864. Clinton, Massachusetts: 1896.

1653. Stowe, Jonathan P. "Life With the 15th Massachusetts." CWTI, 11 [5] [1971]: 4-11, 48-55.

1654. Kirwan, Thomas. MEMORIAL HISTORY OF THE SEVENTEENTH REGIMENT, MASSACHUSETTS VOLUNTEER INFANTRY IN THE CIVIL WAR.... Salem, Massachusetts: 1911.

1655. HISTORY OF THE NINETEENTH REGIMENT, MASSACHUSETTS VOLUNTEER INFANTRY.... By the committee. Salem, Massachusetts: 1906.

1656. Bruce, George A. THE TWENTIETH REGIMENT OF MASSACHUSETTS VOLUNTEER INFANTRY, 1861-1865. Boston, 1906.

1657. Walcott, Charles F. HISTORY OF THE TWENTY-FIRST REGIMENT, MASSACHUSETTS VOLUNTEERS, IN THE WAR FOR THE PRESERVATION OF THE UNION.... Boston, 1882.

1658. PARKER, John L. HENRY WILSON'S REGIMENT. HISTORY OF THE TWENTY-SECOND MASSACHUSETTS INFANTRY, THE SECOND COMPANY SHARPSHOOTERS AND THE THIRD LIGHT BATTERY.... Boston, 1887.

1659. Emmerton, James A. A RECORD OF THE TWENTY-THIRD REGIMENT MASSACHUSETTS VOLUNTEER INFANTRY.... Boston, 1886.

1660. Valentine, Herbert E. STORY OF COMPANY F, 23RD MASSACHUSETTS VOLUNTEERS, IN THE WAR FOR THE UNION.... Boston, 1896.

1661. Roe, Alfred S. THE TWENTY-FOURTH REGIMENT, MASSACHUSETTS VOLUNTEERS ..."NEW ENGLAND GUARD REGIMENT." Worcester, 1907.

1662. Denny, Joseph W. WEARING THE BLUE IN THE TWENTY-FIFTH MASSACHUSETTS VOLUNTEER INFANTRY, WITH BURNSIDE's COAST DIVISION, 18TH ARMY CORPS.... Worcester, 1879.

1663. Putnam, Samuel H. THE STORY OF COMPANY A , TWENTY-FIFTH REGIMENT MASSACHUSETTS VOLUNTEERS.... Worcester, 1886.

1664. Derby, William P. BEARING ARMS IN THE TWENTY-SEVENTH MASSACHUSETTS REGIMENT OF VOLUNTEER INFANTRY.... Boston, 1883.

1665. Osborne, William H. THE HISTORY OF THE TWENTY-NINTH REGIMENT OF MASSACHUSETTS VOLUNTEER INFANTRY.... Boston, 1877.

1666. Howe, Henry W. PASSAGES FROM THE LIFE OF HENRY WARREN HOWE, CONSISTING OF DIARY AND LETTERS WRITTEN DURING THE CIVIL WAR, 1861-1865. A CONDENSED HISTORY OF THE THIRTIETH MASSACHUSETTS REGIMENT.... Lowell, Massachusetts: 1899.

1667. Parker, Francis J. THE STORY OF THE THIRTY-SECOND REGIMENT, MASSACHUSETTS INFANTRY. WHENCE IT CAME: WHERE IT WENT: WHAT IT SAW, AND WHAT IT DID. Boston, 1880.

1668. Boies, Andrew J. RECORD OF THE THIRTY-THIRD MASSACHUSETTS VOLUNTEER INFANTRY FROM AUGUST, 1862, TO AUGUST, 1865. Fitchburg, Massachusetts: 1880.

1669. Underwood, Adin B. THE THREE YEARS' SERVICE OF THE THIRTY-THIRD MASSACHUSETTS INFANTRY REGIMENT.... Boston, 1880.

1670. Clark, William H. REMINISCENCES OF THE THIRTY-FOURTH MASSACHUSETTS VOLUNTEER INFANTRY. Holliston, Massachusetts: 1871.

1671. Lincoln, William S. LIFE WITH THE THIRTY-FOURTH MASSACHUSETTS INFANTRY IN THE WAR OF THE REBELLION. Worcester, 1879.

1672. HISTORY OF THE THIRTY-FIFTH REGIMENT MASSACHUSETTS VOLUNTEERS, 1862-1865. By the committee. Boston, 1884.

1673. HISTORY OF THE THIRTY-SIXTH REGIMENT MASSACHUSETTS VOLUNTEERS, 1862-1865. By the committee. Boston, 1884.

1674. Bowen, James L. HISTORY OF THE THIRTY-SEVENTH REGIMENT, MASSACHUSETTS VOLUNTEERS ... WITH A COMPREHENSIVE SKETCH OF THE DOINGS OF MASSACHUSETTS AS A STATE, AND OF THE PRINCIPAL CAMPAIGNS OF THE WAR. Holyoke, Massachusetts: 1884.

1675. Powers, George W. THE STORY OF THE THIRTY-EIGHTH REGIMENT OF MASSACHUSETTS VOLUNTEERS. Cambridge, Massachusetts: 1866.

1676. Roe, Alfred S. THE THIRTY-NINTH REGIMENT MASSACHUSETTS VOLUNTEERS, 1862-1865. Worcester, 1914.

1677. Bosson, Charles P. HISTORY OF THE FORTY-SECOND REGIMENT INFANTRY, MASSACHUSETTS VOLUNTEERS.... Boston, 1886.

1678. RECORD OF THE SERVICE OF THE FORTY-FOURTH MASSACHUSETTS VOLUNTEER MILITIA IN NORTH CAROLINA, AUGUST 1862 TO MAY 1863. Boston, 1887.

1679. Hubbard, Charles E. THE CAMPAIGN OF THE FORTY-FIFTH REGIMENT, MASSACHUSETTS VOLUNTEER MILITIA. "THE CADET REGIMENT." Boston, 1882.

1680. Mann, Albert W. HISTORY OF THE FORTY-FIFTH REGIMENT, MASSACHUSETTS VOLUNTEER MILITIA.... Boston, 1908.

1681. Plummer, Albert. HISTORY OF THE FORTY-EIGHTH REGIMENT, MASSACHUSETTS VOLUNTEER MILITIA.... Boston, 1907.

1682. Stevens, William B. HISTORY OF THE FIFTIETH REGIMENT, INFANTRY, MASSACHUSETTS VOLUNTEER MILITIA, IN THE LATE WAR OF THE RE-BELLION. Boston, 1907.

1683. Pierce, Charles F. HISTORY AND CAMP LIFE OF COMPANY C, FIFTY-FIRST REGIMENT, MASSACHUSETTS VOLUNTEER MILITIA, 1862-1863. Worcester, 1886.

1684. Moors, John F. HISTORY OF THE FIFTY-SECOND REGIMENT, MASSACHU-SETTS VOLUNTEERS. Boston, 1893.

1685. Wills, Henry A. THE FIFTY-THIRD REGIMENT MASSACHUSETTS VOLUN-TEERS. COMPRISING ALSO A HISTORY OF THE SIEGE OF PORT HUDSON. Fitchburg, Massachusetts: 1889.

1686. Emilio, Luis F. HISTORY OF THE FIFTY-FOURTH REGIMENT OF MASSA-CHUSETTS VOLUNTEER INFANTRY, 1863-1865. Boston, 1891.

1687. Fox, Charles B. RECORD OF THE SERVICE OF THE FIFTY-FIFTH REGI-MENT OF MASSACHUSETTS VOLUNTEER INFANTRY. Cambridge, 1868.

1688. Anderson, John. THE FIFTY-SEVENTH REGIMENT OF MASSACHUSETTS VOLUNTEERS IN THE WAR OF THE REBELLION. ARMY OF THE POTOMAC. Boston, 1896.

Michigan

1689. Belknap, Charles E. HISTORY OF THE MICHIGAN ORGANIZATIONS AT CHICKAMAUGA, CHATTANOOGA AND MISSIONARY RIDGE, 1863. Lansing. 1897.

1690. Williams, Frederick D. MICHIGAN SOLDIERS IN THE CIVIL WAR. Lansing: Michigan Historical Commission, 1960.

1691. Thatcher, Marshall P. A HUNDRED BATTLES IN THE WEST, ST. LOUIS TO ATLANTA, 1861-1865. THE SECOND MICHIGAN CAVALRY.... Detroit, 1884.

1692. Kidd, James H. PERSONAL RECOLLECTIONS OF A CAVALRYMAN WITH CUSTER'S MICHIGAN CAVALRY BRIGADE IN THE CIVIL WAR. Ionia, Michigan: 1908.

1693. Isham, Asa B. AN HISTORICAL SKETCH OF THE SEVENTH MICHIGAN VOL-UNTEER CAVALRY FROM ITS ORGANIZATION IN 1862, TO ITS MUSTER OUT, IN 1865. New York, 1893.

1694. Lee, William O. PERSONAL AND HISTORICAL SKETCHES AND FACIAL HISTORY OF AND BY MEMBERS OF THE SEVENTH REGIMENT MICHIGAN VOLUNTEER CAVALRY, 1862-1865. Detroit, 1902.

1695. Sligh, Charles R. HISTORY OF THE SERVICES OF THE FIRST REGIMENT MICHIGAN ENGINEERS AND MECHANICS, DURING THE WAR, 1861-1865. Grand Rapids, Michigan: White Printing, 1921.

1696. Isham, Frederic S. HISTORY OF THE DETROIT LIGHT GUARD: ITS RECORDS AND ACHIEVEMENTS. Detroit, 1896.

1697. Owen, Charles W. THE FIRST MICHIGAN INFANTRY.... Quincy, Michigan, 1903.

1698. Barrett, Orvey S. REMINISCENCES, INCIDENTS, BATTLES, MARCHES, AND CAMP LIFE OF THE OLD 4TH MICHIGAN INFANTRY IN WAR OF REBELLION, 1861 TO 1864. Detroit, 1888.

1699. Blackburn, George M. "A Michigan Regiment in the Palmetto State." SC HIS MAG, 68 [1967]: 154-164. [8th Michigan]

1700. Bennett, Charles W. HISTORICAL SKETCHES OF THE NINTH MICHIGAN INFANTRY ... FOUR YEARS IN CAMPAIGNING IN THE ARMY OF THE CUMBERLAND. Coldwater, Michigan: 1913.

1701. Hewes, Fletcher W. HISTORY OF THE FORMATION, MOVEMENTS, CAMPS, SCOUTS AND BATTLES OF THE TENTH REGIMENT, MICHIGAN VOLUNTEER INFANTRY. Detroit, 1864.

1702. Cutcheon, Byron M. THE STORY OF THE TWENTIETH MICHIGAN INFANTRY .... Lansing, 1904.

1703. Snook, John H. "Governor Wisner and the Twenty-Second Michigan Volunteer Infantry." MICH HIS, 31 [1947]: 10-20.

1704. Curtis, Orson B. HISTORY OF THE TWENTY-FOURTH MICHIGAN OF THE IRON BRIGADE KNOWN AS THE DETROIT AND WAYNE COUNTY REGIMENT. Detroit, 1891.

1705. Smith, Donald L. THE TWENTY-FOURTH MICHIGAN OF THE IRON BRIGADE. Harrisburg, Pennsylvania: Stackpole, 1962.

1706. Travis, Benjamin F. THE STORY OF THE TWENTY-FIFTH MICHIGAN. Kalamazoo, 1897.

Minnesota

1707. Carley, Kenneth. MINNESOTA IN THE CIVIL WAR. Minneapolis: Ross and Haines, 1961.

1708. Holcombe, Return K. HISTORY OF THE FIRST REGIMENT MINNESOTA VOLUNTEER INFANTRY. Stillwater, Minnesota: Easton and Masterman, 1916.

1709. Imholte, John Q. THE FIRST VOLUNTEERS: HISTORY OF THE FIRST MINNESOTA VOLUNTEER REGIMENT, 1861-1865. Minneapolis: Ross and Haines, 1963.

1710. Bishop, Judson W. THE STORY OF A REGIMENT, BEING A NARRATIVE OF THE SERVICE OF THE SECOND REGIMENT, MINNESOTA VETERAN VOLUNTEER INFANTRY IN THE CIVIL WAR.... St. Paul, 1890.

1711. Carley, Kenneth. "The Second Minnesota in the West." MINN HIS, 38 [1963]: 258-273.

1712. Rezneck, Samuel. "The Civil War Role, 1861-1863, of a Veteran New York Officer, Major John E. Wool [1784-1869]." NY HIS, 38 [1963]: 258-273. [2nd Minnesota]

1713. Simon, Donald J. "The Third Minnesota Regiment in Arkansas, 1863-1865." MINN HIS, 40 [1967]: 281-372.

1714. Brown, Alonzo L. HISTORY OF THE FOURTH REGIMENT OF MINNESOTA INFANTRY VOLUNTEERS DURING THE GREAT REBELLION, 1861-1865. St. Paul, 1892.

Missouri

1715. Petty, A.W.M. A HISTORY OF THE THIRD MISSOURI CAVALRY FROM ITS ORGANIZATION AT PALMYRA, MISSOURI, 1861, UP TO NOVEMBER SIXTH, 1864.... Little Rock, Arkansas: 1865.

1716. Waring, George E. WHIP AND SPUR [FOURTH MISSOURI CAVALRY]. Boston, 1875.

1717. Frost, M.O. REGIMENTAL HISTORY OF THE TENTH MISSOURI VOLUNTEER INFANTRY. Topeka, Kansas: 1892.

1718. Anders, Leslie. THE EIGHTEENTH MISSOURI, Indianapolis: Bobbs-Merrill, 1968.

1719. ———. "Missourians Who Marched Through Georgia." MO HIS R, 59 [1965]: 192-209. [18th Missouri]

1720. ———. THE TWENTY-FIRST MISSOURI: FROM HOME GUARD TO UNION REGIMENT. Westport, Connecticut: Greenwood, 1975.

1721. Neal, William A. AN ILLUSTRATED HISTORY OF THE MISSOURI ENGINEER AND THE 25th INFANTRY REGIMENTS, TOGETHER WITH A ROSTER OF BOTH REGIMENTS.... Chicago, 1889.

1722. Canan, Howard V. "The Missouri Paw Paw Militia of 1863-1864." MO HIS R, 62 [1968]: 431-448.

New Hampshire

1723. Cleveland, Mather. NEW HAMPSHIRE FIGHTS THE CIVIL WAR. London, New Hampshire: Privately printed, 1969.

1724. HISTORY OF THE FIRST NEW HAMPSHIRE BATTERY DURING THE WAR OF THE REBELLION. Manchester, 1878.

1725. Stanyan, John M. A HISTORY OF THE EIGHTH REGIMENT NEW HAMPSHIRE VOLUNTEERS, INCLUDING ITS SERVICE AS INFANTRY, SECOND NEW HAMPSHIRE CAVALRY.... Concord, 1892.

1726. Abbot, Stephen G. THE FIRST REGIMENT NEW HAMPSHIRE VOLUNTEERS IN THE GREAT REBELLION, CONTAINING THE STORY OF THE CAMPAIGN.... Keene, 1890.

1727. Haynes, Martin A. HISTORY OF THE SECOND REGIMENT NEW HAMPSHIRE VOLUNTEERS: ITS CAMPS, MARCHES AND BATTLES. Manchester, 1865.

1728. Eldredge, Daniel. THE THIRD NEW HAMPSHIRE AND ALL ABOUT IT. Boston, 1893.

1729. Child, William. A HISTORY OF THE FIFTH REGIMENT, NEW HAMPSHIRE VOLUNTEERS IN THE AMERICAN CIVIL WAR. Bristol, New Hampshire: 1893.

1730. Richards, Donald H. "The Fifth New Hampshire Volunteer [Light Infantry]." HIS NH, 28 [1973]: 241-261.

1731. Cadwell, Charles K. THE OLD SIXTH REGIMENT, ITS WAR RECORD, 1861-1865. New Haven, Connecticut: 1875.

1732. Jackson, Lyman. HISTORY OF THE SIXTH NEW HAMPSHIRE REGIMENT IN THE WAR FOR THE UNION. Concord, 1891.

1733. Little, Henry F. THE SEVENTH REGIMENT NEW HAMPSHIRE VOLUNTEERS IN THE WAR OF THE REBELLION. Concord, 1896.

1734. Lord, Edward O. HISTORY OF THE NINTH REGIMENT, NEW HAMPSHIRE VOLUNTEERS IN THE WAR OF THE REBELLION. Concord, 1895.

1735. Cogswell, Leander W. A HISTORY OF THE ELEVENTH NEW HAMPSHIRE REGIMENT, VOLUNTEER INFANTRY IN THE REBELLION WAR, 1861-1865. Concord, 1891.

1736. Bartlett, Asa W. HISTORY OF THE TWELFTH REGIMENT, NEW HAMPSHIRE VOLUNTEERS IN THE WAR OF THE REBELLION. Concord, 1897.

1737. Thompson, S.M. THIRTEENTH REGIMENT OF NEW HAMPSHIRE VOLUNTEER INFANTRY IN THE WAR OF THE REBELLION, 1861-1865. Boston, 1888.

1738. Buffrum, Francis H. A MEMORIAL OF THE GREAT REBELLION: BEING A HISTORY OF THE FOURTEENTH REGIMENT NEW HAMPSHIRE VOLUNTEERS .... Boston, 1892.

1739. McGregor, Charles. HISTORY OF THE FIFTEENTH REGIMENT, NEW HAMPSHIRE VOLUNTEERS, 1862-1863. Concord, 1900.

1740. Townsend, Luther. HISTORY OF THE SIXTEENTH REGIMENT, NEW HAMPSHIRE VOLUNTEERS. Washington, D.C.: 1897.

1741. Kent, Charles N. HISTORY OF THE SEVENTEENTH REGIMENT, NEW HAMPSHIRE VOLUNTEER INFANTRY, 1862-1863. Concord, 1898.

1742. Livermore, Thomas L. HISTORY OF THE EIGHTEENTH NEW HAMPSHIRE VOLUNTEERS, 1864-65. Boston, 1904.

New Jersey

1743. Hanifen, Michael. HISTORY OF BATTERY B, FIRST NEW JERSEY ARTILLERY. Ottawa, Illinois: 1905.

1744. Pyne, Henry R. THE HISTORY OF THE FIRST NEW JERSEY CAVALRY [SIXTEENTH REGIMENT, NEW JERSEY VOLUNTEERS]. Trenton, 1871.

1745. Risley, Clyde A. "3rd New Jersey Cavalry Regiment, 1864-1865." MIL COLL HIS, 9 [1957]: 44-46. [1st Regiment, U.S. Hussars]

1746. Baquet, Camille. HISTORY OF THE FIRST BRIGADE, NEW JERSEY VOLUNTEERS, FROM 1861 to 1865.... Trenton, 1910. New edition, 1961.

1747. Drake, James M. THE HISTORY OF THE NINTH NEW JERSEY VETERAN VOLUNTEERS. A RECORD OF ITS SERVICE FROM SEPTEMBER 13, 1861, TO JULY 12TH, 1865.... Elizabeth, New Jersey: 1889.

1748. Everts, Hermann. A COMPLETE AND COMPREHENSIVE HISTORY OF THE NINTH REGIMENT NEW JERSEY VOLUNTEER INFANTRY.... Newark, New Jersey: 1865.

1749. Marbaker, Thomas D. HISTORY OF THE ELEVENTH NEW JERSEY VOLUNTEERS, FROM ITS ORGANIZATION TO APPOMATTOX.... Trenton, 1898.

1750. Haines, William P. HISTORY OF THE MEN OF COMPANY F, WITH DESCRIPTION OF THE MARCHES AND BATTLES OF THE 12TH NEW JERSEY VOLUNTEERS.... Camden, New Jersey: 1897.

1751. Swords, Robert S. HISTORICAL SKETCH OF COMPANY "D," THIRTEENTH REGIMENT NEW JERSEY VOLUNTEERS.... New York, 1875.

1752. Toombs, Samuel. REMINISCENCES OF THE WAR, COMPRISING A DETAILED ACCOUNT OF THE EXPERIENCES OF THE THIRTEENTH REGIMENT NEW JERSEY VOLUNTEERS.... Orange, New Jersey: 1878.

1753. Terrill, John N. CAMPAIGNS OF THE FOURTEENTH REGIMENT NEW JERSEY VOLUNTEERS. New Brunswick, New Jersey: 1884.

1754. Campbell, Edward L. HISTORICAL SKETCH OF THE FIFTEENTH REGIMENT, NEW JERSEY VOLUNTEERS, FIRST BRIGADE, FIRST DIVISION, SIXTH CORPS. Trenton, 1880.

1755. Haines, Alanson A. HISTORY OF THE FIFTEENTH REGIMENT, NEW JERSEY VOLUNTEERS. New York, 1883.

New York

1756. Ames, Nelson. HISTORY OF BATTERY G, FIRST REGIMENT, NEW YORK LIGHT ARTILLERY. Marshalltown, Iowa: 1900.

1757. Remington, Cyrus K. A RECORD OF BATTERY I, FIRST NEW YORK LIGHT ARTILLERY. Buffalo, 1891.

1758. Roback, Henry. THE VETERAN VOLUNTEERS OF HERKIMER AND OTSEGO COUNTIES IN THE WAR OF THE REBELLION. [Second Heavy Artillery and other units.] Utica, New York: 1888.

1759. Kirk, Hyland C. HEAVY GUNS AND LIGHT: A HISTORY OF THE 4TH NEW YORK HEAVY ARTILLERY. New York, 1890.

1760. Murphy, George E., William F. Murphy, and James E. Murphy. "The Eighth New York Heavy Artillery." NIAG FRON, 45 [1963]: 69-91.

1761. Roe, Alfred S. THE NINTH NEW YORK HEAVY ARTILLERY. A HISTORY OF ITS ORGANIZATION.... Worcester, Massachusetts: 1899.

1762. Webb, Edward P. HISTORY OF THE 10TH REGULAR NEW YORK HEAVY ARTILLERY.... Watertown, New York: 1887.

1763. Shaw, Charles A. A HISTORY OF THE 14TH REGIMENT NEW YORK HEAVY ARTILLERY IN THE CIVIL WAR.... Mt. Kisco, New York: 1918.

1764. Smith. James E. A FAMOUS BATTERY AND ITS CAMPAIGNS, 1861-1864 [Fourth New York Independent Battery].... Washington, D.C.: 1892.

1765. Winter, Frank H. and Mitchell R. Sharpe. "Major Lion's Rocketeers: The New York Rocket Battalion." CWTI, 11 [9] [1973]: 10-15.

1766. Merrill, Julian W. RECORDS OF THE 24TH INDEPENDENT BATTERY, NEW YORK LIGHT ARTILLERY.... New York, 1870.

1767. Bowen, James R. REGIMENTAL HISTORY OF THE FIRST NEW YORK DRAGOONS [ORIGINALLY THE 130TH NEW YORK VOLUNTEER INFANTRY].... Battle Creek, Michigan: 1900.

1768. Beach, William H. THE FIRST NEW YORK [LINCOLN] CAVALRY FROM APRIL 19, 1861 TO JULY 7, 1865. New York, 1902.

1769. Stevenson, James H. "BOOTS AND SADDLES." A HISTORY OF THE FIRST VOLUNTEER CAVALRY OF THE WAR, KNOWN AS THE FIRST NEW YORK [LINCOLN] CAVALRY, AND ALSO AS THE SABRE REGIMENT.... Harrisburg, Pennsylvania: 1879.

1770. Glazier, Willard. THREE YEARS IN THE FEDERAL CAVALRY. [Second New York Cavalry] New York, 1874.

1771. Duganne, A.J.H. THE FIGHTING QUAKERS. A TRUE STORY OF THE WAR FOR OUR UNION. [Fourth New York Cavalry] New York, 1866.

1772. Beaudry, Louis N. HISTORIC RECORDS OF THE FIFTH NEW YORK CAVALRY, FIRST IRA HARRIS GUARD.... Albany, New York: 1868.

1773. Foster, Alonzo. REMINISCENCES AND RECORD OF THE 6TH NEW YORK VETERAN VOLUNTEER CAVALRY. Brooklyn, New York: 1892.

1774. Hall, Hillman A. HISTORY OF THE SIXTH NEW YORK CAVALRY [SECOND IRA HARRIS GUARD] SECOND BRIGADE--FIRST DIVISION--CAVALRY CORPS.... Worcester, Massachusetts: 1908.

1775. Norton, Henry. DEEDS OF DARING, OR, HISTORY OF THE EIGHTH NEW YORK VOLUNTEER CAVALRY.... Norwich, New York: 1889.

1776. Cheney, Newel. HISTORY OF THE NINTH REGIMENT, NEW YORK VOLUNTEER CAVALRY.... Poland Center, New York: 1901.

1777. Preston, Noble D. HISTORY OF THE TENTH REGIMENT OF CAVALRY NEW YORK STATE VOLUNTEERS.... New York, 1892.

1778. Smith, Thomas W. THE STORY OF A CAVALRY REGIMENT: "SCOTT'S 900" ELEVENTH NEW YORK CAVALRY, FROM THE ST. LAWRENCE RIVER TO THE GULF OF MEXICO.... Chicago, 1897.

1779. Norton, Chaucey S. "THE RED NECK TIES," OR, HISTORY OF THE FIFTEENTH NEW YORK VOLUNTEER CAVALRY.... Ithaca, New York: 1891.

1780. Hall, Henry. CAYUGA IN THE FIELD. A RECORD OF THE 19TH NEW YORK VOLUNTEERS, ALL THE BATTERIES OF THE 3D NEW YORK ARTILLERY, AND 75TH NEW YORK VOLUNTEERS.... Auburn, New York: 1873.

1781. Thomas, Howard. BOYS IN BLUE FROM THE ADIRONDACK FOOTHILLS.... Prospect, New York: Prospect Books, 1960. [14th, 26th, 34th, 97th, 117th, 121st, 146th, and 152nd regiments]

1782. Clark, Lewis H. MILITARY HISTORY OF WAYNE COUNTY, NEW YORK. THE COUNTY IN THE CIVIL WAR. Sodus, New York: 1883.

1783. Davenport, Alfred. CAMP AND FIELD LIFE OF THE FIFTH NEW YORK VOLUNTEER INFANTRY. [Duryee Zouaves] New York, 1879.

1784. Morris, Gouverneur. THE HISTORY OF A VOLUNTEER REGIMENT. BEING A SUCCINCT ACCOUNT OF ... THE SIXTH REGIMENT NEW YORK VOLUNTEER INFANTRY KNOWN AS WILSON ZOUAVES.... New York, 1891.

1785. Swinton, William. HISTORY OF THE SEVENTH REGIMENT, NATIONAL GUARD, STATE OF NEW YORK.... New York, 1870.

1786. Clark, Emmons. HISTORY OF THE SEVENTH REGIMENT OF NEW YORK, 1806-1889. 2 v. New York, 1890.

1787. Roehrenbeck, William J. THE REGIMENT THAT SAVED THE CAPITAL. [Seventh New York] New York: Yoseloff, 1961.

1788. Graham, Matthew J. THE NINTH REGIMENT, NEW YORK VOLUNTEERS [HAWKINS' ZOUAVES].... New York, 1900.

1789. Whitney, J.H. THE HAWKINS ZOUAVES: [NINTH NEW YORK VOLUNTEERS] THEIR BATTLES AND MARCHES. New York, 1866.

1790. Cowtan, Charles W. SERVICES OF THE TENTH NEW YORK VOLUNTEERS [NATIONAL ZOUAVES].... New York, 1882.

1791. Metcalf, Lewis H. "'So Eager Were We All....'" AM HER, 16 [4] [1965]: 32-41. [11th New York]

1792. Spierl, Charles F. "Patchogue's Kansas Brigade." LONG ISLAND FORUM, 34 [1971]: 242-245, 260-262. [12th New York]

1793. Curtis, Newton M. FROM BULL RUN TO CHANCELLORSVILLE: THE STORY OF THE SIXTEENTH NEW YORK INFANTRY.... New York, 1906.

1794. Mills, John H. CHRONICLES OF THE TWENTY-FIRST REGIMENT, NEW YORK STATE VOLUNTEERS. Buffalo, 1867.

1795. Wingate, George W. HISTORY OF THE TWENTY-SECOND REGIMENT OF THE NATIONAL GUARD OF THE STATE OF NEW YORK, FROM ITS ORGANIZATION TO 1895. New York, 1896.

1796. Snyder, Charles M. "Robert Oliver, Jr., and the Oswego County Regiment." [24th New York Infantry] NYH, 38 [1957]: 276-293.

1797. Fairchild, Charles B. HISTORY OF THE 27TH REGIMENT NEW YORK VOLUNTEERS ... BEING A RECORD OF ITS MORE THAN TWO YEARS OF SERVICE IN THE WAR FOR THE UNION, FROM MAY 21ST, 1861, TO MAY 31ST, 1863.... Binghamton, New York: 1888.

1798. Boyce, Charles W. A BRIEF HISTORY OF THE TWENTY-EIGHTH REGIMENT NEW YORK STATE VOLUNTEERS, FIRST BRIGADE, FIRST DIVISION, TWELFTH CORPS, ARMY OF THE POTOMAC.... Buffalo, 1896.

1799. Judd, David W. THE STORY OF THE THIRTY-THIRD NEW YORK STATE VOLUNTEERS.... Rochester, New York: 1864.

1800. Floyd, Frederick C. HISTORY OF THE FORTIETH [MOZART] REGIMENT, NEW YORK VOLUNTEERS, WHICH WAS COMPOSED OF FOUR COMPANIES FROM NEW YORK, FOUR COMPANIES FROM MASSACHUSETTS AND TWO COMPANIES FROM PENNSYLVANIA. Boston, 1909.

1801. Nash, Eugene A. A HISTORY OF THE FORTY-FOURTH REGIMENT, NEW YORK VOLUNTEER INFANTRY.... Chicago, 1911.

1802. Nichols, James M. PERRY'S SAINTS, OR, THE FIGHTING PARSON'S REGIMENT IN THE WAR OF THE REBELLION. [48th New York] Boston, 1886.

1803. Palmer, Abraham J. THE HISTORY OF THE FORTY-EIGHTH REGIMENT NEW YORK STATE VOLUNTEERS.... Brooklyn, New York: 1885.

1804. Bidwell, Frederick D. HISTORY OF THE FORTY-NINTH NEW YORK VOLUNTEERS. Albany, New York: 1916.

1805. Wheeler, Gerald E. "D'Epineuil's Zouaves." CWH, 2 [1956]: 93-100. [53rd New York]

1806. ——— and A. Stuart Pitt. "The 53rd New York: A Zoo-Zoo Tale." NYH, 37 [1956]: 414-431.

1807. Fisk, Joel C. A CONDENSED HISTORY OF THE 56TH REGIMENT, NEW YORK VETERAN VOLUNTEER INFANTRY, WHICH WAS A PART OF THE ORGANIZATION KNOWN AS THE "TENTH LEGION" IN THE CIVIL WAR.... Newburgh, New York: 1906.

1808. BRASS BUTTONS AND LEATHER BOOTS: SULLIVAN COUNTY AND THE CIVIL WAR. [56th and 143rd New York regiments] South Fallsburg, New York: Steingart Associates, 1963.

1809. Frederick, Gilbert. THE STORY OF A REGIMENT ... THE FIFTY-SEVENTH NEW YORK.... Chicago, 1895.

1810. Eddy, Richard. HISTORY OF THE SIXTIETH REGIMENT NEW YORK STATE VOLUNTEERS.... Philadelphia, 1864.

1811. Whittemore, Henry. HISTORY OF THE SEVENTY-FIRST REGIMENT NATIONAL GUARD STATE OF NEW YORK.... New York, 1886.

1812. Brown, Henri L. HISTORY OF THE THIRD REGIMENT, EXCELSIOR BRIGADE, 72D NEW YORK VOLUNTEER INFANTRY.... Jamestown, New York: 1902.

1813. Tocin, Kerry R. "To Hell and Back: Companies D, E, and H : 72d New York Volunteers, Dunkirk, New York [1861-1864]." NIAG FRON, 21 [1974]: 80-95.

1814. Smith, Abram P. HISTORY OF THE SEVENTY-SIXTH REGIMENT NEW YORK VOLUNTEERS.... Courtland, New York: 1867.

1815. Todd, William. THE SEVENTY-NINTH HIGHLANDERS, NEW YORK VOLUNTEERS.... Albany, New York: 1886.

1816. Gates, Theodore B. THE "ULSTER GUARD" [20TH NEW YORK STATE MILITIA].... [80th New York Infantry] New York, 1879.

1817. Jaques, John W. THREE YEARS' CAMPAIGN OF THE NINTH NEW YORK STATE MILITIA.... [83rd New York Infantry] New York, 1865.

1818. Todd, William, editor. HISTORY OF THE NINTH REGIMENT NEW YORK STATE MILITIA--NATIONAL GUARD STATE OF NEW YORK [EIGHTY-THIRD NEW YORK VOLUNTEERS]. 1845-1888. New York, 1889.

1819. Battillo, Anthony. "'Red-Legged Devils From Brooklyn.'" CWTI, 10 [10]]1972]: 10-16. [84th New York/14th Brooklyn]

1820. Tevis, C.V. THE HISTORY OF THE FIGHTING FOURTEENTH. [84th New York Infantry] New York, 1911.

1821. King, David H. HISTORY OF THE NINETY-THIRD REGIMENT, NEW YORK VOLUNTEER INFANTRY.... Milwaukee, Wisconsin: 1895.

1822. Hall, Isaac. HISTORY OF THE NINETY-SEVENTH REGIMENT, NEW YORK VOLUNTEERS ["CONKLING RIFLES"].... Utica, New York: 1890.

1823. Corell, Philip. HISTORY OF THE NAVAL BRIGADE, 99TH NEW YORK VOLUNTEERS, UNION COAST GUARD. New York, 1905.

1824. Stowits, George H. HISTORY OF THE ONE HUNDREDTH REGIMENT OF NEW YORK STATE VOLUNTEERS.... Buffalo, 1870.

1825. Ford, Henry E. HISTORY OF THE 101ST REGIMENT. Syracuse, New York: 1898.

1826. Kimball, Orville S. HISTORY AND PERSONAL SKETCHES OF COMPANY I, 103 NEW YORK STATE VOLUNTEERS.... Elmira, New York: 1900.

1827. Washburn, George H. A COMPLETE ... RECORD OF THE 108TH REGIMENT NEW YORK VOLUNTEERS.... Rochester, New York: 1894.

1828. Hyde, William L. HISTORY OF THE ONE HUNDRED AND TWELFTH REGIMENT NEW YORK VOLUNTEERS. Fredonia, New York: 1866.

1829. Beecher, Harris H. RECORD OF THE 114TH REGIMENT NEW YORK STATE VOLUNTEERS.... Norwich, New York: 1866.

1830. Pellet, Elias P. HISTORY OF THE 114TH REGIMENT, NEW YORK STATE VOLUNTEERS, CONTAINING A PERFECT RECORD OF ITS SERVICES.... Norwich, New York: 1866.

1831. Clark, James H. THE IRON HEARTED REGIMENT: BEING AN ACCOUNT OF ... THE 115TH REGIMENT NEW YORK VOLUNTEERS.... Albany, 1865.

1832. Clark, Orton S. THE ONE HUNDRED AND SIXTEENTH REGIMENT OF NEW YORK STATE VOLUNTEERS: BEING A COMPLETE HISTORY OF ITS ORGANIZATION AND OF ITS NEARLY THREE YEARS' ACTIVE SERVICE.... Buffalo, 1868.

1833. Mowris, James A. A HISTORY OF THE ONE HUNDRED AND SEVENTEENTH REGIMENT, NEW YORK VOLUNTEERS, [FOURTH ONEIDA,] FROM THE DATE OF ITS ORGANIZATION.... n.p., 1866.

1834. Cunningham, John L. THREE YEARS WITH THE ADIRONDACK REGIMENT, 118TH NEW YORK VOLUNTEER INFANTRY, FROM THE DIARIES AND OTHER MEMORANDA OF JOHN L. CUNNINGHAM, MAJOR 118TH NEW YORK VOLUNTEERS.... Norwood, Massachusetts: Plimpton Press, 1920.

1835. Van Santvoord, Cornelius. THE ONE HUNDRED AND TWENTIETH REGIMENT NEW YORK STATE VOLUNTEERS. Rondout, New York: 1894.

1836. Best, Isaac O. HISTORY OF THE 121ST NEW YORK STATE INFANTRY. Chicago: J.H. Smith, 1921.

1837. Swinfen, David. RUGGLES' REGIMENT: THE 122nd NEW YORK VOLUNTEERS IN THE AMERICAN CIVIL WAR. Hanover, New Hampshire: University Press of New England, 1982.

1838. Morhous, Henry C. REMINISCENCES OF THE 123D REGIMENT, NEW YORK STATE VOLUNTEERS.... Greenwich, New York: 1879.

1839. Weygant, Charles H. HISTORY OF THE ONE HUNDRED AND TWENTY-FOURTH REGIMENT, NEW YORK STATE VOLUNTEERS. Newburgh, New York: 1877.

1840. Simons, Ezra D. A REGIMENTAL HISTORY. THE ONE HUNDRED AND TWENTY-FIFTH NEW YORK STATE VOLUNTEERS. New York, 1888.

1841. Willson, Arabella M. DISASTER, STRUGGLE, TRIUMPH. THE ADVENTURES OF 1000 "BOYS IN BLUE," FROM AUGUST, 1862, TO JUNE, 1865 ... DEDICATED TO THE 126TH REGIMENT OF NEW YORK STATE VOLUNTEERS.... Albany, New York: 1870.

1842. McGrath, Franklin. THE HISTORY OF THE 127TH NEW YORK VOLUNTEERS, "MONITORS".... n.p., 1898.

1843. Hanaburgh, David H. HISTORY OF THE ONE HUNDRED AND TWENTY EIGHTH REGIMENT, NEW YORK VOLUNTEERS.... Pokeepsie, New York: 1894.

1844. Young, Moses G., editor. A CONDENSED HISTORY OF THE 143D REGIMENT NEW YORK VOLUNTEER INFANTRY OF THE CIVIL WAR, 1861-1865. Newburgh, New York: 1909.

1845. McKee, James H. BACK "IN WAR TIMES". HISTORY OF THE 144TH REGIMENT, NEW YORK VOLUNTEER INFANTRY.... New York, 1903.

1846. Brainard, Mary G. CAMPAIGNS OF THE ONE HUNDRED AND FORTY-SIXTH NEW YORK STATE VOLUNTEERS, ALSO KNOWN AS HALLECK'S INFANTRY, THE FIFTH ONEIDA, AND GARRARD'S TIGERS. New York: Putnam, 1915.

1847. Collins, George K. MEMOIRS OF THE 149TH REGIMENT, NEW YORK STATE VOLUNTEER INFANTRY, 3D BRIGADE, 2D DIVISION, 12TH AND 20TH ARMY CORPS. Syracuse, New York: 1891.

1848. Cook, Stephen G. THE "DUTCHESS COUNTY REGIMENT" [150TH REGIMENT OF NEW YORK STATE VOLUNTEER INFANTRY] ... ITS STORY AS TOLD BY ITS MEMBERS.... Danbury, Connecticut: 1907.

1849. Howell, Helena A. CHRONICLES OF THE ONE HUNDRED FIFTY-FIRST REGIMENT NEW YORK STATE VOLUNTEER INFANTRY, 1863-1865, CONTRIBUTED BY ITS SURVIVING MEMBERS.... Albion, New York: 1911.

1850. Dunkelman, Mark H. and Michael J. Winey. THE HARDTACK REGIMENT: AN ILLUSTRATED HISTORY OF THE 154TH REGIMENT NEW YORK STATE INFANTRY VOLUNTEERS. East Brunswick, New Jersey: Fairleigh Dickinson University Press, 1981.

1851. Tiemann, William F. THE 159TH REGIMENT INFANTRY, NEW YORK STATE VOLUNTEERS.... Brooklyn, New York: 1891.

1852. HISTORY OF THE SECOND BATTALION, DURYEE ZOUAVES, ONE HUNDRED AND SIXTY-FIFTH REGIMENT, NEW YORK VOLUNTEER INFANTRY, MUSTERED IN THE UNITED STATES SERVICE AT CAMP WASHINGTON, STATEN ISLAND, NEW YORK.... New York, 1905.

1853. Rogers, William H. HISTORY OF THE ONE HUNDRED AND EIGHTY-NINTH REGIMENT OF NEW YORK VOLUNTEERS. New York, 1865.

Ohio

1854. Davidson, Henry M. HISTORY OF BATTERY A, FIRST REGIMENT OF OHIO VOLUNTEER LIGHT ARTILLERY. Milwaukee, Wisconsin: 1865.

1855. Cutter, Orlando P. OUR BATTERY, OR, THE JOURNAL OF COMPANY B, 1ST OHIO VOLUNTEER ARTILLERY. Cleveland, 1864.

1856. HISTORY OF THE SIXTEENTH BATTERY OF OHIO VOLUNTEER LIGHT ARTILLERY, U.S.A., FROM ENLISTMENT, AUGUST 20, 1861, TO MUSTER OUT, AUGUST 2, 1865. COMPILED FROM THE DIARIES OF COMRADES.... n.p., 1906.

1857. Tracie, Theodore C. ANNALS OF THE NINETEENTH OHIO BATTERY, VOLUNTEER ARTILLERY, INCLUDING AN OUTLINE OF THE OPERATIONS OF THE SECOND DIVISION, TWENTY-THIRD ARMY CORPS.... Cleveland, 1878.

1858. Curry, William L. FOUR YEARS IN THE SADDLE. HISTORY OF THE FIRST REGIMENT, OHIO VOLUNTEER CAVALRY. Columbus, 1898.

1859. Gillespie, Samuel L. A HISTORY OF COMPANY A, 1ST OHIO CAVALRY, 1861-1865. Washington Court House, Ohio: 1898.

1860. Halton, Robert W., editor. "Just a Little Bit of the Civil War As Seen By W.J. Smith, Company M, 2nd Ohio Volunteer Cavalry." OHIO HIS, 84 [1975]: 101-126, 222-242.

1861. Starr, Stephen Z. "The Third Ohio Volunteer Cavalry: A View From the Inside." OHIO HIS, 85 [1976]: 306-318.

1862. Crofts, Thomas. HISTORY OF THE SERVICE OF THE THIRD OHIO VETERAN VOLUNTEER CAVALRY.... Toledo, Ohio: 1910.

1863. Stimmel, Smith. "Experience as a Member of President Lincoln's Bodyguard." ND HIS Q, 1 [1926/1927]: 7-33. [Union Light Guard, Ohio Cavalry]

1864. Kern, Albert. HISTORY OF THE FIRST REGIMENT OHIO VOLUNTEER INFANTRY IN THE CIVIL WAR.... Dayton, Ohio: n.p., 1918.

1865. Kepler, William. HISTORY OF THE THREE MONTHS' AND THREE YEARS' SERVICE ... OF THE FOURTH REGIMENT OHIO VOLUNTEER INFANTRY.... Cleveland, 1886.

1866. Hannaford, Ebenezer. THE STORY OF A REGIMENT: A HISTORY OF THE CAMPAIGNS, AND ASSOCIATIONS IN THE FIELD, OF THE SIXTH REGIMENT OHIO VOLUNTEER INFANTRY. Cincinnati, 1868.

1867. Wilder, Theodore. THE HISTORY OF COMPANY C, SEVENTH REGIMENT, OHIO VOLUNTEER INFANTRY. Oberlin, Ohio: 1866.

1868. Wilson, Lawrence. ITINERARY OF THE SEVENTH OHIO VOLUNTEER INFANTRY, 1861-1865.... New York, 1907.

1869. Wood, George L. THE SEVENTH REGIMENT: A RECORD. New York, 1865.

1870. Sawyer, Franklin. A MILITARY HISTORY OF THE 8TH REGIMENT OHIO VOLUNTEER INFANTRY.... Cleveland, 1881.

1871. Wittke, Carl F. THE NINTH OHIO VOLUNTEERS, A PAGE FROM THE CIVIL WAR RECORD OF THE GERMAN TURNERS OF OHIO. Columbus: F.J. Heer, 1926.

1872. Horton, Joshua H. A HISTORY OF THE ELEVENTH REGIMENT [OHIO VOLUNTEER INFANTRY,] CONTAINING THE MILITARY RECORD ... OF EACH OFFICER AND ENLISTED MAN.... Dayton, Ohio: 1866.

1873. Chase, John A. HISTORY OF THE FOURTEENTH OHIO REGIMENT ... FROM THE BEGINNING OF THE WAR IN 1861 TO ITS CLOSE IN 1865. Toledo, Ohio: 1881.

1874. Entry omitted.

1875. De Velling, Charles T. ... HISTORY OF THE SEVENTEENTH REGIMENT, FIRST BRIGADE, THIRD DIVISION, FOURTEENTH CORPS, ARMY OF THE CUMBERLAND.... Zanesville, Ohio: 1889.

1876. Canfield, Silas S. HISTORY OF THE 21ST REGIMENT OHIO VOLUNTEER INFANTRY.... Toledo, Ohio: 1893.

1877. Williams, T. Harry and Stephen E. Ambrose. "The 23rd Ohio: This Regiment Included Two Future Presidents and an Army Commander." CWTI, 3 [2] [1964]: 22-25.

1878. Culp, Edward C. THE 25TH OHIO VETERAN VOLUNTEER INFANTRY IN THE WAR FOR THE UNION. Topeka, Kansas: 1885.

1879. Se Cheverell, John H. JOURNAL HISTORY OF THE TWENTY-NINTH OHIO VETERAN VOLUNTEERS.... Cleveland, 1883.

1880. Hays, E.Z., editor. HISTORY OF THE THIRTY-SECOND REGIMENT OHIO VETERAN VOLUNTEER INFANTRY. Columbus, 1896.

1881. Kell, Frederick W. THIRTY-FIFTH OHIO. A NARRATIVE OF SERVICE FROM AUGUST, 1861 TO 1864. Fort Wayne, Indiana: 1894.

1882. Beach, John N. HISTORY OF THE FORTIETH OHIO VOLUNTEER INFANTRY. London, Ohio: 1884.

1883. Kimberly, Robert L. THE FORTY-FIRST OHIO VETERAN VOLUNTEER INFANTRY IN THE WAR OF THE REBELLION. Cleveland, 1897.

1884. Mason, Frank H. THE FORTY SECOND OHIO INFANTRY: A HISTORY OF THE ORGANIZATION.... Cleveland, 1876.

1885. Saunier, Joseph A., editor. A HISTORY OF THE FORTY SEVENTH REGIMENT, OHIO VETERAN VOLUNTEER INFANTRY, SECOND BRIGADE, SECOND DIVISION, FIFTEENTH ARMY CORPS. ARMY OF THE TENNESSEE. Hillsboro, Ohio: 1903.

1886. Bering, John A. HISTORY OF THE FORTY-EIGHTH OHIO VETERAN VOLUNTEER INFANTRY GIVING A COMPLETE ACCOUNT OF THE REGIMENT.... Hillsboro, Ohio: 1880.

1887. Stewart, Nixon B. DAN McCOOK'S REGIMENT, 52ND OHIO VOLUNTEER INFANTRY. A HISTORY OF THE REGIMENT, ITS CAMPAIGNS AND BATTLES. FROM 1862 TO 1865. Claysville, Ohio: 1900.

1888. Duke, John K. HISTORY OF THE FIFTY-THIRD REGIMENT OHIO VOLUNTEER INFANTRY.... Portsmouth, Ohio: 1900.

1889. Osborn, Hartwell. TRIALS AND TRIUMPHS: THE RECORD OF THE FIFTY-FIFTH OHIO VOLUNTEER INFANTRY. Chicago, 1904.

1890. Williams, Thomas J. AN HISTORICAL SKETCH OF THE 56TH OHIO VOLUNTEER INFANTRY DURING THE GREAT CIVIL WAR. Columbus, 1899.

1891. Connelly, Thomas W. HISTORY OF THE SEVENTIETH OHIO REGIMENT FROM ITS ORGANIZATION TO ITS MUSTERING OUT. Cincinnati, 1902.

1892. Hurst, Samuel H. JOURNAL-HISTORY OF THE SEVENTY-THIRD OHIO VOLUNTEER INFANTRY. Chillicothe, 1866.

1893. Owens, Ira S. GREENE COUNTY IN THE WAR. BEING A HISTORY OF THE SEVENTY-FOURTH REGIMENT. WITH SKETCHES OF THE TWELFTH, NINETY-FOURTH, ONE HUNDRED AND TENTH, FORTY-FOURTH, AND ONE HUNDRED AND FIFTY-FOURTH REGIMENTS AND THE TENTH OHIO BATTERY.... Xenia, Ohio: 1872.

1894. Stevenson, Thomas M. HISTORY OF THE 78TH REGIMENT OHIO VETERAN VOLUNTEER INFANTRY, FROM ITS "MUSTER-IN" TO ITS "MUSTER-OUT": COMPRISING ITS ORGANIZATION, MARCHES, CAMPAIGNS, BATTLES AND SKIRMISHES. Zanesville, Ohio: 1865.

1895. Chamberlin, William H. HISTORY OF THE EIGHTY-FIRST REGIMENT OHIO INFANTRY VOLUNTEERS, DURING THE WAR OF THE REBELLION. Cincinnati, 1865.

1896. Wright, Charles. A CORPORAL'S STORY. EXPERIENCES IN THE RANKS OF COMPANY C, 81ST OHIO VOLUNTEER INFANTRY, DURING THE WAR FOR THE MAINTENANCE OF THE UNION, 1861-1864. Philadelphia, 1887.

1897. Marshall, Thomas B. HISTORY OF THE EIGHTY-THIRD OHIO VOLUNTEER INFANTRY, THE GREYHOUND REGIMENT. Cincinnati, 1912.

1898. Ashburn, Joseph N. HISTORY OF THE EIGHTY-SIXTH REGIMENT OHIO VOLUNTEER INFANTRY. Cleveland, 1909.

1899. Ewing, Elmore E. BUGLES AND BELLS, OR STORIES TOLD AGAIN. Cincinnati, 1899. [91st Ohio]

1900. Demoret, Alfred. A BRIEF HISTORY OF THE NINETY-THIRD REGIMENT, OHIO VOLUNTEER INFANTRY.... Ross, Ohio: 1898.

1901. RECORD OF THE NINETY-FOURTH REGIMENT, OHIO VOLUNTEER INFANTRY, IN THE WAR OF THE REBELLION. Cincinnati, n.d.

1902. Day, Lewis W. STORY OF THE ONE HUNDRED AND FIRST OHIO INFANTRY. A MEMORIAL VOLUME. Cleveland, 1894.

1903. Greene, Charles R. VOLUNTEER SERVICE IN ARMY OF CUMBERLAND.... Olathe, Kansas: 1914. [101st Ohio]

1904. Schmutz, George S. HISTORY OF THE 102D REGIMENT, OHIO VOLUNTEER INFANTRY. Wooster, Ohio: 1907.

1905. PERSONAL REMINISCENCES AND EXPERIENCES BY MEMBERS OF THE ONE HUNDRED AND THIRD OHIO VOLUNTEER INFANTRY. Oberlin, Ohio: 1900.

1906. Pinney, Nelson A. HISTORY OF THE 104TH REGIMENTAL OHIO VOLUNTEER INFANTRY FROM 1862 TO 1865. Akron, Ohio: 1886.

1907. Tourgee, Albion W. THE STORY OF A THOUSAND. BEING A HISTORY OF THE SERVICE OF THE 105TH OHIO VOLUNTEER INFANTRY.... Buffalo, New York: 1896.

1908. Smith, Jacob. CAMPS AND CAMPAIGNS OF THE 107TH REGIMENT OHIO VOLUNTEER INFANTRY, FROM AUGUST, 1862, TO JULY, 1865. n.p., 1910.

1909. McAdams, Francis M. EVERY DAY SOLDIER LIFE, OR A HISTORY OF THE ONE HUNDRED AND THIRTEENTH OHIO VOLUNTEER INFANTRY. Columbus, 1884.

1910. Wildes, Thomas F. RECORD OF THE ONE HUNDRED AND SIXTEENTH REGIMENT, OHIO INFANTRY VOLUNTEERS IN THE WAR OF THE REBELLION. Sandusky, Ohio: 1884.

1911. Granger, Moses M. THE OFFICIAL WAR RECORD OF THE 122ND REGIMENT OF OHIO VOLUNTEER INFANTRY.... Zanesville, Ohio: 1912.

1912. Keyes, Charles M. THE MILITARY RECORD OF THE 123RD REGIMENT OF OHIO VOLUNTEER INFANTRY. Sandusky, Ohio: 1874.

1913. Lewis, George W. THE CAMPAIGNS OF THE 124TH REGIMENT, OHIO VOLUNTEER INFANTRY, WITH ROSTER AND ROLL OF HONOR. Akron, Ohio: 1894.

1914. Clark, Charles T. OPDYCKE TIGERS, 125TH OHIO VOLUNTEER INFANTRY, A HISTORY OF THE REGIMENT AND THE CAMPAIGNS AND BATTLES OF THE ARMY OF THE CUMBERLAND. Columbus, 1895.

1915. Gilson, John H. CONCISE HISTORY OF THE ONE HUNDRED AND TWENTY-SIXTH REGIMENT OHIO VOLUNTEER INFANTRY. Salem, Ohio: 1883.

1916. Sherman, Sylvester M. HISTORY OF THE 133D REGIMENT, OHIO VOLUNTEER INFANTRY AND INCIDENTS CONNECTED WITH ITS SERVICE DURING THE "WAR OF THE REBELLION." Columbus, 1896.

1917. Perkins, George. A SUMMER IN MARYLAND AND VIRGINIA, OR, CAMPAIGNING WITH THE 149TH OHIO VOLUNTEER INFANTRY.... Chillicothe, Ohio: 1911.

1918. Stipp, Joseph A. THE HISTORY AND SERVICE OF THE 154TH OHIO VOLUNTEER INFANTRY. Toledo, Ohio: 1896.

Pennsylvania

1919. Minnigh, H.N. HISTORY OF COMPANY K [INFANTRY] FIRST PENNSYLVANIA RESERVES. Duncansville, Pennsylvania: 1891. [Also known as 30th Pennsylvania]

1920. Guelzo, Allen C. "The Fighting Philadelphia Brigade." CWTI, 18 [1980]: 12-23.

1921. Ward, George W. HISTORY OF THE SECOND PENNSYLVANIA VETERAN HEAVY ARTILLERY [112TH REGIMENT PENNSYLVANIA VOLUNTEERS] FROM 1861 TO 1866.... Philadelphia, 1904.

1922. Cuffel, Charles A. HISTORY OF DURELL'S BATTERY IN THE CIVIL WAR [INDEPENDENT BATTERY D, PENNSYLVANIA VOLUNTEER ARTILLERY]. A NARRATIVE OF THE CAMPAIGNS AND BATTLES OF BERKS AND BUCKS' COUNTIES ARTILLERISTS.... Philadelphia, 1903.

1923. Clark, William. HISTORY OF HAMPTON BATTERY F, INDEPENDENT PENNSYLVANIA LIGHT ARTILLERY.... Akron, Ohio: 1900.

1924. Lloyd, William P. HISTORY OF THE FIRST REGIMENT PENNSYLVANIA RESERVE CAVALRY, FROM ITS ORGANIZATION, AUGUST, 1861, TO SEPTEMBER, 1864.... Philadelphia, 1864.

1925. HISTORY OF THE THIRD PENNSYLVANIA CAVALRY, SIXTIETH REGIMENT PENNSYLVANIA VOLUNTEERS, IN THE AMERICAN CIVIL WAR, 1861-1865. By the committee. Philadelphia, 1905.

1926. Hyndman, William. HISTORY OF A CAVALRY COMPANY. A COMPLETE RECORD OF COMPANY "A", 4TH PENNSYLVANIA CAVALRY ... IN ALL THE CAMPAIGNS OF THE ARMY OF THE POTOMAC.... Philadelphia, 1870.

1927. Longacre, Edward J. "The Most Inept Regiment of the Civil War." CWTI, 8 [7] [1969]: 4-7. [5th Pennsylvania Cavalry]

1928. Gracey, Samuel L. ANNALS OF THE SIXTH PENNSYLVANIA CAVALRY. Philadelphia, 1868.

1929. Sipes, William B. THE SEVENTH PENNSYLVANIA VETERAN VOLUNTEER CAVALRY: ITS RECORD, REMINISCENCES AND ROSTER.... Pottsville, Pennsylvania: 1905.

1930. Dornblaser, T.F. SABRE STROKES OF THE PENNSYLVANIA DRAGOONS, IN THE WAR OF 1861-1865. Philadelphia, 1884. [7th Pennsylvania Cavalry]

1931. Rowell, John W. YANKEE CAVALRYMEN: THROUGH THE CIVIL WAR WITH THE NINTH PENNSYLVANIA CAVALRY. Knoxville: University of Tennessee Press, 1971.

1932. HISTORY OF THE ELEVENTH PENNSYLVANIA VOLUNTEER CAVALRY, TOGETHER WITH A COMPLETE ROSTER OF THE REGIMENT AND REGIMENTAL OFFICERS. Philadelphia, 1902.

1933. Slease, William D. THE FOURTEENTH PENNSYLVANIA CAVALRY IN THE CIVIL WAR. Pittsburgh: Art Engraving and Printing, 1915.

1934. Carraway, William E. "The Mutiny of the 15th Pennsylvania Volunteer Cavalry." DENVER WESTERNERS' MONTHLY ROUNDUP, 17 [11] [1961]: 5-15.

1935. Kirk, Charles H. HISTORY OF THE FIFTEENTH PENNSYLVANIA VOLUNTEER CAVALRY ... THE ANDERSON CAVALRY.... Philadelphia, 1906.

1936. Wilson, Suzanne C. COLUMN SOUTH: WITH THE FIFTEENTH PENNSYLVANIA CAVALRY FROM ANTIETAM TO THE CAPTURE OF JEFFERSON DAVIS. Flagstaff, Arizona: Colton, 1960.

1937. Moyer, H.P., compiler. HISTORY OF THE SEVENTEENTH REGIMENT PENNSYLVANIA VOLUNTEER CAVALRY, OR ONE HUNDRED AND SIXTY-SECOND IN THE LINE OF PENNSYLVANIA VOLUNTEER REGIMENTS, WAR TO SUPPRESS THE REBELLION.... Lebanon, Pennsylvania, 1911.

1938. HISTORY OF THE EIGHTEENTH REGIMENT OF CAVALRY, PENNSYLVANIA VOLUNTEERS [163D REGIMENT OF THE LINE] 1862-1865.... By the committee. New York, 1909.

1939. Elwood, John W. ELWOOD'S STORIES OF THE OLD RINGGOLD CAVALRY, 1847-1865, THE FIRST THREE YEAR CAVALRY OF THE CIVIL WAR. Coal Center, Pennsylvania: 1914. [22nd Pennsylvania Cavalry]

1940. Farrar, Samuel C. THE TWENTY-SECOND PENNSYLVANIA CAVALRY AND THE RINGGOLD BATTALION, 1861-1865. Akron, Ohio: 1911.

1941. Sypher, Josiah R. HISTORY OF THE PENNSYLVANIA RESERVE CORPS: A COMPLETE RECORD OF THE ORGANIZATION: AND OF THE DIFFERENT COMPANIES, REGIMENTS AND BRIGADES: CONTAINING DESCRIPTIONS OF EXPEDITIONS, MARCHES, SKIRMISHES, AND BATTLES.... Lancaster, Pennsylvania: 1865. [1st-13th Pennsylvania]

1942. Banes, Charles H. HISTORY OF THE PHILADELPHIA BRIGADE. SIXTY-NINTH, SEVENTY-FIRST, SEVENTY-SECOND, AND ONE HUNDRED AND SIXTH PENNSYLVANIA VOLUNTEERS. Philadelphia, 1876.

1943. Copeland, Willis R. THE LOGAN GUARDS OF LEWISTON, PENNSYLVANIA, OUR FIRST DEFENDERS OF 1861: A HISTORY. Lewistown, Pennsylvania: Mifflin County Historical Society, 1962.

1944. Locke, William H. THE STORY OF THE REGIMENT. Philadelphia, 1868. [11th Pennsylvania]

1945. Wray, William J. HISTORY OF THE TWENTY-THIRD PENNSYLVANIA VOLUNTEER INFANTRY. BIRNEYS ZOUAVES: THREE MONTHS AND THREE YEARS SERVICE.... Philadelphia, 1904.

1946. Woodward, Evan M. OUR CAMPAIGNS, OR, THE MARCHES, BIVOUACS, BATTLES, INCIDENTS OF CAMP LIFE AND HISTORY OF OUR REGIMENT DURING ITS THREE YEARS TERM OF SERVICE.... Philadelphia, 1865. [2nd Pennsylvania Reserves/31st Pennsylvania]

1947. ———. HISTORY OF THE PENNSYLVANIA RESERVE: BEING A COMPLETE RECORD OF THE REGIMENT, WITH INCIDENTS OF THE CAMP, MARCHES.... Trenton, New Jersey: 1883. [32nd Pennsylvania]

1948. Hardin, Martin D. HISTORY OF THE TWELFTH REGIMENT, PENNSYLVANIA RESERVE VOLUNTEER CORPS [41ST REGIMENT OF THE LINE], FROM ITS MUSTER INTO THE UNITED STATES SERVICE.... New York, 1890.

1949. Glover, Edwin A. BUCKTAILED WILDCATS, A REGIMENT OF CIVIL WAR VOLUNTEERS. New York: Yoseloff, 1960. [13th Pennsylvania Reserves/42nd Pennsylvania]

1950. Hoffsommer, Robert D. "The Bucktails." CWTI, 4 [9] [1966]: 16-21. [13th Pennsylvania]

1951. Thomson, Osmund R.H. HISTORY OF THE "BUCKTAILS," KANE RIFLE REGIMENT OF THE PENNSYLVANIA RESERVE CORPS.... Philadelphia, 1906. [13th Pennsylvania]

1952. Reinberg, Mark. "Descent of the Raftsmen Guard: A Roll Call." W PA HIS MAG, 53 [1970]: 1-32. [13th Pennsylvania]

1953. Albert, Allen D., editor. HISTORY OF THE FORTY-FIFTH REGIMENT PENNSYLVANIA VETERAN VOLUNTEER INFANTRY, 1861-1865, WRITTEN BY THE COMRADES. Williamsport, Pennsylvania: 1912.

1954. Roberts, Agatha L. AS THEY REMEMBERED. New York: William Frederick, 1964. [45th Pennsylvania]

1955. Bosbyshell, Oliver C. THE 48TH IN WAR. BEING A NARRATIVE OF THE CAMPAIGNS OF THE 48TH REGIMENT, INFANTRY, PENNSYLVANIA VETERAN VOLUNTEERS, DURING THE WAR OF THE REBELLION. Philadelphia, 1895.

1956. Gould, Joseph. THE STORY OF THE FORTY-EIGHTH: A RECORD OF THE CAMPAIGNS OF THE FORTY-EIGHTH REGIMENT PENNSYLVANIA VETERAN VOLUNTEER INFANTRY.... Philadelphia, 1908.

1957. Westbrook, Robert S. HISTORY OF THE 49TH PENNSYLVANIA VOLUNTEERS. Altoona, 1898.

1958. Crater, Lewis. HISTORY OF THE FIFTIETH REGIMENT, PENNSYLVANIA VETERAN VOLUNTEERS, 1861-1865. Reading, Pennsylvania, 1884.

1959. Parker, Thomas H. HISTORY OF THE 51ST REGIMENT OF PENNSYLVANIA VOLUNTEERS AND VETERAN VOLUNTEERS, FROM ITS ORGANIZATION.... Philadelphia, 1869.

1960. Mott, Smith B., compiler. THE CAMPAIGNS OF THE FIFTY-SECOND REGIMENT, PENNSYLVANIA VOLUNTEER INFANTRY, FIRST KNOWN AS "THE LUZERNE REGIMENT".... Philadelphia, 1911.

1961. HISTORY OF THE FIFTY-SEVENTH REGIMENT, PENNSYLVANIA VETERAN VOLUNTEER INFANTRY.... By the committee. Meadville, Pennsylvania: n.d.

1962. Brewer, A.T. HISTORY SIXTY-FIRST REGIMENT PENNSYLVANIA VOLUNTEERS, 1861-1865.... Pittsburgh, 1911.

1963. Hays, Gilbert A. UNDER THE RED PATCH: STORY OF THE SIXTY-THIRD REGIMENT, PENNSYLVANIA VOLUNTEERS, 1861-1864.... Pittsburgh, 1908.

1964. Obreiter, John. THE SEVENTY-SEVENTH PENNSYLVANIA AT SHILOH. Harrisburg, 1905.

1965. Gibson, J.T., editor. HISTORY OF THE SEVENTY-EIGHTH PENNSYLVANIA VOLUNTEER INFANTRY. Pittsburgh, 1905.

1966. Judson, Amos M. HISTORY OF THE EIGHTY-THIRD REGIMENT PENNSYLVANIA VOLUNTEERS. Erie, Pennsylvania: 1865.

1967. Dickey, Luther S. HISTORY OF THE EIGHTY-FIFTH REGIMENT PENNSYLVANIA VOLUNTEER INFANTRY ... COMPRISING AN AUTHENTIC NARRATIVE OF CASEY'S DIVISION AT THE BATTLE OF SEVEN PINES. New York, 1915.

1968. Prowell, George R. HISTORY OF THE EIGHTY-SEVENTH REGIMENT, PENNSYLVANIA VOLUNTEERS.... York, Pennsylvania: 1903.

1969. Vautier, John D. HISTORY OF THE 88TH PENNSYLVANIA VOLUNTEERS IN THE WAR FOR THE UNION, 1861-1865. Philadelphia, 1894.

1970. Mark, Penrose G. RED, WHITE, AND BLUE BADGE, PENNSYLVANIA VETERAN VOLUNTEERS. A HISTORY OF THE 93RD REGIMENT, KNOWN AS THE "LEBANON INFANTRY" AND "ONE OF THE 300 FIGHTING REGIMENTS".... Harrisburg, 1911.

1971. Galloway, George N. THE NINETY-FIFTH PENNSYLVANIA VOLUNTEERS [GOSLINE'S PENNSYLVANIA ZOUAVES] IN THE SIXTH CORPS.... Philadelphia, 1884.

1972. Price, Isaiah. HISTORY OF THE NINETY-SEVENTH REGIMENT, PENNSYLVANIA VOLUNTEER INFANTRY.... Philadelphia, 1875.

1973. Reed, John A. HISTORY OF THE 101ST REGIMENT, PENNSYLVANIA VETERAN VOLUNTEER INFANTRY, 1861-1865. Chicago, 1910.

1974. Dickey, Luther S. HISTORY OF THE 103D REGIMENT, PENNSYLVANIA VETERAN VOLUNTEER INFANTRY, 1861-1865. Chicago, 1910.

1975. Davis, William W.H. HISTORY OF THE 104TH PENNSYLVANIA REGIMENT, FROM AUGUST 22nd, 1861, TO SEPTEMBER 30th, 1864. Philadelphia, 1866.

1976. Scott, Kate M. HISTORY OF THE ONE HUNDRED AND FIFTH REGIMENT OF PENNSYLVANIA VOLUNTEERS.... Philadelphia, 1877.

1977. Ward, Joseph R.C. HISTORY OF THE ONE HUNDRED AND SIXTH REGIMENT, PENNSYLVANIA VOLUNTEERS, 2D BRIGADE, 2D DIVISION, 2D CORPS, 1861-1865. Philadelphia, 1906.

1978. Boyle, John R. SOLDIERS TRUE: THE STORY OF THE ONE HUNDRED AND ELEVENTH REGIMENT PENNSYLVANIA VETERAN VOLUNTEERS AND OF ITS CAMPAIGNS.... New York, 1903.

1979. Mulholland, St. Clair A. THE STORY OF THE 116TH REGIMENT, PENNSYLVANIA INFANTRY.... Philadelphia, 1899.

1980. HISTORY OF THE CORN EXCHANGE REGIMENT, 118TH PENNSYLVANIA VOLUNTEERS, FROM THEIR FIRST ENGAGEMENT AT ANTIETAM TO APPOMATTOX.... By the committee. Philadelphia, 1888.

1981. HISTORY OF THE 121ST REGIMENT PENNSYLVANIA VOLUNTEERS. By the Survivors' Association. Philadelphia, 1893.

1982. Sprenger, George F. CONCISE HISTORY OF THE CAMP AND FIELD LIFE OF THE 122D REGIMENT, PENNSYLVANIA VOLUNTEERS. Lancaster, Pennsylvania: 1885.

1983. Green, Robert M., compiler. HISTORY OF THE ONE HUNDRED AND TWENTY-FOURTH REGIMENT, PENNSYLVANIA VOLUNTEERS IN THE WAR OF THE REBELLION.... Philadelphia, 1907.

1984. Greene, Edward M. "The Huntingdon Bible Company." CWTI, 3 [1] [1964]: 22-24. [125 Pennsylvania]

1985. HISTORY OF THE ONE HUNDRED AND TWENTY-FIFTH REGIMENT, PENNSYLVANIA VOLUNTEERS, 1862-1863. By the committee. Philadelphia, 1906.

1986. HISTORY OF THE 127TH REGIMENT, PENNSYLVANIA VOLUNTEERS, FAMILIARLY KNOWN AS THE "DAUPHIN COUNTY REGIMENT." By the committee. Lebanon, Pennsylvania: 1902.

1987. Orwig, Joseph R. HISTORY OF THE 131ST PENNSYLVANIA VOLUNTEERS, WAR OF 1861-1865. Williamsport, Pennsylvania: 1902.

1988. Lewis, Osceola. HISTORY OF THE ONE HUNDRED AND THIRTY-EIGHTH REGIMENT, PENNSYLVANIA VOLUNTEER INFANTRY. Norristown, Pennsylvania: 1866.

1989. McConnell, Edward N. "A Brief History of Company A, 139th Regiment, Pennsylvania Volunteers." W PA HIS MAG, 55 [1972]: 307-318.

1990. White, Andrew G. HISTORY OF COMPANY F, 140TH REGIMENT, PENNSYLVANIA VOLUNTEERS. Greenville, Pennsylvania: 1908.

1991. Stewart, Robert L. HISTORY OF THE ONE HUNDRED AND FORTIETH REGIMENT PENNSYLVANIA VOLUNTEERS. Philadelphia, 1912.

1992. Craft, David. HISTORY OF THE ONE HUNDRED FORTY-FIRST REGIMENT, PENNSYLVANIA VOLUNTEERS, 1862-1865. Towanda, Pennsylvania: 1885.

1993. Muffly, Joseph W., editor. THE STORY OF OUR REGIMENT: A HISTORY OF THE 148TH PENNSYLVANIA VOLUNTEERS, WRITTEN BY THE COMRADES. Des Moines, Iowa: 1904.

1994. Nesbit, John W. GENERAL HISTORY OF COMPANY D, ONE HUNDRED AND FORTY-NINTH PENNSYLVANIA VOLUNTEERS. Oakdale, California: 1908

1995. Chamberlin, Thomas. HISTORY OF THE ONE HUNDRED AND FIFTIETH REGIMENT, PENNSYLVANIA VOLUNTEERS, SECOND REGIMENT, BUCKTAIL BRIGADE. Philadelphia, 1895.

1996. Kiefer, William R. HISTORY OF THE ONE HUNDRED AND FIFTY-THIRD ... WHICH WAS RECRUITED IN NORTHAMPTON COUNTY, PENNSYLVANIA, 1862-1863. Easton, Pennsylvania: 1909.

1997. UNDER THE MALTESE CROSS, ANTIETAM TO APPOMATTOX, THE LOYAL UPRISING IN WESTERN PENNSYLVANIA, 1861-1865: CAMPAIGNS OF THE 155TH PENNSYLVANIA REGIMENT.... Pittsburgh, 1910.

1998. Gibbs, James M. HISTORY OF THE FIRST BATTALION PENNSYLVANIA SIX MONTHS VOLUNTEERS AND 187TH REGIMENT PENNSYLVANIA VOLUNTEER INFANTRY, SIX MONTHS AND THREE YEARS SERVICE.... Harrisburg, 1905.

1999. Woodward, Evan M. HISTORY OF THE ONE HUNDRED AND NINETY-EIGHTH PENNSYLVANIA VOLUNTEERS, BEING A COMPLETE RECORD OF THE REGIMENT, WITH ITS CAMPS, MARCHES, AND BATTLES.... Trenton, New Jersey: 1884.

Rhode Island

2000. Barker, Harold R. HISTORY OF THE RHODE ISLAND COMBAT UNITS IN THE CIVIL WAR, 1861-1865. Pascoag, Rhode Island: By the author, 1964.

2001. Aldrich, Thomas M. THE HISTORY OF BATTERY A, FIRST REGIMENT RHODE ISLAND LIGHT ARTILLERY IN THE WAR TO PRESERVE THE UNION, 1861-1865. Providence, 1904.

2002. Reichardt, Theodore. DIARY OF BATTERY A, FIRST REGIMENT RHODE ISLAND LIGHT ARTILLERY. Providence, 1865.

2003. Rhodes, John H. THE HISTORY OF BATTERY B, FIRST REGIMENT RHODE ISLAND, LIGHT ARTILLERY, IN THE WAR TO PRESERVE THE UNION, 1861-1865. Providence, 1894.

2004. Sumner, Geroge C. BATTERY D, FIRST RHODE ISLAND LIGHT ARTILLERY, IN THE CIVIL WAR, 1861-1865. Providence, 1897.

2005. Lewis, George. THE HISTORY OF BATTERY E, FIRST REGIMENT RHODE ISLAND LIGHT ARTILLERY.... Providence, 1892.

2006. Fenner, Earl. THE HISTORY OF BATTERY H, FIRST REGIMENT RHODE ISLAND LIGHT ARTILLERY.... Providence, 1894.

2007. Denison, Frederic. SHOT AND SHELL: THE THIRD RHODE ISLAND HEAVY ARTILLERY REGIMENT IN THE REBELLION, 1861-1865.... Providence, 1879.

2008. Burlingame, John K., Compiler. HISTORY OF THE FIFTH REGIMENT OF RHODE ISLAND HEAVY ARTILLERY, DURING THREE YEARS AND A HALF OF SERVICE IN NORTH CAROLINA.... Providence, 1892.

2009. Denison, Frederic. SABRES AND SPURS: THE FIRST REGIMENT RHODE ISLAND CAVALRY IN THE CIVIL WAR, 1861-1865.... Central Falls, Rhode Island: 1876.

2010. Woodbury, Augustus. ... THE CAMPAIGN OF THE FIRST RHODE ISLAND REGIMENT IN THE SPRING AND SUMMER OF 1861.... Providence, 1862.

2011. ———. THE SECOND RHODE ISLAND REGIMENT: A NARRATIVE OF MILITARY OPERATIONS IN WHICH THE REGIMENT WAS ENGAGED.... Providence, 1875.

2012. Allen, George H. FORTY SIX MONTHS WITH THE FOURTH RHODE ISLAND VOLUNTEERS.... Providence, 1887.

2013. Hopkins, William P. THE SEVENTH REGIMENT RHODE ISLAND VOLUNTEERS IN THE CIVIL WAR, 1861-1865. Providence, 1903.

2014. Spicer, William A. HISTORY OF THE NINTH AND TENTH REGIMENTS RHODE ISLAND VOLUNTEERS, AND THE TENTH RHODE ISLAND BATTERY, IN THE UNION ARMY IN 1862. Providence, 1892.

2015. Thompson, John C. HISTORY OF THE ELEVENTH REGIMENT, RHODE ISLAND VOLUNTEERS.... Providence, 1881.

2016. Grant, Joseph W. THE FLYING REGIMENT. JOURNAL OF THE CAMPAIGNS OF THE 12TH REGIMENT RHODE ISLAND VOLUNTEERS. Providence, 1865.

2017. HISTORY OF THE TWELFTH REGIMENT, RHODE ISLAND VOLUNTEERS, IN THE CIVIL WAR.... By the committee. Providence, 1904.

Tennessee [Union Troops]

2018. Carter, William R. HISTORY OF THE FIRST REGIMENT OF TENNESSEE VOLUNTEER CAVALRY IN THE GREAT WAR OF THE REBELLION, WITH THE ARMIES OF THE OHIO AND CUMBERLAND.... Knoxville, 1902.

2019. Scott, Samuel W. HISTORY OF THE THIRTEENTH REGIMENT, TENNESSEE VOLUNTEER CAVALRY, UNITED STATES ARMY, INCLUDING A NARRATIVE OF THE BRIDGE BURNING, THE CARTER COUNTY REBELLION, AND THE LOYALTY, HEROISM AND SUFFERING OF THE UNION MEN AND WOMEN OF CARTER AND JOHNSON COUNTIES.... Knoxville, 1903.

Vermont

2020. Benedict, George G. VERMONT IN THE CIVIL WAR. A HISTORY OF THE PART TAKEN BY THE VERMONT SOLDIERS IN THE WAR FOR THE UNION, 1861-1865. 2 v. Burlington, Vermont: 1886-1888.

2021. Starr, Stephen Z. "The Inner Life of the First Vermont Volunteer Cavalry, 1861-1865." VT HIS, 46 [1978]: 157-174.

2022. Folsom, William R. "Vermont at Bull Run." VT HIS, 19 [1951]: 5-21. [2nd Vermont]

2023. Holbrook, William C. A NARRATIVE OF THE SERVICES OF THE OFFICERS AND ENLISTED MEN OF THE 7TH REGIMENT OF VERMONT VOLUNTEERS [VETERANS], FROM 1862 TO 1865. New York, 1882.

2024. Carpenter, George N. HISTORY OF THE EIGHTH REGIMENT VERMONT VOLUNTEERS, 1861-1865. Boston, Massachusetts: 1886.

2025. Jordan, Holman D. "The Eighth Regiment of Vermont Volunteers in the La Fourche Country, 1862-1863." VT HIS, 31 [1963]: 106-116.

2026. Haynes, Edwin M. A HISTORY OF THE TENTH REGIMENT, VERMONT VOLUNTEERS, WITH BIOGRAPHICAL SKETCHES OF THE OFFICERS WHO FELL IN BATTLE.... Lewiston, Maine: 1870.

2027. Benedict, George G. ARMY LIFE IN VIRGINIA. LETTERS FROM THE TWELFTH VERMONT REGIMENT AND PERSONAL EXPERIENCES OF VOLUNTEER SERVICE IN THE WAR FOR THE UNION.... Burlington, 1895.

2028. Sturtevant, Ralph O. PICTORIAL HISTORY THIRTEENTH REGIMENT VERMONT VOLUNTEERS.... n.p., 1910.

2029. Benedict, George G. A SHORT HISTORY OF THE 14TH VERMONT REGIMENT ... AN ACCOUNT OF THE REUNION HELD JULY 4TH, 1887.... Fair Haven, Vermont: 1887.

West Virginia [Union Troops]

2030. Reader, Francis S. HISTORY OF THE FIFTH WEST VIRGINIA CAVALRY, FORMERLY THE SECOND VIRGINIA INFANTRY, AND OF BATTERY G, FIRST WEST VIRGINIA LIGHT ARTILLERY. New Brighton, Pennsylvania: 1890.

2031. Sutton, Joseph J. HISTORY OF THE SECOND REGIMENT WEST VIRGINIA CAVALRY VOLUNTEERS.... Portsmouth, Ohio: 1892.

2032. Rawling, Charles J. HISTORY OF THE FIRST REGIMENT, VIRGINIA INFANTRY.... [First West Virginia Infantry] Philadelphia, 1887.

2033. Barton, Thomas K. AUTOBIOGRAPHY OF DR. THOMAS H. BARTON ... INCLUDING A HISTORY OF THE FOURTH REGT., WEST VIRGINIA VOL. INF'Y.... Charleston, West Virginia: 1890.

2034. Brown, Genevieve. "A History of the 6th Regular West Virginia Infantry Volunteers." W VA R, 9 [1948]: 315-368.

2035. Matheny, H.E. MAJOR GENERAL THOMAS MALEY HARRIS ... AND ROSTER OF THE 10TH WEST VIRGINIA VOLUNTEER INFANTRY REGIMENT, 1861-1865. Parsons, West Virginia: McClain Printing, 1963.

2036. Hewitt, William. HISTORY OF THE TWELFTH WEST VIRGINIA VOLUNTEER INFANTRY.... Steubenville, Ohio: 1892.

Wisconsin

2037. HISTORY OF THE SERVICES OF THE THIRD BATTERY, WISCONSIN LIGHT ARTILLERY, IN THE CIVIL WAR OF THE UNITED STATES, 1861-1865. By the committee. Berlin, Wisconsin: 1902.

2038. Bryant, Edwin E. HISTORY OF THE THIRD REGIMENT OF WISCONSIN VETERAN VOLUNTEER INFANTRY 1861-1865. Madison, 1891.

2039. Cheek, Philip. HISTORY OF THE SAUK COUNTY RIFLEMEN, KNOWN AS COMPANY "A" SIXTH WISCONSIN.... Madison, 1909.

2040. Driggs, George W. OPENING OF THE MISSISSIPPI, OR TWO YEARS' CAMPAIGNING IN THE SOUTH-WEST. A RECORD OF THE CAMPAIGNS, SIEGES, ACTIONS AND MARCHES IN WHICH THE 8TH WISCONSIN VOLUNTEERS HAVE PARTICIPATED.... Madison, 1864.

2041. Williams, John M. THE "EAGLE REGIMENT," 8TH WISCONSIN INFANTRY VOLUNTEERS.... Belleville, Wisconsin: 1890.

2042. Rood, Hosea W. STORY OF THE SERVICE OF COMPANY E, AND OF THE TWELFTH WISCONSIN REGIMENT OF VETERAN VOLUNTEER INFANTRY.... n.p., 1898.

2043. Houghton, Edgar P. "History of Company I, Fourteenth Wisconsin Infantry, From October 19, 1861--October 9, 1865." WIS MAG HIS, 11 [1927]: 26-49.

2044. Aubery, James M. THE THIRTY SIXTH WISCONSIN VOLUNTEER INFANTRY ... AN AUTHENTIC RECORD OF THE REGIMENT FROM ITS ORGANIZATION TO ITS MUSTER OUT.... Milwaukee, 1900.

2045. Eden, Robert C. THE SWORD AND GUN, A HISTORY OF THE 37TH WISCONSIN VOLUNTEER INFANTRY.... Madison, 1865.

Western States and Territories

[Alphabetically by author]

2046. Adams, Blanche V. "The Second Colorado Cavalry in the Civil War." COL MAG, 8 [1931]: 95-106.

2047. Barbour, Charlotte A. "Quartermastering for the 2nd Colorado Volunteers...." COL MAG, 38 [1961]: 301-366.

2048. Britton, Wiley. THE UNION INDIAN BRIGADE IN THE CIVIL WAR. Kansas City, Missouri: Franklin Hudson, 1922.

2049. Carey, Raymond G. "The 'Bloodless Third' Regiment, Colorado Volunteer Cavalry." COL MAG, 38 [1961]: 275-300.

2050. Clenenden, Clarence C. "The Column From California." CWTI, 9 [9] [1971]: 20-28.

2051. Colwell, Wayne. "The California Hundred." PAC HIS R, 13 [1969]: 63-75.

2052. Cooling, Benjamin F. "The First Nebraska Infantry Regiment and the Battle of Fort Donelson." NEB HIS, 45 [1964]: 131-145.

2053. English, Abner M. "Dakota's First Soldiers." SD HIS COLL, 9 [1918]: 241-307.

2054. Hall, Martin H. "Colorado Volunteers Save New Mexico For the Union." MID AM, 38 [1956]: 195-213.

2055. Hollister, Ovando J. BOLDLY THEY RODE: A HISTORY OF THE FIRST COLORADO REGIMENT OF VOLUNTEERS. Lakewood, Colorado: Golden Press, 1949. A reprint of a 1863 volume.

2056. ———. COLORADO VOLUNTEERS IN NEW MEXICO, 1862. Chicago: Donnelley, 1962.

2057. Hunt, Aurora. "California Volunteers on Border Patrol, Texas and Mexico, 1862-1866. SOUTH CAL HIS SOC Q, 30 [1948]: 265-276.

2058. ———. "The Far West Volunteers." MONTANA, 12 [1962]: 49-61.

2059. Kibby, Leo P. "California Soldiers in the Civil War." CAL HIS SOC Q, 40 [1961]: 343-350.

2060. ———. "Patrick Edward Connor, Commanding General, Third California Infantry: First Gentile of Utah." JW, 2 [1963]: 425-434.

2061. ———. "With Colonel Carleton and the California Column." SOUTH CAL HIS SOC Q, 41 [1959]: 337-344.

2062. McGhee, L.A. "Colorado Pioneers in the Civil War." SW SOC SCI Q, 25 [1944]: 31-42.

2063. Pettis, George H. THE CALIFORNIA COLUMN. Santa Fe, New Mexico: Historical Society of New Mexico, 1908.

2064. ———. FRONTIER SERVICE DURING THE REBELLION. Providence, Rhode Island: 1885.

2065. Rogers, Fred B. SOLDIERS OF THE OVERLAND: BEING SOME ACCOUNT OF THE SERVICES OF GENERAL PATRICK EDWARD CONNOR AND HIS VOLUNTEERS IN THE OLD WEST. San Francisco: Grabhorn, 1938.

2066. Smith, Philip D. "The Sagebrush Soldiers: Nevada's Volunteers in the Civil War." NEB HIS SOC Q, 5 [1962]: 1-87.

2067. Smyrl, Frank H. "Texans in the Union Army, 1861-1865." SW HIS Q, 65 [1961/1962]: 234-250.

2068. Victor, Frances F. "The First Oregon Cavalry." ORE HIS SOC Q, 3 [1902]: 123-163.

2069. Virden, Bill. "The Affair at Minter's Ranch." SD HIS SOC Q, 7 [1961]: 23-25.

2070. Whitford, William C. COLORADO VOLUNTEERS IN THE CIVIL WAR: THE NEW MEXICO CAMPAIGN IN 1862. Denver, Colorado: 1906.

2071. Willard, James F. "The Tyler Rangers: The Black Hawk Company and the Indian Uprising of 1864." COL MAG, 7 [1930]: 147-152.

2072. Williams, Ellen. THREE YEARS AND A HALF IN THE ARMY: OR, HISTORY OF THE SECOND COLORADOS. New York, 1885.

G. CAMPAIGNS AND BATTLES

This category is divided into five sections. The first is "general" which includes works dealing with [a] the activities of federal units and [b] more than one campaign or more than one battle. The second section contains entries on the campaigns and battles listed within the states where they took place. The three final short sections cover the "Scribner Series," maps and national park booklets.

General

2073. Abbot, Willis J. BATTLE FIELDS AND CAMP FIRES. New York, 1890.

An account of military affairs from the Second Bull Run campaign through the battle of Chattanooga.

2074. ———. BATTLE-FIELDS OF '61. New York, 1889.

This volume precedes the above work in time, covering military operations from the outbreak of war through the Peninsular Campaign.

2075. Aldrich, M. Almy. HISTORY OF THE UNITED STATES MARINE CORPS. Boston, 1875.

Details the limited role of the marines in the Civil War.

2076. Anderson, John H. AMERICAN CIVIL WAR. London, 1910.

Written by a British officer this 120-page work covers the first two years of the war in the eastern theater.

2077. Bickham, William D. ROSECRANS' CAMPAIGN WITH THE FOURTEENTH ARMY CORPS. Cincinnati, 1863.

A narrative of the affairs of the Army of the Cumberland. The author was a Cincinnati newspaper correspondent.

2078. Brackett, Albert G. HISTORY OF THE UNITED STATES CAVALRY FROM THE FORMATION OF THE FEDERAL GOVERNMENT TO THE 1ST OF JUNE 1863.... New York, 1865.

This account covers the early years of the war in some detail, focusing largely on the actions of cavalry regiments and their commanders.

2079. Brown, D. Alexander. GALVANIZED YANKEES. Urbana: University of Illinois Press, 1963.

The fascinating story of 6,000 Confederate prisoners of war, who took the oath of allegiance to the Union and were formed into six regiments of United States troops. These units served in the western theater from late 1864 until September 1866. In the last chapter the author discusses "Galvanized Confederates" or those former Yankees who entered service for the South.

2080. Brunker, Howard M.E. STORY OF THE CAMPAIGN IN EASTERN VIRGINIA, APRIL, 1861 TO MAY, 1863. London, 1910.

A brief sketch of campaigning in the East from the outbreak of war through Chancellorsville, written by a British officer.

2081. Buell, Augustus C. "THE CANNONEER." Washington, D.C., 1890.

Opinionated recollections of a "detached volunteer" who had served with the 4th United States Artillery in the Army of the Potomac.

2082. Carter, Samuel. THE LAST CAVALIERS: CONFEDERATE AND UNION CAVALRY IN THE CIVIL WAR. New York: St. Martin's, 1979.

In this story of the lionized, valiant, and eccentric cavalry leaders and their men, every major and most minor cavalry actions of the Civil War are related.

2083. Castel, Albert. "The Guerrilla War." CWTI, 13 [6] [1974]: 3-50.

The entire issue of CIVIL WAR TIMES ILLUSTRATED is devoted to an excellent discussion of the subject.

2084. Curtis, Newton M. FROM BULL RUN TO CHANCELLORSVILLE: THE STORY OF THE SIXTEENTH NEW YORK INFANTRY WITH PERSONAL REMINISCENCES. New York, 1906.

A detailed and readable account of the campaigns of the 16th New York, written by the unit's former commander, who later rose to the rank of general. Curtis thinks very well of McClellan and his achievements.

2085. Elting, John R. "The United States Sharpshooters." MIL COLL HIS, 6 [1954]: 57-61.

Two regiments of "sharpshooters" -- outstanding marksmen -- were organized by the Union army, both of which performed with distinction in the eastern theater.

2086. ——— and Roger D. Sturcke. "The 1st Union Hussar Regiment, 1864-1865." MIL COLL HIS, 30 [1978]: 13-18.

This regiment of mounted troops was recruited in New Jersey.

2087. Embick, Milton A. MILITARY HISTORY OF THE THIRD DIVISION, NINTH CORPS, ARMY OF THE POTOMAC. Harrisburg, 1913.

This 100-page volume contains records of the division's association and addresses delivered at the dedication of statues and monuments.

2088. Fiske, John. THE MISSISSIPPI VALLEY IN THE CIVIL WAR. Boston, 1900.

A widely-read account by one of the most popular historians of the day, although the work has since been superceded by a number of other volumes.

2089. Fout, Frederick W. THE DARK DAYS OF THE CIVIL WAR. St Louis, Missouri: 1904.

The author, who served with the 15th Indiana Artillery Battalion, describes campaigns in West Virginia, Antietam, East Tennessee, and Georgia.

2090. French, Samuel L. THE ARMY OF THE POTOMAC FROM 1861 to 1863. New York, 1906.

An account of the Army of the Potomac under McClellan, Burnside, and Hooker, based on official documents largely, but including pointed opinions of the author.

2091. Gates, Theodore B. THE WAR OF THE REBELLION.... New York, 1884.

The author served with New York's "Ulster Guard" and describes operations in the east from First Bull Run through the Peninsular Campaign.

2092. Goodhart, Briscoe. HISTORY OF THE INDEPENDENT LOUDOUN VIRGINIA RANGERS. Washington, D.C.: 1896.

A straightforward narrative of this United States Volunteer Cavalry unit's operations in northern Virginia from 1862 through the end of the war. Their primary job was to serve as scouts for the Union forces.

2093. Hoole, William S. ALABAMA TORIES, THE 1ST ALABAMA CAVALRY, USA, 1862-1865, Tuscaloosa: Confederate Printing, 1960.

With the federal invasion in 1862, some Alabama citizens who did not hold with secession joined the Union army. The history of the 1st Alabama Cavalry, organized in October 1862, is told in detail.

2094. Hubbell, John T., editor. BATTLES LOST AND WON: ESSAYS FROM CIVIL WAR HISTORY. Westport, Connecticut: Greenwood, 1975.

An anthology of 18 excellent articles on military aspects of the war, which first appeared in the quarterly journal CIVIL WAR HISTORY.

2095. Humphreys, Andrew A. FROM GETTYSBURG TO THE RAPIDAN. New York, 1883.

An 86-page account of the campaigning of the Army of the Potomac from July 1863 to April 1864. This is not part of Scribner's CAMPAIGNS OF THE CIVIL WAR series.

2096. Hyde, Thomas W. FOLLOWING THE GREEK CROSS; OR MEMORIES OF THE SIXTH ARMY CORPS. Boston, 1894.

Hyde was a major with the 7th Maine and fought in the eastern theater. He was breveted brigadier general and also received the Medal of Honor for his bravery at Antietam. This is an excellent, well-written book.

2097. Hyman, Harold M. "Lincoln's Galvanized Yankees." LIN HER, 65 [1963]: 32-36.

The efforts of Lincoln and Stanton to induce captured Confederates to become Union soldiers by taking the oath of loyalty is described. Done largely for propaganda purposes, this plan was only moderately successful.

2098. Irwin, Richard B. HISTORY OF THE NINETEENTH ARMY CORPS. New York, 1892.

A lengthy, useful account of the 19th Corps from the autumn of 1862 to the fall of 1864.

2099. Joinville, Francois F.P.L.M. d'Orleans, Prince de. THE ARMY OF THE POTOMAC: ITS ORGANIZATION, ITS COMMANDER, AND ITS CAMPAIGN. New York, 1862.

A classic account of the Peninsular Campaign by a French nobleman who accompanied McClellan's troops. Sympathetic to the Union cause.

2100. Jones, Paul. THE IRISH BRIGADE. Washington, D.C.: Luce, 1969.

This study is more concerned with Thomas Francis Meagher and his life than the Irish Brigade itself. Meagher led the brigade until May 1863 when he resigned. The author does provide some insight into the political psychology of the Irish immigrants during the war.

2101. Jones, Virgil C. GRAY GHOSTS AND REBEL RAIDERS. New York: Henry Holt, 1956.

An excellent account of the role played by Virginia's partisan rangers in the war. The successful depredations of these Confederate guerrillas, it is argued, may have lengthened the war almost a year.

2102. Kelley, Margaret R. "A Soldier of the Iron Brigade." WIS MAG HIS, 22 [1939]: 286-311.

An account of William Ryan, an Irish immigrant who commanded a company in the Iron Brigade. Ryan was discharged after being wounded in the spring of 1863.

2103. Longacre, Edward G. MOUNTED RAIDS OF THE CIVIL WAR. South Brunswick, New Jersey: Barnes, 1975.

While not containing much new information, this is a good survey of cavalry operations of both Union and Confederate armies.

2104. Lord, Francis A. "Ellet's 'Marine Brigade' of the Federal Army." MIL COLL HIS, 17 [1975]: 159-160.

Operations of a Union amphibious unit in the Mississippi River.

2105. ———. "Killed [Not in Action]." CWTI, 8 [6] [1969]: 30-33.

Author discusses three types of situations under which soldiers were killed other than by enemy action. They were: [a] carelessness, [b] officers and men killed by their own troops, and [c] the killing of prisoners.

2106. Maguire, Thomas M. THE CAMPAIGNS IN VIRGINIA, 1861-1862. London, 1891.

A 70-page narrative written by a British civilian.

2107. McClellan, Carswell. THE PERSONAL MEMOIRS AND MILITARY HISTORY OF U.S. GRANT VERSUS THE RECORD OF THE ARMY OF THE POTOMAC. Boston, 1887.

An unfriendly look at Grant's command in 1864-1865.

2108. McClellan, George B. ... LETTER OF THE SECRETARY OF WAR, TRANSMITTING REPORT ON THE ORGANIZATION OF THE ARMY OF THE POTOMAC .... Washington, D.C.: 1864.

Official report of the Army of the Potomac commander covering the period from July 26, 1861 to November 7, 1862, when he was relieved. An invaluable research tool.

2109. McCormack, John F., Jr. "'Never Were Men So Brave.'" CWTI, 8 [1] [1969]: 36-44.

The title is a quotation from Robert E. Lee describing the Irish Brigade, which suffered very heavy casualties but never lost a battle flag in the war.

MILITARY HISTORICAL SOCIETY OF MASSACHUSETTS, PAPERS OF.

2110. CAMPAIGNS IN VIRGINIA, 1861-1862. Boston, 1895.

2111. THE VIRGINIA CAMPAIGN OF 1862 UNDER GENERAL POPE. Boston, 1895.

2112. CAMPAIGNS IN VIRGINIA, MARYLAND, AND PENNSYLVANIA, 1862-1863.... Boston, 1903.

2113. THE WILDERNESS CAMPAIGN, MAY-JUNE, 1864. Boston, 1905.

2114. ... SHENANDOAH CAMPAIGNS OF 1862 AND 1864 AND THE APPOMATTOX CAMPAIGN, 1865. Boston, 1907.

2115. CAMPAIGNS IN KENTUCKY AND TENNESSEE INCLUDING THE BATTLE OF CHICKAMAUGA, 1862-1864 .... Boston, 1908.

2116. THE MISSISSIPPI VALLEY, TENNESSEE, GEORGIA, ALABAMA, 1861-1864. Boston, 1910.

2117. OPERATIONS ON THE ATLANTIC COAST, 1861-1865. Boston, 1912.

2118. CIVIL WAR AND MISCELLANEOUS PAPERS. Boston, 1918.

Each of the above volumes contains an excellent collection of articles by different authors on the subject indicated. For the most part the contributors participated in the actions they wrote about.

MORGAN'S RAID [June--July 1863]

2119. Benedict, James B., Jr. "General John Hunt Morgan, the Great Indiana--Ohio Raid." FCHQ, 31 [1975]: 147-171.

A satisfactory account of the famous raid, written in the author's senior year [1956] at Phillips Academy, Andover, Massachusetts and submitted in competition for a prize in American history.

2120. Blair, John L. "Morgan's Ohio Raid." FCHQ, 36 [1962]: 242-271.

In addition to reviewing Morgan's raid, the author examines the theory that the raid was designed to spark a pro-Confederate uprising in the Northwest. He concludes that the evidence is inconclusive.

2121. Butler, Lorine L. MORGAN AND HIS MEN. Philadelphia: Dorrance, 1960.

The story of a gallant generous man who was a romantic but controversial figure.

2122. Funk, Arville L. "An Ohio Farmer's Account of Morgan's Raid." OHIO HIS Q, 70 [1961]: 244-246.

A letter from David Hulse describing the passage of Morgan and his men through Sharonville, Ohio. Hulse's main theme is the protection of the horses from both Union and Confederate soldiers.

2123. Gard, Ronald M. MORGAN'S RAID INTO OHIO. Lisbon, Ohio: n.p., 1963.

A 62-page description of Morgan's raid.

2124. Harrison, Lowell A. "A Federal Officer Pursues John Hunt Morgan." FCHQ, 48 [1972]: 129-143.

Ten illuminating letters from Captain Samuel McDowell Starling to his daughters in Kentucky. The letters are written from various places in Kentucky, Indiana, and Ohio, from July 2 to July 28, 1863.

2125. "Hines Raid, Invasion of the State, The." IND HIS BULL, 36 [1959]: 53-56.

Captain Thomas H. Hines ventured into Indiana with 62 men. All but three were captured. Hines managed to evade capture, rejoined Morgan, was captured, and finally escaped with Morgan.

2126. Jordan, Lewis. "Report of Colonel Lewis Jordan, Commanding 6th Regiment Indiana Legion." IND HIS BULL, 38 [1961]: 115-117.

Written on August 11, 1863 by Colonel Jordan, the report summarizes the actions taken against Morgan and his men in July while they were in Indiana.

2127. Keller, Allan. MORGAN'S RAID. Indianapolis: Bobbs-Merrill, 1961.

A readable account of the raid.

2128. Reid, Samuel C. THE CAPTURE AND WONDERFUL ESCAPE OF GENERAL JOHN H. MORGAN, AS REPORTED BY SAMUEL C. REID, JR. OF THE ATLANTA INTELLIGENCER. Joseph G. Mathews, editor. Atlanta, Georgia: Emory University Library, 1947.

A 20-page booklet reprinting an article written by a reporter from the ATLANTA INTELLIGENCER.

2129. Smith, Myron J., Jr. "An Indiana Sailor Scuttles Morgan's Raid." IND HIS BULL, 48 [1971]: 87-98.

Traces the efforts of Commander Leroy Fitch in pursuing the Confederate raiders. Fitch used "tinclads," which were "thinly armored, converted steamers" to pursue the raiders and ultimately thwart their efforts to retreat.

2130. Still, John S. "Blitzkrieg, 1863, Morgan's Raid and Route." CWH, 3 [1957]: 291-306.

A review of Morgan's famous raid and the route of his march. Morgan achieved his military objective, delaying Rosecrans' move toward Chattanooga, but he paid a very high price.

* * *

2131. Morrow, Henry A. "... The Diary of Colonel Henry A. Morrow...." CWTI, 14 [1976]: [9] 12-22; [10] 1-21.

Morrow was a member of the 24th Michigan which was part of the Iron Brigade. Serving in most of the major battles in the east, Morrow was wounded at Gettysburg and again at the Wilderness. His eye-witness accounts are interesting.

2132. Newcomer, Christopher A. COLE'S CAVALRY; OR THREE YEARS IN THE SADDLE IN THE SHENANDOAH VALLEY. Baltimore, 1885.

A discussion of a Maryland cavalry unit in the Union army. There are some brief descriptions of various military activities and good details of army life.

2133. Nolan, Alan T. THE IRON BRIGADE: A MILITARY HISTORY. New York: Macmillan, 1961.

An excellent history of this famous fighting unit composed of troops from Wisconsin, Michigan, and Indiana, and which was one of the few western organizations to fight with the Army of the Potomac.

2134. Powell, William H. THE FIFTH ARMY CORPS. London, England: 1896.

A voluminous, yet solid history of the 5th Corps, Army of the Potomac.

2135. Redway, George W. ... THE WAR OF SECESSION, 1861-1862.... London, England: 1910.

A good study of operations from Bull Run to Malvern Hill by a British scholar.

2136. Rhodes, Charles D. HISTORY OF THE CAVALRY OF THE ARMY OF THE POTOMAC.... Kansas City, Missouri: 1900.

A survey of cavalry operations in the eastern theater.

2137. Ripley, William Y.W. VERMONT RIFLEMEN IN THE WAR FOR THE UNION. Rutland, Vermont: 1883.

A history of Company F of the First United States [Berdan's] Sharpshooters.

2138. Rodenbough, Theophilus F. "The Cavalry of the Civil War, Its Evolution and Influence." ARR, 43 [1911]: 561-570.

This article forms the introductory chapter to a volume in the PHOTOGRAPHIC HISTORY OF THE CIVIL WAR series then being published. Author reviews U.S. cavalry history prior to the Civil War as well as during the war.

2139. Round, Harold F. "Hooker's 'Light Division.'" CWTI, 5 [4] [1966]: 20-23, 25-27.

Author describes the three-month life of a unit organized "to act independently in reconnaissance, outpost duty, skirmishing, and making forced marches" for the Army of the Potomac.

2140. Sheppard, Eric W. THE AMERICAN CIVIL WAR, 1864-1865. London, England: Gale and Polden, 1938.

An able account of the last year of the war written by a British officer.

2141. Smith, Charles. THE HISTORY OF FULLER'S OHIO BRIGADE, 1861-1865. Cleveland, 1909.

A lengthy, but good brigade history, including route of march, roster, portraits, battle maps and biographies. Quite dependent upon the OFFICIAL RECORDS.

2142. Starr, Stephen Z. THE UNION CAVALRY IN THE CIVIL WAR. 2 v. Baton Rouge: Louisiana State University Press, 1979-1981.

This is a carefully-researched, well-documented, and very well-written study of the federal horse soldiers. Author discusses the organization of units, the daily life of officers and men, and campaigns.

2143. Stevens, Charles A. BERDAN'S UNITED STATES SHARPSHOOTERS.... St. Paul, Minnesota: 1892.

Although old, this remains an excellent account of the 1st United States Regiment of Sharpshooters, which served in the Army of the Potomac. Author was a journalist.

2144. Stevens, George T. THREE YEARS IN THE SIXTH CORPS.... New York, 1870.

While this work is over 100 years old it is still helpful for an understanding of operations in the East throughout the war. It provides good glimpses of soldier life.

2145. Stine, James H. HISTORY OF THE ARMY OF THE POTOMAC. Philadelphia, 1892.

This big book has its weaknesses, but it can be a worthwhile source for the reader.

2146. Stuart, Reginald C. "Cavalry Raids in the West: Case Studies of Civil War." TENN HIS Q, 30, [1971]: 259-276.

The author examines three cavalry raids [two South, one North] in Tennessee and Kentucky in the winter of 1862-1863 and concludes that the role of the cavalry was diminishing. Few long raids ever achieved significant lasting results.

2147. Swinton, William. CAMPAIGNS OF THE ARMY OF THE POTOMAC.... New York, 1882.

The reissue of an 1866 volume by a NEW YORK TIMES correspondent, this is a solid narrative of operations in the eastern theater for the entire war.

2148. Tilney, Robert. MY LIFE IN THE ARMY.... Philadelphia, 1912.

A well-written account by an Englishman who served for three and one-half years with the Fifth Corps in the Army of the Potomac from 1862 to 1865.

2149. Van Horne, Thomas B. HISTORY OF THE ARMY OF THE CUMBERLAND.... 2 v. Cincinnati, 1875.

This two-volume work was written at the request of General George H. Thomas and is based largely on his own private and public papers.

2150. Waddle, Angus L. THREE YEARS WITH THE ARMIES OF THE OHIO AND CUMBERLAND. Chillicothe, Ohio: 1889.

The author, an officer in the 33rd Ohio, recalls his experiences while campaigning in the western theater.

2151. Walker, Francis A. HISTORY OF THE SECOND ARMY CORPS IN THE ARMY OF THE POTOMAC. New York, 1891.

A large volume filled with documentary materials. Walker was wounded at Chancellorsville and after the war became a famous economist and educator.

2152. Webb, Willard, editor. CRUCIAL MOMENTS OF THE CIVIL WAR. New York: Fountainhead Publishers, 1961.

A good collection of eyewitness accounts of 18 important battles.

2153. Weinert, Richard W. "A Regiment of Rascals." CWTI. 5 [6] [1966]: 22-24.

A brief account of the 16th Virginia Infantry. The unit, composed chiefly of bounty jumpers, was organized to serve in the defence of the nation's capital.

2154. Williams, Kenneth P. LINCOLN FINDS A GENERAL: A MILITARY STUDY OF THE CIVIL WAR. 5 v. New York: Macmillan, 1949-1959.

A landmark work, distinguished by thoroughgoing scholarship and thoughtful analysis. Author died after carrying the story through the campaigns of 1863. Grant emerges as a superior general.

Campaigns and Battles by States

The following entries include all "major" and many "minor" military actions grouped by state. The term "major" has arbitrarily been determined to refer to those campaigns and battles where the combined casualty numbers [dead, wounded, missing, and taken prisoner] are in excess of 5,000. The major campaigns and battles are listed chronologically at the beginning of each state. Entries for such campaigns and battles are organized alphabetically by author. Following the major campaigns and battles the remaining entries for the particular state are listed alphabetically by author.

Alabama

2155. Bearss, Edwin C. "Rousseau's Raid on the Montgomery and West Point Railroad." ALA HIS Q, 25 [1963]: 7-48.

During the Atlanta Campaign, General Lovell R. Rousseau conducted a cavalry raid along the railroad west of Columbus, Georgia, inflicting heavy damage on the Confederate line. The action occurred from July 9-22, 1864.

2156. Burns, Zed H. "Abel D. Streight Encounters Nathan Bedford Forrest." J MISS HIS, 30 [1968]: 245-259.

From April 11 to May 3, 1863, Streight, who commanded the 51st Indiana, conducted an unsuccessful raid into northwest Georgia for the purpose of cutting the railroad and preventing supplies and reinforcements from reaching Bragg.

2157. Folman, John K. "The War Comes to Central Alabama: Ebenezer Church, April 1, 1865." ALA HIS Q, 26 [1964]: 187-202.

Union general James H. Wilson's famous raid in the spring of 1865 which brought war to an area which had not known it before. Confederate forces failed to stop the federals at Ebenezer Church, where General "Bed" Forrest attempted a futile defence with inadequate troops.

2158. Cook, James F. "The 1863 Raid of Abel D. Streight: Why it Failed." ALA R, 22 [1969]: 254-269.

Author contends that useless ammunition and sheer exhaustion were the decisive factors in Streight's surrender to Forrest.

2159. Johnson, Kenneth R. "Confederate Defenses and Union Gunboats on the Tennessee River: A Federal Raid Into Northwest Alabama." ALA HIS Q, 30 [1968]: 39-60.

A discussion of Confederate defenses on the Tennessee.

2160. Jones, Allen W. "A Federal Raid Into Southern Alabama." ALA R, 14 [1961]: 259-268.

This raid took place in February 1862.

2161. Jones, James P. "Wilson's Raiders Reach Georgia: The Fall of Columbus, 1865." GA HIS Q, 59 [1975]: 313-329.

The culmination of General James H. Wilson's celebrated raid through central Alabama and Georgia in March and April of 1865. Columbus fell April 16 after the war was over.

2162. ———. YANKEE BLITZKRIEG: WILSON'S RAID THROUGH ALABAMA AND GEORGIA. Athens: University of Georgia Press, 1976.

An exhaustive account of the raid which wiped out the "last ditch" of the Confederacy. The 27-year old Wilson led 13,000 cavalrymen in the campaign.

2163. Longacre, Edward G. "'All is Fair in Love and War.'" CWTI, 8 [3] [1969]: 32-40.

In this account of Streight's raid into northwestern Georgia, the author states that the Confederate Forrest convinced Streight he should surrender because his forces were inferior in number to the Confederates.

2164. Roberson, B.L. "The Courthouse Burnin'est General." TENN HIS Q, 23 [1964]: 372-378.

An account of the raids led by Confederate General Hylan B. Lyon against Union railroad and telegraph lines in northern Alabama in the last year of the war.

2165. Trusty, Lance. "Private Smith Takes Mobile: A Soldier's Journal." LIN HER, 80 [1978]: 78-83.

A portion of a Union soldier's journal describing the land assault against Mobile in the spring of 1865.

Arkansas

PEA RIDGE [March 6-8, 1862] [Also called ELKHORN]

2166. Bearss, Edwin C. "The Battle of Pea Ridge." ARK HIS Q, 20 [1961]: 74-94.

A description of the events leading up to the battle and the first day of fighting, March 6, 1862.

2167. ———. "The Battle of Pea Ridge." ANN IOWA, 36 [1963]: 659-689; 37 [1964]: 9-41, 121-155, 207-239, 304-317.

This five-part study is the most thoroughgoing analysis of the battle known as "The Gettysburg of the West."

2168. Brown, D. Alexander. "Pea Ridge: 'The Gettysburg of the West.'" CWTI, 6 [6] [1967]: 4-11, 46-48.

A detailed analysis of this bloody two day decisive battle. Not only did the South lose three generals, but the way was opened for the Union to control Arkansas.

2169. Brown, Walter L. "Pea Ridge, Gettysburg of the West." ARK HIS Q, 15 [1956]: 3-16.

Author argues that the Confederate defeat at Pea Ridge was a major setback. It meant the loss of Missouri--and much more--after which the South must remain on the defensive in the West.

2170. Castel, Albert. "New View of the Battle of Pea Ridge." MO HIS R, 62 [1968]: 136-151.

Author believes that the traditional view, wherein the Confederate failure at Pea Ridge, March 7, 1862, caused the South to abandon the Trans-Mississippi as an important theater of war, is not quite correct. It did become a "secondary" area, but had the general military situation permitted it, stronger efforts would have been made to regain and hold the Trans-Mississippi West.

2171. Edwards, Dale. "Arkansas: Pea Ridge and State Division." JW, 14 [1975]: 167-184.

Discusses the Civil War in Arkansas and the consequences of the Union victory at Pea Ridge.

2172. Ford, Harvey S. "Van Dorn and the Pea Ridge Campaign." A MIL INST J, 3 [1939]: 222-236.

Describes military affairs in Missouri and Arkansas and takes a close look at Pea Ridge.

2173. Ham, Sharon. "End of Innocence." PALIMP, 60 [1979]: 76-97.

Sketches of nine boys from Independence, Missouri, who served in the Union Army. Eight of the nine died at Pea Ridge.

2174. Kerr, Homer L. "Battle of Elkhorn: The Gettysburg of the Trans-Mississippi West." In ESSAYS ON THE CIVIL WAR. William F. Holmes and Harold M. Hollingsworth, editors. Austin: University of Texas Press, 1968.

Federal success in this important struggle for control of Missouri is attributed to a more favorable tactical position, exhaustion of Confederate troops, depletion of supplies and ammunition, and the loss of three Confederate generals.

2175. Moody, Claire M. BATTLE OF PEA RIDGE OR ELKHORN TAVERN. Little Rock, Arkansas: Arkansas Valley Printing, 1956.

A brief examination of this unforgettable encounter.

* * *

2176. Abercrombie, Irene. "The Battle of Prairie Grove." ARK HIS Q, 2 [1943]: 309-315.

An account of a minor but bloody battle which occurred in northwestern Arkansas on December 7, 1862.

2177. Atkinson, J. "The Action at Prairie d'Ann." ARK HIS Q, 19 [1960]: 40-50.

Prairie d'Ann was a four-day battle [April 10-13, 1864] in southwestern Arkansas which prevented Union General Frederick Steele from linking up with Banks' Red River operations.

2178. Bearss, Edwin C. "The Battle of Helena, July 4, 1863." ARK HIS Q, 20 [1961]: 256-297.

The Confederate attack on Helena was a belated and futile attempt to divert attention from Vicksburg, which fell to the Federals the day of this battle.

2179. ———. "The Battle of the Post of Arkansas." ARK HIS Q, 18 [1959]: 237-279.

Arkansas Post [Fort Hindman], a strong Confederate fort 50 miles up the Arkansas River, was seized by General McClernand, January 10-11, 1863.

2180. ———. "Confederate Action Against Fort Smith Post: Early 1864." ARK HIS Q, 29 [1970]: 226-251.

A blow-by-blow account of Confederate efforts to seize the important federal posts of Fort Smith, Van Buren, Roseville, and Clarksville, Arkansas, in the spring of 1864.

2181. ———. "The Federals Capture Fort Smith, 1863." ARK HIS Q, 28 [1969]: 156-190.

A Union offensive into Indian Territory led to the recapture of Fort Smith on September 1, 1863. The campaign ended Confederate activity north of the Arkansas River.

2182. ———. "The Federals Raid Van Buren and Threaten Fort Smith." ARK HIS Q, 26 [1967]: 123-142.

At stake were overland routes from Fort Smith to Missouri.

2183. ———. "The Federals Struggle to Hold On To Fort Smith." ARK HIS Q, 24 [1965]: 149-179.

Fort Smith was located on the Arkansas River as it entered Indian Territory. It was an important Union supply depot for troops in Arkansas and beyond.

2184. ———. "Fort Smith Serves General McCulloch as a Supply Depot." ARK HIS Q, 24 [1965]: 315-347.

Confederate General Benjamin McCulloch commanded Fort Smith while it was in Confederate hands. He was killed at Pea Ridge.

2185. ———. "General Bussey Takes Over At Fort Smith." ARK HIS Q, 24 [1965]: 220-240.

An account of supply problems at Fort Smith in the last months of the war.

2186. ———. "Marmaduke Attacks Pine Bluff." ARK HIS Q, 23 [1964]: 291-313.

Author discusses the causes for Confederate General Marmaduke's unsuccessful move against Pine Bluff in October 1863.

2187. ———. STEELE'S RETREAT FROM CAMDEN AND THE BATTLE OF JENKINS' FERRY. Little Rock, Arkansas: Pioneer Press, 1967.

The final episodes in Steele's belated and unsuccessful efforts to reach Banks.

2188. ——— and Arrell M. Gibson. FORT SMITH: LITTLE GIBRALTAR ON THE ARKANSAS. Norman: University of Oklahoma Press, 1969.

In this informative history of an important frontier post, Indian affairs, the Civil War on the western border, and the development of the Southwest is described. The book covers the period from 1817 when the fort was founded to 1896.

2189. Castel, Albert G. "Fiasco at Helena." CWTI, 7 [5] [1968]: 12-17.

An account of the Confederate failure at Helena, occurring on the day Vicksburg fell.

2190. Davis, William C. "The Battle of Prairie Grove." CWTI, 7 [4] [1968]: 12-19.

Union General James Blunt defeated a superior Confederate force, December 7, 1862 and prevented it from reinforcing the Confederates at Vicksburg.

2191. DeWolf, Charles W. "The Capture of Van Buren, Arkansas, During the Civil War: From the Diary of a Union Horse Soldier." Thomas E. Wright, editor. ARK HIS Q, 38 [1979]: 72-89.

DeWolf participated in the capture of Van Buren in December 1862.

2192. Huff, Leo E. "Guerrillas, Jayhawkers and Bushwackers in Northern Arkansas During the Civil War." ARK HIS Q, 24 [1965]: 127-148.

Guerrilla bands of Jayhawkers [Union] and Bushwhackers [Confederates] brought desolation along the border.

2193. ———. "The Union Expedition Against Little Rock, August-September, 1863." ARK HIS Q, 22 [1963]: 224-237.

General Frederick Steele commanded this successful operation which led to the Confederate loss of northern Arkansas and some of the Trans-Mississippi West.

2194. Huffstot, Robert S. "Post of Arkansas." CWTI, 7 [9] [1969]: 10-19.

An account of the successful Union assault on this Confederate fort which helped restore confidence in the Union war effort after Fredericksburg.

2195. Jones, Allen W. "Military Events in Arkansas During the Civil War, 1861-1865." ARK HIS Q, 22 [1963]: 124-170.

Detailed tables of places, dates, and types of over 800 military events.

2196. McDonald, Harold L. "The Battle of Jenkins' Ferry." ARK HIS Q, 7 [1948]: 57-67.

Union forces were routed in the final battle of the "Camden Expedition," April 30, 1864.

2197. Oates, Stephen P. "The Prairie Grove Campaign, 1862." ARK HIS Q, 19 [1960]: 119-141.

At Prairie Grove, Arkansas early in December 1862 the Confederates failed to drive the Federals out of the state, in a battle which was technically a stalemate, but actually a defeat for the South.

2198. Richards, Ira D. "The Battle of Jenkins' Ferry." ARK HIS Q, 20 [1961]: 3-16.

Jenkins' Ferry was located on the Saline River some miles south of Little Rock.

2199. ———. "The Battle of Poison Spring." ARK HIS Q, 18 [1959]: 338-349.

The Confederates won this minor battle in southwestern Arkansas, April 18, 1864.

2200. ———. "The Engagement of Marks' Mills." ARK HIS Q, 19 [1960]: 51-60.

Confederate cavalry routed a federal wagon train during the Arkansas campaign of April 1864.

2201. Smith, Jodie A. "Battlegrounds and Soldiers of Arkansas, 1861-1865." ARK HIS Q, 6 [1947]: 180-185.

Includes a listing of battles fought in the state of Arkansas.

2202. White, Lonnie J., editor. "A Bluecoat's Account of the Camden Expedition." ARK HIS Q, 24 [1965]: 82-89.

The hardships of the ill-fated Camden Expedition are related in this account written by a white officer in a black regiment.

District of Columbia

2203. Cooling, B. Franklin, III. "Civil War Deterrent: Defenses of Washington." MIL AFF, 29 [1965] 164-178.

With each Confederate move, the defense plan for Washington was reevaluated. The first step was to gain major footholds in Virginia on Arlington Heights and in Alexandria. By the end of the war 68 forts had been constructed surrounding the city and over 800 mounted artillery pieces were in place.

2204. ———. SYMBOL, SWORD AND SHIELD: DEFENDING WASHINGTON DURING THE CIVIL WAR. Hamden, Connecticut: Archon Books, 1975.

A good study of the defense works around Washington, built at a cost of $1,400,000. The extensive field fortifications allowed Washington to emerge from the war unscathed. This book is a more thoroughgoing examination of the defenses of Washington than contained in the previous entry.

2205. Hecks, Frederick C. "Lincoln, Wright and Holmes at Fort Stevens." JISHS, 39 [1946]: 323-332.

Fort Stevens was part of the defense works around Washington, where Lincoln exposed himself to enemy fire at the time of Early's Raid.

2206. Langsdorf, Edgar. "Jim Lane and the Frontier Guard." KAN HIS Q, 9 [1940]: 13-25.

Lane, senator from Kentucky, formed the Frontier Guard as a voluntary unofficial unit. Cameron called on Lane to guard the President, so the unit camped in the East Room of the White House. In spite of the comic opera aspects, these actions made Lane an "intimate" of Lincoln.

2207. Vandiver, Frank E. JUBAL'S RAID: GENERAL EARLY'S FAMOUS ATTACK ON WASHINGTON IN 1864. New York: McGraw-Hill, 1960.

An authoritative account of the celebrated raid on Washington, July 1864, which culminated a one-month campaign designed to secure Lee's communications to the West and clear the Shenandoah Valley of Federals. Author describes in gripping detail the chaos in Washington as Early's forces approached.

Florida

2208. Baltzell, George F. "The Battle of Olustee, Florida." FLA HIS Q, 9 [1930/1931]: 199-223.

The Federals were defeated in this engagement west of Jacksonville, February 20, 1864.

2209. Bearss, Edwin C. "Asboth's Expedition Up the Alabama and Florida Railroad, July 21-25, 1864." FLA HIS Q, 39 [1960/1961]: 159-166.

Union General Alexander Asboth, a native of Hungary, was a divisional commander in the West before assuming command of the District of West Florida in August 1863.

2210. ———. Civil War Operations In and Around Pensacola." FLA HIS Q, 36 [1957/1958]: 125-165; 39 [1960/1961]: 231-255, 330-353.

A detailed three-part study of affairs at Pensacola, Florida and Ft. Pickens, from the time it was seized by authorities of the seceding state of Florida on January 12, 1861, until the time it was retaken by federal forces on May 10, 1862.

2211. ———. "Federal Expedition Against Saint Marks Ends at Natural Bridge." FLA HIS Q, 45 [1967]: 369-390.

Main purpose of this Union amphibious attack on March 4-6, 1865, was to close the Saint Marks River to blockade runners.

2212. ———. "Military Operations on the St. Johns, September-October, 1862." FLA HIS Q, 42 [1963/1964]: 232-247, 331-350.

The first part of this two-part article deals with the failure of the navy to drive the Confederates from St. Johns Bluff. Control of the St. Johns River was essential to the Confederates if Jacksonville was to remain open as a blockade running port. Federal efforts to close the river finally succeeded in the fall of 1862.

2213. Boyd, Mark F. "The Battle of Marianna." FLA HIS Q, 29 [1950/1951]: 225-242.

General Asboth was badly wounded in the face in the battle in northern Florida, September 27, 1864.

2214. Cushman, Joseph D. "The Blockade and Fall of Apalachicola 1861-1862." FLA HIS Q, 41 [1962/1963]: 38-46.

Though possessing a population of only 2,000, Apalachicola was one of the most important seaports in the pre-war South. It was under Union blockade in the early months of the war, but was finally abandoned by the Confederates in March 1862 because of their great need for troops in Tennessee. Oddly enough, for the remainder of the war neither side occupied the city.

2215. Duren, Charles M. "The Occupation of Jacksonville, February 1864, and the Battle of Olustee." FLA HIS Q, 32 [1953/1954]: 262-287.

This is a letter from the author, who was a lieutenant with the federal forces.

2216. East, Omega C. "St. Augustine During the Civil War." FLA HIS Q, 31 [1952/1953]: 75-91.

Federal forces occupied the undefended St. Augustine on March 11, 1862 and held it until the war was over. While the soldiers encountered civilian hostility and guerrilla fighters in the area, they succeeded in their main objective of closing St. Augustine as a blockade-running port for Confederates.

2217. Jones, Allen W. "Military Events in Florida During the Civil War, 1861-1865." FLA HIS Q, 39 [1960/1961]: 42-45.

An alphabetical listing of military events in Florida during the war. The material is organized in three columns: the place of the event, the type of the event, and the date of the event.

2218. Larkin, J.L. "Battle of Santa Rosa Island." FLA HIS Q, 37 [1958/1959]: 372-376.

An account of an unsuccessful attempt by Confederates to oust Union forces from Santa Rosa Island in Pensacola Bay, October 8-9, 1861.

2219. McMurry, Richard. "The President's Tenth and the Battle of Olustee." CWTI, 16 [9] [1978]: 12-24.

The Florida campaign of February 1864 was designed to mobilize political support in Florida for President Lincoln's forthcoming reelection bid.

2220. Swift, Lester L., editor. "Captain Dana in Florida: A Narrative of the Seymour Expedition." CWH, 11 [1965]: 245-256.

Gustavus Sullivan Dana's diary describes the ill-fated Florida expedition of February 1864, which resulted in the Union defeat at Olustee.

Georgia

THE ANDREWS RAID [April 12-13, 1862]

2221. Feuerlicht, Roberta S. ANDREWS' RAIDERS. New York: Collier, 1963.

A colorful dramatic account of the "Great Locomotive Chase."

2222. Folger, Fred J. "The Andrews Raid." NW OHIO Q, 39 [1967]: [1] 10-15; [2] 51-60; [4] 5-14.

In this three-part series, following an account of the raid, author describes the fates of the raiders after their capture.

2223. Grose, Parlee C. THE CASE OF PRIVATE SMITH AND THE REMAINING MYSTERIES OF THE ANDREWS RAID. McComb, Ohio: General Publishing, 1963.

The author does not fully succeed, and he admits it, in clearing up the mystery of what happened to James Smith of the 2nd Ohio and one of the original "raiders." He also analyzes a number of the works which have been published about the raid.

2224. Kartz, Wilbur G. "The Andrews Railroad Raid." CWTI, 5 [1] [1966]: 8-17, 38-43.

Discusses the locomotives which figured in the raid, the "General" and the "Texas" and tells what became of them.

2225. O'Neill, Charles K. WILD TRAIN: THE STORY OF THE ANDREWS RAIDERS. New York: Random House, 1956.

The most detailed, recent account of the raid told through the words of the participants and other contemporaries. The final 100 pages of the book describe the subsequent lives of the 14 [of 22] survivors and the quarrels and disputes which broke out among them. There is some speculation as to who the mysterious "Andrews" was, with no conclusion drawn.

2226. Pittenger, William. CAPTURING A LOCOMOTIVE: A HISTORY OF SECRET SERVICE IN THE LATE WAR. Philadelphia, 1882.

One of eleven later editions of the next entry. The reissue of the book may have triggered the controversy over Pittenger's informing on his fellows.

2227. ———. DARING AND SUFFERING: A HISTORY OF THE GREAT RAILROAD ADVENTURE. Philadelphia, 1863.

An early basic source by one of the "raiders" who was exchanged after his capture. Though awarded the Medal of Honor with other survivors, Pittenger was later accused of having betrayed the eight who were executed. The dispute on this point burst into the open in the 1880s, but was never cleared up.

CHICKAMAUGA [September 19-20, 1963]

2228. Chapin, James. "With the Army of the Cumberland in the Chickamauga Campaign: The Diary of James W. Chapin, Thirty-Ninth Indiana Volunteers." Donald E. Reynolds and Max H. Kels, editors. GA HIS Q, 54 [1975]: 223-242.

Chapin's diary discusses the military strategy of the campaign.

2229. Gracie, Archibald. THE TRUTH ABOUT CHICKAMAUGA. Boston, 1911.

This is a detailed account of the campaign, accompanied by good maps.

2230. Kepler, Virginia. "My God, We Thought You Had a Division Here." CWTI, 5 [9] [1967]: 4-11, 47-49.

Describes the actions of the 21st Ohio at Chickamauga. The unit was equipped with Colt repeating rifles, which were important in saving the Army of the Cumberland.

2231. Livingood, James W. "Chickamauga and Chattanooga National Military Park." TENN HIS Q, 23 [1964]: 3-23.

Describes how two veterans, feeling the battlefield should be preserved, developed the idea that grew into the military park of today.

2232. Martin, John A. "Some Notes of the Eighth Kansas Infantry and the Battle of Chickamauga: Letters of Colonel John A. Martin." KAN HIS Q, 13 [1944]: 139-145.

Three letters from Lieutenant Colonel John A. Martin, the 22-year old commander of the 8th Kansas, to John J. Ingalls, shortly after the battle of Chickamauga. The regiment suffered 65 per cent losses in the battle.

2233. Morgan John M. "Old Steady: The Role of James Blair Steedman at the Battle of Chickamauga." NW OHIO Q, 22 [1950]: 73-94.

A Union general, Steedman saw his division suffer heavy losses while he himself was badly wounded and had his horse shot from beneath him.

2234. Swift, Lester L. "The Preacher Regiment at Chickamauga and Missionary Ridge." LIN HER, 72 [1970]: 51-60

Author describes the participation of the 73rd Illinois in these two campaigns.

2235. Tucker, Glenn. "The Battle of Chickamauga." CWTI, 8 [2] [1969]: 1-50.

The entire issue of CIVIL WAR TIMES ILLUSTRATED is devoted to the battle. Tucker argues that had the Confederates followed up their victory they might have won the war.

2236. ———. CHICKAMAUGA: BLOODY BATTLE IN THE WEST. Indianapolis: Bobbs-Merrill, 1961.

The best and most complete account of the battle. Tucker provides a detailed narrative of the bitter two-day fighting in September 1863 and leaves little to the imagination. It is a story well-told.

2237. Turchin, John B. CHICKAMAUGA. Chicago, 1888.

The author of this thorough but dated work, was formerly an officer in the Russian army, who came to the United States in 1856 and rose to the rank of general in the Union army.

ATLANTA CAMPAIGN [May 1-September 8, 1864]

2238. Adolphson, Stephen J. "An Incident of Valor in the Battle of Peachtree Creek, 1864." GA HIS Q, 57 [1973]: 406-420.

Refers to an incident involving a soldier of the 104th Illinois in the battle east of Atlanta, July 20, 1864.

2239. Breeden, James O. "A Medical History of the Later Stages of the Atlanta Campaign." JSH, 35 [1969]: 31-59.

Author compares Confederate and Union medical statistics for the months of July and August 1864.

2240. Brown, Fred E. "The Battle of Allatoona." CWH, 6 [1960]: 277-297.

The maneuverings of both armies leading to Sherman's victory of May 25, 1864, are described.

2241. Bynum, Hartwell T. "Sherman's Expulsion of the Roswell Women in 1864." GA HIS Q, 54 [1970]: 169-182.

The article deals with Sherman's capture and destruction of the Roswell Factory textile mills and the disposition of approximately 400 female workers.

2242. Carter, Samuel. THE SIEGE OF ATLANTA. New York: St. Martin's, 1973.

Written by a journalist, this book gives the general reader a feeling for life in the besieged city, although a few errors have crept into the account.

2243. Castel, Albert. "Union Fizzle at Atlanta: The Battle of Utoy Creek." CWTI, 16 [10] [1978]: 26-32.

A feud between Generals Palmer and Schofield cost Sherman valuable time in his "pin-wheel" move west of Atlanta, August 5-6, 1864.

2244. Clauss, Errol M. "The Battle of Jonesborough." CWTI, 7 [7] [1968]: 12-23.

A detailed account of the final battle of the Atlanta Campaign, August 31-September 1, 1864.

2245. ———. "Sherman's Failure at Atlanta." GA HIS Q, 53 [1969]: 321-329.

Since Sherman's avowed goal at the beginning of the campaign was the capture of Hood's army and as Hood's army was not taken, the capture of Atlanta, important as it was, remained only a partial success to the general.

2246. ———. "Sherman's Rail Support in the Atlanta Campaign." GA HIS Q, 50 [1966]: 413-420.

The transportation system to supply federal troops was very well organized.

2247. Dodge, Grenville M. THE BATTLE OF ATLANTA AND OTHER CAMPAIGNS .... Denver: Sage Books, 1965.

This reprint of a privately-printed volume of 1910, contains a collection of speeches and writings by the celebrated Union general and engineer. Because of his engineering expertise and military accomplishments, he rose to the rank of major general in Sherman's army.

2248. Hay, Thomas R. "The Atlanta Campaign." GA HIS Q, 7 [1923]: 99-118.

Covers the period from July 22 to the fall of Atlanta. After a brief synopsis, the author analyzes the strategy and points out the errors made in a fourteen page section called "Comments."

2249. Hicken, Victor. "Hold The Fort." CWTI, 7 [3] [1968]: 18-27.

The Federals repelled a strong attack by the Confederates at Allatoona, the important federal supply depot north of Atlanta, October 5, 1864.

2250. Hoehling, Adolph A. LAST TRAIN FROM ATLANTA. New York: Yoseloff, 1958.

A very good narrative of the Atlanta Campaign and of the effect it had on the people.

2251. Howard, O.O. "The Battle About Atlanta." ATLAN MON, 38 [1876]: 385-399, 559-567.

A vivid two-part article covering the campaigning from early July 1864 to the fall of Atlanta two months later, by one of the federal generals on the scene.

2252. Julian, Allen P. "From Dalton to Atlanta: Sherman vs Johnston." CWTI, 3 [4] [1964]: 4-7, 34-41.

General Joseph E. Johnston fought a strategic retreat from Dalton to Atlanta, inflicting far more casualties on Sherman's forces than the Confederates suffered.

2253. Key, William. THE BATTLE OF ATLANTA AND THE GEORGIA CAMPAIGN. New York: Twayne, 1958.

A straightforward account of the Atlanta campaign.

2254. Major, Duncan K. SUPPLY OF SHERMAN'S ARMY DURING THE ATLANTA CAMPAIGN. Fort Leavenworth, 1911.

An account of Sherman's supply system drawn largely from the OFFICIAL RECORDS and written by two army officers.

2255. Mathews, Byron H. THE McCOOK-STONEMAN RAID. Philadelphia: Dorrance, 1976.

Author details the cavalry raid west and south of Atlanta, July 26-31, 1864, which failed of its purpose.

2256. McMurry, Richard M. "The Affair at Kolb's Farm." CWTI, 7 [8] [1968]: 20-27.

This incident, occurring on June 24, 1864 near Marietta, Georgia, is noted for the unhappy partnership between Sherman and Hooker for the North and the unhappy relationship between Johnston and Hood for the South.

2257. ———. "The Atlanta Campaign of 1864: A New Look." CWH, 22 [1976]: 5-15.

Recent scholarship challenges the traditional view that General Joseph Johnston's defensive strategy was sound.

2258. ———. "'The Hell Hole': New Hope Church." CWTI, 11 [10] [1973]: 32-43.

Also known as "Dallas," this battle fought on May 25, 27, 1864, was one of several moves by Sherman to maneuver around Johnston, who was positioned on the railroad to Atlanta.

2259. ———. "Kennesaw Mountain." CWTI, 8 [9] [1970]: 19-33.

The Federals were decisively repulsed at Kennesaw Mountain on June 27, 1864--Sherman's big mistake in the Atlanta Campaign--but the northern lines soon outflanked the Southern lines and the Confederates were forced to surrender the strong defensive position and retreat toward Atlanta.

2260. ———. "The Mackall Journal and Its Antecedents." CWH, 20 [1974]: 311-328.

Author concludes that the "Mackall Journal" dealing with General Johnston and the Atlanta Campaign, as it appeared in the OFFICIAL RECORDS, is partly fraudulent.

2261. ———. "More on 'Raw Courage.'" CWTI, 14 [6] [1975]: 36-38.

A tale about the capture of a Confederate outpost and ferry along the Chattahoochee River by a colonel and ten nude Union soldiers.

2262. ———. "Resaca: "A Heap of Hard Fiten.'" CWTI, 11 [7] [1970]: 4-12, 44-48.

Previews the beginnings of the Atlanta Campaign--from Dalton to Resaca. The battle of Resaca, May 14-15, 1864, was important due to the fact that it was one of the strongest positions between Chattanooga and Atlanta.

2263. Merrill, W.E. "Blockhouses--Federal Means of Protecting Communications." CWTI, 4 [9] [1966]: 34-39.

An account of the steps taken to defend Sherman's rail lines to Atlanta.

2264. Monroe, Haskell. "Federal Raiding in Liberty County, Georgia." GA HIS Q, 44 [1960]: 154-171.

Probes the activities of Union soldiers in a Georgia county in December 1864 and January 1865.

2265. Nye, Wilbur S. "The Battle of Lafayette." CWTI, 5 [3] [1966]: 34-39.

Union cavalry defeated a superior Confederate force, preventing it from disrupting Sherman's communications during the Atlanta Campaign.

2266. Osborn, George C. "The Atlanta Campaign, 1864." GA HIS Q, 34 [1950]: 271-287.

After sketching the background and political situation, the author broadly outlines the campaign. He concludes with the observation that the capture of Atlanta gave new impetus in the North to continue the war.

2267. Read, Ira B. "The Campaign From Chattanooga to Atlanta As Seen by a Federal Soldier." Richard B. Harwell, editor. GA HIS Q, 25 [1941]: 262-278.

Written to an aunt in Hudson, Ohio, this exceedingly long letter covers a period from May 3, 1864 to September 18, 1864. Composed of personal observations since his aunt could read of "the general movements of the army" in the daily papers.

2268. Robbins, Peggy. "Hood vs. Sherman: A Duel of Words." CWTI, 17 [4] [1978]: 22-29.

During the Battle of Atlanta, Hood and Sherman exchanged long and heated letters on "laws" and "rights" in warfare.

2269. Rowell, John W. "McCook's Raid." CWTI, 13 [4] [1974]: 4-9, 42-48.

An account of the McCook-Stoneman raid west of Atlanta in late July 1864.

2270. Secrist, Phillip L. "'Scenes of Awful Carnage.'" CWTI, 10 [3] [1971]: 4-9, 45-48.

The little known battle at Pickett's Mill, May 29, 1864, was an element in Sherman's flanking move west of Allatoona. It was poorly-planned by the Union commanders and resulted in a savage setback.

FROM ATLANTA TO THE SEA [November 15-December 21, 1864]

2271. Bonner, James C. "Sherman at Milledgeville in 1864." JSH, 22 [1956]: 273-291.

A description of the three-day occupation of the state capital and the destruction of everything which might be of material aid to the Confederacy.

2272. Boynton, Henry V. SHERMAN'S HISTORICAL RAID. Cincinnati, 1875.

A critical review of Sherman in Georgia based on War Department records.

2273. Clarke, John T. "The Diary of a Civil War Soldier with Sherman in Georgia. MO HIS SOC BULL, 8 [1952]: 356-370.

Although a slaveowner, author joined the Union army when war broke out because he disapproved of secession. Diary consists of brief entries beginning May 1, 1864 and concluding August 30, 1864.

2274. Conyngham David P. SHERMAN'S MARCH THROUGH THE SOUTH. New York, 1865.

Although old and difficult to obtain, this volume provides a vivid view of the march written by an observant correspondent for the NEW YORK HERALD.

2275. Coulter, Ellis M. "Robert Gould Shaw and the Burning of Darien, Georgia." CWH, 5 [1959]: 363-373.

Colonel James Montgomery ordered the raid on Darien. After securing the town, it was ransacked and looted. Major Robert Shaw of the 54th Massachusetts [the state's first black regiment] protested the orders to burn the town.

2276. Davis, Burke. SHERMAN'S MARCH. New York: Random House, 1980.

Author presents Sherman from the point of view of his men and southerners through eyewitness accounts. He stresses the tragedies on both sides and manages to capture the mood of the soldiers.

2277. De Laubenfels, David J. "Where Sherman Passed By." GA R, 47 [1957]: 381-395.

This study is based on maps drawn by the chief topographical engineer of the Fourteenth Corps.

2278. Dozer, Jesse L. 'Marching With Sherman Through Georgia and the Carolinas: Civil War Diary of Jesse L. Dozer." Wilfred W. Black, editor. GA HIS Q, 52 [1968]: 308-336, 451-479.

An excellent account of the "March to the Sea" and beyond.

2279. Ewing, Charles. "Sherman's March Through Georgia: Letters From Charles Ewing to His Father, Thomas Ewing." George C. Osborn, editor. GA HIS Q, 42 [1958]: 323-327.

Eight letters from Charles Ewing describing the march through Georgia.

2280. Gibson, John M. THOSE 163 DAYS: A SOUTHERN ACCOUNT OF SHERMAN'S MARCH FROM ATLANTA TO RALEIGH. New York: Coward-McCann, 1961.

A southern writer has studied the sources and has rendered judgment on Sherman and his march. It was wrong to wage war in this way, he asserts, and Sherman is found guilty. Despite the partisan view, this is a good book.

2281. Hedley, Fenwick Y. MARCHING THROUGH GEORGIA. Chicago, 1890.

A popular and authoritative volume of "pen-pictures of every day life in General Sherman's army."

2282. Hitchcock, Henry. MARCHING WITH SHERMAN.... New Haven: Yale University Press, 1927.

An important work based on the letters and diaries of the literate Major Hitchcock, who served on Sherman's staff.

2283. Jones, Katharine M. WHEN SHERMAN CAME: SOUTHERN WOMEN AND THE "GREAT MARCH." New York: Bobbs-Merrill, 1964.

A gripping account of the reaction to Sherman's march to the sea and through the Carolinas as told in the words of 45 southern women who lived through the experience. In this well-edited volume of both published and unpublished memoirs. the author has done a first-rate job of compiling and editing the material.

2284. Meade, Rufus. "With Sherman Through Georgia and the Carolinas: Letters of a Federal Soldier." James A. Padgett, editor. GA HIS Q, 32 [1948]: 285-322; 33 [1949]: 49-81.

An excellent account of the march by a well-educated, observant soldier. He retains a sympathetic yet non-partisan view.

2285. Miers, Earl S. THE GENERAL WHO MARCHED TO HELL: WILLIAM TECUMSEH SHERMAN AND HIS MARCH TO FAME AND INFAMY. New Brunswick, New Jersey: Rutgers University Press, 1948.

A well-done study of the most hated and debated campaign of the Civil War, the "March to the Sea." In recreating the atmosphere of the moment, the author culls letters from soldiers, diaries of Georgians, and contemporary newspapers dealing with the march. He is severe with Sherman.

2286. Nichols, George W. THE STORY OF THE GREAT MARCH. FROM THE DIARY OF A STAFF OFFICER. New York, 1865.

A widely-read description of the march by an army major who became a well-known writer of fiction in later years.

2287. Pepper, George W. PERSONAL RECOLLECTIONS OF SHERMAN'S CAMPAIGNS IN GEORGIA AND THE CAROLINAS. Zanesville, Ohio: 1866.

Pepper, who was both a correspondent and an officer in the 80th Ohio, wrote a valuable volume of memoirs of conditions encountered in field and camp.

2288. Rhodes, James F. "Sherman's March to the Sea." AHR, 6 [1901]: 466-474.

A brief account of the famous march. Rhodes commends Sherman for both the conception and execution of the campaign which broke the back of the South.

2289. Rogers, George A. and R. Frank Saunders, Jr. "The Scourge of Sherman's Men in Liberty County." GA HIS Q, 60 [1976]: 356-369.

This Georgian county was occupied by the Federals for approximately six weeks. The destruction of the railroad and the foraging of Sherman's army left a psychological mark on Liberty County [near Savannah].

2290. Rzika, John. "With Sherman Through Georgia: A Journal." David J. de Laubenfels, editor. GA HIS Q, 41 [1957]: 288-300.

The author, a subordinate on Sherman's staff, later changed his name to John Laube de Laubenfels. His journal reveals that the extent of the damage and destruction as a result of the march was less than previously reported.

2291. Sherman, William T. GENERAL SHERMAN'S OFFICIAL ACCOUNT OF HIS GREAT MARCH.... New York, 1865.

The general describes his campaigns from Chattanooga to the end of the war. The volume includes his testimony before a committee of Congress and his rebuttal to charges and criticism from the secretary of war.

2292. Wheeler, Richard, editor. SHERMAN'S MARCH: AN EYEWITNESS HISTORY. New York: Crowell, 1978.

"Eyewitness" accounts are linked with the author's own narrative in this entertaining book.

2293. Upson, Theodore F. WITH SHERMAN TO THE SEA.... Oscar O. Winther, editor. Baton Rouge: Louisiana State University Press, 1943. Reprint 1958.

A valuable collection of letters, diaries, and reminiscences of a man who served with the 100th Indiana.

THROUGH THE CAROLINAS [February 1-March 27, 1865]

2294. Barrett, John G. SHERMAN'S MARCH THROUGH THE CAROLINAS. Chapel Hill: University of North Carolina Press, 1956.

This able study, based on thorough research, provides an almost mile-by-mile record of Sherman's "other" march. Dramatic descriptions and amusing anecdotes appear in abundance. Sherman's belief in "total war" is established as is his concern for those victimized by his method.

2295. ———. "General Sherman's March Through North Carolina." NC HIS R, 42 [1965]: 192-207.

Another discussion of the subject covered in the previous entry.

2296. ———. "Sherman and Total War in the Carolinas." NR HIS R, 37 [1960]: 367-381.

A discussion of Sherman's novel philosophy of total war--destruction of the enemy's economic resources and its will to fight on--as applied to the Carolinas' Campaign.

2297. Chapin, James W. "A Yank in the Carolinas Campaign: The Diary of James W. Chapin, Eighth Indiana Cavalry." Donald E. Reynolds and Max H. Kele, editors. NC HIS R, 46 [1969]: 42-57.

Chapin had served with the 39th Indiana which became the 8th Indiana cavalry after Chickamauga. He was elevated to lieutenant in May 1864 and served with Sherman in Georgia and the Carolinas. The brief diary entries here run from January 28-March 25, 1865.

2298. Keys, Thomas B. "The Federal Pillage of Anderson, South Carolina: Brown's Raid." SC HIS MAG, 76 [1975]: 80-86.

In an attempt to locate Confederate gold and Jefferson Davis, federal troops sacked Anderson, destroyed property, and seized gold and whiskey.

2299. LeConte, Joseph. 'WARE SHERMAN, A JOURNAL OF THREE MONTHS' PERSONAL EXPERIENCE.... Berkeley: University of California Press, 1937.

The author, a famous scientist and southerner, kept a journal during the last months of the war. His daughter wrote an introductory memoir.

2300. Lucas, Marion B. SHERMAN AND THE BURNING OF COLUMBIA. College Station: Texas A. and M. University Press, 1976.

Ever since Columbia, South Carolina was burned on the night of February 17, 1865, a controversy has raged over who did the burning. Author argues that it was probably not Sherman's troops, as southerners believed, but rather it was due to an accident when Confederates sought to burn cotton stock and high winds fed the blaze.

2301. Luvaas, Jay. "Johnston's Last Stand: Bentonville." NC HIS R, 33 [1956]: 332-358.

The last battle in the Carolina Campaign was at Bentonville, North Carolina, March 19, 1865, where Johnston unsuccessfully sought to drive back the Federals.

2302. Rhodes, James F. "Who Burned Columbia?" AHR, 7 [1902]: 485-493.

Author debates the pros and cons of the controversy and concludes that the burning of Columbia was by accident, not design, owing to the reckless drunken behavior of northern troops, liberated northern prisoners, and local blacks and convicts.

2303. Spencer, Cornelia P. THE LAST NINETY DAYS OF THE WAR IN NORTH CAROLINA. New York, 1866.

A useful and discerning account by a very unusual lady.

2304. Yates, Richard E. "Governor Vance and the End of the War in North Carolina." NC HIS R, 18 [1941]: 315-338.

An account of the last days in office of North Carolina's wartime governor, Zebulon Vance. Vance was arrested on May 13, 1865, spent a month and a half in Old Capitol Prison, and was then released.

* * *

2305. Julian, Allen P. "Fort Pulaski." CWTI, 11 [2] [1970]: 8-21.

A detailed description of Ft. Pulaski, which guarded the sea approach to Savannah and the Federals' capture of the fort in a two-day engagement, April 10-11, 1862.

Kansas and Missouri

Because so much of the fighting in Missouri spilled across the border into Kansas, and because so much of the fighting in Kansas spilled across the border into Missouri, the two states have been combined in this section of the bibliography. No "major" battles occurred so the entries are listed alphabetically by author.

2306. Abrahamson, James and Kermit M. Henninger. "The Battle of Westport." WEST HIS Q, 9 [1973]: 48-52.

The Confederate defeat at Westport, Missouri, located on the Kansas border just south of Kansas City, October 23, 1864, was the culminating battle in General Sterling Price's raid into the state. Called the "biggest Civil War engagement west of the Missouri," this marked the end of Confederate activity in the state.

2307. Adamson, Hans C. REBELLION IN MISSOURI: 1861. Philadelphia: Chilton, 1961.

Relates the story of General Nathaniel Lyon "as a daring political and military leader ... during [the] first months of the Civil War." His actions kept Missouri in the Union. Later Congress passed a joint resolution stating that the Battle of Wilson's Creek was a federal victory under Lyon.

2308. Anders, Leslie. "'Farthest North': The Historian and the Battle of Athens." MO HIS R, 69 [1975]: 147-168.

Author rejects the theory that Iowa troops were responsible for the Union victory at Athens in northern Missouri, August 5, 1861 and states that home guards played the central role.

2309. Austin, Robert A. "Battle of Wilson's Creek." MO HIS R, 27 [1932/1933]: 46-49.

The outnumbered federals suffered a bloody defeat at Wilson's Creek in southwestern Missouri, August 10, 1861, which opened up much of the state to Confederate control.

2310. Bearss, Edwin C. "The Army of the Frontier's First Campaign: The Confederates Win at Newtonia." MO HIS R, 60 [1966]: 283-319.

A study of the intricate movements of both armies in this minor engagement on September 30, 1862.

2311. ———. "The Battle of Wilson's Creek." ANN IOWA, 36 [1961/1962]: 81-109, 226-259.

A good two-part account of this early battle for the control of Missouri, in which the federals were routed and General Nathaniel Lyon killed.

2312. ———. "From Rolla to Fayetteville With General Curtis." ARK HIS Q, 19 [1960]: 226-259.

A discussion of the activities of Union General Samuel Curtis, who commanded the Southwestern District of Missouri in 1862.

2313. Berneking, Carolyn. "A Look at Early Lawrence: Letters From Robert Gaston Elliott." KAN HIS Q, 43 [1977]: 282-296.

Letters from an anti-slavery newspaperman, which include his personal account of Quantrill's raid on Lawrence, August 1863.

2314. Britton, Wiley. THE CIVIL WAR ON THE BORDER. 2 v. New York, 1890-1899.

Relying on his own experiences and official papers, the author has painted an important picture of campaigning in the border regions.

2315. ———. MEMOIRS OF THE REBELLION ON THE BORDER. Chicago, 1892.

While an earlier work than the previous entry, this is still a helpful account of border warfare. Britton served with the 6th Kansas Cavalry.

2316. Brown, D. Alexander. "The Battle of Westport." CWTI, 5 [4] [1966]: 4-11, 40-43.

Author describes this major defeat for the Confederates in late October 1864, which closed out the war along the border.

2317. ———. "Wilson's Creek." CWTI, 11 [1] [1972]: 8-18.

This bloody battle in August 1861 was called the "Bull Run of the West."

2318. Brownlee, Richard S. "The Battle of Pilot Knob, Iron County, Missouri, September 27, 1864." MO HIS R, 59 [1964]: 1-30.

Sterling Price was repulsed in this desperate six-hour fight, which saved St. Louis from attack.

2319. Burch, Paul W. "Kansas: Bushwhackers vs. Jayhawkers." JW, 14 [1975]: 83-104.

Despite the continuing warfare between Missourians and Kansans, Kansas survived and prospered, and supported the Union during the Civil War.

2320. Canan, Howard V. "Milton Burch: Anti-Guerrilla Fighter." MO HIS R, 59 [1965]: 223-242.

Assigned to scouting duties, Burch succeeded in dispersing many bands of Confederate sympathizers.

2321. ———. "When Yank Fought Yank: An Incident on the Kansas Border." CWH, 12 [1962]: 143-155.

An account of a raid against Missouri Unionists by a group of Kansas Unionists in November 1862.

2322. Castel, Albert. "The Bloodiest Man in American History." AM HER, 11 [6] [1960]: 22-25, 97-99.

Quantrill's raid on Lawrence, Kansas, August 21, 1863, and his use of cruel and ruthless tactics, is described.

2323. ———. "The Jayhawkers and Copperheads of Kansas." CWH, 5 [1959]: 283-293.

Union General Thomas Ewing attempts to suppress some of the violence along the Kansas-Missouri frontier.

2324. ———. "Kansas Jayhawking Raids into Western Missouri in 1861." MO HIS R, 54 [1959-1960]: 1-11.

Author describes several raids by Kansas Jayhawkers into western Missouri which, in his opinion, were not only unjustified, but also further poisoned relations between the two states.

2325. ———. "Order No. 11 and the Civil War on the Border." MO HIS R, 57 [1963]: 357-368.

On August 25, 1863 General Ewing ordered all families in certain Missouri counties to vacate their homes. The order was designed to deprive the Confederate guerrillas of support and supplies.

2326. ———. "Quantrill's Bushwhacking: A Case Study in Partisan Warfare." CWH, 13 [1967]: 40-50.

An analysis of Quantrill's guerrilla tactics as a model for the study of partisan warfare today.

2327. ———. "Quantrill's Missouri Bushwhackers in Kentucky: The End of the Trail." FCHQ, 38 [1964]: 125-132.

While on his way to Washington after the war ended, Quantrill was killed by federal troops in Kentucky, May 1865.

2328. ———. "The Siege of Lexington." CWTI, 8 [5] [1969]: 4-13.

After his victory at Wilson's Creek in August 1861, Sterling Price moved north and captured Lexington, Missouri, on September 20. Lexington had been a federal strong point on the Missouri River. This triumph had little long-range significance, however.

2329. ———. "War and Politics: The Price Raid of 1864." KAN HIS Q, 24 [1958]: 129-143.

The Sterling Price raid lasted about a month in September and October, 1864 and signalled the end of Confederate influence in the state.

2330. Connelley, William E. QUANTRILL AND THE BORDER WARS. Cedar Rapids, 1910. Reprint 1956.

This probably is still the best account of Quantrill's activities along the border, although the work does have its critics.

2331. Covington, James W. "The Camp Jackson Affair, 1861." MO HIS R, 55 [1961]: 197-212.

An account of a bitter battle between sympathizers from each side for control of the important federal supply depot and arsenal at St. Louis, April-May 1861.

2332. Dixon, Ben F. "Battle on the Border: Athens, Missouri, August 5, 1861." ANN IOWA, 36 [1961/1962]: 1-15.

An account of the threatened secessionist invasion of southern Iowa which was repulsed by Union militia at Athens, Missouri.

2333. Duffner, Robert W. "Guerrilla Victory at Centralia, September 27, 1864." MO HIS SOC BULL, 29 [1973]: 131-144.

Early in the Price Raid, Confederate General "Bloody Bill" Anderson attacked the north central town of Centralia, killing many federal soldiers, terrorizing residents, destroying two trains, and rendering the railroads useless.

2334. Edwards, John N. NOTED GUERRILLAS, OR THE WARFARE OF THE BORDER. Dayton, Ohio: Morningside Bookshop, 1976.

Reprint of an 1877 volume by John Edwards, writer and Confederate officer. He glorifies the deeds of many guerrillas including Quantrill, Anderson, and the James and Younger brothers, most of whom he knew.

2335. Garretson, Owen A. "The Battle of Athens." PALIMP, 8 [1927]: 138-149.

Athens, Missouri was just opposite Croton, Iowa, which was a station on the Des Moines Valley Railroad. Feelings were tense. In a battle for control of Athens, the Confederates were routed.

2336. Goodman, Thomas M. A THRILLING RECORD. Thomas R. Hooper, editor. Maryville, Missouri: By the editor, 1960.

A reprint of an 1868 booklet written by the lone survivor of a massacre of federal troops by drunken bushwhackers at Centralia, Missouri on September 27, 1864 during Price's raid. The story of the massacre is told without elaboration.

2337. Hardman, Nicholas P. "Bushwhacker Activity on the Missouri Border: Letters to Dr. Glen O. Hardeman, 1862-1865." MO HIS R, 58 [1964]: 265-277.

Letters from his wife to a surgeon in the Union army who had been a successful farmer and slaveholder. Letters deal with the operations of the bushwhackers.

2338. Herklotz, Hildegarde R. "Jayhawkers in Missouri, 1858-1863." MO HIS R, 17 [1922]: 266-284; 18 [1923]: 64-101.

Detailed descriptions of the border strife.

2339. Holcombe, Return I. and [ ] Adams. AN ACCOUNT OF THE BATTLE OF WILSON'S CREEK. Fred DeArmond, editor. Springfield, Missouri: Springfield Public Library and Greene County Historical Society, 1961.

This slim but solid military account of the Battle of Wilson's Creek, August 10, 1861, was reissued in 1961 to honor the centennial of the engagement. The work, written by two journalists, originally appeared in 1883 at a reunion of veterans of the fight.

2340. Hulston, John K. "West Point and Wilson's Creek." CWH, 1 [1955]: 333-354.

Author studies the actions of 18 West Point graduates in their first battle. Wilson's Creek served as a proving ground for those who rose to high rank.

2341. Jenkins, Paul B. THE BATTLE OF WESTPORT. Kansas City, Missouri: 1906.

An account of the Confederate raid into Missouri in 1864--known as Price's raid.

2342. Johnson, Harvey. "In Pursuit of Quantrill: An Enlisted Man's Response." William E. Unrau, editor. KAN HIS Q, 39 [1973]: 379-391.

An Ohio soldier, Johnson wrote three letters home describing his participation in an unsuccessful pursuit of Quantrill.

2343. Kurtz, Henry I. "The Battle of Belmont." CWTI, 2 [3] [1963]: 18-24.

At Belmont, Missouri, November 7, 1861, Grant experienced his first real battle. Although he was forced back and committed numerous errors, he achieved his main objective.

2344. Langsdorf, Edgar. "Price's Raid and the Battle of Mine Creek." KAN HIS Q, 30 [1964]: 281-306.

Fought on the day after Westport, October 25, 1864, Price fought this delaying action at Mine Creek in eastern Kansas.

2345. Lobdell, Jared C. "Nathaniel Lyon and the Battle of Wilson's Creek." MO HIS SOC BULL, 17 [1960]: 3-15.

Lyon was killed in this early battle.

2346. Margreiter, John L. "Union Heroism at Pilot Knob Saved St. Louis From Attack." CWTI, 2 [9] [1964]: 10-17.

As Price approached St. Louis he was repulsed at Pilot Knob, September 27, 1864 and turned his attention to central and western Missouri.

2347. McElroy, John. THE STRUGGLE FOR MISSOURI. Washington, D.C.: 1909.

The story of the first year of the war in Missouri by the Washington newspaperman who was the most celebrated survivor of Andersonville Prison.

2348. McGhee, James E. "The Neophyte General: U.S. Grant and the Belmont Campaign." MO HIS R, 67 [1973]: 465-483.

Grant, in a diversionary move against Belmont, was acting on erroneous reports of Confederate movements. He administered some damage before being forced to withdraw.

2349. Mink, Charles R. "General Order No. 11: The Forced Evacuation of Civilians During the Civil War." MIL AFF, 34 [1970]: 132-136.

In an attempt to control guerrillas and to prevent vengeance attacks from Kansas, General Ewing ordered most inhabitants banished from four Missouri counties.

2350. Monaghan, Jay. CIVIL WAR ON THE WESTERN BORDER, 1854-1865. Boston: Little, Brown, 1955.

A good, documented study of the border warfare along the Kansas, Missouri, and Arkansas frontier and told extremely well. The story begins with the struggle over slavery in Kansas in the mid-50s and and continues until the Civil War is over. This tricky subject, with a heavy mix of politics and fighting, is nicely sorted out for the reader.

2351. Monnett, Howard N. ACTION BEFORE WESTPORT, 1864. Kansas City, Missouri: Westport Historical Society, 1964.

A long time student of the engagement at Westport which administered the final blow to Sterling Price and his Missouri campaign, the author briefly traces the background of the battle and then focuses his attention on the battle itself, September 23-24, 1864. Useful maps and illustrations accompany the text.

2352. ———. "The Origins of the Confederate Invasion of Missouri, 1864." MO HIS SOC BULL, 18 [1961/1962]: 37-48.

Although Price's raid failed in its attempt to relieve the pressure on Confederate forces east of the Mississippi, from a logistical standpoint, the number of engagements fought exceeded the number in any other raid of the war.

2353. ———. "The Westport Police Guard in the Civil War." WEST HIS Q, 7 [1971]: 3-6.

A federal volunteer unit helped defeat the Confederate forces.

2354. Mudd, Joseph A. WITH PORTER IN NORTH MISSOURI: A CHAPTER IN THE HISTORY OF THE WAR BETWEEN THE STATES. Washington, D.C.: 1909.

Basically a military history.

2355. Niepman, Ann D. "General Order No. 11 and Border Warfare During the Civil War." MO HIS R, 66 [1972]: 185-210.

Generals Ewing and Schofield concluded that only depopulation of four western Missouri counties or an increase in troops could prevent the loss of life in the region. Since no troops were available, the removal of the civilian population was ordered.

2356. Oates, Stephen B. "Marmaduke's Cape Girardeau Expedition, 1863." MO HIS R, 57 [1962/1963]: 237-247.

Although Confederate General John Marmaduke's raid on the federal supply depot at Cape Girardeau, Missouri, in April 1863, did not achieve its objectives, it provided a useful experience for future raids.

2357. Parrish, William E. "Fremont in Missouri." CWTI, 17 [1] [1978]: 4-10, 40-45.

General John C. Fremont assumed command of the new Department of the West at St. Louis in July 1861. He was to drive Confederates from the state and establish order. The problems were too numerous and when he failed, he was removed.

2358. Peckham, James. GEN. NATHANIEL LYON AND MISSOURI IN 1861. New York, 1866.

A full, early account of Missouri's troubled times in the first year of the war.

2359. Peterson, Cyrus A. PILOT KNOB, THE THERMOPYLAE OF THE WEST. New York, 1914.

An able account of the battle that saved St. Louis in September 1864.

2360. Plummer, Mark A. "Missouri and Kansas and the Capture of General Marmaduke." MO HIS R, 59 [1963/1964]: 90-104.

The controversy attending the capture of Confederate General Marmaduke by a "boy" generated bitter recriminations among Union political and military figures in Missouri and Kansas in 1864 and beyond.

2361. Rampp, Lary C. "Incident at Baxter Springs on October 6, 1863." KAN HIS Q, 36 [1970]: 183-197.

Quantrill's raiders, dressed in federal uniforms, surprised a federal escort accompanying the transfer of General Blunt's headquarters. They routed the party and butchered the corpses.

2362. Robinett, Paul M. "Marmaduke's Expedition Into Missouri: The Battles of Springfield and Hartville, January, 1863." MO HIS R, 58 [1963/1964]: 151-173.

This Confederate raid into central Missouri was designed to force federal units in Arkansas and along the frontier to pull back. It appeared to achieve these goals and temporarily revived the waning hopes for success of pro-Confederate Missourians

2363. Schrantz, Ward L. "The Battle of Carthage." MO HIS R 31 [1937]: 140-149.

A minor engagement early in the war on July 5, 1861, in southwestern Missouri.

2364. Schroeder, L.E. "The Battle of Wilson's Creek and its Effect Upon Missouri." MO HIS R, 71 [1977]: 156-173.

Author argues that despite its victory at Wilson's Creek, the long-range outcome was the loss of the state for the South.

2365. Smith, Harold F. "The 1861 Struggle for Lexington, Missouri." CWH, 7 [1961]: 155-166.

An account of the Confederate siege of Lexington in September 1861, in which General Sterling Price's superior force compelled the Federals to surrender.

2366. Snead, Thomas L. THE FIGHT FOR MISSOURI FROM THE ELECTION OF LINCOLN TO THE DEATH OF LYON. New York, 1888.

The author took part in the early struggle for Missouri and has written a valuable account of it.

2367. Tucker, Samuel. PRICE'S RAID THROUGH LINN COUNTY, KANSAS, OCTOBER 24, 25, 1864. n.p., 1958.

A short account of the effect of the Confederate sweep through eastern Kansas in their retreat following Westport.

2368. Williams, Burton J. "Quantrill's Raid on Lawrence: A Question of Complicity." KAN HIS Q, 34 [1969]: 143-149.

Discusses the possibility that the infamous raid was successful because some of the town's citizens may have given vital information to Quantrill.

2369. Williamson, Hugh P. "The Battle of Moore's Mill." MO HIS R, 66 [1972]: 539-548.

Federal troops defeated a Confederate force in this little known battle in Callaway County, Missouri, July 28, 1862.

Kentucky

2370. Bearss, Edwin C. "The Battle of Hartsville and Morgan's Second Kentucky Raid." KY HIS SOC REG, 65 [1967]: 1-19, 120-123, 239-252.

This three-part series describes Bragg's efforts to force Grant out of Mississippi and Morgan's attempts to cut Rosecrans' lines at Murfreesboro. All this in the 1862 Christmas season.

2371. ———. "Morgan's Second Kentucky Raid, December, 1862." KY HIS SOC REG, 70 [1972]: 200-218; 71 [1973]: 177-188; 426-438.

Another account of Morgan's 1862 "Christmas Raid."

2372. Brown, D. Alexander. "Morgan's Christmas Raid." CWTI, 13 [9] [1975]: 12-19.

Still another look at Morgan's "Christmas Raid," December 21, 1862-January 1, 1863.

2373. DeFalaise, Louis. "General Stephen Gano Burbridge's Command in Kentucky." KY HIS SOC REG, 69 [1971]: 101-127.

Temporarily assigned to a command in Kentucky, Burbridge suppressed disloyalty by coercion and economic pressure. He was relieved of his post for his efforts.

2374. Engerud, H. "The Battle of Munfordville, September 14-17, 1862." IND HIS BULL, 50 [1973]: 127-135.

Bragg seized Munfordville, only 40 miles from Louisville, but unwisely abandoned it to go to Frankfort.

2375. Finley, Luke W. "The Battle of Perryville." SHSP, 30 [1902]: 238-250.

Perryville. October 8, 1862, was the final battle in Bragg's Kentucky campaign. Although the Confederates won a tactical victory they were forced to withdraw to East Tennessee.

2376. Harrison, Lowell H. "Mill Springs, 'The Brilliant Victory.'" CWTI, 10 [9] [1972]: 4-9, 44-47.

The Union victory at Mill Springs, Kentucky, January 19, 1862, under General George H. Thomas, opened up East Tennessee for the North.

2377. Horn, Stanley F. "The Battle of Perryville." CWTI, 4 [10] [1966]: 4-11, 42-47.

Both sides blundered badly, yet both claimed victory in the most important battle fought in Kentucky.

2378. Long, E.B. "The Paducah Affair: Bloodless Action That Altered the Civil War in the Mississippi Valley." KY HIS SOC REG, 70 [1972]: 253-276.

Grant's occupation of Paducah, September 6, 1861, secured control of the mouths of the Tennessee and Cumberland rivers, vital to Union success in the West.

2379. McMurtry, R. Gerald. "Zollicoffer and the Battle of Mill Springs." FCHQ, 29 [1955]: 303-319.

The Confederate general was killed under strange circumstances.

2380. McWhiney, Grady. "Controversy in Kentucky: Braxton Bragg's Campaign of 1862." CWH, 6 [1960]: 5-42.

A sympathetic analysis of Bragg's 1862 Kentucky campaign, in which author urges that in view of the general's various problems, much was accomplished.

2381. Peskin, Allan. "The Hero of the Sandy Valley: James A. Garfield's Kentucky Campaign of 1861-1862." OHIO HIS, 72 [1963]: 3-24, 129-139.

Author describes the future president's achievements, under difficult circumstances, in eastern Kentucky.

2382. Stern, Joseph S., Jr. "The Siege of Cincinnati." HIS PHIL SOC OH BULL, 18 [1960]: 163-186.

An account of the hastily-prepared plans to defend Cincinnati against the threatened Confederate invasion in September 1862.

2383. Tapp, Hamilton. "The Battle of Perryville, 1862." FCHQ, 9 [1935]: 158-181.

A well-written account of "the greatest single military event ever enacted" in Kentucky. Proportionally, it was "one of the bloodiest" of Civil War battles.

2384. Taylor, Robert B. "The Battle of Perryville, October 8, 1862, as Described in the Diary of Captain Robert B. Taylor." Hamilton Tapp, editor. KY HIS SOC REG, 60 [1962]: 255-292.

A detailed, perceptive record of the events leading up to the battle and the battle itself, by a captain of the 22nd Kentucky.

2385. Walker, Peter F. "Holding the Tennessee Line, Winter 1861-1862." TENN HIS Q, 16 [1957]: 228-249.

A description of the Confederate defensive position across southern Kentucky during the fall and winter of 1861-1862. The line collapsed early in 1862.

2386. Whitsell, Robert D. "Military and Naval Activity Between Cairo and Columbus." KY HIS SOC REG, 61 [1963]: 107-121.

Author narrates the military activities of Union forces under Grant and Confederate forces under Leonidas Polk in western Kentucky in the fall of 1861.

Louisiana

RED RIVER CAMPAIGN [March 10-May 22,1864]

2387. Bearss, Edwin C. "The Story of Fort Beauregard." LA STUD, 3 [1964]: 330-384; 4 [1965]: 3-40.

The story of the federal efforts to capture Fort Beauregard on the Washita River in early May 1864.

2388. Benson, Solon F. "The Battle of Pleasant Hill, Louisiana." ANN IOWA, 7 [1906]: 481-522.

Heavy fighting at Pleasant Hill, April 9, 1864, west of Natchitoches, forced the Confederates to withdraw.

2389. Billias, George A. "Maine Lumbermen Rescue the Red River Fleet." NEW ENG SOC STUD BULL, 16 [1958]: 5-8.

Describes the ingenious efforts of Maine regiments, led by Colonel Joseph Bailey, to construct dams along the Red River above Alexandria to permit federal boats to withdraw and escape Confederate capture.

2390. Donnan, William G. "A Reminiscence of the Last Battle of the Red River Expedition." ANN IOWA, 6 [1904]: 241-247.

The "last battle" was near Yellow Bayou on May 18, 1864.

2391. Johnson, Ludwell H. RED RIVER CAMPAIGN: POLITICS AND COTTON IN THE CIVIL WAR. Baltimore: Johns Hopkins University Press, 1958.

The most thorough and best-written account of the campaign, which was intended to procure cotton, as well as secure the Louisana-Arkansas-Texas frontier for the Federals. The author skillfully weaves together the military, political, and economic motivations behind Banks' ill-fated effort.

2392. Landers, H.L. "Wet Sand and Cotton: Banks' Red River Campaign." LA HIS Q, 19 [1936]: 150-195.

The unsuccessful Union effort to open up northern Louisana and Texas in 1864 produced more bitter quarrels and recriminations than any other campaign.

2393. Longacre, Edward G. "Rescue on the Red River." CWTI, 14 [6] [1975]: 4-9,39-42.

Author describes Bailey's spectacular feat of saving the Union fleet by damming the Red River.

2394. Meiners, Fredericka. "Hamilton P. Bee in the Red River Campaign." SW HIS Q, 78 [1974/1975]: 21-44.

Bee commanded a Texas force at Monett's Ferry during the Red River Campaign and was relieved because of poor performance.

2395. Tyson, Carl F. "Highway of War." RED RIVER VALL HIS R, 3 [1978]: 28-51.

A record of the war from the fall of Vicksburg to the end of the Red River Campaign.

2396. Williams, Richard H. "General Banks' Red River Campaign." LA HIS Q, 32 [1949]: 103-144.

Banks is somewhat absolved from responsibility for the failure of the Red River Campaign since he had originally opposed it.

* * *

2397. Boilard, David and Joseph Carvalho, III. "Pvt. John E. Bisbee, the 52nd Massachusetts Volunteers and the Banks Expedition." HIS J W MASS, 3 [1974]: 39-49.

A common man's view of the Banks' expedition of 1862-1863, which led to the capture of Port Hudson.

2398. Booth, George W. "We've Played Cards and Lost." CWTI, 9 [9] [1973]: 17-24.

A northerner in New Orleans describes the last days, April 13-30, 1862, before its capture.

2399. Cunningham, Edward. THE PORT HUDSON CAMPAIGN, 1862-1863. Baton Rouge: Louisiana State University Press, 1963.

Author succeeds in putting the Port Hudson siege in proper perspective with regard to the war in the West. A good account of the battle.

2400. Harrington, Fred H. "Arkansas Defends the Mississippi." ARK HIS Q, 4 [1945]: 109-117.

Arkansas troops played a central role in the defense of Port Hudson, a major Confederate position on the Mississippi below Vicksburg, which fell to federal troops on July 8, 1863.

2401. Jackson, Crawford. "An Account of the Occupation of Port Hudson, Louisiana." ALA HIS Q, 18 [1956]: 474-485.

This account written by a Confederate sergeant is very interesting. It was the first time he had fought against black troops.

2402. Lathrop, Barnes F. "Federals 'Sweep the Coast': An Expedition Into St. Charles Parish, August 1862." LA HIS, 9 [1968]: 62-68.

A narration of a federal expedition along the west bank of the Mississippi between New Orleans and Baton Rouge.

2403. Moore, Waldo W. "The Defense of Shreveport: The Confederacy's Last Redoubt." MIL AFF, 17 [1953]: 72-82.

Shreveport surrendered in late May 1865, seven weeks after Appomattox.

2404. Perrin, William E., Jr. "Civil War Military Operations In and Around Ponchatoula, Louisiana." LA HIS, 12 [1971]: 123-136.

Ponchatoula is just northwest of New Orleans, across Lake Ponchartrain.

2405. Williams, T. Harry and A. Otis Herbert, Jr. THE CIVIL WAR IN LOUISIANA, A CHRONOLOGY. Baton Rouge: Louisiana Civil War Centennial Commission, 1961.

Many minor events are listed here, as well as important military and civil happenings.

2406. Winters, John D. THE CIVIL WAR IN LOUISIANA. Baton Rouge: Louisiana State University Press, 1963.

Details events from Louisiana's secession convention in January 1861 to the surrender of the Confederate naval forces on the Red River in June 1865.

Maryland

ANTIETAM [September 17, 1862] [Also called Sharpsburg]

2407. Allan, William. "Strategy of the Sharpsburg Campaign." MD HIS MAG, 1 [1906]: 247-271.

Written by a former lieutenant colonel and chief ordnance officer of the 2nd Corps, Army of Northern Virginia. The author believes he was justified in dividing his forces to take Harper's Ferry but should not have fought at Sharpsburg, though he thinks he fought rather well there.

2408. Duncan, Richard R. "Marylanders and the Invasion of 1862." CWH, 11 [1965]: 370-383.

An account of the impact of Lee's army on the people of western Maryland during the invasion of September 1862.

2409. Hassler, Warren W. "The Battle of South Mountain." MD HIS MAG, 52 [1957]: 39-64.

South Mountain, a few miles east of Sharpsburg, was the scene of vigorous fighting on September 14, 1862, as Lee tried to delay McClellan's advance.

2410. Heysinger, Isaac W. ANTIETAM AND THE MARYLAND AND VIRGINIA CAMPAIGNS OF 1862.... New York, 1912.

A rather sensational account of the campaigning in Virginia and western Maryland by an army captain who supports McClellan's behavior.

2411. McCormack, John F. "The Harper's Ferry Skedaddlers." CWTI, 14 [1975]: 32-39.

Describes the escape of 1,500 federal cavalry from a Confederate trap and their capture of a supply train, September 14-15, 1862.

2412. Mies, John. "Breakout at Harper's Ferry." CWH, 2 [1956]: 13-28.

Another account of the episode noted in the previous entry. The federal force was led by Benjamin Davis, the only southerner in his West Point class to remain loyal to the Union.

2413. Murfin, James V. THE GLEAM OF BAYONETS: THE BATTLE OF ANTIETAM AND THE MARYLAND CAMPAIGN. New York: Yoseloff, 1965.

A somewhat pedestrian account of the Antietam campaign in which the author is very critical of McClellan--perhaps too much so. Well-researched, but not carefully edited.

2414. Schenck, Martin. "Burnside's Bridge." CWH, 2 [1956]: 5-19.

An account of the heavy fighting at the critical bridge south of Sharpsburg on the afternoon of September 17. The Ninth Corps commander, Burnside, was finally driven back by Confederates newly arrived from Harper's Ferry.

2415. Schildt, John W. SEPTEMBER ECHOES, THE MARYLAND CAMPAIGN OF 1862. Middleton, Maryland: Valley Register, 1960.

Designed more for tourists and Civil War fans than scholars, this 140-page booklet, which draws heavily from standard secondary sources, is a useful handbook on Antietam.

2416. Sears. Stephen W. LANDSCAPE TURNED RED: THE BATTLE OF ANTIETAM. New Haven, Connecticut: Ticknor and Fields, 1983.

A scholarly, well-written study of the "greatest single day's battle of the war." The author takes McClellan to task for missing many golden opportunities to destroy Lee's army before, during, and after the battle.

2417. Stackpole, Edward J. FROM CEDAR MOUNTAIN TO ANTIETAM: AUGUST-SEPTEMBER, 1862. Harrisburg, Pennsylvania: Stackpole, 1959.

An able, highly detailed account of the entire campaign, including the battle of Cedar Mountain, Second Bull Run, Chantilly, Harpers Ferry, South Mountain, and Antietam. The author permits his own military background to allow him to assess the military moves of the two armies and the Federals do not fare very well. Excellent maps.

2418. Teetor, Paul R. A MATTER OF HOURS: TREASON AT HARPER'S FERRY. Rutherford, New Jersey: Fairleigh Dickinson University Press, 1982.

The author seeks to show that Harper's Ferry's commander, Colonel Dixon Miles was a traitor who deliberately betrayed the garrison and exposed it to capture by Stonewall Jackson. The work is weakened by factual and spelling errors and dubious research, and fails entirely to convince the reader. Despite these flaws, it so happens that the editor of this bibliography has in his possession letters from his grandfather, who was captured at Harper's Ferry, strongly stating that Colonel Miles had indeed betrayed the 11,000 troops there.

* * *

2419. Beiley, John W., Jr. "The McNeill Rangers and the Capture of Generals Crook and Kelley." MD HIS MAG, 62 [1967]: 47-63.

A description of the capture of these two federal generals in Cumberland, Maryland, February 22, 1865, by 70 Confederate cavalrymen under the command of Captain John H. McNeill.

2420. Bowman, Forest J. "Capture of Generals Crook and Kelley." CWTI, 7 [10] [1969]: 28-37.

Another account of the incident noted in the previous entry.

2421. Duncan, Richard R. "Maryland's Reaction to Early's Raid in 1864: A Summer of Bitterness." MD HIS MAG, 64 [1969]: 248-279.

Confederate General Jubal Early launched his famous raid from Lynchburg, Virginia, June 27, 1864, and after marauding through the Shenandoah Valley, Maryland, Washington, D.C., and Pennsylvania, returned to Virginia in August. He inflicted substantial damage and experienced no serious resistance.

2422. Morseberger, Robert E. "The Battle That Saved Washington." CWTI, 13 [2] [1974]: 12-17, 20-27.

On July 9, 1864, Early encountered the forces of General Lew Wallace on the Monocacy River, southeast of Frederick, Maryland. Though Wallace was defeated, he had saved Washington by delaying Early's advance.

2423. Stegmaier, Mark J. "The Kidnapping of Generals Crook and Kelley by the McNeill Rangers, February 21, 1865." W VA HIS, 29 [1967]: 13-47.

Another account of this sensational event.

2424. Suppiger, Joseph E. "'In Defense of Washington.'" CWTI, 15 [5] [1976]: 38-45.

Cassius Marcellus Clay, colorful Kentucky abolitionist, raised troops for the defense of Washington April 17-April 25, 1861. Fortunately the "regulars" arrived, and Clay sailed for Russia to take up his appointment as minister to that country.

2425. Worthington, Glenn H. FIGHTING FOR TIME, OR, THE BATTLE THAT SAVED WASHINGTON.... Baltimore: Day Printing, 1932.

A good, detailed account of the Monocacy battle with useful maps and illustrations.

Mississippi

VICKSBURG CAMPAIGN [December 1862-July 4, 1863]

2426. Ambrose, Stephen E. et. al. "Struggle for Vicksburg: The Battles and Siege That Decided the Civil War." CWTI, 6 [4] [1967]: 3-66.

This is another single-campaign issue of the publication. Deals with the initial thrust southward, fighting in the bayous, the battles of Port Gibson, Raymond, Champion Hill and Vicksburg.

2427. Bearss, Edwin C. "The Campaign Culminating in the Fall of Vicksburg, March 29-July 4, 1863." IOWA J HIS, 59 [1961]: 173-180, 238-242.

An account of Iowa troops who participated in the campaign.

2428. ———. DECISION IN MISSISSIPPI: MISSISSIPPI'S IMPORTANT ROLE IN THE WAR BETWEEN THE STATES. Jackson, Mississippi: Mississippi Commission on the War Between the States, 1962.

An expert on warfare along the lower Mississippi, the author has poured almost too much into this account of the Vicksburg campaign.

2429. ———. "Grand Gulf's Role in the Civil War." CWH, 5 [1969]: 5-29.

Grand Gulf, located on the east bank of the Mississippi south of Vicksburg, was evacuated by the Confederates on May 2 as Grant crossed over the river.

2430. ———. REBEL VICTORY AT VICKSBURG. Vicksburg: Vicksburg Centennial Commemoration Commission, 1963.

Author describes the federal failure to capture Vicksburg in the summer and fall of 1862. Naval forces under Farragut, coming up from New Orleans and under Charles Davis, coming down from Memphis, were unable to reduce the city. Although Vicksburg would eventually fall, it is argued that this Confederate victory has been too long ignored.

2431. ———. "Sherman's Demonstration Against Snyder's Bluff." J MISS HIS, 27 [1965]: 168-186.

This assault in the vicinity of Haines' Bluff north of Vicksburg was designed as a diversion while Grant crossed at Port Gibson below Vicksburg. It occurred April 30-May 1.

2432. ———. "The Vicksburg River Defense and the Enigma of 'Whisling Dick.'" J MISS HIS, 19 [1957]: 21-30.

"Whistling Dick" was a famous Confederate artillery piece at Vicksburg, which fell to the Federals on July 4, 1863. However, the name came to be applied loosely to other Confederate guns of the same make.

2433. Bearss, Margie R. "The Capture of Haines' Bluff by the 4th Iowa Cavalry." ANN IOWA, 40 [1970]: 334-343.

Contrary to contemporary accounts, the author argues that the Fourth Iowa Cavalry, not Union gunboats, captured Haines' Bluff.

2434. Bell, John N. "Diary of Captain John N. Bell of Company E, 25th Iowa Infantry at Vicksburg." Edwin C. Bearss, editor. IOWA J HIS, 59 [1961]: 181-221.

The author was a keen observer of what he saw and heard. From this record of his experiences, it is easy to see that Bell was a sentimental, homesick man.

2435. Brinkerhoff, Arch M. "Diary of Private Arch M. Brinkerhoff, Company H, 4th Iowa Infantry, at Vicksburg." Edwin C. Bearss, editor. IOWA J HIS, 59 [1961]: 225-237.

This well-edited diary provides insight into camp life during the siege of Vicksburg.

2436. Brown, D. Alexander. "Battle at Chickasaw Bluffs." CWTI, 9 [4] [1970]: 4-9. 44-48.

An account of Sherman's failure to seize Chickasaw Bluffs north of Vicksburg in December 1862.

2437. Burton, Anthony B. " Lt. Anthony B. Burton's Account of the Activities of the 5th Battery Ohio Light Artillery at Vicksburg." Edwin C. Bearss, editor. LA STUD, 10 [1971]: 274-330.

This record covers the history of the Fifth Ohio Battery from its muster in--September 1861--through the Vicksburg campaign.

2438. Carter, Samuel. THE FINAL FORTRESS: THE CAMPAIGN FOR VICKSBURG. New York: St. Martin's, 1980.

Paints a dramatic, generalized picture of the siege. The author combines the "experiences of ordinary soldiers and noncombatants with the larger strategic events of the episode."

2439. Colby, Carlos W. "Bullets, Hardtack and Mud: A Soldier's View of the Vicksburg Campaign." John S. Painter, editor. JW, 4 [1965]: 129-168.

These thoughtful letters were written between December 19, 1862 and August 5, 1863, while Colby was a member of the 97th Illinois which participated in the entire campaign.

2440. Connelly, Thomas L. "Vicksburg: Strategic Point or Propaganda Device?" MIL AFF, 34 [1970]: 49-53.

Author suggests that to the South the psychological or propaganda loss of Vicksburg was possibly more significant than its economic or strategic impact.

2441. Cunningham, Edward. THE PORT HUDSON CAMPAIGN, 1862-1863. Baton Rouge: Louisiana State University Press, 1963.

Port Hudson, the last Confederate stronghold on the Mississippi, fell July 9, 1863, after withstanding four major federal assaults in a seven week period. Its surrender was the final episode in General Banks' 1863 Red River Campaign. This is a thorough, readable account of this final phase of operations on the Mississippi.

2442. Garland, Hamlin. TRAIL-MAKERS OF THE MIDDLE BORDER. New York: Macmillan, 1926.

Drawing in part on his father's experiences, Garland creates an extensive portrait of Grant while describing the life of the common soldier at the siege of Vicksburg.

2443. Ginder, Henry. "A Louisiana Engineer at the Siege of Vicksburg." L. Moody Simms, editor. LA HIS, 8 [1967]: 371-378.

Written from Vicksburg in June 1863, these letters vividly depict the city and its defenders during the later days of the siege.

2444. Grant, Frederick D. "With Grant at Vicksburg." OUTLOOK, [July 2, 1898]: 533-543.

General Grant's schoolboy son was allowed to accompany his father during the siege. He writes engagingly and with pride of his experiences.

2445. Halsell, Willie D., editor. "The Sixteenth Indiana Regiment in the Last Vicksburg Campaign." IND MAG HIS, 43 [1947]: 67-82.

A collection of ten letters from William H. Jordan, a lieutenant in the 16th Indiana, to his mother. They are dated January 1, 1863-January 5, 1865 while he was stationed at Vicksburg and in the southwestern theater.

2446. Hoehling, A.A., et al. VICKSBURG: 47 DAYS OF SIEGE. Englewood Cliffs: Prentice-Hall, 1969.

This is a social history of Vicksburg during the siege--an account of the people of the city, their ordeal, and their emotional reactions. Work includes letters, diaries, and narratives, and is organized chronologically. A vivid glimpse of Vicksburg in its most critical hour.

2447. Howard, Brett. "The Story of Vicksburg." MANKIND, 1 [2] [1967]: 4-19.

An analysis of the Confederate and Union strategies, which led to the siege and capitulation of the important Confederate river port. Author argues that Grant's methods were unprecedented.

2448. Jones, Archer. "The Vicksburg Campaign." J MISS HIS, 29 [1967]: 12-27.

A study of the attitudes and actions of Generals Johnston and Pemberton and of President Jefferson Davis during the siege of the city.

2449. Kaiser, Leo M. "Beleaguered City: The Vicksburg Campaign as Seen in Unpublished Union Letters.: SOUTH STUD, 17 [1978]: 69-90.

The author paints a picture of the siege through the letters of eight Illinois soldiers.

2450. Longacre, Edward G. "The Port Hudson Campaign." CWTI, 10 [10] [1972]: 20-31, 34.

General Nathaniel Banks, the Massachusetts politician-soldier, commanded the troops that captured Port Hudson.

2451. Myers, John. "Dear and Mutch Loved One: An Iowan's Vicksburg Letters." Edward G. Longacre, editor. ANN IOWA, 43 [1975]: 49-61.

Ten letters from a member of the 28th Iowa to his wife. The author wrote vivid accounts of siege warfare, terrors of battle, and boredom.

2452. Miers, Earl S. THE WEB OF VICTORY: GRANT AT VICKSBURG. New York: Knopf, 1955.

An excellent, readable volume on the siege, in which Grant begins to emerge as a great military leader.

2453. Moore, Ross H. "The Vicksburg Campaign of 1863." J MISS HIS, 1 [1939]: 151-168.

Studies Confederate tactics in an attempt to fix the responsibility for the Confederate defeat.

2454. Raynor, William H. "The Civil War Diary of Colonel William H. Raynor During the Vicksburg Campaign." Edwin C. Bearss, editor. LA STUD, 9 [1970]: 243-300.

The diary of a federal officer of the 56th Ohio who moved with Grant's army from Milliken's Bend to the fall of Vicksburg, April 16-July 3, 1863.

2455. Reynolds, Donald E. "Union Strategy in Arkansas During the Vicksburg Campaign." ARK HIS Q, 29 [1970]: 20-38.

Author analyzes the strategy designed to capture the fortified Post of Arkansas and Little Rock.

2456. Scroggs, Jack B. and Donald E. Reynolds. "Arkansas and the Vicksburg Campaign." CWH, 5 [1959]: 390-401.

Argues that basic weaknesses existed in the Confederate command in the West. The result was hesitation and indecision.

2457. Sherman, William T. "Vicksburg by New Year's." CWTI, 16 [9] [1978]: 44-48.

A letter from General Sherman to Dr. John W. Draper in New York describes his failure at Chickasaw Bluffs in late December 1862.

2458. Walker, Peter F. VICKSBURG: A PEOPLE AT WAR, 1860-1865. Chapel Hill: University of North Carolina Press, 1960.

A good study of Vicksburg society until the city's fall in July 1863. There is little on the last two years of the war. The volume, a revised Ph. D. dissertation has been carefully researched and well-written. One of the most often asked questions--"What did the Vicksburg civilians do during the siege?"--has now been answered.

2459. Warmoth, Henry C. "The Vicksburg Diary of Henry Clay Warmoth." Paul H. Hass, editor. J MISS HIS, 31 [1969]: 334-347; 32 [1970]: 60-74.

Warmoth was an officer in an Illinois unit, who later became famous as the "carpetbag" governor of Louisiana.

2460. Wells, Seth J. THE SIEGE OF VICKSBURG. Detroit: William H. Rowe, 1915.

Based on the diary of the author, who served with the 17th Indiana. Contents cover the period from before the city's fall through the occupation.

2461. Wheeler, Richard. "The Siege of Vicksburg." AM HER, 27 [4] [1976]: 66-75.

Author describes the Vicksburg campaign through the eyes of Union and Confederate officers, newspapermen, and civilians of the city.

2462. Wilcox, Charles E. "With Grant at Vicksburg." Edgar L. Erickson, editor. JISHS, 30 [1938]: 440-503.

Based on the author's diary. He served with the 33rd Illinois.

* * *

2463. Bahr, Howard L. and William K. Duke. "The Wet August: Andrew J. Smith's Mississippi Campaign." CWTI, 16 [7] [1977]: 10-19.

Discusses Union campaign in Mississippi in 1864.

2464. Bearss, Edwin C. "Colonel Streight Drives For the Western and Atlantic Railroad." ALA HIS Q, 26 [1964]: 133-186.

Author complains that military historians have failed to see that Grierson's raid through central Mississippi and Abel Streight's raid in eastern Mississippi in April and May 1863 were part of one grand operation. He demonstrates their relationship here.

2465. ———. "The Great Railroad Raid." ANN IOWA, 40 [1969]: 147-160; 222-239.

A two part account of the federal raid on supply bases in northwestern Mississippi and along the Mississippi Central Railroad in August 1863. The 2nd, 3rd, and 4th Iowa cavalry played an important part in the successful raid.

2466. ———. "McArthur's May Expedition Against the Mississippi Central Railroad." J MISS HIS, 28 [1966]: 1-14.

An account of a Union raid under General John McArthur, wherein the railroad line was cut, but the major objective of the operation was not achieved.

2467. Brooksher, William and David K. Snider. "A Visit to Holly Springs." CWTI, 14 [3] [1975]: 4-17.

Describes an engagement between the Confederate cavalary of General Earl Van Dorn and Grant's forces at Holly Springs, Mississippi, in December 1862.

2468. Brown, D. Alexander. "The Battle of Brice's Cross Roads." CWTI, 7 [1] [1968]: 4-9, 44-48.

On June 10, 1864, General Forrest inflicted a decisive defeat on a much larger Union force in northeastern Mississippi, which led to an investigation by a military board.

2469. ———. GRIERSON'S RAID. Urbana: University of Illinois Press, 1954.

An excellent account of the famous raid through Mississippi led by Union Colonel Benjamin H. Grierson. Leaving northeastern Mississippi on April 17, 1863, the Federals traveled 600 miles in 16 days, tore up 50 miles of railroads and diverted Confederate strength from Vicksburg as Grant was preparing to recross the Mississippi.

2470. ———. "Grierson's Raid. 'Most Brilliant' of the War." CWTI, 3 [9] [1965]: 4-11, 30-32.

In condensing the material from his book, the author tells how Grierson's men contributed heavily to the Union victory at Vicksburg.

2471. Carter, Theodore G. "The Tupelo Campaign...." MISS SOC HIS PUB, 10 [1909]: 91-113.

The Federals were driven from Tupelo, in northeastern Missis-aippi, by Forrest's cavalry.

2472. Castel, Albert. "The Battle Without a Victor ... Iuka." CWTI, 11 [6] [1972]: 12-18.

On September 19 and 20, 1862, a federal force from Corinth moved against Sterling Price at Iuka, in northeastern Mississippi.

2473. Dimick, Howard T. "Motives for the Burning of Oxford, Mississippi, August 22, 1864." J MISS HIS, 8 [1946]: 111-120.

Author contends there were no reasons for burning the city. It was undefended, all stores had been removed, and there were no fortifications.

2474. Dodson, Clyde N. "The Battle of Brice's Crossroads." MIL R, 44 [1964]: 85-98.

An account of the routing of federal forces at this battle on June 10, 1864.

2475. Glenn, Jack W. "The Battle of Iuka." J MISS HIS, 24 [1962]: 142-157.

While the Confederates were repulsed in their attempt to move north at Iuka, September 19, 1862, they were able to get away with their forces relatively intact.

2476. Hartje, Robert. "Van Doren Conducts a Raid on Holly Springs and Enters Tennessee." TENN HIS Q, 18 [1959]: 120-133.

The Confederate cavalry commander assaulted Grant's base as Grant was preparing his first move against Vicksburg.

2477. Koury, Mike. "Union Disaster in Mississippi: The Battle of Brice's Crossroads." BY VALOR AND ARMS, 1 [3] [1975]: 41-47.

Relates the events of the Union defeat at Brice's Crossroads.

2478. Leftwich, William G. "The Battle of Brice's Cross Roads." W TENN HIS SOC PAPERS, 20 [1956]: 5-19.

Author observes that the engagement resulted in a brilliant tactical success for Forrest who, although outnumbered, defeated the mismanaged federal forces under General Samuel Sturgis.

2479. Luckett, William W. "Bedford Forrest in the Battle of Brice's Cross Roads." TENN HIS Q, 15 [1956]: 99-110.

Credits Confederate victory to Forrest's ingenuity and capability.

2480. McMurry, Richard M. "Sherman's Meridian Campaign." CWTI, 14 [2] [1975]: 24-32.

Prior to leaving for his Atlanta Campaign in March, Sherman busied himself with destroying railroads and Confederate resources in central Mississippi in February, 1864.

2481. Shank, George K., Jr. "Meridian: A Mississippi City at Birth, During the Civil War, and in Reconstruction." J MISS HIS, 26 [1964]: 275-282.

An account of the havoc wrought by Sherman's troops when they occupied Meridian.

2482. Stinson, Byron. "Hot Work in Mississippi: The Battle of Tupelo." CWTI, 11 [4] [1972]: 4-9, 46-48.

The Federals attempted to prevent Confederates from destroying the Mobile and Ohio Railroad in this engagement of July 13-15, 1864.

2483. Sunderland, Glenn W. "The Battle of Corinth." CWTI, 6 [1] [1967]: 28-37.

Heavy fighting and casualties marked this successful federal attempt to repulse Confederates anxious to seize the important rail center, October 2-4, 1862.

North Carolina

[See also Georgia: MARCH THROUGH CAROLINAS]

2484. Asprey, Robert C. "The Assault on Fort Fisher." MARINE CORPS GAZETTE, 44 [1966]: 30-31.

Fort Fisher, protecting Wilmington, North Carolina, the last seaport still in Confederate hands, fell on January 15, 1865.

2485. Glazier, James E. "The Roanoke Island Expedition: Observations of a Massachusetts Soldier." James I. Robertson, Jr., editor. CWH, 12 [1966]: 321-346.

A group of letters from Private Glazier of the 23rd Massachusetts which provide a good account of the expedition of February 1862.

2486. Iobst, Richard W. BATTLE OF NEW BERN. Raleigh: North Carolina Centennial Commission, 1962.

This 14-page pamphlet describes the capture of New Bern on Pamlico Sound by Burnside's Expedition, March 14, 1862.

2487. Luvaas, Jay. "Burnside's Roanoke Expedition." CWTI, 7 [8] [1968]: 4-11, 43-48.

Roanoke Island, off the east coast of northern North Carolina, was captured on February 8, 1862, by troops accompanying Burnside's Expedition. The capture of the island led to further victories along the coast which completed the blockade of two-thirds of North Carolin's Atlantic coastline.

2488. ———. "The Fall of Fort Fisher." CWTI, 3 [5] [1964]: 5-9, 31-35.

Amphibious landings spelled the doom of this important Confederate outpost.

2489. Merrill, James M. "The Hatteras Expedition, August 1861." NC HIS R, 39 [1952]: 204-219.

A small federal force captured Forts Hatteras and Clark on August 28-29, 1861.

2490. Paludan, Phillip S. VICTIMS: A TRUE STORY OF THE CIVIL WAR. Knoxville: University of Tennessee Press, 1981.

A collection of essays which show how an isolated incident in the western mountains of North Carolina served as a catalyst to weave individual, community, and nation into a coherent cultural pattern. The incident was the murder of thirteen Unionists by Confederate "Rangers."

2491. Price, Charles L. and Claude C. Sturgill. "Shock and Assault in the First Battle of Fort Fisher." NC HIS R, 47 [1970]: 24-39.

Prior to the fall of Fort Fisher in January 1865, an earlier effort by the Federals to seize the place the previous month had been unsuccessul.

2492. Stick, David. THE OUTER BANKS OF NORTH CAROLINA. Chapel Hill: University of North Carolina Press, 1958.

A solid survey of the history of the many islands and inlets which line the North Carolina coast, including a good account of the Civil War years.

2493. Van Noppen, Ina W. STONEMAN'S LAST RAID. Raleigh, North Carolina: North Carolina State College, 1961.

In March 1865 Stoneman's cavalry was ordered from Tennessee into western North Carolina as a diversion to preoccupy both Lee and Joseph Johnston. He caused considerable damage, but much of it was done after Lee had surrendered.

2494. Whitman, George W. "Civil War Letters of George Washington Whitman From North Carolina." NC HIS R, 50 [1973]: 73-92.

The writer, the younger brother of poet Walt Whitman and a member of the 51st New York, wrote these letters from Roanoke Island and New Bern to his mother.

Pennsylvania

GETTYSBURG CAMPAIGN [June 3-August 1, 1863]

2495. Anthony, William, editor. ANTHONY'S HISTORY OF THE BATTLE OF HANOVER.... Hanover, Pennsylvania: By author, 1945.

A collection of sketches about the cavalry fighting at Hanover, June 30, 1863, preceding the outbreak of the battle at Gettysburg.

2496. Bates, Samuel P. THE BATTLE OF GETTYSBURG. Philadelphia, 1875.

Though old and undocumented, this volume can still be read with profit.

2497. Battine, Cecil W. THE CRISIS OF THE CONFEDERACY: A HISTORY OF GETTYSBURG AND THE WILDERNESS. London, England: 1905.

This is a detailed, useful account of the two battles written by a British officer.

2498. Beale, James, compiler. TABULATED ROSTER OF THE ARMY OF THE POTOMAC AT GETTSBURG.... Philadelphia, 1888.

Designates brigade, division and corps which served during the battle. Arranged by states and regiments.

2499. Beecham, Robert K. GETTYSBURG, THE PIVOTAL BATTLE OF THE CIVIL WAR. Chicago, 1911.

A readable account written in old age by a man who was a young federal officer during the battle. He served with the 2nd Wisconsin.

2500. Bellah, James W. SOLDIERS' BATTLE: GETTYSBURG. New York: David McKay, 1962.

While a well-written book, this volume is largely a re-working of secondary materials. The reader might well argue with the author's basic premise as reflected in the title. Written by an experienced novelist, it shows how the battle might have appeared to the participants--in other words, it is a soldier's view of the battle.

2501. Burrage, Henry S. GETTYSBURG AND LINCOLN: THE BATTLE, THE CEMETERY, AND THE NATIONAL PARK. New York, 1906.

The battle, the establishment of the cemetery and park, and the work of the park commission are the elements comprising this book. Author discusses at some length the Gettysburg address and its variations.

2502. Calderhead, William L. "Philadelphia in Crisis: June-July, 1863." PENN HIS, 28 [1961]: 142-155.

A description of the plans made in Philadelphia in late June and early July 1863 to meet Lee's invasion of Pennsylvania. The drilling of a "home guard" force and the construction of defense works were the chief projects undertaken.

2503. Carpenter, John A. "General O.O. Howard at Gettysburg." CWH, 9 [1963]: 261-276.

A defense of Howard's behavior on the first day of battle.

2504. Chamberlain, Joshua L. "Through Blood and Fire at Gettysburg." HEARST'S MAG, 23 [1913]: 894-909.

The famous commander of the 20th Maine tells of his unit's heroic rescue of Little Round Top on the second day of the battle.

2505. Coddington, Edwin B. THE GETTYSBURG CAMPAIGN: A STUDY IN COMMAND. New York: Scribner's, 1968.

This massive, carefully-researched, and well-written volume should remain the standard work on the subject for some time. Battle accounts are good and judgments are balanced. Good maps and illustrations enhance the book's appeal.

2506. ———. "Lincoln's Role in the Gettysburg Campaign." PENN HIS, 34 [1967]: 250-265.

Author discusses the Halleck-Hooker feud on the eve of the battle, and also deals with Lincoln's view that General Meade had a glorious opportunity to win at Gettysburg, destroy Lee's army, and thus shorten the war.

2507. ———. "Pennsylvania Prepares for Invasion, 1863." PENN HIS, 31 [1964]: 157-175.

There was a general reluctance among the people to volunteer for the defense forces as Lee's invasion was imminent.

2508. Coit, Joseph H. "The Civil War Diary of Joseph H. Coit." James McLachlan, editor. MD HIS MAG, 60 [1965]: 245-260.

The events of June 1863 are recounted by an instructor at the College of Saint James, an Episcopalian preparatory school near Hagerstown, Maryland.

2509. Conquest, Robert. "The Battle of Gettysburg." HIS TOD, 8 [1959]: 177-186.

A British historian holds that Gettysburg was the turning point of the Civil War.

2510. Cowan, Andrew. "Repulsing Pickett's Charge." CWTI, 3 [5] [1964]: 26-35.

An eyewitness account of the most famous episode of the battle based on the author's official report and a speech he made at the dedication of the monument to General Alexander S. Webb.

2511. Doubleday, Abner. GETTYSBURG MADE PLAIN. New York, 1888.

A succinct, 59-page account of the battle by the man who assumed command of the First Corps upon the death of General John Reynolds.

2512. Dowdey, Clifford. DEATH OF A NATION: THE STORY OF LEE AND HIS MEN AT GETTYSBURG. New York: Knopf, 1958.

A well-paced story of the Confederate defeat.

2513. Downey, Fairfax D. CLASH OF CAVALRY: THE BATTLE OF BRANDY STATION, JUNE 9, 1863. New York: David McKay, 1959.

A vivid narrative of the greatest cavalry battle in history to this time, as both armies moved through Virginia northward to their rendezvous at Gettysburg. Confederate General "Jeb" Stuart, shielding Lee's troops, was attacked by General Alfred Pleasonton. Although Stuart held his position, the maligned federal cavalry gained great confidence.

2514. ———. THE GUNS AT GETTYSBURG. New York, David McKay, 1958.

An impressive study of the role of the artillery at Gettysburg, written by an artillery veteran of the two world wars. Downey believes that the importance of artillery in the battle has been overlooked and he meticulously sets the record straight. He expresses praise for General Henry J. Hunt, chief of artillery for the Army of the Potomac, to whose memory he dedicates the book.

2515. Drake, Samuel A. ... THE BATTLE OF GETTYSBURG, 1863. Boston, 1892.

A well-written, useful volume in spite of its age.

2516. ENCOUNTER AT HANOVER: PRELUDE TO GETTYSBURG.... Gettysburg: Times and News Publishing Company, 1963.

A discursive description of the invasion of Pennsylvania with particular reference to the cavalry fight at Hanover on the eve of the battle. A history of the town of Hanover is included.

2517. Frost, Lawrence. "Cavalry Action on the Third Day at Gettysburg: A Case Study." MIL COLL HIS, 29 [1977]: 149-157.

An account of the repulse of Jeb Stuart's forces by Union General David Gregg, east of Gettysburg, on the third day.

2518. Hage, Anne A. "The Battle of Gettysburg as Seen by Minnesota Soldiers." MINN HIS, 38 [1963]: 245-257.

Author draws her account from the diaries and letters of soldiers who fought in the battle.

2519. Hale, Charles A. "With Colonel Cross at the Wheatfield." Edward G. Longacre, editor. CWTI, 13 [5] [1974]: 30-38.

A hitherto unpublished memoir of Charles A. Hale, who served on the staff of Colonel Edward E. Cross, a brigade commander in Hancock's Second Corps. Cross was killed near Devil's Den on the second day.

2520. Haskell, Frank A. THE BATTLE OF GETTYSBURG. Boston: Houghton Mifflin, 1958.

A reprint of a classic report of the battle, written by a staff officer serving with the Iron Brigade in the Second Corps. Haskell wrote the manuscript immediately after the battle and it reflects all the fire, fury, gore, and heroism of the moment. An outstanding soldier, Haskell was killed while leading a brigade at Cold Harbor.

2521. Hassler, Warren W. CITIES AT THE CROSSROADS: THE FIRST DAY AT GETTYSBURG. Tuscaloosa: University of Alabama Press, 1970.

The author, who excels in describing fighting at the unit level, has written a vivid narrative of the first day, a day which he feels has not received the recognition it deserves. The First Corps, with its commander dead, fought well under Doubleday and saved the day for the Federals. Howard, again, had his problems and Lee is faulted for not giving Ewell more specific orders.

2522. ———. "The First Day's Battle of Gettysburg." CWH, 6 [1960]: 259-276.

A shorter, earlier version of the previous title. Author notes again that the first day, although just as important as the second and third days, is often overlooked.

2523. ———. "George G. Meade and His Role in the Gettysburg Campaign." PENN HIS, 32 [1965]: 380-405.

Meade, in the author's view, has been largely neglected. Here he discusses the general's thinking on the eve of and during the battle.

2524. Hoffsommer. Robert D. "This Was: The Aftermath of Gettysburg." CWTI, 2 [4] [1963]: 35-38.

A statistical look at the loss of life in the battle.

2525. Hoke, Jacob. THE GREAT INVASION OF 1863, OR, GENERAL LEE IN PENNSYLVANIA.... Dayton, Ohio: 1887.

A compendium of material on the relative strength of the two armies, their routes of march, the battle itself, and the Confederate retreat, written by a civilian observer. Numerous documents are included.

2526. Hollingsworth, Allan M. and James M. Cox, editors. THE THIRD DAY AT GETTYSBURG: PICKETT'S CHARGE. New York: Henry Holt, 1959.

This volume contains 93 documents drawn chiefly from the OFFICIAL RECORDS pertaining to the culminating event of the battle.

2527. Howard, Oliver O. "The Campaign and Battle of Gettysburg, June and July 1863." ATLAN MON, 38 [1876]: 48-71.

The commander of the Eleventh Corps reviews the battle many years later and defends his role in it.

2528. Jones, Archer. "The Gettysburg Decision." VA MHB, 68 [1960]: 331-343.

Author analyzes the Confederate conferences which led to the decision to invade the North.

2529. ———. "The Gettysburg Decision Reassessed." VA MHB, 76 [1968]: 64-66.

A follow-up of the previous entry.

2530. Kantor, Mackinlay. GETTYSBURG. New York: Random House, 1952.

A volume intended for youthful readers.

2531. Keidel, George C. "Jeb Stuart in Maryland, June, 1863." MD HIS MAG, 34 [1939]: 161-164.

The dashing Confederate cavalry officer went on a raid around Hooker's advancing forces and thus deprived Lee of his "eyes" for most of the Gettysburg battle.

2532. Klein, Frederic S. "Affair at Westminster." CWTI, 7 [5] [1968]: 32-38.

Nearing the end of his Maryland excursion, Stuart's 6,000 troopers clashed with two companies of Delaware cavalry on June 29, 1863. This may have delayed Stuart's arrival at Gettysburg.

2533. ———. "Meade's Pipe Creek Line." MD HIS MAG, 57 [1962]: 133-149.

On June 30 Meade issued the "Pipe Creek Circular," outlining a defensive line for the Federals southeast of Gettysburg protecting the railroads and highways to Baltimore and Washington.

2534. Long, E.B. "The Battle That Almost Was: Manassas Gap." CWTI, 11 [8] [1972]: 20-28.

General William H. French might have ended the war at Manassas Gap, July 15-24, 1863, if he had not delayed in attacking Lee's army on its retreat from Gettysburg.

2535. Longacre, Edward G. "The Battle of Brandy Station: 'A Shock That Made the Earth Tremble.'" VA CAV, 25 [1976]: 136-143.

An analysis of the strategy employed by each side in this tremendous cavalry engagement.

2536. ———. "Henry Whelan's 'Race For Life' At Brandy Station." CWTI, 17 [9] [1979]: 32-38.

A dramatic account of a costly cavalry charge by the 6th Pennsylvania Cavalry at Brandy Station.

2537. Longstreet, Helen D. LEE AND LONGSTREET AT HIGH TIDE: GETTYSBURG IN THE LIGHT OF THE OFFICIAL RECORDS. Gainesville, Georgia: 1904. Reprint 1969.

Confederate General James Longstreet's second wife, Helen, who was born just about the time the Battle of Gettysburg took place and lived to be 99 years old, wrote this spirited defense of the general's actions on the second day.

2538. McLaughlin, Jack. GETTYSBURG: THE LONG ENCAMPMENT. New York: Appleton-Century, 1963.

A lavishly illustrated volume, in which the campaign is gone over and the various reunions of veterans are described. At the fiftieth reunion in 1913 surviving veterans reenacted Pickett's Charge.

2539. McLeod, Martha N., editor. BROTHER WARRIORS: THE REMINISCENCES OF UNION AND CONFEDERATE VETERANS. Washington, D.C.: Darling Printing, 1940.

A sentimental volume of nostalgia gathered from the 75th and last reunion of veterans in 1938.

2540. Miers, Earl S. and Richard A. Brown, editors. GETTYSBURG. New Brunswick, New Jersey: Rutgers University Press, 1948. Reprint 1963.

A collection of close to 100 contemporary accounts of the battle.

2541. Montgomery, James S. THE SHAPING OF A BATTLE: GETTYSBURG. Philadelphia: Chilton, 1959.

An imaginative effort, drawn from secondary sources, to view the battle "in the round," hopping back and forth between the two armies as the fighting unfolds. Author succeeds in keeping the reader's interest. Meade is upgraded. Unfortunately, the Bachelder maps, first issued by the War Department in 1876, do not come out very clearly.

2542. Morse, Charles F. HISTORY OF THE SECOND MASSACHUSETTS REGIMENT OF INFANTRY AT GETTYSBURG. Boston, 1882.

The author was a colonel in the 2nd Massachusetts.

2543. Mosby, John S. STUART'S CAVALRY IN THE GETTYSBURG CAMPAIGN. New York, 1908.

The famed "Gray Ghost" of the Confederacy strongly supports Stuart's actions during the Gettysburg campaign.

2544. Naisawald, L. Van Loan. "Did Union Artillery Make the Difference?" CWTI, 2 [4] [1963]: 30-34.

Author holds that the Union's use of its artillery was decisive in the federal victory.

2545. Nielson, Jon M., editor. "The Prettiest Cavalry Fight You Ever Saw.... " CWTI, 17 [4] [1978]: 4-7, 10-12, 42-43.

An eyewitness account of Brandy Station.

2546. Norton, Oliver W. THE ATTACK AND DEFENSE OF LITTLE ROUND TOP .... New York, 1913.

A detailed discussion of the struggle for Little Round Top, the key to the Federals' left flank on the afternoon of July 2.

2547. ———. STRONG VINCENT AT GETTYSBURG. Chicago, 1909.

A Union general, Vincent ordered his brigade to Little Round Top as it was being assaulted on the second day. Seriously wounded, he urged his men on. He died within a few days.

2548. Nye, Wilbur S. "The Affair at Hunterstown." CWTI, 9 [10] [1971]: 22-25, 28-34.

While Longstreet was mounting his offensive on the Emmitsburg Road on the afternoon of July 2, a fierce cavalry fight broke out at Hunterstown, a small town five miles northeast of Gettysburg.

2549. ———. HERE COME THE REBELS! Baton Rouge: Louisiana State University Press, 1965.

The detailed carefully-woven account of the Confederate move North into Pennsylvania, the parrying thrusts of the Federals, and the "levee en masse" mobilized by state and local authorities to meet the foe. An expert military analyst deals with his subject expertly.

2550. ———. "The Prelude to Gettysburg." CWTI, 2 [4] [1963]: 8-13.

A discussion of the Confederate invasion with an emphasis on Lee's achievements in administration and organization.

2551. Paris, L.P.A. d'Orleans, Comte de. THE BATTLE OF GETTYSBURG.... Philadelphia, 1912.

Good chapters on the battle excerpted from the author's four-volume history of the war.

2552. Pierce, Francis M. THE BATTLE OF GETTYSBURG.... New York, 1914.

A sweeping and interesting account of the campaign.

2553. Purcell, Hugh D. "The Nineteenth Massachusetts Regiment at Gettysburg." ESSEX INST HIS COLL, 99 [1963]: 277-288.

Describes the role of the 19th in holding the line against Pickett's charge.

2554. Rawle, William B. THE RIGHT FLANK AT GETTYSBURG. Philadelphia, 1878.

A 27-page pamphlet recounting General Gregg's repulse of Stuart in the cavalry engagement east of Gettysburg on the afternoon of the third day.

2555. Robertson, James I. Jr. "The Continuing Battle of Gettysburg: American Review Essay." GA HIS Q, 59 [1974]: 278-282.

Critics blame Longstreet while friends praise him, in the search for reasons for the Confederate defeat.

2556. Sauers, Richard A. THE GETTYSBURG CAMPAIGN, JUNE 3-AUGUST 1, 1863: A COMPREHENSIVE, SELECTIVELY ANNOTATED BIBILIOGRAPHY. Westport, Connecticut: Greenwood, 1982.

The volume contains 2757 entries on the campaign, many of which are newspaper and magazine articles. The reader will also find listings of poetry and fiction, biographies of principal figures, and histories of the regiments.

2557. Scott, James K.P. THE STORY OF THE BATTLES AT GETTYSBURG. Harrisburg, Pennsylvania: Telegraph Press, 1927.

An honest but unorganized account of the first day, with numerous maps and illustrations.

2558. Sefton, James E. "Gettysburg: An Exercise in the Evaluation of Historical Evidence." MIL AFF, 28 [1964]: 64-72.

Analyzes the difficulties confronting the military historian in evaluating the accuracy of statements made by military commanders in the heat of battle.

2559. Stackpole, Edward J. "The Battle of Gettysburg." CWTI, 2 [4] [1963]: 3-7, 45-52.

An unplanned meeting on the morning of July 1 between advance units of Lee's infantry and Meade's cavalry on the Chambersburg Pike signaled the beginning of the great battle.

2560. ———. THEY MET AT GETTYSBURG. Harrisburg: Eagle, 1956.

Although without documentation, this is an interesting survey of the campaign and is enhanced by countless excellent maps and illustrations, many drawn from BATTLES AND LEADERS.

2561. ——— and Wilbur S. Nye. THE BATTLE OF GETTYSBURG: A GUIDED TOUR. Harrisburg: Stackpole, 1960.

A fact-filled, 96-page booklet containing just about everything the Gettysburg tourist needs to know. It provides help for auto drivers, describes the battle, and contains useful maps and illustrations.

2562. Stewart, George R. PICKETT'S CHARGE: A MICROHISTORY OF THE FINAL ATTACK AT GETTYSBURG, JULY 3, 1863. Boston: Houghton Mifflin, 1959.

One of the most thoroughgoing account of the famous charge, replete with useful illustrations and maps. It is well written and well researched.

2563. Stonesifer, Roy P. "The Little Round Top Controversy--Gouverneur Warren, Strong Vincent, and George Sykes." PENN HIS, 35 [1968]: 225-230.

In discussing which man was responsible for ordering the critical occupation of Little Round Top on the second day, the author supports the traditional view that Warren has the best claim. The role of the other two was still important, however.

2564. ———. "The Union Cavalry Comes of Age." CWH, 11 [1965]: 274-283.

The cavalry of the Army of the Potomac became the equal of its adversary in the Gettysburg Campaign.

2565. Storrick, William C. GETTYSBURG: THE PLACE, THE BATTLES, THE OUTCOME. Harrisburg: McFarland, 1932. Numerous reprints.

A guidebook, arranged by topic, written by a man who once directed the tour guides at the battlefield.

2566. Stribling, Robert M. GETTYSBURG CAMPAIGN AND CAMPAIGNS OF 1864 AND 1865 IN VIRGINIA. Petersburg, Virginia, 1905.

A useful survey of the last two years of the war in the East written by a former officer of Confederate artillery.

2567. Tilberg, Frederick. "Gettysburg, 1863." AM HER, 5 [Winter 1953-1954]: 28-37.

Author analyzes the response of the leadership on each side to the rapidly changing circumstances of the battle.

2568. Todd, Edward N., editor. "Bishop Whittingham, Mount Calvary Church and the Battle of Gettysburg." MD HIS MAG, 60 [1965]: 325-328.

The church split because of the prayers offered to one side or the other.

2569. Toombs, Samuel. NEW JERSEY TROOPS IN THE GETTYSBURG CAMPAIGN .... Orange, New Jersey: 1888.

The author was a sergeant during the battle, but his account is largely dependent upon secondary materials. The book includes numerous illustrations.

2570. Tremain, Henry E. TWO DAYS OF WAR, A GETTYSBURG NARRATIVE, AND OTHER EXCURSIONS. New York, 1905.

This lengthy work, written by a member of General Dan Sickles' staff, contains many essays pertaining to the battle.

2571. Tucker, Glenn. "The Cavalry Invasion of the North." CWTI, 2 [4] [1963]: 18-22.

Jeb Stuart's liberal interpretation of Lee's orders of June 23, 1863, led him to take his cavalry on a raid through Maryland and Pennsylvania and miss much of the battle of Gettysburg.

2572. ———. HIGH TIDE AT GETTYSBURG. Indianapolis: Bobbs-Merrill, 1958. Reprint 1973.

This is a thorough account of the campaign, replete with anecdotes, and sound in its analyses.

2573. ———. "What Became of Pickett's Report on His Assault at Gettysburg?" CWTI, 6 [6] [1967]: 37-39.

Author speculates about the fate of the report which Pickett wrote to Lee after Gettysburg.

2574. Vanderslice, John M. GETTYSBURG THEN AND NOW.... New York, 1899.

A detailed narrative of how and where the various regiments fought, what positions they held, and where they moved. The work is embellished by 125 full-page illustrations.

2575. Wheeler-Bennett, John. "Why Gettysburg?" HIS TOD, 11 [1961]: 452-459.

An Englishman discusses the events leading up to the battle.

2576. Young, Jesse B. THE BATTLE OF GETTYSBURG: A COMPREHENSIVE NARRATIVE. Dayton, Ohio: Morningside, 1976.

The author, a first lieutenant in the 84th Pennsylvania, was on the staff of General Andrew A. Humphrey, a division commander in the Third Corps, during the battle. An observer rather than a participant, Young wrote an excellent account of the battle, which includes perceptive sketches of a number of the important officers. This is a reprint of the 1913 edition.

2577. Zerbe, Karen. "Call to Arms: Reading's Reaction to the Gettysburg Campaign." BERKS CTY HIS R, 35 [1970]: 137-139, 158-160.

When news of the invasion reached Reading, the city held public meetings, urged enlistments in the army, and appropriated money for defense.

* * *

2578. Baker, Liva. "The Burning of Chambersburg." AM HER, 24 [5] [1973]: 36-39, 97.

On Jubal Early's raid through Maryland to Washington in the summer of 1864, the Confederate general ordered a force to occupy and burn the town if a ransom was not promptly paid. The citizens refused to pay the ransom and two-thirds of Chambersburg was destroyed by fire, July 30, 1864.

2579. Brooksher, William R. and David K. Snider. "Around McClellan Again." CWTI, 13 [5] [1974]: 4-8, 39-48.

An account of Jeb Stuart's second raid around McClellan in October 1862, which took him into Chambersburg, where he sacked the city.

2580. Price, Channing. "Stuart's Chambersburg Raid: An Eyewitness Account." CWTI, 4 [9] [1966]: 8-15, 42-44.

Price, an aide to Stuart, describes the romantic aspects of the raid in a letter to his mother.

South Carolina

[See also Georgia: MARCH THROUGH CAROLINAS]

2581. Barnes, John S. "The Battle of Port Royal From the Journal of John Sanford Barnes, October 8 to November 9, 1861." John D. Hayes, editor. NY HIS SOC Q, 45 [1961]: 365-395.

The useful journal of naval lieutenant John Sanford Barnes, who served on the WABASH in the federal campaign against Port

Royal, South Carolina in the autumn of 1861. With Port Royal's fall on November 8, much of the South Atlantic coast came under federal control.

2582. Burton, E. Milby. THE SIEGE OF CHARLESTON, 1861-1865. Columbia: University of South Carolina Press, 1970.

A fairly good examination of the four year federal effort to blockade and seize Charleston during which 14 different methods of warfare were used. Among the criticisms of the scholarship in this study of the "587 days" is the suggestion that there was no siege at all since Charleston was never cut off on the landward side until the end of the war.

2583. Emilio, Juis F. THE ASSAULT ON FORT WAGNER, JULY 18, 1863. Boston, 1887.

After failing to seize the fort on Morris Island, July 10, another attack led by the 54th Massachusetts Colored Infantry on July 18 captured the fort temporarily. The commander of the 54th, Colonel Robert G. Shaw, was killed. Following a siege the fort was finally taken on September 7, a day after the Confederates evacuated it.

2584. Florance, John E., Jr. "Morris Island, Victory or Blunder." SC HIS MAG, 55 [1954]: 143-152.

Author concludes that federal assault on and capture of Morris Island outside Charleston in September 1862 was a mistake. Union losses were heavy and their army and naval forces were no closer to Charleston than before.

2585. Floyd, Viola C. "The Fall of Charleston." SC HIS MAG, 66 [1965]: 1-7.

Reprint of an article in the NEW YORK TRIBUNE, March 4, 1865, on the occupation of Charleston by federal troops after the city fell February 18, 1865. The report described efforts of the retreating Confederates to destroy military installations, 2,000 bales of cotton, and boats.

2586. Foote, Shelby. "DuPont Storms Charleston." AM HER, 14 [4] [1963]: 28-34.

Union Admiral Samuel F. DuPont failed in his attempt to force an entrance to Charleston Harbor, April 7, 1863.

2587. Gillmore, Quincy A. ENGINEER AND ARTILLERY OPERATIONS AGAINST THE DEFENCES OF CHARLESTON HARBOR IN 1863. New York, 1868.

A detailed, technical account of the unsuccessful efforts to recapture Fort Sumter in the summer of 1863. The volume is illustrated with 83 plates.

2588. Johnson, John. THE DEFENSE OF CHARLESTON HARBOR.... Charleston, 1890.

A valuable work on the defense of Sumter and adjacent islands, including official reports, maps, illustrations, and much else.

2589. Jones, Samuel. THE SIEGE OF CHARLESTON AND THE OPERATIONS ON THE SOUTH ATLANTIC COAST.... New York, 1911.

An important work detailing federal amphibious operations along the South Atlantic coast.

2590. Keith, Willis J. "Fort Johnson." CWTI, 14 [7] [1975]: 32-39.

Author describes two unsuccessful efforts by Union forces to seize Fort Johnson on James Island in Charleston harbor.

2591. Patterson, Gerard and Wilbur S. Nye. "The Battle of Secessionville." CWTI, 7 [6] [1968]: 4-10, 43-47.

In an ill-advised attack 9000 Federals were repulsed by a much smaller force, June 16, 1862. Secessionville was located on James Island in Charleston harbor.

Tennessee

FORTS HENRY, DONELSON [February 6; February 12-16, 1862]

2592. Ambrose, Stephen E. "Fort Donelson: 'Disastrous Blow to South.'" CWTI, 5 [3] [1966]: 4-13, 42-49.

In reviewing the Donelson battle, the author concludes that the northern victory was primarily the result of indecisive generalship of Albert Sidney Johnston.

2593. ———. "The Union Command System and the Donelson Campaign." MIL AFF, 24 [1960]: 78-86.

The problems of a divided Union command in the West are detailed in this article. Happily Grant was able to capture Fort Donelson in spite of the weak command structure.

2594. Bearss, Edwin C. "The Fall of Fort Henry." W TENN HIS SOC PAPERS, 17 [1963]: 85-107.

Describes the attack on the fort by Union forces of Commodore Andrew H. Foote.

2595. ———. "The Iowans at Fort Donelson." ANN IOWA, 36 [1961/1962]: 241-268, 321-243.

Iowans participated in General Charles F. Smith's attack on the Confederate right, February 15.

2596. ——— and Howard P. Nash. "The Attack on Fort Henry." CWTI, 4 [7] [1965]: 9-15.

Bad luck, wet powder, and an accurate bombardment by the Union gunboats helped defeat the Confederates at Ft. Henry.

2597. Churchill, James O. "Wounded at Fort Donelson: A First Person Account." CWTI, 8 [4] [1969]: 18-26.

In a letter of his parents, Churchill, who commanded Company A, 11th Illinois, describes the role his unit played in the battle. Failing to receive orders to retreat, the 11th was cut off, and Churchill himself was wounded.

2598. Cooling, Benjamin E. "The Attack on Dover." CWTI, 2 [5] [1963]: 10-13.

Dover was another name for the Fort Donelson engagement.

2599. ———. "Campaign for Forts Henry and Donelson." CONFLICT, 7 [1974]: 28-39.

Grant's strategy and successes are analyzed.

2600. ———. "The First Nebraska Infantry Regiment and The Battle of Fort Donelson." NEB HIS, 45 [1964]: 131-145.

Men of the 1st Nebraska played an important role in the Union victory at Fort Donelson. It was their first major engagement.

2601. ———. "Virginians and West Virginians at Fort Donelson." W VA HIS, 28 [1967]: 101-120.

The only eastern units present at Fort Donelson came from the Virginias.

2602. Crummer, Wilbur F. "With Grant at Fort Donelson, Shiloh, and Vicksburg." Oak Park, Illinois: Crummer, 1915.

Extols Grant's leadership in these campaigns.

2603. Engerud, H. "General Grant, Fort Donelson and 'Old Brains.'" FCHQ, 39 [1965]: 201-215.

A review of the relationship between Grant and Halleck as the first major campaign in the West shapes up.

2604. Hamilton, James T. THE BATTLE OF FORT DONELSON. New York: Yoseloff, 1968.

A well-written, interesting account of the battle. The only useful full-length study to appear in recent years.

2605. Maihafer, H.J. "The Partnership." US NAV INST PROC, 93 [1967]: 49-57.

Describes the joint Army-Navy operations between Grant and Foote in the Henry and Donelson campaign.

2606. Ripley, C. Peter. "Prelude to Donelson: Grant's January, 1862, March Into Kentucky." KY HIS SOC REG, 68 [1970]: 311-318.

In January 1862 Grant was ordered to move into Kentucky, avoid any major engagement, and prevent reinforcements from reaching Albert Sidney Johnston at Bowling Green. His mission was a success.

2607. Roland, Charles P. "Albert Sidney Johnston and the Loss of Forts Henry and Donelson. JSH, 23 [1957]: 45-69.

A discussion of the strategic choices facing the Confederate command on the eve of the Henry-Donelson campaign.

2608. Simplot, Alex. "General Grant and the Incidents at Dover." WIS MAG HIS, 44 [1960/1961]: 83-84.

Simplot, an Iowan, was a sketch artist and correspondent for HARPER'S WEEKLY. In 1911 He wrote this account of an incident in the Fort Donelson campaign.

2609. Treichel, James A. "Lew Wallace at Fort Donelson." IND MAG HIS, 59 [1963]: 3-18.

Details Wallace's service in the West. As result of his actions at Donelson he was promoted to major-general.

2610. Walker, Peter F. "Command Failure: The Fall of Forts Henry and Donelson." TENN HIS Q, 16 [1957]: 335-360.

Notes that lack of equipment and men were not the only reasons for the fall of the forts. The ineptitude of southern generals involved was "Johnston's severest handicap."

SHILOH [April 6-7, 1862] [Also known as Pittsburg's Landing]

2611. Bearss, Edwin C. "General William Nelson Saves The Day at Shiloh." KY HIS SOC REG, 63 [1965]: 36-69.

An account of the Union troop movements preceding the battle.

2612. Dawes, E.C. "'The Rebels Are Crossing the Field!' First Day at Shiloh: An Eyewitness Account." CWTI, 7 [10] [1969]: 4-9, 44-48.

The author, though a major and adjutant of the 53rd Ohio, had just graduated from college. He describes the action as he saw it, noting the bravery, cowardice, and stupidity.

2613. Deaderick, John B. SHILOH, MEMPHIS, AND VICKSBURG. Memphis: Western Tennessee Historical Society, 1960.

A 32-page pamphlet reviewing the campaigning from Shiloh to Vicksburg.

2614. ———. THE TRUTH ABOUT SHILOH. Memphis, Tennessee: Toof,1942.

Another brief pamphlet summarizing the main events.

2615. Eisenschiml, Otto. "Shiloh: The Blunders and the Blame." CWTI, 2 [1] [1963]: 6-13, 30-34.

Concludes Grant and Sherman deserved to be court-martialed for their actions in this "Battle of Big Blunders." Johnston and Beauregard suffered from conflicting orders as well as bad luck.

2616. ———. THE STORY OF SHILOH. Chicago: Norman Press, 1946.

An 89-page interpretive study which is somewhat biased.

2617. Hurst, T.M. "The Battle of Shiloh." TENN HIS MAG, 5 [1919]: 81-96.

Author believes battle was the "greatest" of the war. He also presents proof Grant was not "under the influence" at any time during the battle.

2618. McDonough, James L. "Glory Can Not Atone: Shiloh, April 6, 1862." TENN HIS Q, 35 [1976]: 279-295.

Using primary materials, author depicts the attitudes and feelings of the participants. He notes their youth and military inexperience and is also impressed by the northerners' optimism and confidence.

2619. ———. SHILOH: IN HELL BEFORE NIGHT. Knoxville: University Tennessee Press, 1977.

Probably the best one volume work on Shiloh. More an overview than a refighting of the battle, in which the terrible confusion and chaos are made clear. The heavy losses indicated that the nature of the war was changing.

2620. Rice, DeLong. THE STORY OF SHILOH. Jackson, Tennessee: McCowat-Mercer, 1924.

A 70-page booklet written by the then superintendent of Shiloh Military Park.

2621. Rich, Joseph W. THE BATTLE OF SHILOH. Iowa City, Iowa: 1911.

Author participated in the battle and discusses the role Iowans played in it.

2622. Roland, Charles P. "Albert Sidney Johnston and the Shiloh Campaign." CWH, 4 [1958]: 355-382.

Stresses the fact that the Confederates scored one of the biggest strategic surprises of the war. Had Johnston not been killed, his prestige would have been greatly enhanced.

2623. Stillwell, Leander. "In the Ranks at Shiloh." JISHS, 15 [1922]: 460-476.

An interesting, fresh account of the battle written by a participant who does not pretend to present the "grand view," but rather the events as viewed by a common soldier.

2624. Sword, Wiley. SHILOH: BLOODLY APRIL. New York: Morrow, 1974.

An admirable study of the hardest two-day battle of the war. The author, using manuscripts and secondary sources, skillfully maneuvers his way across the tricky terrain of Shiloh without faltering. A fair, judicious account.

2625. Throne, Mildred. "Iowa and the Battle of Shiloh." IOWA J HIS, 55 [1957]: 209-248.

A detailed account of Shiloh, seen through the letters, diaries, and reminiscences of Iowa participants. Shiloh brought the horrors of war home for the first time to the people of the West.

2626. ———. "Letters From Shiloh." IOWA J HIS, 52 [1954]: 235-280.

In these letters from Iowans in Grant's army at Shiloh, one can readily grasp the horrors of war. In their confusion and bewilderment, the soldiers blamed their commander.

2627. Wallace, Harold L. "Lew Wallace's March to Shiloh Revisited." IND MAG HIS, 59 [1963]: 19-30.

Wallace arrived after the fighting ended on the first day. His tardiness ended his career as a fighting commander.

MURFREESBORO [December 31, 1862-January 2, 1863]
[Also known as Stones River]

2628. Bearss, Edwin C. "Cavalry Operations in the Battle of Stones River." TENN HIS Q, 19 [1960]: 23-53, 110-144.

Detailed account of cavalry actions, although author concludes the cavalry played a "prominent but not a decisive role."

2629. Brooksher, William R. and David K. Snider. "The 'War Child' Rides." CWTI, 14 [9] [1976]: 4-10, 44-46.

Discusses Rosecrans' handling of his troops. His task was complicated by the problem of disrupted supply lines.

2630. Horn, Stanley F. "The Seesaw Battle of Stones River." CWTI, 2 [10] [1964]: 7-11, 34-36.

Tells of General William S. Rosecrans' first victory as commander of the Army of the Cumberland. The heavy artillery won the battle for the North.

2631. Kniffin, Gilbert C ... ARMY OF THE CUMBERLAND AND THE BATTLE OF STONES RIVER. Washington, D.C.: 1907.

A good, concise paper, 24 pages in length, drawn from a speech made before the Military Order of the Loyal Legion.

2632. McDonough, James L. STONES RIVER: BLOODY WINTER IN TENNESSEE. Knoxville: University of Tennessee Press, 1980.

An outstanding study of the battle. Author holds that it was a far more significant encounter than historians have assumed. The victory was important for national morale--after Fredericksburg--and created problems within the Confederate high command.

2633. Stevenson, Alexander F. THE BATTLE OF STONES RIVER NEAR MURFREESBORO, TENNESSEE. Boston, 1884.

An early narrative of the battle, although it still is of interest to modern readers.

2634. Trenerry, Walter N. "Lester's Surrender at Murfreesboro." MINN HIS, 39 [1965]: 191-197.

Discusses the controversial surrender of Union Colonel Henry C. Lester to Forrest.

CHATTANOOGA [November 23-25, 1863]

2635. Downey, Fairfax D. STORMING OF THE GATEWAY: CHATTANOOGA, 1863. New York: David McKay, 1960.

A well-written, moving account of the action which opened up the southeast to federal forces.

2636. Fitch, Michael H. THE CHATTANOOGA CAMPAIGN.... Madison, Wisconsin: 1911.

A good account of the battle with particular emphasis on the role of Wisconsin troops.

2637. Govan, Gilbert E. and James W. Livingood. "Chattanooga Under Military Occupation, 1863-1865." JSH, 17 [1951]: 23-47.

Describes the many problems facing Chattanooga under federal occupation in the last year and a half of war.

2638. Henry, Robert S. "Chattanooga and the War." TENN HIS Q, 19 [1960]: 222-230.

Points out the importance of Chattanooga as a transportation center and as the key to communication between Virginia and the western South.

2639. Howard, Oliver O. "Chattanooga." ATLAN MON, 38 [1876]: 213-219.

General Howard, who was at Chattanooga, seeks to set the record straight on several controversial features of the battle.

2640. Kniffen, Gilbert C. ... THE ARMY OF THE CUMBERLAND AT MISSIONARY RIDGE. Washington, D.C.: 1900.

An excellent, 28-page pamphlet based on a speech delivered at a meeting of the Military Order of the Loyal Legion.

2641. Searcher, Victor. "An Arkansas Druggist Defeats a Famous General." ARK HIS Q, 13 [1954]: 249-256.

The story of the heroic efforts of General Pat Cleburne in defending Missionary Ridge from the assaults of both Sherman and Thomas.

2642. Smith, William F. ... MILITARY OPERATIONS AROUND CHATTANOOGA, IN OCTOBER AND NOVEMBER, 1863. Wilmington, Delaware: 1886.

In a short personal memoir, "Baldy" Smith, chief engineer for Grant during this campaign, recalls the events prior to and during the battle. He organized the "Cracker Line" which was vital to the reopening of Chattanooga's communications to the outside.

2643. Taylor, Benjamin F. MISSION RIDGE AND LOOKOUT MOUNTAIN WITH PICTURES OF LIFE IN CAMP AND FIELD. New York, 1872.

An able series of articles about the Chattanooga Campaign written by a reporter for the CHICAGO EVENING JOURNAL.

2644. Tucker, Glenn. "The Battles for Chattanooga." CWTI, 10 [5] [1971]: 3-45.

Excellent maps, photographs, and other illustrations accompany this moving narrative. The entire issue of CIVIL WAR TIMES ILLUSTRATED is devoted to Chattanooga.

2645. Turner, Justin G. "O.O. Howard to Henry Wilson." LIN HER, 65 [1963]: 113-115.

A letter from General Howard pertaining to federal military leadership during the Chattanooga Campaign.

FRANKLIN AND NASHVILLE [November and December 1864]

2646. Cox, Jacob D. THE BATTLE OF FRANKLIN, TENNESSEE, NOVEMBER 30, 1864. New York, 1897.

An excellent volume by the able northern general who led a division at Franklin and Nashville. This book is not part of the Scribner series CAMPAIGNS OF THE CIVIL WAR.

2647. Crownover, Sims. "The Battle of Franklin." TENN HIS Q, 14 [1955]: 291-322.

In this bloody battle, Hood "had more men killed ... than died on one side in some of the great conflicts of the war."

2648. Gist, William W. "The Battle of Franklin." TENN HIS MAG, 6 [1924/1925]: 213-265.

A vivid account of the battle by a 15-year old member of the 24th Ohio. After the war Gist became a minister.

2649. Hay, Thomas R. "The Cavalry at Spring Hill." TENN HIS MAG, 8 [1924-1925]: 7-23.

The Federals were able to hold off the Confederates at Spring Hill, south of Franklin, November 29, 1864, long enough to permit Schofield's forces to escape a trap and get back to Franklin.

2650. ———. HOOD'S TENNESSEE CAMPAIGN. New York: Neale, 1929.

A well-done work dealing with Hood's effort to regain ground in Tennessee after the Atlanta Campaign in the fall of 1864.

2651. Horn, Stanley F. THE DECISIVE BATTLE OF NASHVILLE. Baton Rouge: Louisiana State University Press, 1956.

A good description of the battle, carefully planned by both sides, which saw the defeat of "one of the two great armies of the Confederacy" and thus the eventual defeat of the South. A large crowd of "sullen" townspeople flocked from the city to witness the battle.

2652. ———. "Nashville--The Most Decisive Battle of the War." CWTI, 3 [8] [1964]: 4-11, 31-36.

A condensed version of the entry listed above.

2653. ———. "The Spring Hill Legend." CWTI, 8 [1] [1969]: 20-32.

Author rejects the "legend" that Hood missed an excellent opportunity to block Schofield's withdrawal at Spring Hill, November 29, 1864. Hood was never in position with sufficient strength to cut off the Federals.

2654. Lynne, Donald M. "Wilson's Cavalry at Nashville." CWH, 1 [1955]: 141-159.

Author examines the role of the cavalry of General James Wilson in the defeat of Hood at Nashville.

2655. McDonough, James L. "West Point Classmates--Eleven Years Later: Some Observations on the Spring Hill-Franklin Campaign." TENN HIS Q, 28 [1969]: 182-196.

An account of the maneuvering before the battle at Franklin.

2656. Robertson, James I., Jr. "The Human Battle of Franklin." TENN HIS Q, 24 [1965]: 20-30.

A report on the human cost of Franklin.

2657. Scofield, Levi T. THE RETREAT FROM PULASKI TO NASHVILLE.... Cleveland, 1909.

Maps and photos enhance this pamphlet about Franklin.

* * *

2658. Anderson, William M. "A Michigan Artilleryman's View of the Engagement at Thompson's Station. MICH HIS, 60 [1976]: 359-366.

An objective assessment of the disastrous defeat of federal forces at Thompson's Station, March 4-5, 1863.

2659. Fink, Harold S. "The East Tennessee Campaigns and the Battle of Knoxville in 1863." E TENN HIS SOC PROC, 29 [1957]: 79-117.

An interesting account of the events leading up to and including the battle.

2660. Fry, James B. OPERATIONS OF THE ARMY UNDER BUELL FROM JUNE 10th TO OCTOBER 30TH, 1862.... New York, 1884.

A thorough, friendly record of Buell's command, written by his chief of staff, who would shortly become provost marshal general and chief administrator of the Civil War draft.

2661. Hartje, Robert. "The Gray Dragoon Wins His Final Victory." TENN HIS Q, 23 [1964]: 38-58.

Confederate cavalry General Earl Van Dorn routed the federals at Thompson's Station, March 4-5, 1863, in a minor engagement, but one which "typified a new mode of combat." Two months later Van Dorn was killed in the area over a private matter.

2662. Klein, Maury. "The Knoxville Campaign." CWTI, 10 [6] [1971]: 4-10, 40-43.

The story of Longstreet's frustrating and vacillating campaign for Knoxville in the fall of 1863.

2663. Maness, Lonnie E. "Forrest and the Battle of Parker Crossroads." TENN HIS Q, 34 [1975]: 154-167.

A minor engagement, December 31, 1862, in the Murfreesboro campaign, where the Confederate Forrest was routed while trying to disrupt Rosecrans' supply lines.

2664. Melton, Maurice. "Smoke Across the Water." CWTI, 18 [1] [1979]: 4-11, 43-46.

An account of the successful Union campaign under General John Pope at New Madrid, Missouri and Island Number 10, Tennessee, in March-April 1862.

2665. Mullen, Jay C. "Pope's New Madrid and Island Number 10 Campaign." MO HIS R, 59 [1965]: 325-343.

Author argues that New Madrid and Island Number 10 did not have a decisive effect upon the fighting in the Mississippi Valley.

2666. Nash, Howard P. "Island No. 10" CWTI, 5 [8] [1966]: 42-47.

A description of the capture of this Confederate strongpoint by both Union naval and ground forces.

2667. Rowell, John W. "The Battle of Mossy Creek." CWTI, 8 [4] [1969]: 10-16.

An unimportant but bitterly fought cavalry battle northeast of Knoxville on December 29, 1863.

2668. Seymour, Digby G. DIVIDED LOYALTIES: FORT SANDERS AND THE CIVIL WAR IN EAST TENNESSEE. Knoxville: University of Tennessee Press, 1963.

A well-written story of the fighting in East Tennessee, with a special focus on Longstreet's unavailing assault on Fort Sanders, November 29, 1863. This was Burnside's chief defensive position protecting Knoxville.

2669. Sunderland, Glenn W. "The Battle of Hoover's Gap." CWTI, 6 [3] [1967]: 34-41.

An account of the first battle fought with the Spencer repeating rifles.

2670. ———. LIGHTNING AT HOOVER'S GAP. WILDER'S BRIGADE IN THE CIVIL WAR. New York: Yoseloff, 1969.

An accurate, dispassionate account of the famous "Lightning Brigade" of Colonel John T. Wilder. Equipped with Spencer repeating rifles they wrought havoc among the Confederates at Hoover's Gap, Chickamauga, Chattanooga, Atlanta, and Selma.

2671. Willett, Robert L., Jr. "The First Battle of Franklin." CWTI, 7 [10] [1969]: 16-23.

Author describes a hard-fought, though minor, battle at Franklin, April 10, 1863.

2672. Williams, Kenneth P. "The Tennessee River Campaign and Anna Ella Carroll." IND MAG HIS, 46 [1050]: 221-248.

Author dismisses the claim of Anna Ella Carroll that she induced the Union army to launch the Tennessee River campaign which led to the fall of Forts Henry and Donelson.

Vermont

ST. ALBANS RAID [October 19, 1864]

On October 19, 1864, some twenty Confederate cavalrymen crossed the Vermont border from Canada and raided the town of St. Albans, twenty miles inside the state. The objectives of the raid were to raise money for the Confederate cause and divert federal troops from the Virginia front. The Confederates robbed the banks in St. Albans of close to $200,000 and killed one local citizen before fleeing safely back into Canada. They were arrested by Canadian authorities but were later released, having convinced the judge that they had been on an authorized military raid and thus were not subject to extradition, which the American government demanded. The following entries deal with this episode.

2673. Ashley, Robert P. "The St. Albans Raid." CWTI, 6 [7] [1967]: 18-25.

2674. Branch, John. ST. ALBANS RAID, ST. ALBANS, VERMONT, OCTOBER 19, 1864. St. Albans: By the author, 1936.

2675. Gray, Clayton. CONSPIRACY IN CANADA. Montreal, Canada: L'Atelier Press, 1959.

2676. Heth, Gary E. "The St. Albans Raid: Vermont Viewpoint." VT HIS, 33 [1965]: 250-254.

2677. Hill, Richard H. "The Centennial of St. Alban's Raid." FCHQ, 38 [1965]: 353-354.

2678. Kazar, John D., Jr. "The Canadian View of the Confederate Raid on Saint Albans." VT HIS, 33 [1965]: 255-273.

2679. Kinchen, Oscar A. DAREDEVILS OF THE CONFEDERATE ARMY: THE STORY OF THE ST. ALBANS RAID. Boston: Christopher Publishing House, 1959.

2680. ———. "Some Unpublished Documents on the St. Alban's Raid." VT HIS, 32 [1964]: 179-183.

2681. Lindsey, David. "St. Albans Has Been Surprised." A HIS ILL, 10 [9] [1976]: 14-22.

2682. Wilson, Charles M. "The Hit-and-Run Raid." AM HER, 12 [5] [1961]: 28-31, 90-93.

Virginia

FIRST BULL RUN [July 21, 1861] [Also known as First Manassas]

2683. Beatie, Russel H. ROAD TO MANASSAS. New York: Cooper Square, 1961.

Author discusses the development of the Union command in the East from the time of Sumter to First Bull Run.

2684. Beauregard, Pierre G.T. A COMMENTARY ON THE CAMPAIGN AND BATTLE AT MANASSAS.... New York, 1891.

A summary of the Confederate general's response to remarks questioning his handling of troops during the battle, plus a statement on the art of war.

2685. Davis, William C. BATTLE AT BULL RUN: A HISTORY OF THE FIRST MAJOR CAMPAIGN OF THE CIVIL WAR. Garden City, New York: Doubleday, 1977.

Recounts this battle which was the first in which strategic use was made of railroads for troop movements. Gives critical appraisals of the leadership abilities of the officers, "their background and unusual characteristics." The work is well documented and well-written.

2686. ———. "Prelude at Blackburn's Ford." CWTI, 16 [2] [1977]: 10-22.

The Federals tested Confederate strength at Blackburn's Ford, July 18, 1861, three days before the battle, and were repulsed.

2687. Donnelly, Ralph W. "Federal Batteries on the Henry House Hill, Bull Run, 1861." MIL AFF, 21 [1957]: 188-192.

It is argued that two federal batteries [Griffin and Ricket] were not wiped out by the 33rd Virginia, as customarily thought. They were routed, rather, because of the flight of supporting artillery.

2688. Foster, C. Allen. SUNDAY IN CENTREVILLE, THE BATTLE OF BULL RUN, 1861. New York: David White, 1971.

The author has written a narrative account of the first major battle of the war for high school students; it might appeal to some of them.

2689. Fry, James B. McDOWELL AND TYLER AND THE CAMPAIGN OF BULL RUN, 1861. New York, 1884.

A 63-page booklet written by McDowell's chief of staff during this dampaign.

2690. Hanson, Joseph M. BULL RUN REMEMBERS.... Manassas: National Capitol Publishers, 1953.

A collection of useful essays dealing with both Bull Run campaigns by the former battlefield superintendent.

2691. Johnston, Robert M. BULL RUN: ITS STRATEGY AND TACTICS. Boston, 1913.

An excellent study of the planning of the campaign, the details of the action, and the consequences of the battle.

2692. Patterson, Robert. A NARRATIVE OF THE CAMPAIGN IN THE VALLEY OF THE SHENANDOAH, IN 1861. Philadelphia, 1865.

Northern General Patterson was assigned to detain the Confederates at Winchester and thus prevent them from reaching the Bull Run battlefield. He failed and in this short book he tries to explain his actions.

2693. Ramirez, Thomas P. "Bull Run: Battle of a Summer Day." MANKIND, 2 [2] [1969]: 10-17, 49.

A description of the chaos and disorganization in this "Battle of Blunders" by two untrained armies, including the wild retreat to Washington.

SHENANDOAH VALLEY CAMPAIGN [March-June 1862]

2694. Allan, William. STONEWALL JACKSON'S CAMPAIGN IN THE SHENANDOAH VALLEY OF VIRGINIA.... London, England: 1912.

A useful account of Jackson's Valley operations, November 4, 1861 to June 17, 1862, by the ordnance chief of the Second Confederate Corps.

2695. Ashby, Thomas A. THE VALLEY CAMPAIGNS.... New York, 1914.

An intriguing memoir of a non-combatant who lived in the Shenandoah Valley during the war and who describes how the fighting affected the people.

2696. Bushong, Millard K. "Jackson in the Shenandoah." W VA HIS, 27 [1966]: 85-96.

Describes how Jackson's knowledge of geographic features and iron discipline enabled him to tie up close to 100,000 federal troops and thus weaken McClellan's offensive against Richmond.

2697. Goldthorpe, George W. "The Battle of McDowell, Virginia." W VA HIS, 13 [1952]: 159-215.

Jackson routed a federal force at McDowell, May 7-8, 1962, at the southern end of the Valley, west of Staunton, thus preventing an attack on his rear as he again moved north.

2698. Kearsey, Alexander H. A STUDY OF THE STRATEGY AND TACTICS OF THE SHENANDOAH VALLEY CAMPAIGN, 1861-1862. London, England: Gale and Polden, 1930.

With the use of six maps the author illustrates the principles of war as they were employed in the Valley Campaign.

2699. Pierce, John E. "Jackson, Garnett, and 'The Unfortunate Breach.'" CWTI, 12 [6] [1973]: 32-41.

At Kernstown, March 23, 1862, the first battle of the Valley Campaign, Jackson appeared to be carrying the day but shortly was driven back by vastly superior numbers of federal troops.

2700. Pendleton, Sandie. "The Valley Campaign of 1862 as Revealed in Letters of Sandie Pendleton." W.G. Bean, editor. VA MHB, 78 [1970]: 326-364.

"Sandie" Pendleton, brigade ordnance officer for Stonewall Jackson during the Valley Campaign, described his experiences in newly-discovered letters written to his parents and sisters.

2701. Robertson, James I., Jr. "Stonewall in the Shenandoah: The Valley Campaign of 1862." CWTI, 11 [2] [1972]: 3-49.

Another able, single-campaign issue of CIVIL WAR TIMES ILLUSTRATED.

2702. Stackpole, Edward J. "Stonewall Jackson in the Shenandoah." CWTI, 3 [7] [1964]: 4-11, 36-41.

Shy, taciturn, and uncommunicative, Jackson proved himself a master of strategy. He remained steadfast to his own principles and was idolized by those who served under him.

2703. Stone, Louis P. "I Was Completely Surrounded by a Band of Guerrillas.'" CWTI, 10 [8] [1971]: 26-33.

One of Fremont's famed "Jessie Scouts" took part in the latter stages of the Valley Campaign and was captured by Confederates.

2704. Tanner, Robert G. STONEWALL IN THE VALLEY. Garden City, New York: Doubleday, 1976.

This military history covers the action in the "lower" Valley in 1862 in detail. Author believes Jackson "skillfully" bought time for the Confederacy, which was his main objective. Tanner has also given the reader good, perceptive sketches of all the main participants.

2705. ———. "We Are In For It." CWTI, 15 [7] [1976]: 16-29.

A look at the Battle of Kernstown, where the survival of Jackson's entire army was threatened.

2706. Tracy, Albert. "Fremont's Pursuit of Jackson in the Shenandoah Valley: The Journal of Colonel Albert Tracy, March-July, 1862." Francis F. Wayland, editor. VA MHB, 70 [1962]: 165-194, 322-354.

A vivid record of army life in camp, on the march, and in battle, as the Federals vainly sought to capture the elusive Jackson.

PENINSULAR CAMPAIGN [March-July 1862]

2707. Adams, Francis C. THE STORY OF A TROOPER. New York, 1865.

This big book carries interesting accounts of camp life of a New York cavalryman during the Peninsular Campaign.

2708. Angiolillo, Joe. "Road to Richmond: The Peninsular Campaign, May-July, 1862." STRAT TAC, 60 [1977]: 4-18.

Author reviews the several battles in the East from First Bull Run through the Peninsular Campaign.

2709. Barnard, John G. and W.F. Barry. REPORT OF THE ENGINEER AND ARTILLERY OPERATIONS OF THE ARMY OF THE POTOMAC.... New York, 1863.

General Barnard was chief engineer for McClellan. General Barry was McClellan's chief of artillery.

2710. Brooksher, William R. and David K. Snider. "Stuart's Ride: The Great Circuit Around McClellan." CWTI, 12 [1] [1973]: 4-10, 40-47.

An account of Stuart's amazing circumvention of McClellan's army on the Peninsula, June 11-14, 1862, designed to inform Lee of his adversary's strength and position.

2711. Bryan, Charles F., Jr. "Stalemate at Seven Pines." CWTI, 12 [5] [1973]: 4-6, 8-11, 39-47.

In the battle of Seven Pines [known also as Fair Oaks] fought outside Richmond, May 31-June 1, 1862, Confederate General Joseph Johnston was seriously wounded and was replaced by Robert E. Lee. The Confederate effort to drive McClellan away from Richmond failed.

2712. Cullen, Joseph P. "The Battle of Gaines's Mill." CWTI, 3 [1] [1964]: 10-19, 24.

This second engagement of the "Seven Days" was fought north of the Chickahominy, June 27, 1862. The Federals were driven back.

2713. ———. "At Malvern Hill: 'It Was Not War--It was Murder.'" CWTI, 5 [2] [1966]: 4-14.

In the last battle of the "Seven Days," July 1, 1862, Lee made an ill-advised assault against a strong federal position and suffered heavy losses.

2714. ———. "Mechanicsville." CWTI, 5 [7] [1966]: 5-11.

Mechanicsville, June 26, 1862, was the first battle of the "Seven Days."

2715. ———. THE PENINSULAR CAMPAIGN, 1862. Harrisburg, Pennsylvania: Stackpole, 1973.

A good study of the 1862 federal assault on Richmond, which comes down very heavily on both McClellan and Lee. While undocumented, the author knows his subject well, having for years been a National Park Service historian near Richmond.

2716. Dowdey, Clifford. THE SEVEN DAYS: THE EMERGENCE OF LEE. Boston: Little, Brown, 1964.

In this excellent examination of the climax of the Peninsular Campaign, the author has employed modern psychoanalytic techniques. For example, in analyzing Jackson's failure the author concludes that the general was ill from stress and exhaustion and should not have been at the front.

2717. Evans, Thomas H. "At Malvern Hill: A First Person Account." CWTI, 6 [8] [1967]: 38-43.

Now a lieutenant, Evans served for eleven years as an enlisted man in the Regular Army. He gives a brief account of the battle and describes what it was like on the field afterwards.

2718. ———. "There Is No Use Trying To Dodge Shot." CWTI, 6 [5] [1967]: 40-45.

Author describes his role in the bloody battle at Gaines's Mill.

2719. Gerrish, Theodore. ARMY LIFE: A PRIVATE'S REMINISCENCES OF THE CIVIL WAR. Portland, Maine: 1882.

A member of the 20th Maine, Gerrish participated in the Peninsular Campaign. He later became a clergyman.

2720. Harmon, George D. "General Silas Casey and the Battle of Fair Oaks." HISTORY, 4 [1941]: 84-102.

Casey, author of the three-volume INFANTRY TACTICS, commanded the Federal Third Division, Fourth Corps, at Fair Oaks/Seven Pines, and was promoted to major general for his service there.

2721. James, C. Rosser. "An Untold Incident of McClellan's Peninsular Campaign." W PENN MAG HIS, 44 [1961]: 151-157.

Tells the story of James and his mother who were left alone on the plantation and how a Union officer befriended them.

2722. Kent, William C. "Sharpshooting With Berdan." CWTI, 15 [2] [1976]: 4-9, 42-48.

A corporal in Berdan's First United States Sharpshooters Regiment, the author describes his experiences in the "Seven Days" in a series of letters.

2723. Lowe, Thadeus S.C. "Observation Balloon in the Battle of Fair Oaks." ARR, 43 [1911]: 186-190.

A personal recollection by Professor Lowe, some 50 years later, of his experiences in the balloon "Intrepid", as he observed the battle of Fair Oaks/Seven Pines.

2724. Rhodes, James F. "The First Six Weeks of McClellan's Peninsular Campaign." AHR, 1 [1895/1896]: 464-472.

A strong indictment of McClellan's failure to attack the Confederates in the Peninsula in April and May of 1862.

2725. Smith, Gustavus W. THE BATTLE OF SEVEN PINES. New York, 1891.

Smith commanded the Confederate forces briefly at Seven Pines after Johnston was disabled and before Lee arrived. He defends his actions in this work.

2726. SOURCE BOOK OF THE PENINSULA CAMPAIGN.... Fort Leavenworth, Kansas: General Service Schools Press, 1921.

A massive collection of primary materials on the campaign designed for use at the Command and General Staff School at Fort Leavenworth.

2727. Thomas, Emory W. "The Peninsular Campaign." CWTI, 17 [10] [1979]: 4-11, 40-45; 18 [1] 28-35, [2] 12-18, [3] 10-17, [4] 14-24.

A five-part piece recounting various battles during the Peninsular Campaign.

SECOND BULL RUN CAMPAIGN [August-September 1862]

2728. Allan, William. "Lee's Campaign Against Pope in 1862." MAG A HIS, 12 [1884]: 126-147.

Lee demolished Pope's forces in a brilliant campaign, culminating in Second Bull Run, which is described here. Although Fitz-John Porter's vindication was still two years away when this article was written, it states that Porter "was a sacrifice to the blind rage of Pope."

2729. Ambrose, Stephen E. "Henry Halleck and the Second Bull Run Campaign." CWH, 6 [1960]: 238-249.

Author describes Halleck's planned tactics for the Second Bull Run Campaign, a scheme which failed because of the poor cooperation between the forces of Generals McClellan and Pope.

2730. Dougherty, William E. "Eyewitness Account of Second Bull Run." A HIS ILL, 1 [8] [1966]: 31-43.

A condensed version of Dougherty's account of the battle which originally appeared in the UNITED SERVICE MAGAZINE in 1883.

2731. Eisenschiml, Otto. THE CELEBRATED CASE OF FITZ-JOHN PORTER: AN AMERICAN DREYFUS AFFAIR. Indianapolis: Bobbs-Merrill, 1950.

An effective defense for General Fitz-John Porter, who was courtmartialed and dismissed from the Union army for disobeying orders at Second Bull Run. Twenty-five years later he was vindicated and restored to rank.

2732. Gordon, George H. HISTORY OF THE CAMPAIGN OF THE ARMY OF VIRGINIA, UNDER JOHN POPE. Boston, 1880.

The author, an outspoken brigade commander in Pope's short-lived Army of Virginia, wrote a detailed, vivid account of the campaign, in which his dislike of Pope shows through.

2733. Moore, John G. "The Battle of Chantilly." MIL AFF, 28 [1964]: 49-63.

Describes the action fought around Ox Hill, Virginia, September 1, 1862, as Lee unsuccessfully attempted to cut off Pope's retreating army.

2734. Naisawald, L. Van Loan. "The Battle of Chantilly." CWTI, 3 [3]: [1964]: 10-13.

Chantilly set the stage for Lee's first invasion of the North and the battle of Antietam.

2735. ———. "The Fitz-John Porter Case." CWTI, 7 [3] [1968]: 4-11, 42-48.

A discussion of Porter's trial, dismissal from the army, and later reinstatement.

2736. Parker, George C. "I Feel ... Just Like Writing You A Letter." CWTI, 16 [1] [1977]: 12-21.

The author, a member of the 21st Massachusetts, describes Second Bull Run in letters to his mother-in-law.

2737. Porter, Fitz-John. GENERAL FITZ-JOHN PORTER'S STATEMENT OF THE SERVICES OF THE FIFTH ARMY CORP, IN 1862. New York, 1878.

Porter's own defense of his conduct at Second Bull Run. A fairly convincing statement, this was published before his acquittal some eight years hence.

2738. Seaborne, J. Gray. "The Battle of Cedar Mountain." CWTI, 5 [8] [1966]: 28-41.

At Cedar Mountain, just south of the Rapidan in central Virginia, the first battle of the Second Bull Run Campaign was fought, August 9, 1862. The federal attack under Banks was successful at first, but eventually repulsed.

2739. Sheppard, Eric W. ... THE CAMPAIGN IN VIRGINIA AND MARYLAND. New York, 1911.

An excellent account of the campaign, beginning with Pope's appointment to command the Army of Virginia in late June through the Battle of Antietam.

FREDERICKSBURG [December 13, 1862]

2740. Cullen, Joseph. The Battle of Fredericksburg." A HIS ILL, 13 [3] [1978]: 4-9, 38-47.

General Ambrose Burnside's delay in getting his troops across the Rappahannock gave Lee time to command the heights behind the city, a central factor in the Union army's defeat.

2741. Evans, Thomas H. "... The Cries of the Wounded Were Piercing and Horrible." CWTI, 7 [4] [1968]: 28-38.

Author was a member of a unit in General Sykes' division in the Fifth Corps, which participated in the Battle of Fredericksburg.

2742. Gough, John E. FREDERICKSBURG AND CHANCELLORSVILLE, A STUDY OF THE FEDERAL OPERATIONS. London, England: 1913.

A useful work written by a British officer as a study manual for the British army.

2743. Greene, Jacob L. GENERAL WILLIAM B. FRANKLIN AND THE OPERATIONS OF THE LEFT WING AT THE BATTLE OF FREDERICKSBURG. Hartford, Connecticut: 1900.

A 38-page pamphlet describing the unsuccessful efforts of the Federals to capture the heights south of Fredericksburg on the morning of the day of the battle.

2744. Henderson, George F.R. THE CAMPAIGN OF FREDERICKSBURG, NOVEMBER-DECEMBER, 1862.

An excellent account written by the celebrated British military historian for use by British officers.

2745. Redway, George W. ... FREDERICKSBURG, A STUDY IN WAR. New York, 1906.

Another good examination of the battle, designed as a manual for the training of British officers.

2746. Stackpole, Edward J. "The Battle of Fredericksburg." CWTI, 4 [8] [1965]: 4-47.

An excellent issue of CIVIL WAR TIMES ILLUSTRATED devoted entirely to the battle. The narrative is condensed from the author's DRAMA ON THE RAPPAHANNOCK cited next.

2747. ———. DRAMA ON THE RAPPAHANNOCK: THE FREDERICKSBURG CAMPAIGN. Harrisburg: Military Service Publishing, 1957.

Although the work is not documented, it is a good account of the battle and includes useful maps and illustrations.

2748. Teall, William W. "... Ringside Seat at Fredericksburg." Wilbur S. Nye, editor. CWTI, 4 [2] [1965]: 17-34.

The diary of William Teall, a member of General Sumner's staff, who made three balloon ascents with Professor Lowe during the battle of Fredericksburg.

2749. Whan, Vorin E. FIASCO AT FREDERICKSBURG. University Park, Pennsylvania: Penn State University Press, 1961.

Although not overly-long, this volume is the most recent and most thorough work on the Fredericksburg campaign.

CHANCELLORSVILLE [May 1-4, 1863]

2750. Bates, Samuel P. THE BATTLE OF CHANCELLORSVILLE. Meadville, Pennsylvania: 1882.

An old, but still useful study of the battle.

2751. Bigelow, John. THE CAMPAIGN OF CHANCELLORSVILLE.... New Haven, Connecticut: 1910.

Author has written an excellent, documented, and objective account of the battle, which he subtitles a "Strategic and Tactical Study."

2752. Carpenter, John A. "Doubleday's 'Chancellorsville and Gettysburg.'" MIL AFF, 27]1963]: 84-88.

A strong criticism of General Abner Doubleday's 1882 volume CHANCELLORSVILLE AND GETTYSBURG, which was part of the Scribner's series. Author dismisses the Doubleday book as a "polemic of little literary and historical value."

2753. Crowson, E. Thomas. "The High Tide of Confederate Fighting." W VA HIS, 36 [1975]: 140-145.

A glimpse of the Battle of Chancellorsville.

2754. Cullen, Joseph P. "The Battle of Chancellorsville." CWTI, 7 [2] [1968]: 4-50.

Another excellent "single-battle" issue published by CIVIL WAR TIMES ILLUSTRATED. As with other such issues it is filled with good maps, photographs, and illustrations.

2755. Hamlin, Augustus C. ... THE BATTLE OF CHANCELLORSVILLE.... Bangor, Maine: 1896.

A thorough examination of "Stonewall" Jackson's famous flanking movement and assault on the federal Eleventh Corps, May 2, 1863. Actions of Howard, who commanded the Eleventh Corps, are defended.

2756. Nelson, Alanson H. THE BATTLES OF CHANCELLORSVILLE AND GETTYSBURG. Minneapolis, 1899.

An informed look at these two major campaigns by an officer with the 57th Pennsylvania.

2757. Richardson, Charles. THE CHANCELLORSVILLE CAMPAIGN.... New York, 1907.

A 124-page account of the battle, heavily dependent upon official reports.

2758. Stackpole, Edward J. CHANCELLORSVILLE: LEE'S GREATEST BATTLE. Harrisburg: Stackpole Company, 1958.

The author, who makes no attempt at an original, interpretive study of Chancellorsville, has succeeded in achieving his goal of providing a detailed blood-and-guts narrative of the battle. It is well organized and well written, high on Lee and Jackson, low on Hooker.

THE WILDERNESS [May 5-7, 1864]

2759. Alexander, Edward P. "The Wilderness Campaign." AMERICAN HISTORICAL ASSOCIATION, THE ANNUAL REPORT OF, 1908: 225-234.

An analysis of Grant's conduct of the Wilderness Campaign.

2760. Cullen, Joseph P. "Battle of the Wilderness." CWTI, 10 [1] [1971]: 4-11, 42-47.

Grant and Lee met for the first time in the wooded area west of Fredericksburg.

2761. Henderson, George F.R. ... THE CAMPAIGN IN THE WILDERNESS OF VIRGINIA. London, England: 1908.

This is a 40-page pamphlet drawn from a speech Henderson had delivered in 1894. With his usual skill, the author examines the behavior of Lee and Grant.

2762. Melcher, Holman S. "'We Were Cut Off!'" CWTI, 9 [8] [1969]: 10-15.

The memoirs of a company commander of the 20th Maine, which, though cut off, managed to get away and captured 32 Confederates.

2763. Robertson, Robert S. "Into the Furnace of the Wilderness." CWTI, 8 [1] [1969]: 4-9, 45-47.

The author, an aide to a brigade commander in the Second Corps, provides a stirring, first-hand account of the battle, "a battle which no man saw."

2764. Schaff, Morris. THE BATTLE OF THE WILDERNESS. Boston, 1910.

Still a very useful work.

2765. Steere, Edward. THE WILDERNESS CAMPAIGN. Harrisburg: Stackpole, 1960.

A well-written, detailed account of the battle. Although little new material can be found, the author's careful, personal study of the complex terrain has made it possible to trace the movements of key units on both sides.

2766. Vaughan-Sawyer, George H. ... GRANT'S CAMPAIGN IN VIRGINIA, 1864. New York, 1908.

A well-written narrative of the campaign by a British officer.

SPOTTSYLVANIA [May 8-21, 1864]

2767. Cullen, Joseph P. "Spottsylvania." CWTI, 10 [2] [1971]: 4-9, 46-48.

Describes the heavy fighting in the initial phases of the battle, May 10-12.

COLD HARBOR [June 1-3, 1864]

2768. Cleveland, Edmund J. "The Second Battle of Cold Harbor As Seen Through the Eyes of a New Jersey Soldier...." Edmund J. Cleveland, Jr., editor. NJ HIS SOC PROC, 66 [1948]: 25-37.

Private Cleveland, who served with the 9th New Jersey, describes the events of June 1-14, 1864, in this journal.

2769. Cullen, Joseph P. "Cold Harbor." CWTI, 2 [7] [1963]: 11-17.

Details this battle which changed the course of the war in the East. The North lost some 7,000 men within 30 minutes.

2770. Wert, Jeffry D. "One Great Regret: Cold Harbor." CWTI, 17 [10] [1979]: 23-35.

Tells of Grant's regret at ordering the suicidal attack of June 3.

SHENANDOAH VALLEY CAMPAIGN [June-October 1864]

2771. Anderson, David D. "The Second Michigan Cavalry Under Philip H. Sheridan." MICH HIS, 45 [1961]: 210-218.

A study of the campaigns of the Second Michigan Cavalry under Colonel Sheridan's command.

2772. Brice, Marshall M. CONQUEST OF A VALLEY. Charlottesville: University of Virginia Press, 1965.

In this work which describes the federal victory at Piedmont [Staunton, Virginia], June 5, 1864, the author asserts that the battle was of much greater significance than it has traditionally been considered. He almost succeeds in making his point. At any rate, it is a good account of the battle.

2773. Crowninshield, Benjamin W. "Sheridan at Winchester." ATLAN MON, 42 [1878]: 683-691.

A former member of Sheridan's staff defends the general's performance in the Shenandoah Campaign of 1864 against recent criticism.

2774. Cullen, Joseph P. "The Battle of Winchester." CWTI, 6 [2] [1967]: 4-11, 40-44.

The federal victory at Winchester, September 19, 1864 was aided by the division of Jubal Early's Confederate forces.

2775. ———. "Cedar Creek." CWTI, 8 [8] [1969]: 4-9, 42-48.

An account of the culminating battle in the Valley, October 19, 1864, in which the Confederates routed the Federals initially, but failed to press their advantage. Then Sheridan, following his famous ride from Winchester, reorganized his troops and drove the Confederates back in an amazing shift of fortune.

2776. DuPont, Henry A. THE CAMPAIGN OF 1864 IN THE VALLEY OF VIRGINIA.... New York: National Americana Society, 1925.

DuPont served as an officer with the Fifth United States Artillery during this campaign.

2777. Golladay, V. Dennis. "Jubal Early's Last Stand." VA CAV, 20 [1970]: 28-33.

Author describes the battle of Waynesboro, Virginia, March 2, 1865, wherein Sheridan routed Early's outmanned forces and gave the Federals clear supremacy in the Shenandoah.

2778. Haselberger, Fritz and Mark Haselberger. "The Skirmishes at New Creek and Piedmont." W VA HIS, 27 [1966]: 211-219.

In early June 1864, the 1st Pennsylvania Rifles defeated a unit from the 7th Virginia Cavalry, not the 3rd Virginia Cavalry as previously believed, in the Shenandoah Valley.

2779. Kimball, William J. "The 'Outrageous Bungling at Piedmont.'" CWTI, 5 [9] [1967]: 40-46.

The Confederates were defeated at Piedmont, a short distance northeast of Staunton, June 5, 1864. This was preliminary to Early's raid up the Valley and on into Maryland.

2780. Morton, Louis. "Vermonters at Cedar Creek." VT HIS, 33 [1965]: 326-341.

An outline of Sheridan's scorched earth policy in the Valley and the Battle of Cedar Creek.

2781. Nichols, Clifton M. A SUMMER CAMPAIGN IN THE SHENANDOAH VALLEY IN 1864. Springfield, Ohio: 1899.

Author served with the 152nd Ohio as a "100 Days" volunteer in the Shenandoah during 1864. The book is in the form of newspaper dispatches as Nichols was editor of the Springfield DAILY NEWS. He wrote under the pseudonym "Nickliffe."

2782. Stackpole, Edward J. SHERIDAN IN THE SHENANDOAH: JUBAL EARLY'S NEMESIS. Harrisburg: Stackpole, 1961.

A lengthy account of the action in the Valley during the summer and fall of 1864, in which Sheridan's achievements are viewed with favor. The author supplies a traditional version of these events, from which not a great deal of new information can be gleaned.

2783. Turner, Charles W., editor. "General David Hunter's Sack of Lexington, Virginia, June 10-14, 1864." VA MHB, 83 [1975]: 173-183.

Rose Page Pendleton, daughter of Confederate Brigadier General William N. Pendleton, described the damage done by federal troops in Lexington, Virginia, in this memoir of June 18, 1864.

2784. Walker, Aldace F. THE VERMONT BRIGADE IN THE SHENANDOAH VALLEY, 1864. Burlington, Vermont: 1869.

An early, but still useful account of the Valley Campaign of 1864.

PETERSBURG, RICHMOND, AND APPOMATTOX [June 1864-April 1865]

2785. Bond, Brian. "Appomattox: The Triumph of General Grant." HIS TOD, 15 [5] [1965]: 297-305.

A short sketch of the career of Grant, with special attention focused on those qualities which made him an outstanding military leader.

2786. Bowen, George A. "'Boys, Your Work is Done.'" Edward G. Longacre, editor. NJ HIS, 95 [1977]: 101-109.

Excerpts from the Civil War journal of George A. Bowen, commander of Company C, 12th New Jersey. The unit was at Appomattox when Lee surrendered.

2787. Boykin, Edward C. BEEFSTEAK RAID. New York: Funk and Wagnalls, 1960.

Author describes a celebrated cavalry raid by the Confederates under Wade Hampton, September 1864, in the Petersburg area for food supplies. Hampton's men came away with 2,468 badly needed cattle for Lee's starving forces. A dramatic, though undocumented tale.

2788. Cannon, John. HISTORY OF GRANT'S CAMPAIGN FOR THE CAPTURE OF RICHMOND.... London, England: 1869.

An early, lengthy account of the Petersburg-Richmond siege by a British officer, which is still of use.

2789. Cleveland, Edmund J. "The Siege of Petersburg, July 30-September 19, 1864." Edmund J. Cleveland, editor. NJ HIS SOC PROC, 66 [1948]: 176-196.

Cleveland served with the 9th New Jersey. This is a continuation of the journal in Number 2768.

2790. Cullen, Joseph P. "Richmond Falls!" A HIS ILL, 8 [9] [1974]: 10-21.

The capital of the Confederacy is described just before, during, and after its fall.

2791. ———. "The Siege of Petersburg!" CWTI, 9 [5] [1970]: 4-50.

Another excellent single-issue account, profusely illustrated.

2792. Davis, Burke. TO APPOMATTOX: NINE APRIL DAYS, 1865. New York: Rinehart, 1959.

Drawn from over 200 accounts, this intriguing volume provides a day by day description of Grant's pursuit of Lee across southern Virginia.

2793. Davis, William C. "The Campaign to Appomattox." CWTI, 14 [1] [1975].

The entire issue of CIVIL WAR TIMES ILLUSTRATED is devoted to the final month of the war--from the battle of Five Forks to the inevitable end, Appomattox.

2794. Dent, Frederick T. "The Letters of Frederick Dent." CWTI, 17 [1] [1978]: 34-39.

The last weeks of the war are recounted by Lieutenant Colonel Frederick Dent, Grant's brother-in-law, in letters to his wife, December 18, 1864 to April 9, 1865.

2795. Devin, Thomas C. "'Didn't We Fight Splendid.'" CWTI, 17 [8] [1978]: 38-40.

A long letter from Union General Thomas Devin recounting the final phases of the siege of Richmond. Special emphasis is given to Five Forks and Appomattox.

2796. Hannaford, Roger. "Dinwiddie Court House and Five Forks: Reminiscences of Roger Hannaford, Second Ohio Volunteer Cavalry." Stephen Z. Starr, editor. VA MHB, 87 [1979]: 417-437.

The author, who took part in this campaign, relates in detail the problems and hardships his unit experienced.

2797. ———. "The Wilson Raid, June, 1864." A Trooper's Reminiscences." Stephen Z. Starr, editor. CWH, 21 [1975]: 218-241.

Hannaford kept a record of the Wilson raid through southern Virginia, June 21-30, 1864.

2798. Klein, Frederic S. "Bottling Up Butler At Bermuda Hundred." CWTI, 6 [7] [1967]: 4-11, 45-47.

Union General Benjamin Butler bungled his assignment on the Peninsula in the spring of 1864 and found himself "corked up" at Bermuda Hundred.

2799. ———. "Lost Opportunity at Petersburg." CWTI, 5 [5] [1966]: 38-50.

An analysis of the Union move across the James River after the repulse at Cold Harbor. Failure to attack Petersburg at once, in mid-June 1864, resulted in the siege which would last until the war's end.

2800. Kurtz, Henry I. "Five Forks: The South's Waterloo." CWTI, 3 [6] [1964]: 4-11, 28-31.

This crucial battle at the fork of five country roads on April 1, 1865, opened the way to Petersburg resulting in Lee's retreat to Appomattox.

2801. Longacre, Edward G. "Wilson-Kautz Raid." CWTI, 11 [2] [1970]: 32-42.

A partially successful attempt to cut the Southside Railroad, leading west out of Petersburg, was carried out by Union Generals James Wilson and August V. Kautz, June 22-July 1, 1864.

2802. Mahone, William. "On the Road to Appomattox." William C. Davis, editor. CWTI, 9 [9] [1971]: 5-11, 42-47.

A valuable, recently-discovered letter from General William "Little Billy" Mahone to General James Longstreet, who was preparing his memoirs. Written sometime between 1890 and 1894,

2803. Marszalek, John F., Jr. "The Stanton-Sherman Controversy." CWTI, 9 [6] [1970]: 4-12.

Author discusses the dispute which developed between General Sherman and Secretary of War Stanton over Sherman's overly liberal surrender terms offered to Confederate General Joseph Johnston.

2804. Miers, Earl S. THE LAST CAMPAIGN: GRANT SAVES THE UNION. New York: Lippincott, 1972.

A well-written, popular account of the last year of the war in which the author views with favor Lincoln, Grant, and Lee, but is not so sympathetic to Davis.

2805. Naroll, Raoul W. "Lincoln and the Sherman Peace Fiasco: Another Fable?" JSH, 20 [1954]: 459-483.

The widely-held view that Sherman's initial surrender terms to Johnston reflected Lincoln's liberal reconstruction policy is rejected. Lincoln had not sanctioned such proposals.

2806. Patrick, Rembert W. THE FALL OF RICHMOND. Baton Rouge: Louisiana State University Press, 1960.

A volume of lectures, drawn largely from original sources, detailing Richmond's fall, April 2-4, 1865.

2807. Pleasants, Henry, Jr. and George H. Straley. INFERNO AT PETERSBURG. Philadelphia: Chilton, 1961.

An engrossing account of the famous effort to mine the Confederate lines outside Petersburg, which resulted in the disaster known as "The Crater." Pleasants was a cousin of the commander [also named Henry Pleasants] of the 48th Pennsylvania, which constructed the tunnel and planted the mine. This work is more of a biography of Pleasants and his part in planning and construction of the mine.

2808. ———. THE TRAGEDY OF THE CRATER. Boston: Christopher Publishing, 1938.

An earlier, shorter, and less complete account of "The Crater" than the previous entry. The work was probably inspired by the reenactment of the explosion, witnessed by the author, the year before.

2809. Rodick, Burleigh C. APPOMATTOX: THE LAST CAMPAIGN. New York: Philosophical Library, 1965.

A useful, well-written account of the last days of the war, which is probably more helpful to the general reader than to the exacting scholar. The author has nicely recaptured the spirit of the moment.

2810. Schaff, Morris. THE SUNSET OF THE CONFEDERACY. Boston, 1912.

Another look at the retreat to Appomattox, which though rather old, still has appeal.

2811. Sherman, William T. "'To Execute the Terms of Surrender.'" CWTI, 15 [9] [1977]: 34-42.

In a letter to John Draper, Sherman explains the reasons for his lenient terms to Johnston. He had hoped to conclude the fighting, prevent guerrilla warfare, and arrange a truce before news of Lincoln's assassination was made public.

2812. Sommers, Richard J. "The Battle No One Wanted." CWTI, 14 [5] [1975]: 10-18.

Describes an assault along the Confederate lines south and east of Petersburg, which no one in the federal high command seemed to support, except Grant. The results were minimal.

2813. ———. RICHMOND REDEEMED: THE SIEGE AT PETERSBURG. Garden City, New York: Doubleday, 1981.

This history covers in minute detail the period from June 1864 to April 1865. It concentrates on what the author terms "Grant's Fifth Offensive," September 29-October 2, 1864. The last chapter analyzes the commanders involved and the importance of leadership.

2814. Spencer, Warren F. "A French View of the Fall of Richmond: Alfred Paul's Report to Drouyan de Lehuys." VA MHB, 73 [1965]: 178-188.

This dispatch, dated April 11, 1865, was written by the French consular agent to the French foreign minister.

2815. Stern, Philip V. AN END TO VALOR: THE LAST DAYS OF THE CIVIL WAR. Boston: Houghton Mifflin, 1958.

A colorful, readable narrative which concentrates on the period between Lincoln's second inauguration and the final victory march in Washington.

2816. Stickney, Albert. WARREN COURT OF INQUIRY. n.p.: n.d.

The counsel for General Warren presents an able case for the man removed by Sheridan at Five Forks. The 92-page pamphlet was published in the 1880s.

2817. Tomkins, Christopher Q. "The Occupation of Richmond, April 1865: The Memorandum of Events of Colonel Christopher Q. Tompkins." VA MHB, 73 [1965]: 189-198.

A reprint of the colonel's account of the Union occupation of Richmond.

2818. Tremain, Henry E. LAST HOURS OF SHERIDAN'S CAVALRY.... New York, 1904.

The author, an officer on Sheridan's staff, describes the last days of the war. Later, Tremain would receive the Medal of Honor for action at Resaca, Georgia, May 15, 1864.

2819. Warren, Gouverneur K. PROCEEDINGS, FINDINGS, AND OPINIONS OF THE COURT OF INQUIRY.... 3 v. Washington, D.C.: 1883.

All one would ever want to know about the Warren Court of Inquiry and its findings, is in these massive tomes.

2820. Weitzel, Godfrey. RICHMOND OCCUPIED. Richmond: Richmond Civil War Centennial Committee, 1965.

A reprint of the description of the Union occupation of Richmond, April 3, 1865, by the commander of the first federal troops to enter the city.

* * *

2821. Cullen, Joseph P. "When Grant Faced Lee Across the North Anna." CWTI, 3 [10] [1965]: 16-23.

An analysis of Union and Confederate tactics as the two armies sidled in a southeasterly direction toward Richmond in late May 1864.

2822. Crowson, E.T. "The Expedition of Henry Lockwood to Accomac." W VA HIS, 26 [1975]: 202-212.

A Union force under Henry Hayes Lockwood occupied Virginia's Eastern Shore counties without difficulty in 1861 and maintained good relations with the local citizens.

2823. Davis, William C. THE BATTLE OF NEW MARKET. Garden City, New York: Doubleday, 1975.

An excellent account of this dramatic battle, May 15, 1864, where about 250 cadets from the Virginia Military Institute were brought into the fray and helped drive off the Federals. Good maps assist the reader in following the detailed description of the engagement.

2824. ———. "The Day at New Market." CWTI, 10 [4] [1971]: 4-11, 43-47.

A description of the valiant charge by the Virginia Military Institute cadets.

2825. Hassler, William W. "Yellow Tavern." CWTI, 5 [7] [1966]: 4-11, 46-48.

It was at Yellow Tavern, Virginia, May 11, 1864, where the Confederates attempted to block Sheridan's raid toward Richmond and Jeb Stuart was mortally wounded.

2826. Jones, Virgil C. ... EIGHT HOURS BEFORE RICHMOND. New York: Henry Holt, 1957.

The definitive work on the Kilpatrick-Dahlgren federal cavalry raid against Richmond, February 28-March 1, 1864. In the unsuccessful attack, Dahlgren was killed and papers were found upon his body suggesting that the purpose of the raid was to burn Richmond and kill Jefferson Davis.

2827. ———. "The Kilpatrick-Dahlgren Raid: Boldly Planned ... Timidly Executed." CWTI, 4 [1] [1965]: 12-21.

A short account extracted from the author's book.

2828. Kellogg, Sanford C. THE SHENANDOAH VALLEY AND VIRGINIA, 1861 TO 1865: A WAR STUDY. New York, 1903.

This still useful study covers all the campaigning in the Valley, not only the major fighting of 1862 aND 1864 but eveything else also.

2829. Kimball, William J. "The Little Battle of Big Bethel." CWTI, 6 [3] [1967]: 28-32.

One of the early land battles of the war was fought at Big Bethel, June 10, 1861, on the Virginia Peninsula. The Federals were repulsed by much larger forces in this minor engagement, which saw very few casualties.

2830. King, G. Wayne. "General Judson Kilpatrick." NJ HIS, 91 [1973]: 35-42.

This federal cavalry officer had little regard for civilian military control or for orders from his superiors. As an example, the unsuccessful Kilpatrick-Dahlgren raid on Richmond is noted.

2831. Long, John S. "The Gosport Affair, 1861." JSH, 23 [1957]: 155-172.

As the war broke out, Virginia militia attacked and seized the shipbuilding facilities at Gosport, April 20, 1861. The withdrawing Federals unsuccessfully tried to destroy ships and machinery in the yards.

2832. Luvaas, Jay and Wilbur S. Nye. "The Campaign That History Forgot." CWTI, 8 [7] [1969]: 11-42.

A detailed account of a confrontation between Meade and Lee at Mine Run in central Virginia, November 26-December 1, 1863.

Recognizing Lee's strong position, Meade withdrew without attacking and went into winter quarters.

2833. Miller, Samuel H. "Yellow Tavern." CWH, 2 [1956]: 57-81.

A full study of the heavy fighting outside Richmond, May 11, 1864, in which Stuart was killed.

2834. Monaghan, Jay. "Custer's 'Last Stand': Trevilian Station, 1864." CWH, 8 [1962]: 245-258.

In heavy fighting northwest of Richmond following Cold Harbor, June 11-12, 1864, Custer lost 800 horses and his headquarters' wagon. The Federals were unable to cut the railroads west of the capital.

2835. Moore, James O. "Custer's Raid Into Albermarle County: The Skirmish at Rio Hill, February 29, 1864." VA MHB, 79 [1971]: 338-348.

In a raid in the Charlottesville area, General Custer destroyed some Confederate military equipment and three mills, but left untouched a railroad bridge which was his primary objective.

2836. Naisawald, L. Van Loan. "The Battle of Bristoe Station." VA CAV, 18 [1968]: 39-47.

Bristoe Station, in central Virginia, was the scene of an infantry engagement, October 14, 1863, where A.P. Hill's corps was driven back, but eventually the outnumbered Lee compelled Meade to withdraw.

2837. Patch, Joseph D. THE BATTLE OF BALL'S BLUFF. Fitzhugh Turner, editor. Leesburg, Virginia: Potomac Press, 1958.

The well-illustrated, 123-page volume, including official reports and newspaper accounts, deals with the battle of October 21, 1861. Though a minor engagement, the affair had major consequences with the investigation into the death of Senator Edward D. Baker.

2838. Ryckman, E.C. "Clash of Cavalry at Trevilians." VA MHB, 75 [1967]: 443-458.

Sheridan failed in his mission to destroy the Virginia Central Railroad east of Charlottesville in June 1864, but he did preoccupy a portion of Lee's cavalry, thus permitting Grant to move south and east of Richmond undetected.

2839. Stuart, Meriwether. "Colonel Ulric Dahlgren and Richmond's Union Underground, April, 1864. VA MHB, 72 [1964]: 152-204.

An account of the clandestine removal of the body of Ulric Dahlgren--after his death in the Kilpatrick raid of February-

March 1864--from the Oakwood Cemetery in Richmond to a hidden site favored by the Union underground of the city.

2840. Sword, Wiley. "Cavalry on Trial at Kelly's Ford." CWTI, 13 [1] [1974]: 32-40.

An account of a cavalry engagement at Kelly's Ford in central Virginia, March 17, 1863, in which "for the first time in the war a large number of Union cavalry had matched the superb Confederate horsemen of Stuart blow-for-blow in battle."

2841. Thomas, Emory M. "The Kilpatrick-Dahlgren Raid." CWTI, 16 [10] [1978]: 4-9. 46-48; 17 [1] [1978]: 26-33.

A description of the ill-fated raid on Richmond early in 1864. Author comments on the repercussions of the plot revealed in the papers found on Dahlgren's body.

2842. Turner, Edward R. THE NEW MARKET CAMPAIGN, MAY 1864. Richmond, 1912.

A solid study of the famous Confederate victory, which featured the Virginia Military Institute cadets.

2843. Weinert, Richard P. "The Suffolk Campaign." CWTI, 7 [9] [1969]: 31-39.

Treats of General Longstreet's campaign in April-May 1863 against Union forces at Suffolk, Virginia. This was Longstreet's first independent command.

2844. Williams, Robert A. "Haw's Shop: A 'Storm of Shot and Shell.'" CWTI, 9 [9] [1971]: 12-19.

A severe cavalry engagement occurred at Haw's Shop, or Enon Church, Virginia, May 29, 1864, as Grant sidled closer to Richmond.

West Virginia

2845. Askew, Margaret. "Harper's Ferry: Could It Have Been Defended?" VA CAV, 29 [1979]: 14-21.

Author reviews the continual fighting for control of this important point.

2846. Ambler, Charles H. "General Robert E. Lee's Northwest Virginia Campaign." W VA HIS, 5 [1943/1944]: 101-115.

An analysis of Lee's "failure" in Western Virginia in the early months of the war. The failure was due to bad weather, poor transportation facilities, inadequate supplies, and Lee's "excessive consideration for the feelings of others."

2847. Bearss, Edwin C. "War Comes to the Chesapeake and Ohio Canal." W VA HIS, 29 [1968]: 153-177.

After an unprofitable year in 1860, the canal company looked forward to recouping its losses in 1861. Instead, war came and Confederate troops attempted, in the face of persistent federal resistance, to put the canal out of operation. Most of the action occurred around Harper's Ferry.

2848. Boehm, Robert B. "The Battle of Rich Mountain, July 11, 1861." W VA HIS, 20 [1958/1959]: 5-15.

McClellan successfully drove the Confederates out of their position on Rich Mountain in this early campaigning in Western Virginia.

2849. ———. "Battle of Rich Mountain." CWTI, 8 [10] [1970]: 4-15.

This battle gave control of the area to the Union and safeguarded the western section of the B & O Railroad.

2850. ———. "The Jones-Imboden Raid Through West Virginia." CWTI, 3 [2] [1964]: 14-21.

A Confederate cavalry raid destroyed bridges along the B & O Railroad in April 1863.

2851. Carnes, Eva M. "The Battle of Philippi." AM HER, 3 [1952]: 56-59, 76.

An account of the "first land battle" of the Civil War, June 3, 1861, at Philippi, West Virginia.

2852. Cohen, Stan. "Top of Allegheny." W VA HIS, 28 [1967]: 318-323.

Author describes a Civil War campground and battlefield located at "Top of Allegheny" in Pocahontas County in eastern West Virginia.

2853. Conley, Phil. "The First Land Battle of the Civil War." W VA HIS, 20 [1958/1959]: 120-123.

The battle of Philippi, June 3, 1861.

2854. Curry, Richard O. "McClellan's Western Virginia Campaign of 1861." OHIO HIS, 71 [1962]: 83-96.

In addition to an outline of McClellan's campaigns, this article emphasizes the strategic and psychological significance of these early Union victories.

2855. ——— and F. Gerald Ham. "The Bushwhackers' War: Insurgency and Counter-Insurgency in West Virginia." CWH, 10 [1964]: 416-433.

Author describes the bitter guerrilla warfare which raged in West Virginia after the end of formal Union-Confederate hostilities in 1861. Guerrilla activities reached a peak in 1862-1863 with the breakdown of civil government in the central sections of the new state.

2856. Davis, William C. "Massacre at Saltville." CWTI, 9 [10] [1971]: 4-11, 43-48.

After a successful defense of their salt works in western Virginia, October 2, 1864, the victorious Confederates slaughtered 100 helpless black prisoners.

2857. Dayton, Ruth W. "The Beginning: Philippi, 1861." W VA HIS, 13 [1951/1952]: 254-266.

The story of a little town in Western Virginia where occurred the "first land battle of the Civil War."

2858. Hall, Granville D. LEE'S INVASION OF NORTHWEST VIRGINIA IN 1861. Chicago, 1911.

A collection of documents dealing with General Robert E. Lee's unsuccessful efforts to regain control of Western Virginia in the fall of 1861.

2859. Haselberger, Francis E., Jr. "The Battle of Hanging Rocks Pass Near Romney, West Virginia, September 24, 1861." W VA HIS, 25 [1963]: 1-20.

A struggle for control of the gateway for Confederate attacks on the B & O Railroad, which changed hands fifty-six times during the war.

2860. ———. "General Rosser's Raid on the New Creek Depot." W VA HIS, 26 [1965]: 86-109.

Confederate General Thomas Rosser led a successful cavalry raid on the New Creek Depot, on the south branch of the Potomac River in late November 1864. He captured supplies and burned facilities of the B & O Railroad.

2861. ———. "Skirmishes at South Branch and Patterson's Creek, West Virginia." W VA HIS, 25 [1964]: 265-269.

Confederate guerrillas attacked Union troops responsible for protecting the B & O Railroad. The raid took place the first week in July 1864.

2862. Haselberger, Fritz. "The Battle of Blue's Gap." W VA HIS, 28 [1967]: 241-248.

Union forces were based in Romney, West Virginia, to protect the B & O. On January 7, 1862, Confederate forces sought to drive the Federals away. Blue Gap was about 15 miles southeast of Romney.

2863. ———. "Skirmishes at Dan's Run and Kelley's Island." W VA HIS, 26 [1965]: 220-233.

An account of a minor cavalry skirmish between Indiana and Virginia units on an island in the North Branch of the Potomac in June 1861.

2864. ———. "Wallace's Raid on Romney in 1861." W VA HIS, 27 [1966]: 97-110.

A federal force under General Lew Wallace seized Romney on June 12, 1861.

2865. Haselberger, Fritz and Mark Haselberger. "The Battle of Greenland Gap." W VA HIS, 28 [1967]: 285-304.

A Confederate diversionary attack to loosen federal control of the B & O Railroad occurred on April 25, 1863, about 25 miles southwest of the present Keyser.

2866. ———. "The Burning of the 21st Bridge of the Baltimore and Ohio Railroad at New Creek." W VA HIS, 27 [1965]: 56-64.

Confederate troops from Tennessee tore out the railroad tracks, heated them until they were molten, and then twisted them around trees. [June 19, 1861] The bridge crossed the North Branch of the Potomac one and a half miles east of New Creek.

2867. ———. "Kelley's Occupation of Romney in 1861." W VA HIS, 28 [1967]: 121-136.

Federals occupied this key town on the B & O Railroad in the fall and early winter of 1861 and 1862.

2868. ———. "The Skirmishes at New Creek and Piedmont, July 14 and 15, 1861." W VA HIS, 27 [1966]: 211-219.

An account of the role of the 1st Pennsylvania Rifles at the skirmishes at New Creek and Piedmont.

2869. Jones, Allen W. "Military Events in West Virginia During the Civil War, 1861-1865." W VA HIS, 21 [1959/1960]: 186-196.

Although they were overshadowed by the war in Eastern Virginia, more than 500 military actions took place in over 50 different places in West Virginia. Listings are arranged by place, showing type of action and date.

2870. Klement, Frank. "General John B. Floyd and the West Virginia Campaign of 1861." W VA HIS, 8 [1946/1947]: 319-333.

An account of the accomplishments of John B. Floyd and Henry A Wise, Confederate generals, who held independent commands in Western Virginia in 1861.

2871. Nichols, William E. "Fighting Guerrillas in West Virginia." CWTI, 6 [1] [1967]: 20-25.

Letters from the author who was a member of the 153rd Ohio.

2872. Shaffer, Dallas B. "Rich Mountain Revisited." W VA HIS, 28 [1966]: 16-34.

Federal forces under General William Rosecrans made a night march to the top of the mountain, July 11, 1861, and drove the Confederates off after a hot fight.

2873. Summers, Festus P. "The Jones-Imboden Raid." W VA HIS, 1 [1939/1940]: 15-29.

An account of the famous Confederate raid of April 1863, where the objective was to wreck the B & O Railroad, in addition to overthrowing the "reorganized" state government at Wheeling, recruit troops, and collect supplies.

2874. Thomas, Joseph W. "The Campaigns of McClellan and Rosecrans in Western Virginia, 1861-1862." W VA HIS, 5 [1943/1944]: 245-308.

A detailed study of the struggle for Western Virginia drawn almost exclusively from the OFFICIAL RECORDS. Union success was attributed to superiority in numbers, fire power, transport, and leadership.

2875. Webster, Donald B. "The Last Days of the Harpers Ferry Armory." CWH, 5 [1959]: 30-44.

An account of the Confederate seizure of the federal armory at Harpers Ferry in the early days of the war. When Union troops evacuated, they set fire to the arsenal.

2876. Wert, Jeffry D. "Duped in the Mountains of Virginia." CWTI, 17 [8] [1978]: 4-11, 41-44.

An analysis of the importance of Harpers Ferry and the northern Shenandoah valley in early 1861.

Western States and Territories

2877. Archambeau, Ernest R., Jr. "The New Mexico Campaign, 1861-1862." PAN PLAINS HR, 37 [1964]: 3-32.

Confederate forces under General Henry H. Sibley launched a major move against federal troops in New Mexico in the winter of 1861-1862. While enjoying early successes, they were finally forced to withdraw in the face of superior Union numbers.

2878. Armstrong, A.F. "The Case of Major Isaac Lynde." NM HIS R, 36 [1961]: 1-35.

Union Major Isaac Lynde, commanding a 700-man garrison at Fort Fillmore, New Mexico, surrendered to a 200-man Confederate force, July 27, 1861. Shortly thereafter Lynde was dismissed from the army.

2879. Athearn, Robert G. "West of Appomattox: Civil War Beyond the Great River." MON MAG HIS, 11 [1962]: 2-10.

A study of the general impact of the war upon western states and territories.

2880. Barr, Alwyn. "Sabine Pass, September, 1863." TEX MIL HIS, 2 [1962]: 17-22.

In early September 1863, a federal naval force unsuccessfully tried to capture Sabine Pass, an important fort on the east Texas coast.

2881. ———. "Texas Coastal Defenses, 1861-1865." SW HIS Q, 65 [1961/1962]: 1-31.

An examination of the more important military and naval actions along the coast, as the Federals hoped to establish footholds.

2882. Bearss, Edwin C. "The Civil War Comes to Indian Territory, 1861: The Flight of Opothleyoholo." JW, 11 [1972]: 9-42.

The tale of an Indian chief who, although a slaveowner, sided with the North. The article also describes the internal quarrels among the Creeks as the war broke out.

2883. Brophy, A. Blake. "Fort Fillmore, New Mexico, 1861: Public Disgrace and Private Disaster." J ARIZ HIS, 9 [1968]: 195-218.

An account of the ignominious surrender of Major Lynde's forces to the Confederates.

2884. Brown, D. Alexander. "The Million Dollar Wagon Raid." CWTI, 7 [6] [1968]: 12-20.

On September 18, 1864, the Confederates successfully raided a rich Union supply train of 205 wagons in Indian Territory.

2885. Colton, Ray C. THE CIVIL WAR IN WESTERN TERRITORIES: ARIZONA, COLORADO, NEW MEXICO, UTAH. Norman: University of Oklahoma Press, 1959.

A solid, well-written, and carefully researched study of campaigning west of the Mississippi. While not a great deal of new material is brought forth here, the work is a good synthesis of political and military developments. Half the text is devoted to the invasion of New Mexico.

2886. Crimmons, Martin L. "Fort Fillmore." NM HIS R, 6 [1931]: 327-333.

Federal fort in southeastern New Mexico, which fell to the Confederates in late July 1861.

2887. Debo, Angie. "The Site of the Battle of Round Mountain, 1861." CH OK, 28 [1949]: 187-206.

Describes efforts to identify the exact spot of a minor engagement in northeastern Oklahoma, fought on November 19, 1861.

2888. ———. "The Location of the Battle of Round Mountain." CH OK, 41 [1963]: 70-104.

The site of the above-mentioned battle is located along the Salt Creek in northeastern Oklahoma.

2889. Edwards, G. Thomas. "Holding the Far West For the Union: The Army in 1861." CWH, 14 [1968]: 307-324.

A review of military and political events in the Department of the Pacific [chiefly California], from January through September, 1861.

2890. Fischer, LeRoy H. "Quantrill's Civil War Operation in Indian Territory." CH OK, 46 [1968]: 155-181.

Even though Quantrill was in trouble for killing a Confederate officer in Texas, the South still made use of him. His last raid into Indian Territory occurred in April-May 1864. By spreading confusion he "helped shape the course of the war in Indian Territory."

2891. Fitzhugh, Lester N. "Saluria, Fort Esperanza and the Military Operations on the Texas Coast, 1861-1864." SWHQ, 61 [1957/1958]: 66-100.

An account of Confederate efforts to defend the entire Texas coast and the difficulties which this task presented.

2892. Goldman, Henry H. "General James H. Carleton and the New Mexico Indian Campaigns 1862-1866." JW, 2 [1963]: 156-165.

Federal General Carleton, a controversial figure, led two regiments of California volunteers into New Mexico to suppress the Apache and Navajo Indians.

2893. Hall, Martin H. "The Skirmish at Mesilla." ARIZ W, 1 [1959]: 343-351.

The federal failure at Mesilla, July 25, 1861, led to the abandonment of all Union control over southern New Mexico.

2894. ———. "The Skirmish of Picacho." CWH, 4 [1958]: 27-35.

A minor engagement north of Tucson, Arizona, April 15, 1862.

2895. ———. SIBLEY'S NEW MEXICO CAMPAIGN. Austin: University of Texas Press, 1960.

A well-written, thorough account of the Confederate invasion of New Mexico and their eventual withdrawal therefrom, 1861-1862. Political reasons for the invasion and the political results are also discussed.

2896. Heath, Gary N. "The First Federal Invasion of Indian Territory." CH OK, 44 [1967]: 409-419.

The federal victory at Pea Ridge, Arkansas, March 1862, was the turning point in the war for the Indian Territory. As a result of it, Union commanders decided to invade the territory and did so successfully.

2897. Hilleary, William M. A WEBFOOT VOLUNTEER: THE DIARY OF WILLIAM M. HILLEARY, 1864-1866. Herbert B. Nelson and Preston E. Onstad, editors. Corvallis, Oregon: Oregon State University Press, 1965.

The diary of William Hilleary illuminates a phase of the Civil War in the Pacific Northwest dealing with the activities of the Oregon volunteers who protected the northwest from the Indians.

2898. Horn, Calvin and William S. Wallace. UNION ARMY OPERATIONS IN THE SOUTHWEST. Albuquerque, New Mexico: Horn and Wallace, 1961.

Drawn largely from the OFFICIAL RECORDS, this volume covers the war years in the Southwest--from the Battle of Glorieta to the final withdrawal of Confederate forces from the territory.

2899. Hunt, Aurora. THE ARMY OF THE PACIFIC: ITS OPERATIONS IN CALIFORNIA, TEXAS, ARIZONA, NEW MEXICO, UTAH, NEVADA, OREGON, WASHINGTON, PLAINS REGION.... Glendale, California: A.H. Clarke, 1951.

Probably the most detailed study of military operations in the western states and territories, 1860-1866. Although some of the material is drawn from the OFFICIAL RECORDS, the book also contains excerpts from soldiers' letters which "were published in contemporary home-town newspapers."

2900. Ickis, Alonza F. BLOODY TRAILS ALONG THE RIO GRANDE. Nolie Mumey, editor. Denver, Colorado: Old West Publishing, 1958.

The diary of a soldier with the first volunteer regiment to leave the Colorado Territory for the war. The Battle of Valverde, New Mexico, is discussed.

2901. Keleher, William A. TURMOIL IN NEW MEXICO, 1846-1888. Santa Fe, New Mexico: Rydall Press, 1952.

An excellent account of the history of the New Mexico Territory following the Mexican War. Pages 143-274 provide a good description of Sibley's invasion of the territory and the march of General Carleton's "California Column" during the summer of 1862.

2902. Kerby, Robert L. THE CONFEDERATE INVASION OF NEW MEXICO AND ARIZONA, 1861-1862. Los Angeles: Westernlore Press, 1958.

A rather short, but thorough, examination of Sibley's New Mexico campaign. Includes battle statistics and portraits of the commanders.

2903. Lewis, Oscar. THE WAR IN THE FAR WEST: 1861-1863. Garden City, New York: Doubleday, 1961.

An interesting, informal look at affairs between the Rocky Mountains and the Pacific Coast during the war, with special emphasis on California.

2904. McCoy, Raymond. "Arizona: Early Confederate Territory." MON MAG HIS, 12 [1962]: 16-20.

A brief look at Major Isaac Lynde's defeat at Fort Fillmore, July 27, 1861.

2905. McKee, James C. NARRATIVE OF THE SURRENDER OF A COMMAND OF THE UNITED STATES FORCES AT FORT FILLMORE, NEW MEXICO. Houston, Texas: Stagecoach Press, 1960.

This work describes the Confederate capture of Fort Fillmore following Major Lynde's surrender, July 1861. This is a reprint of the 1881 edition.

2906. Muir, Andrew. "Dick Dowling and the Battle of Sabine Pass." CWH, 4 [1958]: 399-428.

After a brief account of Dowling's life as "an early oil operator and a public spirited citizen," there is a discussion of his experiences with the Davis Guard at Sabine Pass.

2907. Rampp, Lary C. and Donald L. Rampp. THE CIVIL WAR IN INDIAN TERRITORY. Austin, Texas: Presidential Press, 1975.

A collection of articles which originally appeared in MILITARY HISTORY OF TEXAS AND THE SOUTHWEST, Volumes 10 and 11. All deal with the action in the Indian Territory.

2908. Santee, J. "The Battle of La Glorieta Pass." NM HIS R, 6 [1931]: 66-75.

An account of the critical battle at Glorieta Pass, New

Mexico Territory in late March 1862, which secured the territory for the Union.

2909. Tolbert, Frank X. DICK DOWLING AT SABINE PASS. New York: McGraw Hill, 1962.

A rather short, not well-done account of the incredible performance by Dick Dowling and his 42 Confederate artillerymen, in turning back a Union fleet of 21 ships on September 8, 1863.

2910. Trickett, Dean. "The Civil War in the Indian Territory." CH OK, 17 [1939]: 315-327, 401-412; 18 [1940]: 142-153, 266-280; 19 [1941]: 55-69, 381-396.

A series of articles discussing the battles, leaders, and the actions of the Indians in territorial campaigning in 1861 and 1862.

2911. Twitchell, Ralph E. "The Confederate Invasion of New Mexico, 1861-1862." OLD SANTA FE, 3 [1916]: 5-43.

Another account of the Sibley invasion of 1861-1862.

2912. Utley, Robert M. "Kit Carson and the Adobe Walls Campaign." AW, 2 [1965]: 4-11, 73-75.

A campaign against unfriendly Indians to keep the important Santa Fe Trail open for supplies to the federal troops in Santa Fe.

2913. Watford, Wilbur H. "The Far Western Wing of the Rebellion, 1860-1865." CAL HIS SOC Q, 34 [1955]: 125-148.

A well-written piece describing military operations in the Far West with special emphasis on California troops.

2914. Westphall, David. "The Battle of Glorieta Pass: Its Importance in the Civil War." NM HIS R, 44 [1969]: 137-154.

A review of this federal victory during the Sibley invasion, which marked Colorado's major military contribution to winning the war.

2915. Whitford, William C. COLORADO VOLUNTEERS IN THE CIVIL WAR: THE NEW MEXICO CAMPAIGN IN 1862. Boulder, Colorado: Pruett Press, 1963.

This is a reprint of a 1906 volume, designed for a popular audience. Concentrates on the role of Colorado volunteers in the actions against Sibley.

2916. Willey, William J. "The Second Federal Invasion of Indian Territory." CH OK, 44 [1967]: 420-430.

The success of the first federal invasion of Indian Territory in 1862 led to no permanent results, so a second invasion was organized, in which Union forces seized control of the entire territory.

2917. Wright, Arthur A. THE CIVIL WAR IN THE SOUTHWEST. Denver, Colorado: Big Mountain Press, 1964.

Author describes the operations of the California volunteers and also notes the efforts made by both sides to win over the Mexican state governments of Chihuahua and Sonora.

2918. ———. "Colonel John P. Slough and the New Mexico Campaign." COL MAG, 39 [1962]: 89-105.

Slough commanded the Colorado volunteers in their New Mexico invasion. He resigned in the field. The Glorieta Pass engagement is described.

The Scribner's Series

CAMPAIGNS OF THE CIVIL WAR

This 13-volume set, published by Charles Scribner's Sons of New York, appeared from 1881 to 1885. The works, a number of which were written by former high-ranking Union officers, are generally of good quality and provide a useful overview of the major campaigns of the war. Volume 13, STATISTICAL RECORD, is not a military history, but it is a standard work on organization, numbers, losses, chronology, and data on general officers.

2919. Volume 1. Nicolay, John G. THE OUTBREAK OF THE REBELLION. 1881.

2920. Volume 2. Force, Manning F. FROM FORT HENRY TO CORINTH. 1882.

2921. Volume 3. Webb, Alexander S. THE PENINSULA. 1885.

2922. Volume 4. Ropes, John C. THE ARMY UNDER POPE. 1881.

2923. Volume 5. Palfrey, Francis W. THE ANTIETAM AND FREDERICKSBURG. 1882.

2924. Volume 6. Doubleday, Abner. CHANCELLORSVILLE AND GETTYSBURG. 1882.

2925. Volume 7. Cist, Henry M. THE ARMY OF THE CUMBERLAND. 1885.

2926. Volume 8. Greene, Francis V. THE MISSISSIPPI. 1882.

2927. Volume 9. Cox, Jacob D. ATLANTA. 1882.

2928. Volume 10. ———. THE MARCH TO THE SEA: FRANKLIN AND NASHVILLE. 1882.

2929. Volume 11. Pond, George E. THE SHENANDOAH VALLEY IN 1864. 1883.

2930. Volume 12. Humphreys, Andrew A. THE VIRGINIA CAMPAIGN OF '64 AND '65. 1883.

Volume 13. Phisterer, Frederick. STATISTICAL RECORD. 1883. [See Number 56]

Maps

2931. Davis, Geoorge B., Leslie J. Perry, and Joseph W. Kirkley. THE OFFICIAL ATLAS OF THE CIVIL WAR. New York: Yoseloff, 1958.

A one volume reprint of the multi-volume ATLAS TO ACCOMPANY THE OFFICIAL RECORDS, published by the War Department, 1891-1895. This huge book contains 821 maps, 106 engravings, and 209 drawings, all very excellently reproduced. The maps are in soft colors. Documents, reports, and other source materials accompany the illustrations.

2932. Esposito, Vincent J., chief editor. THE WEST POINT ATLAS OF AMERICAN WARS. 2 v. New York: Praeger, 1962.

Easily the best collection of Civil War maps extant, prepared by the one-time head of the Department of Military Art and Engineering at the United States Military Academy. Volume one covers the 1689-1900 era, while maps 17 through 154 deal with the Civil War. A good, succinct commentary accompanies the maps.

2933. National Geographic Society. BATTLEFIELDS OF THE CIVIL WAR. James M. Darley, chief cartographer. Washington, D.C.: 1961.

An instructive map in color, 78 by 103 centimeters, drawn especially for the NATIONAL GEOGRAPHIC.

2934. Symonds, Craig L. A BATTLEFIELD ATLAS OF THE CIVIL WAR. Annapolis: Nautical and Aviation Publishing, 1983.

A useful, 106-page volume including 43 full-page maps in color, prepared by the former head of Graphic Arts at the Naval Academy.

2935. United States Coast and Geodetic Survey. SELECTED CIVIL WAR MAPS.... Washington, D.C.: 1961.

A collection of 20 plates, reproduced from originals made by the United States Coast and Geodetic Survey, 1861-1865, showing various cities, forts, and geographic regions.

National Park Booklets

From time to time, the National Park Service has published informational booklets about the many historic parks in the United States. Those booklets pertaining to the Civil War are listed below. They are, generally, of a high quality, amply illustrated, with good maps, and averaging about 50 pages in length.

2936. Baker, Raymond and Edwin C. Bearss. ANDERSONVILLE: THE STORY OF A CIVIL WAR PRISON.

2937. Barnes, Frank. FORT SUMTER NATIONAL MONUMENT. 1952.

2938. Bearss, Edwin C. THE FALL OF FORT HENRY. 1963.

2939. ———. UNCONDITIONAL SURRENDER: THE FALL OF FORT DONELSON. 1962.

2940. Cullen, Joseph. RICHMOND NATIONAL BATTLEFIELD PARK. 1961.

2941. Dillahunty, Albert. SHILOH NATIONAL MILITARY PARK. 1955.

2942. Everhart, William. VICKSBURG. 1954.

2943. Everhart, William and James Sullivan. HARPER'S FERRY NATIONAL HISTORIC PARK.

2944. Luvaas, Jay. APPOMATTOX COURT HOUSE.

2945. Lykes, Richard. CAMPAIGN FOR PETERSBURG. 1970.

2946. McClure, Stanley. FORD'S THEATER AND THE HOUSE WHERE LINCOLN DIED.

2947. McMurry, Richard. KENNESAW MOUNTAIN NATIONAL BATTLEFIELD PARK.

2948. Sullivan, James. CHICKAMAUGA AND CHATTANOOGA BATTLEFIELDS. 1956.

2949. Tilberg, Frederick. ANTIETAM NATIONAL BATTLEFIELD. 1961.

2950. ———. GETTYSBURG NATIONAL MILITARY PARK. 1954.

2951. Wilshin, Francis. MANASSAS. 1953.

H. PRISONS AND PRISONERS

By Harry F. Lupold

2952. Allen, William H. "One Hundred and Ninety Days in Rebel Prisons." ANN IOWA, 38 [1966]: 222-238.

Private Allen wrote this account of his imprisonment 34 years after the event.

2953. Ames, Amos W. "A Diary of Prison Life in Southern Prisons." ANN IOWA, 40 [1969]: 1-19.

Corporal Ames describes life in various prisons.

2954. Baldwin, Terry E. "Clerk of the Dead: Dorance Atwater." CWTI, 10 [6] [1971]: 12-21.

During his imprisonment at Andersonville, Atwater was a clerk in the prison hospital and kept a record of everyone who died.

2955. Baretski, Charles A. "General Albin Francis Schoepf--A Preliminary View." POL AM STUD, 23 [1966]: 93-96.

A sympathetic examination of Schoepf's role at Fort Delaware where 30,000 Confederates were imprisoned at various times.

2956. Bartleson, Frederick A. LETTERS FROM LIBBY PRISON. New York: Greenwich, 1956.

A journal that describes life and prison escapes in Libby Prison during 1864.

2957. Bartlett, Louis. "Captain T.W. Rathbone's 'Brief Diary of Imprisonment,' July 1-November 21, 1864." OHIO HIS, 71 [1962]: 33-56.

Describes Rathbone's capture near North River Mills, West Virginia, his imprisonment, escape, and eventual rescue by a Union naval vessel.

2958. Barziza, Decimus et Ultimus. THE ADVENTURES OF A PRISONER OF WAR, 1863-1864. R. Henderson Shuffler, editor. Austin: University of Texas Press, 1964.

A reprint of the original edition, this vivid description of life on Johnson's Island makes for profitable reading.

2959. Benson, Berry. BERRY BENSON'S CIVIL WAR BOOK. Susan Williams Benson, editor. Athens, Georgia: University of Georgia Press, 1962.

A good, informative introduction to life in Elmira Prison.

2960. Brannon, Peter A. "The Cahaba Military Prison, 1863-1865." ALA R, 3 [1950]: 163-173.

This Alabama cotton shed was converted into a 500-man prison, but eventually housed over 2,000 northern prisoners.

2961. Bray, John. "Escape From Richmond." CWTI, 5 [2] [1966]: 28-33.

An account of Bray's escape from Libby Prison.

2962. Breedon, James O. "Andersonville--A Southern Surgeon's Story." HIS MED BULL, 47 [1973]: 317-343.

The story of Joseph Jones, a surgeon who cared for the Union prisoners in Andersonville.

2963. Burdick, John M. "The Andersonville Journal of Sergeant J.M. Burdick." Ovid L. Futch, editor. GA HIS Q, 45 [1961]: 287-295.

The author, a member of the 21st New York Cavalry, was captured near Lynchburg, Virginia, June 19, 1864. The diary covers a two-month period. Burdick died soon after his release.

2964. Burger, Nash K. "Captain Wirz of Andersonville." CATH DIG, 30 [1966]: 116-119.

Condensation of an article, sympathetic to Wirz, which first appeared in THE NATIONAL OBSERVER, November 8, 1965.

2965. Byrne, Frank L. "Libby Prison: A Study in Emotions." JSH, 24 [1958]: 430-444.

A good study of prison officials who doubted their ability to maintain control of the prison.

2966. Cleary, Ann. "Life and Death in Andersonville Prison." HIS J W MASS, 2 [1973]: 27-42.

An account of the high mortality rate as well as the daily life in this overcrowded prison. Some played cards or chess, some prayed, and some turned craftsmen.

2967. Davidson, Henry M. FOURTEEN MONTHS IN SOUTHERN PRISONS. Milwaukee, 1865.

Author recounts his life in Richmond, Danville, Andersonville, and Savannah prisons.

2968. Dougherty, Michael. DIARY OF A CIVIL WAR HERO. New York: Pyramid Books, 1960.

Dougherty spent several months at Andersonville, but the authenticity of his rather vivid account has been questioned.

2969. Duncan, John E. "The Correspondence of a Yankee Prisoner in Charleston, 1865." SC HIS MAG, 75 [1974]: 215-224.

Duncan describes long marches, inadequate diet, boredom, and frustration, all of which he experienced until his liberation by Sherman's army in 1865.

2970. Eberhart, James W. "Diary of Salisbury Prison by James W. Eberhart." W PA HIS MAG, 56 [1973]: 211-251.

Sergeant Eberhart writes of life in this North Carolina prison.

2971. Emerson, Wilson W. FORT WARREN. Newark: University of Delaware Press.

Based on sound research and written for the general audience, this 32-page booklet is recommended reading.

2972. Foote, Morris C. "Narrative of an Escape From a Rebel Prison Camp." AM HER, 11 [4] [1960]: 65-75.

The account of an escape from Camp Sorghum, near Columbia, South Carolina, in 1864. The author, a lieutenant in the 92nd New York, had been imprisoned for seven months.

2973. Forbes, Eugene. DIARY OF A SOLDIER AND PRISONER OF WAR IN REBEL PRISONS. Trenton, New Jersey: 1865.

This brief memoir is notable for its lack of bitterness and its unusally comprehensive entries.

2974. Francis, David W. "The United States Navy and the Johnson's Island Conspiracy: The Case of John C. Carter." NW OHIO Q, 52 [1980]: 229-243.

John C. Carter was a Union naval officer who violated his orders and pursued a group of conspirators involved in a plot to escape from Johnson's Island prison in 1864. This action ended Carter's active naval career.

2975. Futch, Ovid L. HISTORY OF ANDERSONVILLE PRISON. Gainesville: University of Florida Press, 1968.

The most thorough examination of the infamous Confederate prison, in which the author does not put the entire blame for the tragedy on General Winder and Captain Wirz. However, they might have handled the situation in a better fashion.

2976. Harding, George C. "Prison Life at Camp Pratt." Arthur W. Bergeron, Jr., editor. LA HIS, 14 [1973]: 386-391.

Article contains excerpts from Harding's memoirs dealing with his six-week imprisonment in Louisiana.

2977. Haviland, Thomas P. "A Brief Diary of Imprisonment." VA MHB, 50 [1942]: 230-237.

Haviland, an officer of the 12th Massachusetts, was captured at Second Bull Run and remained a prisoner for a month. He kept a diary during his brief incarceration.

2978. Hesseltine, William B., editor. CIVIL WAR PRISONS. Kent, Ohio: Kent State University Press, 1962.

A collection of eight essays reprinted from CIVIL WAR HISTORY. Prisons covered are Andersonville, Fort Warren, Libby, Elmira, Rock Island, Johnson's Island, and Charleston. Hesseltine has written an excellent introduction to the topic.

2979. ———. CIVIL WAR PRISONS: A STUDY IN WAR PSYCHOLOGY. Columbus: Ohio State University Press, 1930.

In this excellent discussion of military prisons, the author concerns himself with war psychosis and the prisoner exchange controversy. No doubt the best book on the subject.

2980. ———. "Military Prisons of St. Louis, 1861-1865." MO HIS R, 23 [1929]: 380-399.

A scholarly article dealing chiefly with the Gratiot Street Prison.

2981. ———. "The Underground Railroad from Confederate Prisons to East Tennessee." E TENN HIS SOC PUB, 2 [1930]: 55-69.

Some Union soldiers did manage to escape from southern prisons and make their way north. They were aided by the "Sons of America" which was formed to aid Union men as well as by Negros who provided food, clothing, and shelter.

2982. Holmes, Clayton W. THE ELMIRA PRISON CAMP. New York, 1912.

This older work attempts to explain away southern arguments of mistreatment at Elmira prison, by placing the blame on homesickness and climate.

2983. Howard, Harlan S. "Prisoner of the Confederates: Diary of a Union Artilleryman." Warren A. Jennings, editor. W VA HIS, 36 [1975]: 309-323.

Howard tells of his capture at Chickamauga, his imprisonment at Libby, and his escape through West Virginia to Union lines.

2984. Jordon, Phillip D. "Yankee Sailor in Dixieland Jails." PALIMP, 54 [1973]: 2-10.

Recounts the tale of George Collier Remey and his experiences in southern jails after his capture at Fort Sumter.

2985. Kaufold, John. "The Elmira Observatory." CWTI, 16 [4] [1977]: 30-35.

Not only was the Elmira, New York, prison crowded and lice-infested, but some enterprising capitalist built an observation tower adjacent to the camp in 1864. For a nominal fee, sight-seers could observe the prisoners while enjoying refreshments.

2986. Keen, Nancy T. "Confederate Prisoners of War at Fort Delaware." DEL HIS, 13 [1968]: 1-27.

The author based her research on prisoners' accounts. She suggests that Fort Delaware had a reputation as a death trap and was feared above all other Union prison camps.

2987. King, G. Wayne. "Death Camp at Florence." CWTI, 12 [8] [1974]: 34-42; [9] [1974]: 34-74.

Conditions were deplorable at Camp Florence. Eventually in February 1865, the Confederates paroled all the sick prisoners.

2988. King, John R. MY EXPERIENCE IN THE CONFEDERATE ARMY AND IN NORTHERN PRISONS. Clarksburg, West Virginia: United Daughters of the Confederacy, 1917.

Directed toward a popular audience, this memoir concerns life spent in Elmira and Point Lookout prisons.

2989. Kowalewski, John A. "Capt. Mlotkowski of Ft. Delaware." POL AM STUD, 23 [1966]: 89-92.

Diary of an officer of a Pennsylvania artillery unit, which policed the prison camp at Fort Delaware. Mlotkowski was well-regarded by both the prisoners and his own men.

2990. Kurnat, Alan A. "Prison Life at Johnson's Island." WEST RES MAG, [September-October 1981]: 30-34.

A well-written, popular account of the camp established on Johnson's Island in Sandusky Bay, Ohio, for Confederate officers. This prison had the lowest mortality rate of all federal prisons.

2991. Lawrence, F. Lee. CAMP FORD C.S.A. Austin: Texas Civil War Centennial Advisory Committee, 1964.

Based on primary source materials, this is a useful record of Union prisoners in Texas.

2992. Long, E.B. "Camp Douglas: 'A Hellish Den'?" CHI HIS, 1 [1970]: 83-95.

While it was certainly not the best Civil War prison camp and probably was not the worst, Camp Douglas, on Chicago's south side, was not a pleasant place for a southern soldier. Over 30,000 Confederates were imprisoned there, of whom 4,454 died.

2993. Lupold, Harry F. "A Union Medical Officer Views the 'Texians.'" SW HIS Q, 77 [1974]: 481-486.

Letters of an Ohio doctor who was captured during the 1864 Red River Campaign and held prisoner for six weeks.

2994. Mallinson, David L. "The Andersonville Raiders." CWTI 10 [4] [1971]: 24-31.

The "raiders," composed largely of New York bounty jumpers, were as great a threat to the other prisoners as starvation and disease. Eventually they were seized, tried, and six of them were hanged.

2995. Maul, David T. "Five Butternut Yankees." JISHS, 56 [1963]: 177-192.

Members of the Irish Brigade were assigned to guard duty at a camp for Confederate prisoners.

2996. McCaffrey, James M. "The Palmyra Massacre." CWTI, 19 [8] [1980]: 38-43.

Federal General John McNeil ordered the execution of ten Confederate prisoners at Palmyra, Missouri, in October 1862, for questionable Confederate crimes against a Unionist.

2997. McElroy, John. THIS WAS ANDERSONVILLE. Roy Meredith, editor. Bonanza Books, 1957.

The best known work about the horrors of Andersonville, written by a survivor, a member of the 16th Illinois Cavalry. McElroy paints Andersonville as a monstrous tragedy of human depravity. This classic has appeared in several editions.

2998. Mitchell, Leon, Jr. "Camp Ford, Confederate Military Prison." SW HIS Q, 66 [1962-1963]: 1-16.

A description of Camp Ford, a Confederate prison, which was in operation from November 1863 to May 1865, near Tyler, Texas. Over 5,300 federal prisoners were held in this camp, 286 of that number dying.

2999. Monaghan, Jay. "How a Yankee Soldier, Mistaken for the Devil, Escaped From Andersonville Prison." LIN HER, 74 [1972]: 89-91.

An amusing story of a tunnel escape. The prisoners eventually broke through the middle of a campfire, but managed to succeed by playing on the superstitions of a young Confederate soldier.

3000. Moore, Hugh. "Illinois Commentary: A Reminiscence of Confederate Prison Life." Clifford A. Haka, editor. JISHS, 65 [1972]: 451-461.

A colorful account of daily life as well as crime among the prisoners at Andersonville and Florence, South Carolina.

3001. Morseberger, Robert E. and Katherine M. Morseberger. "After Andersonville: The First War Crimes Trial." CWTI, 13 [4] [1974]: 30-41.

A description of the trial of Captain Henry Wirz, commander of Andersonville prison. Wirz is viewed sympathetically and it is suggested that the real culprit was General Winder.

3002. Neal, Harry E. "Rebels, Ropes and Reprieves." CWTI, 14 [10] [1976]: 30-35.

A tale of life in Libby Prison.

3003. Newsome, Edmund. EXPERIENCE IN THE WAR OF THE GREAT REBELLION. Carbondale, Illinois: 1879.

Author details his life in the prisons at Macon, Savannah, Charleston, and Columbia.

3004. Page, James M. THE TRUE STORY OF ANDERSONVILLE PRISON. New York, 1908.

An unusual defense of the Confederates and Wirz by a Michigan cavalry officer who had been imprisoned at Andersonville.

3005. Patterson, Edmund D. YANKEE REBEL: THE CIVIL WAR JOURNAL OF EDMUND DEWITT PATTERSON. John G. Barrett, editor. Chapel Hill: University of North Carolina Press, 1966.

A well-edited edition of an intriguing and highly quotable diary of an Ohioan, who went south as a teenager and became a devoted Confederate. Captured at Gettysburg as a member of the 9th Alabama, he was imprisoned at Johnson's Island. He was visited there by members of an unforgiving family, who did very little to ease his plight.

3006. Perry-Mosher, Kate E. "The Rock Island P.O.W. Camp." CWTI, 8 [4] [1969]: 28-36.

Known as a "Rebel" to prison authorities, Kate Perry-Mosher still managed to provide clothing and tobacco to Confederates in the Rock Island prison. She also established a communications underground and assisted in several escapes.

3007. Putnam, George H. "A Soldier's Narrative of Life at Libby and Danville Prisons. THE OUTLOOK, [March 25, 1911]: 695-704.

An interesting condensation of Major Putnam's account of his life in Libby and Danville prisons during the last year of war.

3008. Ransom, John. JOHN RANSOM'S DIARY. Philadelphia, 1883. Reprint 1963.

A gripping account of life and death at Andersonville by one of its survivors.

3009. Robertson, James I., Jr. "Houses of Horror: Danville's Civil War Prisons." VA MHB, 69 [1961]: 329-345.

Six prisons for federal captives were established in Danville, Virginia, in the fall of 1863. This account, drawn from diaries of Union prisoners, reveals that the prisons were poor to begin with and got progressively worse.

3010. ———. "Old Capitol: Eminence to Infamy." MD HIS MAG, 65 [1970]: 394-412.

Once the home of Congress, later a school and a hotel, "Old Capitol" was converted to a prison in 1861. Known as "The Bastille," it housed both military and political offenders of the North and South.

3011. Ross, Charles. "Diary of Charles Ross 1863." VT HIS, 31 [1963]: 4-64.

The diary of a Vermont soldier who was captured near Petersburg, Virginia. He was later paroled from Andersonville in time for Thanksgiving at home.

3012. Schmitt, Frederick E. "Prisoner of War, Experiences in Southern Prisons." John P. Hunter, editor. WIS MAG HIS, 42 [1958-1959]: 83-93.

The author, a private in the 3rd New Jersey Cavalry, was captured at Ream's Station in June 1864 and spent time in Libby Prison.

3013. Sedgwick, Arthur G. "Libby Prison: The Civil War Diary of Arthur G. Sedgwick." William M. Armstrong, editor. VA MHB, 71 [1963]: 449-460.

The diary of a young lieutenant, fresh from Harvard, who was captured in late July 1864, is the basis for this account of life in Libby Prison.

3014. Shatzel, Albert H. "Imprisoned at Andersonville: The Diary of Albert Harry Shatzel...." Donald F. Danker, editor. NEB HIS, 38 [1957]: 81-125.

Captured in the Wilderness, Shatzel, a private in the 1st Vermont Cavalry, was in Andersonville from May 23 until September 12, 1864. He made daily entries in his diary.

3015. Shewmon, Joe. "The Amazing Ordeal of Pvt. Joe Shewmon." CWTI, 1 [1] [1962]: 45-50.

Author's story of his captures, imprisonments, and escapes, which reveal how his resourcefulness permitted him to survive.

3016. Shriver, Philip R. OHIO'S MILITARY PRISONS IN THE CIVIL WAR. Columbus: Ohio State University Press, 1964.

Another in the series published by the Ohio Civil War Centennial Commission, this is a readable, scholarly view of Camp Chase in Columbus and Johnson's Island in Lake Erie.

3017. Speer, William H. "A Confederate Soldier's View of Johnson's Island Prison." James B. Murphy, editor. OHIO HIS, 79 [1970]: 101-111.

An interesting, but biased account by a North Carolina officer of life on Johnson's Island. In the early years of the war, this was one of the best-managed prisons, thus Speer's complaints are not entirely justified.

3018. Stephens, Alexander H. RECOLLECTIONS OF ALEXANDER H. STEPHENS. Myrta Lockett Avary, editor. New York, 1910.

Some reflections on prison life at Fort Warren, Boston Harbor, 1865, by the Confederate vice-president.

3019. Sterns, Amos E. THE CIVIL WAR DIARY OF AMOS E STERNS, A PRISONER AT ANDERSONVILLE. Leon Basile, editor. Madison, New Jersey: Fairleigh Dickinson University Press, 1981.

A member of the 25th Massachusetts, Sterns was captured in Virginia in May 1864. He blamed the hardships he endured on the war itself rather than evil prison authorities.

3020. Stortz, John. "Experiences of a Prisoner During the Civil War In and Out of the Hands of the Rebels." ANN IOWA, 37 [1964]: 167-194.

Stortz describes his capture, Andersonville, his escape, and the long road back to Union lines.

3021. Sunseri, Alvin R. "Transient Prisoner: The Reminiscences of William H. Gilbert." JISHS, 74 [1981]: 41-50.

Gilbert served with the Chicago Zouaves of the 19th Illinois. He spent seventeen months in prisons at Atlanta, Libby, Pemberton, Andersonville, Charleston, and Florence before his escape on February 22, 1865.

3022. Sweet, A. Porter. "From Libby to Liberty." MIL R, 51 [4] [1971]: 63-70.

Describes the escape attempts of Colonel Thomas E. Rose and 100 soldiers from Libby prison. A day-by-day progress of the escape plan is detailed.

3023. Tuttle, James G. "Recollections of the Civil War." MICH HIS, 31 [1947]: 287-300.

Tuttle was captured near Fairfax Courthouse shortly after the Battle of Bull Run. His recollections concern his stay in various southern prisons and his attempts to escape.

3024. Walker, Theodore R. "Rock Island Prison Barracks." CWH, 8 [1962]: 152-163.

After news of Andersonville got out the situation of the Confederate prisoners became worse.. This prison was the most western of the camps, located on Rock Island in the Mississippi, between Davenport, Iowa, and Moline, Illinois.

3025. Welles, James M. "Tunneling Out of Libby Prison." McCLURE'S MAG, 22 [1902]: 317-326.

Welles tells the story of his imprisonment and daring escape.

3026. White, Raymond D. "Colonel John A. Fite's Letters From Prison." TENN HIS Q, 32 [1973]: 140-147.

This is another account of life in the Union prison camp on Johnson's Island, Sandusky, Ohio.

3027. Wilkins, William D. "Forgotten in the 'Black Hole': A Diary From Libby Prison." CWTI, 15 [3] [1976]: 36-44.

Captain Wilkins was captured at the battle of Cedar Mountain. He, in common with all of "Pope's men" suffered unusually harsh treatment at Libby prison. Journal is articulate and detailed.

3028. Winchell, James. "Wounded and a Prisoner: A First Person Account." CWTI, 4 [5] [1965]: 20-25.

A member of Berdan's 1st U.S. Sharpshooters recalls the medical treatment he received while a prisoner of war.

3029. Winslow, Hattie Lou. CAMP MORTON, 1861-1865. Indianapolis: Indiana HIstorical Society, 1940.

This detailed study is a must for anyone interested in prison camp life at this Indianapolis prison.

I. SPIES AND INTELLIGENCE

3030. Bakeless, John. "Catching Harry Gilmore." CWTI, 10 [1] [1971]: 34-40.

Union Major Harry Young finally snared Confederate spy Harry Gilmore in 1865.

3031. ———. "Lincoln's Private Eye." CWTI, 14 [6] [1975]: 22-30.

The story of William Alvin Lloyd.

3032. ———. "The Mystery of Appomattox." CWTI, 9 [3] [1970]: 18-32.

Major Harry Young and his men played havoc with retreating Confederate forces. By using real or forged telegrams they gained the provisions intended for Lee's forces at Amelia Court House. This may have contributed to the reasons for Lee's surrender.

3033. Baker, Lafayette C. HISTORY OF THE UNITED STATES SECRET SERVICE. Philadelphia, 1867.

A big volume which relates the experiences of General Lafayette Baker, who headed the wartime "Bureau of the National Detective Police." Baker was involved in tracking down spies, conspirators, and bounty jumpers, in the investigation of government departments, and in the capture of John Wilkes Booth. He tells many extravagant stories, some of which historians are inclined to question.

3034. Beymer, William G. ON HAZARDOUS SERVICE; SCOUTS AND SPIES OF THE NORTH AND SOUTH. New York, 1912.

Colorful tales and adventure stories of spies.

3035. Blanton, Margaret G. "Moment of Truth for a Spy." CWTI, 6 [6] [1967]: 2 -23.

Details some of the exploits of three members of "Coleman's Scouts," a federal espionage group.

3036. Boyd, Belle. BELLE BOYD IN CAMP AND PRISON. Curtis C. Davis, editor. New York: Yoseloff, 1968.

A well-edited edition of Belle Boyd's spy memoir, first published in London in 1865. Belle, who served the confederacy with some success, turns out to be not as great a spy as she thought she was.

3037. Brandt, Nat. "New York is Worth Twenty Richmonds." AM HER, 22 [6] [1971]: 74-80. 106-107.

A review of the unsuccessful Confederate plot to burn down New York City in November 1864.

3038. Brockett, Linus P. SCOUTS, SPIES, AND HEROES OF THE GREAT CIVIL WAR. Jersey City, New Jersey: 1892.

A typical "popular" spy book "with songs ... anecdotes ... witty sayings...."

3039. Brown, Spencer K. SPENCER KELLOGG BROWN, HIS LIFE IN KANSAS AND HIS DEATH AS A SPY, 1842-1863.... George G. Smith, editor. New York, 1903.

The edited diary of a very young secret service agent.

3040. Castel, Albert. "Samuel Ruth: Union Spy." CWTI, 14 [10] [1976]: 36-44.

A discussion of Ruth's espionage career and his work on the Richmond, Fredericksburg and Potomac Railroad.

3041. Davis, Curtis C. "The Civil War's Most Over-Rated Spy." W VA HIS, 27 [1965]: 1-9.

Belle Boyd was a colorful and interesting individual, but her work as a spy has been greatly over-rated.

3042. ———. "Companions of Crisis: The Spy Memoir as a Social Document." CWH, 10 [1964]: 385-400.

Analyzes nineteen autobiographies and five biographies and concludes that the "spy memoir" was dull and overly romantic.

3043. Dayton, Ruth W. "The Death of a Famous Spy." AMER, 7 [February 1912]: 154-157.

Traces briefly the career of Pryce Lewis one of the first Union spies. He served under Pinkerton.

3044. Downs, Edward C. FOUR YEARS A SCOUT AND SPY, "GENERAL BUNKER," ONE OF LIEUT. GENERAL GRANT'S MOST DARING AND SUCCESSFUL SCOUTS.... Zanesville, Ohio: 1866.

The highly colorful tale of the author's four years in service.

3045. Ellis, Daniel. THRILLING ADVENTURES OF DANIEL ELLIS, THE GREAT UNION GUIDE OF EAST TENNESSEE.... New York, 1867.

Another overly romantic tale, but a good account of East Tennessee and the divisions within the region.

3046. Fishel, Edwin C. "The Mythology of Civil War Intelligence." CWH, 10 [1964]: 344-367.

Debunks seven myths, derived from improbable spy memoirs, about Civil War "intelligence."

3047. Foster, G.A. THE EYES AND EARS OF THE CIVIL WAR. New York: Criterion Books, 1964.

A brief description of intelligence work during the war with sidelights on communication and observation activity.

3048. ———. "John Scobell, Union Spy in the Civil War...." EBONY, 19 [2] [1963]: 135-138.

Scobell, a freed slave, was one of the few black "full fledged spys." Pinkerton discovered him among the "contrabands."

3049. ———. "The Woman Who Saved the Union Navy." EBONY, 19 [1964]: 48-50.

Mary Louvestre, talented slave seamstress in Norfolk, in an incredible happenstance, copied plans for the renovation of the VIRGINIA into the ironclad MERRIMAC.

3050. Johns, George S. PHILIP HENSON, THE SOUTHERN UNION SPY.... St. Louis, Missouri: 1887.

Although a Union spy, Henson frequently furnished harmless information to the Confederacy. He was "born, reared, and married in the south," and retired to Mississippi.

3051. Kane, Harnett T. SPIES FOR THE BLUE AND GRAY. Garden City, New York: Hanover House, 1954.

This well known writer has written a lively book in which he discusses all of the better known spies of the war.

3052. Kerby, Joseph O. THE BOY SPY: A SUBSTANTIALLY TRUE RECORD OF EVENTS DURING THE WAR OF THE REBELLION. Chicago, 1889.

An exaggerated account, primarily for younger readers.

3053. Kurtz, Wilburg G. "A Federal Spy in Atlanta." ATL HIS BULL, 30 [December 1957]: 13-20.

The story of J. Milton Glass, who spent most of the war years in Atlanta spying for the Union.

3054. Miller, Robert R. "Placido Vega: A Mexican Secret Agent in the United States, 1864-1866." THE AMERICAS, 19 [1962]: 137-148.

General Vega was sent to the United States to secure arms and munitions for Juarez's revolutionary cause in Mexico. In his 28 months in the country he spent over $600,000 for military and propaganda purposes.

3055. Mogelever, Jacob. DEATH TO TRAITORS; THE STORY OF LAFAYETTE C. BAKER.... Garden City, New York: Doubleday, 1960.

An uneven biography of an uneven man.

3056. O'Donnell, J.H. "The 'Accidental' Explosion at City Point, August 9, 1864." VA MHB, 72 [1964]: 356-360.

Deals with the successful effort of Confederate secret service agent John Maxwell to blow up a Union ammunition dump on the James River in August 1864.

3057. Orrmont, Arthur. MR. LINCOLN'S MASTER SPY: LAFAYETTE BAKER. New York: Messner, 1966.

Lafayette Baker, the famous wartime figure but almost forgotten by later generations is dealt with very sympathetically in this biography. A controversial figure, he is given the benefit of the doubt on all matters.

3058. Pike, James. THE SCOUT AND RANGER; BEING THE PERSONAL ADVENTURES OF CORPORAL PIKE, OF THE FOURTH OHIO CAVALRY. Cincinnati, Ohio: 1865.

Prior to the war Pike served as a ranger in Texas. During the war he served under several Union generals. Good reading.

3059. Pinkerton, Allan. THE SPY OF THE REBELLION; BEING A TRUE HISTORY OF THE SPY SYSTEM OF THE UNITED STATES ARMY DURING THE LATE REBELLION.... New York, 1883.

The story of the Secret Service department under McClellan, Pinkerton's own story as one of the top agents, and the stories of other agents. All somewhat exaggerated, no doubt.

3060. Richman, Irwin. "Pauline Cushman: A Personality Profile." CWTI, 7 [10] [1969]: 38-44.

A brief account of "the lady spy of the Cumberland."

3061. Robbins, Peggy. "Allen Pinkerton's Southern Assignment." CWTI, 15 [9] [1977]: 44-47.

Pinkerton, using the name E.J. Allen of Augusta, Georgia, traveled into the Deep South to ascertain the general feelings of the populace. He returned north with much useful information.

3062. Sabine, David B., "Pinkerton's 'Operative': Timothy Webster." CWTI, 12 [5] [1973]:: 32-38.

The story of a Union secret service agent who was eventually caught and executed as a military spy by the Confederates.

3063. Steere, Edward. "Catalyst of Victory." ARMY INFO DIG, 16 [8] [1961]: 90-99.

An account of a number of successes and failures of Civil War intelligence systems. Intelligence was gathered chiefly by the cavalry, spies, and a careful reading of the enemy press.

3064. Stern, Philip Van Doren. SECRET MISSIONS OF THE CIVIL WAR.... Chicago: Rand McNally, 1959.

A collection of accounts of Civil War events "woven into a continuous narrative."

3065. Stone, Louis P. "I Was Completely Surrounded by a Band of Guerrillas." CWTI, 10 [8] [1971]: 26-33.

A report of the author's intelligence operations for the Union in 1862 and his subsequent capture in the Shenandoah Valley.

3066. Stuart, Meriwether. "Operations Sanders: Wherein Old Friends and Ardent Pro-Southerns Prove to be Union Secret Agents." VA MHB, 81 [1973]: 157-199.

The plans to capture George Sanders, a Confederate agent attempting to secure British aid, failed.

3067. Turney, Catherine. "Crazy Betty." MANKIND, 3 [3] [1971]: 58-64.

Elizabeth Van Lew, living in a Richmond mansion, spied for the Union during the war.

3068. Weinert, Richard P., "Federal Spies in Richmond." CWTI, 3 [10] [1965]: 28-34.

Details the activities of Union agents in the Confederate capital.

3069. Young, Henry H. THE CAMPAIGN LIFE OF LT. COLONEL HENRY HARRISON YOUNG.... Providence, Rhode Island: 1882.

Young was an aide to General Sheridan and his chief scout. This work is a brief account of his war experiences.

3070. ———. COLONEL HENRY H. YOUNG IN THE CIVIL WAR. Providence, Rhode Island: 1910.

An even briefer account of Young's wartime record.

J. MEDICAL

3071. Adams, George W. DOCTORS IN BLUE: THE MEDICAL HISTORY OF THE UNION ARMY IN THE CIVIL WAR. New York: Henry Schuman, 1952.

An excellent work based on primary sources. It covers the entire medical field from ambulances and administration to nursing and treatments.

3072. Bacon, Cyrus, Jr. "The Daily Register of Dr. Cyrus Bacon, Jr.; Care of the Wounded at the Battle of Gettysburg." Walter M. Whitehouse and Frank Whitehouse, Jr., editors. MICH ACA, 8 [1976]: 373-386.

Dr. Bacon was stationed at a field hospital on the Taneytown road, southeast of Little Round Top. He comments articulately on almost everything.

3073. ———. "A Michigan Surgeon at Chancellorsville One Hundred Years Ago." Frank Whitehouse, Jr. and Walter M. Whitehouse, editors. UNIV MICH MED BULL, 29 [1963]: 315-331.

Here again the author presents a clear, informative picture of battlefield medicine.

3074. Baird, Nancy D. "The Yellow Fever Plot." CWTI, 13 [7] [1974]: 16-23.

Describes the alleged plot by Dr. Luke Pryor Blackburn to introduce yellow fever into northern cities by means of contaminated clothing. The charges were never proven. He later became governor of Kentucky and was known as the "Good Samaritan."

3075. Barton, Thomas D. AUTOBIOGRAPHY, INCLUDING A HISTORY OF THE FOURTH REGIMENT, WEST VA. VOL. INFANTRY.... Charleston, West Virginia: 1890.

Deals briefly with medical treatment in the field.

3076. Baxter, J.H., compiler. STATISTICS, MEDICAL AND ANTHROPOLOGICAL OF THE PROVOST-MARSHAL-GENERAL'S BUREAU. 2 v. Washington, D.C.: 1875.

Includes 100 reports about the health of draftees and volunteers from enrollment board surgeons. Volume two consists of elaborate statistical charts drawn from data in Volume one.

3077. Bickel, R.J. "The Estes House." ANN IOWA, 60 [1970]: 427-444.

The account of a military hospital in Keokuk, Iowa.

3078. Billings, John S. "A Billings Manuscript of Civil War Recollections: An Evening on a Hospital Boat...." NY PUB LIB BULL, 69 [1965]: 307-313.

Billings was one of the first medical men to volunteer in 1861. This is a sketch of a journey from City Point, Virginia, to Washington D.C. on a hospital boat on a night in August 1864, just after the battle at Petersburg.

3079. Breeden, James O. "A Medical History of the Later Stages of the Atlanta Campaign." JSH, 75 [1969]: 31-59.

A statistical and descriptive analysis of the heavy inroads made on the armies of both Sherman and Hood by injury and disease.

3080. Brieger, Gert H. "Therapeutic Conflicts and the American Medical Profession in the 1860's." HIS MED BULL, 41 [1967]: 215-222.

A discussion of the controversy which followed the May 1863 order from Surgeon General William A. Hammond which forbade the use of calomel and tartar emetic by army doctors in the field.

3081. Brinton, Daniel G. "From Chancellorsville to Gettysburg: A Doctor's Diary." D.G. Brinton Thompson, editor. PA MHB, 89 [1965]: 292-315.

Dr. Brinton, Chief Surgeon, Eleventh Corps of the Army of the Potomac, was a witness to the crushing of Howard at Chancellorsville and the heavy fighting on the first day from Cemetery Ridge at Gettysburg.

3082. ———. "Dr. Daniel Garrison Brinton with the Army of the Cumberland." D. G. Brinton Thompson, editor. PA MHB, 90 [1966]: 466-490.

After Gettysburg, Brinton was transferred to the western theater and observed the fighting around Chattanooga.

3083. Brinton, John H. PERSONAL MEMOIRS OF JOHN H. BRINTON, MAJOR AND SURGEON U.S.V., 1861-1865. New York, 1914.

The celebrated surgeon and scholar presents a good insight into medical practices during the war.

3084. Brooks, Stewart. CIVIL WAR MEDICINE. n.p.: C.C. Thomas, 1966.

Although brief, this study is very useful to an understanding of the subject. Good photos, fast-moving narrative covering all aspects of medicine.

3085. Burr, Bell, compiler. MEDICAL HISTORY OF MICHIGAN. 2 v. Minneapolis, Minnesota: Bruce Publishing, 1930.

Contains brief biographical sketches and notes on the Civil War medical records of Michigan men who served in the Medical Corps.

3086. Burton, Elijah P. DIARY OF E.P. BURTON, SURGEON.... Des Moines, Iowa: The Historical Records Survey, 1939.

A mimeographed project by the W.P.A.

3087. Carrigan, Jo Ann. "Yankees Versus Yellow Jack in New Orleans, 1862-1865." CWH, 9 [1963]: 248-260.

Describes how yellow fever was controlled following the federal occupation of New Orleans in 1862. General Ben Butler is praised for his work.

3088. Clements, Bennett A. MEMOIR OF JONATHAN LETTERMAN. New York, 1883.

The record of the Medical Director of the Army of the Potomac is praised.

3089. Conn, Granville P. HISTORY OF THE NEW HAMPSHIRE SURGEONS IN THE WAR OF THE REBELLION. Concord, New Hampshire: 1906.

Brief biographical sketches of surgeons serving in New Hampshire regiments.

3090. Cunningham, Horace H. FIELD MEDICAL SERVICES AT THE BATTLES OF MANASSAS [BULL RUN]. Athens, Georgia: University of Georgia Press, 1968.

A study of the ineffective Union and Confederate ambulance services, field hospitals, and treatment of casualties at 1st and 2nd Bull Run and how this led to reforms in the North but not in the South. A medical history of more than average interest to even a lay reader.

3091. De Channal, General. "Good Order and Cleanliness: A French Report on Federal Hospitals." CWTI, 6 [6] [1967]: 40-44.

Excerpts of a report by General Du Channal of the French army, on conditions observed in the Union army in 1863 and 1864.

3092. Diffenbaugh, Willis G. "Military Surgery in the Civil War." MIL MED, 130 [1965]: 490-496.

This discussion of the most prevalent types of wounds and how they affected different parts of the body is accompanied by several revealing drawings.

3093. DiMeglio, John E. "Calamity and Sanitation: Medical Affairs In the Union in the Early War Years." SOC STUD, 65 [2] [1974]: 75-82.

Unhealthy sanitary conditions in Union military camps were studied by a commission and, as a result, a military policy on medicine and sanitation slowly improved.

3094. Duncan, Louis C. THE MEDICAL DEPARTMENT OF THE UNITED STATES ARMY IN THE CIVIL WAR. Washington, D.C.: n.d.

Only the Army of the Potomac is covered in this series of magazine articles which were reprinted in book form. Duncan was an officer in the Medical Corps.

3095. Farmer, Phoebe W. "Military Medicine in Occupied New Orleans, 1863." Edward McMillan, editor. LA HIS, 8 [1967]: 198-204.

A letter by Phoebe W. Farmer, who served as a volunteer nurse in the Union hospitals in New Orleans. She severely criticized the medical care and sanitary conditions in the hospitals.

3096. Flint, Austin, editor. CONTRIBUTIONS RELATING TO THE CAUSATION AND PREVENTION OF DISEASE AND TO CAMP DISEASES.... New York, 1867.

Published by the United States Sanitary Commission, this report includes a study of the diseases contracted by the Andersonville prisoners.

3097. Freeman, Julia S. THE BOYS IN WHITE; THE EXPERIENCE OF A HOSPITAL AGENT IN AND AROUND WASHINGTON. New York, 1870.

Federal hospital life is depicted very clearly.

3098. Fuller, William. "Many ... Diseases Are ... Feined." Albert Castel, editor. CWTI, 16 [5] [1977]: 29-32.

Surgeon Fuller wrote an article in 1864 on the prevalence and nature of fake illnesses and injuries employed by soldiers to win a discharge.

3099. Gill, John C. "An Ohio Doctor Views Campaigning on the White River, 1864." Harry F. Lupold, editor. ARK HIS Q, 34 [1975]: 333-351.

Dr. Gill, with an Ohio infantry regiment, wrote letters discussing troop movements, family matters, life in service, the White River region, a need for money and clothing, medical affairs, and Confederate guerrilla resistance.

3100. ———. "A Union Medical Officer Views the 'Texans.'" Harry F. Lupold, editor. SW HIS Q, 77 [1974]: 481-486.

Dr. John C. Gill, a Cleveland surgeon, wrote a series of

letters home as a Confederate prisoner of war after the abortive Red River campaign. Gill was held captive six weeks and left some interesting observations of his Texan captors.

3101. ———. "A Union Surgeon Views the War From Kentucky, 1862." Harry F. Lupold, editor. KY HIS SOC REG, 72 [1974]: 272-275.

A letter from a Cleveland, Ohio, surgeon describing his experiences while campaigning with the 65th Ohio in Kentucky in March 1862.

3102. Grace, William. THE ARMY SURGEON'S MANUAL, FOR THE USE OF MEDICAL OFFICERS, CADETS, CHAPLAINS, AND HOSPITAL STEWARDS.... New York, 1865.

Contains all the general orders from the War Department and the regulations of the Medical Department.

3103. Hammond, William A., editor. MILITARY MEDICAL AND SURGICAL ESSAYS.... Philadelphia, 1864.

Prepared for the United States Sanitary Commission, this set of essays depicts the state of medicine during the war.

3104. ———. A STATEMENT OF THE CAUSES WHICH LED TO THE DISMISSAL OF SURGEON-GENERAL WILLIAM A. HAMMOND FROM THE ARMY.... New York, 1864.

The surgeon-general was dismissed from service in August 1864 for irregularities in liquor contracts. He was vindicated and restored to rank of Brigadier General in 1879. After the war he was prominent in research on nervous disorders.

3105. Harrison, Dr. Samuel A. "The Civil War Diary of Dr. Samuel A. Harrison." Charles A. Wagandt, editor. CWH, 13 [1967]: 131-146.

Excerpts from the journal of a Maryland doctor who supported the Union, but resided among many secessionists.

3106. Heaton, Leonard D. and Joe M. Blumberg. "Lt. Colonel Joseph J. Woodward [1833-1884]: U.S. Army Pathologist-Researcher-Photomicroscopist." MIL MED, 131 [1966]: 530-538.

Dr. Joseph Woodward, a medical pioneer, was the first person to develop the technique of photomicrography for medical purposes during the war. He also played an important part in developing the Army Medical Museum.

3107. HOSPITAL DIRECTORIES OF THE CIVIL WAR 1862-1865. Boston: G.K. Hall, 1962.

A reproduction of the United States Sanitary Commission records. Lists all hospitalized soldiers from all branches of service--by state and by regiment.

3108. Jarche, Saul. "Edwin Stanton and American Medicine." HIS MED BULL, 45 [1971]: 153-158.

For various reasons Secretary of War Stanton was somewhat hostile to the operations of the Army Medical Corps. The conflict between the two lasted through most of the war.

3109. Johnson, Charles B. MUSKETS AND MEDICINE.... Philadelphia: F.A. Davis, 1917.

Recollections of hospital service with the 130th Illinois.

3110. Jones, Gordon W. "The Medical History of the Fredericksburg Campaign: Course and Significance." J HIS MED ALL SCI, 18 [1963]: 241-256.

A study of the medical history of the battle of Fredericksburg, a turning point in the care of the wounded.

3111. ———. "Sanitation in the Civil War." CWTI, 5 [7] [1966]: 12-18.

The article surveys the problems of mass hygiene. A study of Civil War medicine is a study of men's resistance to infection. Many illnesses and resultant deaths were caused by the lack of cleanliness in camps and hospitals.

3112. ———. "Sheridan's Medical Service in the Shenandoah." CWTI, 3 [5] [1964]: 16-21.

Surgeon James T. Ghiselin organized the medical services in the Shenandoah Valley. His first problem was the correction of inefficient handling of the wounded.

3113. ———. "Wartime Surgery." CWTI, 2 [2] [1963]: 7-9, 28-30.

"The American Civil War was a medical hell." During the four years of war, only a few advances were made in the medical field.

3114. Jordan, Philip D. "The Career of Henry M. Farr, Civil War Surgeon." ANN IOWA, 44 [3] [1978]: 191-211.

As surgeon with the 25th Iowa volunteer infantry, Farr participated in campaigns in Tennessee and in the march on Atlanta. He describes the day-to-day routine of army surgeons during the war.

3115. Kennedy, Gerald. "U.S. Army Hospital: Keokuk, 1862-1865." ANN IOWA, 42 [1962]: 118-136.

Article describes all aspects of wartime operations, medical services, patients served, and routines at the army hospital in Keokuk, Iowa.

3116. Key, Jack D. "U.S. Army Medical Department and Civil War Medicine." MIL MED, 133 [1968]: 181-192.

The Army Medical Department was totally unprepared to handle the demands made on it with the outbreak of the Civil War. Through the efforts of Surgeon-General William A. Hammond and Medical Director of the Army of the Potomac Jonathan Letterman, many administrative and organizational changes were made, greatly improving the department's operations.

3117. Letterman, Jonathan. MEDICAL RECOLLECTIONS OF THE ARMY OF THE POTOMAC. New York, 1866.

Dr. Letterman was medical director of the Army of the Potomac. The memoirs of this outstanding medical innovator are both interesting and informative.

3118. Lewis, John B. "Reminiscences of a Civil War Surgeon, John B. Lewis." Stanley B. Weld and David A. Soakis, editors. J HIS MED ALL SCI, 21 [1] [1966]: 47-58.

Reminiscences of Dr. Lewis, a Connecticut surgeon. He describes the unpreparedness of the nation as a whole in 1861 and attributes the high mortality rate to inadequate facilities.

3119. Lind, John Y. "The Civil War Letters of John Young Lind." Willard Wight, editor. J PRES HIS SOC, [June 1961].

Some inspired letters written by a U.S. Army surgeon.

3120. Margreiter, John L., Jr. "Anesthesia in the Civil War." CWTI, 6 [2] [1967]: 22-25.

Chloroform and ether were the most common anesthetics used during the war. A sampling shows the death rate was 5.4 per thousand for chloroform and 3.0 per thousand for ether.

3121. Mayer, Nathan. "A Connecticut Surgeon in the Civil War: The Reminiscences of Dr. Nathan Mayer." J HIS MED ALL SCI, 19 [1964]: 272-286.

Dr. Mayer served as a medical officer in the Union army. He wrote his memoirs some forty years later.

3122. Oblensky, Florence E. "Jonathan Letterman, 11 Dec. 1824-15 March, 1872." MIL MED, 133 [1968]: 312-315.

A brief account of the life of the medical director of the Army of the Potomac.

3123. Olmsted, Frederick L. compiler. HOSPITAL TRANSPORTS. Boston, 1863.

Provides a vivid description of the tragedy involved in the embarkation of the wounded during the Peninsular Campaign.

3124. Ordronaux, John. MANUAL OF INSTRUCTIONS FOR MILITARY SURGEONS, ON THE EXAMINATION OF RECRUITS AND DISCHARGE OF SOLDIERS. New York, 1863.

Includes the official regulations of the Provost Marshal General's bureau regarding requirements for discharge of recruits.

3125. Otis, George A. ... REPORTS ON THE EXTENT AND NATURE OF MATERIALS AVAILABLE FOR THE PREPARATION OF A MEDICAL AND SURGICAL HISTORY OF THE REBELLION. Philadelphia, 1865.

Printed for the surgeon general's office, contains a list of the many records available.

3126. Patten, James C. "An Indiana Doctor Marches with Sherman: The Diary of James Comfort Patten." Robert G. Athearn, editor. IND MAG HIS, 49 [1953]: 405-422.

Good descriptions by an observant and articulate writer who did not like the southern climate, cavalry, or "institutions."

3127. Perry, John G. LETTERS FROM A SURGEON OF THE CIVIL WAR.... Martha D. Perry, compiler. Boston, 1906.

Describes hospital service in Virginia.

3128. Plaisance, Aloyius F. and Leo F. Schelver, III. "Federal Military Hospitals in Nashville, May and June 1863." TENN HIS Q, 29 [1970]: 166-175.

With the occupation of Nashville and heavy fighting in the area, the city soon became a major supply base and hospital center. Comfortable quarters were provided.

3129. Redding, Joseph S. and John C. Matthews. "Anesthesia During the American Civil War." CLINICAL ANESTHESIA, 11 [1968]: 1-18.

A discussion of the various types of anesthesia used during the war, chloroform and ether being the most popular.

3130. Reed, William H. HOSPITAL LIFE IN THE ARMY OF THE POTOMAC. Boston, 1866.

An excellent work for information on hospitals, patient care, as well as army life.

3131. Reedy, Michael J. "Army Doctor: Four Short Term Chiefs." MIL MED, 132 [1967]: 188-194.

Deals primarily with Clement Alexander Finley, Surgeon General of the United States from May 15, 1861 to April 14, 1862.

3132. Rein, David M. "S. Weir Mitchell, Pioneer Psychiatrist in the Civil War." TOPIC, 2 [Fall 1961]: 65-71.

This pioneer concentrated on wounds of the nerves during the war. He worked on the boundary line between physiology and psychology. After the war, Mitchell established what was probably the first clinic for nervous disorders in the country.

3133. Shands, A.R., Jr. "William Ludwig Detmold: America's First Orthopaedic Surgeon." MIL MED, 133 [1968]: 563-569.

The German-born Detmold played an important role in the Federal Army Medical Services in the first year of the war. He was an expert amputator, removing 75 limbs on the day after First Bull Run. He developed an eating knife for one-armed men. He later became a professor at Columbia's College of Physicians and Surgeons.

3134. Shryock, Richard H. THE DEVELOPMENT OF MODERN MEDICINE: AN INTERPRETATION OF THE SOCIAL AND SCIENTIFIC FACTORS INVOLVED. Philadelphia: University of Pennsylvania Press, 1936.

Of immense interest to anyone who wants a better understanding of the role of medicine in society.

3135. ———. "A Medical Perspective of the Civil War." AQ, 14 [1962]: 161-173.

Writing during the Civil War Centennial, the author suggests there might not be so much celebrating if one took into account the thousands of lives lost because of the primitive state of medical science.

3136. Smith, George W. MEDICINES FOR THE UNION ARMY.... Madison, Wisconsin: American Institute for the History of Pharmacy, 1962.

Discusses the army's efforts to make the much needed drugs required in the hospitals. Also concentrates on the laboratories at Astoria and Philadelphia. A knowledge of pharmacology would be helpful for the reader.

3137. Steiner, Paul E. PHYSICIAN-GENERALS IN THE CIVIL WAR; A STUDY IN NINETEENTH MID-CENTURY AMERICAN MEDICINE. Springfield, Illinois: C.C. Thomas, 1966.

Discusses medicine and also sketches the lives of 33 generals "who relinquished medical careers for field commands." Good bibliography.

3138. ———. DISEASE IN THE CIVIL WAR: NATURAL BIOLOGICAL WARFARE IN 1861-1865. Springfield, Illinois: C.C. Thomas, 1968.

An account of the effects of disease on eight major battles, noting the inferior state of medical science at the time. More deaths were caused by disease than by enemy fire.

3139. ———. MEDICAL-MILITARY PORTRAITS OF UNION AND CONFEDERATE GENERALS. Philadelphia: Whitmore, 1968.

A pathologist examines the medical history of ten Union and Confederate generals, attempting to show how their ailments effected the course of the war. While Steiner's review of their military careers is traditional, his probing into their medical records breaks new ground.

3140. Stevenson, Benjamin F. LETTERS FROM THE ARMY. Cincinnati, Ohio: 1884.

This surgeon served with the 22nd Kentucky, primarily in Mississippi and Louisiana.

3141. Stinson, Byron. "'The Army Disease.'" A HIS ILL, 6 [8] [1971]: 10-17.

Soluble morphine and the hypodermic syringe together served as the panacea for the sick and injured during the Civil War. The morphine was used for everything from severe injuries to pleurisy. The result of such wholesale "giving" was drug addiction for many.

3142. ———. "'Battle Fatigue' and How It Was Treated in the Civil War." CWTI, 4 [7] [1965]: 40-44.

Psychiatric casualties of the war are discussed and the methods used to cure and prevent recurrence are described.

3143. ———. "Scurvy in the Civil War." CWTI, 5 [5] [1966]: 20-25.

A description of the frequency and treatment of scurvy in the Union army and among Union prisoners of war.

3144. Thrall, Seneca E. "An Iowa Doctor in Blue: The Letters of Seneca E. Thrall." Mildred Throne, editor. IOWA J HIS, 58 [1960]: 97-188.

The letters of a doctor in the 13th Iowa.

3145. Trowbridge, Silas T. "Saving a General." CWTI, 11 [4] [1972]: 20-25.

Excerpts from the autobiography of Dr. Trowbridge telling how his treatment saved Union General Richard James Ogelsby, wounded at Corinth, Mississippi.

3146. Turner, William. "Diary of W. W. Turner, D.C., 1863." Mildred Throne, editor. IOWA J HIS, 48 [1950]: 267-282.

Dr. William H. Turner kept a detailed diary from March to May 1863, while he served aboard the CITY OF MEMPHIS, a hospital ship handling sick and wounded troops fighting in the Vicksburg Campaign.

3147. U.S. Surgeon-General's Office. THE MEDICAL AND SURGICAL HISTORY OF THE WAR OF THE REBELLION. 3 v. Washington, D.C.: 1870-1888.

Statistical reports on diseases and casualties of the war.

3148. U.S. Sanitary Commission. SURGICAL MEMOIRS OF THE WAR OF THE REBELLION. 2 v. New York: 1870-1871.

A study of surgical procedures.

3149. ———. MILITARY, MEDICAL AND SURGICAL ESSAYS PREPARED FOR THE UNITED STATES SANITARY COMMISSION. 1863-1864. Washington, D.C.: 1865.

Covers all aspects of the medical side of the war.

3150. Vickery, Richard. "On the Duties of the Surgeon in Action: Surgeon Richard Vickery...." Albert Castel, editor. CWTI, 17 [3] [1978]: 12-23.

Vickery left medical school at the University of Michigan to enlist in the "hospital corps" of the 2nd Michigan. He returned to school in 1864.

3151. Watson, William. LETTERS OF A CIVIL WAR SURGEON. Paul Fatout, editor. West Lafayette, Indiana: n.p., 1961.

A slim volume of letters written by the surgeon of the 105th Pennsylvania.

3152. Whitman, Walt. THE WOUND DRESSER. Richard M. Bucke, editor. New York: Bodley Press, 1949.

This collection of newspaper articles and letters to his mother provides a unique personal account of life in northern military hospitals where Whitman served as a volunteer nurse. While the letters tend to be self-promoting, they nonetheless capture the pathos of the scene and also record Whitman's response to major wartime events.

IV

NAVY

By Fraser G. MacHaffie

The Union navy has already attracted the attention of bibliographers. The work of Myron J. Smith, Jr., AMERICAN CIVIL WAR NAVIES: A BIBLIOGRAPHY [1972], has the navy as its sole focus while the two-volume CIVIL WAR BOOKS: A CRITICAL BIBLIOGRAPHY [1967-1969], edited by Nevins, Robertson and Wiley, has a section by Thomas Wells, "The Navies." Seeing no need to reinvent the wheel, I have concentrated on recent articles and monographs while including representative items already covered by either Smith or Wells.

With several exceptions, it is hoped that all aspects of the Union navy's involvement is covered. For the most part, I have avoided nineteenth century citations. I have also not used foreign titles or manuscript collections. Lastly, references to blacks serving in the navy will not be found here, but rather in the section on BLACKS AND EMANCIPATION.

Journals which continue to include occasional articles on the Union navy and which deserve watching are CIVIL WAR HISTORY, CIVIL WAR TIMES ILLUSTRATED and the UNITED STATES NAVAL INSTITUTE PROCEEDINGS.

3153. Adams, Scarritt. "The Miracle That Saved the Union." AM HER, 27 [1] [1975]: 73-78.

An illustrated account of engineer John Ericsson's remarkable work of launching his MONITOR within 101 days of receiving the go-ahead from the Union Navy's Ironclad Board.

3154. Adams, W.T. "The Birth of the Aircraft Carrier." US NAV INST PROC, 93 [1967]: 162-163.

Adams sees the balloon ship as the precursor of aircraft carriers, in this survey of the work of balloonists J. LaMountain and Thaddeus S.C. Lowe. The potential of "Chief Aeronaut" Lowe's balloon corps was not recognized; it collapsed after Lowe's resignation in May 1862.

3155. ———. "RED ROVER: First Hospital Ship of the U.S. Navy." US NAV INST PROC, 94 [1968]: 149-151.

This ship was captured in April 1862 and converted to a hospital ship to attend the needs of the sick and wounded on the

Western Gunboat Flotilla ships. Its staff included Sisters of the Holy Cross and other female nurses.

3156. Anderson, Bern. BY SEA AND BY RIVER: THE NAVAL HISTORY OF THE CIVIL WAR. New York: Knopf, 1962.

Author discusses operations on the Gulf, the Mississippi River and its tributaries, the blockade, and the naval action on the coasts of Virginia and the Carolinas. He sees the blockade as the most important contribution of the Union navy. The book has an emphasis on strategy with personalities and anecdotes kept to a minimum.

3157. Anderson, Stuart. "1861: Blockade vs. Closing the Confederate Ports." MIL AFF, 41 [1977]: 190-194.

An analysis of Lincoln's decision to blockade the Confederate ports, rather than close them. The probable unfriendly reaction in Britain and France were the prime considerations.

3158. Baxter, James P., III. INTRODUCTION OF THE IRONCLAD WARSHIP. Cambridge: Harvard University Press, 1933.

A good discussion of the changes in naval architecture during the war and beyond.

3159. Bearss, Edwin C. HARDLUCK IRONCLAD: THE SINKING AND SALVAGE OF THE CAIRO. Baton Rouge: Louisiana State University Press, 1966.

The ironclad CAIRO was sunk in the Yazoo River near Vicksburg, Mississippi, on December 12, 1862. Her remains were located in 1956 and salvage operations commenced in 1963. The article describes the construction and operations of the ship, as well as the problems of raising it and what to do with it once it was raised.

3160. ———. "The Ironclads at Fort Donelson." KY HIS SOC REG, 74 [1976]: 1-9, 73-84, 167-191.

The quick success of the ironclads at Fort Henry was not repeated at Fort Donelson. The primary reason was the higher elevation of the Confederate guns. Author gives a detailed account from both sides of the engagement.

3161. Besse, Sumner B. C.S. IRONCLAD VIRGINIA AND U.S. IRONCLAD MONITOR, WITH DATA AND REFERENCES FOR SCALE MODELS. Newport News, Virginia: Mariners Museum, 1978.

A reprint of two booklets originally published in 1936 and 1937. It contains a brief history, illustrations and plans of both craft, written with model builders in mind.

3162. Bolander, Louis H. "The ALLIGATOR, First Federal Submarine of the Civil War." US NAV INST PROC, 44 [1938]: 844-854.

An account of the engineer-inventor de Villeroi's first and second submarines, the latter becoming known as the ALLIGATOR while in Union service. The vessel disappeared on April 2, 1863, when a tow rope parted off Cape Hatteras.

3163. Boyer, Samuel P. NAVAL SURGEON: THE DIARY OF DR. SAMUEL PELLMAN BOYER. Elinor and James A. Barnes, editors. Bloomington: Indiana University Press, 1963.

Dr. Boyer served as medical officer on the U.S.S. FERNANDINA and the U.S.S. MATTABASSET. He spent several years with the blockading squadron off the South Atlantic coast. Diary contains interesting material on medical practices of the day.

3164. Boynton, Charles B. THE HISTORY OF THE NAVY DURING THE REBELLION. 2 v. New York, 1867-1868.

For many years this work was considered one of the best accounts of naval action in the war, although it has since been superceded.

Brother, Charles. [See number 3252]

3165. Browne, Henry R. and Symmes E. Browne. FROM FRESH WATER NAVY, 1861-1864: THE LETTERS OF ACTING MASTER'S MATE HENRY R. BROWNE AND ACTING ENSIGN SYMMES E. BROWNE. John D. Milligan, editor. Annapolis: United States Naval Institute, 1970.

These letters, written while the two brothers were serving on western waters, cover the entire span of the war. Among the events described are the expeditions against Vicksburg and the disastrous Red River expedition.

3166. Bruzek, Joseph C. "The U.S. Schooner Yacht 'AMERICA.'" US NAV INST PROC, 93 [1967]: 159-187.

An account of the performance of the AMERICA, with particular emphasis on her service with the Union navy during the war.

3167. Buhl, Lance C. "Mariners and Machines: Resistance to Technological Change in the American Navy, 1865-1869." JAH, 61 [1974]: 703-727.

Author develops the thesis found in Elting E. Morison, MEN, MACHINES, AND MODERN TIMES, where the resistance to change is described as purely psychological or intellectual. He examines the heated debates over technological change and status among engineers and between engineers and line officers that followed the ending of the war.

3168. Burns, Zed H. "Ship Island: An Annotated Bibliography." J MISS HIS, 33 [1970]: 147-151.

Brief notes on 38 government, newspaper, and secondary sources concerning Ship Island, Mississippi.

3169. Burpo, Robert S. "Notes on the First Fleet Engagement in the Civil War." AM NEP, 19 [1959]: 265-273.

A description of the largest gunboat engagement to this time, May 10, 1862. It took place at Plum Point [Fort Pillow] on the Mississippi River.

3170. Callahan, Edward W. LIST OF OFFICERS OF THE NAVY OF THE UNITED STATES AND OF THE MARINE CORPS FROM 1775 TO 1900. New York: Haskell House, 1969.

3171. Canfield, Eugene B. CIVIL WAR NAVAL ORDNANCE. Washington, D.C.: Navy Department, 1969.

This 24-page booklet discusses the contributions of Ulric Dahlgren, Robert Parrott, and J.M. Brooke to Union navy ordnance. It is well illustrated with diagrams, several from the 1866 Ordnance Manual. Tables give specifics for various guns.

3172. ———. NOTES ON NAVAL ORDNANCE OF THE AMERICAN CIVIL WAR, 1861-1865. Washington, D.C.: American Ordnance Association, 1960.

3173. ———. "Porter's Mortar Schooners." CWTI, 6 [6] [1967]: 28-36.

Commander David D. Porter sought to destroy Forts Jackson and St. Philip, guarding the mouth of the Mississippi River, with a flotilla of 21 mortar schooners in April 1862. Success would open a clear route for Farragut to move against New Orleans. In the five-day engagement, Porter's mortars failed to do the job, but Farragut got through anyhow.

3174. Carrison, Daniel J. THE NAVY FROM WOOD TO STEEL, 1860-1890. New York: Franklin Watts, 1965.

Largely an uncritical account of the Union navy's role in the Civil War.

3175. Carse, Robert. BLOCKADE: THE CIVIL WAR AT SEA. New York: Rinehart, 1958.

A rather pedestrian study with more of the focus on indiviuals than the general effect of the blockade itself.

3176. Christley, James L. "The ALLIGATOR: The North's Underwater Threat, A Product of One Man's Imagination." CWTI, 19 [10] [1981]: 26-31.

A brief history of the ALLIGATOR, a 45-foot submarine, built to the design of French engineer Brutus DeVilleroi. The craft was built in Philadelphia, but no use could be found for it. It sank off the Carolina coast in April 1863.

3177. Church, Frank L. CIVIL WAR MARINE: A DIARY OF THE RED RIVER EXPEDITION, 1864. James P. Jones and Edward F. Keuchel, editors. Washington, D.C.: U.S. Marine Corps, 1975.

One of the few sources on the service by marines in the war. The journal of Second Lieutenant Church covers the spring of 1864 when he was commander of the marine guard participating in the Red River expedition.

3178. Coggins, Jack. "Civil War Naval Ordnance." CWTI, 4 [7] [1965]: 16-20.

A description of gunnery techniques during the war. The ordnance developed at the time foreshadowed that of modern naval warfare.

3179. ———. "New Guns and Projectiles Ended the Reign of Wooden Warships." CWTI, 4 [6] [1965]: 22-25.

An account of the development and characteristics of naval ordnance. Types of cannon, carriages, projectiles, detonators, propellants, and fuses are discussed.

3180. Crandall, Warren D. and Isaac D. Newall. HISTORY OF THE RAM FLEET AND THE MISSISSIPPI MARINE BRIGADE IN THE WAR FOR THE UNION AND THE MISSISSIPPI AND ITS TRIBUTARIES: THE STORY OF THE ELLETS AND THEIR MEN. St. Louis, Missouri: 1907.

This detailed account was penned by two participants in the events described. Extensive use is made of official correspondence, which shows, for example, the energy of Charles Ellet, Jr. in building the ram fleet and the problems caused by the unwillingness of the fleet commander to cooperate with this unconventional force. The second part of the volume describes the establishment of the Mississippi Marine Brigade and concludes with 250 portraits of officers and men of the brigade.

3181. Currie, George E. WARFARE ALONG THE MISSISSIPPI: THE LETTERS OF LIEUTENANT COLONEL GEORGE E. CURRIE. Norman E. Clarke, Sr., editor. Mount Pleasant, Michigan: Central Michigan University Press, 1961.

Currie served with the Marine Ram Brigade on the Mississippi River and wrote twelve detailed letters about his experiences.

3182. Dalzell, George W. THE FLIGHT FROM THE FLAG. Chapel Hill: University of North Carolina Press, 1940.

Author explores a somewhat neglected topic, the Confederate attacks on the North's merchant marine and the consequences for the Union.

3183. Davis, William C. DUEL BETWEEN THE FIRST IRONCLADS. Garden City, New York: Doubleday, 1975. Reprint 1981.

An excellent account in which the salvage of the MERRIMAC and its conversion to the VIRGINIA is recounted alongside the planning and building of the MONITOR. A nice blending of technical material and personal accounts. The book also considers the consequences for naval architecture flowing from the engagement between the two vessels.

3184. DICTIONARY OF AMERICAN NAVAL FIGHTING SHIPS. 8 v. Washington, D.C.: Navy Department, 1963-1983.

Union navy vessels are included in this massive compilation.

3185. Dillon, John F. "The Role of Riverine Warfare in the Civil War." NAV WAR COLL R, 25 [1973]: 58-78.

A discussion of the importance of inland naval campaigning--"riverine warfare"--to federal success in the Civil War. Growing out of the needs of the moment, the collaboration between Union military and naval forces on the Mississippi hastened northern victory.

3186. Dufour, Charles L. THE NIGHT THE WAR WAS LOST. Garden City, New York: Doubleday, 1960.

A solid study of Farragut's running the forts on the lower Mississippi, which led to the federal capture of New Orleans. This is viewed as a critical setback for the Confederates.

3187. Edge, Frederick M. AN ENGLISHMAN'S VIEW OF THE BATTLE BETWEEN THE ALABAMA AND THE KEARSARGE: AN ACCOUNT OF THE NAVAL ENGAGEMENT IN THE BRITISH CHANNEL ON SUNDAY, JUNE 19, 1864. New York, 1864.

A 47-page booklet containing eyewitness accounts from officers of both ships, as well as extracts from the log of the KEARSARGE. Author concludes that the Union victory was due to superior gun power.

3188. Ely, Robert B. "This Filthy Ironpot." AM HER, 19 [2] [1968]: 108-111.

The author was an officer on the U.S.S. MANHATTAN, a monitor which participated in the Battle of Mobile Bay. His journal contains useful social commentary about life aboard a war vessel--the eccentricities of officers and men, their complaints, joys, and their reactions to life on an almost uninhabitable vessel.

3189. Falero, Frank. "Naval Engagements in Tampa Bay, 1862." FLA HIS Q, 46 [1967]: 134-140.

Three naval clashes occurred in Tampa Bay during the war.

3190. Fessenden, B.L. "The Yankee Clipper and the Cape Cod Boy." AM NEP, 23 [1963]: 264-269.

An account of two voyages made by the author, who commanded the clipper ship JACOB BELL. The vessel was seized and burned by the Confederate raider FLORIDA in February 1863.

3191. Foote, Shelby. "DuPont Storms Charleston." AM HER, 14 [4] [1963]: 23-24, 89-92.

An account of the failure of Union ironclads to successfully assault Charleston, South Carolina in April 1863.

3192. Gilbert, Benjamin F. "Lincoln's Far Eastern Navy." JW, 8 [1969]: 355-368.

In the summer of 1863 a demonstration of naval power was staged by western nations including the United States off the coast of Japan, during which various Japanese ships, land batteries, and the city of Kagoshima were heavily damaged.

3193. Goldberg, Mitchell S. "A Federal Navy Raid Into Galveston Harbor, November 7-8, 1861: What Really Happened?" SW HIS Q, 76 [1972]: 58-70.

Article contains three letters discussing the northern blockade of Confederate ports.

3194. ———. "Naval Operations of the United States Pacific Squadron in 1861." AM NEP, 33 [1973]: 41-51.

Of the six federal naval squadrons operating away from the east coast in 1861, only the Pacific Squadron remained on station. A major concern was the safety of gold shipments from California to the Isthmus of Panama en route to the northeast.

3195. Goodman, Richard F. "Yankee Paymaster." Robert J. Plumb, editor. US NAV INST PROC, 103 [1977]: 50-57.

In February 1864 Richard French Goodman was appointed acting assistant paymaster and saw service on the NIGHTINGALE and MIAMI. Extracts from his journal relate his impressions, experiences, and some candid comments on his accounting ability--he was five dollars short at the end of the first day.

3196. Gordon, Arthur. "The Great Stone Fleet: Calculated Catastrophe." US NAV INST PROC, 94 [1968]: 72-82.

In the winter of 1861-1862, before the Union blockade had become effective, an attempt to block the approaches to Charleston and Savannah was made by a fleet of 45 old whaling ships loaded with stones. A miserable failure, the episode only further strained Anglo-American relations, already in a bad way because of the TRENT affair.

3197. Gosnell, H. Allen. GUNS ON THE WESTERN WATERS: THE STORY OF RIVER GUNBOATS IN THE CIVIL WAR. Baton Rouge: Louisiana State University Press, 1949.

A fairly good, though undocumented account of this important phase of the naval war. Extensive use is made of eyewitness observations, some not readily available elsewhere. An introductory section discusses naval science, marine engines, ordnance, and gunnery.

3198. Greene, S. Dana. "'I Fired the First Gun and Thus Commenced the Great Battle.'" AM HER, 8 [4] [1957]: 10-13, 102-105.

A letter home from a sailor who took part in the MONITOR-MERRIMAC duel.

3199. Haberlein, Charles R., Jr. "Damn the Torpedoes." In THE IMAGE OF WAR, 1861-1865: Volume 6, THE END OF AN ERA, pp. 86-121. Garden City, New York: Doubleday, 1984.

A brief but detailed and lively account of Admiral David G. Farragut's celebrated assault at Mobile Bay in August 1864. Although the city remained in Confederate hands until almost the war's end, its value to the South was gone. The operation demonstrated the importance of the new ironclads and the benefits of joint army-navy operations.

3200. Hanford, Franklin. "How I Entered the Navy." US NAV INST PROC, 91 [1965]: 75-87.

Memoir of a recent United States Naval Academy midshipman, who entered the navy in 1862. Hanford later became a rear admiral.

3201. Hart, John E. "Commanding the U.S.S. ALBATROSS." CWTI, 15 [4] [1976]: 28-35.

This letter from the commander of the ALBATROSS to his wife provides an insight into the daily life and loneliness aboard the vessel.

3202. Hayes, John D. "Sea Power in the Civil War." US NAV INST PROC, 87 [1961]: 60-69.

Initially, the Civil War was expected to be fought on land. This was not the case, and the article discusses the emerging strategic value of the navy. However, the author may be going too far when he claims, "In the end, sea power prevailed and brought about the downfall of the Confederacy."

3203. Heffernan, John D. "The Blockade of the Southern Confederacy: 1861-1865." SMITH J HIS, 11 [1967/1968]: 23-44.

Heffernan is critical of the navy department's handling of the blockade, arguing that more might have been achieved had attention been paid to the opinions of those on the spot, such as Farragut and DuPont.

3204. Heitzman, William R. "The Ironclad WEEHAWKEN in the Civil War." AM NEP, 42 [1982]: 193-202.

A well-researched account of the brief life of this coastal

monitor. Under the command of Captain [later Rear Admiral] John Rodgers, the WEEHAWKEN participated in the attack on Fort Sumter in April 1863 and the capture of the Confederate raider ATLANTA in June 1863. It sank on December 6, 1863.

3205. Hoehling, A.A. THUNDER AT HAMPTON ROADS. Englewood Cliffs: Prentice-Hall, 1976.

A detailed reconstruction of the two day battle between the MONITOR and the MERRIMAC. Maritime and shipping problems of both the Union and the Confederacy are discussed. The final chapter tells the story of the discovery of the sunken wreck of the MONITOR and the up-to-date techniques employed in the search.

3206. Horstman, Ronald. "The Loss of Government Greenbacks on the Steamer RUTH." MO HIS R, 70 [1975]: 87-89.

Built in 1862, the RUTH was used as a transport for Union forces in the West. On August 4, 1863, while loaded with over 200 passengers and carrying $2,600,000 in greenbacks to pay Grant's troops, it was set fire by a Confederate agent near Cairo, Illinois. The ship burned and sank with the loss of practically everyone on board.

3207. Huffstot, Robert D. "The CARONDELET." CWTI, 6 [5] [1967]: 5-11, 46-48.

The CARONDELET was a Union ironclad that ran the Confederate batteries at Island Number 10 to shield federal troops crossing near that point. Its action compelled the Confederates to withdraw.

3208. Hunt. Aurora. "The Civil War on the Western Seaboard." CWH, 9 [1963]: 178-186.

At the outbreak of war, the Union's Pacific Squadron consisted of six small wooden vessels. But in 1863, when a Confederate privateer, J.M. CHAPMAN, planned to seize one of the Pacific mail steamers with its cargo of gold, it was captured by the Pacific Squadron as it sailed mischief-bent from San Francisco.

3209. Johnson, Ludwell H. "A Campaign That Failed." In THE IMAGE OF WAR, 1861-1865: Volume 5, THE SOUTH BESIEGED, pp. 346-377. Garden City, New York: Doubleday, 1983.

An account of the unsuccessful Union Red River Campaign of March-April, 1864. The article deals with the battle between Banks and Taylor, but also describes the retreat of Admiral Porter's Mississippi Squadron back down the river.

3210. Johnson, Robert E. "Investment By Sea: The Civil War Blockade." AM NEP, 32 [1972]: 45-57.

The Union blockade was very successful, although it was plagued by a shortage of men and ships.

3211. Jones, Virgil C. "The Battle of Galveston Harbor." CWTI, 5 [10] [1967]: 28-38.

An account of a coordinated land and sea attack on New Year's Day, 1863, by Confederate forces which temporarily broke the Union blockade of the island port. For the Federals, it was "the most disgraceful affair that has occurred to our navy."

3212. ———. THE CIVIL WAR AT SEA. 3 v. New York: Holt, Rinehart, and Winston, 1960-1962.

One reviewer wrote of this trilogy, "Generally sound as history, but above all, is readable." Author concentrates on overall planning and strategy. The set remains an excellent, detailed survey of the naval aspects of the war.

3213. ———. "The Navies Begin: Improvisation and Innovative Technology Clash on the Water." In THE IMAGE OF WAR, 1861-1865: Volume 1, SHADOWS OF THE STORM, pp. 217-263. Garden City, New York: Doubleday, 1981.

This article examines the development of both the Union and Confederate navies from the outbreak of the war up to the capture of Fort Clark, Fort Hatteras, and Port Royal.

3214. ———. "Preparation Paid Off For Farragut At Mobile Bay." CWTI, 3 [2] [1964]: 6-13, 28-31.

A sketch of the Union admiral.

3215. ———. "'We Are Useless': Mr. Lincoln's Blockade." CWTI, 10 [8] [1971]: 10-24.

Describes the frustration of the sailors and officers with the almost impossible task of blockading 3,500 miles of coastline. The Union did not have enough ships and the blockade runners of the Confederacy proved themselves to be both creative and inventive.

3216. Jones, Virgil C. and Harold L. Peterson. THE STORY OF A CIVIL WAR GUNBOAT, U.S.S. CAIRO, COMPRISING "A NARRATIVE OF HER WARTIME ADVENTURES".... Washington: National Park Service, 1971.

James B. Eads built a fleet of ironclads for the Mississippi River, including the CAIRO. It took part in engagements at Fort Pillow and Memphis, but was sunk on the Yazoo in December 1862. Located in 1956 the wreck was raised in 1964.

3217. Kaplan, Hymen R. "The U.S. Coast Guard and the Civil War." US NAV INST PROC, 86 [1960]: 40-50.

The author traces the record of the Coast Guard during the war.

3218. Keeler, William F. ABOARD THE U.S.S. FLORIDA: THE LETTERS OF

PAYMASTER WILLIAM FREDERICK KEELER, U.S. NAVY, TO HIS WIFE, ANNA. Annapolis, Maryland: United States Naval Institute, 1968.

A well-edited collection of lively letters describing service with the federal blockading squadron off Wilmington, North Carolina.

3219. Kemp, Daniel F. "Gunboat War at Vicksburg." John D. Milligan, editor. AM HER, 29 [5] [1978]: 62-67.

Kemp was a gun crew member of the U.S.S. CINCINNATI, which served in western waters. In his memoirs, written in 1927, he described Steele's Bayou Expedition as "one of the great mistakes of the Civil War." Kemp participated in the attack on Vicksburg during which the CINCINNATI was sunk.

3220. Kenney, Edward C. "From the Log of the RED ROVER, 1861-1865: A History of the First United States Navy Hospital Ship." MO HIS R, 10 [1965]: 31-49.

The RED ROVER was a captured vessel which was re-outfitted as a summer hospital ship. It provided accommodations for nearly 2,500 patients.

3221. Knapp, David, Jr. "The Rodney Church Incident." J MISS HIS, 32 [1970]: 245-249.

A short account of the activities of the Union vessel RATTLER in Arkansas and Mississippi waters from November 1862 to September 1863.

3222. Laas, Virginia J. "Sleepless Sentinels: The North Atlantic Blockading Squadron, 1863-1864." CWH, 31 [1985]: 24-38.

Central focus is on Rear Admiral Samuel Phillips Lee, commander of the squadron from July 1862. The author discusses the evolution of the blockading strategy and includes a useful discussion of adjudication of prizes and the distribution of prize money.

3223. LIST OF LOGBOOKS OF UNITED STATES NAVY SHIPS, STATIONS, AND MISCELLANEOUS UNITS, 1801-1947. Washington, D.C.: National Archives and Records Service, 1978.

This publication includes many logbooks of Union ships.

3224. Long, E.B. "Plum Run Bend: The Forgotten Battle." CWTI, 11 [3] [1972]: 4-11, 40-45.

This engagement on May 10, 1862, is described by the author as "one of the two largest fleet actions by gunboats on rivers in the entire history of warfare."

Lonn, Ella. FOREIGNERS IN THE UNION ARMY AND NAVY. [See number 5377].

3225. MacBride, Robert. CIVIL WAR IRONCLADS: THE DAWN OF NAVAL ARMOR. Philadelphia: Chilton, 1962.

This is a ship-by-ship survey of the ironclads in both Union and Confederate navies. The writer is a commercial artist and the book contains many fine drawings.

3226. Macartney, Clarence E. MR. LINCOLN'S ADMIRALS. New York: Funk and Wagnalls, 1956.

Useful sketches of a dozen or so Civil War naval figures, intended for the general reader.

3227. Marchand, John B. CHARLESTON BLOCKADE: THE JOURNALS OF JOHN B. MARCHAND, U.S. NAVY, 1861-1862. Craig L. Symonds, editor. Newport, Rhode Island: Naval War College Press, 1976.

Marchand commanded the U.S.S. JAMES ADGER and for a time was senior officer of the blockading squadron off Charleston.

3228. McArthur, Henry S. "A Yank at Sabine Pass." CWTI, 12 [8] [1973]: 38-43.

Author was a member of the 75th New York which was assigned to the gunboat CLIFTON when it attacked Sabine Pass, September 7-8, 1863. The attack failed and McArthur was captured.

3229. McCordock, Robert S. THE YANKEE CHEESE BOX. Philadelphia: Dorrance, 1938.

An account of the MONITOR and MERRIMAC. Drawing largely on the OFFICIAL RECORDS, newspapers, and private correspondence, the author discusses the construction of the two vessels, the battle, and the subsequent scramble to build ironclads.

3230. McCormack, John F., Jr. "Sabine Pass." CWTI, 12 [8] [1973]: 4-9, 34-37.

An account of the unsuccessful Union gunboat assault on Fort Griffin at Sabine Pass, Texas, September 7-8, 1863.

3231. Melton, Maurice. "From Vicksburg to Port Hudson: Porter's River Campaign." CWTI, 12 [10] [1974]: 26-37.

A description of Admiral David Porter's campaign along the lower Mississippi in 1862.

3232. Merli, Frank J. "Squadron of the South." In THE IMAGE OF WAR: Volume 5, THE SOUTH BESEIGED, pp. 99-152. Garden City, New York: Doubleday, 1983.

A good overview of the work of the South Atlantic Blockading Squadron with useful descriptions of the capture of Fort Pulaski and the failure to take Fort Sumter and Charleston. Author wonders if the blockade along the South Atlantic coast was not a "waste of resources and opportunities." The Union ships could have been better employed in the Mississippi region.

3233. Merrill, James M. BATTLE FLAGS SOUTH: THE STORY OF THE CIVIL WAR NAVIES ON WESTERN WATERS. Rutherford, New Jersey: Fairleigh Dickinson University Press, 1970.

In this account of the struggle for control of the Mississippi and its tributaries, the author portrays forcefully the frustration of naval commanders on both sides, in trying to organize a freshwater navy with little cooperation or support from the distant bureaucracies. Not much analysis of strategy or policy.

3234. ———. "The Hatteras Expedition, August, 1861." NC HIS R, 29 [1952]: 204-219.

A combined Union army and navy force won an early victory for the North with the capture of Forts Clark and Hatteras along the North Carolina coast, in August 1861.

3235. ———. "Men, Monotony, and Mouldy Beans--Life on Board Civil War Blockaders." AM NEP, 16 [1956]: 49-59.

Making extensive use of contemporary correspondence and diaries, the author describes what conditions were like aboard the ships of the Union's blockading squadrons.

3236. ———. THE REBEL SHORE. Boston: Little, Brown, 1957.

One of the first attempts to give an account of the Union navy's affairs from the capture of Forts Clark and Hatteras onward. The book is written in an easy, popular style.

3237. ———. "Strangling the South." In THE IMAGE OF WAR, 1861-1865: Volume 3, THE EMBATTLED CONFEDERACY, pp. 102-183. Garden City, New York: Doubleday, 1982.

A good survey of the work of the North Atlantic Blockading Squadron. Action at Forts Clark, Hatteras, and Fisher is recounted, while a useful description may be found of the unsuccessful engagement at Drewry's Bluff when the Union navy attempted to reach Richmond. Merrill writes of the day-to-day blockading duty --the boredom and frustration as well as the prospect of prize money.

3238. ———. "Strategy Makers in the Union Navy Department, 1861-1865. MID AM, 44 [1962]: 19-32.

Gustavus Vasa Fox, Assistant Secretary of the Navy, is seen as the principal agent of change in taking the navy from wood and sail to iron and steam. If the author is correct, Fox's zeal for the single-handed success of the navy must have been a serious impediment to inter-service cooperation.

3239. ———. "Union Shipbuilding on Western Rivers During the Civil War." SMITH J HIS, 3 [1968/1969]: 17-44.

A well-documented and illustrated account of the work of a number of people in the purchase, conversion, and building of the Mississippi River flotilla of tinclads, ironclads, and rams based at Cairo, Illinois. The flotilla was very successful in preventing supplies from the trans-Mississippi West from reaching the Confederate armies, capturing Confederate forts, transporting troops, and destroying Confederate shipping on the Mississippi.

3240. Miller, Robert R. "The 'CAMANCHE': First Monitor of the Pacific." CAL HIS SOC Q, 45 [1966]: 113-124.

The problems of constructing an ironclad in San Francisco Bay and devising harbor defenses are analyzed.

3241. Milligan, John D. "Charles Ellet and His Naval Steam Ram." CWH, 9 [1963]: 121-132.

Secretary of War Stanton saw an opportunity to use Ellet's idea of a steam ram on the Mississippi where it was feared the Confederates were preparing ironclads. Though successful in an engagement with the Confederates at Memphis, the ram's importance declined with the improvement in gunnery capabilities.

3242. ———. GUNBOATS DOWN THE MISSISSIPPI. Annapolis, Maryland: United States Naval Institute, 1965.

A good account of the key role of the Union navy's Mississippi operations in bringing the river and its tributaries under federal control.

3243. Millis, Walter. "The Iron Sea Elephants." AM NEP, 10 [1950]: 15-32.

In reaction to the MONITOR-MERRIMAC clash, the Union ordered the construction of some 30 vessels designed on the MONITOR principle. Author describes the project and gives an overview of the MONITOR class ships.

3244. Minich, Rachael. "New York Ferryboats in the Union Navy." NY HIS SOC Q, 46 [1962]: 422-436; 47 [1963]: 173-219; 49 [1965]: 52-87.

Several ferryboats were purchased by the Union in the early desperate days of war. They served with some distinction in the Potomac flotilla and the various blockading squadrons, as their shallow draft and maneuverability proved assets.

3245. THE MONITOR, ITS MEANING AND FUTURE: PAPERS FROM A NATIONAL CONFERENCE. Washington, D.C.: Preservation Press, 1978.

A discussion of what should be done with the MONITOR, the wreck of which was found in 1973. Also a broader debate on the pros and cons of salvaging sunken Civil War ships.

3246. Nash, Howard P. "A Civil War Legend Examined." AM NEP, 23 [1963]: 197-203.

Author seeks to explode the legend that John Ericsson designed the MONITOR and rushed her to completion just in time to meet and defeat the MERRIMAC.

3247. ———. "The Ignominious Stone Fleet." CWTI, 3 [3] [1964]: 44-49.

An account of the unsuccessful effort to block the entrance to Charleston harbor by sinking an old ship loaded with stones.

3248. ———. A NAVAL HISTORY OF THE CIVIL WAR. New York: Barnes, 1972.

A general survey of the Union and Confederate navies, in which the author concludes that Union naval superiority won the war for the North. The biggest element in this was the success of the federal blockade of the South. A popular work, the book provides a good introduction to this aspect of the war.

3249. Newcomer, Lee N. "The Battle of the Rams." AM NEP, 25 [1965]: 128-139.

Naval war on the Mississippi in the spring of 1862 with the federal defeat at Plum Run Bend and federal victory at Memphis is recounted. Charles Ellet's rams are featured and the efforts of two of them at Memphis swung the balance of the battle to the Union's favor.

3250. Newton, John G. "How We Found the MONITOR." NG, 147 [1] [1975]: 48-61.

Tells of the discovery off Cape Hatteras in August 1973 of the remains of the gunboat MONITOR by a team from Duke University. Illustrated by a series of remarkable photographs taken in April 1974 by the United States Navy. The article also contains a brief history of the ship and its loss.

3251. Nichols, Sayres O. "Fighting in North Carolina Waters." Roy F. Nichols, editor. NC HIS R, 40 [1963]: 75-84.

Through the letters of 17-year-old Sayres Ogden Nichols, a surgeon's steward on the U.S.S. MIAMI, naval action along the North Carolina coast is depicted.

3252. O'Connell, John C. and Charles Brother. TWO NAVAL JOURNALS, 1864: THE JOURNAL OF MR. JOHN C. O'CONNELL, C.S.N., ON THE C.S.S. TENNESSEE AND THE JOURNAL OF PVT. CHARLES BROTHER, U.S.M.C., ON THE U.S.S. HARTFORD, AT THE BATTLE OF MOBILE BAY. C. Carter Smith, Jr., editor. Chicago: Wyvern Press, 1964. Reprint, 1969.

"Brother's Journal is the diary of a young New Yorker who served as a member of the United States Marine Guard aboard the U.S.S. HARTFORD."

OFFICIAL RECORDS OF THE UNION AND CONFEDERATE NAVIES IN THE WAR OF THE REBELLION. [See number 52]

3253. O'Flaherty, Daniel. "The Blockade That Failed." AM HER, 6 [5] [1955]: 36-41, 104-105.

Author discusses why he feels the northern blockade was not successful.

3254. Paist, Paul H. "The Keokuk Guns." US NAV INST PROC, 92 [1966]: 174-177.

An account of the problems overcome by Confederate engineers in salvaging two guns from the wreck of the KEOKUK, which sank in shallow water following the unsuccessful attack on Fort Sumter in April 1863.

3255. Parker, John C. "With Farragut at Port Hudson: First Person Account." CWTI, 7 [7] [1968]: 42-49.

The author was the executive officer of the ESSEX, the only ironclad in Farragut's little fleet.

3256. Paullin, Charles O. "President Lincoln and the Navy." AHR, 14 [1908/1909]: 284-303.

Author praises Lincoln for his able handling of naval matters at a time when a reevaluation in naval architecture was taking place and the navy was engaged in its most elaborate operations in history--the blockade.

3257. Peterkin, Ernest. "Building a Behemoth." CWTI, 20 [4] [1981]: 12-21.

The article covers the career of inventor John Ericsson and the building of the MONITOR.

3258. Porter, David D. THE NAVAL HISTORY OF THE CIVIL WAR. New York, 1886.

A massive history of the naval war as viewed by one of the North's most distinguished admirals. Most of the material is devoted to actions in which Porter himself participated.

3259. Pratt, Fletcher. CIVIL WAR ON WESTERN WATERS. New York: Henry Holt, 1956.

This book recounts the shipbuilding and amphibious operations undertaken by the Union navy, army, and Naval Brigade to regain control of the Mississippi and its tributaries. The inter-personal "chemistry" of Farragut and Davis, Porter and Sherman is discussed in a very folksy style.

3260. Pullar, Walter S. "Abe Lincoln's Brown Water Navy." NAV WAR COLL R, 21 [1969]: 71-88.

An account of the Mississippi Squadron. The poor state and performance of the Union navy in the early days of the war are attributed to the promotion system and long period of peace from 1812. Author concludes that the commanders in the Mississippi campaigning did better than the average.

3261. Rae, Thomas W. "The Little MONITOR Saved our Lives." A HIS ILL, 1 [4] [1966]: 32-39.

An eyewitness account of the confrontation between the U.S.S. MINNESOTA and the MERRIMAC, written by the third assistant engineer of the MINNESOTA.

3262. Ramseur, Stephen D. "'The Fight Between the Two Iron Monsters': The MONITOR Versus the VIRGINIA as Described By Major Stephen Dodson Ramseur, C.S.A." CWH, 30 [1984]: 268-271.

An eyewitness report from a letter written by Ramseur to his brother-in-law.

3263. Reed, Rowena. COMBINED OPERATIONS IN THE CIVIL WAR. Annapolis: Naval Institute Press, 1978.

Author says that General McClellan developed the idea of "combined operations," that is, operations involving cooperation between naval and land forces under separate command. The claim is made that had McClellan's strategy been fully employed the war would have ended in 1862.

3264. Reynolds, Clark G. "The Great Experiment: Hunter's Horizontal Wheel." AM NEP, 24 [1964]: 5-24.

Lieutenant William W. Hunter attempted to adapt steam power to naval usage through paddle wheels attached horizontally to the bottom of the vessel. The attempt was made to do this, but it proved unsuccessful.

3265. ———. "Yankee Supership? Sortie of SPUYTEN DUYVIL." AM NEP, 42 [1982]: 85-100.

Originally named the STROMBOLI, this vessel was the only true torpedo boat built from the keel up. Article describes its construction. The SPUYTEN DUYVIL saw action on the James River in late 1864.

3266. Riggs, David F. "Sailors of the U.S.S. CAIRO: Anatomy of a Gunboat Crew." CWH, 28 [1982]: 266-273.

An examination of the muster roll for the CAIRO illustrates the vocational backgrounds and the varied geographic and ethnic origins of the crew. Few had any prior steamboat experience while one-third of the crew were not American citizens.

3267. Roberts, John C. and Richard H. Webber. "Gunboats in the River War, 1861-1865." US NAV INST PROC, 91 [1965]: 83-99.

Authors describe some of the less well-known happenings in the western river fighting. They down play the amphibious nature of most engagements.

3268. Sandefer, H.L. and Archie P. McDonald. "Sabine Pass: David and Goliath." TEXANA, 7 [1979]: 177-188.

The heroic story of Lieutenant Dick Dowling, who fought off the federal invasion fleet at Sabine Pass with only one company of Confederates and six guns. The Union strategy and tactics are criticized.

3269. Saunders, Herbert. "The Civil War Letters of Herbert Saunders." Ronald K. Huch, editor. KY HIS SOC REG, 69 [1971]: 17-29.

Saunders, a carpenter's mate on the Union gunboat PEOSTA for three years, writes of his experiences during 1864.

3270. Shier, Maynard J. "Hatteras Inlet: The First Revenge." CWTI, 17 [7] [1978]: 4-11, 44-47.

A description of the federal capture of Forts Clark and Hatteras on the North Carolina coast in August 1861.

3271. Sloan, Edward William, III. BENJAMIN FRANKLIN ISHERWOOD, NAVAL ENGINEER: THE YEARS AS ENGINEER IN CHIEF, 1861-1869. Annapolis: United States Naval Institute, 1965.

This biography is especially valuable for information on the conflicts between Isherwood and the navy men still fighting wars with sailing ships, between a civilian marine engineer and line officers, and between the engineer Isherwood and the inventor Ericsson.

3272. Smith, David R. THE MONITOR AND THE MERRIMAC: A BIBLIOGRAPHY. Los Angeles: University of California Library, 1968.

A 35-page annotated booklet, listing all published and private material pertaining to this famous sea battle.

3273. Smith, Myron J., Jr. AMERICAN CIVIL WAR NAVIES: A BIBLIOGRAPHY. Metuchen, New Jersey: Scarecrow Press, 1972.

The beginning point for any serious, as well as not so serious, Civil War naval research. The bibliography contains over 2,800 citations, many with brief annotations. Inevitably a few minor errors have crept in, but the book remains an excellent source.

3274. ———. "Gunboats in a Ditch: The Steele's Bayou Expedition, 1863." J MISS HIS, 37 [1975]: 165-186.

In March 1863 Admiral Porter planned a "novel" means of taking Vicksburg from the rear. His fleet of five ironclads, four mortars and, four tugboats traversed part of the distance up the Yazoo Delta, but was soon blocked by overhanging saplings and

Confederate troops. Forced to withdraw, Porter was barely able to escape and only managed to pull out because of help from Sherman's forces.

3275. Stanley, Henry. "Henry Stanley's Mess Book: Offenses and Punishments Aboard the ETHAN ALLEN." Leon Basile, editor. CWH, 23 [1977]: 69-79.

Stanley, master of arms, kept a 33-page journal of offenses and punishments on his ship between August 25, 1863 and April 6, 1865. The most common offenses were insolence and disobedience. The record indicates harsh and brutal punishment.

3276. Stedman, Charles E. THE CIVIL WAR SKETCHBOOK OF CHARLES ELLERY STEDMAN, SURGEON UNITED STATES NAVY. Jim Dan Hill, editor. San Rafael, California: Presidio Press, 1976.

Built around letters, this biography provides a detailed, personal, and romanticized view of life in the Union navy. Stedman experienced the boredom of the blockade on the U.S.S. HURON and the human cost of action on the monitor NAHANT.

3277. Still, William N., Jr. "A Naval Sieve: The Union Blockade in the Civil War." NAV WAR COLL R, 36 [1983]: 38-45.

Author argues that the effect of the blockade on the South has been overstated and sees the employment of hundreds of ships on blockade duty as wasteful. A greater contribution to victory would have been made by concentrating on combined operations on the coast and inland rivers.

3278. ———. "The New Ironclads: Invention Went Wild in the Race For Newer and More Powerful Iron Behemoths." In THE IMAGE OF WAR, 1861-1865: Volume 2, THE GUNS OF '62, pp. 49-85. Garden City, New York: Doubleday, 1982.

A brief but informative discussion of the development of ironclads--Union and Confederate. The text is profusely illustrated, including interior and engine room views, not published before.

3279. ———. "Technology Afloat." CWTI, 14 [7] [1975]: 4-9, 40-47.

A discussion of naval technological improvements--steel plating, steam engines, torpedoes, submarines, ordnance--brought about by the war.

SULTANA

The SULTANA was a troopship plying the Mississippi River from early 1863 to the end of the war. Its capacity was 376 passengers plus a complement of 85 officers and men. On April 21, 1865, it left New Orleans on a regular run to Vicksburg, Memphis, Cairo, Evansville, and Cincinnati. On the night of April 24 it reached Vicksburg, where many thousands of repatriated federal prisoners, who lived in the Midwest, were being processed. So eager were many of these soldiers to get home that they began pouring on to the SULTANA in such numbers that it was impossible to stop them. The total passenger count was in excess of 2,300. The vastly overcrowded ship, with leaking boilers, left Vicksburg and reached Memphis on the evening of April 26. After a stop to discharge some cargo and to repair the boilers, it resumed its trip north.

About ten miles north of Memphis early on the morning of April 27, the boilers exploded, fire broke out, and the ship began to sink. Passengers and wreckage were blown all over the adjacent waters; many of the men were badly burned, hundreds more were drowned. Those still on the ship jumped in the water to avoid the fire; most were unable to save themselves because of their weakened physical condition. The final death toll is only approximate, about 1,700, since there was no record of who had come aboard at Vicksburg. A few hundred survivors formed the Sultana Survivors Society. William F. Dixon, below, was one of the survivors. The following entries deal with the "SULTANA Disaster."

3280. Berry, Chester D. LOSS OF THE SULTANA AND REMINISCENCES OF SURVIVORS. Lansing, Michigan: 1902.

3281. Dixon, William F. "Aboard the SULTANA." CWTI, 12 [10] [1974]: 38-39.

3282. Elliott, James W. TRANSPORT TO DISASTER. New York: Holt, Rinehart and Winston, 1962.

3283. Floyd, William B. "The Burning of the SULTANA." WIS MAG HIS, 11 [1927]: 70-76.

3284. Larson, Cedric A. "Death on the Dark River." AM HER, 6 [6] [1955]: 48-51, 98.

3285. Talkington, Robert. "A Survivor From the SULTANA." IND HIS BULL, 32 [1955]: 123-125.

3286. Walker, John L. CAHABA PRISON AND THE SULTANA DISASTER. Eva D. Walker, editor. Hamilton, Ohio: 1910.

3287. Yager, Wilson M. "The SULTANA Disaster." TENN HIS Q, 35 [1976]: 306-325.

* * *

3288. Thompson, Edgar K. "The U.S. Monitor PATAPSCO." US NAV INST PROC, 94 [1968]: 148-149.

The PATAPSCO was one of the PASSAIC class of monitors built and launched by John Ericsson in 1862. She hit a mine a half-mile from Fort Sumter on January 15, 1865, and sank in seconds.

3289. Turner, Maxine. "Naval Operations on the Apalachicola and Chattahoochee Rivers, 1861-1865." ALA HIS Q, 36 [1974]: 189-266.

A year-by-year description of naval activity by both sides on these rivers in Florida, Georgia, and Alabama.

3290. UNIFORMS OF THE UNITED STATES NAVY, 1776-1898. Washington, D.C.: Office of the Chief of Naval Operations, 1966.

This includes changes made by Secretary of the Navy Gideon Welles in July 1862, May 1863, and January 1864. The text is accompanied by twelve large color drawings, two of which refer to the Civil War period.

3291. Wade, Norman. "Letters of Norman Wade." Leone B. Cousins, editor. NOVA SCOTIA HIS Q, 4 [1974]: 117-146.

A Nova Scotian, Wade entered the Union navy and rose to the rank of captain. He died aboard ship at the age of 25.

3292. ———. "A Nova Scotian in the Union Navy: The Letters of Norman Wade." Leone B. Cousins, editor. CANADA, 2 [1975]: 58-73.

An introductory note sketches Wade's life. He served aboard the Union ship CYRENE.

3293. Webber, Richard H., editor. MONITORS OF THE U.S. NAVY, 1861-1937. Washington, D.C.: Navy Department, 1969.

The 48-page booklet contains a detailed description of all monitors, including a facsimile of the contract for the building of the ironclad MONITOR. About nine pages are devoted to monitors built after the Civil War.

3294. Wegner, Dana M. "Commodore William D. Porter." CWTI, 11 [4] [1972]: 26-35.

A sketch of the life of "Dirty Bill" Porter, controversial commander of the U.S.S. ESSEX.

3295. ———. "The WEEHAWKEN'S 'Fearful Accident.'" CWTI, 11 [8] [1972]: 4-9. 46-47.

Assigned to bombard Charleston, the U.S.S. WEEHAWKEN filled with water and sank at anchor.

Wells, Thomas. "The Navies." In CIVIL WAR BOOKS. [See Number 47]

3296. West, Richard S., Jr. "Gunboats in the Swamps: The Yazoo Pass Expedition." CWH, 9 [1963]: 157-166.

An unsuccessful effort to take Vicksburg by an amphibious force moving across the northern part of the Yazoo Delta in the spring of 1863.

3297. ———. MR. LINCOLN'S NAVY. New York: Longmans, Green, 1957.

A solid survey of all the Union navy's operations.

3298. White, Oliver. PENCIL SKETCHES OF SERVICE IN THE MARINE ARTILLERY.... Toulon, Illinois: 1863.

Though an ancient publication, this 86-page memoir is one of the few detailing Civil War service in the Marine Corps.

3299. White, William C. and Ruth White. TIN CAN ON A SHINGLE. New York: Dutton, 1957.

A review of events before and after the battle between the MERRIMAC and the MONITOR, as well as a report of the engagement itself.

The Scribner's Series

THE NAVY IN THE CIVIL WAR

As a companion set to its 13-volume CAMPAIGNS OF THE CIVIL WAR [see numbers 2919-2930] Charles Scribner's Sons published a three-volume THE NAVY IN THE CIVIL WAR. They are good works, compatible in quality to the volumes in the army series.

3300. Volume 1. Soley, James R. THE BLOCKADE AND THE CRUISERS. 1883.

3301. Volume 2. Ammen, Daniel. THE ATLANTIC COAST. 1883.

3302. Volume 3. Mahan, Alfred T. THE GULF AND INLAND WATERS. 1883.

V

LINCOLN

The material on Lincoln has been organized into two categories: "General" and "Assassination." The reader may also wish to consult the several journals which deal exclusively with Lincolniana. Numerous entries are drawn from the these journals, with the exception of LINCOLN LORE, a four-page monthly pamphlet issued by the Lincoln National Life Foundation of Fort Wayne, Indiana. Other periodicals which are cited in the pages that follow are the ABRAHAM LINCOLN QUARTERLY, a scholarly journal published by the Abraham Lincoln Association, and the LINCOLN HERALD, published by the Lincoln Memorial University at Harrowgate, Tennessee.

A. GENERAL

3303. Abbott, Lyman. "Lincoln as a Labor Leader." OUTLOOK, [February 27, 1909]: 499-505.

The editor of OUTLOOK discusses Lincoln's views on labor, namely that any labor system which denied the right of the worker, of whatever color, the opportunity to rise as far as his abilities permitted him, was inherently wrong.

3304. Agar, Herbert. ABRAHAM LINCOLN. New York: Macmillan, 1952.

A striking portrait of Lincoln, although necessarily short to conform to the BRIEF LIVES series format designed for English readers. The author did as much as could be done in the space he had.

3305. Ambrose, Stephen E. "The Savior of His Country." CWTI, 6 [10] [1968]: 26-33.

This "appraisal" summarizes the traits that earned Lincoln the title, "Savior of his Country." Among the many traits listed are his humanity, self-confidence, political pragmatism, and above all his vision and belief in America.

3306. Ander, O. Fritiof, editor. LINCOLN IMAGES: AUGUSTANA COLLEGE CENTENNIAL ESSAYS. Rock Island, Illinois: Augustana College Library, 1960.

This thought-provoking volume evaluates some of Lincoln's problems through essays by outstanding Lincoln scholars of today. It also contains a bibliography of Augustana's large Lincoln collection.

3307. Anderson, David. ABRAHAM LINCOLN. New York: Twayne, 1970.

An analysis of Lincoln's literary style as it developed from the early years to the Gettysburg Address and the Second Inaugural. In the latter two, he went beyond the meaning of the war and touched on the meaning of life and the human condition.

3308. ———. "Abraham Lincoln, Man of Letters." UNIV COLL Q, 12 [2] [1967]: 3-8.

Analyzes the Gettysburg Address, the letter to Mrs. Bixby, and the Second Inaugural Address, all of which establish for Lincoln a secure literary reputation. Author believes that without them "it would be minor."

3309. ———. "Emerson and Lincoln." LIN HER, 60 [1958]: 123-128.

Emerson had misgivings about Lincoln's slavery position at first, but later came to view him as the "Great Man of his age."

3310. Anderson, Dwight G. ABRAHAM LINCOLN: THE QUEST FOR IMMORTALITY. New York: Knopf, 1982.

A psychological study wherein Lincoln's obsession with death moved him to press for "political immortality" comparable to Washington's.

3311. Anderson, Frank M. THE MYSTERY OF A "PUBLIC MAN." Minneapolis: University of Minnesota Press, 1948.

A fascinating historical detective story attempting to identify the diarist who said Douglas held Lincoln's hat and cane during the inaugural ceremonies. But no one has successfully revealed who the "Public Man" was.

3312. Anderson, Ken. "The Role of Abraham Lincoln and Members of His Family in the Charleston Riots During the Civil War." LIN HER, 79 [1977]: 53-60.

Lincoln ordered the release of a number of pro-Confederate sympathizers arrested following the bloody Charleston, Illinois, [Coles County] riot of March 28, 1864. It is believed he did this--although his motives can never be fully known--because his family lived in Coles County, he was related to two of the prisoners, and he knew several of the others.

3313. Angle, Paul M., editor. CREATED EQUAL? Chicago: University of Chicago Press, 1958.

This work contains the complete texts of speeches in the Lincoln-Douglas debates.

3314. ———. "HERE I HAVE LIVED": A HISTORY OF LINCOLN'S SPRINGFIELD, 1821-1865. New Brunswick: Rutgers University Press, 1950.

A valuable history of the Springfield Lincoln knew, by one of the foremost Lincoln scholars. This work, a reprint of a 1935 edition, is also useful as an early example of "urban history."

3315. ———, editor. THE LINCOLN READER. New Brunswick: Rutgers University Press, 1947.

An excellent view of Lincoln drawn from the writings of 65 experts.

3316. ———. NEW LETTERS AND PAPERS OF LINCOLN. Boston: Houghton Mifflin, 1930.

A well-edited volume by this well-known Lincoln scholar, which includes 430 Lincoln items not previously published.

3317. ———, editor. A PORTRAIT OF ABRAHAM LINCOLN IN LETTERS BY HIS ELDEST SON. Chicago: Chicago Historical Society, 1969.

A collection of 80 letters written by Robert Todd Lincoln to Isaac Markens, 1908-1924. While no major revelations are to be found here, interesting insights into Lincoln's life can be. The letters also reveal Robert Lincoln in a different light than that in which he is normally viewed.

3318. ———. A SHELF OF LINCOLN BOOKS: A CRITICAL, SELECTIVE BIBLIOGRAPHY OF LINCOLNIANA. New Brunswick: Rutgers University Press, 1946.

An excellent and critical appraisal of 81 books about Lincoln. An average of one and one-half pages is devoted to each work.

3319. ——— and Earl Schenck Miers, editors. THE LIVING LINCOLN: THE MAN, HIS MIND, HIS TIMES, AND THE WAR HE FOUGHT, RECONSTRUCTED FROM HIS OWN WRITINGS. New Brunswick: Rutgers University Press, 1955.

An excellently edited and annotated collection of Lincoln's writings, which shows the development of Lincoln's thought on crucial issues.

3320. Arnold, Isaac N. THE LIFE OF ABRAHAM LINCOLN. Chicago, 1885.

This work smoothed the feathers ruffled by the Ward Hill Lamon biography of 1872. It is still of interest because author knew Lincoln intimately for 25 years. Written in the "filio-pietistic" spirit, it deals only sketchily with Lincoln's private life.

3321. Ashton, J. Hubley. "Lincolniana: A Glimpse of Lincoln in 1864." JISHS, 69 [1976]: 67-69.

An incident occurred during the time Ashton was assistant attorney general which illustrates Lincoln's sense of justice and his kind heart.

3322. Baber, Adin and Mary E. Lobb. "How a Railroader Saw Lincoln Leave Illinois in 1861." LIN HER, 68 [1966]: 121-129.

A discussion of railroad arrangements for Lincoln's trip from Springfield to Washington to assume the presidency.

3323. ———. "The Lincoln Log Cabins." LIN HER, 71 [1969]: 19-26.

A study of the literature on the Lincoln log cabin homes when the family lived in Indiana. Author suggests they may have had two cabins side-by-side.

3324. Baker, Monty R. "Abraham Lincoln in Theses and Dissertations." LIN HER, 74 [1972]: 107-111.

Although dated, this is a good listing for those interested in the field of Lincolniana.

3325. Ballard, Colin R. THE MILITARY GENIUS OF ABRAHAM LINCOLN.... Cleveland, Ohio: World, 1952.

An American edition of a 1926 work written by a British officer. It provides a good study of the important military operations of the war and expresses a favorable view of Lincoln's understanding of military matters.

3326. Baringer, William E. A HOUSE DIVIDING: LINCOLN AS PRESIDENT-ELECT. Springfield, Illinois: Abraham Lincoln Association, 1945.

A good account of how the cabinet was selected, with a discussion of some of the personal and factional hostilities within it. A sequel to the next entry.

3327. ———. LINCOLN'S RISE TO POWER. Boston: Little, Brown, 1937.

A detailed and well-written account of Lincoln's emergence as a national figure from the "House Divided" speech in June 1858 to the presidential nomination in June 1860.

3328. ———. LINCOLN'S VANDALIA: A PIONEER PORTRAIT. New Brunswick: Rutgers University Press, 1949.

An excellent account of Lincoln's first four years in the Illinois legislature in the mid- to later 1830s, when Vandalia was still the state capital. The reader is left to determine for himself if the youthful congressman was already demonstrating the talents which would carry him to the White House.

3329. ——— and Earl S. Miers, editors. LINCOLN DAY-BY-DAY: A CHRONOLOGY, 1809-1865. 2 v. Washington: Lincoln Sesquicentennial Commission, 1960.

These works constitute a revision and enlargement of the earlier volumes of Angle, Thomas, and Pratt. They are invaluable to anyone engaged in Lincoln research. [See number 3493]

3330. Barton, William E. A BEAUTIFUL BLUNDER: THE TRUE STORY OF LINCOLN'S LETTER TO MRS. LYDIA A. BIXBY. Indianapolis: Bobbs-Merrill, 1926.

After thorough research, author concludes that the "Widow" Bixby lost two, not five, sons in the war and that despite its nobility, Lincoln's famous letter was a "beautiful blunder."

3331. ———. THE LIFE OF ABRAHAM LINCOLN. 2 v. Indianapolis: Bobbs-Merrill, 1925.

This biography is somewhat superficial except in those portions based on the author's own research. A clergyman, Barton brought out new material pertaining to Lincoln's family and background. For example, he was the first to question the authenticity of the Ann Rutledge legend.

3332. ———. LINCOLN AT GETTYSBURG: WHAT HE INTENDED TO SAY; WHAT HE SAID; WHAT HE WAS REPORTED TO HAVE SAID; WHAT HE WISHED HE HAD SAID. Indianapolis: Bobbs-Merrill, 1930. Reprint 1950.

This is a somewhat heavy, yet thorough analysis of the contradictory evidence pertaining to the writing and delivery of the Gettysburg Address and the reaction to it.

3333. ———. THE LINEAGE OF LINCOLN. Indianapolis: Bobbs-Merrill, 1929.

Probably the most thoroughgoing study of the Lincoln and Hanks families yet to appear. The work includes over 100 pages of documents and an extensive bibliography.

3334. ———. THE PATERNITY OF LINCOLN.... New York: George H. Doran, 1920.

An exhaustive study of the legitimacy of Lincoln, which concludes that Thomas was Abraham's father and that Abraham was born in wedlock.

3335. ———. THE SOUL OF ABRAHAM LINCOLN. New York: George H. Doran, 1920.

Perhaps the best study of Lincoln's religious beliefs.

3336. ———. WOMEN LINCOLN LOVED. Indianapolis: Bobbs-Merrill, 1927.

In this volume of dubious value, the author discusses a number of women who had an important influence on Lincoln's life, such as his mother, grandmother, sister, wife, and a few friends.

3337. Basler, Roy P., editor. ABRAHAM LINCOLN: HIS SPEECHES AND WRITINGS. New York: Grosset and Dunlap, 1946. Reprint 1962.

An excellent one-volume collection of Lincoln's public works. The book contains 228 entries with helpful editorial comments.

3338. ———, editor. THE COLLECTED WORKS OF ABRAHAM LINCOLN. 9 v. New Brunswick: Rutgers University Press, 1953-1955.

The most recent and most authoritative collection of Lincoln materials.

3339. ———. THE LINCOLN LEGEND: A STUDY IN CHANGING CONCEPTIONS. Boston: Houghton Mifflin, 1935.

A thoughtful analysis of the "Lincoln Legend" as it appeared in biography, poetry, fiction, and sculpture over the years.

3340. ———. A TOUCHSTONE FOR GREATNESS: ESSAYS, ADDRESSES AND OCCASIONAL PIECES ABOUT ABRAHAM LINCOLN. Westport, Connecticut: Greenwood, 1973.

A collection of speeches and writings about Lincoln, bringing together the results of the author's 40 year study of the president. Basler discusses many of the controversial elements in Lincoln's life and concludes with reflections on the sources of his greatness.

3341. Bass, Henry B. "In Search of Lincoln's English Ancestors." LIN HER, 72 [1970]: 3-9.

A report of a fun trip to several villages northeast of London, where Lincoln's ancestors had lived. Not much was known about the ancestors before this visit and nothing new was learned as a result of it, though a good time was had by all.

3342. Bates, David H. LINCOLN IN THE TELEGRAPH OFFICE. New York, 1907.

The impressions of Lincoln by the young telegraph operators during his regular visits to the telegraph office in the war department.

3343. Bernard, Kenneth. "Lincoln and the Civil War as Viewed by a Dissenting Yankee of Connecticut." LIN HER, 74 [1974]: 208-215.

Richard Harvey Phelps, businessman, farmer, and life-long Democrat, believed the war was the work of abolitionist clergy, the Emancipation Proclamation was "monstrous", and Lincoln was a scoundrel.

3344. Betts, William W., Jr. LINCOLN AND THE POETS. Pittsburgh: University of Pittsburgh Press, 1965.

Contains 40 Lincoln-inspired poems. Editor has provided introductory statements on each of the 23 American poets.

3345. Beveridge, Albert J. ABRAHAM LINCOLN, 1809-1858. 2 v. Boston: Houghton Mifflin, 1928.

Although this work has since been superceded, for many years it was the standard biography on Lincoln through the debates with Douglas. Beveridge was the first to apply the technique of a trained historian, although he himself was not one, to the study of Lincoln. His work carries one of the fullest accounts of Lincoln's Illinois political career.

3346. Blankenship, Jane. "State Legislator as Debater: Lincoln, 1834-1842." AFAJ, 2 [1965]: 28-32.

A study of Lincoln's speeches during his years as state legislator reveals that he was developing a knowledge of "the minds of men and the strategies of persuasion" which would help him on the road to the White House.

3347. Blegen, Theodore C. LINCOLN'S IMAGERY: A STUDY IN WORD POWER. La Crosse, Wisconsin: Sumac Press, 1954.

An excellent analysis of Lincoln's figures of speech which aids our understanding of the man.

3348. Boritt, G.S. LINCOLN AND THE ECONOMICS OF THE AMERICAN DREAM. Memphis, Tennessee: Memphis State University Press, 1978.

Attempts to establish that Lincoln's actions were an extension of his "American Dream." He believed that the growth of the economy should be fostered by sound government policies, that an individual had the right to the fruits of his labor, and that a person could rise by his own efforts.

3349. ———. "Lincoln's Opposition to the Mexican War." JISHS, 67 [1974]: 79-100.

Author rejects the Herndon-Beveridge "political suicide" theory on Lincoln's opposition to the Mexican War. Rather than risking his political future by his anti-war position, Lincoln's stand was well-supported by his constituents and his political future was certainly not jeopardized.

3350. ———. "Lincoln and Taxation During His Illinois Legislative Years." JISHS, 61 [1968]: 365-373.

The Panic of 1837 and the need for "internal improvements" within the state converted Lincoln from a "no tax" man to a "high tax man at the state level."

3351. Brewer, W.M. "Lincoln and the Border States." JNH, 34 [1949] 46-72.

In addition to describing the economic, social, and political make up of the Border states, the author demonstrates how Lincoln, a Border state product himself, ably grasped the importance of the region and handled the sensitive relations between the government and the Border states with great skill.

3352. Brice, Marshall M. "Lincoln and Rhetoric." COLL COMP COM, 17 [1966]: 12-14.

Analyzes Lincoln's rhetoric. Concludes with a plea for rhetoric as a formal discipline in the schools today. Author believes a feeling for language must be restored.

3353. Brogan, Denis W. ABRAHAM LINCOLN. New York: Schocken Books, 1963.

The reissue of this slim volume first published in the 1930s reveals some changes in the author's thought, but not many. The war is less avoidable here than before, for example, and Douglas and McClellan do not fare quite so well. Grant has improved some. However, Lincoln is as great as ever.

3354. Browne, Francis F., editor. THE EVERY-DAY LIFE OF ABRAHAM LINCOLN. New York, 1886. Chicago, 1913. [Second edition]

Author draws from over 500 sources, mainly people who knew Lincoln, in developing a personality portrait of the president. The second edition is a tighter book than the first.

3355. Bullard, F. Lauriston. ABRAHAM LINCOLN AND THE WIDOW BIXBY. New Brunswick: Rutgers University Press, 1946.

A review of the evidence--pro and con--about the letter to the Widow Bixby, which the author feels is a "minor footnote to history." "A notable piece of detection work."

3356. ———. LINCOLN IN MARBLE AND BRONZE. New Brunswick: Rutgers University Press, 1952.

A handsome, illustrated volume containing 68 essays, each of which discusses a statue erected in Lincoln's honor.

3357. Canby, Courtlandt, editor. LINCOLN AND THE CIVIL WAR: A PROFILE AND A HISTORY. New York: Braziller, 1960.

A good collection of writings about Lincoln.

3358. Cannon, Foster. "The Early Manuscripts of the Gettysburg Address." LIN HER, 58 [1957]: 18-24.

A study of the "first" and "second" drafts of the address.

3359. Carpenter, Francis B. THE INNER LIFE OF ABRAHAM LINCOLN: SIX MONTHS AT THE WHITE HOUSE WITH ABRAHAM LINCOLN. THE STORY OF A PICTURE. New York, 1866.

A young artist, Carpenter, won the chance to paint a picture of Lincoln reading the Emancipation Proclamation. For half a year he went as he pleased in the White House and had many opportunities to observe Lincoln and other important persons. He reported what he saw and heard in the popular, well-done book.

3360. Carson, Herbert L. "Nor Long Remember: Lincoln at Gettysburg." PENN HIS, 28 [1961]: 365-371.

Gives the general background of this approximately three minute speech which was virtually ignored at the time.

3361. Charnwood, Lord [Godfrey R. Benson]. ABRAHAM LINCOLN. London, England: 1916.

This book which "lifted the whole field of LIncoln studies to an international plane," was a best seller when it first appeared and remains an excellent work 70 years later, particularly in dealing with Lincoln's character and in analyzing the reasons for his actions. An introspective rather than a factual study.

3362. Coddington, Edwin B. "Lincoln's Role in the Gettysburg Campaign." PENN HIS, 34 [1967]: 250-265.

Lincoln maintained that the Gettysburg victory should have been as decisive as the one at Vicksburg. He believed Meade could have trapped Lee. Author examines this premise.

3363. Cooke, John W. "Freedom in the Thought of Abraham Lincoln." LIN HER, 72 [1970]: 10-16.

Drawing on the natural rights philosophy, Lincoln adopted a more radical concept of freedom than did his contemporaries.

3364. Cope, F.D. "The Military Role of Lincoln in the War of Secession." LIN HER, 72 [1970]: 20-26.

Author concludes that Lincoln firmly grasped the essential purpose of the war and the necessity for a non-vindictive restoration of the Union.

3365. Cortada, James W. "Spanish Views on Abraham Lincoln, 1861-1865." LIN HER, 76 [1974]: 80-85.

The Spanish minister in Washington, Gabriel Garcia Tassara, kept Madrid well posted on the progress of the Civil War and Lincoln's views about it.

3366. Cramer, John H. "Lincoln in Ohio." OSAHQ, 54 [1945]:149-168.

The text of Lincoln's speech in Cincinnati in September 1859 is reproduced as well as the newspaper response to it. In addition, the substance of his little-known remarks at Hudson and Alliance while on his way to the inauguration is noted.

3367. ———. LINCOLN UNDER ENEMY FIRE. Baton Rouge: Louisiana State University Press, 1948.

An account of an occasion when Lincoln "exposed his tall form" to enemy fire at Fort Stevens, a defensive work in the District of Columbia, which was under Confederate attack in July 1864.

3368. Crissey, Elwell. LINCOLN'S LOST SPEECH. New York: Hawthorn Books, 1967.

An examination of all the materials pertaining to Lincoln's "lost speech" at the Illinois Republican convention in Bloomington, May 29, 1856. The author believes that this speech, for which there was no text and no written transcript, set in motion the chain of events which would lead Lincoln to the presidency.

3369. Current, Richard N. THE LINCOLN NOBODY KNOWS.... New York: McGraw-Hill, 1958.

The author investigates and judiciously evaluates eleven controversies surrounding Lincoln, such as his views on race and religion, his military capacity, his statesmanship, whether he provoked war at Ft. Sumter, and the truth about Ann Rutledge. While there are no conclusive answers to many of these questions, Current offers his own interpretation.

3370. Dahl, Curtis. "Lincoln Saves A Reformer." AM HER, 23 [6] [1972]: 74-78.

Lincoln pardons Franklin W. Smith, a Boston merchant, who was unjustly convicted of naval contract frauds.

3371. Davis, Machael. THE IMAGE OF LINCOLN IN THE SOUTH. Knoxville: University of Tennessee Press, 1971.

Although considered by southerners to be a monster during the Civil War and Reconstruction, Lincoln had risen in the South's estimation by the turn of the century. His character, humor, and non-vindictiveness explain this reversal in thinking within a generation's time and Lincoln's emergence as a southern hero.

3372. Dodge, Daniel K. ABRAHAM LINCOLN, MASTER OF WORDS. New York: Appleton, 1924.

An able exposition of Lincoln's literary skill, as reflected in his speeches and writings.

3373. Donald, David. LINCOLN RECONSIDERED: ESSAYS ON THE CIVIL WAR ERA. New York: Knopf, 1956.

An interesting collection of nine essays loosely centered on the Lincoln theme. While they are well done and make for pleasurable reading, there is not a great deal which is really new in these pages.

3374. Dorfman, Maurice. "Lincoln's Arithmetic Education: Influence on His Life." LIN HER, 68 [1966]: 61-80, 108-120.

Lincoln kept a "sum book" in the mid-1820s and author uses this to analyze Lincoln's understanding of arithmetic. His mastery of the subject proved of great help to him in his political career.

3375. Dorris, Jonathan T. PARDON AND AMNESTY UNDER LINCOLN AND JOHNSON. Chapel Hill: University of North Carolina Press, 1953.

This is an exhaustive study of the pardon policy of chiefly President Andrew Johnson with respect to former Confederate civil and military leaders. Lincoln believed in a lenient approach and his successor moved ahead on the same lines, so that most disabilities were removed by 1868. A masterful treatment of a difficult subject.

3376. Duff, John H. A. LINCOLN, PRAIRIE LAWYER. New York: Rinehart, 1960.

The author, a lawyer, has provided a detailed record of Lincoln's professional career on the Illinois circuit, 1837-1860. This definitive account emphasizes the life-long influence that law had on Lincoln.

3377. Edwards, Herbert J. and John E. Hawkins. LINCOLN THE WRITER: THE DEVELOPMENT OF HIS LITERARY STYLE. Orono, Maine: University of Maine Press, 1962.

In this slim volume, the authors analyze Lincoln's growth as a writer and affirm his status as an immortal in literature as well as in politics.

3378. Eisendrath, Joseph L. "Lincoln's First Appearance on the National Scene, July 1847." LIN HER, 76 [1974]: 59-62.

Lincoln's first major public appearance occurred at a Rivers and Harbors convention in Chicago in 1847.

3379. Eisenschiml, Otto. "Two Curious Facets of Lincoln's Character." LIN HER, 63 [1961]: 85-88.

Although Lincoln's integrity was beyond question, the author believes his conduct at times was both contradictory and unpredictable. The inconsistencies were, perhaps, due to the fact that he was an unimaginative man.

3380. Endy, Melvin B., Jr. "Abraham Lincoln and American Civil Religion: A reinterpretation." CH HIS, 44 [1975]: 229-241.

Author modestly challenges some of the recent claims to Lincoln's greatness as a prophet of an "American civil religion."

3381. Erickson, Gary. "The Graves of Ann Rutledge and the Old Concord Burial Ground." LIN HER, 71 [1969]: 90-107.

In 1890 Ann Rutledge's remains were moved from the New Salem cemetery to the Petersburg, Illinois cemetery.

3382. ———. "Lincoln's Civil Religion and the Lutheran Heritage." LIN HER, 75 [1973]: 158-171.

Resolutions dealing with national social issues were adopted by the Evangelical Lutheran Church in 1862 and presented to Lincoln. The resolutions and the president's response are included here.

3383. Evans, William A. MRS. ABRAHAM LINCOLN.... New York: Knopf, 1932.

An early effort at "psycho-history" by a medical doctor who wanted to know what innate social and cultural forces made Mary Todd Lincoln the way she was. While useful in its day, the book has been superceded by Ruth Randall's work.

3384. Fehrenbacher, Don E. "The Historical Significance of the Lincoln-Douglas Debates." WIS MAG HIS, 42 [1959]: 193-199.

Had the Republican party not decided to throw its support behind a candidate of their own rather than the "Little Giant," the party would have been wiped out in Illinois.

3385. ———. "Lincoln, Douglas, and the 'Freeport Question.'" AHR, 66 [1961]: 599-617.

The Douglas pronouncement at Freeport on August 27, 1858, secured his re-election to the Senate, but destroyed his support in the South and divided the Democratic party.

3386. ———. "Lincoln and Judicial Supremacy: A Note on the Galena Speech of July 23, 1856." CWH, 16 [1970]: 197-204.

Author challenges traditional view that Lincoln favored judicial disposition of the problem of slavery in the territories.

3387. ———. "Lincoln and the Weight of Responsibility." JISHS, 68 [1975]: 45-56.

Lincoln had no "love affair with power" in the White House. Instead, he felt only "a burden of responsibility terrifying in its dimension" because it often meant choosing between life and death for others.

3388. ———. "Origins and Purpose of Lincoln's 'House-Divided" Speech." MVHR, 46 [1960]: 615-643.

Author argues that it was the growing Republican attachment to Douglas after the latter denounced the Lecompton Constitution that prompted the speech. Lincoln believed that Republican support of Douglas would destroy the Republican party.

3389. ———. PRELUDE TO GREATNESS: LINCOLN IN THE 1850s. Stanford: Stanford University Press, 1962.

In a well-done collection of seven essays, the author examines the traditional, the revisionist, and the most recent scholarship and restores Lincoln to a position of primacy in Illinois Republican politics.

3390. ———, editor. THE LEADERSHIP OF ABRAHAM LINCOLN. New York: Wiley, 1970.

A "problems" book in which 18 Civil War scholars analyze Lincoln's leadership skills in different areas.

3391. Feinstein, Howard M. "The Chronicles of Reuben: A Psychological Test of Authenticity." AQ, 18 [1966]: 637-654.

Author suggests that the controversial "Chronicles of Reuben," popularized by Herndon, but dismissed as fraudulent by most historians, should not be so quickly abandoned. Using the psychoanalytic approach it appears that Lincoln might well have authored the document.

3392. Fesler, J.W. "Lincoln's Gettysburg Address." IND MAG HIS, 40 [1944]: 209-222.

Describes how the speech was generally regarded as a "failure" by the men on the platform. For the public, it was over before they had settled down to listen to it.

3393. Fortenbaugh, Robert. "Abraham Lincoln at Gettysburg...." PENN HIS, 5 [1938]: 223-244.

Chronicles the changes made in the various copies of the speech. Lincoln made three changes himself.

3394. Frank, John P. LINCOLN AS A LAWYER. Urbana: University of Illinois Press, 1961.

John P. Frank, a Yale law professor with an interest in history as well as law, studied Lincoln's legal career for a number of years. A series of lectures at the University of Illinois resulted in this book. While Lincoln was not a great lawyer, his skill in communication, his keen memory, and his ability to see the practical issues in a given case made him a good one.

3395. Franklin, John H. "Lincoln and Public Morality." TOPIC, 5 [9] [1965]: 27-43.

Morality in public service is difficult, but Lincoln faced the problem honestly and realistically.

3396. Futrell, Roger H. "Zachariah Riney: Lincoln's First Schoolmaster." LIN HER, 74 [1972]: 136-142.

Riney taught Lincoln, who was seven years old at the time, in a log cabin school in Hardin County, Kentucky.

3397. George, Joseph, Jr. "'Abraham Africanus I': President Lincoln Through the Eyes of a Copperhead Editor." CWH, 14 [1968]: 226-239.

A glimpse at the writing of C. Chauncey Burr, an anti-Lincoln editor.

3398. Goodhart, Arthur L. "Lincoln and the Law." A BAR ASSN J, 50 [1964]: 433-441.

Author believes the fact that Lincoln was a practicing lawyer almost until his inauguration gave him a facility with words, an insight into problems, and the vision to stretch the law to meet the demands of the day.

3399. Graebner, Norman A. THE ENDURING LINCOLN. Urbana: University of Illinois Press, 1959.

The central theme in this work, based on four lectures delivered at the University of Illinois in February 1959, is pragmatism. The lectures were delivered by T. Harry Williams, Roy Basler, David Donald, and the editor.

3400. Grimsley, Elizabeth T. "Six Months in the White House." JISHS, 19 [1926]: 43-73.

This favorite cousin of Mrs. Lincoln provides interesting sidelights from "inside" the White House. She accompanied the pair to Washington in February 1861.

3401. Gunderson, Robert G. "'Stoutly Argufy': Lincoln's Legal Speaking." WIS MAG HIS, 46 [1963]: 109-117.

Although Lincoln's preparation as a speaker was severely limited primarily by his backwoods heritage, he excelled at being able to talk sense to a jury, and his ideas were always arranged in an orderly manner.

3402. Hackensmith, C.W. "Family Background and Education of Mary Todd." KY HIS SOC REG, 69 [1971]: 187-196.

Genealogical information on the Todds is covered briefly. Mrs. Lincoln attended an exclusive boarding school before making her debut in society.

3403. ———. "Lincoln's Family and His Teachers." KY HIS SOC REG, 57 [1969]: 317-334.

Traces Lincoln's ancestry from Samuel Lincoln born in England in 1620 to Thomas [Abe's father]. The paternal side of the Hanks' family proving difficult to trace, author concentrates on the maternal [Shipley] side of the family.

3404. ———. "The Much Maligned Mary Todd Lincoln." FCHQ, 44 [1970]: 282-292.

Author believes Mary Todd Lincoln was ill-treated and after all her losses, people took advantage of her. Herndon's lectures in 1873 did not help matters.

3405. Hamilton, Charles and Lloyd Ostendorf. LINCOLN IN PHOTOGRAPHS: AN ALBUM OF EVERY KNOWN POSE. Norman: University of Oklahoma Press, 1963.

The volume includes 119 photographs of Lincoln, from the earliest daguerreotype in 1846 until the final death posture. The photos show the president with a beard and without the beard. Also included are a number of pictures of Lincoln's family, friends, and advisers.

3406. Harnsberger, Caroline T. THE LINCOLN TREASURY. Chicago: Wilcox and Follett, 1950.

Discusses many matters which reflect Lincoln's thinking, although not in his own words.

3407. Hattaway, Herman and Archer Jones. "Lincoln as Military Strategist." CWH, 26 [1980]: 293-303.

Authors give Lincoln high marks as a strategist. They emphasize his friendly relationship with Grant.

3408. Heckman, Richard A. LINCOLN v DOUGLAS: THE GREAT DEBATES CAMPAIGN. Washington, D.C.: Public Affairs Press, 1967.

In this detailed analysis of each of the seven debates, the author argues that although Lincoln and Douglas were not too far apart on the issue of slavery, they adopted divergent stands to win votes. This helped polarize public opinion and made it more difficult to avoid war.

3409. Helm, Katherine. TRUE STORY OF MARY, WIFE OF LINCOLN. New York: Harper, 1928.

Written by Mary Todd Lincoln's niece [her mother, Emilie Todd Helm was Mrs. Lincoln's sister], this volume attempts to redraw the picture of Mrs. Lincoln in a more favorable light. It is not certain that she succeeded. Enough of the material is fabricated as to raise the question whether this is biography or fiction.

3410. Herndon, William and Jesse W. Weik. HERNDON'S LINCOLN: THE TRUE STORY OF A GREAT LIFE.... 3 v. Chicago, 1889. Reprint 1929, 1949.

Lincoln's law partner and young friend, Herndon, gathered a mass of material about Lincoln soon after his death, some of which was used by Lamon in his 1872 biography. He had nourished but almost abandoned the idea of a biography of his own when he met Jesse Weik, a young writer. Weik diligently put Herndon's material together in book form. Although many of Herndon's opinions and analyses have been found incorrect, his personal observations of Lincoln have proven essential to any understanding of the man.

3411. Hertz, Emanuel. ABRAHAM LINCOLN: A NEW PORTRAIT. 2 v. New York: Liveright, 1931.

A loose compilation of Lincoln materials and the author's speeches about Lincoln. A number of new items can be found here, but the work suffers from careless editing.

3412. ———, editor. THE HIDDEN LINCOLN, FROM THE LETTERS AND PAPERS OF WILLIAM H. HERNDON. New York: Viking Press, 1938.

Based on the Herndon Papers in the Library of Congress, the work includes recollections about Lincoln's childhood and other things. While a useful source book, it is not very satisfactorily edited.

3413. ———, editor. LINCOLN TALKS: A BIOGRAPHY IN ANECDOTE. New York: Viking Press, 1939.

A biography told through memoirs, letters, newspapers, and people reporting from memory. More a reference book of "Lincoln stories," most of which have a foundation in fact but are somewhat open to debate.

3414. Hickey, James T., editor. "Impressions of Herndon and Lincoln by Charles S. Zane." JISHS, 64 [1971]: 206-209.

Zane became Herndon's law partner after Lincoln's election and inauguration.

3415. Hirschfield, Robert S. "Lincoln and the Crisis Presidency." LIN HER, 64 [1962]: 15-25.

Lincoln's unprecedented use of the power of the presidency has special meaning to modern Americans living in an age of crisis.

3416. Hofstadter, Richard. THE AMERICAN POLITICAL TRADITION. New York: Knopf, 1948.

Lincoln is one of a number of famous political figures discussed in this work. His political philosophy is examined on pages 92-134.

3417. Holland, Josiah G. LIFE OF ABRAHAM LINCOLN. Springfield, Massachusetts, 1886. Reprint 1961.

The first major biography of Lincoln is still of value although it presents the mid-Victorian view of the man who was a model youth who rose to the top by force of his ideals. Author's emphasis on Lincoln as an orthodox Christian touched off a lively controversy. Holland was a noted Springfield editor and writer who interviewed a number of Lincoln's contemporaries.

3418. Holzer, Harold. "The Bearding of the President, 1860: The Portraitists Put on Hairs." LIN HER, 78 [1976]: 95-102.

Lincoln began growing his beard after his election and by inauguration time he had a full one. Caught unprepared, artists and portraitists added ridiculous beards to old prints and passed them off as new pictures of the president.

3419. ———. "Lincoln and the Printmakers." JISHS, 68 [1975]: 74-84.

During Lincoln's presidency American printmakers had to contend with changes in Lincoln's actual appearance. Meeting the great demand for Lincoln prints tested the skills, efficiency, and even the artistic integrity of the printmakers.

3420. Horner, Harlan H. THE GROWTH OF LINCOLN'S FAITH. New York: Abingdon, 1939.

Shows that although Lincoln cared little for creeds and dogmas, his chief reliance was on God. His faith grew during his presidential years.

3421. Howells, William D. LIFE OF ABRAHAM LINCOLN. Springfield, Illinois: Abraham Lincoln Association, 1938.

This celebrated author, in 1860 a young writer for a Columbus, Ohio newspaper, wrote the only campaign biography of Lincoln. Although a slim book, it profits from Lincoln's own corrections.

3422. Hubbard, George U. "Abraham Lincoln As Seen By the Mormons." UTAH HIS Q, 31 [1963]: 91-108.

Mormonism impacted on Lincoln periodically throughout his political career. At times they held each other in disfavor, but by 1865 the Mormons had developed a high opinion of Lincoln.

3423. Hynd, Alan. "The Other Plot to Kill Lincoln." READERS DIG, 88 [February 1966]: 92-97.

The story of the Baltimore plot which was born at the Barnum Hotel bar. Fernandina, the hotel's head bartender was in on it.

3424. Jaffa, Harry V. CRISIS OF THE HOUSE DIVIDED. Garden City, New York: Doubleday, 1959.

Analyzes congressional documents as well as earlier speeches and writings of Lincoln and Douglas to support his interpretation. Jaffa believes that although differences of opinion existed, there was a real threat of a Lincoln-Douglas coalition. Lincoln's firm stand plus his conviction that slavery would spread prevented such a coalition.

3425. ——— and Robert W. Johannsen, editors. IN THE NAME OF THE PEOPLE. Columbus: Ohio State University Press, 1959.

The speeches and writings of Lincoln and Douglas in the Ohio campaign of 1859.

3426. Jennison, Keith W. THE HUMOROUS MR. LINCOLN. New York: Bonanza Books, 1965.

Lincoln's story as told through his own anecdotes, jokes, witticisms, and stories, all of which reflect the changing use of humor in Lincoln's life. The author chose the versions which he preferred.

3427. Jervey, Edward D. "A Study of the Gettysburg Address." LIN HER, 61 [1959]: 20-22.

A comparison of the fifth version of the speech with the original one.

3428. Johannsen, Robert W. "In Search of the Real Lincoln, or Lincoln at the Crossroads." JISHS, 61 [1968]: 229-247.

The study of Lincoln is changing, and only through the "historical truth" rather than the myth can the "real Lincoln" be found.

3429. Jones, Edgar D. LINCOLN AND THE PREACHERS. New York: Harper, 1948.

An excellent study of Lincoln's relations with the men of the cloth.

3430. Keiser, David S. "Quaker Ancestors for Lincoln." LIN HER, 63 [1961]: 134-137.

Lincoln claimed his ancestors were Quakers from Berks County, Pennsylvania. Keiser states he has solved the question. Lincoln's great-great-grandparents were Quakers.

3431. Kempf, Edward Jr. ABRAHAM LINCOLN'S PHILOSOPHY OF COMMON SENSE: AN ANALYTICAL BIOGRAPHY OF A GREAT MIND. 3 v. New York: New York Academy of Sciences, 1965.

A "psychobiological analysis of the development of the mind and personality of Abraham Lincoln...." The author presents the thesis that Lincoln's melancholia resulted in his greatness.

3432. Kibby, Leo P. "Lincoln Belongs to the Ages." JW, 7 [1968]: 456-460.

The effects of Lincoln's life and works on generations of Americans.

3433. King, Willard. "Riding the Circuit With Lincoln." AM HER, 6 [2] [1955]: 48-49. 104-109.

An account of the vicissitudes of life and travel while

"riding the circuit" in Illinois in the 1840s and 1850s. Drawn from the letters of Judge David Davis, a close friend of Lincoln.

3434. Klein, Frederic S. "On Trial." CWTI, 7 [9] [1969]: 40-46.

Lincoln commuted the sentences of many soldiers doomed to be executed.

3435. Klement, Frank. "Lincoln, the Gettysburg Address, and Two Myths." BG MAG, 2 [1984]: 7-11.

Author demonstrates that two widely-held beliefs about the Gettysburg Address were false. The first was that Lincoln composed the message while on the train from Washington to Gettysburg. The second was that it was received in utter silence.

3436. ———. SEVEN WHO WITNESSED LINCOLN'S GETTYSBURG ADDRESS. Madison, Wisconsin: Lincoln Fellowship of Wisconsin, Historical Bulletin Number 40, 1984.

Fascinating sketches of seven people who were either on the platform or near it when Lincoln delivered the Gettysburg Address. All seven were closely connected with the planning of the festivities.

3437. Kooker, Arthur R. "Abraham Lincoln, Spokesman for Democracy." JW, 4 [1965]: 260-271.

Author discusses the results of his studies on Lincoln's life and works.

3438. Kranz, Henry B., editor. ABRAHAM LINCOLN: A NEW PORTRAIT. New York: Putnam, 1959.

A collection of articles about Lincoln by [a] writers of the 1950s and 1960s, [b] his contemporaries, and [c] Lincoln himself. The idea was to approach Lincoln's personality from as many different angles as possible to form a composite picture. Two-thirds of the work is composed of 22 essays by modern writers, while the remaining material is drawn from Lincoln and his contemporaries.

3439. Lamon, Ward H. THE LIFE OF ABRAHAM LINCOLN: FROM HIS BIRTH TO HIS INAUGURATION AS PRESIDENT. Boston, 1872.

Herndon gathered his material shortly after Lincoln's death, but had no time then to write a biography. In 1872 he sold his data to Ward Lamon, Lincoln's old friend and bodyguard, who enlisted Chauncey Black to ghost write this book for him. This is really Herndon's book, to be superceded by his own work in 1889. The work has been described as the first challenge to the "filio-pietistic" school of Lincoln historiography. Though an intimate of Lincoln's, Lamon made no effort to disguise the president's flaws and indiscretions.

3440. Lapsley, Arthur B. THE WRITINGS OF ABRAHAM LINCOLN. 8 v. New York, 1905. Reprint 1923.

An early compendium of Lincoln's writings, but inferior to the "Tandy Edition" of Nicolay and Hay's "Complete Works," released the same year.

3441. Learned, Marion D. ABRAHAM LINCOLN, AN AMERICAN MIGRATION.... Philadelphia, 1909.

In disposing of the popular theory that Lincoln was of German ancestry, the author establishes his English roots.

3442. "Lincoln Celebration, The." OUTLOOK, [February 20, 1909]: 363-365.

Accounts of celebrations throughout the country on the centenial of Lincoln's birth.

3443. Lincoln, Waldo. HISTORY OF THE LINCOLN FAMILY.... Worcester, Massachusetts: Commonwealth Press, 1923.

The author traces the line of descent of the Samuel Lincoln family in Worcester, Massachusetts, 1627-1920.

3444. Lorant, Stefan. ABRAHAM LINCOLN, HIS LIFE IN PHOTOGRAPHS. New York: Duell, Sloan, and Pearce, 1941.

Over 400 pictures--and good ones, too--are included in this work, which is essentially directed at younger readers.

3445. ———. LINCOLN: A PICTURE STORY OF HIS LIFE. New York: McGraw-Hill, 1952.

This is a good short biography, well-illustrated with many photographs of the president, a number of them appearing for the first time. It is a revision of the previous entry.

3446. Luthin, Reinhard H. THE REAL ABRAHAM LINCOLN: A COMPLETE ONE VOLUME HISTORY OF HIS LIFE AND TIMES. Englewood Cliffs, New Jersey: Prentice-Hall, 1960.

In this reworking of standard material, the author seeks to present Lincoln as he exactly was, shorn of myth and legend. The resulting portrait is not a flattering one, at least for the pre-presidential years. The war brought out Lincoln's greatness, but he was far from perfect.

3447. Mabie, Hamilton W. "Lincoln as a Literary Man." OUTLOOK, [February 5, 1898]: 321-327.

The author notes that although Lincoln had few of the educational opportunities afforded the literary giants of the day, he was able to develop a style and technique superior to all others by wide reading, self-education, and a unique talent.

3448. Mallam, William D. "Lincoln and the Conservatives." JSH, 28 [1962]: 31-45.

The conservative Republicans of 1862 were men of very strong convictions. Rather than abandon these convictions, they would prefer to leave politics. They had little zeal for abolishing slavery and supported the war largely to preserve the Union.

3449. Massey, Mary Elizabeth. "Mary Todd Lincoln." A HIS ILL, 10 [2] [1975]: 4-9.

Over 100 years after the death of Mary Todd Lincoln, the enigma of "the most studied, controversial, maligned First Lady in the nation's history" remains.

3450. McClure, Alexander K. ABRAHAM LINCOLN AND MEN OF WAR TIME.... Philadelphia, 1892. Reprint 1962.

A valuable collection of reminiscences about the great and near great in wartime Washington by a prominent Pennsylvanian who knew Lincoln well.

3451. Mearns, David C. THE LINCOLN PAPERS: THE STORY OF THE COLLECTION, WITH SELECTIONS TO JULY 4, 1861. 2 v. Garden City, New York: Doubleday, 1948.

An account of the Lincoln manuscripts in the Robert Todd Lincoln Collection, first opened in July 1947. Although only a small portion of the total collection--18,000 manuscripts--were opened at this time, this set has been called "one of the most important Lincoln books ever published."

3452. Meserve, Frederick H. HISTORICAL PORTRAITS AND LINCOLNIANA: INDEX OF A PART OF THE COLLECTION OF AMERICANA OF.... New York, 1915.

Meserve amassed the greatest collection of Lincoln photographs. This volume lists 8,000 of them, as well as a few items which do not pertain to Lincoln.

3453. ——— and Carl Sandburg. THE PHOTOGRAPHS OF ABRAHAM LINCOLN. New York: Harcourt, Brace, 1944.

Carl Sandburg has written a series of able essays accompanying this collection of photographs of Lincoln, his family, friends, and government and army officials.

3454. Miers, Earl S. and C. Percy Powell. LINCOLN DAY BY DAY: A CHRONOLOGY, 1809-1865. 3 v. Washington: Lincoln Sesquicentennial Commission, 1960.

A scholarly source of details on Lincoln's daily life. Documentation is based on manuscripts, newspapers, writings, and court records. It includes an exhaustive subject index and a bibliography of sources.

3455. Milgrim, James W. ABRAHAM LINCOLN ILLUSTRATED ENVELOPES AND LETTER PAPER, 1860-1865. Northbrook, Illinois: Northbrook Publishing, 1985.

This lavishly illustrated work will delight philatelists and Lincolnophiles. Among other things, it contains chapters on the history of political campaigns and patriotic stationery.

3456. Minger, Ralph E. "Abraham Lincoln: His Philosophy of Politics and His Leadership Qualities." JW, 4 [1965]: 272-276.

The pragmatic Lincoln believed in four fundamental principles: the idea of the American Union, an individual's right to own property, that man had a higher nature, and that Providence had a controlling voice in the affairs of man.

3457. Mitgang, Herbert, editor. ABRAHAM LINCOLN, A PRESS PORTRAIT. Chicago: Quadrangle, 1971.

This reprint of the 1956 edition provides a good, factual portrayal of the president as he appeared in the contemporary press. Lincoln was not popular with many editors and writers. The material is drawn from numerous magazines and 78 newspapers.

3458. Monaghan, Jay, compiler. LINCOLN BIBLIOGRAPHY, 1839-1939. 2 v. Springfield: Illinois Historical Library, 1943-1945.

A project of the Illinois State Historical Library, this standard, but dated work lists 3,958 books, pamphlets, programs, speeches, and other items pertaining to Lincoln. The volumes are arranged chronologically by date of publication. Foreign language titles are listed separately.

3459. Morgenthau, Hans J. and David Hein. ESSAYS ON LINCOLN'S FAITH AND POLITICS. Lanham, Maryland: University Press of America, 1983.

In this fine volume, one in a series on the American presidency, Morgenthau analyzes Lincoln's thought from the perspective of a political scientist, Hein from the position of a theologian and religious historian.

3460. Morison, Samuel E. "Mr. Lincoln Attends Church." MD HIS MAG, 57 [1962]: 47-55.

The president-elect attended St. John's Church in Washington, D.C., on Sunday, February 24, 1861, shortly after he arrived in town. The event is recalled in this address by Morison at the same church on February 26, 1961.

3461. Morse, John T., Jr. ... ABRAHAM LINCOLN. Boston, 1893.

This early work was one of the few studies of Lincoln which dealt with the president in a straightforward, balanced manner. It can still be read with profit.

3461a. Murph, David R. "Abraham Lincoln and Divine Providence." LIN HER, 73 [1971]: 8-15.

Author argues that too many students of Lincoln's religious thought have failed to recognize that his whole life represented a developing awareness of the unmistakable role of Divine power in the lives of men.

3462. Neely, Mark E., Jr. THE ABRAHAM LINCOLN ENCYCLOPEDIA. New York: McGraw-Hill, 1982.

In approximately 300 topical entries, this unique source provides a state-of-the-art picture of Lincoln's life, thoughts, politics, biographers, background, and legacy. Brief bibliographies follow the entries. Of the thousands of books on Lincoln, this volume ranks among the best for its scholarship, readability, and wealth of information.

3463. Nelson, Paul D. "From Intolerance to Moderation: The Evolution of Abraham Lincoln's Racial Views." KY HIS SOC REG, 72 [1974]: 1-9.

Although racist in his early views, Lincoln gradually changed in his thinking to a degree. He became more flexible but died "still a racist and proud of being a Southerner by birth."

3464. Nevins, Allan. "Hiram Barney and Lincoln: Three Unpublished Documents." HUNT LIB BULL, 26 [1962/1963]: 1-10.

Documents of Barney, a close personal friend of Lincoln, recounting confidences between the two on matters of state.

3465. ———, editor. LINCOLN AND THE GETTYSBURG ADDRESS: COMMEMORATIVE PAPERS BY JOHN DOS PASSOS AND OTHERS. Urbana: University of Illinois Press, 1964.

An excellent collection of essays.

3466. ———. "Lincoln's Ideals of Democracy." TOPIC 5 [9] [1965]: 11-26.

Taken from LINCOLN: A CONTEMPORARY PORTRAIT. [See number 3467] Lincoln firmly believed in democracy "of the people, by the people."

3467. ——— and Irving Stone, editors. LINCOLN: A CONTEMPORARY PORTRAIT. Garden City, New York: Doubleday, 1962.

A collection of 13 essays in which various aspects of Lincoln's life are analyzed. Some of his beliefs were intuitive, but his approach was often pragmatic.

3468. Newman, Ralph G. "Basic Lincolniana." CWH, 3 [1957]: 199-208.

Author lists 106 "basic" Lincoln books, noting their different editions. Many are coded to Monaghan's LINCOLN BIBLIOGRAPHY. A good beginning list.

3469. ———, editor. LINCOLN FOR THE AGES. Garden City, New York: Doubleday, 1960.

An excellent collection of essays. The idea behind it is to find out what made Lincoln great. Contributors are noteworthy.

3470. Newton, Joseph F. LINCOLN AND HERNDON. Cedar Rapids, Iowa: 1910.

Consists of a voluminous correspondence between Herndon and Theodore Parker, 1854-1859. This well-edited work illuminates aspects of the lives of both Herndon and LIncoln.

3471. Nicolay, Helen. PERSONAL TRAITS OF ABRAHAM LINCOLN. New York, 1912.

A glimpse of Lincoln from the viewpoint of his two secretaries. A valuable collection of anecdotes and stories illustrating the personal side of Lincoln drawn largely from unused notes of the author's father, John Nicolay.

3472. Nicolay, John G. A SHORT HISTORY OF LINCOLN. New York, 1902.

A useful condensation of the 10 volume work [see next entry], focusing on the presidential years. While superceded by modern writings, the book is still of interest.

3473. ——— and John Hay. ABRAHAM LINCOLN: A HISTORY. 10 v. New York, 1890.

A monumental work written by Lincoln's two private secretaries. Although Robert Todd Lincoln permitted the use of his collection and censored all that was written as a condition of its use, the biography is surprisingly frank. It is indispensable for any in-depth understanding of Lincoln, the man.

3474. ———. ABRAHAM LINCOLN: A HISTORY. Paul M. Angle, editor. Chicago: University of Chicago Press, 1966.

A good, handy abridgment of the ten-volume work.

3475. ———. ABRAHAM LINCOLN, COMPLETE WORKS.... 2 v. New York, 1894.

The first effort to bring together Lincoln's speeches, writings, and state papers. Consisting of 1,736 items, the volumes were adequate for their time.

3476. ———. COMPLETE WORKS OF ABRAHAM LINCOLN. 12 v. New York, 1905.

A more elaborate version of the above entry, the "Tandy Edition" contains 518 additional entries and the first bibliography of works about Lincoln.

3477. Northrup, Jack. "Gov. Richard Yates and Pres. Lincoln." LIN HER, 70 [1968]: 193-206.

An analysis of the relationship between Illinois Governor Yates and Lincoln with respect to both military and political matters in Illinois during the war. Yates was a strong supporter of the administration.

3478. Oates, Stephen B. "'Why Should the Spirit of Mortal be Proud?'" A HIS ILL, 11 [1] [1976]: 32-41.

A look at Lincoln's law career.

3479. ———. "Wilderness Fugue: Lincoln's Journey to Manhood on the Kentucky and Indiana Frontier." AW, 13 [2] [1976]: 4-13.

An almost year-by-year record of Lincoln's physical and mental growth in Kentucky and Indiana prior to his settling in Illinois in 1830.

3480. Ostendorf, Lloyd. "Lincoln in Stereo." CWTI, 14 [10] [1976]: 4-9.

Describes various photographic equipment such as the 2-lens stereoscopic camera and a multiple 4-lens camera which made "duplicate" prints. Tells how author obtained the only known "pair of stereographic images of a close-up of Lincoln."

3481. ———. "The Lost Lincoln Photographs." A HIS ILL, 3 [10] [1968]: 34-43.

Author speculates on the fate of at least a dozen Lincoln photographs which are known to exist but which have never been located.

3482. ———. "The Photographs of Mary Todd Lincoln." JISHS, 61 [1968]: 269-332.

A collection of 26 photographs of Mary Todd Lincoln.

3483. ———. A PICTURE STORY OF ABRAHAM LINCOLN. New York: Lathrop, Lee and Shepard, 1962.

Consists of 160 ink drawings of Lincoln from birth to death. Primarily for younger readers, but adults can enjoy it as well.

3484. ———. "The Story of the 'Tired Lincoln' Photograph." JISHS, 57 [1964]: 400-405.

This old photograph is unusual in that it is probably the most unflattering portrait of Lincoln ever taken.

3485. Pargellis, Stanley. "Lincoln's Political Philosophy." ALQ, 3 [1945]: 275-290.

In this analysis Lincoln is considered a conservative.

3486. Petersen, William F. LINCOLN-DOUGLAS: THE WEATHER AS DESTINY. Springfield, Illinois: C.C. Thomas, 1943.

The author is a medical doctor who, after a diligent study of weather data and contemporary records, explains why a person of Lincoln's elongated physique behaved as he did under different climatic conditions.

3487. Phillips, Isaac H. ABRAHAM LINCOLN BY SOME MEN WHO KNEW HIM. Bloomington, Illinois: 1910.

A small book which contains thoughtful appraisals by five young friends of Lincoln, who knew the president as a man 20-25 years their senior.

3488. Plowden, David. LINCOLN AND HIS AMERICA. New York: Viking Press, 1970.

A large absorbing book of illustrations and drawings which tells the Lincoln story without embellishment.

3489. Poland, Charles P. "Abraham Lincoln and Civil Liberties: A Reappraisal." LIN HER, 76 [1974]: 119-132.

An analysis of Lincoln's views on the Constitution in wartime. He believed that it could not apply with the same force as in peacetime, that it must be stretched at times to preserve the Union.

3490. Powell, C. Percy, compiler. LINCOLN DAY BY DAY.... Volume III: 1861-1865. Earl S. Miers, editor-in-chief. Washington, D.C.: Lincoln Sesquicentennial Commission, 1960.

A scholarly source of details on the last 1,566 days of Lincoln's life. Documentation is based on manuscripts, newspapers, and writings. Covers not only Lincoln but his family as well. [See number 3329]

3491. Pratt, Harry E. CONCERNING MR. LINCOLN.... Springfield, Illinois: Abraham Lincoln Association, 1944.

Letter-writers of his own day describe the president.

3492. ———. THE PERSONAL FINANCES OF ABRAHAM LINCOLN. Springfield, Illinois: Abraham Lincoln Association, 1943.

An important book on an overlooked subject. Author shows that Lincoln was not reared in "abject poverty" and that he accumulated a goodly competence from his professional and presidential efforts and husbanded his resources wisely.

3493. ———, Paul M. Angle and Benjamin P. Thomas. LINCOLN DAY-BY-DAY. 4 v. Springfield, Illinois: Abraham Lincoln Association, 1933-1941,

A massive blow-by-blow chronology of Lincoln's activities

from his birth to the presidency. Volumes One and Two by Pratt carry the story through 1846. Volume Three by Thomas covers the years 1847-1853, and Volume Four by Angle covers the years 1854-1861. Based on original materials, the compilation corrects a number of errors committed by earlier writers on Lincoln. This is an invaluable source for Lincoln scholars. Now updated. [See number 3329 and number 3490]

3494. Pressly, Thomas J. "Bullets and Ballots: Lincoln and the 'Right of Revolution.'" AHR, 67 [1962]: 647-662.

In his earlier years Lincoln had upheld the "right of revolution," but as president his views changed, and he considered secession as illegal.

3495. Randall, James G. "Has the Lincoln Theme Been Exhausted?" AHR, 41 [1936]: 270-294.

Despite the plethora of writings on Lincoln pouring from the presses, the author feels that the subject still has not been fully milked and points the directions which future research should take.

3496. ———. LINCOLN AND THE SOUTH. Baton Rouge: Louisiana State University Press, 1946.

Four thought-provoking essays on Lincoln's thinking concerning Reconstruction of the Union. Emphasized is Lincoln's practicality and his continuing sympathy for his "native" South.

3497. ———. LINCOLN THE LIBERAL STATESMAN. New York: Dodd, Mead, 1947.

One of the best collections of essays on the subject. These eight selections relate the past to the present and cover the important and controversial aspects of Lincoln's career. Although judicious and moderate, they make a case for "Lincoln the Liberal Statesman."

3498. ———. LINCOLN, THE PRESIDENT. 4 v. New York: Dodd, Mead, 1945-1955.

The first professional historian to apply the tools of his trade to the subject, Randall has produced what probably will remain the definitive study of Lincoln. [The last volume, edited by Richard Current, was published posthumously.] The president is treated honestly, yet sympathetically, while many of the hoary legends are expertly analyzed. From these pages "Lincoln emerges unscathed as a folk-hero fully worthy of the magic he created."

3499. Randall, Ruth P. THE COURTSHIP OF MR. LINCOLN. Boston: Little Brown, 1957.

Mrs. Randall has written a solid, scholarly study of a somewhat "elusive theme." There are no notes, but a useful bibliography is included.

3500. ———. LINCOLN'S SONS. Boston: Little, Brown, 1956.

A successful effort to recapture the personalities and the characters of the four Lincoln boys. It is a perceptive study of family relationships and a pleasure to read.

3501. ———. MARY LINCOLN: BIOGRAPHY OF A MARRIAGE. Boston: Little, Brown, 1953.

This is an excellent, well-researched biography of the often maligned wife of President Lincoln. The author, while fully demolishing the falsehoods propagated by Herndon about Mary Lincoln which have been widely-accepted, recognizes that the president's lady had a bad temper and must have been a difficult woman to get along with.

3502. Rawley, James A. "The Nationalism of Abraham Lincoln. CWH, 9 [1963]: 283-298.

Author seeks to demonstrate that "Abraham Lincoln is the supreme nationalist in the history of the United States."

3503. Raymond, Henry J. THE LIFE AND PUBLIC SERVICES OF ABRAHAM LINCOLN.... New York, 1865.

An early attempt to collect all of Lincoln's speeches, letters, and proclamations, but much is left out.

3504. Reep, Thomas P. LINCOLN AT NEW SALEM. Petersburg, Illinois: Old New Salem League, 1927.

An interesting study of New Salem, which includes sketches of many of the settlers who knew Lincoln well. Author was a lawyer who grew up in the area.

3505. Reilly, Tom. "Early Coverage of a President-Elect: Lincoln at Springfield, 1860." JOUR Q, 49 [1972]: 469-479.

The record of the work of Henry Villard, sent by the NEW YORK HERALD to cover Lincoln's activities in Springfield between the election and the time he left for Washington. This represented a new concept in journalism.

3506. Rice, Allen T. REMINISCENCES OF ABRAHAM LINCOLN BY DISTINGUISHED MEN OF HIS TIME. New York, 1909.

This revised edition of an 1886 volume contains the recollections of a number of men--most of whose names were better known in their own time than today--about their varied relationships with Lincoln.

3507. Riddle, Donald W. CONGRESSMAN ABRAHAM LINCOLN. Urbana: University of Illinois Press, 1957.

A carefully-researched work covering Lincoln's career from his election to Congress in 1846 to his unsuccessful Senate bid in 1855. Lincoln was a serious public servant, but his opposition to the Mexican War and fuzzy thinking on slavery led to his temporary political eclipse. This is not a flattering picture overall, Lincoln being the opportunist that he was.

3508. ———. LINCOLN RUNS FOR CONGRESS. New Brunswick: Rutgers University Press, 1948.

Good research, but a weak literary style mark this volume which precedes the above and takes the story through Lincoln's successful congressional bid in 1846.

3509. Rietveld, Ronald D. "Lincoln and the Politics of Morality." JISHS, 68 [1975]: 27-43.

A study of the evolution of Lincoln's thought on the morality of slavery. As a young man he did not view it as a moral wrong, but as he grew and re-emerged in politics he concluded that it was wrong.

3510. Robbins, Peggy. "The Lincolns and Spiritualism." CWTI, 15 [5] [1976]: 4-10, 46-47.

After the death of Willie, Mrs. Lincoln became involved in spiritualism. Lincoln also attended seances, but whether he was a "believer" is debatable. They held a "spiritual soiree" at the White House, making no effort to hide their interest in it.

3511. Robinson, Luther E. ABRAHAM LINCOLN AS A MAN OF LETTERS. Chicago: Reilley & Lee, 1918.

A meticulous and effective analysis of Lincoln's evolution as a literary artist from his early days at Salem through Gettysburg and the Second Inaugural.

3512. Rolle, Andrew, "The Books About Lincoln." CATH DIG, 28 [1964]: 63-66.

An excellent short discussion of the subject.

3513. Ross, Ishbel. THE PRESIDENT'S WIFE: MARY TODD LINCOLN. New York: Putnam, 1973.

This is a readable biography of Mary Lincoln which stresses her personal life and attempts to separate fact from myth.

3514. Ross, Rodney A. "Mary Todd Lincoln, Patient at Bellevue Place, Batavia." JISHS, 63 [1970]: 5-34.

Describes Mrs. Lincoln's sojourn at the sanitarium from

May 20, 1875 to September 10, 1875. The experience was very humiliating, but not restrictive. She was declared sane in June 1876.

3515. Ryan, Daniel J. "Lincoln and Ohio." OSAHQ, 32 [1923]: 7-281.

A lengthy account of Lincoln's relations with Ohioans and Ohio. His visit to the state in 1855 and 1859 are chronicled as well as the speeches he made on those occasions. A section is devoted to Vallandigham and the ceremonies in Ohio memorializing Lincoln's death.

3516. Sandburg, Carl. ABRAHAM LINCOLN. 6 v. [PRAIRIE YEARS, 2 v.; WAR YEARS, 4 v.] New York: Harcourt, Brace, 1926-1939.

The noted Illinois poet drew on his magnificent literary skills to paint an unforgettable portrait of Lincoln. Some critics have argued that the early volumes were more literature than history, but either way Sandburg has written an epic of the man and his times.

3517. ———. LINCOLN COLLECTOR: THE STORY OF OLIVER R. BARRET'S GREAT PRIVATE COLLECTION. New York: Harcourt, Brace, 1950.

An excellent source book, consisting of copies and transcripts of the more important items in Barret's fine collection.

3518. ——— and Paul Angle. MARY LINCOLN, WIFE AND WIDOW. New York: Harcourt, Brace, 1932.

A still useful, well-documented study which discounts Herndon's story about the Lincoln courtship. Relying largely on primary materials, the authors explore the complex psychology of the president's volatile wife.

3519. Schiffer, Saul S. THE AMERICAN CONSCIENCE: THE DRAMA OF THE LINCOLN-DOUGLAS DEBATES. New York: Horizon, 1973.

After a review of slavery, a comparison of Lincoln and Douglas, and an account of the debates, the author concludes that Lincoln won, having occupied a higher moral position.

3520. Schurz, Carl. ABRAHAM LINCOLN: AN ESSAY. New York, 1891.

Schurz, who had many meetings with Lincoln, outdid Herndon in creating a believable figure. The president's faults are neither ignored nor exaggerated.

3521. Schwartz, Harold. "Abraham Lincoln and the Marfan Syndrome." JAMA, 187 [1964]: 473-479.

From the physical descriptions of Lincoln and from the fact that the Marfan Syndrome was found in a Lincoln descendant, the author suggests the Marfan Syndrome was also present in Lincoln. The syndrome is described as a "hereditary disarrangement of connective tissue, affecting one or more of three systems--skeletal, visual, and cardiovascular." Hence the president's elongated limbs, long narrow face, etc.

3522. Searcher, Victor. LINCOLN'S JOURNEY TO GREATNESS. Philadelphia: Winston, 1960.

Author describes the president-elect's trip from Springfield to Washington prior to assuming office.

3523. ———. LINCOLN TODAY. New York: Yoseloff, 1970.

Divided into two parts, the work covers "Books About Lincoln" and "Lincoln in the Lively Arts." This is a good collection of annotated titles under the two headings, demonstrating Lincoln's continuing importance in American life.

3524. Segal, Charles M., editor. CONVERSATIONS WITH LINCOLN. New York: Putnam, 1961.

The story of Lincoln as portrayed in his conversations with over 100 people from the time of his nomination until his death. A well-edited work, it provides a good glimpse of the personal side of the president.

3525. Shaw, Albert. ABRAHAM LINCOLN: A CARTOON HISTORY. 2 v. New York: Review of Reviews, 1929.

A good collection of cartoons, drawings, and photographs, but the rather wordy text takes the story only to Lincoln's first inauguration.

3526. Shaw, Archer, editor. THE LINCOLN ENCYCLOPEDIA: THE SPOKEN AND WRITTEN WORDS OF A. LINCOLN ARRANGED FOR READY REFERENCE. New York: Macmillan, 1950.

This book may be of use to some people--it contains 5,000 alleged excerpts from Lincoln's speeches and writins--but it is marred by the inclusion of forged documents and false quotations.

3527. Shutes, Milton H. "Lincoln and Elizabeth Morgan McElrath." LIN HER, 62 [1960]: 66-69.

Partial text of an interview with the president by a woman who wished to go home to the South.

3528. ———. LINCOLN AND THE DOCTORS. New York: Pioneer Press, 1933.

A medical biography of the president.

3529. ———. "The Tears of Lincoln." PAC HIS, 14 [1970]: 20-31.

An attempt to document each time Lincoln cried.

3530. Simmons, Dawn L. A ROSE FOR MRS. LINCOLN: A BIOGRAPHY OF MARY TODD LINCOLN. Boston: Beacon, 1970.

In this sympathetic study, the author argues that Mary Todd Lincoln was victimized by a hostile press, partly induced by her refusal to accommodate reporters on her various visitations. The biggest culprit in shaping her unfavorable image, however, was Herndon.

3531. Simon, Paul. LINCOLN'S PREPARATION FOR GREATNESS: THE ILLINOIS LEGISLATIVE YEARS. Norman: University of Oklahoma Press, 1965.

A readable account of Lincoln's formative years.

3532. Smith, E.B. "Abraham Lincoln: Realist." WIS MAG HIS, 52 [1969]: 158-168.

Lincoln, ever the realist, understood his America and his humanitarianism gave him a total view of the tragedy of slavery to both black and white alike.

3533. Smith, R.N. "Lincolns in Southern Kentucky." KY HIS SOC REG, 68 [1970]: 231-238.

Tends to refute the idea that Lincoln was born in Cumberland County, Kentucky, even though his father owned land there.

3534. Smith, T.V. ABRAHAM LINCOLN AND THE SPIRITUAL LIFE. Boston: Beacon, 1952.

A philosopher examines one of the less well-known aspects of Lincoln's being. He is viewed as a moralist, one who strictly adhered to the truth, and who loved beauty much as an artist does.

3535. Sparks, Edwin E., editor. THE LINCOLN-DOUGLAS DEBATES OF 1858. Springfield, Illinois: 1909.

Full texts of all the speeches are included in this volume.

3536. Stanton, Robert L. "Robert Livingston Stanton's Lincoln." Dwight L. Smith, editor. LIN HER, 76 [1974]: 172-181.

A memoir of Robert L. Stanton and his friendship with Lincoln. Stanton was a Presbyterian minister and college president, who visited the White House a number of times.

3537. Starr, John W. LINCOLN AND THE RAILROADS: A BIOGRAPHICAL STUDY. New York: Dodd, Mead, 1927.

Anything and everything pertaining to Lincoln's connection with railroads seems to have been assembled here. His views about railroads as an attorney, his attitude toward railroad legislation as president, and his experiences on railroad trips occupy most of the space.

3538. Steiner, Edward A. "Abraham Lincoln in Hungary." OUTLOOK, [May 21, 1910]: 122-124.

The poignant tale of a young Hungarian Jew, who came to the United States, lost an arm and a leg as a Union soldier, and returned to Hungary to die. He took a picture of Abraham Lincoln and an American flag with him and was buried in the flag.

3539. Stephenson, Nathaniel W. LINCOLN.... Indianapolis: Bobbs-Merrill, 1922.

While this early effort at "psycho-history" is unconvincing today, the author deals with Lincoln's presidency in masterful fashion.

3540. Stern, Philip Van Doren, editor. THE LIFE AND WRITINGS OF ABRAHAM LINCOLN. New York: Random House, 1940.

This "giant" in the Modern Library series includes a good biographical sketch of Lincoln. It is more suited for the non-specialist than the multi-volume works. Contains 274 entries.

3541. Stoddard, William O. INSIDE THE WHITE HOUSE IN WAR TIMES. New York, 1890.

The president as one of his secretaries saw him.

3542. Strickland, Arvarh E. "The Illinois Background of Lincoln's Attitude Toward Slavery and the Negro." JISHS, 56 [1963]: 474-494.

While opposing slavery and its effects, Lincoln could not condemn southern people for not freeing their slaves because he had no solutions for the problems which would follow emancipation. This was his position during the Illinois years.

3543. Symonds, Craig L. "Lincoln and the Strategy of Union." NAV WAR COLL R, 27 [1975]: 63-70.

Lincoln's genius as a political leader was demonstrated during the war by his able managing of diverse military, economic, political, and social factors in order to preserve the Union.

3544. Tarbell, Ida M. IN THE FOOTSTEPS OF THE LINCOLNS. New York: Harper, 1924.

Although the early sections describe the locale and environment where Lincoln's six ancestral generations lived, the bulk of the book contains a useful study of the president.

3545. ———. THE LIFE OF ABRAHAM LINCOLN.... 2 v. New York, 1900.

A carefully-researched, well-written biography by one of the famous journalist-muckrakers of the day. Author uncovered new material by interviewing people who knew Lincoln and was the first writer to recognize the pioneer and frontier influence on the formation of Lincoln's character. The work was very popular and did much to spread an interest in Lincoln. It ran through 11 editions.

3546. Temple, Wayne C. "Abraham Lincoln and Others at the St. Nicholas." LIN HER, 70 [1968]: 79-124.

A detailed account of the planning and construction of the St. Nicholas Hotel in Springfield, Illinois in the 1850s. The hotel became a stopping place for famous visitors in Lincoln's time and remains so today.

3547. ———. "Lincoln and Bennett: The Story of a Store Account." LIN HER, 69 [1967]: 107-115.

A sketch of John Thomas Bennett, a storekeeper-politician and friend of Lincoln in the 1830s. Lincoln's account at Bennett's store from February 1836-April 1837 is examined.

3548. ———. "Lincoln's Arms and Dress in the Black Hawk War." LIN HER, 71 [1969]: 145-149.

Not having time to secure a uniform, Lincoln wore a calico shirt, blue denims, a buckskin coat, and an "old slouch wool hat." He used a flintlock musket and rode on a borrowed horse.

3549. ———. "Lincoln as Seen From the Kitchen." DAR MAG, 97 [1963]: 119-122.

Eating regular meals did not rate high on Lincoln's list of priorities. He "ate to live instead of living to eat." Upon occasion he forgot to eat at all.

3550. ———. "Lincoln in the Census." LIN HER, 68 [1966]: 135-140.

The article contains census data on the Lincoln family from 1810 through 1860.

3551. ———. "Lincoln's Military Service in the Black Hawk War." LIN HER, 72 [1970]: 87-89.

Recent discovery of a clerk's error in spelling Lincoln's name shows that Lincoln was re-commissioned a captain in the 31st Illinois militia in December 1832, five months after his military career was supposed to have ended.

3552. ———. "Lincoln, Scouting, and Religion." LIN HER, 72 [1970]: 27-34.

Author searches Lincoln's thought and character to see what parallels there are with the Boy Scout creed.

3553. ———. "When Lincoln Left Town With Another Woman." LIN HER, 68 [1966]: 175-185.

When Lincoln traveled east in 1860 for his Cooper Union address he was accompanied by Mrs. Stephen Smith, a Springfield neighbor.

3554. Thomas, Benjamin P. ABRAHAM LINCOLN, A BIOGRAPHY. New York: Knopf, 1952.

Thomas was the first biographer to have full access to the Robert Todd Lincoln Collection and produced the best one volume life of Lincoln yet written. An excellent bibliographic essay accompanies the text.

3555. ———. LINCOLN'S NEW SALEM. Springfield, Illinois: Abraham Lincoln Association, 1934. Revised 1954.

An excellent study of this important period in Lincoln's early life, as well as an account of the restoration of New Salem by the state of Illinois. However, most of this material may be found in the author's biography, listed above.

3556. ———. PORTRAIT FOR POSTERITY: LINCOLN AND HIS BIOGRAPHERS. New Brunswick: Rutgers University of Press, 1947.

Based on letters of various Lincoln biographers discussing their work, the author has composed a number of essays shedding new light on the feuds and intrigues behind the writing of the Lincoln biographies.

3557. Tice, George. LINCOLN. New Brunswick: Rutgers University Press, 1984.

A collection of copies of 47 celebrated Lincoln photographs, in a twelve-inch by twelve-inch format, taken by George Tice to commemmorate Lincoln's 175th birthday.

3558. Tilley, John S. LINCOLN TAKES COMMAND. Chapel Hill: University of North Carolina Press, 1941.

An unfriendly interpretation of the early months of Lincoln's presidency. Author blames Lincoln for "firing the first shot" and thus for bringing about war.

3559. Townsend, William H. LINCOLN AND HIS WIFE'S HOME TOWN. Indianapolis: Bobbs-Merrill, 1929.

A fairly successful effort to show how Lincoln's views on slavery were partly shaped by his visits to Mary Todd's home town, Lexington, Kentucky. The work also has value in its discussion of an important Border state.

3560. ———. LINCOLN AND LIQUOR. New York: Press of the Pioneers, 1934.

This work covers all that anyone needs to know about a rather common matter.

3561. ———. "Lincoln's Rebel Niece--Katherine Helm, Artist and Author." LIN HER, 47 [1945]: 2-12.

Tells the story of Mrs. Lincoln's favorite niece, Katherine Helm, daughter of Emilie Todd Helm and Confederate General Ben Hardin Helm. Katherine became a noted artist and it is her picture of Mary Lincoln that is in the White House collection.

3562. Tracy, Gilbert A. UNCOLLECTED LETTERS OF ABRAHAM LINCOLN. Boston: Houghton Mifflin, 1917.

The author has compiled 359 letters, telegrams, and other writings which did not appear in THE COLLECTED WORKS. The volume is well-edited and a useful commentary accompanies many of the entries.

3563. Trueblood, Elton. ABRAHAM LINCOLN: THEOLOGIAN OF AMERICAN ANGUISH. New York: Harper & Row, 1973.

In this study of Lincoln's religious thought and wartime spiritual growth, not a great deal that is new can be found, but it is a well-written, worthwhile book.

3564. Tucker, Glenn. "Was Lincoln a Converted Christian?" LIN HER, 78 [1976]: 102-108.

The story about how Colonel James F. Jaquess, commander of the 73rd Illinois, the "Preacher's Regiment," may have converted Lincoln to the Christian faith during one of his sermons in Springfield in 1847. Jaquess spoke out after the war, at a reunion of his old regiment, to refute current charges that Lincoln was an agnostic.

3565. Turner, Justin G. "Lincoln and the Cannibals." PAC HIS R, 31 [1962]: 31-39.

In August of 1865, a letter addressed to Lincoln was delivered to the state department from a Hawaiian missionary. The last half of the letter contains a modest account of the rescue of an American sailor from a group of cannibals the year before.

3566. ——— and Linda L. Turner. MARY TODD LINCOLN: HER LIFE AND LETTERS. New York: Knopf, 1972.

A revealing biography of Lincoln's wife, woven around more than 600 of her letters. The letters reveal a very insecure person who depends on intimidation and promise of political appointment to get whatever she wanted. She had a desperate need for friends.

3567. U.S. Library of Congress. A CATALOG OF THE ALFRED WHITAL STERN COLLECTION OF LINCOLNIANA IN THE LIBRARY OF CONGRESS. Washinton, D.C.: Library of Congress, 1960.

A list, in library catalog format, of approximately 7,000 items by, or about, Lincoln and Lincoln-associated ephemera. This outstanding collection also includes reference to some rare items.

3568. Wakefield, Sherman. HOW LINCOLN BECAME PRESIDENT. New York: Wilson-Erickson, 1936.

An interesting look at the town of Bloomington, Illinois and the role its citizens played in assisting Lincoln along the road to the White House. The role of Jesse Fell is stressed.

3569. Warren, Louis A. LINCOLN'S PARENTAGE AND CHILDHOOD. New York: Century, 1926.

A study of Lincoln's Kentucky years which gives a more favorable view of Thomas Lincoln. Author attempts to prove Nancy Hanks was legitimate and claims Lucy Hanks was a widow when "she married Henry Sparrow after Nancy's birth."

3570. ———. LINCOLN'S YOUTH ... 1816-1830. New York: Appleton, 1960.

Covers each year of Lincoln's life in Indiana from the age of seven to his 21st birthday. It contains much information on the family and "for almost the first time the public gets a picture of his sister Sarah." A laudatory account.

3571. ——— and Frederick Tilberg. "Have We Done Lincoln Justice at Gettysburg? No, Says Dr. Louis Warren; Yes, Says Dr. Frederick Tilberg." CWTI, 15 [4] [1976]: 10-17.

Warren argues Lincoln did not deliver his famous address at the present site of the Soldiers' National Monument. Tilberg maintains it is the correct site. Both present evidence to prove their hypotheses.

3572. Washington, John E. THEY KNEW LINCOLN. New York: Dutton, 1942.

"A collection of memories of Abraham Lincoln gathered from the Negro men and women who knew him personally."

3573. Watson, Stuart L. and others. "Lincoln Lives in Appalachia." LIN HER, 75 [1973]: 56-76.

A collection of articles about Lincoln Memorial University, located in Harrowgate, Tennessee, and its vast collection of Lincolniana. The institution was founded in 1897 as a result of the efforts of General O.O. Howard. It publishes the LINCOLN HERALD.

3574. Wefer, Marion. "Another Assassination, Another Widow, Another Embattled Book." AM HER, 18 [5] [1967]: 79-88.

Excerpts from Elizabeth Keckley's 1868 book about her four years as Mary Lincoln's dressmaker.

3575. Weik, Jesse W. "A Law Student's Recollection of Abraham Lincoln." OUTLOOK, [February 11, 1911]: 311-314.

A young law student, Jonathan Birch, recalls fondly several

stories about his friend Abraham Lincoln. Later, through Birch's intercession, the president revoked an unjustified death sentence on a soldier in Birch's regiment, the 63rd Indiana.

3576. ———. "Personal Recollections of Abraham Lincoln." OUTLOOK, [February 13, 1909]: 345-348.

Once a youthful lawyer who knew Lincoln and collaborated with William Herndon in the famous biography, Weik discusses several of the president's unique qualities. The article appeared during the centennial of Lincoln's birth.

3577. ———. THE REAL LINCOLN: A PORTRAIT. Boston: Houghton Mifflin, 1922.

Acting on a suggestion from Leonard Swett many years before, Weik drew heavily on Herndon's manuscripts to amplify aspects of Lincoln's private life and legal career, which were not given detailed treatment by Herndon.

3578. Weisenburger, Francis P. "Lincoln and His Ohio Friends." OHIO HIS Q, 68 [1959]: 223-256.

A thorough look at the relationships between Lincoln and various Ohioans both before and during the presidency.

3579. Werstein, Irving. ABRAHAM LINCOLN VERSUS JEFFERSON DAVIS. New York: Crowell, 1959.

A rather shallow study in which the qualities of the two presidents are compared.

3580. Wheare, Kenneth C. ABRAHAM LINCOLN AND THE UNITED STATES. New York: Macmillan, 1949.

Intended to familiarize Britishers with Lincoln, this volume does little more than touch on the highlights of the man and his times. But the author does very well what he attempts to do.

3581. Whitney, Henry C. LIFE ON THE CIRCUIT WITH LINCOLN.... Boston, 1892.

Although the author wanders frequently from the main subject, he writes knowledgeably and entertainingly of those five or six fascinating years on the circuit. He knew Lincoln well and shared many experiences with him. A new edition, edited by Paul Angle, appeared in 1940.

3582. Williams, Wayne C. A RAIL SPLITTER FOR PRESIDENT. Denver: University of Denver Press, 1951.

In material drawn from more than 50 newspapers, we see Abraham Lincoln as he appeared to his contemporaries on the eve of becoming president. The well-selected quotations impart the feeling of the frenzied enthusiasm of one of our most crucial elections.

3583. Wilson, Charles R. "New Light on the Lincoln-Blair-Fremont Bargain." AHR, 42 [1936]: 71-78.

An analysis of the mystery attending Fremont's withdrawal from the presidential race on September 22, 1864 and the dismissal of Montgomery Blair from Lincoln's cabinet the following day. Author concludes that no deal was struck pertaining to these two events, as has been traditionally held. Fremont was finished well before his letter of withdrawal, and Blair would have been fired anyhow.

3584. Wilson, Rufus R. INTIMATE MEMORIES OF ABRAHAM LINCOLN. Elmira, New York: Primavera, 1945.

A collection of over 80 reminiscences of Lincoln's friends and contemporaries--a sequel to the following entry--which include among them, many not readily found elsewhere.

3585. ———. LINCOLN AMONG HIS FRIENDS. Caldwell, Idaho: Caxton, 1942.

While many of the 53 memoirs included in this work contain familiar material, there are a number more which are of interest. Some should be read with caution.

3586. ———. LINCOLN IN CARICATURE: A HISTORICAL COLLECTION.... Elmira, New York: Primavera, 1945. Reprint 1953.

An annotated volume of 165 cartoons and illustrations pertaining to the president.

3587. Wilson, William E. "'There I Grew Up.'" AM HER, 17 [5] [1966]: 30-31, 98-102.

An account of Lincoln's harsh Indiana boyhood.

3588. Winstead, Mrs. Thomas D. "Thomas Lincoln." KY HIS SOC REG, 71 [1973]: 189-193.

Author refutes the idea that Thomas Lincoln was a "no-good, poverty stricken" drunkard. He was, rather, thrifty, hard-working, and resourceful paying 118 pounds cash for land in 1803. He also served on juries time after time.

3589. Woldman, Albert A. LAWYER LINCOLN. Boston: Houghton Mifflin, 1936.

A thorough examination of all phases of Lincoln's legal career--his training, his practice, his partners, his cases, riding the circuit, and much more.

3590. Wolf, William J. THE ALMOST CHOSEN PEOPLE. Garden City, New York: Doubleday, 1959.

Religion was a part of Lincoln's social conscience, and his

religious development was a continuing process. He was also free of sectarianism. Author proves his thesis through Lincoln's words, character, and life. The volume is both interesting and impartial.

3591. Wrone, David R. "Abraham Lincoln's Idea of Property." SCI SOC, 33 [1969]: 54-70.

Lincoln never developed a clear concept concerning the idea of property, that is whether ownership of it might be a force for evil by the exploitation of society and the unpropertied. The Industrial Revolution had not progressed sufficiently in his lifetime for such an issue to become clearly defined.

3592. Wynne, Patricia H. "Lincoln's Western Image in the 1860 Campaign." MD HIS MAG. 59 [1964]: 165-181.

Lincoln's image as a westerner carved in the heroic mold of the pioneers who built a society out of the wilderness helped win support for him in the 1860 campaign.

3593. Zall, P.M., editor. ABE LINCOLN LAUGHING. Berkeley: University of California Press, 1982.

Consists of a collection of some 300 anecdotes by or about Lincoln. Arranged chronologically.

3594. Zilversmit, Arthur, editor. LINCOLN ON BLACK AND WHITE: A DOCUMENTARY HISTORY. Malabar, Florida: Krieger, 1983.

A collection of documents which contain various statements of Lincoln on the issue of race. While the data here may conflict, the reader has the opportunity to decide for himself if the president was a "racist" or not. This is a reprint of the 1971 edition.

B. ASSASSINATION

3595. Bishop, Jim. THE DAY LINCOLN WAS SHOT. New York: Harper, 1955.

A carefully-researched, well-written, "blow-by-blow" account of Lincoln's last day. One of the better books dealing with the subject.

3596. Brooks, George R. "Lincoln's Funeral Arrangements." MO HIS SOC BULL, 22 [1966]: 211-214.

A short note based on the papers of George R. Harrington, a treasury official who was selected to arrange the state funeral.

3597. Bryan, George S. THE GREAT AMERICAN MYTH. New York: Carrick and Evans, 1940.

After a careful review of the evidence, the author concludes that the "official" version of the assassination is the correct one. There was no conspiracy.

3598. Cochran, Hamilton. "Booth's Other Pistol." CWTI, 13 [9] [1975]: 20-24.

Author relates story of a small derringer with Booth's name carved on it which was supposedly found on the floor of the stage at Ford's Theater. He raises several questions. How did it get there? Did Booth have two pistols?

3599. Cottrell, John. THE ANATOMY OF AN ASSASSINATION: THE MURDER OF ABRAHAM LINCOLN. New York: Funk and Wagnalls, 1968.

A somewhat pedestrian and flawed recounting of the assassination story, in which a good deal of credence is given to the conspiratorial theories involving Secretary of War Stanton.

3600. DeWitt, David M. THE ASSASSINATION OF ABRAHAM LINCOLN.... New York, 1909.

An early, careful study in which some awkward questions about the conduct of the investigation, the assassination, the trial, and the execution of the conspirators are asked. Although new information has become available since this book was published, it remains one of the most reliable accounts.

3601. Eisenschiml, Otto. IN THE SHADOW OF LINCOLN'S DEATH. New York: W. Funk, 1940.

Author examines the subject most thoroughly, introduces new data, and speculates on Stanton's involvement.

3602. ———. WHY WAS LINCOLN MURDERED? Boston: Little, Brown, 1937.

In a piece of exhaustive research, the author raises many more awkward questions about the assassination than did DeWitt [number 3600] and practically charges certain people in high places--such as Stanton--with complicity in the plot. He concedes, however, that his conclusions are drawn from purely circumstantial evidence.

3603. Fleet, Betsy, editor. "A Chapter on Unwritten History: Richard Baynham Garrett's Account of the Flight and Death of John Wilkes Booth." VA MHB, 71 [1963]: 387-407.

Booth was apprehended on Garrett's farm near Fredericksburg, Virginia.

3604. Harbin, Billy J. "Laura Keene at the Lincoln Assassination." ED THEA J, 18 [1966]: 47-54.

Author seriously questions the story of Laura Keene, supported by alleged eye-witnesses in their later testimony, that the actress rushed to Lincoln's box at the Ford Theater after he was shot and held his head in her arms. However, the truth of the matter will probably never be known.

3605. Jones, James P. "Lincoln's Avengers: The Assassination and Sherman's Army. LIN HER, 64 [1962]: 185-190.

Describes the reaction of Sherman, his staff, and Joseph Johnston to the news.

3606. Kunhardt, Dorothy M. and Philip B. Kunhardt, Jr. TWENTY DAYS: A NARRATIVE IN TEXT AND PICTURES OF THE ASSASSINATION OF ABRAHAM LINCOLN.... New York: Harper and Row, 1965.

An outstanding illustrated history of the period of Lincoln's murder and the days following. Excellent photographs accompany a well-written text. Mrs. Kunhardt was able to draw on the fine collection of her father, Frederick Hill Meserve.

3607. Lattimer, John K. "The Wound That Killed Lincoln." JAMA, 187 [1964]: 480-489.

Had modern medical and surgical knowledge and techniques been available in 1865, Booth's shot still would have killed Lincoln.

3608. Levin, Alexandra L. "Who Hid John H. Surratt, The Lincoln Conspiracy Case Figure?" MD HIS MAG, 60 [1965]: 175-184.

Surratt is brought to trial.

3609. Lewis, Lloyd. MYTHS AFTER LINCOLN. New York: Harcourt, Brace, 1929.

Author builds on the tragic act of assassination in describing the emergence of Lincoln as a folk hero, an "American god."

3610. Markowitz, Arthur M. "Lincolniana: Tragedy of an Age: An Eyewitness Account of Lincoln's Assassination." JISHS, 66 [1973]: 205-211.

Roeliff Brinkerhoff, a captain in the Quartermaster's Corps, was present at the theater the night of Lincoln's assassination. In this account he relates his impressions of that fateful evening and conveys the sense of grief he and his contemporaries experienced upon the death of Lincoln.

3611. Pittman, Benn. THE ASSASSINATION OF PRESIDENT LINCOLN AND THE TRIAL OF THE CONSPIRATORS. Philip Van Doren Stern, editor. New York: Funk and Wagnalls, 1954.

A reprinting of the trial record prepared by Benn Pittman, the official trial recorder. Pittman's was the best of several versions of the trial proceedings which were published. While it is helpful to historians to have this scarce document again available, this edition is a photographic reproduction of the original and may require the use of a magnifying glass to read.

3612. Planck, Gary R. "Lincoln Assassination: The 'Forgotten' Litigation--Shuey v. United States [1875]." LIN HER, 75 [1973]: 86-92.

Shuey, executor of the man who informed the American government that Lincoln assassin John H. Suratt was a Swiss guard at the papal palace, sued the United States when the reward money was cancelled. He lost his case.

3613. ———. "Lincoln's Assassination: More 'Forgotten' Litigation, Ex parte Mudd [1868]." LIN HER, 76 [1974]: 86-90.

Dr. Samuel Mudd was sentenced to hard labor for life, but gained his release from President Johnson for the services he rendered during a yellow fever epidemic.

3614. Rietvald, Ronald D., editor. "An Eyewitness Account of Abraham Lincoln's Assassination." CWH, 22 [1976]: 60-69.

A previously unpublished memoir of an eyewitness, Frederick A. Sawyer, who was sitting in the orchestra seats below the presidential box.

3615. Roscoe, Theodore. THE WEB OF CONSPIRACY: THE COMPLETE STORY OF THE MAN WHO MURDERED ABRAHAM LINCOLN. Englewood Cliffs: Prentice-Hall, 1959.

An exhaustive study of the Lincoln assassination plot, which includes much familiar and some novel materials and interpretations. But withal, the mystery still remains a mystery.

3616. Searcher, Victor. THE FAREWELL TO LINCOLN. New York: Abingdon, 1965.

An unhurried trip on the Lincoln funeral train from Washington to Springfield. There are stops en route to reflect on Lincoln, his administration, and his place in American history.

3617. Sedgwich, Paul J. "Some Legal Aspects of the Trial of the Lincoln Conspirators." LIN HER, 68 [1966]: 3-10.

Author argues that a military commission was the proper tribunal to try the Lincoln assassins.

3618. Starr, John W. LINCOLN'S LAST DAY. New York: Stokes, 1922.

A microscopic study, virtually minute-by-minute, of Lincoln's last day. The conversations Lincoln had, the stories he told, and the business he transacted from the time he arose in the morning until he left for the theater are described.

3619. Stern, Philip Van Doren. THE MAN WHO KILLED LINCOLN. New York: Random House, 1939. Reprint 1955.

A literary hybrid, this extensively researched account of

Booth's role in the assassination plot draws a thin line between fiction and historical biography.

3620. Steward, Charles J. "Lincoln's Assassination and the Protestant Clergy of the North." JISHS, 54 [1961]: 268-293.

Thirty ministers in the North gave eleven theological justifications for the assassination of Lincoln, five of which pertained to Reconstruction. The majority called for an end to the lenient policies of Lincoln.

3621. Trefousse, Hans L. "Belated Revelations of the Assassination Committee." LIN HER, 58 [1956]: 13-16.

Extracts from material gathered by the committee to investigate the assassination.

3622. Turner, Thomas R. "Public Opinion and the Assassination of Abraham Lincoln." LIN HER, 78 [1976]: 17-24, 66-76.

Author concludes that Lincoln's contemporaries did not share the view of recent writers that the president was the victim of a conspiracy involving Secretary of War Stanton.

3623. Van Wenden, Kathy. "The Assassination of Abraham Lincoln: Its Effects in California." JW, 4 [1965]: 211-230.

An account of the reaction of the people--"shock and grief"--to news of the assassination. Article includes descriptions of various memorial services.

3624. Weichmann, Louis J. A TRUE HISTORY OF THE ASSASSINATION OF ABRAHAM LINCOLN AND OF THE CONSPIRACY OF 1865. Floyd E. Risvold, editor. New York: Knopf, 1975.

Weichmann, who was privy to the plot against Lincoln, became a government witness at the trial and provided the testimony victimizing Mary Surratt. To defend himself against such charges, which haunted him the rest of his life, he prepared a manuscript published here for the first time. The editor seems to support Weichmann's argument.

3625. Whiteman, Maxwell. WHILE LINCOLN LAY DYING. Philadelphia: Union League, n.d.

James "Corporal" Tanner, who later gained fame as pension commissioner and head of the GAR, lived next door to the Peterson house where Lincoln was taken after being shot. He was summoned to the scene to take shorthand notes of all conversations and interviews which took place while the president was dying. This book is a published version of Tanner's notes.

VI

BIOGRAPHIES AND PERSONAL ACCOUNTS

This section includes biographies, autobiographies, memoirs, reminiscences, papers, letters, journals, and diaries of significant civil and military persons, arranged alphabetically by subject. Comparable materials for officers beneath the rank of lieutenant-colonel and enlisted men will be found in SOLDIER LIFE. Biographies of blacks, women, writers, journalists, and artists will be found in the sections dealing with those subjects.

CHARLES FRANCIS ADAMS

3626. Adams, Charles F., Jr. CHARLES FRANCIS ADAMS. Boston, 1900.

A personal view of wartime diplomacy. Needs to be read along with later works.

3627. Duberman, Martin B. CHARLES FRANCIS ADAMS, 1807-1886. Boston: Houghton Mifflin, 1960.

This is, perhaps, the best study of Adams' life. It is based on the Adams' family papers.

3628. Ford, Worthington C., editor. A CYCLE OF ADAMS LETTERS, 1861-1865. 2 v. Boston: Houghton Mifflin, 1920.

An excellent collection of wartime letters between Charles Francis Adams and his two sons, Charles Francis Adams, Jr. and Henry Adams.

HENRY ADAMS

3629. Adams, Henry. THE EDUCATION OF HENRY ADAMS. Ernest Samuels, editor. Boston: Houghton Mifflin, 1973.

As secretary to his father Charles Francis Adams, special Minister to Great Britain, Henry Adams viewed the war from England and hence provides a memoir account of English diplomacy and popular opinion. Adams' personal response, written in retrospect, suggests his distaste for military action but also his desire that the Confederacy and slavery be abolished.

3630. ———. THE LETTERS OF HENRY ADAMS. Volume I. J.C. Levenson, et al., editors. Cambridge, Massachusetts: Belknap, 1982.

An extensive array of letters which cover the political crisis of 1860-1861 [written in Washington, D.C.] as well as the British diplomatic and popular reaction to the war from 1861-1865 [written in London]. The bulk of the letters are written to Henry's brother Charles Francis Adams, Jr., who served as a Union officer. A valuable insight into a Boston Brahmin's perspective on the war.

3631. Samuels, Ernest. THE YOUNG HENRY ADAMS. Cambridge: Harvard University Press, 1948.

Covered here are Adams' experiences as Washington correspondent for the BOSTON ADVERTISER just prior to the war and as London correspondent for the NEW YORK TIMES during the war. This offers an effective description of anti-slavery Unionist politics. See especially Chapters Three and Four.

ANDREW JONATHAN ALEXANDER

3632. Wilson, James H. THE LIFE AND SERVICES OF BREVET BRIGADIER GENERAL ANDREW JONATHAN ALEXANDER. New York, 1887.

This volume, published in the year of his death, is based on family letters and public records. Alexander, a Regular Army man, served on Bank's staff in Washington, with McClellan's on the Peninsula, and as chief of staff to General James H. Wilson.

ADELBERT AMES

3633. Ames, Blanche. ADELBERT AMES 1835-1933, GENERAL, SENATOR, GOVERNOR.... North Easton, Massachusetts: n.p., 1964.

A sympathetic biography written by Ames' wife, who was the daughter of Major-General Benjamin F. Butler. Ames served as colonel of the famous 20th Maine.

3634. Buice, S. David. "The Military Career of Adelbert Ames." SOUTH Q, 2 [1964]: 236-246.

The unjust criticism of Ames as a Mississippi "carpetbagger" during Reconstruction has blotted out his distinguished record as a Union officer in the Civil War. A West Point graduate, Ames commanded the 20th Maine and later led a brigade in the Eleventh Army Corps. Long after the war he was awarded the Medal of Honor for heroism at First Bull Run.

JOHN A. ANDREW

3635. Browne, Albert G. SKETCH OF THE OFFICIAL LIFE OF JOHN A. ANDREW AS GOVERNOR OF MASSACHUSETTS. New York, 1868.

Author was Andrew's secretary and based his account on personal observations and records.

3636. Chandler, Peleg W. MEMOIR OF GOVERNOR ANDREW. Boston, 1880.

A favorable account, including the author's own recollections.

3637. Pearson, Henry G. THE LIFE OF JOHN A. ANDREW, GOVERNOR OF MASSACHUSETTS, 1861-1865. 2 v. Boston, 1904.

Author relies principally on Andrew's private and official correspondence dealing mainly with his years as war governor.

CHRISTOPHER C. ANDREWS

3638. Andrews, Alice E., editor. CHRISTOPHER C. ANDREWS ... GENERAL IN THE CIVIL WAR: RECOLLECTIONS, 1829-1922. Cleveland, Ohio: Arthur H. Clarke, 1928.

Memories of his service in the Civil War, including his imprisonment in the South.

JOHN W.M. APPLETON

3639. Bailey, Kenneth R. "One of the Famous 54th Massachusetts: A Short Biography of General John W.M. Appleton." W VA HIS, 31 [1970]: 161-179.

A sketch of the military and business career of John Appleton, who for nearly two years served as an officer in the all-black 54th Massachusetts regiment. After the war he moved to West Virginia, where he was active in the coal business and rose to the rank of general in the state's National Guard.

SAMUEL CHAPMAN ARMSTRONG

3640. Talbot, Edith. SAMUEL CHAPMAN ARMSTRONG: A BIOGRAPHICAL STUDY. New York, 1904.

Armstrong was an officer in the 125th New York and later commanded Colored infantry regiments. This volume includes passages from a number of his letters home.

GEORGE ARROWSMITH

3641. Applegate, John S. REMINISCENCES AND LETTERS OF GEORGE ARROWSMITH. Red Bank, New Jersey: 1893.

A sympathetic account of a lieutenant colonel of the 157th New York, who was killed at Gettysburg.

DAVID RICE ATCHISON

3642. Parrish, William E. DAVID RICE ATCHISON OF MISSOURI: BORDER POLITICIAN. Columbia: University of Missouri Press, 1961.

Despite a stated bias in favor of his subject, the author presents a complete, balanced study of Atchison.

WILLIAM WOODS AVERELL

3643. Boehm, Robert B. "The Unfortunate Averell." CWTI, 5 [5] [1966]: 30-36.

A "personality profile" of the Union cavalry leader who was removed from his command for lack of aggressiveness.

3644. Eckert, Edward K. and Nicholas J. Amato, editors. "'A Long and Perilous Life': The Memoirs of William W. Averell." CWTI, 16 [1972]: [6] 22-30; [7] 36-41.

An account of Averell's adventures early in the war, carrying dispatches from St. Louis to Fort Arbuckle, Indian Territory, 300 miles beyond the western boundary of Arkansas.

WILLOUGHBY M. BABCOCK

3645. Babcock, Willoughby M. SELECTIONS FROM THE LETTERS AND DIARIES OF BREVET-BRIGADIER GENERAL WILLOUGHBY BABCOCK.... Albany: University of the State of New York, 1922.

A slim volume of letters and diaries from the commander of the 75th New York, which served in Florida and elsewhere. A good glimpse of camp life and the daily routine of the soldier in the Union army.

ABSOLOM BAIRD

3646. Baird, John A., Jr. "'For Gallant and Meritorious Service': Major General Absolom Baird." CWTI, 15 [3] [1976]: 4-9, 45-48.

A general account of the military career of the Union general who received the Medal of Honor for his actions at Jonesboro.

EDWARD D. BAKER

3647. Baltz, John D. HON. EDWARD D. BAKER, U.S. SENATOR FROM OREGON ... COLONEL E.D. BAKER'S DEFENSE IN THE BATTLE OF BALL'S BLUFF. Lancaster, Pennsylvania: 1888.

A sympathetic look at Baker's role in the battle of Ball's Bluff, fought at Leesburg, Virginia, October 21, 1861.

3648. Blair, Harry C. and Rebecca Tarshis. THE LIFE OF COLONEL EDWARD D. BAKER. Portland, Oregon: n.p., 1960.

Although this is not a very substantial work, it contains a good bit of material on California during the war.

NATHANIEL P. BANKS

3649. Harrington, Fred H. FIGHTING POLITICIAN, MAJOR GENERAL N.P. BANKS. Philadelphia: University of Pennsylvania Press, 1948.

In this solid biography, Banks' Civil War service is emphasized. All available material on the subject has been utilized.

3650. McDowell, John E. "Nathaniel P. Banks: Fighting Politico." CWTI, 11 [9] [1973]: 4-9, 44-47.

Although lacking in education and in military skill, Banks had one major ambition--to become president. The failure of the Red River expedition put an end to his presidential hopes. "The story of a successful failure."

WILLIAM FRANCIS BARTLETT

3651. Palfrey, Francis W. MEMOIR OF WILLIAM FRANCIS BARTLETT. Boston, 1878.

A Union general, Bartlett was a regimental and later a divisional commander. He was wounded at Yorktown, Port Hudson [twice], the Wilderness, and the Crater, where he was taken prisoner.

EDWARD BATES

3652. Beale, Howard K., editor. THE DIARY OF EDWARD BATES, 1859-1866. Washington, D.C.: U.S. Government Printing Office, 1933. Reprint 1971.

A well-edited diary which provides a useful look inside Lincoln's cabinet.

3653. Cain, Marvin R. LINCOLN'S ATTORNEY GENERAL: EDWARD BATES OF MISSOURI. Columbia: University of Missouri Press, 1965.

Author has written a good biography of Bates who was loyal to Lincoln, but who finally quit the cabinet, considering Lincoln a weak president. Bates was mediocre, dull, and had little or no influence on Lincoln and his administration.

3654. Frank, John P. "Edward Bates, Lincoln's Attorney General." A J LEG HIS, 10 [1966]: 34-50.

A sketch of Edward Bates, Lincoln's modest, inconspicuous attorney general [1861-1864] and his method of administering his office. He gave 154 opinions on various matters during his service.

JOHN BEATTY

3655. Beatty, John. THE CITIZEN-SOLDIER; OR, MEMOIRS OF A VOLUNTEER. Cincinnati, Ohio: 1879.

A Union general with the Army of the Cumberland, Beatty provides an excellent account of army life from an officer's point of view. Includes useful details on promotion and review boards and the daily routine of the officers.

JAMES ADDAMS BEAVER

3656. Burr, Frank A. LIFE AND ACHIEVEMENTS OF JAMES ADDAMS BEAVER. Philadelphia, 1882.

A thorough study of the life of the colonel of the 148th Pennsylvania and later governor of the state.

HIRAM G. BERRY

3657. Gould, Edward K. MAJOR GENERAL HIRAM G. BERRY.... Rockland, Maine: 1899.

An able study of the diverse career of a Union general, which includes his wartime correspondence. Berry was killed leading a bayonet attack at Chancellorsville.

JOHN BIGELOW

3658. Clapp, Margaret A. FORGOTTEN FIRST CITIZEN: JOHN BIGELOW. Boston: Little, Brown, 1947.

An excellent biography of the American minister to France during the war.

HORACE BINNEY

3659. Binney, Charles C. THE LIFE OF HORACE BINNEY. Philadelphia, 1903.

Biography of the well-known Pennsylvania attorney who ably defended some of Lincoln's controversial constitutional moves.

JAMES GILLESPIE BIRNEY

3660. Fladeland, Betty. JAMES GILLESPIE BIRNEY: SLAVEHOLDER TO ABOLITIONIST. Ithaca: Cornell University Press, 1955.

Excellent biography of an important abolitionist. As executive secretary of the American Anti-Slavery Society he favored political action rather than military action.

DAVID BELL BIRNEY

3661. Davis, Oliver W. LIFE OF DAVID BELL BIRNEY, MAJOR GENERAL UNITED STATES VOLUNTEERS. Philadelphia, 1867.

Son of James Gillespie Birney, David Birney served in several important command positions with the Army of the Potomac until dying of malaria in October 1864.

JEREMIAH SULLIVAN BLACK

3662. Black, Chauncey F. ESSAYS AND SPEECHES OF JEREMIAH S. BLACK. New York, 1885.

This work includes a biographical sketch of Black, who was a cabinet officer in the Buchanan administration. From Pennsylvania, Black was appointed Secretary of State in 1860.

3663. Brigance, William N. JEREMIAH SULLIVAN BLACK, A DEFENDER OF THE CONSTITUTION.... Philadelphia: University of Pennsylvania Press, 1934.

A straightforward account with little evaluation of Black's achievements.

JAMES GILLESPIE BLAINE

3664. Blaine, James G. TWENTY YEARS OF CONGRESS. 2 v. Norwich, Connecticut: 1884-1886.

Only four chapters of Blaine's autobiography deal with the Civil War years.

AUSTIN BLAIR

3665. Fennimore, Jean J.L. "Austin Blair: Civil War Governor, 1861-1864." MICH HIS, 49 [1965]: 193-227, 344-369.

The problems confronting the wartime governor of Michigan are revealed in these articles.

BLAIR FAMILY

3666. Smith, William E. THE FRANCIS PRESTON BLAIR FAMILY IN POLITICS. 2 v. New York: Macmillan, 1933. Reprint 1969.

A useful work dealing with the affairs of the important Missouri family which played an influential role in wartime politics.

FRANK BLAIR

3667. Wurthman, Leonard B. "Frank Blair: Lincoln's Congressional Spokesman." MO HIS R, 64 [1970]: 263-288.

Frank Blair, who served in Congress during the war, effectively set forth the President's views and defended his policies.

JAMES GILPATRICK BLUNT

3668. Blunt, James G. "General Blunt's Account of His War Experiences." KAN HIS Q, 1 [1932]: 211-265.

A report to the Adjutant General of Kansas written by Blunt in 1866 in which he relates many of his war experiences. He also "abuses" many of his contemporaries.

GEORGE W. BOOTH

3669. Booth, George W. "Running the Inland Blockade." CWH, 11 [1972]: 12-19.

A New Jersey hat manufacturer, Booth traveled by road, river, and train through the Confederate blockade to inspect his brother's branch office in New Orleans. A very interesting account.

JOHN WILKES BOOTH

3670. Cheney, Thomas E. "Facts and Folklore in the Story of John Wilkes Booth." W FOLK, 22 [1963]: 171-177.

After Booth died his body was preserved and eventually put on display [in a railroad car] by Bill Evans, carnival king. In 1933 it was bought for $5,000. What happened after this is anybody's guess.

ARTHUR INGRAHAM BOREMAN

3671. Woodward, Isaiah A. "Arthur Ingraham Boreman: A Biography." W VA HIS, 31 [1969/1970]: 206-269; 32 [1970/1971]: 10-48.

A sketch of West Virginia's first governor.

EDWARD BOUTON

3672. Bouton, Edward. EVENTS OF THE CIVIL WAR. Los Angeles, 1906.

A personal account by a Union officer who rose from captain to brigadier general. He was provost marshal at Memphis following its capture in 1862.

GEORGE SEWALL BOUTWELL

3673. Boutwell, George A. REMINISCENCES OF SIXTY YEARS IN PUBLIC AFFAIRS. 2 v. New York, 1902.

Useful memoirs, including numerous documents, by the commissioner for internal revenue.

EDWARD STUYVESANT BRAGG

3674. Hardgrove, J.G. "General Edward S. Bragg Reminisces." WIS MAG HIS, 33 [1950]: 281-309.

Anecdotes from the life of General Edward S. Bragg, lawyer, soldier, statesman, diplomat, who commanded a Wisconsin unit in the Army of the Potomac. The account is based on Bragg's own recollections as told to a former law partner late in life.

JOHN BRECKINRIDGE

3675. Davis, William C. BRECKINRIDGE: STATESMAN, SOLDIER, SYMBOL. Baton Rouge: Louisiana State University Press, 1974.

This is the first thorough, scholarly study of the man who was vice-president under Buchanan at the time of secession and who became a Confederate general.

ROBERT J. BRECKINRIDGE

3676. Gilliam, Will D., Jr. "Robert J. Breckinridge: Kentucky Unionist." KY HIS SOC REG, 69 [1971]: 362-385.

A sketch of Kentucky's best known Unionist, who was a clergyman, slaveholder, emancipationist, editor, and educator.

BENJAMIN HELM BRISTOW

3677. Webb, Ross A. "A Yankee From Dixie: Benjamin Helm Bristow." CWH, 10 [1964]: 80-94.

Author argues that a majority of Kentuckians were Unionists, like Bristow.

B. GRATZ BROWN

3678. Peterson, Norman L. FREEDOM AND FRANCHISE: THE POLITICAL CAREER OF B. GRATZ BROWN. Columbia: University of Missouri Press, 1965.

A respectable biography of the Missouri wartime Radical, postwar conservative, and Liberal Republican vice-presidential nominee. Emphasis is placed on Missouri state politics in the Civil War and Reconstruction. The work grew out of the author's doctoral dissertation.

ORVILLE HICKMAN BROWNING

3679. Baxter, Maurice G. ORVILLE H. BROWNING, LINCOLN'S FRIEND AND CRITIC. Bloomington: Indiana University Press, 1957.

A scholarly well-written account of Lincoln's friend from his Illinois days, although not a great deal of new material is to be found here. One-third of the book covers Browning's career up to 1861, one-third covers the war and early Reconstruction period, while he was United States senator and cabinet officer, and the final third stresses his later years as a successful lawyer. Browning the person is not easily picked out in this.

3680. Pease, Theodore C. and James G. Randall. THE DIARY OF ORVILLE HICKMAN BROWNING. 2 v. Springfield: Illinois State Historical Library, 1925-1933.

While this is a detailed and informative set, the going is a little heavy at times.

WILLIAM G. BROWNLOW

3681. Coulter, Ellis M. WILLIAM G. BROWNLOW, FIGHTING PARSON OF THE SOUTHERN HIGHLANDS. Chapel Hill: University of North Carolina Press, 1937.

Standard study of the fierce Unionist from East Tennessee. Few secessionists could control this sharp-tongued editor-minister.

WILLIAM CULLEN BRYANT

3682. Bryant, William Cullen II and Thomas G. Goss, editors. THE

LETTERS OF WILLIAM CULLEN BRYANT. 4 v. New York: Fordham University Press, 1984.

Volume Four of this excellently edited series covers the years 1858-1864, the high point of Bryant's influence on public affairs.

JAMES BUCHANAN

3683. Klein, Philip S. PRESIDENT JAMES BUCHANAN: A BIOGRAPHY. University Park: Pennsylvania State University Press, 1962.

A sympathetic study of the much-maligned president who presided over secession. The author succeeds, in some degree, in improving the reputation of Buchanan.

WILLIAM A. BUCKINGHAM

3684. Buckingham, Samuel G. THE LIFE OF WILLIAM A. BUCKINGHAM, THE WAR GOVERNOR OF CONNECTICUT. Springfield, Massachusetts: 1894.

More than a biography, this work, drawn from private sources as well as public documents, is also an account of the activities of Connecticut troops during the war.

JOHN BUFORD

3685. Weigley, Russell F. "John Buford." CWTI, 5 [3] [1966]: 14-23.

Author argues that Buford's role on the first day at Gettysburg has been exaggerated.

MILTON BURCH

3686. Canan, Howard V. "Milton Burch: Anti-Guerrilla Fighter." MO HIS R, 59 [1963]: 223-242.

Burch is described as the hero of the Missouri state militia in its fight against guerrillas.

JOHN W. BURGESS

3687. Maness, Lonnie E. "John W. Burgess: A Unionist in Tennessee." TENN HIS Q, 36 [1977]: 352-366.

At the age of 18 in 1861, this future professor of political science at Columbia University, fled to West Tennessee to join the Union army.

AMBROSE E. BURNSIDE

3688. Cullen, Joseph P. "'The Very Beau Ideal of a Soldier': A Personality Profile of Ambrose Burnside." CWTI, 16 [5] [1977]: 4-10, 38-44.

Author analyzes Burnside's character and seeks to explain his failure.

3689. Poore, Benjamin P. THE LIFE AND PUBLIC SERVICES OF AMBROSE E. BURNSIDE, SOLDIER, CITIZEN, STATESMAN. Providence, 1882.

An early effort to reestablish Burnside's reputation, although much of the book deals with his life after the war.

BENJAMIN FRANKLIN BUTLER

3690. Butler, Benjamin F. AUTOBIOGRAPHY AND PERSONAL REMINISCENCES OF MAJOR GENERAL BENJ. F. BUTLER. Boston, 1892.

In this massive memoir, Butler defends all of his legal, political, and military activities.

3691. ———. PRIVATE AND OFFICIAL CORRESPONDENCE OF GEN. BENJAMIN F. BUTLER DURING THE PERIOD OF THE CIVIL WAR. Jessie A. Marshall, editor. 5 v. Norwood, Massachusetts: Plimpton Press, 1917.

This comprehensive group of papers was collected and published by the Butler family as a defense of Butler's wartime actions.

3692. Harmond, Richard. "'The Beast' in Boston: Benjamin F. Butler as Governor of Massachusetts." JAH, 55 [1968]: 266-280.

Butler was governor during the 1880s.

3693. Holzman, Robert S. STORMY BEN BUTLER. New York: Macmillan, 1954.

A fairly good, sympathetic study, which views Butler as a statesman rather than a demagogue. However, this book adds little that is new.

3694. Horowitz, Murray M. "Ben Butler and the Negro: 'Miracles Are Occurring.'" LA HIS, 17 [1976]: 159-186.

Describes how Butler's wartime experience converted him from a pro-slavery to an anti-slavery supporter.

3695. Nash, Howard P. STORMY PETREL: THE LIFE AND TIMES OF GENERAL BENJAMIN F. BUTLER, 1818-1893. Rutherford, New Jersey: Fairleigh Dickenson University Press, 1969.

A rather standard biography of Butler, drawing heavily on secondary sources and while not offering a great deal that is new, stresses Butler's positive accomplishments.

3696. Russell, Francis. "Butler the Beast?" AM HER, 19 [3] [1969]: 48-53, 76-80.

An understanding sketch of Butler which notes his forgotten virtues in addition to his well-remembered faults.

3697. Trefousse, Hans L. BEN BUTLER, THE SOUTH CALLED HIM BEAST! New York: Twayne, 1957.

This is the most scholarly work on Butler which stresses his worthwhile accomplishments in the field of reform.

3698. Werlich, Robert. "BEAST" BUTLER: THE INCREDIBLE CAREER OF MAJOR GENERAL BENJAMIN FRANKLIN BUTLER. Washington, D.C.: Quaker Press, 1962.

A brief, undocumented, popular work which might be of interest to people who like brief, undocumented, popular works.

3699. West, Richard S. LINCOLN'S SCAPEGOAT GENERAL: A LIFE OF BENJAMIN F. BUTLER, 1818-1893. Boston: Houghton Mifflin, 1965.

A good study of the politician turned general, who continually infuriated his superiors and frequently embarrassed the government.

DANIEL BUTTERFIELD

3700. Butterfield, Julia L., editor. A BIOGRAPHICAL MEMORIAL OF GENERAL DANIEL BUTTERFIELD. New York, 1904.

The extensive correspondence of the general presents him in a favorable light.

3701. Patterson, Gerard. "Daniel Butterfield." CWTI, 12 [7] [1973]: 12-19.

An examination of General Hooker's much disliked chief of staff. In spite of his unpopularity, Butterfield rose rather rapidly through the ranks and became a major general.

SIMON CAMERON

3702. Bradley, Erwin S. SIMON CAMERON, LINCOLN'S SECRETARY OF WAR: A POLITICAL BIOGRAPHY. Philadelphia: University of Pennsylvania Press, 1966.

This well-researched work seeks to revise the traditional, unfavorable view of Lincoln's first and short-lived war secretary.

HENRY WARD CAMP

3703. Trumbull, Henry C. THE KNIGHTLY SOLDIER: A BIOGRAPHY OF MAJOR HENRY WARD CAMP, TENTH CONN. VOLS. Boston, 1865.

Still a useful account of military service in Virginia and North Carolina derived from letters and diaries.

EDWARD R.S. CANBY

3704. Heyman, Max L., Jr. PRUDENT SOLDIER: A BIOGRAPHY OF MAJOR GENERAL E.R.S. CANBY. Glendale, California: Arthur H. Clarke, 1959.

An authoritative biography of the general who commanded the Union forces in New Mexico during the Confederate invasion. In 1862 Canby turned his command over to Carleton and returned east. Also deals with the actions of the California Volunteers in the Southwest.

LeGRAND BOUTON CANNON

3705. Cannon, LeGrand B. PERSONAL REMINISCENCES OF THE REBELLION, 1861-1866. New York, 1895.

This officer's memoirs cover affairs in eastern Virginia in the early part of the war, when he served under the command of General John Wool.

JAMES HENRY CARLETON

3706. Clendenen, Clarence C. "General James Henry Carleton." NM HIS R, 30 [1955]: 23-43.

Carleton organized the California Volunteers in 1862 and proceeded to occupy New Mexico.

3707. Hunt, Aurora. MAJOR GENERAL JAMES HENRY CARLETON.... Glendale, California: Arthur H. Clarke, 1958.

An account of the man who commanded the California Column. Much of this had already appeared in author's THE ARMY OF THE PACIFIC. [See 2899]

JOSHUA LAWRENCE CHAMBERLAIN

3708. Chamberlain, Joshua L. THE PASSING OF THE ARMIES: AN ACCOUNT OF THE FINAL CAMPAIGN OF THE ARMY OF THE POTOMAC. New York, 1915. Reprint 1975.

An interesting personal account of the final fighting in Virginia written long after the war. The passage of time may have obscured some of the details.

3709. Wallace, Willard M. SOUL OF THE LION: A BIOGRAPHY OF GENERAL JOSHUA L. CHAMBERLAIN. New York: Nelson, 1960.

Chamberlain commanded the famous 20th Maine, which performed so heroically at Little Round Top. This is a good, substantive biography of the man who later was governor of Maine and president of Bowdoin College. During the war he fought in 24 major engagements, was wounded six times, and awarded the Medal of Honor for Little Round Top.

ZACHARIAH CHANDLER

3710. Harris, Wilmer C. PUBLIC LIFE OF ZACHARIAH CHANDLER, 1851-1875. Lansing, Michigan: Michigan Historical Commission, 1917.

A very unsatisfactory resume of Chandler's political career, although the author attempted to study his subject with "reasonable impartiality."

SALMON PORTLAND CHASE

3711. Chase, Salmon P. DIARY AND CORRESPONDENCE OF SALMON P. CHASE. Washington, D.C.: 1903.

Covers Chase's career from 1846 to 1870.

3712. Donald, David, editor. INSIDE LINCOLN'S CABINET: THE CIVIL WAR DIARIES OF SALMON P. CHASE. New York: Longmans, Green, 1954.

An excellent edition of Chase's diaries, accompanied by extensive notes and a useful introduction.

3713. Hart, Albert B. SALMON PORTLAND CHASE. Boston, 1899.

An early, though still useful, biography derived from Chase's papers and diaries.

3714. Schuckers, Jacob W. THE LIFE AND PUBLIC SERVICES OF SALMON PORTLAND CHASE. New York, 1874.

An even earlier, eulogistic biography drawn from Chase's papers and public statements.

3715. Warden, Robert B. AN ACCOUNT OF THE PRIVATE LIFE AND PUBLIC SERVICES OF SALMON PORTLAND CHASE. Cincinnati, Ohio: 1874.

Another early, lengthy, laudatory biography.

AUGUSTUS LOUIS CHETLAIN

3716. Chetlain, Augustus L. RECOLLECTION OF SEVENTY YEARS. Galena, Illinois: 1899.

Chetlain was a brigadier general who served throughout the war. The book recalls his military service and much else.

JOHN M. CHIVINGTON

3717. Craig, Reginald S. THE FIGHTING PARSON: BIOGRAPHY OF COLONEL JOHN M. CHIVINGTON. Los Angeles: Western Lore Press, 1959.

A revisionist biography of the architect of the "Sand Creek Massacre," in which the author seeks to restore Chivington's reputation and good name.

BRUTUS J. CLAY

3718. Hood, James L. "The Union and Slavery: Congressman Brutus J. Clay of the Bluegrass." KY HIS SOC REG, 75 [1977]: 214-221.

Elected to Congress in 1863 as a War Democrat, Clay supported much of the Republican program, which eventually cost him his seat.

CASSIUS MARCELLUS CLAY

3719. Clay, Cassius M. THE LIFE OF CASSIUS MARCELLUS CLAY.... 2 v. Cincinnati, 1886.

This autobiography, drawn from the author's memoirs, writings, and speeches, covers his public service before, during, and after the war. There is considerable material of value on his wartime diplomatic service in Russia.

3720. Richardson, H. Edward. CASSIUS MARCELLUS CLAY: FIREBRAND OF FREEDOM. Lexington: University of Kentucky Press, 1976.

A contribution to the Kentucky Bicentennial Bookshelf, this short biography is a somewhat thin portrayal of the wartime minister to St. Petersburg.

3721. Smiley, David L. LION OF WHITEHALL: THE LIFE OF CASSIUS M. CLAY. Madison: University of Wisconsin Press, 1962.

Cassius M. Clay, a hard-nosed, stubborn Kentuckian, was active in politics for over 50 years, but never obtained the high public office he sought. During the Civil War he was American minister to the Russian court, but this did not satisfy his ambition. A good biography of a man and his long life of frustration.

GUSTAVE PAUL CLUSERET

3722. Blaisdell, Lowell L. "A French Civil War Adventurer: Fact and Fancy." CWH, 12 [1966]: 246-257.

Cluseret was a French soldier of fortune who served as a Union officer in the Valley Campaign.

SCHUYLER COLFAX

3723. Moore, Ambrose Y. THE LIFE OF SCHUYLER COLFAX. Philadelphia, 1868.

A campaign biography to accompany Colfax's 1868 bid for the vice-presidency.

3724. Smith, Willard H. SCHUYLER COLFAX: THE CHANGING FORTUNES OF A POLITICAL IDOL. Indianapolis: Indiana Historical Bureau, 1952.

An excellent biography based on all relevant materials.

ELBRIDGE J. COPP

3725. Copp, Elbridge J. REMINISCENCES OF THE WAR OF THE REBELLION, 1861-1865. Nashua, New Hampshire: 1911.

Copp claimed to be "the youngest commissioned officer in the Union Army," but his failing memory led to many errors and unbalanced judgments.

JACOB DOLSON COX

3726. Cox, Jacob D. MILITARY REMINISCENCES OF THE CIVIL WAR. 2 v. New York, 1900.

A valuable memoir by a veteran general officer who saw extensive action. Fletcher Pratt called Cox a "universal genius." A lawyer, he later became governor of Ohio and was a member of Grant's cabinet for a brief time.

SAMUEL SULLIVAN COX

3727. Cox Samuel S. EIGHT YEARS IN CONGRESS, FROM 1857 TO 1865. New York, 1865.

"Sunset" Cox's stand as a War Democrat is brought out in this large collection of his speeches and memoirs.

3728. Lindsey, David. "'Sunset' Cox." CWTI, 4 [6] [1965]: 17-21.

Author traces efforts of Cox to defend freedom of expression in wartime.

3729. ———. "SUNSET" COX, IRREPRESSIBLE DEMOCRAT. Detroit: Wayne State University Press, 1959.

A Democrat, Cox sought to prevent secession and war, but supported the Union war effort. He opposed confiscation and emancipation, but supported the 13th Amendment.

3730. ———. "'Sunset' Cox, Leader of Lincoln's Loyal Opposition, 1861-1865." MID AM, 37 [1955]: 3-30.

Summarizes the main themes of the above entry.

JAMES CRAIG

3731. Robinett, Paul M. "The Military Career of James Craig." MO HIS R, 66 [1971]: 49-75.

A lawyer and Democratic congressman from Missouri, Craig became a brigadier general in 1862 and held commands in Nebraska, Kansas, and Missouri.

SAMUEL J. CRAWFORD

3732. Plummer, Mark A. FRONTIER GOVERNOR: SAMUEL J. CRAWFORD OF KANSAS. Lawrence: University Press of Kansas, 1971.

Crawford arrived in Kansas in 1859, served in the legislature after statehood, commanded a black regiment during the war, and was governor in the early years of Reconstruction. This is a competent biography of a relatively minor figure.

HENRY HUSTON CRITTENDEN

3733. Crittenden, Henry H. THE CRITTENDEN MEMOIRS. New York: Putnam, 1936.

Reader can obtain an idea of Civil War Missouri and the lawlessness which dominated the state.

JOHN JORDON CRITTENDEN

3734. Kirwan, Albert D. JOHN J. CRITTENDEN: THE STRUGGLE FOR THE UNION. Lexington: University of Kentucky Press, 1962.

An excellent biography of Kentucky's foremost political figure, based primarily on manuscript material. Crittenden supported Lincoln's administration and opposed secession.

GEORGE CROOK

3735. Schmitt, Martin F., editor. GENERAL GEORGE CROOK, HIS AUTOBIOGRAPHY. Norman: University of Oklahoma Press, 1946.

This celebrated Indian fighter devotes very little space to his Civil War experiences.

WILLIAM HENRY CROOK

3736. Gerry, Marguerita S., editor. THROUGH FIVE ADMINISTRATIONS: REMINISCENCES OF COLONEL WILLIAM H. CROOK. New York, 1910.

Although Crook was a bodyguard for Lincoln, most of this memoir is devoted to the post-Civil War years.

JOHN THOMAS CROXTON

3737. Miller, Rex. "John Thomas Croxton: Scholar, Lawyer, Soldier, Military Governor, Newspaperman, Diplomat, and Mason." KY HIS SOC REG, 74 [1976]: 281-299.

A Kentucky Unionist, Croxton served with distinction in the Union army and was active in Republican politics after the war.

SHELBY MOORE CULLOM

3738. Cullom, Shelby M. FIFTY YEARS OF PUBLIC SERVICE: PERSONAL RECOLLECTIONS OF SHELBY M. CULLOM, SENIOR UNITED STATES SENATOR FROM ILLINOIS. Chicago, 1911.

Cullom's memoir provides a valuable source for the study of politics during the war.

ANDREW GREGG CURTIN

3739. Albright, Rebecca G. "The Civil War Career of Andrew Gregg Curtin." W PA HIS MAG, 47 [1964]: 323-341; 48 [1965]: 19-42, 151-173.

A sketch of the Pennsylvania governor during the war. An active supporter of the Union, he was known not only for the support the state gave to the war effort, but also for his efforts on behalf of soldiers' dependents.

3740. Beers, Paul P. "Andrew Gregg Curtin." CWTI, 6 [2] [1967]: 12-20.

A brief profile of this independent governor of Pennsylvania. His real interest lay in education, and he signed the bill creating the first free public libraries in the state.

3741. Egle, William H., editor. ANDREW GREGG CURTIN: HIS LIFE AND SERVICES. Philadelphia, 1895.

While this work suffers the shortcomings of any anthology to which a number of writers contributed, it remains one of the few full treatments of Pennsylvania's wartime governor.

GEORGE WILLIAM CURTIS

3742. Norton, Charles E., editor. ORATIONS AND ADDRESSES OF GEORGE WILLIAM CURTIS. 3 v. New York, 1894.

A collection of speeches on issues of the day, including many besides those dealing with the Civil War, by one of the leading, contemporary orators and men of letters.

WILLIAM B. CUSHING

3743. Roske, Ralph J. and Charles Van Doren. LINCOLN'S COMMANDO: THE BIOGRAPHY OF COMMANDER W.B. CUSHING, U.S.N. New York: Harper, 1957.

An undocument biography of Cushing, a Union naval hero, who lived a life of reckless daring.

GEORGE ARMSTRONG CUSTER

3744. Custer, George A. CUSTER IN THE CIVIL WAR: HIS UNFINISHED MEMOIRS. John M. Carroll, editor. San Rafael, California: Presidio Press, 1977.

A reprint of seven short chapters written by Custer which were published in GALAXY magazine in 1876. Includes Custer's reports on his activities at Gettysburg. Of interest to Custer fans is the bibliography which is very good.

3745. Hofling, Charles K. "George Armstrong Custer." MONTANA, 21 [2] [1971]: 32-43.

A "psychoanalytic approach," written by a doctor, makes interesting reading.

3746. Kinsley, D.A. FAVOR THE BOLD: CUSTER, THE CIVIL WAR YEARS. New York: Holt, Rinehart & Winston, 1967.

Popular, undocumented account which covers only Custer's wartime service. "Novelized."

3747. Merington, Marguerite, editor. THE CUSTER STORY: THE LIFE AND INTIMATE LETTERS OF GENERAL GEORGE A. CUSTER AND HIS WIFE ELIZABETH. New York: Devin-Adair, 1950.

The letters of George and Elizabeth Custer present an interesting view of the war and soldiering. They also provide an "on-the-spot" account of the general's various activities.

3748. Monaghan, Jay. CUSTER: THE LIFE OF GENERAL GEORGE ARMSTRONG CUSTER. Boston: Little, Brown, 1959.

This is a good biography, which covers chiefly the Civil War years. The author paints the reckless, carefree Custer in vivid tones, perfectly in keeping with the general's personality and character.

3749. Russell, Don. "Custer's First Charge." BY VALOR AND ARMS, 1 [1] [1974]: 20-29.

Discusses Custer's Civil War career. He took part in every battle in which the Army of the Potomac participated with one exception.

3750. Urwin, Gregory J.W. CUSTER VICTORIOUS: THE CIVIL WAR BATTLES OF GENERAL GEORGE ARMSTRONG CUSTER. Rutherford, New Jersey: Fairleigh Dickinson Press, 1982.

Details Custer's Civil War battles. Inclined to be too sympathetic and oversimplified. Says "thanks to Custer and the Michigan Brigade as much as to any" the Union won at Gettysburg.

3751. Van de Water, Frederic F. GLORY-HUNTER: A LIFE OF GENERAL CUSTER. Indianapolis: Bobbs-Merrill, 1934.

The egotism of Custer is brought out in this well-reseached biography.

EPHRAIM CUTLER

3752. Cutler, Julia Perkins, editor. LIFE AND TIMES OF EPHRAIM CUTLER. Cincinnati, Ohio: 1890.

A worthwhile volume, drawn from the journals and correspondence of the Ohio congressman.

ULRIC DAHLGREN

3753. Dahlgren, John A.B. MEMOIR OF ULRIC DAHLGREN. Philadelphia, 1872.

A factual, although too uncritical account of the Union officer, written by his father, Rear Admiral John A.B. Dahlgren.

3754. Stuart, Meriwether. "Colonel Ulric Dahlgren and Richmond's Union Underground." VA MHB, 72 [1964]: 52-204.

The body of Colonel Dahlgren, who was killed in the Kilpatrick-Dahlgren raid of January 1864, was secretly buried by Confederate authorities. Union sympathizers removed and hid the body.

CHARLES A. DANA

3755. Dana, Charles A. RECOLLECTIONS OF THE CIVIL WAR. New York, 1902.

A well-written collection of reminiscences authored by the former managing editor of Greeley's NEW YORK TRIBUNE. He served as assistant secretary of war in 1863-1864. He later became owner of the NEW YORK SUN.

CHARLES HENRY DAVIS

3756. Davis, Charles H. LIFE OF CHARLES HENRY DAVIS, REAR ADMIRAL, 1807-1877. Boston, 1899.

A satisfactory biography of the Union naval officer, written by his son.

DAVID DAVIS

3757. King, Willard L. LINCOLN'S MANAGER, DAVID DAVIS. Cambridge: Harvard University Press, 1960.

A scholarly biography which sheds light on an ignored figure of the Civil War and Reconstruction, who was Lincoln's campaign manager in 1860--the big fight of his life--a Supreme Court Justice, and a United States Senator. There may be more on Lincoln than Davis here, at least until the assassination.

HENRY WINTER DAVIS

3758. Davis, Henry W. SPEECHES AND ADDRESSES DELIVERED IN THE CONGRESS OF THE UNITED STATES. New York, 1867.

This is one of the best collections of primary materials on the Radical Republican from Maryland.

3759. Henig, Gerald S. HENRY WINTER DAVIS: ANTEBELLUM AND CIVIL WAR CONGRESSMAN FROM MARYLAND. New York: Twayne, 1973.

Based on a thorough study of the sources, this work while a

sympathetic treatment, notes Davis's vanity, vindictiveness, and self-righteousness.

3760. Steiner, Bernard C. LIFE OF HENRY WINTER DAVIS. Baltimore: John Murphy, 1916.

Drawing heavily on Davis's speeches, the author does not probe too deeply into his subject matter.

3761. Tyson, Raymond W. "Henry Winter Davis: Orator for the Union." MD HIS MAG, 58 [1963]: 1-19.

Author concentrates on Davis's superb oratorical skills.

3762. ———. "A Southerner Who Spoke for the Union." SOUTH SPEECH J, 30 [1965]: 117-132.

Although criticizing the Republicans, Davis was strong pro-Union. He died at the age of 48 in 1864.

JEFF C. DAVIS

3763. Jones, James P. "General Jeff C. Davis, USA, and Sherman's Georgia Campaign." GA HIS Q, 47 [1963]: 231-248.

A look at the performance of one of Sherman's ablest lieutenants during the Georgia campaign of 1864.

RUFUS R. DAWES

3764. Dawes, Rufus R. SERVICE WITH THE SIXTH WISCONSIN VOLUNTEERS. Marietta, Ohio: 1890. Reprint 1962.

An excellent personal narrative based on the author's diary and letters.

HENRY CLAY DEAN

3765. Beisel, Suzanne. "Henry Clay 'Dirty' Dean." ANN IOWA, 36 [1963]: 502-524.

A look at the celebrated Iowa copperhead.

PHILIP REGIS DENIS DeTROBRIAND

3766. DeTrobriand, Regis D. FOUR YEARS WITH THE ARMY OF THE POTOMAC. Boston, 1889.

The author came to the United States from France before the war, married, and became an American citizen. After war broke out, he became colonel of the 55th New York. Later he was a divisional commander in the Army of the Potomac, rising to the rank of major general at the close of the war. He continued in the regular army after the war. This is one of the better histories of the war.

JOHN ADAMS DIX

3767. Dix, Morgan, editor. MEMOIRS OF JOHN ADAMS DIX. 2 v. New York, 1883.

Edited by his son, these memoirs of a "politician-general" contain only one chapter on the Civil War. That one is useful for the New York Draft Riots of 1863.

3768. Turner, Justin G. "General Dix and the American Flag." MANU, 21 [1] [1969]: 17-23.

Dix coined the phrase, "If anyone attempts to haul down the American flag, shoot him on the spot."

GRENVILLE M. DODGE

3769. Dugan, Ruth E. "Grenville Mellen Dodge." PALIMP, 11 [1930]: 160-171.

A brief biographical account of this soldier, frontiersman, and railroad engineer. A colonel in the 4th Iowa, he was promoted to brigadier general after the battle of Pea Ridge.

3770. Hirschson, Stanley P. GRENVILLE M. DODGE, SOLDIER, POLITICIAN, RAILROAD PIONEER. Bloomington, Indiana University Press, 1967.

Numerous mistakes and a lack of balance mar this biography of an unusual man.

3771. Mauck, Genevieve P. "Grenville Mellen Dodge, Soldier-Engineer." PALIMP, 47 [1966]: 433-475.

A sketch of aspects of Dodge's life, covering military service, construction of the Union Pacific, erection of his home in Council Bluffs, Iowa, and retirement years.

3772. Perkins, Jacob R. TRAILS, RAILS AND WAR: THE LIFE OF GENERAL G.M. DODGE. Indianapolis: Bobbs Merrill, 1929.

A sympathetic study, but somewhat unreliable.

STEPHEN A. DOUGLAS

3773. Capers, Gerald M. STEPHEN A. DOUGLAS: DEFENDER OF THE UNION. Boston: Little, Brown, 1959.

This is an excellent, factual account of Douglas's career While admittedly pro-Douglas, it is very thought-provoking.

3774. Johannsen, Robert W., editor. THE LETTERS OF STEPHEN A. DOUGLAS. Urbana: University of Illinois Press, 1961.

Probably the definitive collection of Douglas's letters. Unfortunately, speeches, legal briefs, and legislation he sponsored are not included.

3775. Johnson, Allen. STEPHEN A. DOUGLAS: A STUDY IN AMERICAN POLTICS. New York, 1908.

A substantial biography which remains useful many years later.

3776. Milton, George F. EVE OF CONFLICT: STEPHEN A. DOUGLAS AND THE NEEDLESS WAR. Boston: Houghton Mifflin, 1934. Reprint 1964.

This biography of Douglas based on thousands of newly available Douglas documents, postulates the "needless war" theory and argues that had Douglas's leadership been followed, peace would have prevailed.

3777. Wells, Damon. STEPHEN DOUGLAS: THE LAST YEARS, 1857-1861. Austin: University of Texas Press, 1971.

A useful study of the final four frustrating years of Douglas's life. His aims were to preserve the Union and attain the presidency, but because of the force of circumstances neither goal was realistic.

FREDERICK DOUGLASS

3778. Douglass, Frederick. LIFE AND TIMES OF FREDERICK DOUGLASS. Hartford, Connecticut: 1881.

An excellent autobiography, although only two chapters cover the Civil War.

3779. Foner, Philip S. THE LIFE AND WRITINGS OF FREDERICK DOUGLASS. 4 v. New York: International Publishers, 1950-1955.

There may be a few gaps in this set, but not very many.

3780. Holland, Frederic M. FREDERICK DOUGLASS: THE COLORED ORATOR. New York, 1895.

An early, friendly biography.

3781. Quarles, Benjamin. FREDERICK DOUGLASS. Washington, D.C.: Associated Publishers, 1948.

The definitive biography of the famous black fighter for the rights of black people.

3782. Washington, Booker T. FREDERICK DOUGLASS. Philadelphia, 1907.

A sympathetic but honest biography of Douglass by the man who became his most famous successor in the fight for the rights of black people.

NEAL DOW

3783. Dow, Neal. THE REMINISCENCES OF NEAL DOW, RECOLLECTIONS OF EIGHTY YEARS. Portland, Maine: 1898.

Dow, a brigadier general was wounded at Port Hudson, captured, and lodged in Libby prison. The wartime reminiscences of the "Father of Prohibition" make interesting reading.

WILLIAM FRANKLIN DRAPER

3784. Draper, William F. RECOLLECTIONS OF A VARIED CAREER. Boston, 1908.

Draper, an officer in the 36th Massachusetts who rose to the rank of brigadier general, devotes a good bit of his autobiography to the war years.

JOHN VAN DEUSEN DU BOIS

3785. Du Bois, John. "The Civil War Journals and Letters of Colonel John Van Deusen Du Bois, April 12, 1861 to October 16, 1862." Jared C. Lobdell, editor. MO HIS R, 60 [1966]: 436-459; 61 [1967]: 21-50.

An excellent personal account of early campaigning in the western theater. The battles of Wilson's Creek, Shiloh, and Corinth are described in detail.

SAMUEL FRANCIS DuPONT

3786. DuPont, Samuel F. SAMUEL FRANCIS DuPONT: A SELECTION FROM HIS CIVIL WAR LETTERS. 3 v. John D. Hayes, editor. Ithaca: Cornell University Press, 1969.

An excellent record of service in the navy by the Union admiral, in these voluminous letters to his wife.

WILDER DWIGHT

3787. Dwight, Wilder. LIFE AND LETTERS OF WILDER DWIGHT.... Boston, 1868.

A fine collection of letters from the lieutenant colonel of the 2nd Massachusetts, who was killed at Antietam. This is a good source written by an articulate and perceptive person.

ELMER E. ELLSWORTH

3788. Ettlinger, John R. "A Young Hero--Elmer Ellsworth, 1837-1861." BOOKS AT BROWN, 19 [1963]: 23-68.

A sketch of the first northern officer killed in action.

3789. Ingraham, Charles. ELMER E. ELLSWORTH AND THE ZOUAVES OF '61. Chicago: University of Chicago Press, 1925.

Rather short and too laudatory.

3790. Patterson, Richard K. "'The Greatest Little Man I Ever Met.'" A HIS ILL, 6 [8] [1971]: 30-40.

This 22-year-old federal officer was almost like a son to Lincoln and was virtually a member of the Lincoln family.

3791. Randall, Ruth P. COLONEL ELMER ELLSWORTH: A BIOGRAPHY OF LINCOLN'S FRIEND AND FIRST HERO OF THE CIVIL WAR. Boston: Little, Brown, 1960.

A carefully researched and sympathetic study, using the story of Ellsworth to recreate the atmosphere surrounding the people who first responded to the call to arms. Ellsworth was killed at Alexandria, Virginia and his regiment was confined to prevent them from burning Alexandria to the ground.

JOHN ERICSSON

3792. Church, William C. THE LIFE OF JOHN ERICSSON. 2 v. New York, 1890.

This is a good biography based on Ericsson's private papers.

3793. White, Ruth. YANKEE FROM SWEDEN: THE DREAM AND THE REALITY IN THE DAYS OF JOHN ERICSSON. New York: Holt, 1960.

An undocumented biography of the man who designed and built the MONITOR and also invented the screw propeller.

WILLIAM M. EVARTS

3794. Barrows, Chester L. WILLIAM M. EVARTS: LAWYER, DIPLOMAT, STATESMAN. Chapel Hill: University of North Carolina Press, 1941.

A critical appraisal of one of the foremost lawyers of the period.

3795. Dyer, Brainerd. THE PUBLIC CAREER OF WILLIAM M. EVARTS. Berkeley: University of California Press, 1933.

An important study of a major political and legal figure, during the Civil War and after. He was a special agent in Europe in wartime.

ERASTUS FAIRBANKS

3796. Newell, Graham S. "Erastus Fairbanks." VT HIS, 32 [1964]: 59-64.

Sketch of the first Civil War governor of Vermont.

DAVID GLASGOW FARRAGUT

3797. Lewis, Charles L. DAVID GLASGOW FARRAGUT. 2 v. Annapolis: United States Naval Institute, 1941-1943.

A comprehensive two volume work dealing with the life of Farragut, He was the first man to hold the rank of admiral in the United States navy.

JOSIAH M. FAVILL

3798. Favill, Josiah. THE DIARY OF A YOUNG OFFICER SERVING WITH THE ARMIES OF THE UNITED STATES.... Chicago, 1909.

A detailed record of service from the beginning of the war through Spottsylvania by an officer of the 57th New York, who rose to the rank of colonel at the close of the war.

WILLIAM PITT FESSENDEN

3799. Fessenden, Francis. LIFE AND PUBLIC SERVICES OF WILLIAM PITT FESSENDEN.... 2 v. Boston, 1907. Reprint 1970.

A thoroughgoing study of an important figure who was twice United States senator from Maine and secretary of the treasury, written by his son who was a colonel in the 25th Maine.

3800. Jellison, Charles A. FESSENDEN OF MAINE: CIVIL WAR SENATOR. Syracuse: Syracuse University Press, 1962.

A carefully-researched work, this is the first scholarly biography of Fessenden, who represented Maine in the United States Senate from 1854-1869. Author views his subject as a moderate or conservative, rather than a Radical Republican as he is often classified.

STEPHEN J. FIELD

3801. Swisher, Carl B. STEPHEN J. FIELD, CRAFTSMAN OF THE LAW. Washington, D.C.: Brookings Institution, 1930.

An excellent biography of an important Supreme Court Justice.

HORACE NEWTON FISHER

3802. Fisher, Horace C. THE PERSONAL EXPERIENCES OF COLONEL HORACE NEWTON FISHER IN THE CIVIL WAR: A STAFF OFFICER'S STORY. Boston: Thomas Todd, 1960.

Fisher was an inspector general in the western theater. This biography contains many extracts from his letters.

CLINTON BOWEN FISK

3803. Kirby, James E. "How To Become a Union General Without Military Experience." MO HIS R, 66 [1972]: 360-376.

Author describes how Fisk, the founder of Fisk University and a St. Louis businessman, raised a regiment.

MICHAEL HENDRICK FITCH

3804. Fitch, Michael H. ECHOES OF THE CIVIL WAR AS I HEAR THEM. New York, 1905.

Fitch was an officer in a Wisconsin unit which served in the western theater.

GEORGE ALEXANDER FORSYTH

3805. Forsyth, George A. THRILLING DAYS IN ARMY LIFE. New York, 1900.

Memoirs of a Union officer who rose from the rank of private to a brigadier general.

GUSTAVUS VASA FOX

3806. Thompson, Robert M. and Richard Wainwright. CONFIDENTIAL CORRESPONDENCE OF GUSTAVUS VASA FOX, ASSISTANT SECRETARY OF THE NAVY, 1861-1865. 2 v. New York: De Vinne Press, 1918-1920.

This is a basic source for the study of Union naval operations.

3807. Merrill, James M. "Strategy Makers in the Union Navy Department." MID AM, 44 [1962]: 19-32.

The author credits Fox for a major role in the direction of Union naval operations.

JOHN FRASER

3808. Coleman, Helen T.W. "Brigadier General John Fraser ... in the Union Army." W PA HIS MAG, 44 [1961]: 257-260.

A Scottish born Jefferson College professor, Fraser held a command in the Army of the Potomac.

JOHN C. FREMONT

3809. Bartlett, Ruhl J. JOHN C. FREMONT AND THE REPUBLICAN PARTY. Columbus: Ohio State University Press, 1930.

This study is devoted largely to Fremont's political career.

3810. Davis, William C. "John C. Fremont." A HIS ILL, 5 [2] [1970]: 4-11, 44-47.

Davis points out that Fremont lacked "common sense, judgment, humility, and even integrity on occasion," although no one can doubt his courage.

3811. Nevins, Allan. FREMONT, PATHMARKER OF THE WEST. New York: Appleton-Century, 1939.

This is <u>the</u> authoritative biography of Fremont in war and peace. Fremont had a varied life. Most of it was devoted to western exploration, some to politics. As a consequence, only about 100 pages of this big, scholarly work deals with the war years. This is an updated version of the author's earlier two volume, illustrated biography.

HENRY SANFORD GANSEVOORT

3812. Hoadley, John C., editor. MEMORIAL OF HENRY SANFORD GANSEVOORT, ... COLONEL 13TH NEW YORK STATE VOLUNTEER CAVALRY. Boston, 1875.

Contains correspondence of Gansevoort who rose from the rank of private to brigadier general.

JAMES ABRAM GARFIELD

3813. Garfield, James A. THE WILD LIFE OF THE ARMY: CIVIL WAR LETTERS OF JAMES A. GARFIELD. Frederick D. Williams, editor. East Lansing, Michigan: Michigan State University Press, 1964.

By his judicious editing and annotating, the author has enhanced the value of this important work. The letters provide good glimpses of camp life and the daily military routine in both theaters of war from an officer's perspective.

3814. Marshall, S.L.A. "Garfield as a General." CWTI, 6 [9] [1968]: 4-9, 45-47.

General Marshall, a military historian, concludes that Garfield was a "model, the ideal type of American civilian soldier."

3815. Norris, James D. and James K. Martin, editors. "Three Civil War Letters of James A. Garfield." OHIO HIS, 74 [1965]: 247-252.

Three letters written by Garfield to Major Frederick A. Williams. They deal with local and national politics, Fort Sumter, and Garfield's promotion.

3816. Peskin, Allan. GARFIELD. Kent, Ohio: Kent State University Press, 1978.

A prize-winning study of Garfield's diversified career.

JOHN WHITE GEARY

3817. Beers, Paul. "A Profile of John W. Geary." CWTI, 11 [3] [1970]: 10-16.

A sketch of the Union major general who served in many of the major campaigns, both in the East and West. Twice wounded, he became Republican governor of Pennsylvania after the war.

JOHN GIBBON

3818. Gibbon, John. PERSONAL RECOLLECTIONS OF THE CIVIL WAR. New York: Putnam, 1928.

Excellent memoirs of one of the ablest Union generals. He served as one of the surrender commissioners at Appomattox.

WILLIAM HARVEY GIBSON

3819. Bigger, David D. OHIO'S SILVER-TONGUED ORATOR: LIFE AND SPEECHES OF GENERAL WILLIAM H. GIBSON. Dayton, Ohio: 1901.

Useful materials pertaining to Gibson's service with the 49th Ohio are included in this volume.

ALFRED WEST GILBERT

3820. Smith, William E. and Ophea D. Smith, editors. COLONEL A.W. GILBERT, CITIZEN-SOLDIER OF CINCINNATI. Cincinnati: Historical and Philosophical Society of Ohio, 1934.

This work includes an account of the campaigns of 1861-1862 while Gilbert was in service with the 39th Ohio.

LOUIS M. GOLDSBOROUGH

3821. Still, William N., Jr. "Admiral Goldsborough's Feisty Career." CWTI, 17 [10] [1979]: 12-20.

Admiral Goldsborough served well in North Carolina waters, but was blamed unfairly for his cautious policy in the Peninsular Campaign.

GEORGE HENRY GORDON

3822. Gordon, George H. BROOK FARM TO CEDAR MOUNTAIN IN THE WAR OF THE GREAT REBELLION, 1861-1862. Cambridge, Massachusetts: 1883.

One of several volumes of wartime memoirs by the Union general who served in the eastern theater. This book covers the first two years of war. An opinionated officer, Gordon wrote vivid prose reflecting his views.

3823. ———. A WAR DIARY OF EVENTS IN THE WAR OF THE GREAT REBELLION, 1863-1865. Boston, 1882.

A good account of Gordon's service along the South Atlantic and Gulf Coasts in the last two years of the war. Gordon's qualities, noted in the previous entry, are also apparent in this work.

LEWIS ADDISON GRANT

3824. Keyes, Charles. "Major General Lewis Addison Grant." ANN IOWA, 12 [1921]: 511-532.

A sketch of the schoolteacher-lawyer turned soldier, who was wounded on several occasions and won the Medal of Honor. He was a native of Vermont. After the war he served as assistant secretary of war under Harrison.

ULYSSES SIMPSON GRANT

3825. Badeau, Adam. MILITARY HISTORY OF ULYSSES S. GRANT, FROM APRIL 1861 to APRIL 1865. 3 v. New York, 1885.

Badeau, who served as Grant's secretary, wrote this exhaustive and friendly study of Grant's war years.

3826. Bond, Brian. "Appomattox: The Triumph of General Grant." HIS TOD, 15 [1965]: 297-305.

Notes Grant's development as a military leader and compares him to his contemporaries.

3827. Brooks, William E. GRANT OF APPOMATTOX: A STUDY OF THE MAN. Indianapolis: Bobbs-Merrill, 1942.

A good general biography which divides Grant's life into two phases. From childhood to 1863 when he took command before Vicksburg, and from Vicksburg to Appomattox.

3828. Bryson, Thomas A. "Walter George Smith and General Grant's Memoirs." PA MHB, 94 [1970]: 233-244.

Smith was a young Philadelphia lawyer, whose career was enhanced because of his role in litigation concerning the sale of Grant's memoirs.

3829. Carpenter, John A. ULYSSES S. GRANT. New York: Twayne, 1970.

Author believes Lincoln was slow "to give recognition to Grant." Although this work is brief and somewhat superficial, it is sufficiently well-done to satisfy the general reader. The main focus is on Grant's post-war years.

Catton, Bruce. [See numbers 192, 193, 198, 205, 206, 214.]

3830. Coolidge, Louis A. ULYSSES S. GRANT. Boston: Houghton, Mifflin, 1917.

This book is friendly and thorough, but less than half of the contents deal with the war years.

3831. Coppee, Henry. GRANT AND HIS CAMPAIGNS: A MILITARY BIOGRAPHY. New York, 1886.

This is an early "official" biography, which is not as well done as many of the later ones.

3832. Crane, James L. "Grant From Galena." CWTI, 18 [4] [1979]: 26-29.

A flattering description of Grant by the chaplain of the 21st Illinois based on his observations in 1861.

3833. Dana, Charles A. and James H. Wilson. THE LIFE OF ULYSSES S. GRANT, GENERAL OF THE ARMIES OF THE UNITED STATES. Springfield, Massachusetts: 1868.

This book suffers the weaknesses of most campaign biographies.

3834. Deming, Henry C. THE LIFE OF ULYSSES S. GRANT, GENERAL UNITED STATES ARMY. Hartford, Connecticut: 1868.

Another campaign biography.

3835. Edmonds, Franklin S. ULYSSES S. GRANT. Philadelphia: G.W. Jacobs, 1915.

While rather old, this is still a balanced biography.

3836. Garland, Hamlin. ULYSSES S. GRANT: HIS LIFE AND CHARACTER. New York, 1898.

The celebrated writer composed a friendly, readable, but not necessarily scholarly study of the general-president.

3837. Grant, Ulysses S. PERSONAL MEMOIRS OF U.S. GRANT. 2 v. New York: 1885-1886. Reprint 1952.

Composed while Grant was at death's door, this autobiography is of great value for the study of the war.

3838. Grant, Ulysses S., III. "Civil War: Facts and Fiction." CWH, 2 [1956]: 29-40.

The grandson defends his grandfather from "unfounded," but oft repeated criticisms.

3839. ———. ULYSSES S. GRANT: WARRIOR AND STATESMAN. New York: Morrow, 1969.

Although written by Grant's grandson and overly sympathetic, this is still a book of interest. No really new material is to be found here. The purpose is to refute "incorrect" accounts of Grant's career.

3840. Green, Horace. GENERAL GRANT'S LAST STAND: A BIOGRAPHY. New York: Scribners, 1936.

A fairly successful attempt to review Grant's life, as Grant himself remembered it.

3841. Headley, Joel T. THE LIFE OF ULYSSES S. GRANT, EX-PRESIDENT OF THE UNITED STATES AND GENERAL OF THE UNITED STATES ARMY. New York, 1885.

This is a lengthy, laudatory, and not very scholarly work.

3842. Hesseltine, William B. ULYSSES S. GRANT, POLITICIAN. New York: Dodd, Mead, 1935.

Author examines Grant's career in politics with a view to improving his reputation.

3843. King, Charles. THE TRUE ULYSSES S. GRANT. Philadelphia, 1914.

This volume is an effort to "accentuate the positive" in Grant, something which the author feels had not been done before.

3844. Lewis, Lloyd. CAPTAIN SAM GRANT. Boston: Little, Brown, 1950.

An excellent, friendly study of Grant's career up to the beginning of the Civil War. This is the first volume of the trilogy which was completed by Bruce Catton. [See numbers 192 and 193]

3845. Mansfield, Edward D. A POPULAR AND AUTHENTIC LIFE OF ULYSSES S. GRANT. Cincinnati, 1868.

Another campaign biography which focuses chiefly on Grant during the war.

3846. Marshall-Cornwell, Sir James. GRANT AS MILITARY COMMANDER. New York: Van Nostrand Reinhold, 1970.

A good introductory, though lightly documented, study of Grant as a commander by a British general, geographer, and military historian.

3847. McCormick, Robert R. ULYSSES S. GRANT, THE GREAT SOLDIER OF AMERICA. New York: Appleton-Century, 1934.

This favorable study of Grant by the publisher of the CHICAGO TRIBUNE concentrates on the period of the war.

3848. McFeely, William S. GRANT: A BIOGRAPHY. New York: Norton, 1981.

This is the most recent and best biography of Grant. Carefully researched and well-written, it might be classed as a work of psycho-history. Grant's strengths as well as weaknesses are pointed out, but confidence in his own ability never wavered. Only in the midst of war and when writing his memoirs did he find personal fulfillment.

3849. Meredith, Roy, editor. MR. LINCOLN'S GENERAL: U.S. GRANT--AN ILLUSTRATED AUTOBIOGRAPHY. New York: Dutton, 1959.

Employing Grant's own words, accompanied by close to 300 illustrations, the editor has put together an intriguing volume.

3850. Nye, Wilbur S. "Grant--Genius or Fortune's Child." CWTI, 4 [3] [1965]: 4-15, 43-44.

A favorable view of Grant the man and general.

3851. Palmer, Loomis T. THE LIFE OF GENERAL U.S. GRANT, HIS EARLY LIFE, MILITARY ACHIEVEMENTS.... Chicago, 1885.

This is a lengthy, uncritical work, which dwells largely on Grant's post-presidential travels around the globe.

3852. Pitkin, Thomas M. THE CAPTAIN DEPARTS. Carbondale, Illinois: Southern Illinois University Press, 1973.

A brief but moving book dealing with Grant's last fight--his efforts to complete his memoirs before overtaken by death in 1885. Wiped out by business failure, Grant struggled heroically to finish the book and thus provide an income for his family. He succeeded as the memoir became a best seller.

3853. Porter, Horace. CAMPAIGNING WITH GRANT. New York, 1897. Several reprints.

Porter, who was an aide and confidant of Grant, wrote a compelling and informed study of the man in action.

3854. Richardson, Albert D. A PERSONAL HISTORY OF ULYSSES S. GRANT. Hartford, 1868.

Another campaign biography.

3855. Simon, John Y. THE PAPERS OF ULYSSES S. GRANT. 8 v. Carbondale: Southern Illinois University Press, 1967 - .

This definitive collection of Grants works--15 volumes are projected--is marked by careful documentation and general scholarly excellence. Eight volumes were published as of 1982.

3856. ———. "From Galena to Appomattox: Grant and Washburne." JISHS, 58 [1965]: 165-189.

Author describes the close relationship between Grant and Washburne, noting the importance of the congressman to Grant for his return to military respectability. The close ties were broken in an unpleasant 1880 dispute over the Republican presidential nomination.

3857. ———. ULYSSES S. GRANT CHRONOLOGY. Columbus, Ohio: Ohio Historical Society, 1963.

A scholarly convenient reference covering the years 1822 to 1902.

3858. Smith, Nicholas. GRANT, THE MAN OF MYSTERY. Milwaukee, 1909.

Assuming there was a "mystery" in Grant's character, the author seeks to unravel it.

3859. Wilson, James G. THE LIFE AND PUBLIC SERVICES OF ULYSSES SIMPSON GRANT.... New York, 1885.

A revised and enlarged edition of an 1868 campaign biography, which includes Grant's presidential years and beyond. Wilson was a brigadier general in the war, one of the "boy wonders," a major general within five years of his graduation from West Point. Later he became a well-known writer and editor.

3860. Wister, Owen. ULYSSES S. GRANT. Boston, 1901.

A short, but enjoyable study written by a popular writer of the day.

3861. Woodward, William E. MEET GENERAL GRANT. New York: Liveright, 1928.

A popular, highly readable biography.

WALTER QUINTIN GRESHAM

3862. Gresham, Matilda. LIFE OF WALTER QUINTIN GRESHAM, 1832-1895. 2 v. Chicago: Rand, McNally, 1919.

As a young man, the future federal judge and secretary of state served with the 33rd Indiana. Some of his wartime letters are included in this biography.

JOSIAH BUSHNELL GRINNELL

3863. Grinnell, Josiah B. MEN AND EVENTS OF FORTY YEARS. Boston, 1891.

This valuable autobiography by an important Iowa political figure covers the years from 1850 to 1890.

ADAM GUROWSKI

3864. Fischer, Leroy H. LINCOLN'S GADFLY, ADAM GUROWSKI. Norman: University of Oklahoma Press, 1964.

While this is not quite a biography, the author corrects many of Gurowski's excessive judgments. Gurowski exercised more influence on Radical Republicans than on Lincoln with whom he had little contact.

3865. Gurowski, Adam. DIARY. 3 v. Boston, 1862-1866.

Arriving from eastern Europe at the outbreak of the Civil War, Gurowski became a self-appointed propagandist for the Radical Republicans. His outspoken journals contain criticism of many things and people.

HENRY WAGER HALLECK

3866. Ambrose, Stephen E. HALLECK: LINCOLN'S CHIEF OF STAFF. Baton Rouge: Louisiana State University Press, 1962.

A scholarly, well-written biography of one of the most unpopular figures in the Union's high military echelon. Yet, in this sympathetic study, Halleck emerges as a capable administrator who made his nebulous general-in-chief position into an important part of the developing modern command system.

3867. Shutes, Milton H. "Henry Wager Halleck, Lincoln's Chief of Staff." CAL HIS Q, 16 [1937]: 195-208.

Halleck was one of four major generals who came from California. Prior to military service he had been active in financial and civic affairs in the new state and helped frame its first constitution.

JAMES ALEXANDER HAMILTON

3868. Hamilton, James A. REMINISCENCES OF JAMES A. HAMILTON.... New York, 1869.

Hamilton, whose autobiography covers more than half a century, was active in politics in New York during the war.

WILLIAM DOUGLAS HAMILTON

3869. Hamilton, William D. RECOLLECTIONS OF A CAVALRYMAN OF THE CIVIL WAR AFTER FIFTY YEARS, 1861-1865. Columbus, Ohio: Heer, 1915.

This memoir provides many valuable views of the daily routine of the cavalryman. Hamilton was a major, lieutenant-colonel, and colonel of the 9th Ohio Cavalry from 1862 to 1865.

HANNIBAL HAMLIN

3870. Hamlin, Charles E. THE LIFE AND TIMES OF HANNIBAL HAMLIN. Cambridge, Massachusetts: 1899.

Written by the grandson of Lincoln's first vice-president, this work has its shortcomings, but remains a useful biography of the man.

3871. Hunt, H. Draper. HANNIBAL HAMLIN OF MAINE: LINCOLN'S FIRST VICE-PRESIDENT. Syracuse: Syracuse University Press, 1969.

This effort to elevate the reputation of the forgotten wartime vice-president is only partially successful. Hamlin played a traditional, passive role as vice-president and was dropped from the Union ticket in 1864 in the interests of expediency. Not a great deal of material on the non-vice-presidential years is to be found here.

3872. McMurtry, R. Gerald. "Hannibal Hamlin--Lincoln's Vice President." LIN LORE, Number 1617 [1972]: 1-3.

A brief sketch of Hamlin, who found the office of vice-president a frustrating one.

3873. Weisenberg, Leonard A. "Hamlin of Maine." CWTI, 10 [8] [1971]: 35-44.

An account of the unhappy experience of Hannibal Hamlin, who left a strong senate seat to become an ignored vice-president. He was dropped from the ticket in 1864 only to see his successor shortly become president.

WINFIELD SCOTT HANCOCK

3874. Brisbin, James S. A SOLDIER'S STORY OF A SOLDIER'S LIFE: WINFIELD SCOTT HANCOCK. Philadelphia, 1880.

A brief campaign biography for Hancock and William H. English, Democratic candidates for president and vice-president in 1880.

3875. Forney, John W. LIFE AND MILITARY CAREER OF WINFIELD SCOTT HANCOCK. Boston, 1880.

A weak campaign biography.

3876. Hancock, Almira. REMINISCENCES OF WINFIELD SCOTT HANCOCK. New York, 1887.

This memoir by a worshipful wife contains less on the Civil War than one might expect.

3877. Junkin, David X. THE LIFE OF WINFIELD SCOTT HANCOCK: PERSONAL, MILITARY, AND POLITICAL. New York, 1880.

In spite of what has been said about campaign biographies, this is a respectable one, with emphasis on the war years.

3878. Taylor, John M. "General Hancock: Soldier of the Gilded Age." PENN HIS, 32 [1965]: 187-196.

A sketch of General Hancock, who was highly esteemed for his wartime record but whose post-war years were marked by disappointments--in the army and in politics.

3879. Tucker, Glenn. HANCOCK THE SUPERB. Indianapolis: Bobbs-Merrill, 1960.

An excellent biography which covers Hancock's wartime and post-war years very well. The dashing 2nd Corps commander is praised for his heroics at Williamsburg, the Wilderness, Spotsylvania, and Cold Harbor. The author's flair for writing exciting military history is apparent in the first modern study of Hancock.

3880. ———. "Winfield S. Hancock: A Personality Profile." CWTI, 7 [5] [1968]: 5-11, 45-48.

Hancock is viewed as perhaps the greatest Union soldier on the firing line.

3881. Walker, Francis A. GENERAL HANCOCK. New York, 1894.

A non-scholarly study by a man who served under Hancock. In later life, Walker was president of M.I.T. and became recognized as an outstanding educator, economist, and statistician.

HENRY EBENEZER HANDERSON

3882. Cummer, Clyde L., editor. YANKEE IN GRAY: THE CIVIL WAR MEMMOIRS OF HENRY E. HANDERSON, WITH A SELECTION OF HIS WARTIME LETTERS. Cleveland, Ohio: Western Reserve University Press, 1962.

Handerson was an Ohioan who served with a Confederate unit, the 9th Louisiana, in the eastern theater.

DOUGLAS HAPEMAN

3883. Adolphson, Steven J. "'Our Little Colonel': Douglas Hapeman." LIN HER, 75 [1972]: 18-28.

Hapeman, who commanded the 104th Illinois, was an outstanding battlefield commander and won the Medal of Honor at the age of 23.

JAMES HARLAN

3884. Brigham, Johnson. JAMES HARLAN. Iowa City, Iowa: 1913.

A solid biography of an Iowan who resigned from the United States Senate to serve briefly as Lincoln's secretary of interior.

WALTER HARRIMAN

3885. Hadley, Amos. LIFE OF WALTER HARRIMAN. Boston, 1898.

Harriman served as colonel of the 11th New Hampshire and was active in the state's politics.

BENJAMIN HARRISON

3886. Sievers, Harry, Jr. BENJAMIN HARRISON: HOOSIER WARRIOR. 2 v. Chicago: Regnery, 1952, 1959. Reprint 1960.

The first volume of this two volume biography of Harrison deals with his wartime career. The future president had a distinguished war record and nine chapters in the book deal with it. Harrison commanded the 70th Indiana which saw action in Kentucky, Tennessee, and the Atlanta Campaign.

JOHN FREDERICK HARTRANFT

3887. Barrett, Eugene A. "The Civil War Services of John F. Hartranft." PENN HIS, 32 [1965]: 166-186.

A lawyer and political figure, Hartranft enlisted in the Union army and rose to the rank of major general. He was awarded the Medal of Honor and was governor of Pennsylvania in the 1870s.

JAMES E. HARVEY

3888. Crofts, Daniel W. "James E. Harvey and the Secession Crisis." PA MHB, 103 [1972]: 177-195.

Harvey, who struggled for compromise, was named minister to Portugal in 1861. His peace policy was viewed as treasonable and destroyed his career.

FRANK ARETAS HASKELL

3889. Byrne, Frank L. and Andrew T. Weaver, editors. HASKELL OF GETTYSBURG: HIS LIFE AND CIVIL WAR PAPERS. Madison: State Historical Society of Wisconsin, 1970.

An excellent edition of all of Haskell's papers plus a biographical sketch. In addition to his memorable BATTLE OF GETTYSBURG, other perceptive letters analyzing campaigns and generals are also included here. A brilliant young officer, Haskell was cut down at Cold Harbor.

HERMAN HAUPT

3890. Flower, Frank A., editor. REMINISCENCES OF GENERAL HERMAN HAUPT.... Milwaukee, Wisconsin: 1901.

Haupt graduated from West Point in 1835 and became a very successful railroad engineer. He served in the Union army for less than two years, during most of which time he was in charge of military railroads. He authored many engineering books.

3891. Ward, James A. THAT MAN HAUPT: A BIOGRAPHY OF HERMAN HAUPT. Baton Rouge: Louisiana State University Press, 1973.

An exhaustive study of engineer Herman Haupt who had three significant careers in addition to his management of the federal railroad system in the Civil War. The detail may be too much for some, but everything you will ever want to know about Haupt is here.

JOSEPH ROSWELL HAWLEY

3892. Hawley, Joseph R. MAJOR GENERAL JOSEPH R. HAWLEY ... CIVIL WAR MILITARY LETTERS. Albert D. Putnam, editor. Hartford: Connecticut Civil War Centennial Commission, 1964.

A brief, but valuable, collection of letters by Hawley who served throughout the war. He was governor of Connecticut in 1866-1867 and later served as United States Congressman and Senator.

JOHN HAY

3893. Dennett, Tyler. JOHN HAY: FROM POETRY TO POLITICS. New York: Dodd, Mead, 1933.

A solid biography of John Hay, but suprisingly, Hay's years as one of Lincoln's secretaries does not receive a great deal of space.

3894. Hay, John. LINCOLN AND THE CIVIL WAR IN THE DIARIES AND LETTERS OF JOHN HAY. Tyler Dennett, editor. New York: Dodd, Mead, 1939.

A well-edited volume based on the wartime letters and diaries of John Hay. The selection is excellent.

RUTHERFORD BIRCHARD HAYES

3895. Barnard, Harry. RUTHERFORD B. HAYES AND HIS AMERICA. Indianapolis: Bobbs-Merrill, 1954.

A low-key, uninspired lawyer, Hayes was transformed by war into the dashing commander of the 23rd Ohio. he practically invited the Confederates to shoot him, which they did at South Mountain. The Civil War rounded out the personality and character of the future president and gave him full faith in himself.

3896. Davison, Kenneth E. THE PRESIDENCY OF RUTHERFORD B. HAYES. Wesport, Connecticut: Greenwood, 1972.

An excellent biography of Hayes as president, but only one page is devoted to Hayes' Civil War service.

3897. Hayes, Rutherford B. DIARY AND LETTERS OF RUTHERFORD BIRCHARD HAYES, NINETEENTH PRESIDENT OF THE UNITED STATES. 5 v. Charles R. Williams, editor. Columbus: Ohio State Archaeological and Historical Society, 1922-1926.

Hayes commanded the 23rd Ohio. Material on this experience is found in Volume Two of this set.

3898. Williams, T. Harry. HAYES OF THE TWENTY-THIRD: THE CIVIL WAR VOLUNTEER OFFICER. New York: Knopf, 1965.

This excellent biography of Hayes's military career is drawn largely from his letters and diaries. The 23rd Ohio spent much of the war in western Virginia which did not allow for many heroics, but its record was a good one. Author analyzes carefully the relative merits of commanders who had West Point training and those who did not--the "amateurs."

ALEXANDER HAYS

3899. Fleming, George T. LIFE AND LETTERS OF ALEXANDER HAYS. Pittsburgh: n.p., 1919.

Although not well-known, this is an excellent collection of Civil War letters. Hays rose to the rank of major general and commanded units in the Army of the Potomac from 1861 until his death in the Wilderness Campaign.

WILLIAM BABCOCK HAZEN

3900. Hazen, William B. A NARRATIVE OF MILITARY SERVICE. Boston, 1885.

A West Pointer, General Hazen served throughout the war in the western theater and later accompanied Sherman on his march to the sea and through the Carolinas.

WILLIAM H. HERNDON

3901. Donald, David. LINCOLN'S HERNDON. New York: Knopf, 1948.

An outstanding study of Lincoln's first and foremost biographer. Reader obtains a real insight into the character of Lincoln's law partner.

THOMAS H. HICKS

3902. Radcliffe, George L.P. GOVERNOR THOMAS H. HICKS OF MARYLAND AND THE CIVIL WAR. Baltimore, 1901.

A brief and sympathetic look at the governor of a critical state at the time of the outbreak of war. After a period of doubt Hicks came over to the support of the Union.

HENRY LEE HIGGINSON

3903. Perry, Bliss. LIFE AND LETTERS OF HENRY LEE HIGGINSON. 2 v. Boston: Atlantic Monthly Press, 1921.

About 100 pages are devoted to the war experiences of Higginson, who served with the 1st Massachusetts cavalry.

THOMAS WENTWORTH HIGGINSON

3904. Edelstein, Tilden G. STRANGE ENTHUSIASM: A LIFE OF THOMAS WENTWORTH HIGGINSON. New Haven: Yale University Press, 1968.

This is the most recent biography of the commander of the First South Carolina volunteers, the first all-black unit raised in the Civil War. It is an excellent though unflattering account of Higginson's life.

3905. Higginson, Mary T., editor. LETTERS AND JOURNALS OF THOMAS WENTWORTH HIGGINSON, 1846-1906. Boston: Houghton Mifflin, 1921. Reprint 1969.

Higginson's second wife compiled this volume which contains only one chapter on the Civil War.

3906. ———. THOMAS WENTWORTH HIGGINSON: THE STORY OF HIS LIFE. Boston, 1914.

This wifely biography draws heavily on Higginson's private papers.

3907. Meyer, Howard N. COLONEL OF THE BLACK REGIMENT: THE LIFE OF THOMAS WENTWORTH HIGGINSON. New York: Norton, 1967.

While undocumented and sympathetic, this is a thorough and balanced study of the abolitionist colonel.

3908. Wells, Anna M. DEAR PRECEPTOR: THE LIFE AND TIMES OF THOMAS WENTWORTH HIGGINSON. Boston: Houghton Mifflin, 1963.

A solid biography of this noted abolitionist. Higginson was one of the men who helped finance John Brown when he hoped to instigate a slave insurrection in Virginia. The attempt failed with Brown's capture at Harpers Ferry.

SAMUEL S. HILDEBRAND

3909. Evans, James W. and A. Wendell Keith, editors. AUTOBIOGRAPHY OF SAMUEL S. HILDEBRAND, THE RENOWNED MISSOURI "BUSHWACKER." Jefferson City, Missouri: 1870.

Hildebrand's memoirs, while not entirely dependable, provide a dramatic glimpse of warfare on the Missouri-Kansas frontier.

ETHAN ALLEN HITCHCOCK

3910. Hitchcock, Ethan A. FIFTY YEARS IN CAMP AND FIELD. W.V. Croffet, editor. New York, 1909.

This volume of memoirs was published by the author's descendants long after his death. Hitchcock served mainly as a staff officer in the war and was also involved in the prisoner exchange process.

FREDERICK LYMAN HITCHCOCK

3911. Hitchcock, Frederick L. WAR FROM THE INSIDE, OR PERSONAL EXPERIENCES, IMPRESSIONS.... Philadelphia, 1904.

Colonel of the 132nd Pennsylvania, Hitchcock wrote a useful memoir.

FREDERICK HOLBROOK

3912. Moore, Kenneth A. "Frederick Holbrook." VT HIS, 32 [1964]: 65-77.

Holbrook was the second Civil War governor of Vermont.

OLIVER WENDELL HOLMES, JR.

3913. Holmes, Oliver W., Jr. TOUCHED WITH FIRE: CIVIL WAR LETTERS AND DIARY OF OLIVER WENDELL HOLMES, JR. 1861-1864. Mark D. Howe, editor. Cambridge: Harvard University Press, 1946.

A valuable collection of letters from the future Supreme Court justice, supplying glimpses of the military routine from an officer's point of view. He served with the 20th Massachusetts.

3914. Howe, Mark D. JUSTICE OLIVER WENDELL HOLMES. Cambridge: Harvard University Press, 1957.

In this first of a multi-volume biography, the future jurist's Civil War experiences are catalogued.

JOSEPH HOOKER

3915. Hassler, William W. "'Fighting Joe' Hooker." CWTI, 14 [5] [1975]: 4-9, 36-46.

In this sketch of Hooker's war career, the author has supplied a friendly, but balanced glimpse of the tempestuous Union commander.

3916. Hebert, Walter H. FIGHTING JOE HOOKER. Indianapolis: Bobbs-Merrill, 1944.

A substantial, well-researched biography.

3917. Shutes, Milton H. "'Fighting Joe' Hooker." CAL HIS SOC Q, 16 [1937]: 304-320.

A friendly sketch of the Union general who was born and grew up in California. Author contends that despite his failure at Chancellorsville, Hooker was "one of the top generals of the Northern Armies."

OLIVER OTIS HOWARD

3918. Carpenter, John A. SWORD AND OLIVE BRANCH: OLIVER OTIS HOWARD. Pittsburgh: University of Pittsburgh Press, 1964.

A thorough, balanced biography of the Union general who failed at Chancellorsville, but succeeded with the Freedmen's Bureau. Throughout his lifetime of public service, Howard deserves high marks as the "Christian Soldier"--a crusader for racial equality--but who innocently became the target of a number of legal inquiries and investigations.

3919. ———. "O.O. Howard: General at Chancellorsville." CWH, 3 [1957]: 48-63.

Author evaluates the role of the unfortunate Howard at Chancellorsville.

3920. Howard, Oliver O. AUTOBIOGRAPHY OF OLIVER OTIS HOWARD, MAJOR GENERAL, UNITED STATES ARMY. 2 v. New York, 1907.

Generally, this is a good memoir by the commander of the 11th Corps. His recollections are both interesting and pertinent, although at times the author is inclined to wordiness.

3921. Holloway, Laura C. HOWARD, THE CHRISTIAN HERO. New York, 1885.

This early biography has been replaced by later works.

3922. McFeely, William S. YANKEE STEPFATHER, GENERAL O.O. HOWARD AND THE FREEDMEN. New Haven: Yale University Press, 1968.

A good, readable, and popular account of the Commissioner of the Freedmen's Bureau. Emphasis is on the post-war years.

LUCIUS F. HUBBARD

3923. Hubbard, Lucius F. "Letters of a Civil War Officer: L.F. Hubbard and the Civil War." N.B. Martin, editor. MINN HIS, 35 [1957]: 313-319.

A revealing set of letters from an articulate Union officer, who served with the 5th Minnesota and was breveted a brigadier general.

ANDREW ATKINSON HUMPHREYS

3924. Humphreys, Henry H. ANDREW ATKINSON HUMPHREYS. Philadelphia: Winston, 1924.

General Humphreys was an excellent topographical engineer, serving on McClellan's staff in 1862 and later becoming Meade's chief of staff. A man of wide scientific and literary interests, he wrote two books on the Civil War himself.

DANIEL E. HUNGERFORD

3925. Murphy, I.I. LIFE OF COLONEL DANIEL E. HUNGERFORD. Hartford, Connecticut: 1891.

Hungerford served with the 36th New York.

HENRY JACKSON HUNT

3926. Longacre, Edward G. THE MAN BEHIND THE GUNS: A BIOGRAPHY OF GENERAL HENRY JACKSON HUNT, CHIEF OF ARTILLERY, ARMY OF THE POTOMAC. South Brunswick, New Jersey: Barnes, 1977.

This is a solid biography of the argumentative, yet honest chief of artillery. Hunt should probably receive much more credit than has been accorded him to date.

3927. ———. "The Soul of Our Artillery." CWTI, 12 [3] [1973]: 4-7, 10-11, 42-47.

A sketch of Hunt's career summarized from previous entry.

DAVID HUNTER

3928. Longacre, Edward G. "A Profile of Major General David Hunter." CWTI, 16 [9] [1978]: 4-9, 38-43.

A look at the man and his Civil War service. He sanctioned the first black regiment and Congress upheld him.

3929. Schenck, Robert C. "Major General David Hunter." MAG A HIS, 17 [1887]: 138-152.

A eulogistic, biographical tribute to General Hunter, who had recently died, written by a good friend. The author is fearful that Hunter's greatness will be lost to the younger generation if it is not reminded of his fine record.

BENJAMIN FRANKLIN ISHERWOOD

3930. Sloan, Edward W. BENJAMIN FRANKLIN ISHERWOOD, NAVAL ENGINEER: THE YEARS AS ENGINEER IN CHIEF, 1861-1869. Annapolis: U.S. Naval Institute, 1966.

A well-researched biography of the top naval engineer.

OSCAR LAWRENCE JACKSON

3931. Jackson, Oscar L. THE COLONEL"S DIARY: JOURNALS KEPT BEFORE AND DURING THE CIVIL WAR. Sharon, Pennsylvania: n.p., 1922.

A useful memoir by the colonel of the 63rd Ohio.

ANDREW JOHNSON

3932. Hall, Clifton R. ANDREW JOHNSON, MILITARY GOVERNOR OF TENNESSEE. Princeton: Princeton University Press, 1916.

Covers Johnson's years as military governor, 1862-1864.

3933. Johnson, Andrew. THE PAPERS OF ANDREW JOHNSON. Leroy P. Graf, Ralph W. Haskins, and Patricia P. Clark, editors. Volumes 4 and 5. Knoxville: University of Tennessee Press, 1976, 1979.

These two volumes of Johnson's papers cover the years 1860-1862. Well-edited works, they are indispensable for a study of Johnson's wartime service.

3934. Stryker, Lloyd P. ANDREW JOHNSON: A STUDY IN COURAGE. New York: Macmillan, 1929.

A good biography of Lincoln's successor in the White House. Johnson was the only United States senator from a seceding state, Tennessee, who remained loyal to the Union. For this he was name military governor of Tennessee and was later put on the "Union" ticket in 1864.

RICHARD W. JOHNSON

3935. Johnson, Richard W. A SOLDIER'S REMINISCENCES IN PEACE AND WAR. Philadelphia, 1886.

A Union brigadier general from Kentucky, Johnson served chiefly in the western theater. After the war he was a professor of military science, an author, and a Democratic politician.

JOHN ALEXANDER JOYCE

3936. Joyce, John A. A CHECKERED LIFE. Chicago, 1883.

The author was a colonel with the 24th Kentucky [Union] regiment.

GEORGE WASHINGTON JULIAN

3937. Julian, George W. POLITICAL RECOLLECTIONS, 1840 TO 1872. Chicago, 1884.

One of the most valuable memoirs on 19th century politics available. Julian was nominated as vice-president on the "Free Soil" ticket in 1852.

3938. Riddleberger, Patrick W. GEORGE WASHINGTON JULIAN, RADICAL REPUBLICAN: A STUDY IN NINETEENTH-CENTURY POLITICS AND REFORM. Indianapolis: Indiana Historical Bureau, 1966.

A good biography of the Indiana radical turned conservative. Opinionated and outspoken, he played a significant role in state and national politics in the middle years of the 19th century.

PHILIP KEARNY

3939. Cunningham, John T. "Phil Kearny: Greater Than Legend." NJ HIS SOC PROC, 79 [1961]: 149-160.

A sketch of the distinguished Union general, who was killed at Chantilly.

3940. De Peyster, John W. PERSONAL AND MILITARY HISTORY OF PHILIP KEARNY. New York, 1869.

The author was Kearny's cousin and wrote a laudatory biography, but a useful one.

3941. Kearny, Thomas. GENERAL PHILIP KEARNY, BATTLE SOLDIER OF FIVE WARS.... New York: Putnam, 1937.

This authoritative, friendly biography was written by Kearny's grandson.

3942. Werstein, Irving. KEARNY THE MAGNIFICENT: THE STORY OF GENERAL PHILIP KEARNY, 1815-1862. New York: John Day, 1962.

The most recent biography of Kearny is an interesting, although undocumented account. In some respects, it is a rather cursory survey of this ill-fated general's life.

JOSEPH WARREN KEIFER

3943. Keifer, Joseph W. SLAVERY AND FOUR YEARS OF WAR. 2 v. New York, 1900.

Keifer, who served with the 3rd Ohio, rose to the rank of brigadier general. After the war he was a member of Congress, became Speaker of the House of Representatives, and was a major general in the Spanish-American War.

HUGH JUDSON KILPATRICK

3944. King, G. Wayne. "General Judson Kilpatrick." NJ HIS, 91 [1973]: 35-52.

A sketch of the celebrated and reckless federal cavalry commander.

3945. Moore, James. KILPATRICK AND OUR CAVALRY.... New York, 1865.

An early description of Kilpatrick's cavalry "raids, engagements and operations."

SAMUEL JORDAN KIRKWOOD

3946. Clark, Dan E. SAMUEL JORDAN KIRKWOOD. Iowa City: State Historical Society of Iowa, 1917.

A good biography of Iowa's wartime governor.

3947. Lathrop, Henry W. THE LIFE AND TIMES OF SAMUEL J. KIRKWOOD, IOWA'S WAR GOVERNOR. Iowa City, 1893.

Based on Kirkwood's papers, this early biography was endorsed by the war governor.

WILLIAM J. KOUNTZ

3948. Parker, Theodore R. "William J. Kountz, Superintendent of River Transportation Under McClellan, 1861-1862." W PA HIS MAG, 21 [1938]: 237-254.

McClellan, in charge of the Department of the Ohio, called on Kountz, an outstanding steamboat man, for assistance. Fighting graft, corruption, but mostly army officers, Kountz was induced to give up his job in 1862 and remained a civilian for the rest of the war.

WILLIAM KREUTZER

3949. Kreutzer, William. NOTES AND OBSERVATIONS MADE DURING FOUR YEARS OF SERVICE.... Philadelphia, 1878.

Kreutzer was a colonel with the 98th New York.

JAMES H. LANE

3950. Stephenson, Wendell H. THE POLITICAL CAREER OF GENERAL JAMES H. LANE. Topeka: Kansas State Printing Plant, 1930.

A solid, graphic account of Lane's and Kansas' wartime experiences.

JAMES H. LEDLIE

3951. McWhiney, Grady and Jack J. Jenkin. "The Union's Worst General: James H. Ledlie." CWTI, 14 [3] [1975]: 30-39.

Author claims Ledlie's "actions at the Battle of the Crater probably prolonged the war."

WILLIAM GATES LE DUC

3952. Le Duc, William G. RECOLLECTIONS OF A CIVIL WAR QUARTERMASTER: THE AUTOBIOGRAPHY OF WILLIAM G. LE DUC. St. Paul, Minnesota: North Central Publishing, 1963.

Le Duc had extensive service as a quartermaster under McClellan, Hooker, Sherman, and Thomas. These memoirs were written late in life and suffer as a consequence.

ABRAHAM LINCOLN
[See Section V]

THOMAS LEONARD LIVERMORE

3953. Livermore, Thomas L. DAYS AND EVENTS, 1860-1866. Boston: Houghton, Mifflin, 1920.

Livermore was colonel of the 18th New Hampshire. His autobiography is excellent.

JOHN ALEXANDER LOGAN

3954. Andrews, Byron. A BIOGRAPHY OF GEN. JOHN A. LOGAN, WITH AN ACCOUNT OF HIS PUBLIC SERVICES IN PEACE AND IN WAR. New York, 1884.

An Illinois pre-war Democrat, Logan became a brigadier general in March 1862, later commanding units at the brigade, division, and corps level in the western theater. This volume is a campaign biography when Logan was James G. Blaine's running mate on the Republican ticket in 1884.

3955. Brinkman, E.C. "They Wronged John A. Logan." FCHQ, 41 [1967]: 154-168.

Author argues that General Logan should have been given permanent command of the Army of the Tennessee upon General James McPherson's death in the Battle of Atlanta. He was entitled to it by merit, tradition, and according to his wife, Sherman's promise, but O.O. Howard was given the post.

3956. Castel, Albert. "'Black Jack' Logan." CWTI. 15 [7] [1976]: 4-10, 41-45.

Author discusses Logan's work as a commander.

3957. Dawson, George F. LIFE AND SERVICES OF GEN. JOHN A. LOGAN.... Chicago, 1887.

A laudatory study, written shortly after Logan's death, which deals only sketchily with the war years.

3958. Dickinson, John N. "The Civil War Years of John Alexander Logan." JISHS, 56 [1963]: 212-232.

Stunned by public reports of his disloyalty, Logan, then a Democratic congressman from southern Illinois, raised and led the 31st Illinois into battle.

3959. Jones, James P. 'BLACK JACK' JOHN A. LOGAN AND SOUTHERN ILLINOIS IN THE CIVIL WAR. Tallahassee: Florida State University Press, 1967.

A solid study of the subject matter. Author considers Logan the Union's most able political general. Southern Illinois is not brought into the biography as much as the book's title suggests.

3960. Logan, John A. THE VOLUNTEER SOLDIER OF AMERICAN. Chicago, 1887.

This work is subtitled, "With Memoir of the author and military reminiscences from General Logan's private journal." The author probably exaggerates his own role in the events he describes.

CHARLES RUSSELL LOWELL

3961. Emerson, Edward W. LIFE AND LETTERS OF CHARLES RUSSELL LOWELL .... Boston, 1907.

This volume contains the valuable 1851-1864 letters of Lowell, who served as a captain in the 6th United States cavalry, colonel of the 2nd Massachusetts cavalry, and brigadier general of the United States volunteers.

THEODORE LYMAN

3962. Lyman, Theodore. MEADE'S HEADQUARTERS, 1863-1865.... George R. Agassiz, editor. Boston: Atlantic Monthly Press, 1922.

A valuable collection of letters, covering the period from the Wilderness to Appomattox, written by a colonel on Meade's staff.

NATHANIEL LYON

3963. Adamson, Hans C. REBELLION IN MISSOURI, 1861: NATHANIEL LYON AND HIS ARMY OF THE WEST. Philadelphia: Chilton, 1961.

A lively, readable biography of the man who "saved" Missouri for the Union in the tempestuous days of 1861.

3964. Child, Martha F. "The Lionhearted General." NEW ENG GAL, 12 [2] [1970]: 40-48.

A sketch of Lyon, who was killed in the Battle of Wilson's Creek, Missouri, in August 1861.

3965. Oates, Stephen B. "Nathaniel Lyon: A Personality Profile." CWTI, 6 [10] [1968]: 14-25.

Contentious throughout his military career, Lyon viewed everything as a contest between right and wrong.

3966. Parrish, William E. "General Nathaniel Lyon, a Portrait." MO HIS R, 49 [1954/1955]: 1-18.

While praising many of Lyon's qualities, the author feels that the general blundered in seizing Fort Jackson in St. Louis. This act weakened the Unionist cause, strengthened the Confederate cause, and precipitated four years of civil war in Missouri.

3967. Woodward, Ashbel. LIFE OF GENERAL NATHANIEL LYON. Hartford, Connecticut: 1862.

This warm memorial was written too soon after Lyon's death to be of great value.

WILLIAM PENN LYON

3968. Lyon, William P. REMINISCENCES OF THE CIVIL WAR. San Jose, California: 1907.

Lyon commanded the 13th Wisconsin. These memoirs are drawn from his war correspondence and the letters and diary of his wife, who lived in the South during the war. Author's son gathered the material and published the book.

ROBERT McALLISTER

3969. McAllister, Robert. THE CIVIL WAR LETTERS OF GENERAL ROBERT McALLISTER. James I. Robertson, Jr., editor. New Brunswick, New Jersey: Rutgers University Press, 1965.

A valuable collection of 936 personal letters written by the commander of the 11th New Jersey. He was later a brigade commander in both the 2nd Corps and the 3rd Corps.

ALFRED B. McCALMONT

3970. McCalmont, Alfred B. EXTRACTS FROM LETTERS FROM THE FRONT DURING THE WAR OF THE REBELLION. Franklin, Pennsylvania: 1908.

McCalmont, colonel of the 208th Pennsylvania and later a divisional commander, wrote a group of revealing letters about campaigning in Virginia in the latter part of the war.

GEORGE BRINTON McCLELLAN

3971. Campbell, James H. McCLELLAN: A VINDICATION OF THE MILITARY CAREER OF GENERAL GEORGE B. McCLELLAN. New York: Neale, 1916.

A strong defense of the most controversial of all Union commanders.

3972. Castel, Albert. "George B. McClellan: 'Little Mac.'" CWTI, 13 [2] [1974]: 4-11, 44-45.

A brief account of McClellan's military career. Author speculates that "had he won the presidency, the Union cause probably would have been lost."

3973. Curtis, George T. McCLELLAN'S LAST SERVICE TO THE REPUBLIC.... New York, 1886.

An early defense which appeared shortly after the general's death.

3974. Eckenrode, Hamilton and Bryan Conrad. GEORGE B. McCLELLAN, THE MAN WHO SAVED THE UNION. Chapel Hill: University of North Carolina Press, 1941.

This is a more scholarly defense of McClellan than those mentioned above. Lincoln receives considerable criticism.

3975. Hagerman, Edward. "The Professionalization of George B. McClellan and Early Civil War Field Command: An Institution Perspective." CWH, 21 [1975]: 113-135.

A technical study of McClellan's West Point training and how it affected his performance in the field.

3976. Harsh, Joseph L. "On the McClellan-Go-Round." CWH, 19 [1973]: 101-118.

Author urges that a re-evaluation of McClellan is necessary if the real man is to emerge.

3977. Hassler, Warren W. GENERAL GEORGE B. McCLELLAN, SHIELD OF THE UNION. Baton Rouge: Louisiana State University Press, 1957.

A scholarly, friendly biography which covers chiefly the war years. Author admits the various charges that have been made against McClellan and seeks to answer each one. The Peninsular

Campaign was, strategically, a sound concept. The repulse of Lee at Antietam ended the Confederacy's hopes for victory, and McClellan was the victim of Radical Republican politics. Still, "Little Mac's" critics are not likely to remain silent.

3978. Hilliard, George S. LIFE AND CAMPAIGNS OF GEORGE B. McCLELLAN, MAJOR GENERAL U.S. ARMY. Philadelphia, 1864.

This was written as a campaign biography when McClellan was the Democratic candidate for president.

3979. Macartney, Clarence E. LITTLE MAC: THE LIFE OF GENERAL GEORGE B. McCLELLAN. Philadelphia: Dorrance, 1940.

Another defense of McClellan which comes down hard on the Lincoln administration.

3980. McClellan, George B. McCLELLAN'S OWN STORY: THE WAR FOR THE UNION.... New York, 1887.

This is McClellan's own defense of his military leadership while in command of the Army of the Potomac from August 1861 to November 1862.

3981. Michie, Peter S. GENERAL McCLELLAN. New York, 1901.

Michie graduated from West Point in 1863 and served with distinction in the remaining two years of the war. Later he became a professor at the Academy and the author of several books. This is a friendly, but balanced, biography of McClellan.

3982. Montgomery, Horace. "The Newspaper Petticoat Fans of General George B. McClellan." WASH ST UNIV RES STUD, 36 [1968]: 173-176.

Several young ladies of the Ontario Female Seminary at Canandaigua, New York, who were devoted admirers of General McClellan and angry at his removal from command in November 1862, sent him a warm letter of support. To conserve clothing, the girls had fabricated paper petticoats, which rattled in the classroom.

3983. Myers, William S. A STUDY IN PERSONALITY: GENERAL GEORGE BRINTON McCLELLAN. New York: Appleton-Century, 1934.

In this understanding study the author seeks to answer the questions concerning McClellan's behavior by examining his personality.

ROBERT L. McCOOK

3984. Barnett, James. "Crime and No Punishment: The Death of Robert L. McCook." CIN HIS SOC BULL, 22 [1964]: 29-37.

Author describes the death of Brigadier General McCook, killed in cold blood by a band of Confederate guerrillas. The subsequent life of one of the murderers, Frank B. Gurley, is traced.

McCOOK FAMILY

3985. Rodabaugh, James H. "The Fighting McCooks." CWH, 3 [1957]: 287-290.

A sketch of the families and military service of Daniel McCook of Carrollton, Ohio [9 sons] and his brother John McCook of Steubenville, Ohio [5 sons]. The "Tribe of Dan" produced four generals, two colonels, and two majors, while the "Tribe of John" claimed two generals, two lieutenants, and one chaplain.

HUGH McCULLOCH

3986. McCulloch, Hugh. MEN AND MEASURES OF HALF A CENTURY. New York, 1888. Reprint 1970.

Ponderous memoirs of Lincoln's treasury secretary's long public life, but not very much space is devoted to the war years.

IRVIN McDOWELL

3987. Longacre, Edward G. "Fortune's Fool." CWTI, 18 [2] [1979]: 20-31.

Author sketches the career of "one of the Union's hard luck" officers. McDowell was credited with the loss at First Bull Run.

JOHN S. McHENRY, JR.

3988. Potter, Hugh O. "Colonel John S. McHenry, Jr.: Union Soldier-Owensboro Lawyer." FCHQ, 39 [1965]: 128-134.

Colonel McHenry was dismissed from the army in December 1862, probably wrongly, for returning runaway slaves to their owners without first securing an oath of loyalty to the Union from the owners.

WILLIAM McKINLEY

3989. McKinley, William. "A Civil War Diary." H. Wayne Morgan, editor. OHIO HIS Q, 69 [1960]: 272-290.

The fragmentary diary of the eighteen-year-old McKinley, recording events during the first few months of the war.

JUSTUS McKINSTRY

3990. Longacre, Edward G. "A Profile of Justus McKinstry." CWTI, 17 [4] [1978]: 14-21.

General McKinstry used his position as chief supply officer at St. Louis to defraud the Quartermaster Corps of hundreds of thousands of dollars.

JAMES B. McPHERSON

3991. Hassler, William W. "James Birdseye McPherson: A Personality Profile." CWTI, 6 [7] [1967]: 36-44.

A sketch of the fine young Union general who was killed at the Battle of Atlanta, July 22, 1864, while commander of the Army of the Tennessee.

3992. Whaley, Elizabeth J. FORGOTTEN HERO: GENERAL JAMES B. McPHERSON, THE BIOGRAPHY OF A CIVIL WAR GENERAL. New York: Exposition, 1955.

While this work does have some value, it is not a good biography of McPherson.

GEORGE GORDON MEADE

3993. Bache, Richard M. LIFE OF GENERAL GEORGE GORDON MEADE, COMMANDER OF THE ARMY OF THE POTOMAC. Philadelphia, 1897.

A friendly biography of the commander of the Union forces at Gettysburg, based partly on author's acquaintanceship with the general.

3994. Cleaves, Freeman. MEADE OF GETTYSBURG. Norman: University of Oklahoma Press, 1960.

A scholarly, well-researched biography, which treats Meade with sympathy and fairness. However, as one reviewer noted, "Meade remains a shadow this book cannot disturb."

3995. Cullen, Joseph P. "George Gordon Meade." CWTI, 14 [2] [1975]: 4-10, 41-46.

Meade's role at Gettysburg is stressed in this sketch.

3996. Hassler, Warren W. "George G. Meade and His Role in the Gettysburg Campaign." PENN HIS, 32 [1965]: 380-405.

Author analyzes the problem of the neglect of General Meade, commander of the victorious federal forces at Gettysburg. Actually Meade did quite well, having been in command only a few days and is deserving of greater recognition.

3997. Meade, George G. THE LIFE AND LETTERS OF GEORGE GORDON MEADE. 2 v. George G. Meade, editor. New York, 1913.

An excellent source for the study of Meade and his army based on his many letters to his wife. The narrative ties the material together.

3998. Pennypacker, Isaac. GENERAL MEADE. New York, 1901.

This is not considered a very satisfactory biography of the general.

THOMAS FRANCIS MEAGHER

3999. Cavanagh, Michael. MEMOIRS OF GEN. THOMAS FRANCIS MEAGHER.... Worcester, Massachusetts: 1892.

Banished from his native Ireland for sedition, Meagher came to the United States, where he raised and led New York City's Irish Brigade. He later served with Sherman in the Georgia campaign.

MONTGOMERY C. MEIGS

4000. Weigley, Russell F. QUARTERMASTER GENERAL OF THE UNION ARMY: A BIOGRAPHY OF M.C. MEIGS. New York: Columbia University Press, 1959.

A scholarly study of the North's able quartermaster general, who served throughout the Civil War and well beyond. Using primarily the hitherto neglected Meigs papers, the author establishes Meigs as a master in getting the necessary supplies and transportation where they were most needed in the field.

4001. ———. "Montgomery Meigs." CWTI, 3 [7] [1964]: 42-48.

Author describes Meigs' efforts to organize northern productivity for the war, but also notes his inability to forgive his enemies after the war.

NELSON A. MILES

4002. Miles, Nelson. A. PERSONAL RECOLLECTIONS AND OBSERVATIONS OF GENERAL NELSON A. MILES. Chicago, 1896.

Entering the Union army in September 1861, Miles fought in all the major battles in the East, was twice wounded, and was awarded the Medal of Honor for Chancellorsville. He was commander-in-chief of the army in the late 1890s, served in the Spanish-American War, and retired in 1903.

4003. Tolman, Newton F. THE SEARCH FOR GENERAL MILES. New York: Putnam, 1968.

The author is upset that General Nelson Miles, who had such a long and distinguished military career, has been practically ignored by historians and everyone else. He demands that this neglect be terminated at once.

ROBERT HORATIO GEORGE MINTY

4004. Vale, Joseph G. MINTY AND THE CAVALRY.... Harrisburg, 1886.

Minty was a cavalry commander in the West with Sherman. This work is composed largely of letters he wrote to his daughter about his experiences and observations. [It also includes the 4th Michigan, 7th Pennsylvania, 9th Pennsylvania, and 4th United States Cavalry rosters of officers.]

EDWIN D. MORGAN

4005. Rawley, James A. EDWIN D. MORGAN, 1811-1883: MERCHANT IN POLITICS. New York: Columbia University Press, 1955.

The definitive study of one of New York's wartime senators and national chairman of the Republican party from 1856 to 1864.

JUSTIN SMITH MORRILL

4006. Parker, William B. THE LIFE AND PUBLIC SERVICES OF JUSTIN SMITH MORRILL. Boston: Houghton, Mifflin, 1924.

A useful study of the influential senator from Maine, drawn largely from his personal papers.

CHARLES F. MORSE

4007. Morse, Charles F. LETTERS WRITTEN DURING THE CIVIL WAR, 1861-1865. Boston, 1898.

The author was a colonel in the 2nd Massachusetts and served in both theaters.

OLIVER PERRY MORTON

4008. Foulke, William D. LIFE OF OLIVER P. MORTON. 2 v. Indianapolis, 1899.

Morton's wartime governorship of Indiana is covered in the first volume of this sympathetic biography.

4009. Walker, Charles M. SKETCH OF THE LIFE, CHARACTER, AND PUBLIC SERVICES OF OLIVER P. MORTON. Indianapolis, 1878.

Too brief and overly-friendly to be of great value. It was written following Morton's death.

ALBERT JAMES MYER

4010. Wiggin, Bernard L. "Albert J. Myer: Pioneer Meteorologist." NIAG FRON, 17 [1970]: 92-99.

A sketch of the Union army's chief signal officer.

THOMAS A.R. NELSON

4011. Alexander, Thomas B. THOMAS A.R. NELSON OF EAST TENNESSEE. Nashville: Tennessee Historical Commission, 1956.

A well-done story of a Unionist from East Tennessee.

WILLIAM NELSON

4012. Peckham, Howard H. "I Have Been Basely Murdered." AM HER, 14 [5] [1963]: 88-92.

Author describes the murder, on September 29, 1862, of the gigantic Major General Nelson by Union General Jeff C. Davis. Davis was not convicted.

JOHN G. NICOLAY

4013. Nicolay, Helen. LINCOLN'S SECRETARY: A BIOGRAPHY OF JOHN G. NICOLAY. New York: Longmans, Green, 1949.

Based on Nicolay's papers, this friendly biography makes delightful reading. It helps complete the overall picture of Lincoln's "official family." Concentrates on the war years. Book needed as Nicolay was a retiring type.

WILLIAM W. ORME

4014. Orme, William W. CIVIL WAR LETTERS OF BRIGADIER GENERAL WILLIAM WARD ORME, 1862-1866. Springfield, Illinois: Schnepp and Barnes, 1930.

Orme was a colonel of the 94th Illinois and later a divisional commander in the West. These letters are reprinted from JISHS, 23 [1930].

PATRICK H. O'RORKE

4015. Maihafer, Harry J. "The Decision of Paddy O'Rorke." MIL R, 46 [1] [1966]: 66-76.

Author traces the career of a Union commander, a West Point graduate, who became colonel of the 140th New York at a very young age.

JOHN McAULEY PALMER

4016. Palmer, George T. A CONSCIENTIOUS TURNCOAT: THE STORY OF JOHN M. PALMER, 1817-1900. New Haven: Yale University Press, 1941.

A well-written biography of a Union general who commanded in the western theater of operations. Later he was governor of Illinois and in 1896 was the "Gold Democrat" candidate for president.

4017. Palmer John M. PERSONAL RECOLLECTIONS OF JOHN M. PALMER: THE STORY OF AN EARNEST LIFE. Cincinnati, Ohio: 1901.

Palmer's own account of his military and political career. Although a Democratic legislator he became one of the early Republicans. Palmer later returned to the Democratic fold.

DAVID BIGELOW PARKER

4018. Parker, David B. A CHAUTAUQUA BOY IN '61 AND AFTERWARD: REMINISCENCES.... Torrance Parker, editor. Boston, 1912.

Parker served with the 72nd New York, but was better known as chief post office inspector.

ELY SAMUEL PARKER

4019. Brown, D. Alexander "One Real American." A HIS ILL, 4 [7] [1969]: 13-21.

Parker was a Seneca Indian who rose to the rank of brevet brigadier general. He served briefly on Grant's staff.

MARSENA RUDOLPH PATRICK

4020. Longacre, Edward G. "Mr. Lincoln's Policeman." CWTI, 9 [7] [1970]: 22-31.

An 1835 graduate of West Point, Patrick, a hard-nosed, blunt martinet, served as provost marshal general of the Army of the Potomac from 1862 until the end of the war.

4021. Patrick, Marsena R. INSIDE LINCOLN'S ARMY: THE DIARY OF MARSENA RUDOLPH PATRICK, PROVOST MARSHAL GENERAL, ARMY OF THE POTOMAC. David S. Sparks, editor . New York: Yoseloff, 1964.

The famous and invaluable diary of the provost marshal general of the Army of the Potomac has been carefully edited. The tough outspoken Patrick kept a voluminous journal and his personality is well-reflected in this volume, which contains the most essential matter of the original document.

4022. Sparks, David S. "General Patrick's Progress: Intelligence and Security in the Army of the Potomac." CWH, 10 [1964]: 371-384.

Traces the career of this reluctant but conscientious man and details the changing character of Patrick's duties.

GALUSHA PENNYPACKER

4023. Round, Harold F. and William C. Davis. "Galusha Pennypacker." CWTI, 8 [8] [1969]: 16-23.

Sketch of Pennypacker, who became the youngest general officer in American history. Enlisted at 16, was captain of the 97th Pennsylvania at 17, led his unit at Fort Fisher for which he received the Medal of Honor, was wounded seven times, and attained the rank of major general at the age of 20.

JAMES LOUIS PETIGRU

4024. Carson, James P. LIFE, LETTERS AND SPEECHES OF JAMES LOUIS PETIGRU. Washington, D.C.: Lowdermilk, 1920.

These papers of a Unionist from South Carolina were arranged by Petigru's grandson.

JOHN WOLCOTT PHELPS

4025. McClaughry, John. "John Wolcott Phelps: The Civil War General Who Became a Forgotten Presidential Candidate in 1880." VT HIS, 38 [1970]: 263-290.

A Vermont abolitionist writer, Phelps was in the 1836 class at West Point and was with Butler in New Orleans. He was declared an "outlaw" by the Confederacy for his plan to organize slaves for military service. In 1880 he was the American Party candidate for president.

WENDELL PHILLIPS

4026. Austin, George L. THE LIFE AND TIMES OF WENDELL PHILLIPS. Boston, 1888.

An early, laudatory biography.

4027. Bartlett, Irving H. WENDELL PHILLIPS, BRAHMIN RADICAL. Boston: Beacon Press, 1962.

Author has written a balanced biography of the celebrated abolitionist, covering his entire career.

4028. Sherwin, Oscar. PROPHET OF LIBERTY: THE LIFE AND TIMES OF WENDELL PHILLIPS. New York: Bookman Associates, 1958.

A sympathetic but careful study of the man and the events through which he lived. Well-researched and exhaustive in scope.

FRANCIS H. PIERPONT

4029. Ambler, Charles H. FRANCIS H. PIERPONT, UNION WAR GOVERNOR OF VIRGINIA AND FATHER OF WEST VIRGINIA. Chapel Hill: University of North Carolina Press, 1937.

An excellent biography of the man who played a major role in the withdrawal of the 55 western counties from Virginia and the formation of the new state.

HAZEN S. PINGREE

4030. Holli, Melvin G. "Hazen S. Pingree: A Saga of Success." DET HIS SOC BULL, 24 [5] [1968]: 4-11.

A sketch of the man who later became the mayor of Detroit and governor of Michigan during the 1890s. Pingree served with the 1st Massachusetts Heavy Artillery.

ALFRED PLEASONTON

4031. Longacre, Edward C. "Alfred Pleasonton: 'The Knight of Romance.'" CWTI, 13 [8] [1974]: 10-23.

A sketch of the Union cavalry commander, who served in the eastern theater until the spring of 1864 and in the western theater after that.

JOHN POPE

4032. Suppiger, Joseph E. "Lincoln and Pope." LIN HER, 77 [1975]: 218-222.

After Pope was relieved of his command of the Army of Virginia following Second Bull Run, he was sent to Minnesota to suppress the Sioux uprising.

DAVID DIXON PORTER

4033. Lewis, Paul. YANKEE ADMIRAL. New York: David McKay, 1968.

A good biography of David Dixon Porter, Union admiral, which covers the pre-war and post-war years as well as the war years.

4034. Porter, David D. INCIDENTS AND ANECDOTES OF THE CIVIL WAR. New York, 1885.

A useful volume of memoirs by the Union admiral who served in the western river campaigns and later with the North Atlantic Squadron. After the war he was superintendent of the Naval Academy for a time.

4035. Still, William N. "'Porter ... is the Best Man': This Was Gidion Welles' View of the Man He Chose to Command the Mississippi Squadron." CWTI, 16 [2] [1977]: 4-9, 44-47.

A survey of the career of the man who was considered the most successful officer of the Union navy.

4036. West, Richard S., Jr. THE SECOND ADMIRAL: A LIFE OF DAVID DIXON PORTER. New York: Coward-McCann, 1937.

A well-balanced naval hero's biography. This volume does much to restore Porter's reputation which post-war controversies with some generals had belittled.

HORACE PORTER

4037. Mende, Elsie P. AMERICAN SOLDIER AND DIPLOMAT: HORACE PORTER. New York: Stokes, 1927.

A touching biography of General Porter written by his daughter. Space is devoted largely to Porter's Civil War years, his association with Grant, and his diplomatic service in France.

GEORGE HAVEN PUTNAM

4038. Putnam, George H. MEMORIES OF MY YOUTH, 1844-1865. New York, 1914.

The Civil War years are covered on pages 220-442. Putnam served with the 176th New YOrk.

4039. ———. SOME MEMORIES OF THE CIVIL WAR. New York: Putnam, 1924.

This is a collection of articles about significant events and people of the war. Included among the nine essays are letters which Putnam wrote while in a Confederate prison.

WILLIAM CLARKE QUANTRILL

4040. Breihan, Carl W. QUANTRILL AND HIS CIVIL WAR GUERRILLAS. Denver: Sage Books, 1959.

A rather short, but good account of the subject.

4041. Castel, Albert E. WILLIAM CLARKE QUANTRILL: HIS LIFE AND TIMES. New York: Fell, 1962.

A solid study of the Ohio schoolteacher who became the Confederacy's most renown bushwhacker on the Missouri "border." Quantrill was killed in Kentucky by federal troops in May 1864, while on his way to Washington to assassinate Lincoln.

NOTE: For more material on Quantrill and his guerrilla activities see "Kansas-Missouri" in CAMPAIGNS AND BATTLES. [See above, pages 269-277]

JOHN A. RAWLINS

4042. Long, E.B. "John A. Rawlins: Staff Officer Par Excellence." CWTI, 13 [3] [1974]: 10-18.

A sketch of one of the chief members of Grant's staff.

4043. Wilson, James H. THE LIFE OF JOHN A. RAWLINS.... New York: Neale, 1916.

A useful biography of Grant's chief of staff. He also served briefly as Grant's secretary of war.

JOHN FULTON REYNOLDS

4044. Longacre, Edward G. "John F. Reynolds, General." CWTI, 11 [5] [1972]: 26, 35-43.

A sketch of this highly-respected general who was killed on the first day of battle at Gettysburg.

4045. Maloney, Mary R. "General Reynolds and 'Dear Kate.'" AM HER, 15 [1] [1963]: 62-65.

A brief account of Catherine Hewitt's relations with the family of General John Reynolds.

4046. Nichols, Edward J. TOWARD GETTYSBURG: A BIOGRAPHY OF GENERAL JOHN F. REYNOLDS. University Park, Pennsylvania: Penn State University Press, 1958.

Based on the available materials, this substantial biography of a "soldier's general" portrays the ambitious Reynolds in human terms. The Union corps commander was cut down on the morning of the first day at Gettysburg.

4047. Sharp, Arthur G. "Reynolds' Regrets." CWTI, 16 [8] [1977]: 22-33.

Reynolds commanded a battalion of marines at First Bull Run. His unit had the unenviable distinction of being the only such group in Marine Corps history to ever flee the enemy.

ALBERT GALLATIN RIDDLE

4048. Riddle, Albert G. RECOLLECTIONS OF WAR TIMES: REMINISCENCES OF MEN AND EVENTS IN WASHINGTON, 1860-1865. New York, 1895.

Excellent memoirs of an Ohio congressman.

EDWARD HASTINGS RIPLEY

4049. Eisenschiml, Otto, editor. VERMONT GENERAL: THE UNUSUAL WAR EXPERIENCES OF EDWARD HASTINGS RIPLEY, 1862-1865. New York: Devin-Adair, 1960.

Ripley commanded the 9th Vermont and left an impressive collection of over 500 revealing letters. A general at the age of 25, Ripley saw a great deal of action and led the Union troops into Richmond.

GEORGE F. ROBINSON

4050. Cooney, Charles F. "Seward's Savior: George F. Robinson." LIN HER, 75 [3] [1973]: 93-96.

Robinson, a night nurse, helped ward off the assassination attempt against Secretary of State Seward on the night of April 14, 1865.

JACOB ROEMER

4051. Roemer, Jacob. REMINISCENCES OF THE WAR OF THE REBELLION, 1861-1865. L.A. Furney, editor. Flushing, New York: 1897.

Fairly good volume of recollections although they were written many years after the events described took place.

WILLIAM S. ROSECRANS

4052. Lamers, William M. THE EDGE OF GLORY: A BIOGRAPHY OF GENERAL WILLIAM S. ROSECRANS, U.S.A. New York: Harcourt, Brace, and World, 1961.

A thoughtful study of the ill-fated Union general based on extensive research. Author views Rosecrans as a man of some ability, but whose tactlessness and short temper brought him down.

JAMES FOWLER RUSLING

4053. Rusling, James F. MEN AND THINGS I SAW IN THE CIVIL WAR DAYS. New York, 1914.

This is a revised edition of an earlier work, relating the New Jersey officer's career, in which he rose from first lieutenant to brigadier general. Based on his own letters and memoirs, plus published works.

ALEXANDER SCHIMMELFENNIG

4054. Raphelson, Alfred C. "The Unheroic General." A GER R, 29 [1962]: 26-29.

A sketch of Schimmelfennig, a Prussian who became a Union general. He was a capable officer who generally seemed to be in unheroic circumstances at critical times during the war.

4055. ———. "Alexander Schimmelfennig: A German-American Campaigner in the Civil War." PA MHB, 87 [1963]: 156-181.

Schimmelfennig's experiences at Second Bull Run and Gettysburg, where he hid from the enemy in a barn for three days, are recounted.

JOHN McALLISTER SCHOFIELD

4056. McDonough, James L. SCHOFIELD: UNION GENERAL IN THE CIVIL WAR AND RECONSTRUCTION. Tallahassee: Florida State University Press, 1972.

This is not a very thorough biography of Schofield.

4057. ———. "'And All For Nothing.' Early Experiences of John M. Schofield in Missouri." MO HIS R, 64 [1970]: 302-321.

Schofield spent the first three years of the war in the western theater and received the Medal of Honor for his service at Wilson's Creek.

4058. ———. "John McAllister Schofield." CWTI, 13 [5] [1974]: 10-17.

A sketch of the general's career.

4059. Schofield, John M. FORTY-SIX YEARS IN THE ARMY. New York, 1897.

Schofield published his memoirs shortly after retiring as commander-in-chief of the army.

CARL SCHURZ

4060. Schurz, Carl. THE REMINISCENCES OF CARL SCHURZ. 3 v. New York, 1907-1908. One volume abridgment 1961.

An emigre from revolution-wracked Germany, Schurz had a long and distinguieshed career in American public life. He was a Union officer for two years during the war and commanded a division of the Ninth Corps at Chancellorsville.

4061. ———. INTIMATE LETTERS OF CARL SCHURZ, 1841-1869. Joseph Schafer, editor. Madison: State Historical Society of Wisconsin, 1928. Reprint 1970.

Translated from the German, this volume contains less than 100 pages on the war.

4062. Trefousse, Hans L. CARL SCHURZ: A BIOGRAPHY. Knoxville: University of Tennessee Press, 1982.

An excellent study of Schurz which may lead to a reassessment of his place in American history. He may not emerge quite as famously as he once was regarded.

WINFIELD SCOTT

4063. Elliott, Charles W. WINFIELD SCOTT, THE SOLDIER AND THE MAN. New York: Macmillan, 1937.

An excellent biography of the celebrated general whose career spanned the era from the War of 1812 to the Civil War.

4064. Smith, Arthur D. OLD FUSS AND FEATHERS: THE LIFE AND EXPLOITS OF LT. GENERAL WINFIELD SCOTT. New York: Greystone, 1937.

A popular account, but not equal to that of Elliott's noted above.

BENJAMIN FRANKLIN SCRIBNER

4065. Scribner, Benjamin F. HOW SOLDIERS WERE MADE: OR, THE WAR AS I SAW IT UNDER BUELL, ROSECRANS, THOMAS, GRANT, AND SHERMAN. New Albany, Indiana: 1887.

Colonel of the 38th Indiana, Scribner describes his experiences in the western theater.

JOHN SEDGWICK

4066. Jurgen, Robert J. MAJOR GENERAL JOHN SEDGWICK, U.S. VOLUNTEER. Hartford: Connecticut Civil War Centennial Commission, 1963.

A good brief sketch of the no-nonsense commander of the Sixth Corps, who did his duty as he saw it.

4067. Round, Harold F. "'Uncle John' Sedgwick." CWTI, 5 [8] [1966]: 13-21.

A personality file on "one of the best-loved generals in the Army of the Potomac."

4068. Sedgwick, John. CORRESPONDENCE OF JOHN SEDGWICK, MAJOR GENERAL. 2 v. New York, 1902-1903.

The war letters of Sedgwick who was killed at Spottsylvania, will be found in Volume 2.

WILLIAM HENRY SEWARD

4069. Bancroft, Frederic. THE LIFE OF WILLIAM H. SEWARD. 2 v. New York, 1900.

At one time the standard biography of the wartime secretary of state.

4070. Coulter, E. Merton. "Seward and the South: His Career as a Georgia Schoolmaster." GA HIS Q, 53 [1969]: 147-164.

An account of Seward's "escape" from his father's domineering attitude to a job as a schoolmaster in Georgia. The incident was used by Seward's enemies both in the North and South in an attempt to discredit him.

4071. Hale, Edward E. WILLIAM H. SEWARD. Philadelphia, 1910.

This readable biography by one of the country's outstanding men of letters is drawn largely from secondary sources.

4072. Lothrop, Thornton K. WILLIAM HENRY SEWARD. Boston, 1896.

A good, early biography. While undocumented, it contains a useful discussion of foreign policy issues during the war.

4073. Seward, William. THE WORKS OF WILLIAM H. SEWARD. 5 v. George E. Baker, editor. New York: 1853-1884.

Volume 5 of Seward's collected works contains an excellent treatment of the diplomacy of the Civil War.

4074. Van Deusen, Glyndon G. WILLIAM HENRY SEWARD. New York: Oxford University Press, 1967.

In this carefully-researched volume, the best biography of Seward, the secretary of state's reputation is properly restored to a place of distinction in American history. Essentially a moderate, Seward got the reputation of being a radical because of two unfortunate verbal slips. His handling of foreign policy was quite correct.

HORATIO SEYMOUR

4075. Mitchell, Stewart. HORATIO SEYMOUR OF NEW YORK. Cambridge: Harvard University Press, 1938.

This is the definitive biography of New York's Democratic wartime governor. Mitchell assesses the importance of "lame duck" congressmen in deciding the outcome of the Enrollment Act. In presenting a very favorable view of Seymour in quelling the draft riots, this revisionist interpretation contrasts sharply with the one presented in Murdock's "Horatio Seymour and the 1863 Draft." [See number 1274]

4076. Wall, Alexander J. A SKETCH OF THE LIFE OF HORATIO SEYMOUR, 1810-1886.... New York: n.p., 1929.

A brief sketch of New York's wartime governor, including many of his public papers.

ROBERT GOULD SHAW

4077. Riley, Stephen T. "A Monument to Colonel Robert Gould Shaw." MASS HIS SOC PROC, 75 [1963]: 27-38.

An account of the efforts to erect a statue on Boston Common to Shaw, who commanded the 54th Massachusetts, the first all-black regiment raised in the North.

PHILIP HENRY SHERIDAN

4078. Faulkner, Joseph. THE LIFE OF PHILIP HENRY SHERIDAN, THE DASHING, BRAVE AND SUCCESSFUL SOLDIER. New York, 1888.

This early work is a little too brief and eulogistic to be a very helpful biography of the famous Union cavalry commander.

4079. Hergesheimer, Joseph. SHERIDAN: A MILITARY NARRATIVE. Boston: Houghton, Mifflin, 1939.

This "military narrative" is undocumented and suffers in organization, but is the only study of the famous general to appear between the previous and the following entries. A reasonably successful and detailed work, the writing is good and the treatment is balanced. Questions have been raised whether the author was sufficiently familiar with the war to undertake such a study.

4080. O'Connor, Richard. SHERIDAN, THE INEVITABLE. Indianapolis: Bobbs-Merrill, 1953.

An interesting biography. Carefully-researched and well-written, this work stands as the best study of Sheridan yet to appear. Sheridan was an outstanding military figure, imaginative, resourceful, and possessing a thorough grasp of the principles of modern warfare.

4081. Sheridan, Philip H. PERSONAL MEMOIRS OF PHILIP HENRY SHERIDAN. 2 v. New York, 1902.

Another of the classic recollections by one of the Union's outstanding generals. This is an enlarged edition of the earlier work. Edited by Michael V. Sheridan, it updates the story from 1871 until the general's death in 1888.

4082. Weigley, Russell F. "Philip H. Sheridan: A Personality Profile." CWTI, 7 [4] [1968]: 5-11, 46-48.

Author notes that Sheridan had a streak of cruelty and brutality in him.

WILLIAM TECUMSEH SHERMAN

4083. Ambrose, Stephen E. "William T. Sherman." A HIS ILL, 1 [9] [1967]: 4-12.

A sketch of the North's second most famous general.

4084. Athearn, Robert G. WILLIAM TECUMSEH SHERMAN AND THE SETTLEMENT OF THE WEST. Norman: University of Oklahoma Press, 1956.

Author traces Sherman's career as military commander in the Great Plains and Rocky Mountain regions in the years after the Civil War.

4085. Bowman, Samuel M. SHERMAN AND HIS CAMPAIGNS: A MILITARY BIOGRAPHY. New York, 1865.

An early work in which Sherman's premature peace with General Joseph Johnston is defended.

4086. Boyd, James P. THE LIFE OF GENERAL WILLIAM T. SHERMAN. Philadelphia, 1891.

One of the good, early biographies.

4087. Burt, Jesse C. "Sherman, Railroad General." CWH, 2 [1956]: 45-54.

Author discusses Sherman's life-long interest in railroads and his effective use of them during the war.

4088. Castel, Albert. "William Tecumseh Sherman. Part I: The Failure." CWTI, 18 [4] [1979]: 4-7, 42-46.

This is an account of Sherman's lackluster antebellum career, noting his feeling of despondency and sense of failure in 1861.

4089. ———. "William Tecumseh Sherman. Part II: The Subordinate." CWTI, 18 [5] [1979]: 12-23.

Sherman's rise to command, with Grant's support, is traced.

4090. ———. "William Tecumseh Sherman. Part III: The Conqueror." CWTI, 18 [6] [1979]: 10-21.

Author describes Sherman's famous Atlanta Campaign, the March to the Sea, and the culminating drive through the Carolinas.

4091. Coulter, Ellis M. "Sherman and the South." GA HIS Q, 15 [1931]: 28-45.

After his West Point graduation, Sherman was stationed in the South for six years and learned to love it. He did an "about face" during the war. When the war was over his liberal surrender terms to Joseph Johnston caused some in the North to call him a traitor.

4092. Cresto, Kathleen M. "Sherman and Slavery." CWTI, 17 [7] [1978]: 12-21.

Sherman fought for the Union, not necessarily for emancipation. Yet he freed many slaves, while opposing their use as front line troops.

4093. Detzler, Jack J. "The Religion of William Tecumseh Sherman." OHIS HIS, 75 [1967]: 26-34, 68-70.

Relates the continuing conflict between Sherman and his wife, Ellen, a devout Roman Catholic, over his faith and "state of grace."

4094. Eisenschiml, Otto. "Sherman: Hero or War Criminal?" CWTI, 2 [9] [1964]: 7-9, 29-36.

Discusses the many facets of Sherman's character--from his great intelligence to his mental cowardice. Concludes there were three Shermans and that in the final analysis, Sherman did not conduct himself as a gentleman during the war.

4095. Fletcher, Thomas C. LIFE AND REMINISCENCES OF GENERAL WM. T. SHERMAN. Baltimore, 1891.

A eulogistic survey of Sherman's life, including many words of praise by those who knew him and served with him.

4096. Force, Manning F. GENERAL SHERMAN. New York, 1899.

This volume, which is devoted to the war years, still makes good reading.

4097. Hart, B.H. Liddell. "Sherman--Modern Warrior." AM HER, 13 [5] [1962]: 20-23, 102-106.

An analysis of Sherman, the man and his methods, drawn from the author's 1958 book SHERMAN. The general's adaptation to new weapons and changed conditions, and his recognition of the concept of "total war" are praised.

4098. ———. SHERMAN: SOLDIER, REALIST, AMERICAN. New York: Praeger, 1959.

An excellent biography, laudatory though scholarly, of one of the greatest, if not the greatest soldier to emerge from the war. Emphasizes Sherman as a railroad general and believes the war was won in the western theater, particularly by Sherman's campaign. A reprint of the 1929 edition.

4099. Jacobs, Victor L. "Was Uncle Billy Off His Rocker?" MANU, 17 [3] [1965]: 21-27.

Lincoln's friend, Joshua F. Speed, contends that "Uncle Billy" was the victim of bad press relations and not insane, as some argued.

4100. Johnson, Willis F. LIFE OF WM. TECUMSEH SHERMAN. Philadelphia, 1891.

While this account has impressive testimonials to Sherman's greatness, it is not a very satisfying biography.

4101. Lewis, Lloyd. SHERMAN, FIGHTING PROPHET. New York: Harcourt, Brace, 1932. Reprint 1958.

This is a fighting, friendly, and readable biography of the general, written by a respected newsman.

4102. Merrill, James M. WILLIAM TECUMSEH SHERMAN. Chicago: Rand-McNally, 1971.

This is the first Sherman biography to benefit from the availability of much new archival material. Still, it is not the definitive study. The emphasis is more on the man's entire life rather than on the narrower confines of the Civil War. Sherman's fits of depressions, misfortunes, and frustrations make it clear he did not have a happy life.

4103. Murray, Robert K. "General Sherman, the Negro, and Slavery: The Story of an Unrecognized Rebel." NEG HIS BULL, 22 [6] [1959]: 125-130.

Sherman believed in the supremacy of the white race. After the war he backed Andrew Johnson's policies and opposed Radical Reconstruction.

4104. Robbins, Edward. WILLIAM T. SHERMAN. Philadelphia, 1905.

Still a satisfactory though friendly interpretation.

4105. Sherman, John. JOHN SHERMAN'S RECOLLECTIONS OF FORTY YEARS IN THE HOUSE, SENATE, AND CABINET: AN AUTOBIOGRAPHY. 2 v. Chicago, 1895.

The lengthy memoirs of General Sherman's younger brother, who served many years in Congress and was very close to "Cump."

4106. Sherman William T. and John Sherman. THE SHERMAN LETTERS: CORRESPONDENCE BETWEEN GENERAL AND SENATOR SHERMAN FROM 1837 TO 1891. Rachel S. Thorndike, editor. New York, 1894. Reprint 1984.

An excellent source for the study of the very famous brothers. Almost two-thirds of the letters cover the years between 1861-1877.

4107. ———. HOME LETTERS OF GENERAL SHERMAN. M.A. De Wolfe Howe, editor. New York, 1909.

Revealing letters written by the general to his wife.

4108. ———. MEMOIRS OF GENERAL WILLIAM T. SHERMAN. 2 v. New York, 1875. Reprint 1957.

Another set of valuable war memoirs by the distinguished Civil War general. Sherman not only could fight, he could write.

4109. Walters, John B. "General William T. Sherman and Total War." JSH, 14 [1948]: 447-480.

Sherman's concept of "total war"--war waged against civilians and their property as well as against armies--began to develop when he was in command at Memphis in 1862. Confederate guerrilla attacks and the firing on unarmed federal ships convinced him the war must be brought home to the people at large.

4110. ———. MERCHANT OF TERROR: GENERAL SHERMAN AND TOTAL WAR. Indianapolis: Bobbs-Merrill, 1973.

The story of the famous march and the man behind it. This unfriendly account seeks to answer such questions as why the march came about and why Sherman changed in his views on war.

ISAAC R. SHERWOOD

4111. Sherwood, Isaac R. MEMORIES OF THE WAR. Toledo, Ohio: Chittenden, 1923.

In recalling his war experience in old age, General Sherwood became too dependent on various published materials. An editor and local politician before the war, he later served several terms in Congress from Ohio.

JAMES SHIELDS

4112. Condon, William H. LIFE OF MAJOR GENERAL JAMES SHIELDS, HERO OF THREE WARS AND SENATOR FROM THREE STATES. Chicago, 1900.

Shields, an Illinois Democrat, once challenged Lincoln to a duel, which never took place. He was a division commander in the Valley Campaign of 1862. He had served in the Black Hawk and Mexican Wars, and at one time or another was a senator from Oregon, Minnesota, and Illinois.

DANIEL EDGAR SICKLES

4113. Pinchon, Edgecumb. DAN SICKLES, HERO OF GETTYSBURG AND "YANKEE KING OF SPAIN." New York: Doubleday, Doran, 1945.

A novelized biography of the embattled Third Corps commander who lost a leg at Gettysburg and later received the Medal of Honor for his service there.

4114. Swanberg, W.A. SICKLES THE INCREDIBLE. New York: Scribner, 1956.

Probably the best biography of the colorful general who either almost lost or almost saved the Union left on the second day of Gettysburg. But Sickles' career embraced so much more than his war experiences that it is not easy to contain everything in one book. The author has done this fairly and fully.

HENRY WARNER SLOCUM

4115. Slocum, Charles E. THE LIFE AND SERVICES OF MAJOR GENERAL HENRY WARNER SLOCUM. Toledo, Ohio: 1913.

A West Point graduate in 1852, Slocum commanded the Twelfth Corps at Fredericksburg, Chancellorsville, and Gettysburg. Transferred to the west, he commanded the Twentieth Corps in the Atlanta, Georgia, and Carolinas campaigns. Served three terms in Congress.

ABNER RALPH SMALL

4116. Small, Abner R. THE SIXTEENTH MAINE REGIMENT IN THE WAR OF THE REBELLION, 1861-1865. Portland, Maine: 1886.

Small was a major and describes his own experience while serving with the 16th Maine.

GERRIT SMITH

4117. Smith, Gerrit. SPEECHES AND LETTERS OF GERRIT SMITH.... 2 v. New York, 1864-1865.

Smith was a celebrated abolitionist preacher. His public papers for the last two years of the war are included in these volumes.

JOHN GREGORY SMITH

4118. Bowden, Albert R. "John Gregory Smith." VT HIS, 32 [1964]: 79-97.

Sketches life of John G. Smith who was elected governor of Vermont in 1863 on the single plank of upholding the national government. Also details conditions in Vermont at the outbreak of war. "Vermont's problems were legion and varied...."

JOHN H. SMITH

4119. Smith, John H. "The Civil War Diary of Colonel John Henry Smith." David Smith, editor. IOWA J HIS, 48 [1949]: 140-170.

Originally captain of Company 2, 16th Iowa, Smith began his diary when his unit joined the Army of the Tennessee. It covers the Atlanta Campaign, his imprisonment, and his eventual escape.

THOMAS KILBY SMITH

4120. Smith, Walter G. LIFE AND LETTERS OF THOMAS KILBY SMITH.... New York, 1898.

This is a good collection of correspondence of General Smith who served in the western theater throughout the war. This volume was prepared by his son.

WILLIAM FARRAR SMITH

4121. Smith, William F. FROM CHATTANOOGA TO PETERSBURG UNDER GENERALS GRANT AND BUTLER.... Boston, 1893.

General "Baldy" Smith had uncommon ability but was regularly in trouble for criticizing his commanding officers. He defends his behavior in these memoirs.

4122. Longacre, Edward G. "'A Perfect Ishmaelite.'" CWTI, 15 [5] [1976]: 10-20.

A sketch of the war career of General "Baldy" Smith.

DAVID SLOANE STANLEY

4123. Stanley, David S. PERSONAL MEMOIRS OF MAJOR GENERAL D.S. STANLEY. Cambridge: Harvard University Press, 1917.

Interesting memoirs by an Ohio general who was in the 1852 class at West Point. Stanley served in the western theater and was with Sherman in the Atlanta campaign. He received the Medal of Honor for actions at the Battle of Franklin.

EDWIN McMASTERS STANTON

4124. Flower, Frank A. EDWIN McMASTERS STANTON, THE AUTOCRAT OF REBELLION, EMANCIPATION, AND RECRONSTRUCTION. Akron, Ohio: 1905.

An early, friendly work which makes fairly good use of available materials.

4125. Gorham, George C. LIFE AND PUBLIC SERVICES OF EDWIN M. STANTON. 2 v. Boston, 1899.

The most important early biography of Lincoln's irascible, but valuable secretary of war.

4126. Pratt, Fletcher. STANTON: LINCOLN'S SECRETARY OF WAR. New York: Norton, 1953.

A popular, readable book which attempted a re-appraisal of Stanton, but did not completely succeed in doing that.

4127. Thomas, Benjamin P. and Harold M. Hyman. STANTON: THE LIFE AND TIME OF LINCOLN'S SECRETARY OF WAR. New York: Knopf, 1962.

An excellent, scholarly, and well-written biography. Stanton's strengths and weaknesses are carefully demonstrated. The secretary's work is put in correct perspective.

THADDEUS STEVENS

4128. Brodie, Fawn. THADDEUS STEVENS: SCOURGE OF THE SOUTH. New York: Norton, 1959.

Probably the best of the many biographies of this most famous Radical Republican. In this well-written work the author incorporates the latest research on Stevens and corrects common misinformation about him.

4129. Current, Richard N. OLD THAD STEVENS, A STORY OF AMBITION. Madison: University of Wisconsin Press, 1942.

A good biography of the tempestuous Radical Republican from Pennsylvania.

4130. Korngold, Ralph. THADDEUS STEVENS: A BEING DARKLY WISE AND RUDELY GREAT. New York: Harcourt, Brace, 1955.

A readable study of Stanton covering the war and post-war years. The author presents a strong defense of Stevens and his opinions; perhaps he is a little too defensive.

4131. McCall, Samuel W. THADDEUS STEVENS. Boston, 1899.

Old but good.

4132. Miller, Alphonse B. THADDEUS STEVENS. New York: Harper, 1939.

A sympathetic treatment of Stevens written in a somewhat journalistic style.

4133. Singmaster, Elsie. I SPEAK FOR THADDEUS STEVENS. Boston: Houghton, Mifflin, 1947.

This is biography as fiction and is written in a manner favorable to Stevens.

4134. Woodburn, James A. THE LIFE OF THADDEUS STEVENS: A STUDY IN AMERICAN POLITICAL HISTORY.... Indianapolis, 1913.

A friendly study which focuses on the war and Reconstruction eras.

4135. Woodley, Thomas F. THADDEUS STEVENS. Harrisburg, Pennsylvania: Telegraph Press, 1934.

Another sympathetic biography.

ALBAN C. STIMERS

4136. Wegner, Dana. "Ericsson's High Priest." CWTI, 13 [10] [1975]: 26-34.

A sketch of the life and work of the chief engineer of the navy, who promoted the MONITOR.

CHARLES P. STONE

4137. Longacre, Edward G. "Charles P. Stone and the 'Crime of Unlucky Generals.'" CWTI, 13 [7] [1974]: 4-9, 38-41.

Suspected of treason following the disaster at Ball's Bluff in October 1861, Stone was arrested, jailed, and then released six months later with no charges ever being filed. He served in minor command positions for the rest of the war.

GEORGE TEMPLETON STRONG

4138. Strong, George T. THE DIARY OF GEORGE TEMPLETON STRONG. 4 v. Allan Nevins and Milton Halsey, editors. New York: Macmillan, 1952.

Volume Three of this fascinating and long neglected diary covers the war years. An excellent editing job, plus the work's inherent value, provides a choice glimpse of New York City during the war.

DAVID HUNTER STROTHER

4139. Eby, Cecil D., Jr. PORTE CRAYON: THE LIFE OF DAVID HUNTER STROTHER. Chapel Hill: University of North Carolina Press, 1960.

Presents the life of this many faceted man. Born in Virginia, he rose to the rank of federal brigadier general, contributed to HARPERS, and eventually was named consul general to Mexico.

4140. ———. "'Porte Crayon' Meets General Grant." JISHS, 52, [1959]: 229-247.

Strother was serving as United States consul general in Mexico City, when Grant visited in February 1880. Article contains excerpts from Strother's journal about his friendly relations with the ex-president during this trip.

4141. Strother, David H. A VIRGINIA YANKEE IN THE CIVIL WAR: THE DIARIES OF DAVID HUNTER STROTHER. Cecil D. Eby., Jr., editor. Chapel Hill: University of North Carolina Press, 1961.

These diaries rank among the best of the war. As a journalist, Strother's writing is excellent. Entering the army as a topographer, he rose to the rank of brigadier general and served on the staffs of Generals Banks, McClellan, Hunter, and Pope. His cogent diaries all convey the feeling of the moment.

CHARLES SUMNER

4142. Chaplin, Jeremiah and J. D. Chaplin. THE LIFE OF CHARLES SUMNER. Boston, 1874.

An early, sympathetic work which came out shortly after the Massachusetts senator's death.

4143. Dawes, Anna L. CHARLES SUMNER. New York, 1892.

Friendly but superficial.

4144. Donald, David H. CHARLES SUMNER AND THE COMING OF THE CIVIL WAR. New York: Knopf, 1960.

A Pulitzer Prize-winning, though controversial, biography of Sumner up to the outbreak of war.

4145. ———. CHARLES SUMNER AND THE RIGHTS OF MAN. New York: Knopf, 1970.

The second volume in Donald's biography of Sumner is an outstanding work. In the view of one critic, it is "a model of the biographic art." Sumner's impact on American foreign policy, including his roles on the Senate Foreign Relations Committee and in the resolution of the TRENT affair are examined.

4146. Haynes, George H. CHARLES SUMNER. Philadelphia, 1909.

A well-written, favorable study of Sumner's life, which may appeal more to younger readers. While a thorough treatment, the book brings forth very little that is new on Sumner.

4147. Lester, Charles E. LIFE AND PUBLIC SERVICES OF CHARLES SUMNER. New York, 1874.

Released soon after Sumner's death, this work is too laudatory as well as being too early.

4148. Pierce, Edward L. MEMOIR AND LETTERS OF CHARLES SUMNER. 4 v. Boston, 1877-1893.

Remains a valuable set of primary source materials.

4149. Sefton, James E. "Charles Sumner for Our Time: An Essay Review." MD HIS MAG, 66 [1971]: 456-461.

As essay review of Number 4145, listed above. Donald's book is not only a political history but an intellectual history as well.

4150. Shotwell, Walter G. LIFE OF CHARLES SUMNER. New York, 1910.

A ponderous but thorough work.

4151. Storey, Moorfield. CHARLES SUMNER. Boston, 1900.

A fairly useful biography, but very biased toward Sumner. One critic said the book reflected "the flavor of the times."

ROGER BROOKE TANEY

4152. Lewis, Walker. WITHOUT FEAR OR FAVOR: A BIOGRAPHY OF CHIEF JUSTICE ROGER BROOKE TANEY. Boston: Houghton, Mifflin, 1965.

A lengthy and sympathetic study, but it is somewhat weak in dealing with wartime matters. Taney was chief justice of the Supreme Court from 1835 until his death in 1864,

4153. Smith, Charles W. ROGER B. TANEY: JACKSONIAN JURIST. Chapel Hill: University of North Carolina Press, 1936. Reprint 1973.

Contains a short sketch of Taney's life, but is more concerned with his thinking on constitutional issues of the day.

4154. Steiner, Bernard C. LIFE OF ROGER BROOKE TANEY, CHIEF JUSTICE OF THE UNITED STATES SUPREME COURT. Baltimore: Williams and Wilkins, 1922.

A thorough account of Taney's performance on the bench.

4155. Swisher, Carl B. ROGER B. TANEY. New York: Macmillan, 1935.

A scholarly examination of Taney as chief justice by one of the best known constitutional historians.

4156. Tyler, Samuel. MEMOIR OF ROGER BROOKE TANEY.... Baltimore, 1872. Reprint 1972.

An elaborate defense of Taney against criticism of some of his rulings.

CHARLES FREDERICK TAYLOR

4157. Hobson, Charles F. and Arnold Shankman. "Colonel of the Bucktails: Civil War Letters of Charles Frederick Taylor." PA MHB, 97 [1973]: 333-361.

Drawn from 16 of Taylor's letters, this sketch focuses on the campaigns in which he participated and his ambitions for promotion.

WILLIAM RUFUS TERRILL

4158. Hillard, James M. "You Are Strangely Deluded." CWTI, 13 [10] [1975]: 12-18.

A sketch of Brigadier General William Terrill, class of 1853 at West Point, who came from Virginia but sided with the Union. He was killed at Perryville, October 8, 1862. Terrill's brother, James, became a Confederate general and was killed at Bethesda Church in May 1864.

GEORGE HENRY THOMAS

4159. Cleaves, Freeman. ROCK OF CHICKAMAUGA, THE LIFE OF GENERAL GEORGE H. THOMAS. Norman: University of Oklahoma Press, 1948.

A good, solid biography of the man who saved the day at Chickamauga in September 1863.

4160. Coppee, Henry. GENERAL THOMAS. New York, 1893.

An early, laudatory study of Thomas.

4161. Johnson, Richard W. MEMOIR OF MAJOR GENERAL GEORGE H. THOMAS. Philadelphia, 1881.

Johnson, who was a division commander under Thomas, wrote a friendly account of "the Rock." In later years Johnson was a professor, politician, and author.

4162. McKinney, Francis F. EDUCATION IN VIOLENCE: THE LIFE OF GEORGE H. THOMAS AND THE HISTORY OF THE ARMY OF THE CUMBERLAND. Detroit: Wayne State University Press, 1961.

Although based largely on published materials, this is one of the best biographies of Thomas. Author may have leaned too heavily in the general's favor in rating him the equal of Grant.

4163. O'Connor, Richard. THOMAS, ROCK OF CHICKAMAUGA. New York: Prentice-Hall, 1948.

This first modern biography of Thomas makes for good reading, but it has its flaws.

4164. Piatt, Donn. GENERAL GEORGE H. THOMAS: A CRITICAL BIOGRAPHY. Cincinnati, Ohio: 1893.

An early detailed account, presenting a strong defense of the general against his critics.

4165. Thomas, Wilbur. GENERAL GEORGE H. THOMAS, INDOMITABLE WARRIOR: A BIOGRAPHY. New York: Exposition, 1964.

A fairly good biography in which Thomas is called the "greatest general of the Civil War ... of the world." However, too much reliance is based on biased materials in arriving at this judgment.

4166. Tucker, Glenn. "George H. Thomas." CWTI, 5 [1] [1966]: 28-37.

Author rates Thomas as the most capable Union general, noting that his achievements at Chickamauga and Franklin were vital to the North's success.

4167. Van Horne, Thomas B. THE LIFE OF MAJOR GENERAL GEORGE H. THOMAS. New York, 1882.

An early defensive study of the general.

BENJAMIN W. THOMPSON

4168. Thompson, Benjamin W. "Personal Narrative of Experiences in the Civil War, 1861-1865." CWTI, 12 [1973]: [5] 12-21; [6] 12-23; [7] 28-39; [8] 24-33.

A valuable and articulate war memoir by a New Yorker who was forced to move to Florida for his health in the 1850s and then compelled to flee to the North when the war broke out. He became an officer with the Army of the Potomac, commanding a black regiment, among other things, and finally was in charge of Jefferson Davis after his capture.

ALBION WINEGAR TOURGEE

4169. Gross, Theodore L. ALBION W. TOURGEE. New York: Twayne, 1963.

In this volume, Number 39 in the Twayne United States Author Series, the purpose is to analyze the literary works of Tourgee, the carpetbagger governor of North Carolina, who found that radical reform would not work. His writings interpreted the Reconstruction in the South for the North.

4170. Olenick, Monte M. "Albion W. Tourgee: Radical Republican Spokesman of the Civil War Crusade." PHYLON, 23 [1962]: 332-345.

Sketch of the Ohio soldier, judge, writer, editor, and lawyer, who became a carpetbagger in North Carolina in Reconstruction.

4171. Olson, Otto H. CARPETBAGGER'S CRUSADE: THE LIFE OF ALBION WINEGAR TOURGEE. Baltimore: Johns Hopkins University Press, 1965.

A reliable, readable study of the Ohioan who served in the Civil War and then became a celebrated carpetbagger and author. This work focuses chiefly on the Reconstruction era.

EDWARD D. TOWNSEND

4172. Townsend, Edward D. ANECDOTES OF THE CIVIL WAR IN THE UNITED STATES. New York, 1883.

A potpourri of recollections by a man who served most of the war as Acting Adjutant General of the Army.

LYMAN TRUMBULL

4173. Krug, Mark M. LYMAN TRUMBULL, CONSERVATIVE RADICAL. New York: Barnes, 1965.

A carefully-researched, "revisionist" view of the Illinois senator.

4174. White, Horace. THE LIFE OF LYMAN TRUMBULL. Boston, 1913.

A friend of Trumbull, White wrote a friendly review of the senator's years in Congress.

JOHN BASIL TURCHIN

4175. Parry, Albert. "More on General Turchin." RUSS R, 14 [1955]: 19-23.

The Russian-born Turchin came to the United States after the Crimean War and was a division commander with the Army of the Ohio. Court-martialed and dismissed from the service in 1862 for the looting by his troops of Athens, Alabama, he was restored to his command by Lincoln and took part in the fighting in Tennessee.

MASON WHITING TYLER

4176. Tyler, Mason W. RECOLLECTIONS OF THE CIVIL WAR.... William S. Tyler, editor. New York, 1912.

A useful and well-edited journal of the colonel of the 37th Massachusetts, which fought with the Army of the Potomac. Includes letters, diary excerpts, and editor's narrative.

EMORY UPTON

4177. Ambrose, Stephen E. "A Theorist Fights: Emory Upton in the Civil War." CWH, 9 [1963]: 341-364.

A survey of the war years of the great military thinker.

4178. ———. UPTON AND THE ARMY. Baton Rouge: Louisiana State University Press, 1964.

An excellent study of the life of the man who contributed greatly to the development of the modern American army.

4179. Michie, Peter S. THE LIFE AND LETTERS OF EMORY UPTON.... New York, 1885.

Based on Upton's papers and the OFFICIAL RECORDS, only one-fourth of this work covers the Civil War years. Graduating from West Point in May 1861, he rose quickly in rank. After the war he continued in the regular army and served as commandant at West Point.

JOHN PALMER USHER

4180. Richardson, Elmo R. and Alan W. Farley. JOHN PALMER USHER.... Lawrence: University of Kansas Press, 1960.

A carefully-researched and well-written biography of the man who was Lincoln's secretary of interior in the last two years of the war. While Usher was not a colorful personality and his office was not the most glamorous, he did a solid, workmanlike job which this book demonstrates. He succeeded Caleb B. Smith, who had died in office.

CLEMENT LEWIS VALLANDIGHAM

4181. Klement, Frank L. THE LIMITS OF DISSENT: CLEMENT L. VALLANDIGHAM AND THE CIVIL WAR. Lexington: University of Kentucky Press, 1970.

A thorough and valuable biography of the Civil War's most notorious dissenter. The foremost revisionist of Copperheadism, the author enters the troubled thicket of dissent in wartime and emerges with only a few scratches. Vallandigham is no longer the "traitor" he was so often alleged to be.

4182. Vallandigham, James L. A LIFE OF CLEMENT L. VALLANDIGHAM. Baltimore, 1872.

A eulogistic biography of the famous Copperhead by a devoted brother. A minister of the gospel, James, in preparing this book, relied heavily on Clement's speeches and letters.

BENJAMIN FRANKLIN WADE

4183. Land, Mary. "'Bluff' Ben Wade's New England Biography." NEQ, 27 [1954]: 484-509.

Traces the New England heritage of the Ohio senator, who was one of the foremost Radical Republicans during the war and Reconstruction.

4184. Riddle, Albert G. THE LIFE OF BENJAMIN F. WADE. Cleveland, Ohio: 1887.

A laudatory study of Wade by a fellow Ohio politician.

4185. Trefousse, Hans L. BENJAMIN FRANKLIN WADE: RADICAL REPUBLICAN FROM OHIO. New York: Twayne, 1963.

In this new study of the famous radical, Ben Wade emerges as a much more heroic figure than portrayed in earlier writings. Here he is a great crusader for human freedom. Probably the best biography of Wade yet to appear.

JAMES S. WADSWORTH

4186. Pearson, Henry G. JAMES S. WADSWORTH OF GENESEO.... New York, 1913.

A good biography of the New York Republican who became a division commander in the Army of the Potomac and was killed in the Wilderness fighting in 1864.

CHARLES S. WAINWRIGHT

4187. Wainwright, Charles S. A DIARY OF BATTLE: THE PERSONAL JOURNALS OF COLONEL CHARLES S. WAINWRIGHT, 1861-1865. Allan Nevins, editor. New York: Harcourt, Brace and World, 1962.

A valuable journal of a Union artillery commander who fought throughout the war in the eastern theater. A man of strong convictions, he thought highly of McClellan, but lowly of Lincoln and Stanton.

LEWIS WALLACE

4188. Crecelius, Owen. "Lew Wallace." IND HIS BULL, 43 [1966]: 115-125.

A sketch of the Indiana lawyer, writer, legislator, and general, best known for his novel BEN HUR.

4189. McKee, Irving. "BEN-HUR" WALLACE: THE LIFE OF GENERAL LEW WALLACE. Berkeley: University of California Press, 1947.

Probably the best study of Wallace.

4190. Miller, Robert R. "Lew Wallace and the French Intervention in Mexico." IND MAG HIS, 59 [1963]: 31-50.

Wallace supported the liberals in Mexico after the Civil War and played an important role in gaining American support for the Juarez regime.

4191. Treichel, James A. "Lew Wallace at Fort Donelson." IND MAG HIS, 59 [1963]: 3-18.

Wallace should receive "nothing but credit" as a division commander at Fort Donelson.

4192. Wallace, Harold L. "Lew Wallace's March to Shiloh Revisited." IND MAG HIS, 59 [1963]: 19-30.

Author seeks to modify the critical view of Wallace's performance at Shiloh.

4193. Wallace, Lewis. LEW WALLACE: AN AUTOBIOGRAPHY. 2 v. New York, 1908.

A skillfully written set of recollections, although the war years are not described in as much detail as one would like.

GOUVERNEUR KEMBLE WARREN

4194. Ferris, Loraine. "Gouverneur Kemble Warren the Man." NEB HIS MAG, 19 [1938]: 341-353.

A sketch of the Union general, chief of topographical engineers from the Army of the Potomac, who saved Little Round Top on the second day at Gettysburg. Relieved of his command by Sheridan at Five Forks, Warren was "professionally ruined," although cleared 14 years later.

4195. Taylor, Emerson G. GOUVERNEUR KEMBLE WARREN: THE LIFE AND LETTERS OF AN AMERICAN SOLDIER, 1830-1882. Boston: Houghton-Mifflin, 1932.

A good friendly biography of the man who saved the day at Little Round Top. However, the author appears to have misstated the findings of the Warren Court of Inquiry, when he says the court fully vindicated the general.

ELIHU WASHBURNE

4196. Hess, Stephen. "An American in Paris." AM HER, 18 [2] [1967]: 18-27, 71-73.

A sketch of the career of Elihu Washburne of Illinois through whose influence Grant was restored to high military rank and who, in turn, was named minister to France by President Grant. Washburne performed distinguished service in Paris, particularly during the Franco-Prussian War and the Commune uprising.

4197. Simon, John Y. "From Galena to Appomattox: Grant and Washburne." JISHS, 58 [1965]: 165-189.

A sketch of Washburne, the Illinois congressman, who was influential in Grant's military rise.

JAMES MOORE WAYNE

4198. Lawrence, Alexander A. JAMES MOORE WAYNE, SOUTHERN UNIONIST. Chapel Hill: University of North Carolina Press, 1943.

Wayne served on the Supreme Court during Taney's tenure.

ALEXANDER STEWART WEBB

4199. New York Monuments Commission. IN MEMORIAM: ALEXANDER STEWART WEBB, 1835-1911. Albany: Lyon, 1916.

Webb commanded a Second Corps brigade at Gettysburg, where he was wounded and for which he received the Medal of Honor. This is a tribute to his service.

THURLOW WEED

4200. Van Deusen, Glyndon G. THURLOW WEED: WIZARD OF THE LOBBY. Boston: Little, Brown, 1947.

A scholarly study of the New York politician, who aided the Lincoln administration in prosecuting the war, but who probably was more concerned with making a financial gain out of it.

4201. Weed, Thurlow. LIFE OF THURLOW WEED INCLUDING HIS AUTOBIOGRAPHY AND A MEMOIR. 2 v. Boston, 1884.

Still of some use, but considerably out of date.

STEPHEN MINOT WELD

4202. Weld, Stephen M. WAR DIARY AND LETTERS OF STEPHEN MINOT WELD, 1861-1865. Cambridge, Massachusetts: 1912.

An excellent collection of letters by a Union officer who was a divisional commander in the eastern theater. He was captured at Gaines' Mill and later at the Battle of the Crater.

GIDEON WELLES

4203. Niven, John. GIDEON WELLES: LINCOLN'S SECRETARY OF THE NAVY. New York: Oxford University Press, 1973.

A solid, thorough biography of an important figure. Although there is heavy emphasis on the pre-war years and the background to Welles' service as navy secretary, the war itself is the main focal point. An absorbing study.

4204. Welles, Gideon. DIARY OF GIDEON WELLES, SECRETARY OF THE NAVY UNDER LINCOLN AND JOHNSON. 3 v. Howard K. Beale and Alan W. Brownsword, editors. New York: Norton, 1960.

An annotated revised edition [first edition 1911], this is an indispensable work for an understanding of the Lincoln administration. It reveals what changes were made at the time the diary was first issued and what comments Welles added after the war.

4205. ———. SELECTED ESSAYS OF GIDEON WELLES. 2 v. Albert Mordell, compiler. New York: Twayne, 1959-1960.

Important additional material to the diaries.

4206. West, Richard S. GIDEON WELLES, LINCOLN'S NAVY DEPARTMENT. Indianapolis: Bobbs-Merrill, 1943.

A very good work.

CHARLES WHITTLESEY

4207. Whittlesey, Charles. WAR MEMORANDA. CHEAT RIVER TO THE TENNESSEE, 1861-1862. Cleveland, Ohio: 1884.

Colonel Whittlesey describes his experiences in the western theater early in the war.

JOHN T. WILDER

4208. Williams, Samuel E. GENERAL JOHN T. WILDER, COMMANDER OF THE LIGHTNING BRIGADE. Bloomington: Indiana University Press, 1936.

A brief sketch of the man whose forces in the western theater were the first to use the Spencer repeating rifle.

ALEXANDER WILKIN

4209. Hubbs, Ronald M. "The Civil War and Alexander Wilkin." MINN HIS, 39 [1965]: 173-190.

These recently-discovered letters provide sensitive personal insights on the waging of a war. Colonel Wilkin commanded several different Minnesota regiments but did not survive the war.

ORLANDO BOLIVAR WILLCOX

4210. Stille, Glenn G. "A Michigan Hero." DET HIS SOC BULL, 24 [1968]: 19.

Colonel Willcox held commands in both the eastern and western theaters and received the Medal of Honor for services at First Bull Run, where he was wounded and captured.

ALPHEUS STARKEY WILLIAMS

4211. Williams, Alpheus S. FROM THE CANNON'S MOUTH: THE CIVIL WAR LETTERS OF GENERAL ALPHEUS STARKEY WILLIAMS. Milo Quaife, editor. Detroit: Wayne State University Press, 1959.

An excellent, well-edited collection of letters from a man who served in both the eastern and western theaters and commanded the Twentieth Corps in Sherman's southern campaigns.

THOMAS WILLIAMS

4212. Delaney, Norman C. "General Thomas Williams." CWTI, 14 [4] [1975]: 4-9, 36-47.

Sketch of a Union general whose reputation as a commander and administrator has been criticized.

CHARLES WRIGHT WILLS

4213. Wills, Charles W. ARMY LIFE OF AN ILLINOIS SOLDIER ... LETTERS AND DIARY OF THE LATE CHARLES W. WILLS.... Mary E. Kellogg, compiler. Washington, D.C.: 1906.

An interesting collection of materials about a man who rose from private to lieutenant colonel in Illinois units, compiled by his sister. He served in the western theater and then accompanied Sherman in Georgia.

HENRY WILSON

4214. McKay, Ernest. HENRY WILSON, PRACTICAL RADICAL: PORTRAIT OF A POLITICIAN. Port Washington, New York: Kennikat, 1971.

A useful biography of Massachusetts Senator Henry Wilson, a major political figure during the war.

4215. Nason, Elias and Thomas Russell. THE LIFE AND PUBLIC SERVICES OF HENRY WILSON, LATE VICE-PRESIDENT OF THE UNITED STATES. Philadelphia, 1876.

An early, laudatory biography. Includes numerous excerpts from Wilson's papers.

JAMES HARRISON WILSON

4216. Longacre, Edward G. FROM UNION STARS TO TOP HAT: A BIOGRAPHY OF THE EXTRAORDINARY GENERAL JAMES HARRISON WILSON. Harrisburg: Stackpole, 1972.

A substantial, well-written biography of the dashing, egotistical "boy" cavalry general. He helped revitalize the cavalry branch and led the famous raid through Alabama at the end of the war.

4217. Wilson, James H. "'Your Left Arm': James H. Wilson's Letters to Adam Badeau." James Jones, editor. CWH, 12 [1966]: 230-245.

A collection of six letters written by Wilson to his friend Badeau, Grant's military secretary in the spring of 1865. Letters deal with Wilson's Alabama raid and the capture of Jefferson Davis.

4218. ———. UNDER THE OLD FLAG: RECOLLECTIONS OF MILITARY OPERATIONS IN THE WAR FOR THE UNION.... 2 v. New York, 1912.

Memoirs of over 40 years' service by an important officer and prolific writer.

FERNANDO WOOD

4219. Pleasants, Samuel A. FERNANDO WOOD OF NEW YORK. New York: Columbia University Press, 1948.

A good biography of the wartime, Copperhead mayor of New York City.

JOHN ELLIS WOOL

4220. Rezneck, Samuel. "The Civil War Role, 1861-1863, of a Veteran New York Officer, Major General John E. Wool. NY HIS, 44 [1963]: 237-257.

A sketch of the New York general who had served in the War of 1812 and was 72 when the Civil War broke out. He was in command of the Department of the East during the 1863 Draft Riots in New York City.

JOHN L. WORDEN

4221. Jones, James P. "Lincoln's Courier: John L. Worden's Mission to Fort Pickens." FLA HIS Q, 41 [1962/1963]: 145-153.

A sketch of Worden who delivered special orders to Fort Pickens, was captured when he attempted to return to the North, and later commanded the MONITOR.

PERCY WYNDHAM

4222. Longacre, Edward G. "Sir Percy Wyndham." CWTI, 7 [8] [1968]: 12-19.

Sir Percy was a soldier of fortune who fought in the Valley Campaign, at Second Bull Run, and at Brandy Station. He began his "professional" career at the age of 15.

RICHARD YATES

4223. Northrup, Jack. "The Education of a Western Lawyer." A J LEG HIS, 12 [1968]: 294-305.

A Kentucky lawyer, Yates served in the state legislature and became governor of Illinois in 1860. He retained that office throughout the war, playing an important role in the raising of troops and the suppressing of dissenters.

4224. ———. "Richard Yates: A Personal Glimpse of the Illinois Soldiers' Friend." JISHS, 56 [1963]: 121-138.

Yates' efforts to promote welfare of Illinois soldiers involved him in controversy.

4225. Yates, Richard and Catharine Y. Pickering. RICHARD YATES, CIVIL WAR GOVERNOR. John H. Krenkel, editor. Danville, Illinois: Interstate Printers, 1966.

Although the manuscript of Illinois wartime governor was written by Yates' son and granddaughter in the 1930s, it has been polished and documented by the editor. However, the devotion of the authors to their subject leads to distortions in explaining Yates' life and record. Still it makes for good reading.

MULTIPLE BIOGRAPHIES

[By author]

4226. Bartlett, John R. MEMOIRS OF RHODE ISLAND OFFICERS WHO WERE ENGAGED IN THE SERVICE OF THEIR COUNTRY DURING THE GREAT REBELLION.... Providence, Rhode Island: 1867.

A sketch of the 1st Rhode Island is accompanied by short biographies of 109 Rhode Island officers.

4227. Bradford, Gamaliel. UNION PORTRAITS. Boston: Houghton Mifflin, 1961.

The lives of a number of leading political and military figures are traced.

4228. Brockett, Linus P. OUR GREAT CAPTAINS. GRANT, SHERMAN, THOMAS, SHERIDAN, AND FARRAGUT.... New York, 1865.

An early, outdated book of praise.

4229. Dodge, Grenville M. PERSONAL RECOLLECTIONS OF PRESIDENT ABRAHAM LINCOLN, GENERAL ULYSSES S. GRANT AND GENERAL WILLIAM T. SHERMAN. Council Bluffs, Iowa: 1914.

The author served in the western theater, commanding divisions and corps under both Grant and Sherman. Later he was the chief engineer in the construction of the Union Pacific railroad and was an active Republican.

4230. Harrison, Lowell H. "Kentucky-Born Generals in the Civil War." KY HIS SOC REG, 64 [1966]: 129-160.

A sketch of each of the generals from Kentucky, which supplied more Civil War generals than any other state save Virginia and New York.

4231. Hassler, Warren W., Jr. COMMANDERS OF THE ARMY OF THE POTOMAC. Baton Rouge: Louisiana State University Press, 1962.

A series of sketches of Generals McDowell, McClellan, Pope, Burnside, Hooker, Meade, and Grant. It is an interesting account for the casual reader, but adds nothing new for the serious student.

4232. Headley, Joel T. GRANT AND SHERMAN: THEIR CAMPAIGNS AND GENERALS. New York, 1866.

An early, outdated work by "the most popular and graphic writer of military history of modern times...."

4233. Hellie, Richard. "General of Iowa Civil War Regiments." ANN IOWA, 36 [1963]: 498-504.

Biographical sketches of Iowa's generals with a collective portrait.

4234. Korngold, Ralph. TWO FRIENDS OF MAN: THE STORY OF WILLIAM LLOYD GARRISON AND WENDELL PHILLIPS AND THEIR RELATIONSHIP WITH ABRAHAM LINCOLN. Boston: Little, Brown, 1950.

An interesting work although there is little documentation and casual errors have crept in.

4235. Oates, Stephen B. OUR FIERY TRIAL: ABRAHAM LINCOLN, JOHN BROWN, AND THE CIVIL WAR ERA. Amherst: University of Massachusetts Press, 1979.

Ten essays dealing with slavery, the Civil War, Lincoln, Brown, and Nat Turner. Shows how these three men are frequently perceived.

4236. Piatt, Donn. MEMORIES OF THE MEN WHO SAVED THE UNION. New York, 1887.

Brief, laudatory biographies of a number of leading political and military figures.

4237. Sheppard, E.W. "Generals of the American Civil War. I. The Northern Generals." ARMY QDJ [Britain], 86 [1963]: 171-181.

McDowell, McClellan, Burnside, Hooker, Meade, Grant, Halleck, Buell, Rosecrans, Sherman, Grant, and Sheridan are analyzed. Sheridan has been overrated, while Sherman and Grant were the "real conquerors of the Confederacy."

4238. Warner, Ezra J. GENERALS IN BLUE: LIVES OF UNION COMMANDERS. Baton Rouge: Louisiana State University Press, 1964.

Book contains sketches of the lives of 583 men, concentrating on their Civil War years but also includes a useful discussion of the ante-bellum careers of each of them. A good reference volume. A list of 1,367 breveted generals is also included.

VII

SOLDIER LIFE

By Robert J. Fryman

Camp life in the Union army is perhaps best summarized by Sergeant Samuel Cormany's diary entry of October 5, 1863, in which he states, "O how dull camp life is compared with being in Front--doing things to make a fellow tingle all through...." This sentiment was quickly shared by all enlisted men and many commissioned officers, shortly after the realities of military life became apparent. Instead of numerous dress reviews before cheering crowds, periodically punctuated by brief but victorious exploits on the battlefield, the common soldier found himself subjected to a daily routine consisting of seemingly endless hours of drill, fatigue duty, poor food, and sheer boredom, only to be interrupted infrequently by moments of sheer terror in combat.

The following bibliography is a selection of sources which best illustrate the camp and field life of the Union soldier from 1861 to 1865. It is more representative than comprehensive in nature, focusing rather on those works which are considered to be exemplary of the daily routine of the northern enlisted man and officer [below rank of lieutenant-colonel] during the conflict. The majority of the references which follow consist of personal accounts--letters, diaries and journals, written by participants in the conflict, thus imparting a personal character to the selections it contains. The bibliography also includes syntheses which are useful in studying the life of the common Union soldier.

It is highly recommended that the reader examine the 1863 REVISED U.S. ARMY REGULATIONS and William J. Hardee's 1855 RIFLE AND LIGHT INFANTRY TACTICS prior to using the references listed below. These two works formed the basis for the military routine experienced by the Union volunteer and will greatly enhance the reader's understanding and appreciation of camp life in the armies of the United States during the Civil War.

4239. Acton, Edward A. "'Dear Molly.' Letters of Captain Edward A. Acton to his Wife, 1862." Mary A. Hammond, editor. PA MHB, 89 [1965]: 3-51.

The author, who commanded companies in the 5th New Jersey, describes the details of camp life and soldiering, comments on politics and politicians, and expresses his concern for family and friends at home.

4240. Affeld, Charles E. "Pvt. Charles E. Affeld Describes the Mechanicsburg Expeditions." Edwin C. Bearss, editor. JISHS, 56 [1963]: 233-256.

This well-edited selection of diary entries provides some very valuable glimpses into conditions of life during a campaign.

4241. ———. "Pvt. Charles E. Affeld Reports Action West of the Mississippi." Edwin C. Bearss, editor. JISHS, 60 [1967]: 267-296.

A good account of military life in the field and camp in Union operations in the trans-Mississippi region.

4242. Allen, John F. MEMORIAL OF PICKERING DODGE ALLEN. Boston, 1867.

In a memorial to his son, the author includes a good collection of the soldier-son's letters from Louisiana and Mississippi.

4243. Alley, Charles. "Excerpts From the Civil War Diary of Lieutenant Charles Alley...." John S. Ezell, editor. IOWA J HIS, 49 [1951]: 241-256.

Excerpts from the excellent diary of Charles Alley, an Irish immigrant who rose from private to second lieutenant. He served in Company C, 5th Iowa Cavalry.

4244. Alvord, Henry E. "A New England Boy in the Civil War." Caroline B. Sherman, editor. NEQ, 5 [1932]: 310-344.

Thirty-one letters from Henry Elijah Alvord, who entered the army as a teenager and served as a cavalryman throughout the war, first with the 7th Rhode Island Cavalry and then with the 20th Massachusetts Cavalry. After the war he was very active in agricultural education.

4245. Andrus, Onley. THE CIVIL WAR LETTERS OF SGT. ONLEY ANDRUS. Fred A. Shannon, editor. Urbana: University of Illinois Press, 1947.

A useful collection of letters which provide interesting details of camp life and campaign settings in the West.

4246. Arbuckle, John C. CIVIL WAR EXPERIENCES OF A FOOT SOLDIER WHO MARCHED WITH SHERMAN.... Columbus, Ohio: n.p., 1930.

The adventures of an infantryman in Company K, 4th Iowa.

4247. Bailey, George W. A PRIVATE CHAPTER OF THE WAR. St.Louis, 1880.

Useful for information about camp life as seen by an officer.

4248. Barber, Lucius W. ARMY MEMOIRS OF LUCIUS BARBER. Chicago, 1894. Reprint 1984.

This work ranks as one of the most valuable in regard to camp life. The author vividly describes many aspects of the military during the course of the war, providing the reader with an excellent glimpse of the life of the average soldier.

4249. Bardeen, Charles W. A LITTLE FIFER'S WAR DIARY. Syracuse, 1910.

An excellent description of camp and field life with the 1st Massachusetts. The book contains 17 maps, 60 portraits, and over 240 other illustrations.

4250. Bartmess, Jacob W. "Jacob W. Bartmess' Civil War Letters...." Donald F. Carmony, editor. IND MAG HIS, 52 [1956]: 49-74, 157-186.

These letters of an Indiana soldier reflect his unhappiness with the army which he regarded as a "cesspool of corruption."

4251. Barton, Michael. GOODMEN: THE CHARACTER OF CIVIL WAR SOLDIERS. University Park: Pennsylvania State University Press, 1981.

A short, but excellent work on the mores and norms of the Victorian Civil War soldier. The author examines 16 character values of soldiers, both North and South, drawn from the diaries and letters of over 400 men.

4252. Bates, Gilbert H. SERGEANT BATES' MARCH.... New York, 1868.

A member of a Wisconsin artillery unit describes his life and the long march from Vicksburg to Washington.

4253. Bear, Henry C. THE CIVIL WAR LETTERS OF HENRY C. BEAR, A SOLDIER IN THE 116TH ILLINOIS.... Wayne C. Temple, editor. Harrogate, Tennessee: Lincoln Memorial University Press, 1961.

These letters from an Illinois soldier who participated in the Vicksburg and other campaigns in the southwest, describe the conditions of camp life.

4254. Beck, Stephen C. A TRUE SKETCH OF HIS ARMY LIFE. Edgar, Nebraska: 1914.

Beck served in the lower Mississippi with the 124th Illinois.

4255. Bellard, Alfred. GONE FOR A SOLDIER: CIVIL WAR MEMOIRS OF PRIVATE ALFRED BELLARD. David H. Donald, editor. Boston: Little, Brown, 1975.

An illustrated diary kept by a member of the 5th New Jersey. Published 15 years after the war was over, Bellard's descriptions of the battles are most vivid. Much of the diary reflects the great concern the soldier had for food.

4256. ———. "Personal Recollections of the War." AM HER, 26 [5] [1975]: 10-15.

This article consists of a sample of Bellard's drawings depicting life in the Union army. The illustrations of military justice are of particular interest.

4257. Bernadete, Doris, editor. CIVIL WAR HUMOR. Mount Vernon, New York: Peter Pauper Press, 1963.

A short volume drawing on the writings of Petroleum Nasby, Josh Billings, and other humorists of the time.

4258. Benedict, George G. ARMY LIFE IN VIRGINIA. LETTERS FROM THE TWELFTH VERMONT IN THE WAR FOR THE UNION, 1862-1863. Burlington, Vermont: 1895.

A very good series of letters which provide interesting insights into the life of the Union soldier on the march and in camp.

4259. Bennett, Edwin C. MUSKET AND SWORD, OR THE CAMP, MARCH, AND FIRING LINE IN THE ARMY OF THE POTOMAC. Boston, 1900.

Useful descriptions of camp life by a soldier who fought through many of the campaigns in the East.

4260. Bensell, Royal A. ALL QUIET ON THE YAMHILL: THE CIVIL WAR IN OREGON. Gunter Barth, editor. Eugene: University of Oregon Books, 1959.

A well-edited edition of Corporal Bensell's two year journal. He joined a California regiment to fight Confederates in Virginia and wound up watching Indians in Oregon. If you are curious to know what it was like watching Indians in wartime Oregon, this is your book.

4261. Benson, William C. "Civil War Diary of William C. Benson." IND MAG HIS, 23 [1927]: 333-364.

Brief one or two line entries on activities of the day. The final entry on March 10, 1865 reads "was mortally wounded and taken back to field hospital." He died the next day.

4262. Benton, Charles E. AS SEEN FROM THE RANKS: A BOY IN THE CIVIL WAR. New York, 1902.

One of the better accounts of soldier life with respect to training and general camp activities. The author served with Sherman in Georgia and the Carolinas.

4263. Bigelow, Edwin B. "Edwin B. Bigelow: A Michigan Sergeant in the Civil War." Frank L. Klement, editor. MICH HIS, 38 [1954]: 193-252.

Author, a member of the Michigan cavalry brigade, kept a diary from January 1, 1863-June 14, 1864, reprinted here. A sketch of Bigelow precedes the diary entries.

4264. Biggert, Florence E. "Some Leaves From A Civil War Diary." Harry R. Beck, editor. W PA HIS MAG, 42 [1959]: 363-382.

After the state militia was absorbed into federal service, Pennsylvania organized a homeguard. The guard was called up three times, and this article covers Biggert's diary of these musters. It is interesting because he was not a soldier in the real sense of the word.

4265. Billings, John D. HARDTACK AND COFFEE, OR, THE UNWRITTEN STORY OF ARMY LIFE.... Boston, 1887. Many reprints; most recent, 1982.

Billings was an artillerist with the 10th Independent Battery of Massachusetts Artillery. This is one of the best and most widely-quoted works on the life of the Union soldier. The volume provides details on life in camp and insights into the attitudes of soldiers. It is written with wit and style. Humorously illustrated. A classic.

4266. Blake, Henry N. THREE YEARS IN THE ARMY OF THE POTOMAC. Boston, 1865.

A captain of the 11th Massachusetts, Blake did not enjoy army life. He was court-martialed, although acquitted, for bitterly attacking his superior officers. Wounded at Spottsylvania, he was honorably discharged a month later.

4267. Boeger, Palmer H. "Hardtack and Burned Beans." CWH, 4 [1958]: 73-92.

Interesting account of life in the army. Privates, by army regulation, had to cook their own food. Unfortunately the commissary department did not teach recruits what to do with raw pork and beans.

4268. Boney, E.N. "The Conqueror: Sergeant Mathew Woodruff in War and Peace, 1861-1865." ALA R, 23 [1970]: 193-211.

In this summary of the career of Sergeant Woodruff, an infantryman from Missouri, the author points out the soldier's strong anti-Negro bias.

4269. Boots, E.N. "Civil War Letters of E.N. Boots." Wilfred M. Black, editor. VA MHB, 69 [1961]: 194-209.

Boots belonged to a very religious Pennsylvania family. His letters describe general conditions of army service.

4270. Borton, Benjamin. ON THE PARALLELS: OR, CHAPTERS OF INNER HISTORY: A STORY OF THE RAPPAHANNOCK. Woodstown, New Jersey: 1903.

A very general and often sketchy description of camp life. Quite useful for glimpses of picket duty. A New Jerseyite, Borton took part in the Fredericksburg campaign.

4271. Botkin, Benjamin A., editor. A CIVIL WAR TREASURY OF TALES, LEGENDS, AND FOLKLORE. New York: Random House, 1960. Reprint, 1981.

A collection of more than 300 stories, legends, anecdotes, and what-have-you reflecting the war in human as well as humane terms. The material is organized year-by-year.

4272. Brainard, Orson. "Orson Brainard: A Soldier in the Ranks." Wilfred W. Black, editor. OHIO HIS Q, 76 [1967]: 54-72.

Article provides brief, though interesting, notes on cooking, rations, and picket duty as seen in the 51st Ohio.

4273. Brett, David. "MY DEAR WIFE ...:" THE CIVIL WAR LETTERS OF DAVID BRETT, 9TH MASSACHUSETTS BATTERY, UNION CANNONEER. Frank P. Deane, editor. Little Rock, Arkansas: Pioneer Press, 1964.

Among other things, this work is useful in describing how soldiers viewed the army sutler and the various prices they were charged for the goods they purchased.

4274. Bright, Adam S. "RESPECTS TO ALL": LETTERS OF TWO PENNSYLVANIA BOYS IN THE WAR OF THE REBELLION. Aida Truxall, editor. Pittsburgh: University of Pittsburgh Press, 1962.

The early letters of Adam S. and Michael S. Bright supply insight into a recruit's first views of military routine.

4275. Bright, Thomas R. "Yankee in Arms: The Civil War as a Personal Experience." CWH, 19 [1973]: 197-218.

Based on their letters home, the article discusses how the war experience changed two Massachusetts soldiers of differing backgrounds.

4276. Brobst, John F. WELL, MARY: CIVIL WAR LETTERS OF A WISCONSIN VOLUNTEER. Margaret B. Roth, editor. Madison: University of Wisconsin Press, 1960.

An able compilation of well-written, witty letters from a soldier who campaigned with Sherman. A member of the 25th Wisconsin, his convictions and strength of character helped him.

4277. Brown, Edwin W. "Reminiscences of an Ohio Volunteer." Philip D. Jordan and Charles M. Thomas, editors. OHIO HIS Q, 48 [1939]: 304-323.

Brown served with the 20th Ohio.

4278. Brown, William H. "Soldier of the 92nd Illinois: Letters of William H. Brown and His Fiancee, Emma Jane Frazey." Vivian C. Hopkins, editor. NY PUB LIB BULL, 73 [1969]: 114-136.

Article includes twelve letters from William to Emma Jane and ten letters from Emma Jane to William. The infrequent correspondence began in September 1862 and concluded in May 1867.

4279. Bull, Rice C. SOLDIERING: THE CIVIL WAR DIARY OF RICE C. BULL, 123RD NEW YORK VOLUNTEER INFANTRY. K. Jack Bauer, editor. San Rafael, California: Presidio Press, 1977.

An enjoyable account of one man's experience in the Civil War, encompassing both eastern and western theaters. Of particular appeal are the description of the "comforts" of camp life.

4280. Burcher, William M. "A History of Soldier Voting in the State of New York." NYH, 25 [1944]: 459-481.

Six pages of this article are devoted to a brief synopsis of soldier voting in New York in the Civil War.

4281. Butler, Jay C. LETTERS HOME BY JAY CALDWELL BUTLER, CAPTAIN, 101ST OHIO VOLUNTEER INFANTRY, ARRANGED BY HIS SON.... Binghamton, New York: Privately printed, 1930.

This 153-page volume contains numerous letters of interest from an officer who campaigned in the West and before Atlanta.

4282. Cain, Marvin. "A 'Face of Battle' Needed: An Assessment of Motives and Men in Civil War Historiography." CWH, 28 [1982]: 5-27.

An overview of the "psyche" of the soldier in the war, the article discusses the reasons why many men, both Union and Confederate, decided to fight.

4283. Campbell, Henry. "Civil War Letters and Diaries." CWTI, 2 [7] [1963]: 26-29, 42-45; 2 [9] [1964]: 34-37, 46-48.

Campbell was a teenage bugler in the 18th [Lilly's] Indiana Battery, who wrote about campaigning in Tennessee in 1863.

4284. Campbell, John Q.A. "The Civil War Diary of Lieutenant John Q.A. Campbell, Company B, 5th Iowa Infantry." Edwin C. Bearss, editor. ANN IOWA, 39 [1969]: 519-541.

The author describes the progress of the siege of Vicksburg, May 19-June 22, 1863.

4285. Carter, Robert G. FOUR BROTHERS IN BLUE OR SUNSHINE AND SHADOWS OF THE WAR OF THE REBELLION: A STORY OF THE GREAT CIVIL WAR FROM BULL RUN TO APPOMATTOX. Austin: University of Texas Press, 1978.

An excellent series of letters of four brothers from Bradford, Massachusetts, providing an intriguing account of fatigue duty, punishment, and camp life generally. At least one of the brothers was engaged in every major battle of the war.

4286. Castle, Henry A. THE ARMY MULE, AND OTHER WAR SKETCHES. Indianapolis, Indiana: 1898.

A collection of diverse, humorous anecdotes of army life, including "The Army Mule," "The Sutler," and "Dress Parade."

4287. Chadwick, Wallace W. "Into the Breach, Civil War Letters of Wallace W. Chadwick." Mabel W. Mayer, editor. OHIO HIS Q, 52 [1943]: 158-180.

Chadwick served with the 138th Ohio.

4288. Chase, Charles. "Letters of a Maine Soldier Boy." Norman C. Delaney, editor. CWH, 5 [1959]: 45-61.

A series of letters home--with connected narrative--of Charles Chase, a private in the 23rd Maine serving in the eastern theater. Chase was killed at Cold Harbor.

4289. Chase, Charles M. "A Union Band Director Views Camp Rolla 1861." Donald H. Welsh, editor. MO HIS R, 55 [1961]: 307-343.

Chase and his brass band enlisted in the 13th Illinois early in July 1861, on a special three-month contract. In his diary which ran from July 21 to October 10 when the band was discharged, he comments freely on army life and on the Rolla, Missouri community.

4290. Clark, George W. "Civil War Letters of George W. Clark." KY HIS SOC REG, 62 [1964]: 307-317.

These are letters from a poorly-educated soldier whose disenchantment with army life and whose longing for family and his Indiana home transcended all interest in military affairs.

4291. Cody, Darwin. "Civil War Letters of Darwin Cody." Stanley P. Wasson, editor. OHIO HIS Q, 68 [1959]: 371-407.

A well-edited article. Detailed footnotes elaborate on the text.

4292. Coe, Hamlin A. MINE EYES HAVE SEEN THE GLORY: COMBAT DIARIES OF UNION SERGEANT HAMLIN ALEXANDER COE. David Coe, editor. Rutherford, New Jersey: Fairleigh Dickinson University Press, 1975.

In these excerpts from the author's diaries, one gets a good glimpse of the rigors of campaign life.

4293. Comte, Victor. "Detroit's Little French Corporal." F. Clever Bald, editor. MICH HIS, 46 [1962]: 126-146.

A teenager in the 5th Michigan Cavalry, Comte wrote 50 newsy and cheerful letters to his wife. A happy warrior, he complained about very little.

4294. Connolly, James A. THREE YEARS IN THE ARMY OF THE CUMBERLAND: THE LETTERS AND DIARY OF MAJOR JAMES A. CONNOLLY. Paul H. Angle, editor. Bloomington: Indiana University Press, 1959.

In this meaty book, the author wrote perceptively of army life in the western theater and of the daily routine of the camp.

4295. Coon, David. "Letters From A Soldier." Katrina Bennett, editor. WIS THEN NOW, 12 [10] [1966]: 1-5.

A collection of 35 letters from the author, a Wisconsin farmer, to his wife and seven children, written during his service with the 36th Wisconsin in 1864. Coon died in a Confederate prison.

4296. Cooney, Charles F. "Engineers and Entertainment." CWTI, 15 [7] [1976]: 12-15.

In order to alleviate the boredom of winter headquarters, an engineering battalion at Brandy Station decided to form "a dramatic club and ... to build a theater."

4297. Cormany, Samuel. THE CORMANY DIARIES: A NORTHERN FAMILY IN THE CIVIL WAR. James C. Mohr and Richard E. Winslow III, editors. Pittsburgh: University of Pittsburgh Press, 1982.

An excellent collection of diary entries of Cormany and his wife Rachel. He served with the 16th Pennsylvania Cavalry from 1862-1865, and his diaries reveal valuable scenes of camp life as well as battles of the eastern theater. She lived in Chambersburg, and her writings reflect the spirit of the home front.

4298. Cort, Charles E. "DEAR FRIENDS": THE CIVIL WAR LETTERS AND DIARY OF CHARLES EDWIN CORT. Helyn W. Tomlinson, editor. n.p.: n.p., 1962.

A well-edited body of material, with a useful commentary, from a man who served in the western theater with the 92nd Illinois.

4299. Cox, Charles H. "The Civil War Letters of Charles Harding Cox." Lorna L. Sylvester, editor. IND MAG HIS, 68 [1972]: 24-78.

Cox, a member of the 17th Indiana, wrote engagingly about everything he saw and experienced--camp life, mail delivery, foraging, disease, lady visitation--and his letters reflect an elemental excitement concerning army life.

4300. Cox, Jabez T. "Civil War Diary of Jabez Thomas Cox." IND MAG HIS, 28 [1932]: 40-54.

The diary of Cox, May 12 - August 29, 1864, a member of the 133rd Indiana which campaigned in Tennessee.

4301. Cramer, Richard S. "The Civil War Had Jokes, Too." SAN JOSE STUD, 1 [1975]: 86-92.

Cramer records anecdotes repeated by soldiers of both sides as a relief from the horror and chaos of war.

4302. Crane, James. "'Constantly on the Lark': The Civil War Letters of a New Jersey Man." Michael Barton, editor. MANU, 30 [1978]: 12-20.

Four letters from James Crane, a typical private, sometimes brave, oftentimes troublesome, but always attempting to survive the rigors of war.

4303. Crary, Jerry. JERRY CRARY, 1842-1936: TEACHER, SOLDIER, INDUSTRIALIST. Warren, Pennsylvania: Newell Press, 1960.

A brief volume covering the wartime experiences of a member of the 143rd New York.

4304. Crippen, Edward W. "The Diary of Edward W. Crippen...." Robert J. Kerner, editor. ILL ST HIS SOC TRAN, 10 [1909]: 220-282.

Crippen, a private in the 27th Illinois, kept a thoughtful diary from August 7, 1861 to September 19, 1863.

4305. Cronin, David E. THE EVOLUTION OF A LIFE, DESCRIBED IN THE MEMOIRS OF SETH EYLAND.... New York, 1884.

Using a pseudonym, Cronin wrote an excellent volume of recollections. He played a dual role of cavalryman and artist for HARPERS WEEKLY.

4306. Crotty, Daniel. FOUR YEARS CAMPAIGNING IN THE ARMY OF THE POTOMAC. Grand Rapids, Michigan: 1874.

Written by an enlisted man in the 3rd Michigan, these memoirs add little new.

4307. Crumrine, Bishop. "Corporal Crumrine Goes to War." Walter S. Sanderlich, editor. TOPIC 2 [Fall, 1961]: 48-64.

Excerpts from 35 letters written by a young Pennsylvania soldier to his brother, from August 1862 to June 1865. Crumrine was a member of the Pittsburg Heavy Artillery, who spent his entire service in garrison duty at Fort Delaware.

4308. Cunningham, David. "Major Cunningham's Journal, 1862." W VA HIS, 34 [1973]: 187-211.

Cunningham kept a daily journal of his experiences, which included the Antietam campaign and Union operations in southern West Virginia.

4309. Dalzell, James M. PRIVATE DALZELL: HIS AUTOBIOGRAPHY, POEMS AND COMIC WAR PAPERS. Cincinnati, Ohio: 1888.

Sections on the sketches of the war contain some of the most amusing incidents of camp life.

4310. Dana, Gustavus S. "The Recollections of a Signal Officer." Lester L. Swift, editor. CWH, 9 [1963]: 36-54.

Dana served as a flagman during the Port Royal expedition and other operations along the southeastern coast.

4311. ———. "'Bully For the First Connecticut!' The Recollections of a Three-Month Volunteer." Lester L. Swift, editor. LIN HER, 67 [1965]: 72-82.

Dana's recollections of service with Company A, 1st Connecticut, which took part in First Bull Run.

4312. ———. "'A Hartford Boy in a Waterbury Company': The Adventures of a Connecticut Volunteer." Lester L. Swift, editor. LIN HER, 68 [1966]: 20-35.

Dana also served with Company B of the 6th Connecticut, assigned to the Department of the South.

4313. Dannett, Sylvia G. A TREASURY OF CIVIL WAR HUMOR. New York: Yoseloff, 1963.

This illustrated volume includes material found in the contemporary journals.

4314. Davis, Burke. OUR INCREDIBLE CIVIL WAR. New York: Holt, Rinehart, and Winston, 1960.

An entertaining collection of countless odds and ends of Civil War minutiae which had managed to avoid being included in other books on the subject.

4315. Davis, Charles L. "A Signal Officer With Grant...." Wayne C. Temple, editor. CWH, 7 [1961]: 428-437.

Three letters and a brief journal, 1864-1865, from the chief signal officer of the Army of the Potomac. Davis, a captain when discharged, liked the army so much that he rejoined and died a brigadier general.

4316. Davis, Washington. CAMP-FIRE CHATS OF THE CIVIL WAR: BEING THE INCIDENT, ADVENTURE AND WAYSIDE EXPLOIT OF THE BIVOUAC AND BATTLE FIELD.... Chicago, 1884.

A large gathering of stories and legends, somewhat romanticized, as told by members of the Grand Army of the Republic.

4317. Day, David L. MY DIARY OF RAMBLES WITH THE 25TH MASSACHUSETTS VOLUNTEER INFANTRY, WITH BURNSIDE'S COAST DIVISION, 18TH ARMY CORPS, AND ARMY OF THE JAMES. Milford, Massachusetts: 1884.

A short, but intriguing book of memoirs.

4318. DeForest, John W. A VOLUNTEER'S ADVENTURE: A UNION CAPTAIN'S RECORD OF THE CIVIL WAR. James H. Croushere, editor. New Haven: Yale University Press, 1948.

This brings together DeForest's vividly realistic personal recollections of his service as a Union officer with the occupation forces at New Orleans and in battles such as those at Port Hudson and Cedar Creek. Sharp accounts of camp life, combat conditions, and the characters of troops and officers abound. A useful companion piece to DeForest's 1867 novel MISS RAVENEL'S CONVERSION.

4319. Dodd, Ira S. THE SONG OF THE RAPPAHANNOCK: SKETCHES OF THE CIVIL WAR. New York, 1898.

The author, who served with Company F, 26th New Jersey, writes descriptively about various aspects of army life.

4320. Donaghy, John. ARMY EXPERIENCE OF CAPTAIN JOHN DONAGHY, 103RD PENNSYLVANIA VOLUNTEERS, 1861-1864. DeLand, Florida: Painter, 1926.

A valuable record of army experiences by a Pennsylvania officer.

4321. Dority, Orin G. "The Civil War Diary of Orin G. Dority." Marian Glann, editor. NW OHIO Q, 37 [1965]: 7-26, 105-115.

On-the-spot observations by an Ohio artillerist, who served in most of the campaigns in the eastern theater.

4322. Dougherty, William. "Civil War Diary of an Ohio Volunteer." Donald J. Coan, editor. W PA HIS MAG, 50 [1967]: 171-186.

Excerpts from the Dougherty diary provide illuminating insights into the daily routine of the soldier.

4323. Downing, Alexander G. DOWNING'S CIVIL WAR DIARY, BY ALEXANDER G. DOWNING, COMPANY E, ELEVENTH IOWA INFANTRY.... Olynthus B. Clark, editor. Des Moines: Historical Department of Iowa, 1916.

A valuable account of western service covering the period from August 1861 to July 1865.

4324. Driggs, George. OPENING OF THE MISSISSIPPI; OR TWO YEARS CAMPAIGNING IN THE SOUTHWEST. Madison, Wisconsin: 1864.

The author, a member of the 8th Wisconsin, used newspaper articles which he had written during the war, to tell the story of his experiences in the Far West.

4325. Dunham, Abner. "Civil War Letters of Abner Dunham." Mildred Throne, editor. IOWA J HIS, 53 [1955]: 303-340.

Dunham enlisted in the 12th Iowa in October 1861. He wrote to his parents describing his experiences in a number of battles in the West. Captured at Shiloh, he was paroled, and later served at Vicksburg and Nashville.

4326. Dunham, Alburtis. THROUGH THE SOUTH WITH A UNION SOLDIER. Arthur H. DeRosier, Jr., editor. Johnson City, Tennessee: East Tennessee State University Research Advisory Council, 1969.

A well-edited collection of letters from Alburtis and Laforest Dunham of Pontiac, Illinois, who were with the 129th Illinois in Tennessee, Georgia, and the Carolinas. Alburtis died of encephalitis four months after he entered the army. Younger brother Laforest served throughout the war and wrote spiritedly about both military and non-military matters.

4327. Eberhart, James W. "Diary of Salisbury Prison by James W. Eberhart, Sergt Co G 8th Pa Res Corps...." Florence McLaughlin, editor. W PA HIS MAG, 36 [1973]: 211-251.

A prisoner from August 1864 to March 1865, Eberhart wrote a diary which reveals a strong will to survive a terrible ordeal.

4328. Ely, Ralph. WITH THE WANDERING REGIMENT: THE DIARY OF CAPTAIN RALPH ELY OF THE EIGHTH MICHIGAN CAVALRY. George M. Blackburn, editor. Mount Pleasant, Michigan: Central Michigan University Press, 1965.

The entries in this journal are brief. Ely summarized bloody Antietam in eight or nine lines. A useful book, nonetheless.

4329. Farrington, Josiah. "Josiah Farrington's Civil War Diary and Letters." Myron Bradley, editor. NW OHIO Q, 49 [1977]: 87-97.

Farrington describes conditions with the 14th Ohio, campaigning in Tennessee.

4330. Ferguson, Leonard C. "The Civil War Diaries of Leonard C. Ferguson." William A. Hunter, editor. PENN HIS, 14 [1947]: 196-224, 289-313.

A private in the Pennsylvania 57th, Ferguson was captured at Petersburg and sent to Andersonville in June 1864, where he remained until it was closed. The diary runs from January 19, 1864 through April 15, 1865. Entries were made almost every day, but they are brief and non-committal.

4331. Fletcher, Stephen K. "The Civil War Journal of Stephen Keyes Fletcher." Perry McCandless, editor. IND MAG HIS, 54 [1958]: 141-190.

Fletcher, a sergeant in the 33rd Indiana, was a keen observer of the human condition and reports thoughtfully on the pleasures and hardships of army life.

4332. Fletcher, W.B. "The Civil War Journal of William B. Fletcher." Loriman S. Brigham, editor. IND MAG HIS, 57 [1961]: 41-76.

The author, a member of the 6th Indiana, ably describes campaigning in western Virginia, discusses Union spying, and provides thoughtful sketches of persons and places.

4333. Francis, Charles L. NARRATIVE OF A PRIVATE SOLDIER IN THE VOLUNTEER ARMY OF THE UNITED STATES DURING A PORTION OF THE PERIOD COVERED BY THE GREAT WAR OF THE REBELLION OF 1861. Brooklyn, 1879.

A valuable account of army life in 1861 and 1862. Humorous and well-written, the book provides a glimpse of camp life in both the East and West.

4334. Fuller, Charles A. PERSONAL RECOLLECTIONS OF THE WAR OF 1861.... Shelburne, New York: 1906.

The author rose from private to lieutenant in the 61st New York. Late in life he compiled this short, but good book based on his wartime letters.

4335. Gardner, Henry R. "A Yankee in Louisiana: Selections From the Diary and Correspondence of Henry R. Gardner, 1862-1865." Kenneth E. Shewmaker and Andrew Prinz, editors. LA HIS, 5 [1964]: 271-295.

The author served with both the 18th New York Light Artillery and the 10th United States Colored Heavy Artillery. A very good collection of writings.

4336. Gardner, Ira B. RECOLLECTIONS OF A BOY MEMBER OF COMPANY I, FOURTEENTH MAINE VOLUNTEERS, 1861 TO 1865. Lewiston, Maine: 1902.

A short, but readable memoir of service in the southwest.

4337. Gay. Samuel F. "The Gay Letters: A Civil War Correspondence." Max L. Heyman, Jr., editor. JW, 9 [1970]: 377-412.

The author, who joined the 7th Massachusetts as a 19-year old in June 1863, expresses mixed feelings about army life in these letters to his father.

4338. Gillet, Orville. "Diary of Lieutenant Orville Gillet, United States Army, 1864-1865." Ted R. Worley, editor. ARK HIS Q, 17 [1958]: 164-204.

A useful diary of a young officer who served with the 3rd Michigan Cavalry.

4339. Glazier, Willard. THREE YEARS IN THE FEDERAL CAVALRY. New York, 1870.

An excellent account of army life in the cavalry. The early chapters are good on training, fatigue duty, and general camp life.

4340. Glover, Amos. "Diary of Amos Glover." Harry J. Carman, editor. OAHSQ, 44 [1935]: 258-272.

Glover organized and became captain of Company F of the 15th Ohio at the beginning of the war. The regiment served in the western theater. The diary runs from September 16, 1861 until July 25, 1863 and consists of brief, daily entries.

4341. Goodhue, Benjamin W. INCIDENTS OF THE CIVIL WAR. Chicago, 1890.

A modest potpourri of stories, poems, and folklore, some of which are embellished.

4342. Goss, Warren L. RECOLLECTIONS OF A PRIVATE. A STORY OF THE ARMY OF THE POTOMAC. New York, 1890.

One of the most widely quoted accounts of army and camp life. The narrative provides one of the more readable descriptions of soldier life in the eastern army.

4343. Griner, Joseph A. "The Civil War of a Pennsylvania Trooper." Daniel H. Woodward, editor. PA MHB, 87 (1963]: 39-62.

Selected quotations from 123 letters, written by a Pennsylvania cavalryman to his mother and sister. Griner participated in all major eastern campaigns.

4344. Gulick, William O. "The Journal and Letters of Corporal William O. Gulick." Max H. Guyer, editor. IOWA J HIS, 28 [1930]: 194-267, 390-455, 543-603.

Gulick joined the 1st Iowa Cavalry in 1861 and served in the western theater throughout the war. He was mustered out early in 1866 in Texas, where he was with the "Army of Occupation."

4345. Hadley, John V. "An Indiana Soldier in Love and War: The Civil War Letters of John V. Hadley." James I. Robertson, Jr., editor. IND MAG HIS, 59 [1963]: 189-288.

The letters describe the wartime career of a Hoosier soldier who later became a justice of the Indiana Supreme Court. Hadley was at Port Republic, Second Bull Run, Fredericksburg, and Chancellorsville. He provides a glimpse of social life in and out of camp.

4346. Hagadorn, Henry J. "On the March With Sibley in 1863: The Diary of Private Henry J. Hagadorn." ND HIS Q, 5 [1930/1931]: 103-129.

Author provides perceptive insights, not found elsewhere, on army life in the Dakotas while serving with the 7th Minnesota. He participated in General Henry Hastings Sibley's campaign against the Sioux in 1863.

4347. Hannaford, Roger. "Winter Quarters Near Winchester, 1864-1865: Reminiscences of Roger Hannaford, Second Ohio Volunteer Cavalry." Stephen Z. Starr, editor. VA MHB, 86 [1978]: 320-338.

Three years after the war, Hannaford wrote of his cavalry service and his stay near Winchester, Virginia, during January and February, 1865.

4348. Helmon, Howard A. "A Young Soldier in the Army of the Potomac: Diary of Howard Helmon, 1862." Arthur W. Thurner, editor. PA MHB, 87 [1963]: 139-155.

The diary is of value as a simple account of camp life and daily experiences. Of particular interest is the decline in the author's spirits as time passes. He was only 17 years old and served with the 131st Pennsylvania.

4349. Hilleary, William M. A WEBFOOT VOLLUNTEER: THE DIARY OF WILLIAM M. HILLEARY, 1864-1866. Herbert B. Nelson and Preston E. Onstad, editors. Corvallis: Oregon State University Press, 1965.

Hilleary, a corporal in the 1st Oregon, kept a journal for 19 months about his unexciting service in Oregon. While of some interest, the volume is not as entertaining as that of Royal Bensell. [See number 4260]

4350. Hinkley, Julian W. ... A NARRATIVE OF SERVICE WITH THE THIRD WISCONSIN INFANTRY. Madison, 1912.

A well put together account by an experienced soldier, drawn from his wartime writings.

4351. Hinman, Wilbur F. CAMP AND FIELD. SKETCHES OF ARMY LIFE WRITTEN BY THOSE WHO FOLLOWED THE FLAG. Cleveland, 1892.

A readable collection of anecdotes and sketches, perhaps a bit romanticized, of soldier life in the western armies.

4352. ———. THE STORY OF THE SHERMAN BRIGADE. THE CAMP, THE MARCH, THE BIVOUAC, THE BATTLE: AND HOW "THE BOYS" LIVED AND DIED DURING FOUR YEARS OF ACTIVE FIELD SERVICE. Alliance, Ohio: 1897.

This narrative ranks as one of the most outstanding accounts of soldier life. It is highly recommended reading for all who may be interested in the life of the Union soldier, from reveille through inspection.

4353. Hitchcock, Frederick L. WAR FROM THE INSIDE: THE 132ND REGIMENT OF PENNSYLVANIA VOLUNTEER INFANTRY IN THE WAR FOR THE SUPPRESSION OF THE REBELLION, 1862-1863. Philadelphia, 1903.

Good for insights on the rigors of army life during a field campaign. A 1904 edition carried a slightly different title.

4354. Hoag, Levi L. "The Civil War Diary of Sgt. Levi L. Hoag." Edwin C. Bearss, editor. ANN IOWA, 39 [1968]: 168-193.

Author served with the 24th Iowa in the southwestern theater. Diary begins on April 1, 1863, and ends on July 4, 1863, the day Vicksburg fell.

4355. Hodges, Leigh M., editor. "The Tail of the Army Calls on Lincoln." OUTLOOK, [February 15, 1922]: 256-258.

An incredible story about a sergeant on leave who drops in on Lincoln and has a stimulating interview with the president.

4356. Hopkins, Owen J. UNDER THE FLAG OF THE NATION: DIARIES AND LETTERS OF A YANKEE VOLUNTEER DURING THE CIVIL WAR. Otto F. Bond, editor. Columbus: Ohio State University Press, 1961.

A colorful account of military life and battles in the western armies from 1862 to 1865; particularly good with reference to garrison duty on the Mississippi with the 42nd Ohio.

4357. Horton, Dexter. "Diary of an Officer in Sherman's Army, Marching Through the Carolinas." Clement Eaton, editor. JSH, 9 [1943]: 238-254.

Captain Horton excels in describing the destructive techniques of Sherman's forces and in observing social conditions within the interior of the Confederacy.

4358. Hough, Alfred L. SOLDIER IN THE WEST: THE CIVIL WAR LETTERS OF ALFRED LACEY HOUGH. Robert G. Athearn, editor. Philadelphia: University of Pennsylvania Press, 1957.

A close look at military life as seen from the commissary department of the Army of the Cumberland.

4359. Houghton, Henry. "The Ordeal of Civil War: A Recollection." VT HIS, 41 [1973]: 30-49.

A record of Houghton's service with the 3rd Vermont, which fought in the Shenandoah Valley and eastern Virginia, 1863-1865.

4360. Howe, Daniel W. CIVIL WAR TIMES, 1861-1865. Indianapolis, 1902.

An Indiana soldier, Howe kept a diary of his service in the Army of the Cumberland.

4361. Hughes, Frank. "Diary of Lieutenant Frank Hughes." Norman Niccum, editor. IND MAG HIS, 45 [1949]: 275-284.

Hughes reports on conditions in the Confederate prisons where he was confined, the beauty of southern towns, and the flora and fauna of the South.

4362. Hull, Lewis B. "Soldiering on the High Plains: The Diary of Lewis Byram Hull." Myra E. Hull, editor. KAN HIS Q, 7 [1938]: 3-53.

Captured at Harper's Ferry in 1862, Hull was mustered out under parole not to fight again. In 1864 enlisted to serve in the Indian campaigns.

4363. Ibbetson, William H. "William H.H. Ibbetson, Company D, 122nd Regular Illinois." ILL ST HIS LIB PUB, 7 [1930]: 236-273.

The author kept a useful diary of his service from October 8, 1862, to August 8, 1864.

4364. Irwin, Samuel S. "Excerpts From the Diary of Samuel S. Irwin, July 5, 1863 to July 17, 1863." James Monahan, editor. J MISS HIS, 27 [1965]: 390-394.

A brief record of a lieutenant with the 2nd Illinois Cavalry following the fall of Vicksburg.

4365. Jackson, Harry F. and Thomas F. O'Donnell. BACK HOME IN ONEIDA: HERMAN CLARKE AND HIS LETTERS. Syracuse: Syracuse University Press, 1965.

An historical account constructed around 72 letters by a member of the 117th New York. The letters are perceptive, well-written documents, and the narrative history is well done.

4366. Jackson, Isaac. SOME OF THE BOYS: THE CIVIL WAR LETTERS OF ISAAC JACKSON, 1862-1865. Joseph O. Jackson, editor. Carbondale: Southern Illinois University Press, 1960.

A worthwhile record of army life along the Mississippi by this Wisconsin man who was a member of the 83rd Ohio. The Vicksburg letters are especially interesting.

4367. Jacques, John W. THREE YEAR'S CAMPAIGN OF THE NINTH, NEW YORK STATE MILITIA, DURING THE SOUTHERN REBELLION. New York, 1865.

A valuable diary, which contains many scenes of army life and intimate glimpses into the daily routine of the soldier.

4368. James, Frederic A. FREDERIC AUGUSTUS JAMES'S CIVIL WAR DIARY, SUMTER TO ANDERSONVILLE. Jefferson J. Hammer, editor. Rutherford, New Jersey: Fairleigh Dickinson University Press, 1973.

An informative diary of a carpenter's mate, who was captured in September 1863 following his ship's [USS HOUSATONIC] unsuccessful attack on Ft. Sumter. James spent the remaining year of his life in Confederate prisons, dying in Andersonville in September 1864. His diary began in February 1864 and reveals an observant, articulate, and sensitive young man.

4369. Jeffries, Lemuel. "'The Excitement Had Begun!' The Civil War Diary of Lemuel Jeffries, 1862-1863." Jason H. Silverman, editor. MANU, 38 [1978]: 265-278.

The author rose from private to lieutenant and his diaries effectively reveal the life of a common soldier.

4370. Joel, Joseph A. and Lewis R. Stegman. RIFLE SHOTS AND BUGLE NOTES.... New York, 1884.

A thick, intriguing volume of folklore, in which some of the material is true and some embellished.

4371. Johnson, Benjamin C. A SOLDIER'S LIFE: THE CIVIL WAR EXPERIENCES OF BEN C. JOHNSON. Alan S. Brown, editor. Kalamazoo: Western Michigan University Press, 1962.

An interesting, frank account of war in the Department of the Gulf. A member of the "Saline Sharpshooters" of the 6th Michigan, Johnson paints a vivid picture of swamps, fever, and southern life. It is especially noteworthy considering that the 6th Michigan "lost more men from disease than did any other" Michigan unit.

4372. Johnson, Charles F. THE LONG ROLL: BEING A JOURNAL OF THE CIVIL WAR, AS SET DOWN DURING THE YEARS 1861-1863.... East Aurora, New York: 1911.

A well-illustrated book of memories of campaigning in North Carolina with the 9th New York.

4373. Jones, Jenkins L. ... AN ARTILLERYMAN'S DIARY. Madison, Wisconsin: 1914.

A full and vivid record of campaigning with Sherman before Atlanta.

4374. Kaser, David. BOOKS AND LIBRARIES IN CAMP AND BATTLE. Westport, Connecticut: Greenwood, 1984.

A volume which notes that the majority of Union soldiers who could read, read [a] good, well-known works, [b] religious tracts, [c] newspapers and magazines, and [d] escapist novels. There was plenty of leisure time in which to read, and ample material was supplied by the government, commercial publishers, and religious and charitable organizations.

4375. Kelly, Seth. "The 1864 Diary of Corporal Seth Kelly." Anne E. Hemphill, editor. KAN HIS, 1 [1978]: 189-210.

A sketch of army life by a member of the 9th Kansas Cavalry. Discusses the books he read.

4376. Kelsey, Charles C. TO THE KNIFE: THE BIOGRAPHY OF MAJOR PETER KEENAN, 8TH PENNSYLVANIA CAVALRY. Ann Arbor: University of Michigan Press, 1964.

A brief sketch of Keenan, which includes material from his wartime correspondence.

4377. Kelsey, D.M. DEEDS OF DARING BY BOTH BLUE AND GRAY.... Philadelphia, 1883.

A thick, amusing volume of dubious validity.

4378. Kidd, James H. PERSONAL RECOLLECTIONS OF A CAVALRYMAN: WITH CUSTER'S MICHIGAN CAVALRY BRIGADE IN THE CIVIL WAR. Ionia, Michigan: 1908.

A valuable description of camp life in the famed Michigan Cavalry Brigade. The first chapters are particularly useful for information on the training and early camp life experiences of the cavalryman.

4379. King, William C. and W.P. Derby. CAMP-FIRE SKETCHES AND BATTLE-FIELD ECHOES OF THE REBELLION. Springfield, Massachusetts: 1887.

A large, meaty volume of folklore.

4380. Kingsbury, Allen A. THE HERO OF MEDFIELD: CONTAINING THE JOURNALS AND LETTERS OF ALLEN ALONZO KINGSBURY.... Boston, 1862.

A moving memoir of a boy bugler of the 1st Massachusetts, who was killed at Yorktown, Virginia, April 26, 1862.

4381. Lane, David. A SOLDIER'S DIARY: THE STORY OF A VOLUNTEER, 1862-1865.... Jackson, Michigan: 1905.

A solid, daily record of soldier life in the 17th Michigan.

4382. Lansing, Frank E. "'Your Affectionate Son': The Civil War Letters of Frank E. Lansing." Abbott M. Gibney, editor. MICH HIS, 78 [1974]: 25-53.

A keen and perceptive observer of military life, Lansing wrote some 50 letters about his service with the 20th Michigan. He campaigned in both the eastern and western theaters and was imprisoned at Andersonville.

4383. Levey, William T. THE BLUE AND THE GRAY: A SKETCH OF SOLDIER LIFE IN CAMP AND FIELD.... Schenectady, New York: 1904.

A 53-page pamphlet describing the author's experiences as a member of the 134th New York.

4384. Lewis, Andrew. "The Civil War Letters of Captain Andrew Lewis and His Daughter." Michael Barton, editor. W PA HIS MAG, 60 [1977]: 371-390.

In letters to his daughter, the author supplies insights into camp life.

4385. Lockley, Frederick E. "Letters of Fred Lockley, Union Soldier, 1864-1865." John E. Pomfret, editor. HUNT LIB Q, 16 [1952/1953]: 75-112.

The author of these letters served with the 7th New York Heavy Artillery in 1864-1865.

4386. Lord, Francis A. THE FEDERAL VOLUNTEER SOLDIER IN THE AMERICAN CIVIL WAR. Ph.D. Dissertation, University of Michigan, 1949.

This study examines certain patterns common to the experience of Union volunteers. Among the subjects covered are morale and the reasons for enlisting.

4387. ———. "Some Close Shaves." CWTI, 7 [5] [1968]: 40-44.

Fifteen cases are discussed where belt buckles, swords, or prayer books are credited with stopping bullets and saving lives.

4388. Lovett, Robert W. "The Soldiers' Free Library." CWH, 8 [1962]: 54-63.

A library consisting of 1500 books and 800 magazines was donated for the edification of soldiers during the war.

4389. Lowrey, Roland. "Coffee: This Invaluable Beverage." CWTI, 14 [6] [1975]: 10-11.

A brief, but interesting, article on a highly prized and important commodity of camp life.

4390. Lucid, Robert F. "Civil War Humor: Anecdotes and Recollections." CWH, 2 [1956]: 29-48.

Author analyzes a number of volumes of Civil War anecdotes from both the North and the South.

4391. Lusk, William T. WAR LETTERS OF WILLIAM THOMPSON LUSK, CAPTAIN, ASSISTANT ADJUTANT-GENERAL, UNITED STATES VOLUNTEERS, 1861-1863.... New York, 1911.

An excellent group of letters written by an articulate officer serving along the southeastern coast.

4392. Lutz, Earle. "The STARS AND STRIPES of Illinois Boys in Blue." JISHS, 46 [1953]: 132-141.

Illinois soldiers published 26 of some 300 unit newspapers for northern troops, many of which no longer exist. They also claim primacy in the use of the patriotic title of STARS AND STRIPES.

4393. Luvaas, Jay, editor. A SOLDIER'S VIEW: A COLLECTION OF CIVIL WAR WRITINGS. Chicago: University of Chicago Press, 1958.

A useful collection of letters and diary excerpts which describe life in the field and in camp.

4394. Mackley, John. "The Civil War Diary of John Mackley." Mildred Throne, editor. IOWA J HIS, 48 [1950]: 141-168.

The author, a member of the 2nd Iowa, recorded his service in the western theater, from April 18, 1861, to March 28, 1862.

4395. Macy, William M. "The Civil War Diary of William Madison Macy." IND MAG HIS, 30 [1934]: 181-197.

An illuminating journal written by a member of the 94th Illinois.

4396. Mahon, Samuel. "The Civil War Letters of Samuel Mahon." John K. Mahon, editor. IOWA J HIS, 51 [1953]: 233-266.

Mahon, who commanded Company F of the 7th Iowa, reports in detail on Fort Donelson, Shiloh, and service with Sherman in Georgia.

4397. Marshall, Albert O. ARMY LIFE. FROM A SOLDIER'S JOURNAL ... INCIDENTS, SKETCHES AND RECORD OF A UNION SOLDIER'S ARMY LIFE .... Joliet, Illinois: 1886.

A 100-page memoir of the life of a soldier in the western theater, 1861-1864.

4398. Maslowski, Peter. "A Study of Morale in Civil War Soldiers." MIL AFF, 34 [1970]: 122-126.

This article draws some interesting comparisons between the attitudes of American soldiers who served in World War II and their predecessors in the Civil War.

4399. Matthews, James L. "Civil War Diary of Sergeant James Louis Matthews." Roger C. Hackett, editor. IND MAG HIS, 24 [1928]: 306-316.

This diary, by a member of Company F, 12th Indiana Battery, covers the last six months of the war. Entries are brief.

4400. Mattison, Edwin. "Waiting for the War to Come: Union Camp Life in 1861-1862." Theodore Kornweibel, Jr., editor. NIAG FRON, 22 [1975]: 87-97.

A collection of letters, with good descriptions of camp life and army equipment, written by a member of the 83rd Pennsylvania.

4401. Mayfield, Leroy S. "A Hoosier Invades the Confederacy." John D. Barnhart, editor. IND MAG HIS, 39 [1943]: 144-191.

Written by an articulate, observant young college student, who enlisted in July 1861. Neither letters nor diaries reflect any complaint even though the author lay wounded on the battlefield for 36 hours. Mayfield "saw his duty and he done it."

4402. McClure, William T. and Joseph L. McClure. "Civil War Letters of Brothers William T. McClure and Joseph Lewis McClure of the Fifteenth Kentucky Volunteer Infantry." C. Glenn Clift, editor. KY HIS SOC REG, 60 [1962]: 209-232.

A collection of 14 letters from two brothers in the 15th Kentucky from December 22, 1861 to August 10, 1862. The letters are written from camps in Kentucky and Tennessee. William died from typhoid fever in July 1862.

4403. McGregor, Frank R. "Dearest Susie: A Civil War Infantryman's Letters to His Sweetheart." Carl E. Hatch, editor. New York: Exposition, 1971.

An intelligent, literate member of the 83rd Ohio expresses informative opinions on army life in general and astute remarks about the Red River Campaign in particular.

4404. McIntyre, Benjamin F. FEDERALS ON THE FRONTIER: THE DIARY OF BENJAMIN F. McINTYRE, 1862-1864. Nannie M. Tilley, editor. Austin: University of Texas Press, 1963.

A well-edited diary of an Iowan who rose from sergeant to second lieutenant, while serving in the western theater. Very good on social history. McIntyre was in the Missouri campaigning early in the war, at the siege of Vicksburg, and was stationed for a time at Brownsville, Texas, a blockade-running center.

4405. McKell, William J. "The Journal of Sergeant William James McKell." Watt P. Marchman, editor. CWH, 3 [1957]: 315-339.

A member of the 89th Ohio, McKell was a first cousin of Lucy Webb Hayes, wife of the future president. He was captured at Chickamauga and died at Andersonville.

4406. McLaughlin, Jacob. "'Dear Sister Jennie--Dear Brother Jacob': The Correspondence Between a Northern Soldier and His Sister in Mechanicsburg, Pennsylvania, 1861-1864." Florence C. McLaughlin, editor. W PA HIS MAG, 60 [1977[: 109-143, 203-240.

Interesting letters between brother and sister, which reflect conditions both on the home front and the battle front. They cover the period from May 1861 through December 1864.

4407. McMillen, George W. and Jefferson O. McMillen. "Civil War Letters of George Washington McMillen and Jefferson O. McMillen, 122nd Regiment, Ohio Volunteer Infantry." W VA HIS, 32 [1971]: 171-193.

While these letters have only limited reference to camp life, they do provide valuable insights into why the brothers and other Union soldiers enlisted. Jefferson died at Monocacy; George served time in Andersonville, but escaped.

4408. McCrea, Tully. DEAR BELLE: LETTERS FROM A CADET AND OFFICER TO HIS SWEETHEART, 1858-1865. Catherine S. Crary, editor. Middletown, Connecticut: Wesleyan University Press, 1965.

A good collection of letters from an artillery officer with the Army of the Potomac. As a West Point cadet McCrea roomed with George Custer.

* * *

THE MILITARY ORDER OF THE LOYAL LEGION [MOLLUS]

The Military Order of the Loyal Legion [MOLLUS] was formed by Union officers at the time the war ended. The first commandery was in Washington, D.C., but soon state commanderies were established throughout the entire North. In 1885 they were federated into a national organization with Winfield Scott Hancock as the first commander. In 1888 a War Museum and Library was founded in Philadelphia, which 100 years later contains one of the most valuable collections of Civil War materials to be found anywhere.

One of the purposes of MOLLUS was to encourage its members to prepare papers based on their own wartime experiences and read them at the group's meetings. In time, state commanderies began publishing large volumes of "war sketches" or "war papers" based on these talks. Between 1886 and 1912 37 volumes of these recollections appeared in print. Ohio and Minnesota led the list with six each. While these papers deal with many subjects, a great number of them are concerned with soldier life. Although no citations from MOLLUS publications are included in this bibliography, the curious might wish to examine those volumes.

* * *

4409. Miller, James C. "Civil War Diary of James Cooper Miller." CWTI, 8 [2,4,5,6] [1969]: 24-30, 37-41, 42-48, 35-44.

Author, who served with the 9th Pennsylvania Cavalry, saw action in the Peninsular Campaign, in Tennessee, and with Sherman in the Carolinas. Following the Sherman-Johnston truce, he discusses fraternization between the two armies.

4410. Mitchell, Joseph B. BADGE OF GALLANTRY: RECOLLECTIONS OF CIVIL WAR CONGRESSIONAL MEDAL OF HONOR WINNERS. LETTERS FROM THE CHARLES KOHEN COLLECTION. New York, Macmillan, 1968.

This work is based on recollections of over 300 Civil War soldier and sailor recipients of the Medal of Honor. The material was collected by means of letters and questionnaires in the 1890s for a book that was not published until this time. An excellent narrative accompanies the compilation. Of particular interest today is data on 20 blacks who received the medal.

4411. Mockett, Richard H. "The Richard H. Mockett Diary." James L. Sellers, editor. MVHR, 26 [1939]: 233-240.

The author served with the 43rd Wisconsin.

4412. Monaghan, Jay. "Civil War Slang and Humor." CWH, 3 [1957]: 125-133.

A miniature dictionary of Civil War slang filled with fascinating information.

4413. Moore, Frank. ANECDOTES, POETRY, AND INCIDENTS OF THE WAR, NORTH AND SOUTH, 1860-1865. New York, 1867.

An excellent collection of diverse items which reflect the humor of the war.

4414. Morgan, John S. "Diary of John S. Morgan, Company G, Thirty-third Iowa Infantry." ANN IOWA, 13 [1923]: 483-508, 570-610.

Morgan saw action around Vicksburg, although his unit did not participate in the siege. Diary includes a record of regimental movements, letters received, and personal finances.

4415. Morse, Bliss. CIVIL WAR DIARIES. Loren J. Morse, editor. Pittsburg, Kansas: Pittcraft, 1964.

A short, but useful war record written by a member of the 105th Ohio.

4416. Morton, Joseph W., editor ... SPARKS FROM THE CAMP FIRE: OR, TALES OF THE OLD VETERANS. THRILLING STORIES OF HEROIC DEEDS .... Philadelphia, 1893.

A stimulating anthology of "true stories" told by veterans a number of years later.

4417. Nardin, James T. "Civil War Humor: The War in 'Vanity Fair.'" CWH, 2 [1956]: 67-85.

An examination of Civil War humor as it appeared in the pages of VANITY FAIR.

4418. NATIONAL TRIBUNE SCRAP BOOK. Washington, D.C.: 1909.

A voluminous accumulation of stories and anecdotes about life in camp, on the march, in battle, and in prison, as told by a number of reminiscing veterans.

4419. Newton, James A. A WISCONSIN BOY IN DIXIE: THE SELECTED LETTERS OF JAMES A. NEWTON. Stephen E. Ambrose, editor. Madison: University of Wisconsin Press, 1961.

A volume of useful, personal glimpses of army life from the writings of a Wisconsin volunteer.

4420. Nichols, Norman K. "The Reluctant Warrior: The Diary of Norman K. Nichols." CWH, 3 [1957]: 17-39.

Nichols' military goals were to stay out of harm's way, get plenty to eat, make some money, and enjoy the war.

4421. Nisbet, James C. FOUR YEARS ON THE FIRING LINE. Bell I. Wiley, editor. Jackson, Tennessee: McCowat-Mercer Press, 1963.

An excellent, annotated edition of a good Civil War diary.

4422. Noble, Sylvester. "Vett Noble of Ypsilanti: A Clerk for General Sherman." Donald W. Disbrow, editor. CWH, 14 [1968]: 15-39.

A narrative of the career of Sylvester "Vett" Noble of the 14th Michigan, based on his letters home.

4423. Norton, Oliver W. ARMY LETTERS, 1861-1865. BEING EXTRACTS FROM PRIVATE LETTERS TO RELATIVES AND FRIENDS FROM A SOLDIER IN THE FIELD.... Chicago, 1903.

A revealing record of war service in the eastern theater. Norton was a private in the 83rd Pennsylvania, who rose to the rank of lieutenant in the 8th United States Colored Troops.

4424. Nott, Charles C. SKETCHES OF THE WAR: A SERIES OF LETTERS TO THE NORTH MOORE STREET SCHOOL OF NEW YORK. New York, 1865.

An entertaining account of camp life and campaigning by a cavalryman. The chapter dealing with foraging is particularly enlightening. Nott was a captain of the 5th Iowa cavalry and a trustee of public schools in New York.

4425. Oliver, Robert, Jr. "Robert Oliver, Jr., and the Oswego County Regiment." NY HIS, 38 [1957]: 276-293.

Article includes excerpts from letters, books, and diaries of the author, who served in the Army of the Potomac.

4426. Onderdonk, James H. "A Civil War Diary." Dino Fabris, editor. NY HIS, 49 [1968]: 76-89.

The diary of Onderdonk, who died in 1863, illustrates the many personal tragedies of the war.

4427. Osborne, Vincent B. "Vincent B. Osborne's Civil War Experiences." Joyce Farlow and Louise Barry, editors. KAN HIS Q, 20 [1952]: 108-133, 187-223.

Osborne served in the 2nd Kansas Infantry and 2nd Kansas Cavalry. He saw considerable action in the western theater and was twice wounded. A leg was amputated in January 1865.

4428. Owens, John A. SWORD AND PEN: OR, VENTURES AND ADVENTURES OF WILLARD GLAZIER ... IN WAR AND LITERATURE.... Philadelphia, 1881.

Soldier-author Glazier served with the 2nd New York Cavalry. [See number 4339]

4429. Packard, Lionel B. "'Furlough in the Morning': An Ohio Private in the Civil War." Philip Sturm, editor. J W VA HIS ASSN, 2 [1978]: 56-63.

Excerpts from letters written by Lionel Belton Packard to his family describing army life while he awaited assignment to combat duty. However, he died before he saw any action.

4430. Pattison, John J. "With the United States Army Along the Oregon Trail, 1863-1866: Diary by Jno. J. Pattison." NEB HIS MAG, 15, [1934]: 79-93.

A member of the 7th Iowa Cavalry, Pattison began his diary on July 17, 1863, and continued it into 1866. Useful comments on army life as well as the weather.

4431. Pearson, Benjamin F. "Benjamin F. Pearson's War Diary." ANN IOWA, 15 [1925/1927]: 83-129, 194-222, 281-305, 433-463, 507-563.

An excellent, detailed diary, it is of particular interest and value for the events at Vicksburg. The first entry is dated July 22, 1862, and the final entry May 20, 1865.

4432. Peck, George W. HOW PRIVATE GEO. W. PECK PUT DOWN THE REBELLION: OR THE FUNNY EXPERIENCES OF A RAW RECRUIT. Chicago, 1890.

To the compiler of the present bibliography, George W. Peck's book of tongue-in-cheek war memoirs is the most hilariously funny volume to come out of the conflict. The reader should expect something witty from the author of PECK'S BAD BOY--and later governor of Wisconsin--and he is not disappointed. Perhaps some stories are embellished, but it would not be easy to invent most of what has been written here.

4433. PERSONAL NARRATIVES OF EVENTS IN THE WAR OF THE REBELLION.... 100 v. in 10. Providence, Rhode Island: 1878-1915.

A voluminous and outstanding collection of soldiers' and sailors' memoirs.

4434. Pfeifer, James A. "The Military Experiences of James A. Pfeifer, 1861-1865." George D. Harmon, editor. NC HIS R, 32 [1955]: 385-409, 544-572.

Pfeifer enlisted in April 1861 in the 1st Pennsylvania. The letters contain vivid descriptions and cogent comments on the battles of the day, politics, and rebels. After a hospital stay in November 1863, Pfeifer joined the 46th Pennsylvania and was shipped to the western theater.

4435. Phillips, John W. "The Civil War Diary of John Wilson Phillips." Robert G. Athearn, editor. VA MHB, 62 [1954]: 95-123.

The author, a lieutenant colonel of the 18th Pennsylvania, served from July 1862 to the end of the war in Virginia. His full diary runs from February 28th to December 9, 1864.

4436. Pitts, Florisan D. "The Civil War Diary of Florisan D. Pitts." Leo M. Kaiser, editor. MID AM, 40 [1958]: 22-63.

A well-edited, abridged version of a diary kept by an Illinois soldier.

4437. Pomeroy, Randolph C. "The Civil War Diary of Randolph C. Pomeroy." NW OHIO Q, 19 [1947]: 129-156.

A member of the 18th Michigan, Pomeroy wrote eloquently of the everyday life of the common soldier. The reader becomes aware of the horrors of war as well as the long periods of inactivity.

4438. Poor, Walter S. "A Yankee Soldier in a New York Regiment." James J. Heslin, editor. NY HIS SOC Q, 50 [1966]: 109-149.

The author draws a good picture of army life with the 10th New York in letters to his sister.

4439. Post, Lydia M., editor. SOLDIERS' LETTERS FROM CAMP, BATTLEFIELD, AND PRISON.... New York, 1865.

A big book compiled from over 200 Union soldiers' letters on many subjects for the United States Sanitary Commission.

4440. Quenzel, Carrol H. "Books for the Boys in Blue." JISHS, 44 [1951]: 218-230.

Although not very effective at first, agencies to supply reading materials for northern soldiers improved later. The Loan Library System, organized by the United States Christian Commission, distributed 300,000 volumes in the course of the war.

4441. Rathbun, Isaac R. "A Civil War Diary: The Diary of Isaac R. Rathbun, Co. D, 86th N.Y. Volunteers, Aug. 23, 1861-Jan. 20, 1863." Lawrence R. Cavanaugh, editor. NY HIS, 36 [1955]: 336-345.

Diary of a soldier who was wounded and captured at Second Bull Run, but who was allowed to walk back to Washington. In the course of this, he survived a near shipwreck and a train wreck.

4442. Rauscher, Frank. MUSIC ON THE MARCH, 1862-1865, WITH THE ARMY OF THE POTOMAC. Philadelphia, 1892.

A good record, drawn from a diary and letters, of camp life in the eastern theater with the 114th Pennsylvania.

4443. Ray, George B. "Journal of George B. Ray...." HIS PHIL SOC OH PUB, 57 [1926]: 57-73.

The author served as a musician in Company H of the 5th Ohio from April 1861 to April 1863. The diary runs from July 1, 1861 to January 1, 1863.

4444. Reid, Harvey. THE VIEW FROM HEADQUARTERS: CIVIL WAR LETTERS OF HARVEY REID. Frank L. Byrne, editor. Madison: State Historical Society of Wisconsin, 1965.

A collection of articulate and informative letters from a

young Wisconsin schoolteacher who joined the 22nd Wisconsin in the summer of 1862. Reid served for three years in the western theater and with Sherman.

4445. Reynolds, Nathaniel M. "The Civil War Letters of Nathaniel M. Reynolds." James Barnett, editor. LIN HER, 65 [1963]: 199-203.

These letters from a member of the 30th Indiana describe camp conditions, battle operations, and family problems.

4446. Richards, David A. "The Civil War Diary of David Allen Richards." Frederick D. Williams, editor. MICH HIS, 39 [1955]: 183-220.

The diary depicts the drudgery of the unglamorous but essential work of a male nurse in a hospital behind the lines. Also in the middle of his training for combat, author begins to question his ability to become an effective soldier.

4447. Robertson, Melville C. "Journal of Melville Cox Robertson." IND MAG HIS, 28 [1932]: 116-137.

Robertson, a member of the 93rd Indiana, spent much of his one year of army service in Confederate prisons. While surviving months of prison life, he died shortly after being paroled April 22, 1865.

4448. Rogers, Richard, John Rogers, and Theodore Rogers. "Two Brothers' Civil War Letters: A Psychological Interpretation." Michael Barton, editor. MANU, 29 [1977]: 94-101.

Three bothers enlisted in the 93rd Pennsylvania in October 1861. Their letters to their parents provide insight into a soldier's thoughts. John died at Seven Pines, while Richard was killed at Spotsylvania Court House.

4449. Rollins, George S. "'Give My Love to All': The Civil War Letters of George S. Rollins." Gerald S. Henig, editor. CWTI, 11 [7] [1972]: 16-28.

A young private in the 3rd Maine saw a great deal of fighting in the first two years of the war in the East.

4450. Rolph, Gerald V. and Noel Clark. THE CIVIL WAR SOLDIER. Washington, D.C.: Historical Impressions, 1961.

A 24-page booklet, illustrating a soldier's accoutrements.

4451. Root, William H. "The Experiences of a Federal Soldier in Louisiana in 1863." LA HIS Q, 19 [1936]: 635-637.

Root served with the 75th New York.

4452. Ross, Charles. "Diary of Charles Ross, 1862." VT HIS 30 [1962]: 35-148.

A good journal on soldier life written by a member of the 11th Vermont.

4453. Rumpel, John. "Ohiowa Soldier." H.E. Rosenberger, editor. ANN IOWA, 36 [1961]: 111-148.

Excerpts from the wartime diary and letters of John Rumpel, of the 55th Ohio, edited by a nephew. Rumpel served in Virginia in the first two years of the war, was at Gettysburg, then at Chattanooga, and accompanied Sherman to Atlanta and the Sea. After the war Rumpel and other Ohioans settled in Iowa and formed the "Ohiowa Veterans" organization.

4454. Sanford, George B. FIGHTING REBELS AND REDSKINS. E.R. Hagemann, editor. Norman: University of Oklahoma Press, 1969.

Sanford was a cavalryman and frequently a staff officer. His comments on the various commanders are informative. Two-thirds of the book devoted to the war years. Makes interesting and lively reading.

4455. Schreel, Charles. "Charles Schreel's Book: A Diary of a Union Soldier on Garrison Duty in Tennessee." Edward F. Keuchel and James P. Jones, editors. TENN HIS Q, 36 [1977]: 197-207.

An Ohio farm boy, Schreel volunteered enthusiastically, but the glamour quickly evaporated. In his account of camp life he discusses boredom, drinking, fighting, and poor discipline.

4456. Shannon, Fred A. "The Life of the Common Soldier in the Union Army, 1861-1865." MVHR, 13 [1927]: 465-482.

That the life of a Union soldier was a difficult one is the main point of this article. Shannon attributes the problem to a variety of factors such as weak discipline under state-appointed officers, poor equipment, and the monotony of camp life.

4457. Sheldon, Charles L. "The Diary of a Drummer." John L. Melton, editor. MICH HIS, 43 [1959]: 315-348.

Author provides a good insight into a little-known figure in the war--the military musician. He also describes life in the occupied South in the last days of the war.

4458. Sloan, Hugh. "Full Measure of Devotion: The Ordeal of Private Hugh Sloan." Richard K. Darr and Floyd E. Overly, editors. MO HIS R, 60 [1966]: 149-161.

Serving with the 3rd Wisconsin, Sloan describes the routine of army life in letters to his wife.

4459. Small, Abner R. THE ROAD TO RICHMOND: THE CIVIL WAR MEMOIRS OF MAJOR ABNER R. SMALL OF THE SIXTEENTH MAINE VOLUNTEERS.... Harold A. Small, editor. Berkeley, California: University of California Press, 1939. Reprint 1959.

An excellent record of the soldier in wartime by an articulate officer who kept good notes and who also maintained a diary while a prisoner of war. First published in 1898.

4460. Smith, Benjamin T. PRIVATE SMITH'S JOURNAL: RECOLLECTIONS OF THE LATE WAR. Clyde C. Walton, editor. Chicago: Donnelley, 1963.

A well-edited edition of a good journal written by a member of the 51st Illinois, who served in the western theater.

4461. Smith, George G. LEAVES FROM A SOLDIER'S DIARY. Putnam, Connecticut: 1906.

Smith was a member of the 1st Regular United States Infantry, which served in the Gulf Department from the capture of New Orleans to the close of the war.

4462. Smith, W.J. "Just A Little Bit of the Civil War, As Seen By W.J. Smith, Company M, 2nd Ohio Cavalry." Robert W. Halton, editor. OHIO HIS, 84 [1975]: 101-126, 222-242.

An interesting record of cavalry service in the western theater, and then in the last year of the war in the East. Prior to mustering out in St. Louis, Smith and his colleagues took part in the capture of Quantrill's gang in Kentucky.

4463. Snowden, George R. "Home to Franklin! Excerpts From the Civil War Diary of George Randolf Snowden." W PA HIS MAG, 54 [1971]: 158-166.

The author, a Union captain in the 142nd Pennsylvania, describes his journey home from Washington to Franklin, Pennsylvania.

4464. Spangler, Edward W. MY LITTLE WAR EXPERIENCE. WITH HISTORICAL SKETCHES AND MEMORABILIA. York, Pennsylvania: 1904.

Vivid accounts of the fighting at Antietam and Fredericksburg may be found in this diary of a soldier of the 130th Pennsylvania.

4465. Speed, Thomas. "The Civil War Memoirs of Captain Thomas Speed." James R. Bentley, editor. FCHQ, 44 [1970]: 235-272.

The author, a Union officer and Kentucky Unionist, saw action at Knoxville, Kennesaw Mountain, Fort Fisher, and other places. He was a member of the 8th Kentucky Cavalry.

4466. Spencer, Melton. "The Letters of Private Melton Spencer, 1862-1865: A Soldier's View of Military Life on the Northern Plains." ND HIS, 37 [1970]: 233-269.

A valuable account of camp life on the forgotten western frontier.

4467. Stem, Leander. "Stand By the Colors: The Civil War Letters of Leander Stem." John T. Hubbell, editor. KY HIS SOC REG, 73 [1975]: 171-194, 291-313, 396-415.

Stem commanded the 101st Ohio in Kentucky and Tennessee. His letters express a desire for success and occasional feelings of inadequacy.

4468. Stern, Philip Van Doren, editor. SOLDIER LIFE IN THE UNION AND CONFEDERATE ARMIES. Greenwich, Connecticut: Fawcett. 1961.

A well-written work, providing useful information on soldier life in both armies and comparisons between the two. Author uses material from the writings of John Billings [Union] and Carlton McCarthy [Confederate].

4469. Stewart, Alexander M. CAMP, MARCH AND BATTLE-FIELD: OR THREE YEARS AND A HALF WITH THE ARMY OF THE POTOMAC. Philadelphia, 1865.

A very good account of army life in the eastern theater. Particularly good for descriptions of fatigue duty and the daily routine. Author was chaplain of the 13th Pennsylvania.

4470. Stewart. William S. "William S. Stewart Letters, January 13, 1861, to December 4, 1862." Harvey L. Carter and Norma L. Peterson, editors. MO HIS R, 61 [1967]: 187-228, 303-320, 463-488.

A member of the 1st and 11th Missouri, Stewart describes the Camp Jackson affair, the Island Number 10 campaign, and the battles of Iuka and Corinth. The last two battles transformed the 11th regiment into a confident, experienced unit.

4471. Stillwell, Leander. THE STORY OF A COMMON SOLDIER: ARMY LIFE IN THE CIVIL WAR, 1861-1865. Erie, Kansas: Erie Record Press, 1917. Reprint 1983.

A thorough and well-written personal account of the war, replete with revealing views of camp life. The work is based on the author's letters and diary.

4472. Stockwell, Elisha. PRIVATE ELISHA STOCKWELL, JR., SEES THE CIVIL WAR. Byron R. Abernethy, editor. Norman: University of Oklahoma Press, 1958.

A surprisingly useful diary of a lad who enlisted in the 14th Wisconsin at the age of 15 in 1862 and took part in much of the action in the western theater.

4473. Stone, Edwin W. RHODE ISLAND IN THE REBELLION. Providence, Rhode Island: 1864.

A well-done record of one man's service in the eastern theater, but it only covers the first year of the war.

4474. Strong, Robert H. A YANKEE PRIVATE'S CIVIL WAR. Ashley Halsey, editor. Chicago: Regnery, 1961.

This well-edited diary of a member of the 105th Illinois has worthwhile descriptions of army life in the western theater under Sherman.

4475. Sunderland, Glenn W. FIVE DAYS TO GLORY. Brunswick, New Jersey: Barnes, 1970.

An intriguing narrative of campaigning in the West, based on over 200 letters of Sergeant Tilghman Jones of the 59th Illinois. Jones died in the Battle of Nashville in 1864.

4476. Sweet, Benjamin F. "Civil War Experience." Vivian K. McLarty, editor. MO HIS R, 43 [1948/1949]: 237-250.

Although the author, a member of the 27th Ohio, wrote this memoir from memory 40 years later, it is still a good one.

4477. Switzer, Jacob C. "Reminiscences of Jacob Carroll Switzer...." Mildred Throne, editor. IOWA J HIS, 55 [1957]: 319-350; 56 [1958]: 37-76.

A member of the 22nd Iowa, Switzer also wrote his memoirs late in life. And he wrote well, recalling with spirit the incidents of high drama and low comedy.

4478. Sword, Wiley. "How it Felt to Be Shot at in the Civil War." A HIS ILL, 2 [6] [1967]: 26-31.

Drawing on personal comments from soldiers on both sides, Sword describes the feeling of being shot at. While some were cowards and retreated, others stood their ground with iron discipline.

4479. Taylor, A. Reed. "The War History of Two Soldiers: A Two-Sided View of the Civil War." ALA R, 23 [1970]: 83-109.

Author compares such issues as camp life, war attitudes and personal characteristics through the letters of a Union soldier John F. Brobst and a Confederate soldier W. Anderson Stephens.

4480. Taylor, Isaac L. "Campaigning With the First Minnesota, a Civil War Diary." Hazel C. Wolf, editor. MINN HIS, 25 [1944]: 11-39, 117-152, 224-257, 342-361.

Taylor enlisted with the 1st Minnesota early in the war and began his diary on January 1, 1862. He wrote regularly in the diary until July 2, 1863, the day he fell at Gettysburg.

4481. Theaker, James G. THROUGH ONE MAN'S EYES: THE CIVIL WAR EXPERIENCES OF A BELMONT COUNTY VOLUNTEER: LETTERS OF JAMES G. THEAKER. Paul E. Rieger, editor. Mount Vernon, Ohio: Printing Arts, 1974.

Volume contains 95 thoughtful letters from a captain of the 50th Ohio, which performed logistical duties in Kentucky, Ohio, and Tennessee.

4482. Thompson, William G. "Civil War Letters of Major William Thompson." ANN IOWA, 38 [1966]: 431-455.

A Marion, Iowa lawyer and politician in peacetime, the author wrote these letters to his wife between August and December 1862.

4483. Tourgee, Albion W. "A Civil War Diary of Albion W. Tourgee." Dean H. Keller, editor. OHIO HIS, 74 [1965]: 99-131.

The famous post-war novelist and North Carolina "carpetbagger," kept a diary of his service with the 105th Ohio in Tennessee in 1863.

4484. Van Alstyne, Lawrence. DIARY OF AN ENLISTED MAN. New Haven, Connecticut: 1910.

A helpful journal on camp life by an enlisted man who served with the 128th New York and the 90th United States Colored Infantry.

4485. Van Deusen, Ira. "Ira Van Deusen: A Federal Volunteer in North Alabama." Ron Bennett, editor. ALA HIS Q, 27 [1965]: 199-211.

As he campaigned from Kentucky southward to Alabama, the author, in letters to his wife, described the country through which he marched and the battles in which he fought.

4486. Wallace, William. "William Wallace's Civil War Letters: The Virginia Campaign." John O. Holzheuter, editor. WIS MAG HIS, 58 [1973]: 28-59.

A member of the 3rd Wisconsin, Wallace wrote expressively of both the commonplace and the technical in his letters from the Virginia front in 1861-1862.

4487. Ward, Lester F. YOUNG WARD'S DIARY.... Bernhard J. Stern, editor. New York: Putnam, 1935.

The pioneer sociologist of post-war years, served in the ranks with the 141st Pennsylvania. His military service, pages 115-154, makes good reading.

4488. Weinert, Richard P. "The South Had Mosby: The Union: Major Henry Young." CWTI, 3 [1] [1964]: 38-42.

Describes the rise of Henry Young to rank of major and his exploits as a leader of scouts for General Sheridan.

4489. Wheeler, William. ... LETTERS OF WILLIAM WHEELER OF THE CLASS OF 1855.... Cambridge, Massachusetts: 1875.

Valuable letters home from a "Yalie," who served in both the eastern and western theaters and died before Atlanta.

4490. White, Thomas B. "Down the River: Civil War Diary of Thomas Benton White." KY HIS SOC REG, 67 [1969]: 134-74.

An intriguing account of army life in the 42nd Ohio. This is particularly useful for a glimpse at the military routine in the western armies.

4491. Whitman, Walt. "'Our Veteran Mustering Out': Another Newspaper Article by Walt Whitman About His Soldier-Brother." Jerome M. Loving, editor. YALE UNIV LIB GAZ, 49 [1974]: 217-224.

The noted poet wrote two anonymous articles about his brother, who rose to major in the 51st New York and fought in numerous battles.

4492. Wightman, Edward. "The Roughest Kind of Campaigning: Letters of Sergeant Edward Wightman, Third New York Volunteers, May-July 1864." Edward G. Longacre, editor. CWH, 28 [1982]: 324-350.

A vivid record of camp life and battle during Grant's assault against Richmond.

4493. Wilcox, Charles E. "Hunting for Cotton in Dixie...." Edgar L. Erickson, editor. JSH, 4 [1938]: 493-513.

Excerpts from the diary of a soldier serving with the 33rd Illinois.

4494. Wiley, Bell I. THE LIFE OF BILLY YANK: THE COMMON SOLDIER OF THE UNION. Indianapolis: Bobbs-Merrill, 1952.

The classic work on the common soldier, against which all others will be judged. The work draws on a vast collection of letters, diaries and journals, both published and unpublished. It is highly recommended for anyone interested in exploring the details of camp life in the Union army. It is a fit companion piece to Wiley's esteemed THE LIFE OF JOHNNY REB, published in 1943.

4495. ———. "The Common Soldier of the Civil War." CWTI, 12 [4] [1973].

The entire issue of CIVIL WAR TIMES ILLUSTRATED is given over to condensed versions of Wiley's two excellent books mentioned above.

4496. Wiley, Harvey W. "Corporal Harvey W. Wiley's Civil War Diary." William L. Fox, editor. IND MAG HIS , 51 [1955]: 139-162.

This diary of an articulate 17-year old Indianan, covers the period from May to September 1864. In later life, Wiley became chief of the Bureau of Chemistry of the United States Department of Agriculture and played an influential role in the passage of the Pure Food and Drug Act in 1906.

4497. Wilkeson, Frank. RECOLLECTIONS OF A PRIVATE SOLDIER IN THE ARMY OF THE POTOMAC. New York, 1887.

A lad of 16, Wilkeson ran away from his farm to enlist in the 11th New York Artillery. He describes with vividness the trials of being shipped south with a gang of cutthroats and bounty jumpers.

4498. Williams, Edward P. EXTRACTS FROM LETTERS TO A.B.T. FROM EDWARD P. WILLIAMS, DURING HIS SERVICE IN THE CIVIL WAR, 1862-1864. New York, 1903.

A collection of well-written, thoughtful letters by an officer of the 100th Indiana.

4499. Wilson, Ephraim A. MEMOIRS OF THE WAR. Cleveland, 1893.

A thick book of stimulating recollections by an officer of the 10th Illinois.

4500. Wilson, Peter. "Peter Wilson in the Civil War." IOWA J HIS, 40 [1942]: 153-203, 261-320, 339-419.

A group of newsy, observant letters. The first batch covers his training through February 1962. The second deals with Forts Henry and Donelson. He was captured in 1864 and there are no letters after this.

4501. Wise, George M. "Civil War Letters of George M. Wise." Wilfred W. Black, editor. OHIO HIS Q, 65 [1956]: 53-81; 66 [1957]: 187-195.

Letters give good descriptions of activities in the West from New Madrid to the siege of Savannah. He also deals with the vengeful attitude of northern troops and places the blame for the devastation wrought in the Carolinas at Sherman's doorstep.

4502. Woodruff, Mathew. A UNION SOLDIER IN THE LAND OF THE VANQUISHED: THE DIARY OF SERGEANT MATHEW WOODRUFF, JUNE-DECEMBER, 1865. F.N. Boney, editor. University, Alabama: University of Alabama Press, 1969.

A useful, six month journal of a Union soldier of the 21st Missouri on occupation duty in Pascagoula, Mississippi, and Mobile, Alabama. Unfortunately, Woodruff did not decide to keep a diary until the fighting was over, although he had served throughout the war in the western theater. He depicts the boredom of post-war occupation service.

4503. Woodruff, Montgomery S. "The Civil War Notebook of Montgomery Schuyler Woodruff." Frederick M. Woodruff, editor. MO HIS SOC BULL, 29 [1973]: 163-188.

Author was a member of the 2nd Missouri Cavalry and in his journal he reports on campaigning in Arkansas in 1864.

4504. Woolworth, Solomon. EXPERIENCES IN THE CIVIL WAR. Newark, New Jersey: 1903.

A slim book of recollections by a member of the 113th Illinois.

4505. Young, Jesse B. WHAT A BOY SAW IN THE ARMY: A STORY OF SIGHT-SEEING AND ADVENTURE IN THE WAR FOR THE UNION. New York, 1894.

A weak volume of personal experiences as far as the text is concerned. What makes this work important are the sketches by Frank Beard who gained fame as an artist after the war.

VIII

THE WRITTEN WORD

A. LITERATURE

By Charles T. Pridgeon

The following section on literature of the Civil War is divided into four units which focus on [1] fiction, [2] poetry, [3] drama and [4] comment and criticism. Each unit offers a selective rather than a comprehensive bibliography and is designed to serve the researcher whose primary interest is historical or historiographical rather than literary.

[1] Selections in the unit on fiction have been made first of all to provide a representative range of works which portray actual battles and campaigns, leaders and personalities, wartime conditions in the field and on the home front, and debate over political and military issues. Attention has been accorded both to works of special literary distinction or historical note and to works of lesser merit which nonetheless have in important ways shaped public perception of the war and its issues. With this key shaping role of literature in mind, an attempt has been made to include representative selections written for juveniles. The listing of fiction published in the twentieth century is more inclusive than that of the nineteenth only because changing literary standards toward realistic treatment of combat and in some cases characterization as well as the perspective provided by sophisticated historical study have increased the number of works noteworthy for their depictions of the war. In most cases the original publication of a work is listed and the availability of modern editions is mentioned. Specific modern editions are listed when they offer extraordinary editorial commentary, textual variations, or documentation. For other bibiliographies of Civil War fiction, the researcher should consult the works cited in Unit 4 under the Gerhardstein, Lively, McGarry, and Baker entries.

[2] The unit on poetry concentrates on special collections and anthologies of Civil War verse. The war poems of most of the major writers [for example those listed in the entry for Francis F. Browne's BUGLE CALLS] would also be available in appropriate volumes of their collected works. The Dornbusch entry in Unit 4 provides a source of war poetry collections published in the nineteenth century and not listed here.

[3] The dramatic selections included in the third unit are all major plays of the nineteenth and twentieth century legitimate theater and were chosen for their availability in script form. For other titles, the researcher should consult the works cited in the Quinn, Theodore, Brockett, Bloomfield, Welsh, and Whitney entries in Unit 4.

[4] Dominant in the unit on comment and criticism are articles and book-length studies which analyze the ways in which Civil War subjects are developed in literary works or examine biographical background which helps to explain a writer's literary responses to the war. For a representative listing of book reviews, consult the BOOK REVIEW DIGEST [1905-], the BOOK REVIEW INDEX [1965-], and AN INDEX TO BOOK REVIEWS IN THE HUMANITIES [1960-].

1. Fiction

4506. Adams, William T. THE YOUNG LIEUTENANT. Boston, 1865.

Known as "Oliver Optic," Adams was perhaps the most prolific writer for juveniles in the 19th century.

4507. Alger, Horatio. FRANK'S CAMPAIGN. Boston, 1864.

Written by one of the most popular novelists for juveniles, this work dramatizes how young males could reinforce the Union cause on the home front.

4508. Allen, Hervey. ACTION AT AQUILA. New York: Farrar and Rinehart, 1938.

This novel features a Union colonel who with misgivings helps to carry out Sheridan's dictum to devastate the Shenandoah Valley.

4509. Altsheler, Joseph A. IN CIRCLING CAMPS. New York, 1900.

Written by one of the best early 20th century authors of juvenile fiction, this novel relates the adventures of a young Kentuckian who joins the Union cause.

4510. Auchincloss, Louis. WATCHFIRES. Boston: Houghton Mifflin, 1982.

This novel puts military events in the background but effectively illustrates that the quality of personal relationships as much as socio-political views shaped an individual's stance on Civil War and Reconstruction issues.

4511. Bacheller, Irving. FATHER ABRAHAM. Indianapolis: Bobbs-Merrill, 1925.

The moral character of Lincoln influences the relationship between a Union soldier and his southern relatives.

4512. Becker, Stephen. WHEN THE WAR IS OVER. New York: Random House, 1969.

Battlefield panorama is subordinated to an incident between a Union officer and a Confederate soldier which conveys anti-war undertones.

4513. Bierce, Ambrose. AMBROSE BIERCE'S CIVIL WAR. William McCann, editor. Chicago: Gateway, 1956.

This includes all 15 stories contained in IN THE MIDST OF LIFE [1896] but also gathers 5 other pieces of fiction and a set of memoirs which recounts Bierce's experiences as a topographical officer in several major campaigns and battles [Nashville and Atlanta, Shiloh, Chickamauga, Pickett's Mill, Kenesaw Mountain]. An introduction summarizes Bierce's military career.

4514. ———. THE COLLECTED WORKS OF AMBROSE BIERCE. Volume II. New York: Gordian Press, 1966.

This contains 15 Civil War stories originally published under the titles TALES OF SOLDIERS AND CIVILIANS [1892] and IN THE MIDST OF LIFE [1896]. Grim, ironic accounts which contrast characters' romantic expectations with the realities of combat and military policy, these tales feature classic war confrontations between father and son, lover and rival, brother and brother; some are set during battles in which Bierce participated [e.g. Shiloh, Chickamauga, Kennesaw Mountain].

4515. Boyd, James. MARCHING ON. New York: Scribners, 1927.

Set in the Confederacy and written by an author associated with the South. Yet Boyd's ancestry, birth, and education was northern, a fact which some critics feel produced a dualism apparent in this best-selling novel which deals significantly with economic causes and motives.

4516. Branson, Henry C. SALISBURY PLAIN. New York: Dutton, 1965.

This unusual novel narrates the experiences of a Union captain as if they are a Civil War version of the Arthurian legend.

4517. Brick, John. JUBILEE. New York: Doubleday, 1956.

Accurate historical detail and well-drawn battle tactics mark this story of a New York regiment's valor at Gettysburg, Lookout Mountain, and Atlanta.

4518. Brier, Royce. BOY IN BLUE. London: Appleton-Century, 1937.

This extensively details Union military maneuvers and the life of the common soldiers through the battles of the Cumberland Valley.

4519. Burchard, Peter. RAT HELL. New York: Coward, McCann and Geoghegan, 1971.

Written for children, this narrates the escape of Union officers from a Richmond prison camp and their trek through enemy territory.

4520. Caldwell, Taylor. DYNASTY OF DEATH. London: Scribners, 1938. Reprint 1980.

This family saga includes a substantial treatment of munitions manufacturing during the Civil War.

4521. Castor, Henry. THE SPANGLERS. New York: Doubleday, 1948.

Members of a Pennsylvania Dutch family ably defend the Union and suffer imprisonment at Andersonville.

4522. Catton, Bruce. BANNERS AT SHENANDOAH. New York: Doubleday, 1955.

Writing for the adolescent reader, Catton fictionalizes the exploits of Sheridan's cavalry.

4523. Churchill, Winston. THE CRISIS. New York, 1901.

A best-selling romance by one of America's most popular historical novelists offers an authentic social and political portrait of St. Louis before and during the war and interesting portrayals of figures like Lincoln and Sherman. The romantic plot and the border setting of St. Louis are utilized to celebrate a reconciliation of southern and northern cultures.

4524. Crane, Stephen. THE RED BADGE OF COURAGE. AN EPISODE OF THE AMERICAN CIVIL WAR. In THE WORKS OF STEPHEN CRANE. Volume II. Fredson Bowers, editor. Charlottesville, Virginia: University Press of Virginia, 1975.

Originally published in 1896, this landmark novel portrays a youthful soldier who resurges from humiliating cowardice to bravery and heroism. The transformation is not treated romantically, but rather as the consequence of mass battlefield psychology. The narrative emphasizes the confusion of the individual combatant and underplays the rationales of military tactics and strategy. The setting is not named but apparently is Chancellorsville. This edition includes an early draft manuscript and an extensive introduction by L.C. Levenson.

4525. ———. TALES OF WAR. In THE WORKS OF STEPHEN CRANE. Volume VI. Fredson Bowers, editor. Charlottesville, Virginia: University Press of Virginia, 1975.

Among the works in this volume are those originally contained in THE LITTLE REGIMENT AND OTHER EPISODES OF THE AMERICAN CIVIL WAR published in 1897. Written after the success of THE RED BADGE OF COURAGE, these tales feature ironic wartime experiences of combatants and civilians. This volume includes an introduction by James P. Colvert.

4526. DeForest, John W. MISS RAVENEL'S CONVERSION FROM SECESSION TO LOYALTY. New York, 1867.

In scope this is the most important 19th century novel on the war. Pioneering in its realistic depictions of battlefield conditions and the venal politics of military life, it develops northern and southern characters fully and without ideological bias. DeForest served as an officer in the Union army. Modern editions are available.

4527. Devon, Louis. AIDE TO GLORY. New York: Crowell, 1952.

This biographical novel dramatizes the relationship between Grant and his aide-de-camp John Rawlins.

4528. Eliot, George F. CALEB PETTENGILL, U.S.N. New York: Messner, 1956.

Eliot, the military historian, elaborately recreates naval combat and the strategies of the Union blockade.

4529. Erdman, Loula G. ANOTHER SPRING. New York: Dodd, 1966.

Portraying an unusual sociological offshoot of the war, this describes the cooperative efforts of both rich and poor, white and black to survive against the marauding of both armies on the western Missouri border.

4530. Frederic, Harold. THE COPPERHEAD. New York, 1893.

A realistic character study of a farmer whose southern sympathies affront his upstate New York neighbors and bring about his decline from pillar of the community to persecuted outcast. Modern editions available.

4531. Haycox, Ernest. LONG STORM. Boston: Little, Brown, 1946.

The political passions of the war reach the Northwest in this effective story of Copperhead attempts to wrest Oregon from the Union.

4532. Howells, William D. A HAZARD OF NEW FORTUNES. New York, 1889.

An interesting retrospect is conveyed through two veterans, one a southern aristocrat, the other a northern socialist, who link the war to the commercial, capitalistic excesses of the Gilded Age. Modern editions are available.

4533. Jakes, John. NORTH AND SOUTH. New York: Harcourt, Brace, 1982.

South Carolina and Pennsylvania families are contrasted culturally and ideologically as their relationship is traced through the years leading to and during the Civil War.

4534. Kantor, MacKinlay. ANDERSONVILLE. Cleveland: World, 1955.

This winner of a 1956 Pulitzer Prize lengthily narrates the lives of northern prisoners, southern prison officials, and local Georgia citizens against the sordid backdrop of conditions of the Andersonville Prison. Critics are divided in the evaluations; some admonish Kantor for faulty research and distorted interpretation of sources, others congratulate him for writing an outstanding historical novel.

4535. ———. IF THE SOUTH HAD WON THE CIVIL WAR. New York: Bantam, 1961.

The Confederacy wins at Gettysburg and goes on to win the war in this fantasy.

4536. ———. LONG REMEMBER. New York: Coward McCann, 1934.

Set during the battle of Gettysburg, this is a detailed depiction of combat horrors and their demoralizing impact on civilian life. By de-emphasizing a socio-political context, the story underscores the senselessness of war.

4537. Keneally, Thomas. CONFEDERATES. New York: Harper and Row, 1980.

This unusually strong novel concentrates on southern characters but extensively portrays the failure of northern leadership at Second Bull Run and Antietam and develops as a main character a Boston-born widow of a Confederate officer who spies for the Union. Elaborately realistic battle detail mingles with complex characterizations. A brief bibliography of Keneally's background sources is included.

4538. Kirkland, Joseph. THE CAPTAIN OF COMPANY K. Chicago, 1891.

Detailed, realistic handling of infantry combat at Fort Donelson, Shiloh, and Vicksburg combines with a trite love affair and a tale of courage conquering cowardice to make this a notable 19th century representative of "popular" Civil War fiction. A modern edition is available.

4539. Lancaster, Bruce. NIGHT MARCH. Boston: Little, Brown, 1958.

Cavalry action abounds in this tale of the Kilpatrick-Dahlgren raid on Richmond.

4540. ———. ROLL, SHENANDOAH. Boston: Little, Brown, 1956.

Mosby is played down, while Sheridan's scorched-earth campaign in the Shenandoah Valley is portrayed as essential military strategy.

4541. Lentz, Perry. THE FALLING HILLS. New York: Scribners, 1967.

Warfare and racial relations receive realistic treatment in this story which climaxes in the Fort Pillow massacre of black troops.

4542. Lockridge, Ross, Jr. RAINTREE COUNTY. Boston: Houghton Mifflin, 1947.

This noteworthy epic, set in 1892, uses a complex of flashbacks to contrast the golden days of ante-bellum life in a rural Indiana town to the more corrupt commercial atmosphere of the post-war era. Interspersed throughout are episodes featuring Civil War battles including Chickamauga.

4543. Longstreet, Stephen. GETTYSBURG. New York: Farrar, Straus, 1961.

An interesting companion to Kantor's LONG REMEMBER, this episodic novel captures a sense of civilians' life and point of view as the battle rages near their homes.

4544. Mason, F. Van Wyck. ARMORED GIANTS. Boston: Little, Brown, 1980.

Covered here are the construction and performance of the MONITOR and the naval campaign for supremacy on the Mississippi.

4545. ———. BLUE HURRICANE. Philadelphia: Lippincott, 1954.

The river naval battles of 1861-1862 are featured in this occasionally melodramatic adventure by a well-known popular historical novelist.

4546. Medary, Marjorie. COLLEGE IN CRINOLINE. New York: Longmans, 1937.

Written for adolescents, this novel offers an unusual picture of 19th century education as it portrays the attitudes of young Iowans toward the Civil War.

4547. Mitchell, S. Weir. A DIPLOMATIC ADVENTURE. New York, 1906.

Narrated by a secretary to the American legation in Paris, this novel focuses on Napoleon III's attempts to generate English support for the Confederate cause.

4548. Morford, Henry. THE DAYS OF SHODDY: A NOVEL OF THE GREAT REBELLION IN 1861. Philadelphia, 1963.

One of three novels Morford published during the war, this lambastes war profiteering and generally discovers greed behind abolitionist sentiments.

4549. Morrison, Gerry. UNVEXED TO THE SEA. New York: St. Martins, 1961.

The intricacies of the Vicksburg campaign are looked at from both sides.

4550. Morrow, Honore. WITH MALICE TOWARD NONE. New York: Morrow, 1928.

This critically acclaimed portrait of Lincoln and his wrangling with Sumner during 1864-1865 contrasts interestingly to Vidal's 1984 fictional interpretation.

4551. O'Connor, Richard. COMPANY Q. New York: Doubleday, 1957.

Biographer of Civil War generals, O'Connor tells the unusual story of a Union punishment battalion at the siege of Atlanta.

4552. Pennell, Joseph S. THE HISTORY OF ROME HANKS. New York: Scribners, 1944.

A graphic and anti-heroic account of carnage at Shiloh and Gettysburg is linked to the portrayal of a main character whose venality, cowardice, and incompetence take him from battlefield commander to secretary of war.

4553. Pulse, Charles K. JOHN BONWELL. New York: Farrar, Strauss, 1952.

Much historical detail on subjects like the Free Soil movement and the Underground Railroad distinguishes this novel set in the Ohio Valley before and during the Civil War.

4554. Reed, Ishmael. FLIGHT TO CANADA. New York: Random House, 1976.

Through parody and satire as well as anachronisms, Reed takes a comic iconoclastic approach to the Civil War, Lincoln, the issue of slavery, and the standards of traditional historical novels.

4555. Rhodes, James A. and Dean Jauchius. JOHNNY SHILOH. Indianapolis: Bobbs-Merrill, 1959.

This is noteworthy insofar that it portrays the battle experiences of Johnnie Clem, the famous drummer boy and youngest soldier to serve in the war.

4556. Robertson, Constance N. THE GOLDEN CIRCLE. New York: Random House, 1951.

Morgan's raids provide the military action, the activities of Vallandigham and the Knights of the Golden Circle supply the politics, in this extensively documented story of Copperhead attempts to subvert Ohio from the Union cause.

4557. ———. THE UNTERRIFIED. New York: Henry Holt, 1946.

This details Peace Democrat politics and the Copperhead activities of a fictitious New York senator and his family.

4558. Robertson, Don. BY ANTIETAM CREEK. Englewood Cliffs, New Jersey: Prentice-Hall, 1960.

The collapse of strategy and the failure of leadership, especially McClellan's, are set against vividly realistic battle detail and the human touches of individuals' lives.

4559. ———. THE RIVER AND THE WILDERNESS. New York: Doubleday, 1962.

Poor leadership at Frederickoburg and in the Wilderness is the theme of this work.

4560. ———. THE THREE DAYS. Englewood Cliffs, New Jersey: Prentice-Hall, 1959.

Personal stories and military strategy mix effectively in this realistic account of Gettysburg.

4561. Scott, Evelyn. THE WAVE. New York: Jonathan Cape and Harrison Smith, 1929.

A fragmented narration swings panoramically from dramatic scenes, to mental musings, to excerpts from letters and newspapers in order to evoke a hectic picture of life in battle and on the home front.

4562. Shaara, Michael. THE KILLER ANGELS. New York: McKay, 1974.

The impact of topography on military tactics receives notable attention in this Pulitzer Prize winning account of Gettysburg which tends to emphasize the officers' point of view.

4563. Sinclair, Harold. THE HORSE SOLDIERS. New York: Harpers, 1956.

Based authentically on Grierson's raid through Mississippi in April 1863, this understated story portrays Illinois and Iowa cavalry penetrating 200 miles behind Confederate lines.

4564. Sinclair, Upton. MANASSAS: A NOVEL OF THE WAR. New York, 1904.

A northern-educated southerner joins a Union regiment in a novel which portrays Bull Run battle scenes vividly and provides an early economic interpretation of the war. Extensively researched by Sinclair who reveals his usual interest in political and social issues.

4565. Singmaster, Elsie. BOY AT GETTYSBURG. Boston: Houghton Mifflin, 1924.

This and other Singmaster works effectively illustrate how the Civil War has been fictionally packaged for children.

4566. Smith, Chard. ARTILLERY OF TIME. London: Scribners, 1939.

Life in upstate New York before and during the Civil War is captured in elaborate detail.

4567. Stacton, David. THE JUDGES OF THE SECRET COURT. New York: Pantheon, 1961.

The atmosphere in Washington during the spring of 1865 comes alive more effectively than Booth's or Lincoln's characters in this account of the Lincoln assassination plot and the subsequent trial.

4568. Stevenson, Janet. WEEP NO MORE. New York: Viking, 1957.

Espionage in Richmond is featured in this adventure based on the life of abolitionist heroine Elizabeth Van Leu.

4569. Stoddard, W.O. THE BATTLE OF NEW YORK. New York, 1892.

One of several war novels written by Stoddard for juveniles, this dramatizes the New York draft riots and offers a warning about the dangers of anarchy.

4570. Stowe, Harriet B. UNCLE TOM'S CABIN. Boston, 1852.

Popularly identified as a "cause" of the Civil War, this novel attracted international attention and was a crucial factor in defining slavery as a moral and humanitarian issue. Stowe defended the accuracy of her portrayal in A KEY TO UNCLE TOM'S CABIN [1853] and published a companion piece DRED [1856]. Numerous modern editions available.

4571. Toepperwein, Herman. REBEL IN BLUE. New York: Morrow, 1963.

German settlers support the Union cause in Civil War Texas.

4572. Vidal, Gore. LINCOLN. New York: Random House, 1984.

Covering 1861-1865, this novel offers a provocative account of Lincoln's devotion to unionist ideology as well as an intricate portrayal of wartime politics. Battles are viewed from the Washington vantage point, but a solid sense of the progress of the war and of the large picture of military strategy comes across.

4573. Wallace, Willard. THE RAIDERS. Boston: Little, Brown, 1970.

The sinking of the ALABAMA and the capture of Fort Fisher are portrayed in this story of a Union sailor who infiltrates the Confederate navy.

4574. Warren, Robert P. WILDERNESS. New York: Random House, 1961.

Warren uses Civil War battles such as Chancellorsville, Gettysburg, and Antietam as circumstances to develop a psychological study of an idealistic Jewish immigrant who joins the Union army. Characterization dominates historical setting; but this is a strong novel by a literary giant whose interest in the Civil War is sophisticated and long-standing.

4575. Wicker, Tom. UNTO THIS HOUR. New York: Viking, 1984.

An elaborate fictional recreation of the Second Battle of Bull Run which impressively portrays military movements and strategy as well as the dramas of individuals involved or affected. Narration moves between both Union and Confederate characters, some historical, some fictional, but includes significant treatment of McClellan and Pope.

4576. Wood, Ben. FORT LAFAYETTE; OR LOVE AND SECESSION. New York, 1862.

Written by the brother of the famous Copperhead Fernando Wood, this work is weak from a literary standpoint. Ben Wood, who was as bitter toward the Lincoln administration as Fernando, uses the device of fiction to express his resentment toward the Lincoln "dictatorship." [See number 1100]

4577. Zara, Louis. REBEL RUN. New York: Crown, 1951.

This is a fictional version of the 1862 Union raid which attempted to cut the railroad lines between Atlanta and Chattanooga.

2. Poetry

4578. Benet, Stephen V. JOHN BROWN'S BODY. Garden City, New York: Doubleday, 1928.

Epic in scope, this Pulitzer Prize-winning, stylistically diverse poetic narrative covers the era of 1859-1865 and develops historical figures like Grant, Lincoln, Lee, Davis, and Brown himself; a wide range of fictional characters representing regional, racial, and socio-economic types; and the major battles of the war [including an extensive treatment of Gettysburg]. Blending both realistic and romantic elements, Benet portrays the southern culture more subtly and richly than the northern, but while successfully communicating the complexity of the roots and "causes" of the war, suggests an ultimate reconciliation achieved, apparently, in the spirit of egalitarianism of a modern industrial order. The twenty-first edition [1941] published by Rinehart includes an introduction and annotations.

4579. Browne, Francis F., editor. BUGLE-ECHOES. POETRY OF THE CIVIL WAR. New York, 1886.

Of historical interest, this collection assembled by a Union veteran mingles verse from North and South to celebrate the war that proved the nation's mettle and to signal the emergence of a common patriotism and spirit of reconciliation. Among the major northern writers represented are Walt Whitman, James Russell Lowell, John Greenleaf Whittier, Oliver Wendell Holmes, Henry Wadsworth Longfellow, William Cullen Bryant, William Dean Howells, and Bret Harte. Among others are those whose reputations were more noteworthy in the 19th century, such as Richard Henry Stoddard, J.G. Holland, Thomas Bailey Aldrich, Charles G. Halpine, Joaquin Miller, and Bayard Taylor.

4580. Capps, Claudius M., editor. THE BLUE AND THE GRAY; THE BEST POEMS OF THE CIVIL WAR. Freeport, New York: Books for Libraries Press, 1969.

A reprint of a 1943 edition, this anthology includes over 150 poems by more than 120 writers, both well-known and obscure, selected, mainly to represent most of the warring states, North and South. This volume includes many fewer poems by accomplished writers than the Browne anthology noted above and offers only a brief introduction and no background notes.

4581. Lowell, James Russell. THE BIGLOW PAPERS, SECOND SERIES [1862-1866]. In THE WRITINGS OF JAMES RUSSELL LOWELL. 10 v. Boston, 1890.

Originally published in the ATLANTIC, these humorous verse "letters" from a fictional character express northern sentiments on a variety of subjects including the Mason-Slidell affair, Jefferson Davis, and the prospects for Reconstruction. An effective combination of political satire and humor derived from the use of dialect, the "letters" were widely read during the war.

4582. Lowell, Robert. FOR THE UNION DEAD. New York: Farrar, Straus, and Giroux, 1965.

One of the best known and best poems on the war written in this century, the popular title piece of this volume reflects on the ironic connection between Boston's monument to Colonel Robert Shaw's black regiment and the surrounding evidence of new modern forms of slavery to technology.

4583. Melville, Herman. THE BATTLE-PIECES OF HERMAN MELVILLE. Henig Cohen, editor. New York: Yoseloff, 1963.

Completed just after the fall of Richmond and published in 1866, this important collection of 72 poems conveys a humanistic perspective while it captures in graphic images the cataclysmic nature of the war. Many of the poems deal with specific land and naval battles and, while portraying both naive and heroic valor, perceptively characterize the modern, mechanistic quality of Civil War combat.

Moore, Frank. THE REBELLION RECORD.... [See number 46]

4584. Steinmetz, Lee, editor. THE POETRY OF THE AMERICAN CIVIL WAR. Ann Arbor: Michigan State University Press, 1960.

Usefully bolstered by editorial commentary and a bibliography of primary sources, this collection clusters poems under subjects which range from personal responses to battlefield events to social and political assessments of the war. Emphasis falls on now little known poets who gave voice to popular attitudes.

4585. Whitman, Walt. DRUM-TAPS. In LEAVES OF GRASS. Harold W. Blodgett and Sculley Bradley, editors. New York: New York University Press, 1965.

A collection of over 40 poems published in 1865 which captures both the exciting tumult of the war spirit and the depressing reality of the battlefield, the hospital, and the war-struck home front. Illustrated are Whitman's eye for detail, his compassion, and his perception of the war as an event of massive historical significance. This is the most important collection of poems by a single author to come out of the war. Other modern editions are available.

4586. Whittier, John Greenleaf. THE COMPLETE POETICAL WORKS OF JOHN GREENLEAF WHITTIER. Boston, 1894.

Whittier's abolitionist sentiments and Quaker point of view are apparent in a wide range of works including those written for IN TIME OF WAR AND OTHER POEMS [1863].

3. Drama

4587. Aiken, George. UNCLE TOM'S CABIN. In DRAMAS FROM THE AMERICAN THEATER, 1762-1909. Richard Moody, editor. Cleveland: World, 1966.

Appearing in 1852, this extremely popular play, based on the Harriet Beecher Stowe novel, offered a clear moral statement on the slavery issue to pre-war audiences and is thought to have helped shape abolitionist trends in the 1850s. A substantial introduction is included here. Other modern editions are available.

4588. Belasco, David. THE HEART OF MARYLAND. In AMERICA'S LOST PLAYS. Volume 17. Robert H. Ball, editor. Bloomington, Indiana: University of Indiana Press, 1965.

A highly successful melodrama, Belasco's play, performed first in 1895, underscores a key convention in Civil War dramas, that where men usually place duty and country above romance, women do not. Other modern editions are available.

4589. Boucicault, Dion. BELLE LAMAR. In PLAYS FOR THE COLLEGE THEATER. Garrett H. Leverton, editor. New York: Samuel French, 1937.

One of the earliest post-war melodramas [1874], this does not express the reconciliatory message of plays produced later in the century but rather presents a northern hero and southern villain.

4590. Dixon, Thomas. A MAN OF THE PEOPLE. New York: Appleton, 1920.

Lincoln's handling of a Copperhead conspiracy in 1864 provides a central plot for a play that depicts the beleaguered President's confrontations with Stanton, McClellan, and hostile Republican committees.

4591. Drinkwater, John. ABRAHAM LINCOLN. In THE PLAYS OF JOHN DRINKWATER. Volume 2. Grosse Point, Michigan: Scholarly Press, 1968.

Achieving popularity in both England and the United States, this English play includes scenes which emphasize Lincoln's tragic and humane sense of the war as well as his strength and determination in dealing with an intractable cabinet and does not attempt to capture a sharp historical sense of the times. Earlier editions are available.

4592. Fitch, Clyde. BARBARA FRIETCHIE. In PLAYS BY CLYDE FITCH. Volume 2. Montrose Moses and Virginia Gerson, editors. Boston: Little, Brown, 1915.

This popular 1899 play enhances the famous Civil War legend which celebrates Barbara Frietchie's devotion to both lover and country and does so with no concern for historical facts.

4593. Gillette, William. SECRET SERVICE. In PLAYS BY WILLIAM HOOKER GILLETTE. Rosemary Cullen and Don B. Wilmeth, editors. Cambridge: Cambridge University Press, 1983.

Presented first in 1895, this popular, classic drama of spying and the conflict of love and duty is set in Richmond during the last days of the siege and is marked by effective portrayal of military intelligence activities and the disruption of domestic life in the beleaguered city. This includes a helpful introduction. Other modern editions are available.

4594. Howard, Bronson. SHENANDOAH. In DRAMAS FROM THE AMERICAN THEATER, 1762-1909. Richard Moody, editor. Cleveland: World, 1966.

Presented successfully in 1899, Howard's play combines standard romance, spectacular military effects, and reconciliatory tone to become one of the most popular Civil War dramas. This includes an informative introduction. Other modern editions are available.

4595. Levitt, Saul. THE ANDERSONVILLE TRIAL. In AMERICA ON STAGE. Stanley Richards, editor. Garden City, New York: Doubleday, 1976.

Performed first in 1959, this critically acclaimed play, based partly on government documents, portrays the trial of Henry Wirz, commandant of Andersonville Prison, and develops the clash between conscience and obligation to authority. An introduction is included. Other editions are available.

4596. Lewis, Sinclair and Lloyd Lewis. JAYHAWKER. Garden City, New York: Doubleday, 1935.

Expressing a realistic anti-war point of view, this drama [not a critical success] features a free soil Kansan who first takes advantage of the war spirit to gain political power and then, disillusioned by the carnage, collaborates with a southern general in an attempt to end the conflict.

4597. Thomas, Augustus. THE COPPERHEAD. In LONGER PLAYS BY MODERN AUTHORS. Helen L. Cohen, editor. New York: Harcourt, Brace, 1922.

Featuring a main character who poses as a Copperhead to spy for the Union, this critically respected 1918 drama offers war-related local color scenes set during and 40 years after the conflict.

4598. Van Doren, Mark. THE LAST DAYS OF LINCOLN. In AMERICA ON STAGE. Stanley Richards, editor. Garden City, New York: Doubleday, 1976.

Lincoln confers with Union and Confederate leaders as he charitably ponders a post-war policy in this critically praised drama first performed in 1961. A helpful introduction is included. Other editions are available.

4. Comment and Criticism

4599. Aaron, Daniel. THE UNWRITTEN WAR: AMERICAN WRITERS AND THE CIVIL WAR. New York: Knopf, 1973.

In this important study, Aaron scrutinizes the personal, political, and philosophical disposition of both 19th and 20th century writers as he assesses reasons for the shortage of first-rate literary treatments of the Civil War as well as the failure of the works that were written to address certain crucial subjects such as racism, draft evasion, and anti-war sentiments. Aaron is careful to emphasize, however, that a dearth of excellent literary production does not mean that the war failed to deeply touch writers of both North and South. While analyzing in depth over a dozen northern authors, he concludes: "Our untidy and unkempt war still confounds interpreters."

4600. Abel, Darrel. "The American Renaissance and the Civil War: Concentric Circles." EMER SOC Q, 44 [3] [1966]: 86-91.

This surveys the impact of the war on literary forms and tastes and on the hopeful nationalistic spirit expressed by major writers who had established their reputations in the 1840s and 1850s.

4601. Adler, Joyce S. "Melville and the Civil War." NEW LETTERS, 45 [Winter 1973]: 99-117.

The poetry in BATTLE-PIECES is fired by a dread of the war, but also by a sense of its moral necessity and the justice of its cause. In the prose "Supplement" to the volume, however, Melville is blind to the injustices that will be committed against the freed blacks and seems unable to project his tragic vision into the future to foresee the moral atmosphere of the era of Reconstruction.

4602. Allen, Gay W. THE SOLITARY SINGER: A CRITICAL BIOGRAPHY OF WALT WHITMAN. New York: Macmillan, 1955.

This provides the most extensive biographical account of the wartime experiences of Walt Whitman as well as substantial discussion of poems comprising DRUM-TAPS. Allen examines the way in which Whitman worked themes developed earlier into his war pieces and how he revised earlier poems to incorporate his impressions of the war.

4603. ———. WALDO EMERSON. A BIOGRAPHY. New York: Viking, 1981.

"The war was never far from Emerson's mind." Allen's study solidly recounts Emerson's responses to the military conduct of the war and discusses his powerful interest in the issues of slavery and abolition and ultimately in Lincoln's handling of emancipation.

4604. Anderson, David D. "Lincoln and Emerson." LIN HER, 60 [1958]: 123-128.

Journal entries and public addresses reveal that Emerson found Lincoln's handling of the abolition issue to be uncertain and his character lacking a sense of decorum; but, by the close of the war he felt Lincoln had grown in stature to fit the definition of greatness set forth in REPRESENTATIVE MEN [1850].

4605. Axelrod, Steven. "Colonel Shaw in American Poetry: 'For the Union Dead' and its Precursors." AQ, 24 [1972]: 523-537.

The fate of Robert G. Shaw and his black regiment has inspired a large number of poems which tend to use the subject to comment on American political policy. Special attention is accorded to the poems of James Russell Lowell, William Vaughan Moody, John Berryman, and Robert Lowell.

4606. Baker, Ernest. A GUIDE TO HISTORICAL FICTION. London, 1914.

Useful in locating fiction published before 1913, this descriptive bibliography divides material into helpful subject categories [e.g., "Military Operations of 1862," "The Naval Side of the War," and "The Life of Non-combatants"]. Listing of juvenile fiction is included.

4607. Barton, William E. ABRAHAM LINCOLN AND WALT WHITMAN. Port Washington, New York: Kennikat, 1965.

A reissue of a 1928 publication, Barton's study dismisses those accounts which argue that Lincoln admired Whitman. But in analyzing Whitman's adulation of Lincoln during and after the Civil War, he provides an elaborate and intriguing comparison of the two men's experiences and characters.

4608. Basler, Roy P. "Lincoln in Literature." JISHS, 52 [1959]: 33-44.

Basler surveys literature, from biography to folk tale, to explain why Lincoln is a subject irresistible to the poetic and creative imagination which fashions legend as part of a people's search for national identity.

4609. Bloom, Robert L. "The Battle of Gettysburg in Fiction." PENN HIS, 43 [1976]: 309-327.

A survey of fictionalized accounts of Gettysburg reveals that writers at times carelessly distort or ignore historical records but at their best offer provocative interpretations as well as a concrete sense of personal involvement in events which is not offered by most historians.

4610. Bloomfield, Maxwell. "Wartime Drama: The Theater in Washington, 1861-1865." MD HIS MAG, 64 [1969]: 396-411.

The swelling wartime population spurred the building of a wide variety of theaters and production of many plays and extravaganzas which portrayed military exploits, promoted abolitionism, and ridiculed government bureaucracy.

4611. Brockett, O.G. and Lenyth Brockett. "Civil War Theater: Contemporary Treatments." CWH, 1 [1955]: 229-280.

The authors correct a misperception, reinforced by standard histories of the theater, that few dramatic projections on the subject of the war were presented between 1861 and 1865. While lacking in artistic merit, many plays, burlesques, tableaus, panoramas, and pageants dealt with fictitious or authentic war figures and battles and often appeared soon after actual events thus functioning as "newsreels."

4612. Chase, Richard. WALT WHITMAN RECONSIDERED. New York: Sloane, 1955.

Chapter Four concludes that the poems in DRUM-TAPS reflect a "crisis of the imagination" brought on by the trauma of the Civil War apparent in much American literature of the era.

4613. Cohn, Jan. "The Negro Character in Northern Magazine Fiction of the 1860's." NEQ, 43 [1970]: 572-592.

Popular literature during and just after the war suggests that "the North remained complacently racist, if nobly abolitionist."

4614. Cox, James. "Walt Whitman, Mark Twain, and the Civil War." SEWANEE R, 69 [1961]: 185-204.

Cox compares the ways by which the two writers work out their ambivalent feelings toward the war in their literature.

4615. Crawford, Barholow V. "The Civil War and American Literature." EMER SOC Q, 44 [3] [1966]: 91-94.

The central concern here is selecting works for a literature course which would combat cliched and oversimplified notions about the Civil War.

4616. Dandurand, Karen. "New Dickinson Civil War Publications." A LIT, 56 [1984]: 17-27.

Only a handful of Emily Dickinson's poems were published in her lifetime, but four of those appeared in DRUM BEAT, a New

York newspaper designed to raise money for Union medical supplies. This contradicts the inference that Dickinson was indifferent to the Civil War.

4617. Day, Frank L. "Melville and Sherman March to the Sea." AMERICAN NOTES AND QUERIES, 2 [1964]: 134-136.

A representative source study, this demonstrates that Melville drew information for his poetry from the first hand account, THE STORY OF THE GREAT MARCH by George Ward Nichols.

4618. DeVoto, Bernard. "Fiction Fights the Civil War." SAT R LIT, [December 18, 1937]: 3-4.

This brief seminal article offers an early critical assessment of war fiction noting in particular the emergence of works which viewed the war from the common soldiers' perspective.

Dornbusch, Charles E. MILITARY BIBLIOGRAPHY OF THE CIVIL WAR. Volume 3. [See number 16]

4619. Duberman, Martin. JAMES RUSSELL LOWELL. Boston: Houghton Mifflin, 1966.

Chapter Ten offers a substantial account of Lowell's favorable attitude toward Lincoln as well as his literary and journalistic responses to the war.

4620. Eby, Cecil D., Jr. "'The Real War' and the Books." SWR, 47 [1962]: 259-264.

Echoing the lament that little first-rate literature or any masterpieces on the Civil War have been produced, Eby argues that personal narratives should receive more attention as a literary genre and explains why southern narratives are superior to those of the North.

4621. Fatout, Paul. "Ambrose Bierce, Civil War Topographer." A LIT, 26 [1954]: 391-400.

A technical look at Bierce's service as surveyor, draftsman, and mathematician, from Shiloh through the Atlanta campaign.

4622. Fenton, Charles A. STEPHEN VINCENT BENET. New Haven: Yale University Press, 1958.

Two chapters discuss the composition and both public and critical reception of Benet's popular Civil War epic, JOHN BROWN'S BODY [1928].

4623. Fogle, Richard H. "Melville and the Civil War." TULANE STUD ENG, 9 [1959]: 61-89.

This extensive analysis of the poems and prose supplement comprising BATTLE-PIECES assesses Melville's philosophical interpretation of the war and concludes that he was a skeptical patriot who hoped the inevitable conflict would serve as an object lesson calling attention to moral and political weaknesses in the national character.

4624. Ford, Thomas W. "Emily Dickinson and the Civil War." UNIV R [Kansas City], 31 [1965]: 199-203.

Dickinson's well-known preoccupation with death as well as her creative talents were in part nurtured by the Civil War when she wrote more than 850 poems.

4625. Gargano, James W. "A Thematic Analysis of Miss Ravenel's Conversion." TOPIC, 1 [1] [1961]: 40-47.

John W. DeForest's 1867 novel is a landmark not merely because of its realistic portrayal of the war but more importantly because it successfully integrates a conventional love plot with sophisticated characterization and treatment of the ideological conflict between southern and northern cultures. Moreover, the novel avoids "pat didacticism" and implicitly explains the outcome of the war in terms of current evolutionary theory.

4626. Gerber, John. "Mark Twain's 'Private Campaign.'" CWH, 1 [1955]: 37-60.

Twain's account of his brief Civil War experience "is primarily a literary rather than an historical document." The complete memoir which originally appeared in CENTURY MAGAZINE accompanies this article.

4627. Gerhardstein, Virginia B. DICKINSON'S AMERICAN HISTORICAL FICTION. Metuchen, New Jersey: Scarecrow, 1981.

Complementing Lively's bibliography, this valuable resource provides brief annotations for over 200, mainly 20th century, works of Civil War fiction. Sections on Abolition and Reconstruction fiction are also helpful. This is the fourth edition of the work.

4628. Glicksburg, Charles I., editor. WALT WHITMAN AND THE CIVIL WAR: A COLLECTION OF ORIGINAL ARTICLES AND MANUSCRIPTS. Philadelphia: University of Pennsylvania Press, 1933.

This pioneering work brings together and comments upon newspaper articles, diary entries, letters, and poems in an attempt to define Whitman's connection with and perception of the Civil War.

4629. Hanchett, William. IRISH: CHARLES G. HALPINE IN CIVIL WAR AMERICA. Syracuse, New York: Syracuse University Press, 1970.

This biography includes a study of journalist Halpine's popular fictional character Private Miles O'Reilly whose adventures are rich in war-era background.

4630. Handlin, Oscar. "The Civil War as Symbol and as Actuality." MASS R, 3 [1961]: 133-143.

This essay, written at the outset of the Centennial addresses questions crucial to the study of Civil War literature. Handlin first assesses the idealistic and romantic myths that commemorate the war as a positive experience which strengthened sectional character and unity and thus obscured its reality; he then surveys the complex of political and military miscalculations and the savage hatreds which make up the "actuality" of the conflict.

4631. Hayes, John D. and Doris D. Maguire. "Charles Graham Halpine: Life and Adventures of Miles O'Reilly." NY HIS SOC Q, 51 [1967]: 326-344.

An Irish immigrant, Halpine became a journalist and publicist and during the war rose to the rank of brigadier general. He wrote sketches under the pseudonym of Miles O'Reilly.

4632. Helmick, Evelyn T. "The Civil War Odes of Lowell and Tate." GA R, 25 [1971]: 51-55.

Despite being thought of as expressions of two regional cultures, the themes, structure, and images of Robert Lowell's FOR THE UNION DEAD are similar to and derived from those of Allen Tate's ODE TO THE CONFEDERATE DEAD.

4633. Hibler, David J. "Drum-Taps and Battle-Pieces: Melville and Whitman on the Civil War." THE PERSONALIST, 50 [1969]: 130-147.

Whitman's compassionate, optimistic response to the war contrasts with Melville's darker pessimistic outlook.

4634. Howard, Leon. HERMAN NELVILLE. Berkeley: University of California Press, 1951.

Chapter 11 includes an account of Melville's visit to the war front near Leesburg, Virginia, and discusses the composition of poems which were to make up BATTLE-PIECES.

4635. Howell, Elmo. "Mark Twain and the Civil War." BALL ST UNIV F, 13 [Autumn 1972]: 53-61.

Twain's self-image and writing were crucially affected by misgivings over his failure to fight in the Civil War.

4636. Hungerford, Harold R. "'That Was at Chancellorsville'; The Factual Framework of THE RED BADGE OF COURAGE." A LIT, 34 [1963]: 520-531.

Comparison with factual accounts argues that the unnamed battle in the novel is Chancellorsville and that Crane researched the event carefully.

4637. Ives, C.B. "'The Little Regiment' of Stephen Crane at the Battle of Fredericksburg." MIDWEST Q, 8 [1967]: 247-260.

The unnamed battle in this story closely parallels that of Fredericksburg and the unnamed unit featured would appear to be the 69th New York. Crane uses the battle and the regiment to offer a more positive portrayal of courage than that in THE RED BADGE OF COURAGE.

4638. Kaplan, Justin. WALT WHITMAN. New York: Simon and Schuster, 1980.

Whitman's impressions of wartime Washington, his work in the army hospitals, his visits to the front, and his personal and literary responses to the war are given extensive treatment, especially in Chapter 14.

4639. Kavanagh, Paul. "The Nation Past and Present: A Study of Robert Lowell's 'For the Union Dead.'" J AM STUD, 5 [1971]: 93-101.

A comparison of Robert Lowell's poem on Colonel Robert Shaw and another by his ancestor James Russell Lowell illustrates crucial differences in attitude between 19th and 20th century social liberalism.

4640. Kazin, Alfred. "And the War Came." REPORTER, 24 [May 11, 1961]: 36-43.

Kazin, deploring the "frigid emptiness" of the Centennial celebration, provides a compact survey of the impassioned literary responses to the issues and events of the Civil War.

4641. Kroeger, Frederick P. "Longfellow, Melville and Hawthorne: The Passage into the Iron Age.: ILL Q, 33 [December 1970]: 30-41.

All three of these writers reflected on the advent of ironclad ships, but where Longfellow romantically treated the sinking of the CUMBERLAND by the MERRIMAC as an event of heroism, Hawthorne and Melville portrayed the battle of the MERRIMAC and MONITOR as the opening of a new era when engineering design would replace heroic men as the decisive factor in naval warfare.

4642. Leighead, J. Edward. "The Civil War in Dime Novels." A BOOK COLL, 21 [1970]: 35-41.

A narrative bibliography of dime novels about the Civil War which appeared from 1883 to 1904.

4643. Leisy, Ernest E. THE AMERICAN HISTORICAL NOVEL. Norman: University of Oklahoma Press, 1950.

A chapter traces the historical development of the Civil War novel and provides helpful descriptive and critical commentary on major 19th and 20th century examples. This is a standard study of the historical novel; but it does not significantly compare the literary treatment of the Civil War with that of other historical eras, nor does it offer an extensive bibliography of novels. While this should not be overlooked, it is less valuable than Lively's book.

4644. Levy, Leo B. "Hawthorne, Melville, and the MONITOR." A LIT, 37 [1965]: 33-40.

Levy suggests that both writers used the Union ironclad to symbolize the emergence of an impersonal mode of warfare and more generally of a mechanized society.

4645. Light, James. JOHN WILLIAM DeFOREST. New York: Twayne, 1965.

DeForest's experiences with the 12th Connecticut and later with the Freedman's Bureau are recounted in some detail; and the connection between the autobiographical A VOLUNTEER'S ADVENTURES and the fictional MISS RAVENEL'S CONVERSION is discussed.

4646. Lindeman, Jack. "Herman Melville's Civil War." MODERN AGE, 9 [1965]: 387-398.

In some sense the record of a "poet-journalist," the poems in BATTLE-PIECES provide a vivid, concrete, chronological account of the war.

4647. Lively, Robert A. FICTION FIGHTS THE CIVIL WAR. Chapel Hill: University of North Carolina Press, 1957.

This valuable resource examines both novels of literary merit and the much larger array of popular romances. Lively discusses the problems of transforming Civil War issues, personages, and events into fictional stories and characters and provides an intelligent comparison of the historian's and novelist's approach to history. A chapter "The North Examines Itself" links the portrayal of the war to the tradition of literary realism. A bibliography lists 512 19th and 20th century novels [including juvenile fiction] and an extensive array of secondary sources.

4648. Martin, John S. "Henry Adams on War: The Transformation of History into Metaphor." ARIZ Q, 24 [1968]: 350-360.

Adams' personal and philosophical interpretation of the Civil War helped to shape his "dynamic theory of history" and clarified his understanding of the role of faith and leadership in the historical process.

4649. Mattson, J. Stanley. "Mark Twain on War and Peace: The Missouri Rebel and 'The Campaign That Failed.'" AQ, 20 [1968]: 783-794.

An ironic installment in CENTURY MAGAZINE'S "Battles and Leaders of the Civil War" series, Twain's sketch is a sardonic indictment of war.

4650. McGarry, Daniel and Sarah H. White. HISTORICAL FICTION GUIDE. New York: Scarecrow, 1963.

Brief descriptions of content accompany 238 Civil War entries in this bibliography.

4651. Miller, Wayne C. AN ARMED AMERICA: ITS FACE IN FICTION. New York: New York University Press, 1970.

The chapter "The Civil War and American Realism" provides solid commentary on DeForest, Bierce, Crane, and other lesser writers.

4652. Montague, Gene B. "Melville's BATTLE-PIECES." UNIV TEXAS STUD ENG, 30 [1956]: 106-115.

Melville's sustained experiment in the poetic medium reiterated themes already developed in his prose works and expresses his view that the war was fought out of practical necessity and that its victims deserved sympathy.

4653. Mumford, Lewis. HERMAN MELVILLE. New York: Harcourt, Brace, 1929.

Chapter 11 interprets Melville's response to the Civil War as an illustration of a larger collective response, a sense that the conflict had dealt a fatal blow to the hopes of a "provincial" America for a unified national culture carrying out the principles of the Constitution.

4654. Nelles, William. "Saving the State in Lowell's 'For the Union Dead.'" A LIT, 55 [1983]: 639-642.

This note departs from the popular interpretation of the poem and argues that Lowell uses Colonel Robert Shaw and his black troops to symbolize the futility of military action to serve an ideal and the state.

4655. O'Brien, Matthew C. "Ambrose Bierce and the Civil War." A LIT, 48 [1976]: 377-381.

Official records and handwriting discrepancies in a notebook alleged to be Bierce's suggest that he was not with Sherman's army in 1865.

4656. O'Connor, Richard. AMBROSE BIERCE. Boston: Little, Brown, 1967.

Describing Bierce, a topographical engineer from 1861 to 1865, as "the only writer of note to have served in the Civil War armies," O'Connor argues that war experiences focused Bierce's talents and produced the short stories which along with Grant's MEMOIRS are "the only literary works of classic proportions that came out of the Civil War."

4657. Patten, Irene M. "Civil War as Romance of Noble Warriors and Maidens Chaste." AM HER, 22 [3] [1971]: 48-53.

A study of the Civil War romance novels of George Ward Nichols and John Esten Cooke.

4658. Pickering, Sam. "A Boy's Own War." NEQ, 47 [1975]: 362-367.

Horatio Alger, Charles Fosdick, and William T. Adams, three of the North's most prolific writers for juveniles, produced many novels which "reveal a great deal about New England attitudes toward both the war and children's literature."

4659. Pollard, John A. JOHN GREENLEAF WHITTIER: FRIEND OF MAN. Boston: Houghton Mifflin, 1949.

Chapters 11 and 12 substantially discuss Whittier's anti-slavery attitude and his response to the war in the light of his Quaker heritage. Attention is paid to works in IN TIME OF WAR AND OTHER POEMS, including the famous BARBARA FRIETCHIE.

4660. Quinn, Arthur H. A HISTORY OF THE AMERICAN DRAMA FROM THE CIVIL WAR TO THE PRESENT DAY. New York: Appleton-Century, 1964.

Issued first in 1927, this venerable study surveys plays produced between 1861 and 1865 as well as those written later by dramatists such as Belasco, Gillette, Howard, and Fitch.

4661. Ravitz, Abe C. "Harold Frederic's Venerable Copperhead." NY HIS, 41 [1960]: 35-48.

Frederic's novel THE COPPERHEAD expresses his admiration for the moral courage and political integrity of the governor of New York, Horatio Seymour, who like the main character of the novel remained firm in his Copperhead stance during the war.

4662. Reardon, William R. "Civil War Theater: Formal Organization." CWH, 1 [1955]: 205-227.

The development of a highly commercial theater and changes in casting, production, theater design, and acting style are discussed and occasionally loosely tied to socio-economic factors generated by the Civil War.

4663. Richardson, Mary L. "The Historical Authenticity of John Brown's Raid in Stephen Vincent Benet's 'John Brown's Body.'" W VA HIS, 24 [1963]: 168-175.

No clear conclusion is reached in this point-by-point comparison of Benet's poetic version of Brown's raid with accounts in biographies and histories.

4664. Scholnick, Robert J. "Politics and Poetics: The Reception of Melville's Battle-Pieces and Aspects of the War." A LIT, 49 [1977]: 422-430.

The poor sales of Melville's collection of Civil War poetry can in part be attributed to unfavorable reviews by the Radical Republican press which disliked his political conservatism.

4665. Shain, Charles E. "The English Novelists and the American Civil War." AQ, 14 [1962]: 399-421.

An examination of the pattern of attitudes in the literature of Great Britain during and after the Civil War and the reasons why it took a strong pro-South position.

4666. Small, Miriam R. OLIVER WENDELL HOLMES. New York: Twayne, 1962.

This provides a compact survey of Holmes' Harvard class poems and other writings in which he normally expressed strong Unionist sentiments.

4667. Solomon, Eric. "The Bitterness of Battle: Ambrose Bierce's War Fiction." MIDWEST Q, 5 [1964]: 147-165.

In his TALES OF SOLDIERS Bierce expresses his ironic sense of the futility of combat and with a "compressed force" that has "never been equalled" and foreshadows the modern realistic attitude towards war. One of the most effective analyses of Bierce's Civil War stories.

4668. ———. "Stephen Crane's War Stories." TEXAS STUD LIT LANG, 3 [1961]: 67-80.

This examines Crane's evolving attitude toward war and places his Civil War pieces in the spectrum of his other war fiction.

4669. Steinmetz, Lee. "Shadows Have Darkly Fallen: The Poetic Aftermath of the Civil War." CEN R, 5 [1961]: 85-105.

Sectional poets "found themselves farther apart immediately after Appomattox than before."

4670. Stewart, Randall. "Hawthorne and the Civil War." STUD PHIL, 34 [1937]: 91-106.

His growing belief that the dissolution of the Union was inevitable and his apparent association with the unpopular war views of his friend Franklin Pierce put Hawthorne in an awkward political situation and caused stress which "crippled his creative faculties and hastened his death."

4671. Stone, Albert E., Jr. "Best Novel of the Civil War." AM HER, 13 [3] [1962]: 84-88.

Realistic battle scenes, a concern for complex economic causes, and a de-emphasis on sectionalism made John W. DeForest's MISS RAVENEL'S CONVERSION [1867] a pioneering fictional treatment of the war for which the contemporary reading public was not ready.

4672. Stroud, Parry. STEPHEN VINCENT BENET. New York: Twayne, 1962.

Chapter Two provides a lengthy, solid discussion of Benet's epic poem of the Civil War, JOHN BROWN'S BODY [1928].

4673. Theodore, Terry. "The Civil War on the New York Stage from 1861-1900." LIN HER, 74 [1972]: 34-40.

First of a useful four-part series, this surveys the theatrical treatment of Civil War figures and reports that Grant was portrayed the most extensively and favorably and Lincoln was virtually ignored. [The other articles in the series, listed directly below, have the same general title. Consequently, only the sub-titles are given.]

4674. ———. "Civil War Drama, 1861-1865." LIN HER, 74 [1972]: 203-211.

Second in the series, this examines the popular theater's treatment of major wartime issues [the draft, emancipation, prison camp conditions] and its use of timely character types [the negro, the spy, and the female in war settings]. A gauge of public attitude, the productions tended to reinforce patriotism and either evade or view negatively the question of abolition.

4675. ———. "Civil War Drama, 1865-1877." LIN HER, 75 [1973]: 29-34.

Third in the series, this article focuses on Reconstruction drama, both the pageant type which tended to feature a single battle and the chronicle type which tended to trace the course of the entire war. Attention is paid to the melodramatic elements of the play and the transition from strong Unionist themes to more conciliatory emphasis on individual heroism and the conflict of love and duty.

4676. ———. "Civil War Drama 1878-1900." LIN HER, 75 [1973]: 115-122.

During a late 19th century resurgence of interest in the Civil War in the American theatre, the predominant message was sectional reconciliation and the key strategy, the avoidance of all substantive issues. This is the final article of the series.

4677. Turner, Arlin. NATHANIEL HAWTHORNE. New York: Oxford University Press, 1980.

A chapter entitled "A Divided Nation and Divided Minds" substantially examines Hawthorne's ambivalent stance on the moral, political, and military issues of the war as well as "Chiefly About War Matters," an article he wrote for the ATLANTIC.

4678. Wagenknecht, Edward. WILLIAM DEAN HOWELLS; THE FRIENDLY EYE. New York: Oxford University Press, 1969.

Chapter Four provides a critical examination of Howell's attitudes toward the Civil War as expressed in writings produced both during and after the war.

4679. Welsh, Willard. "The War in Drama." CWH, 2 [1955]: 251-280.

This article provides a helpful survey of Civil War drama through 1955 and, from each of the five chronological categories it establishes, examines representative plays in some detail.

4680. Wertheim, Stanley. "THE RED BADGE OF COURAGE and Personal Narratives of the Civil War." A LIT REAL, 6 [Winter 1973]: 61-65.

Source studies have not pointed out that "literally dozens" of personal narratives published during Crane's formative years most likely provided him with both plot and authentic detail for his novel.

4681. Whitman, Walt. SPECIMEN DAYS. In PROSE WORKS. Volume 1. Floyd Stovall, editor. New York: New York University Press, 1963.

A volume of autobiographical narrative which includes Whitman's impressions of the Civil War. Some accounts record home front responses to major battles like First Bull Run, others Whitman's own experiences as a nurse in hospitals both in Washinton, D.C. and the field. Anecdotes and commentary cover a wide range of subjects and describe wartime conditions and attitudes.

4682. ———. WALT WHITMAN'S CIVIL WAR. Walter Lowenfels, editor. New York: Knopf, 1960.

An extensive compilation of Whitman's newspaper articles, journal entries, letters, and poems. Fourteen categories of material treat a wide-variety of war-related topics such as medical care, Negro army troops, generals and public officials, prison camps, the southern character, and President Lincoln. Evident in these writings is Whitman's concern for the war as it was lived by the common people.

4683. Whitney, Blair. "Lincoln's Life as Dramatic Art." JISHS, 61 [1980]: 335-349.

Dividing Lincoln plays into southern hate literature, early idolatry plays, pageants, and works of enduring value, Blair concludes that no drama has successfully united "the historical Lincoln with the symbolic, mythical Lincoln."

4684. Wilson, Edmund. PATRIOTIC GORE. STUDIES IN THE LITERATURE OF THE AMERICAN CIVIL WAR. New York: Oxford University Press, 1962.

Partially self-psychoanalytical, Wilson's study examines northern and southern literary responses as it speculates on the complex cultural origins of attitudes toward the war and its presumed causes. Central to the argument is the thesis that a genteel, repressive, female-dominated social climate combined with male readers' uninterest in literature to prohibit a healthy and incisive literary treatment of the war. What has instead emerged,

Wilson complains, is a body of literature which has transformed the war into myth and perpetuated sectional biases and preconceptions. The discussion can be sprawling and loose; but this is a crucial thought-provoking resource.

4685. Wilt, Napier. "Ambrose Bierce and the Civil War." A LIT, 1 [1929]: 268-285.

This compares Bierce's autobiographical sketches of his Civil War experiences with the events as described in the Rolls of his regiment, the 9th Indiana.

4686. Woodruff, Stuart C. THE SHORT STORIES OF AMBROSE BIERCE: A STUDY IN POLARITY. Pittsburgh: University of Pittsburg Press, 1964.

Through the portrayal of frustrated heroism and nobility, Bierce's Civil War tales illustrate the author's own inability to reconcile his romantic tendency with his harsh realistic vision.

4687. Zweig, Paul. WALT WHITMAN: THE MAKING OF A POET. New York: Basic Books, 1984.

In this helpful study, Zweig identifies the Civil War as "the great event of Whitman's life" which brought to fulfillment the poet's genius. Ironically, though, while his wartime experiences helped Whitman to live out the values he expressed in his poetry, they also caused the decline of his physical and artistic powers.

B. JOURNALISM

4688. Anderson, David B. "The Odyssey of Petroleum Vesuvius Nasby." OHIO HIS, 74 [1965]: 232-246, 279.

A summary of attitudes expressed by David Ross Locke [Nasby] in his widely-read articles. Much of his anger was directed against pro-southern sympathizers in the North.

4689. Andrews, J. Cutler. THE NORTH REPORTS THE CIVIL WAR. Pittsburgh: University of Pittsburgh Press, 1955.

This work deals primarily with the coverage and reporting of combat operations. An excellent study of the men who wrote the stories and the various problems they encountered. It also lists over 300 reporters and the newspapers for which they worked.

4690. ———. "The Pennsylvania Press During the Civil War." PENN HIS, 9 [1942]: 22-36.

An excellent short survey of Pennsylvania newspapers and the men who edited them during the war.

4691. ———. "The Press Reports the Battle of Gettysburg." PENN HIS, 31 [1964]: 176-198.

Summarizes the reporting of the Battle of Gettysburg by the northern, southern, and English press. Despite the terrain, the wide area of the conflict, and problems with telegraph communication, the battle was well reported.

4692. ———. "Writing History From Civil War Newspapers." W PA HIS MAG, 54 [1971]: 1-14.

Author describes the methods used to reconstruct ideas and attitudes of the era through newspapers.

4693. Austin, James C. PETROLEUM V. NASBY. New York: Twayne, 1965.

Extensive coverage is given to both the subject matter and humor of the Civil War era writings attributed to Petroleum V. Nasby, Locke's fictional character. Special attention is paid to the satire resulting from Nasby's portrayal as an illogical and semi-literate Copperhead.

4694. Beales, Benjamin B. "The SAN JOSE MERCURY and the Civil War." CAL HIS SOC Q, 22 [1943]: 223-234, 355-364.

Discusses the role of the newspaper during the war years and gives some insight into contemporary political activities in California.

4695. Blackman, Robert E. "Noah Brooks: Reporter in the White House." JOUR Q, 32 [1955]: 301-310, 374.

Blackman examines the work of the famous Washington correspondent for the SACRAMENTO UNION during the Civil War.

4696. Brooks, Noah. MR. LINCOLN'S WASHINGTON: SELECTIONS FROM THE WRITINGS OF NOAH BROOKS, CIVIL WAR CORRESPONDENT. New York: Barnes, 1967.

Brooks, who used the pen name "Castine," was a personal friend of President Lincoln. This work contains about 25 per cent of his wartime dispatches to his newspaper in Sacramento.

4697. ———. WASHINGTON IN LINCOLN'S TIME. New York, 1895.

Vivid reminiscences of wartime Washington by the celebrated writer. Brooks provides insights into the Lincoln White House.

4698. Brown, Ernest F. RAYMOND OF THE TIMES. New York: Norton, 1951.

Not only is this a good biography of the first editor of the NEW YORK TIMES, but it ably explores Republican party politics and campaign strategies of the 1850s and 1860s. Published in the centennial year of the newspaper's birth, the book recognizes the contributions of Edward B. Wesley, one of the TIMES' three founders, which have often been overlooked.

4699. Browne, Charles F. ARTEMUS WARD: HIS BOOK. Santa Barbara, California: Wallace Hebbard, 1964.

This reprint of an 1862 volume contains the adventures of the traveling showman, Artemus Ward, the pseudonym for the author.

4700. Bullard, Frederic L. FAMOUS WAR CORRESPONDENTS. Boston, 1914.

The story of some of the famous war correspondents with useful insights into the techniques they employed.

4701. Burnett, Alfred. INCIDENTS OF THE WAR: HUMOROUS, PATHETIC, AND DESCRIPTIVE. Cincinnati, 1863.

Revealing incidents written by a reporter for the CINCINNATI TIMES. The articles are primarily about army life in Kentucky in 1862.

4702. Cadwallader, Sylvanus. THREE YEARS WITH GRANT AS RECALLED BY WAR CORRESPONDENT SYLVANUS CADWALLADER. P. Thomas, editor. New York: Knopf, 1955.

The reissue of an intimate book on Grant written by a war correspondent for the CHICAGO TIMES and the NEW YORK HERALD. Cadwallader was almost an unofficial aide to Grant, sitting in on conferences, running errands, and working endlessly to control the general's liking for liquor. Because of his privileged relationship with Grant, Cadwallader enhanced his own reputation and that of the HERALD as a major source for war news.

4703. Carlson, Oliver. THE MAN WHO MADE NEWS: JAMES GORDON BENNETT. New York: Duell, Sloan, and Pearce, 1942.

A well-written biography of the founder of the NEW YORK HERALD. Bennett was probably one of the most hated, but most widely-read editors of his day. Author captures not only the man, but also the times in which he lived.

4704. Carter, L. Edward. "The Revolution in Journalism During the Civil War." LIN HER, 73 [1971]: 229-241.

The Civil War changed the newspaper business from one where opinions were freely stated to one where there was greater emphasis on the news.

4705. Cary, Edward. ... GEORGE WILLIAM CURTIS. Boston, 1894.

A biography of the famous writer and editor of HARPERS WEEKLY for 30 years, which appeared shortly after his death.

4706. Catlin, George B. "Little Journeys in Journalism: Wilbur F. Storey." MICH HIS, 10 [1926]: 515-533.

Before he became editor of the anti-administration CHICAGO TIMES in June 1861, Storey was editor of the DETROIT FREE PRESS. He was opposed to the administration at the outbreak of war, too, as this article reveals.

4707. Christie, Trevor L. "Generals and the News 'Spy.'" SAT R, [July 8, 1967]: 60-61, 65.

The story of the arrest and court-martial of Thomas W. Knox, reporter for the NEW YORK HERALD by General Sherman in January 1863 near Memphis. Knox was cleared of being a spy, but was banished from the front lines. He was the only correspondent ever to experience an army court-martial.

4708. Chu, James C.Y. "Horace White: His Association with Abraham Lincoln, 1854-1860." JOUR Q, 49 [1972]: 51-60.

Horace White, a young Illinois reporter who later became a famous editor, observed Lincoln closely and wrote extensively about his speeches and activities in the years before he became president.

4709. Coffin, Charles C. THE BOYS OF '61: OR, FOUR YEARS OF FIGHTING .... Boston, 1896.

Coffin was one of the few correspondents who covered the entire war, from First Bull Run to the fall of Richmond.

4710. Congdon, Charl s T. TRIBUNE E SAYS: LEADING ARTICLES CONTRIBUTED TO THE NEW YORK TRIBUNE FROM 1857 TO 1863. New York, 1869.

A collection of the best-known editorials and articles written by the "right hand man" of the editor of the TRIBUNE, Horace Greeley.

4711. Cornell, William M. THE LIFE AND PUBLIC CAREER OF HON. HORACE GREELEY. Boston, 1872.

A campaign biography. Greeley was a candidate for the presidency on the Liberal Republican party ticket in 1872. He died three weeks after his defeat.

4712. Cortissoz, Royal. THE LIFE OF WHITELAW REID. 2 v. New York: Scribners, 1921.

An important study of the man who succeeded Greeley as editor of the TRIBUNE and whose journalistic and editorial career spanned nearly half a century. Reid was a young correspondent for the CINCINNATI GAZETTE during the Civil War and covered several major battles.

4713. Croffut, William A. AN AMERICAN PROCESSION.... Boston: Little, Brown, 1931.

"A personal chronicle of famous men" by a reporter for the NEW YORK HERALD, who describes many important Union figures and military actions.

4714. Crounse, Lorenzo L. "The Army Correspondent." HARP MON, 27 [1863]: 627-633.

An excellent report of a war correspondent's personal experiences in covering the Army of the Potomac in the first two years of the war. A war correspondent shares all the dangers, hardships, and excitement of troops in the line.

4715. Crozier, Emmet. YANKEE REPORTERS, 1861-1865. New York: Oxford University Press, 1956.

A well-written, vivid narrative based largely on the files of leading northern newspapers and published accounts by well-known reporters. The book captures the excitement and adventure which correspondents experienced in their quest for the news.

4716. Curl, Donald W., editor. "Sidelights: A Report from Baltimore." MD HIS MAG, 64 [1969]: 280-287.

Halstead, young Republican editor of the CINCINNATI COMMERCIAL, sent dispatches from Baltimore relating the conditions of the Ohio Volunteers who were stationed there. He voiced concern for the city which was torn by conflict.

4717. Curry, Roy W. "The Newspaper Press and the Civil War in West Virginia." W VA HIS, 6 [1945]: 226-264.

The war in West Virginia [including civilian and military atrocities] as seen in the pages of the Wheeling DAILY INTELLIGENCER, NEW YORK HERALD, and the CINCINNATI COMMERCIAL.

4718. Dana, Charles A. RECOLLECTIONS OF THE CIVIL WAR.... New York, 1898.

A newspaperman and government official, Dana provides much information on Washington officials. His observations from the field are acute and perceptive.

4719. EVENING STAR, Washington D.C. MIRROR OF WAR: THE WASHINGTON STAR REPORTS THE CIVIL WAR. John W. Stepp and I. William Hill, editors and compilers. Englewood Cliffs, New Jersey: Prentice-Hall, 1961.

A well-edited, informative group of articles from the paper's Civil War editions.

4720. Everett, Edward G. "Pennsylvania Newspapers and Public Opinion 1861-1862." W PA HIS MAG, 44 [1961]: 1-11.

During the first year of the war the newspapers proved active in uniting the people behind the Union. As the war developed, Democratic papers had a difficult time even though they supported the war effort.

4721. Fahrney, Ralph R. HORACE GREELEY AND THE TRIBUNE IN THE CIVIL WAR. Cedar Rapids, Iowa: Torch, 1936. Reprint 1970.

A sympathetic study of "one of the most mystifying personalities in the history of journalism and politics." The TRIBUNE was a major factor in the lives of the people from 1860-1865.

It was said there were "three readers for every subscriber" and that the paper "exerted a greater influence on public opinion than any other paper in America during the Civil War years."

4722. Fiske, Stephen R. "Gentlemen of the Press." HARP MON, 26 [February 1863]: 361-367.

A description of the organization of newspaper staffs both in the United States and Europe. A brief report on the performance of journalists covering the Civil War may be found at the end of the article.

4723. Freidel, Frank. "The Loyal Publication Society: A Pro-Union Propaganda Agency." MVHR, 26 [1939/1940]: 359-376.

A description of the organization and work of The Loyal Publication Society, a privately-operated pro-Union propaganda group. In its three year existence, 1863-1866, it published hundreds of thousands of copies of some 90 pamphlets which promoted the northern cause.

4724. ———, editor. UNION PAMPHLETS OF THE CIVIL WAR. 2 v. Cambridge, Massachusetts: Harvard University Press, 1967.

Fifty-two selected, hard-to-find letters, articles, and pamphlets written by distinguished public and private persons. A useful explanatory note precedes each document. An excellent collection.

4725. Gardner, Joseph L. "'Bull Run' Russell." AM HER, 13 [4] [1962]: 59-61, 78-83.

An account of William Howard Russell's coverage of the First Bull Run battle.

4726. Geary, James W. "Examining Societal Attitudes Through Satire: Petroleum Vesuvius Nasby Fights the Civil War." ILL Q, 44 [1982]: 29-37.

Examines selected letters of Nasby. The author argues that scholars should use satirically-based source material for a better understanding of the attitudes of the Civil War generation.

4727. George, Joseph, Jr. "Philadelphia's CATHOLIC HERALD: The Civil War Years." PA MHB, 103 [1979]: 196-221.

The CATHOLIC HERALD AND VISITOR was suspicious of Republicans and unsympathetic to blacks. It did, however, support the war and tried to avoid excessive partisanship.

4728. Glenn, William. BETWEEN NORTH AND SOUTH: A MARYLAND JOURNALIST VIEWS THE CIVIL WAR: THE NARRATIVE OF WILLIAM WILKINS GLENN. B. Ellen Marks and Mark N. Schatz, editors. Rutherford, New Jersey: Fairleigh Dickinson University Press, 1976.

Underscores the blind provincialism of so many pro-southern

sympathizers in the North and in the Border states, as well as giving insights into Maryland's war-time politics. Glenn's biased views left him open to charges of Copperheadism.

4729. Godkin, Edwin L. LIFE AND LETTERS OF EDWIN LAWRENCE GODKIN. 2 v. Rollo Ogden, editor. New York, 1900. Reprint 1907.

Irish born Godkin came to this country in 1856 and became the first editor of the weekly NATION in 1865. His Civil War reporting and activities do not receive much attention in this biography.

4730. Goldsmith, Adolph O. "Reporting the Civil War: Union Army Press Relations." JOUR Q, 33 [1956]: 478-487.

Recounts the problems arising from "modern" reporting, touches on attempts at government censorship, and discusses the relations between reporters and commanding generals.

4731. Greeley, Horace. RECOLLECTIONS OF A BUSY LIFE. New York, 1868.

Founder of the NEW YORK TRIBUNE, Greeley was one of the founders of the Republican party and a radical antislavery man. This book is based on a series of articles which first appeared in his newspaper.

4732. Griffis, William E. CHARLES CARLETON COFFIN, WAR CORRESPONDENT, TRAVELLER, AUTHOR, AND STATESMAN. Boston, 1898.

A laudatory biography of the celebrated war correspondent who reported the war for four years.

4733. Guback, Thomas H. "General Sherman's War on the Press." JOUR Q, 36 [1959]: 171-176.

Sherman distrusted reporters and ordered them to stay away during the Vicksburg campaign. When Thomas Knox disobeyed the order and then wrote an article blaming Sherman for the Vicksburg failure, the general had him court-martialed.

4734. Hale, William H. HORACE GREELEY, VOICE OF THE PEOPLE. New York: Harper, 1950.

A good, readable biography of the eccentric editor of the NEW YORK TRIBUNE, although the reader may have difficulty detecting that Greeley was one of the greatest, if not the greatest, of all American newspaper editors.

4735. Harper, Robert S. LINCOLN AND THE PRESS. New York: McGraw-Hill, 1951.

Unstinting research marks this study of Lincoln's relationship with the press from 1836 onward, although major emphasis is on the war years. His most troubling dilemma was how to deal with the bitterly oppositionist newspapers. Against his will, he opted for suppression of those newspapers which he felt were endangering the war effort.

4736. ———. "The Ohio Press in the Civil War." CWH, 3 [1957]: 221-252.

Written by the staff executive of Ohio's Civil War Centennial Commission, this article presents good coverage of the subject. The article was reprinted as a separate pamphlet [Publication Number 3] in a series of 13 publications about Ohio in the Civil War by the state centennial commission.

4737. Harrison, John M. THE MAN WHO MADE NASBY, DAVID ROSS LOCKE. Chapel Hill: University of North Carolina Press, 1969.

Although the life of the creator of Petroleum Nasby is an interesting one, Nasby emerges much more clearly in this study than does Locke. The book provides a substantial study of the origins of Locke's famous fictional character as well as the politics, subject matter, style of humor, and popularity of the Petroleum V. Nasby letters.

4738. Hindes, Ruthanna. GEORGE ALFRED TOWNSEND, ONE OF DELAWARE'S OUTSTANDING WRITERS. Wilmington, Delaware: Hambleton, 1946.

The career of a famous war correspondent is detailed in this 72-page booklet.

4739. Holzer, Harold. "Lincoln and the Printmakers." JISHS, 68 [1975]: 74-84.

A look at the circumstances under which the numerous wartime Lincoln portraits were produced.

4740. Hooper, Osman C. THE CRISIS AND THE MAN, AN EPISODE IN CIVIL WAR JOURNALISM. Columbus: Ohio State University Press, 1929.

This brief volume introduces the reader to Samuel Medary, editor of the Columbus CRISIS, the celebrated Copperhead newspaper.

4741. Horner, Harlan H. LINCOLN AND GREELEY. Urbana: University of Illinois Press, 1953.

A study of the relationship between Lincoln and Greeley, this book tends to be wordy and contains some errors. The interest of the author in his subject is apparent.

4742. Keller, Morton. THE ART AND POLITICS OF THOMAS NAST. New York: Oxford University Press, 1968.

A collection of over 240 cartoons reflecting Nast's outstanding abilities as a political cartoonist. The author provides informative commentary for each cartoon. After serving abroad as artist for the ILLUSTRATED LONDON NEWS, he returned to the United States in 1861 and became staff artist for HARPERS WEEKLY.

4743. Knox, Thomas W. CAMPFIRE AND COTTON-FIELD: SOUTHERN ADVENTURE IN TIME OF WAR: LIFE WITH THE UNION ARMIES, AND RESIDENCE ON A LOUISIANA PLANTATION. New York, 1865. Reprint 1969.

An excellent account and very readable book by a HERALD correspondent. Deals with life in the Mississippi theater. Knox was one of the rare, if not the only, journalists court-martialed by the army. General Sherman did the court-martialing.

4744. Langley, Peter III. "Pessimism-Optimism of Civil War Military News: June 1863-March 1865." JOUR Q, 49 [1972]: 74-78.

The trends of "pessimism-optimism" as expressed in the NEW YORK TIMES and the RICHMOND DISPATCH during the war are examined.

4745. Linn, William A. HORACE GREELEY, FOUNDER AND EDITOR OF THE NEW YORK TRIBUNE. New York, 1903.

A solid biography but it has very limited coverage of Greeley's Civil War activities.

4746. Locke, David R. CIVIL WAR LETTERS OF PETROLEUM V. NASBY. Harvey S. Ford, compiler. Columbus: Ohio State University Press, 1962.

A series of 17 "so-called letters" which prove very entertaining. Nasby was Lincoln's favorite humorist. Thirty-four pages only.

4747. ———. THE STRUGGLES OF PETROLEUM V. NASBY. Joseph Jones and Gunther Barth, editors. Boston: Beacon, 1963.

A well-selected collection of some of the best of Nasby's entertaining letters. The volume is enhanced by the illustrations of the cartoonist, Thomas Nast. The work was originally published in 1872.

4748. Marszalek, John F., Jr. "The Knox Court-Martial: W.T. Sherman Puts the Press on Trial [1963]." MIL LAW R, 59 [1973]: 197-214.

Reporter Thomas Knox of the NEW YORK HERALD was the only newspaperman of record to be court-martialed in American history. General Sherman charged Knox with being a spy and giving intelligence to the enemy. The court acquitted Knox of spying, but ordered his banishment from the area.

4749. ———. SHERMAN'S OTHER WAR: THE GENERAL AND THE CIVIL WAR PRESS. Memphis: Memphis State University Press, 1981.

Sherman blamed the press for his early life failure. The press, in turn, charged that Sherman while in command in Kentucky was insane. Author examines the theory and convicts the press of exaggeration. Sherman's anti-press views were striking, but he believed that any criticism of the war effort gave "aid and comfort" to the enemy.

4750. ———. "William T. Sherman and The Verbal Battle of Shiloh." NW OHIO Q, 4 [1970]: 78-85.

An account of the controversial letters and articles which appeared in Ohio newspapers after Shiloh.

4751. Mathews, Joseph J. REPORTING THE WARS. Minneapolis: University of Minnesota Press, 1957.

Views the total picture of wartime reporting--official sources, censorship, etc. Also presents an analysis of the beginning and "the evolution and the present status of war news."

4752. Matthews, Sidney T. "Control of the Baltimore Press During the Civil War." MD HIS MAG, 36 [1941]: 150-170.

Because of strong secessionist opinion in Maryland, nine Baltimore newspapers were suppressed during the course of the war, either temporarily or permanently. Three loyal newspapers continued to be published without interference.

4753. Milne, Gordon. GEORGE WILLIAM CURTIS AND THE GENTEEL TRADITION. Bloomington: Indiana University Press, 1956.

Curtis was the editor of HARPERS and an active antislavery reformer. A good biography.

4754. Monaghan, Jay. THE MAN WHO ELECTED LINCOLN. Indianapolis: Bobbs-Merrill, 1956.

A very interesting and at times exciting study of Dr. Charles Henry Ray, editor of the pro-Lincoln CHICAGO TRIBUNE, 1855-1863. While Ray hardly "elected" Lincoln, he played an important behind-the-scenes role in assisting Lincoln's rise in the late 1850s and at the 1860 convention.

4755. Mott, Frank L. AMERICAN JOURNALISM. New York: Macmillan, 1962.

Though somewhat old, this work remains the best survey of the American press. This is the third and final edition.

4756. Page, Charles A. LETTERS OF A WAR CORRESPONDENT." James R. Gilmore, editor. Boston, 1899.

This special correspondent for the NEW YORK TRIBUNE offers a few tantalizing glimpses of life in army camps.

4757. Paine, Albert B. TH. NAST: HIS PERIOD AND HIS PICTURES. New York, 1904.

A good, balanced account of the life of the "father of the American cartoon," 1860-1896. A pictorial history of the day through hundreds of Nast's drawings, as well.

4758. Parton, James. THE LIFE OF HORACE GREELEY, EDITOR OF "THE NEW YORK TRIBUNE," FROM HIS BIRTH TO THE PRESENT TIME. Boston, 1872.

The author revised and enlarged his original biography of Greeley for this presidential election year edition.

4759. Peters, E.T. "Quilldriving." CWTI, 18 [3] [1979]: 38-39.

Cites the complaints made by generals against the press and describes the conditions under which the newspapermen worked.

4760. Poore, Benjamin P. PERLEY'S REMINISCENCES OF SIXTY YEARS IN THE NATIONAL METROPOLIS.... 2 v. New York, 1886.

An interesting commentary on public men by a well-known writer of the day. The second volume deals with the Civil War.

4761. Pullen, John J. "Artemus Ward: The Man Who Made Lincoln Laugh." SAT R, [February 7, 1976]: 19-24.

Charles Brown, associate editor of the CLEVELAND PLAIN DEALER, prepared a letter from a fictitious Artemus Ward just to fill up his column and his reputation was made. His Artemus Ward stories provided humorous relief for Lincoln throughout the war. Brown died in 1867 at the age of 33.

4762. Randall, J.G. "The Newspaper Problem ... During the Civil War." AHR, 23 [1918]: 303-323.

Randall analyzes the problems which an unfettered newspaper press caused the government during the war. Although there was some censorship, newspapers generally printed just about what they wished. The most serious problem arose over the publication of military information helpful to the enemy.

4763. Ransome, Jack C. "David Ross Locke: Civil War Propagandist." NW OHIO Q, 20 [1948]: 4-19.

Journalist Locke's humorous creation, Petroleum V. Nasby, satirized Copperheads and in doing so provided strong support for the Union cause and the Republican administration as well as personal comfort to Lincoln.

4764. Reed, John Q. "Civil War Humor: Artemus Ward." CWH, [2] [1956]: 87-101.

A study of Ward's wartime humor.

4765. Reed, Ronald F. "Newspaper Responses to the Gettysburg Address." Q J SPEECH, 53 [1967]: 50-60.

An account of some 260 newspapers' reactions to the speeches of Edward Everett and Abraham Lincoln at Gettysburg. The author concludes that "newspaper reactions to Gettysburg oratory varied markedly."

4766. Reid, Whitelaw. A RADICAL VIEW: THE "AGATE" DISPATCHES OF WHITELAW REID, 1861-1865. 2 v. James G. Smart, editor. Memphis: Memphis State University Press, 1976.

These two volumes, based on the Reid papers in the Library of Congress and issues of the CINCINNATI GAZETTE, contain about ten per cent of the total "Agate" dispatches. The dispatches represent a penetrating, critical analysis of the Union war effort by a Union supporter.

4767. Richmond, Robert W. Humorist on Tour: Artemus Ward in Mid-America, 1864." KAN HIS Q, 33 [1967]: 470-480.

An account of Brown"s "Ward" lectures as he toured the West from October 1863 to March 1864.

4768. Russell, William H. MY DIARY NORTH AND SOUTH. 2 v. London, 1863.

The first nine months of the war are dealt with in this book by the famous English reporter. Fletcher Pratt edited a new, shortened edition of the work in 1954.

4769. Samuels, Ernest. THE YOUNG HENRY ADAMS. Cambridge: Harvard University Press, 1948.

Covered here are Adams' experiences as Washington correspondent for the BOSTON ADVERTISER just prior to the war and as London correspondent for the NEW YORK TIMES during the war.

4770. Saum, Lewis O. "Colonel Custer's Copperhead: The 'Mysterious' Mark Kellogg." MON, 28 [1978]: 12-25.

Anti-Civil War Unionist, anti-Reconstruction Democrat, Copperhead, journalist--these terms describe Mark Kellogg, who went with Custer and died with him at the Little Big Horn massacre.

4771. Seitz, Don C. HORACE GREELEY, FOUNDER OF THE NEW YORK TRIBUNE. Indianapolis: Bobbs-Merrill, 1926.

A popular, well-written biography of the famous editor from his early adventures in journalism in the 1830s until his unsuccessful bid for the presidency and death in 1872.

4772. Shankman, Arnold. "Converse, THE CHRISTIAN OBSERVER and Civil War Censorship." J PRES HIS, 52 [1974]: 227-244.

THE CHRISTIAN OBSERVER was the only newspaper published both in the North and South.

4773. ———. "Freedom of the Press During the Civil War: The Case of Albert D. Boileau." PENN HIS, 42 [1975]: 305-315.

Few arbitrary arrests caused as great a stir as the jailing of Boileau, editor of the PHILADELPHIA EVENING JOURNAL in June 1863. Instead of silencing the Pennsylvania Democrats, this episode made them more vocal than ever.

4774. Smith, George W. "Broadsides for Freedom: Civil War Propaganda in New England." NEQ, 21 [1948]: 291-312.

An account of the work of the New England Loyal Publication Society. Under the leadership of Charles Eliot Norton, the society issued thousands of broadsides supporting and promoting the Union cause.

4775. Starr, Louis M. BOHEMIAN BRIGADE: CIVIL WAR NEWSMEN IN ACTION. New York: Knopf, 1954.

Correspondents in the field and managing editors are the focus of this well-written survey of northern wartime journalism. Use of the papers of Sydney Howard Gay, managing editor of the NEW YORK TRIBUNE, enhances the work. The volume was reissued in 1962 under a new title, REPORTING THE CIVIL WAR.

4776. St. Hill, Thomas N. "The Life and Death of Thomas Nast." AM HER, 22 [6] [1971]: 81-96.

This article contains excerpts from a biographical memoir by the grandson of the noted political cartoonist.

4777. Stoddard, Henry L. HORACE GREELEY, PRINTER, EDITOR, CRUSADER. New York: Putnam, 1946.

A sympathetic, though not definitive, study of the founder of the TRIBUNE, in which the author uses "guarded interpretations."

4778. Swett, Herbert E. "AP Coverage of the Lincoln Assassination." JOUR Q, 47 [1970]: 157-159.

Author contends that the Associated Press "deserves most of the credit" for accurately circulating news about the murder of the president at the time it occurred.

4779. Tarbell, Ida M. A REPORTER FOR LINCOLN: THE STORY OF HENRY E. WING. New York: Macmillan, 1927.

A readable volume describing the war experiences of Henry E. Wing, young reporter for the NEW YORK TRIBUNE in 1864-1865. The author interviewed Wing and drew on his own writings to paint a vivid picture of a man who saw much and knew Lincoln well.

4780. Taylor, John. "You Are ... The Enemy of Our Set." CWTI, 18 [3] [1979]: 28-37.

Describes the anti-press feelings of federal generals Meade and Sherman, as well as other officers.

4781. Temple, Wayne C. and Justin G. Turner. "Lincoln's 'Castine': Noah Brooks." LIN HER, 72 [1970]: 113-124, 148-189; 73 [1971]: 27-45, 78-117, 163-180, 205-228; 74 [1972]: 3-28; 92-106, 143-168, 214-216.

A biography of the noted journalist, Noah Brooks, an intimate friend of the president. It includes a useful bibliography of Brooks' writings.

4782. Thompson, William F. THE IMAGE OF WAR: THE PICTORIAL REPORTING OF THE AMERICAN CIVIL WAR. New York: Yoseloff, 1960.

Work details the propaganda use of sketches as well as pictorial reporting. Not a picture book.

4783. ———. "Pictorial Propaganda and the Civil War." WIS MAG HIS, 46 [1962/1963]: 21-31.

Efforts to gain and preserve support in the North for the war led to the use of highly exaggerated cartoons showing atrocities committed by the Confederates.

4784. Townsend, George A. RUSTICS IN REBELLION: A YANKEE REPORTER ON THE ROAD TO RICHMOND, 1861-1865. Chapel Hill: University of North Carolina Press, 1950.

First published in 1866 under the title CAMPAIGNS OF A NON-COMBATANT, RUSTICS IN REBELLION is an excellent work by a young war correspondent. Townsend immersed himself in front line action and wrote with a balance and maturity which belied his 22 years. However, most of the fighting he witnessed occurred in the first year of the war.

4785. Trietsch, James A. THE PRINTER AND THE PRINCE: A STUDY OF THE INFLUENCE OF HORACE GREELEY UPON ABRAHAM LINCOLN AS CANDIDATE AND PRESIDENT. New York: Exposition, 1955.

In an exhaustive study of secondary materials, the author--who was blind from the age of six--has written a useful analysis of the relationship between the president and the country's most influential editor. But despite his continuous efforts, Greeley had little impact on shaping the administration's policies.

4786. Turner, John J. and Michael D'Innocenzo. "The President and the Press: Lincoln, James Gordon Bennett and the Election of 1864." LIN HER, 76 [1974]: 63-69.

The editor of the NEW YORK HERALD, normally hostile to the administration, supposedly moderated his criticism during the 1864 campaign in exchange for the offer of the ambassadorship to France. Even if true, Bennett did little to help Lincoln win votes in New York City.

4787. Van Deusen, Glyndon G. HORACE GREELEY, NINETEENTH-CENTURY CRUSADER. Philadelphia: University of Pennsylvania Press, 1953.

A good, detailed account of Greeley the crusader for many causes. His strengths and weaknesses are there for all to see, although the Greeley who emerges is still the same old Greeley. However, not as much as might be expected can be found on Greeley the editor.

4788. Villard, Henry. MEMOIRS OF HENRY VILLARD.... Boston, 1904.

The recollections of a very observant war correspondent.

4789. Vinson, J. Chal. THOMAS NAST: POLITICAL CARTOONIST. Athens: University of Georgia Press, 1967.

Author contends that Nast, who gained fame for the first time as propagandist for the Union, was "sui generis" as a political cartoonist. Lincoln considered Nast the Union's best recruiting sergeant. 154 cartoons accompany the text.

4790. Virden, John M. "[Civil War] Correspondents Cover the Battle." ARMY INFO DIG, 16 [8] [1961]: 84-89.

Although there was no press censorship during the war, relations between reporters and field commanders were hardly happy ones. Overall, however, the wartime media arrangements worked out surprisingly well.

4791. Wall, Joseph F. HENRY WATTERSON, RECONSTRUCTED REBEL. New York: Oxford University Press, 1956.

A very good, readable biography of the famous Louisville editor.

4792. Walsh, Justin E. TO PRINT THE NEWS AND RAISE HELL: A BIOGRAPHY OF WILBUR F. STOREY. Chapel Hill: University of North Carolina Press, 1968.

A well-written, readable biography of one of the most famous Copperhead editors of the war years. However, there is fairly little in the book on the crusade of Storey and his CHICAGO TIMES against the Lincoln administration. The work is geared more to journalism history than Civil War history.

4793. Watterson, Henry. "MARSE HENRY"; AN AUTOBIOGRAPHY. New York: George H. Doran, 1919.

In his autobiography, Watterson spends little time or effort on his wartime career.

4794. Westwood, Howard C. "A Scoop for the TRIBUNE." CWTI, 16 [6] [1977]: 32-38.

Discusses the young NEW YORK TRIBUNE reporter, Henry E. Wing, who brought back the first news of the Battle of the Wilderness.

4795. Weisberger, Bernard A. "McClellan and the Press." S ATL Q, 51 [1952]: 383-392.

McClellan, unlike most northern generals, had good personal relations with reporters, and they were sorry to see him go in November 1862. "Little Mac" actually leaked highly classified information to the NEW YORK HERALD, which he refused to give to either Lincoln or Congress.

4796. ———. REPORTERS FOR THE UNION. Boston: Little, Brown, 1953.

A useful, analytical study of the newspaper profession. The author, one of the foremost students of Civil War journalism, develops the theory that reporters became professionals in the 1850s and 1860s, particularly during the war.

4797. ———. "Reporters for the Union." S ATL Q, 76 [1977]: 396-408.

The war made newspaper reporters a powerful force in the land, combining the partisanship of American politics with the high idealism of American reform movements.

4798. Wiley, Bell I. "Soldier Newspapers of the Civil War." CWTI, 16 [4] [1977]: 20-29.

Informal soldier newspapers dealing primarily with camp life are analyzed here. These papers bolstered morale on both sides.

4799. Wilkie, Franc B. PEN AND POWDER. Boston, 1888.

This book contains the wartime observations of reporter Fran Wilkie, who covered the action from Wilson's Creek to Vicksburg.

4800. Wilson, James H. THE LIFE OF CHARLES A. DANA. New York, 1907.

A sympathetic, though good biography of a famous editor, based largely on family papers and documents.

4801. Young, John R. MEN AND MEMORIES: PERSONAL REMINISCENCES. 2 v. May D. Russell Young, editor. New York, 1901.

Young, who later became a very famous newspaperman, served as a wartime reporter. He also founded the Union League of Philadelphia.

IX

THE ARTS

A. PICTORIAL

4802. AMERICAN CIVIL WAR BOOK AND GRANT ALBUM.... Boston, 1894.

"A portfolio of half-tone reproductions" of Grant and events in which he participated, "designed to perpetuate the memory of General Ulysses S. Grant."

4803. AMERICAN HERITAGE CENTURY COLLECTION OF CIVIL WAR ART. S.W. Sears, editor. New York: American Heritage, 1974.

Over 300 sketches and water colors commissioned by the editors of CENTURY magazine after the war. Originally published in 1888 in four volumes, the work contains the contributions of over 50 artists. Beautiful reproductions of these originals are to be found in this new one volume edition.

4804. AMERICAN HERITAGE PICTURE HISTORY OF THE CIVIL WAR. Richard M. Ketchum, editor. New York: American Heritage, 1960.

A large, beautiful volume of 836 illustrations compiled in classic AMERICAN HERITAGE style. Works of all the great photographers and artists will be found here. Military scenes predominate, but the home front is not neglected. A wonderful Bruce Catton narrative brings the illustrative matter to life.

4805. Angle, Paul M. A PICTORIAL HISTORY OF THE CIVIL WAR YEARS. Garden City, New York: Doubleday, 1967.

Contains many sketches and photographs, several never before published, accompanied by a well-written summary of military events.

4806. Ballard, Michael H. "Sculptor for the Union." A HIS ILL, 10 [2] [1975]: 22-30.

John Rogers was the "sculptor for the Union." Although only a minority of his subjects were "war-oriented," they proved to be most popular during the war and again after 1870.

4807. Barnard, George N. PHOTOGRAPHIC VIEWS OF SHERMAN'S CAMPAIGN. Mineola, New York: Dover, 1984.

This reprint of the 1866 edition, contains 61 photographs by the official photographer of the Military Division of the Mississippi. Taken in the field, these photographs provide a vivid record of Sherman's operations.

4808. Blay, John S. THE CIVIL WAR, A PICTORIAL PROFILE. New York: Crowell, 1958.

A collection of 365 illustrations from LESLIE'S and HARPER'S weekly newsmagazines.

4809. Cohen, Stan. THE CIVIL WAR IN WEST VIRGINIA: A PICTORIAL HISTORY. Charleston, West Virginia: Pictorial Histories, 1984.

A lavishly illustrated, oversized picture book.

4810. Commager, Henry S., editor. ILLUSTRATED HISTORY OF THE CIVIL WAR. New York: Simon and Schuster, 1984.

A large pictorial history with beautiful colored illustrations.

4811. Cooney, Charles F. "War Letters From an Artist." CWTI, 14 [2] [1975]: 34-40.

Charles W. Reed, a gifted young man who enlisted with the 9th Massachusetts Light Artillery in August 1862, illustrated his letters home. After the war he became a celebrated artist who made a career out of a camp pastime. Reed also illustrated his diary and kept several sketchbooks. This article includes 12 of his drawings and examples from his letters.

4812. Dammann, Gordon. PICTORIAL ENCYCLOPEDIA OF THE CIVIL WAR. Missoula, Montana: Pictorial Histories, 1983.

Excellent illustrations of medical instruments and equipment.

4813. Dannett, Sylvia G.L. "Artist in Arms During the Civil War." LIN HER, 68 [1966]: 186-189.

Describes the war activities of several painters and sculptors.

4814. Donald, David, editor. DIVIDED WE FOUGHT: A PICTORIAL HISTORY OF THE WAR, 1861-1865. Hirst D. Milhollen and Milton Kaplan, picture editors. New York: Macmillan, 1952.

An excellent volume of illustrations drawn largely from THE PHOTOGRAPHIC HISTORY OF THE CIVIL WAR, but including many new photographs and outstanding drawings by famous Civil War artists. The accompanying text is well-meshed with the pictorial matter.

4815. Eaton, Edward B. ORIGINAL PHOTOGRAPHS TAKEN ON THE BATTLEFIELDS DURING THE CIVIL WAR OF THE UNITED STATES.... Hartford, 1907.

Book includes photographs by Mathew Brady and Alexander Gardner from the collection of Edward B. Eaton.

4816. Egan, Joseph B. and Arthur W. Desmond, editors. THE CIVIL WAR, ITS PHOTOGRAPHIC HISTORY.... 2 v. Wellesley Hills, Massachusetts: Character Building Publications, 1941.

A collection of photographs taken in the field by Brady and others.

4817. Elson, Henry W. THE CIVIL WAR THROUGH THE CAMERA.... New York, 1912.

Brady photographs and 16 paintings feature this excellent early picture book, which was originally published in 16 parts.

4818. ———, editor. DECISIVE BATTLES. New York, 1911.

A good collection of photographs taken on the battlefield by Mathew Brady, Timothy O'Sullivan, Alexander Gardner, and others. Focus is on the later phases of the war.

4819. "Faces North and South: A Civil War Portrait Gallery." A HIS ILL, 9 [9] [1975]: 39-41.

A collection of photographs of Civil War soldiers.

4820. Forbes, Edwin. "As An Artist Saw Gettysburg." J.E.K. Ahrens, editor. CWTI, 8 [6] [1967]: 28-37.

One of the few glimpses of combat drawn by a professional artist. Forbes sketched many major battle scenes from 1862 to 1864.

4821. ———. A CIVIL WAR ARTIST AT THE FRONT.... William F. Dawson, editor. New York: Oxford University Press, 1957.

Artist Forbes captures the day-to-day life of the Union soldier. The work contains over 40 of his illustrations.

4822. ———. LIFE STUDIES OF THE GREAT ARMY. San Francisco: Dunderave, 1975.

In this reprint of an 1876 volume, there are 40 of Forbes' best etchings of soldier life. A descriptive essay explains each etching.

4823. ———. THIRTY YEARS AFTER. 2 v. New York, 1890.

Late in life Forbes gathered together over 300 of his etchings depicting soldier life in the field.

4824. FRANK LESLIE'S ILLUSTRATED HISTORY OF THE CIVIL WAR. Louis S. Moat, editor. New York, 1895.

A large collection of sketches from LESLIE'S WEEKLY is included in this volume. The text is "a concise history ... being official data secured from the war records."

4825. FRANK LESLIE'S PICTORIAL HISTORY OF THE AMERICAN CIVIL WAR. Ephraim G. Squier, editor. 2 v. New York, 1861-1862.

This is the earliest pictorial history of the war.

4826. FRANK LESLIE'S SCENES AND PORTRAITS OF THE CIVIL WAR.... New York, 1894.

Contains works of such artists as Becker, Crane, and Beard. Twenty-six of the 30 "parts" of this volume are devoted to illustrations, the other four parts are text.

4827. Frassanito, William A. ANTIETAM: THE PHOTOGRAPHIC LEGACY OF AMERICA'S BLOODIEST DAY. New York: Scribners, 1978.

A recreation of the most savage day of the war through the photographs of the best cameramen of that time. The author successfully employs the technique used in his earlier work on Gettysburg. [See next entry]

4828. ———. GETTYSBURG: A JOURNEY IN TIME. New York: Scribners, 1975.

An exhaustive compilation of Gettysburg photographs, carefully arranged to give an appearance of the progress of the battle. A number of pictures, formerly incorrectly identified, are now properly described. Modern photographs taken from the same locations as those taken during the battle give the tourist a sense of proximity to the actual events.

4829. ———. "The Photographers of Antietam." CWTI, 17 [5] [1978]: 7-20.

A discussion of the photography of Alexander Gardner and J. Gibson at the battle of Antietam.

4830. Frost, Lawrence A. THE PHIL SHERIDAN ALBUM. Seattle: Superior Publishing, 1968.

A good volume of photographs and drawings, many of them rarely seen, focused on the career of General Sheridan, in war and peace. The accompanying text does not measure up to the illustrations.

4831. ———. U.S. GRANT ALBUM: A PICTORIAL BIOGRAPHY OF ULYSSES S. GRANT FROM LEATHER CLERK TO THE WHITE HOUSE. Seattle: Superior Publishing, 1966.

A good and entertaining picture book of Grant. The photographs are clear and carefully placed. However, the text suffers by comparison.

4832. Gardner, Alexander. GARDNER'S PHOTOGRAPHIC SKETCH BOOK OF THE WAR. Mineola, New York: Dover, 1959.

A one volume reprint of a two volume 1865 publication. The text as well as the photographs, by Gardner and others, make this a work of considerable interest. The reprint is not as good as the original.

4833. Grossman, Julian. ECHO OF A DISTANT DRUM: WINSLOW HOMER AND THE CIVIL WAR. New York: Harry N. Abrams, 1974.

A large collection of Homer's Civil War drawings and paintings, arranged chronologically. Brief notes are included.

4834. Guernsey, Alfred H. and Henry M. Alden. HARPER'S PICTORIAL HISTORY OF THE GREAT REBELLION. 2 v. New York, 1866-1868.

Volume One covers the war to the close of the Peninsular Campaign. Volume Two closes with Reconstruction.

4835. Horan, James D. MATHEW BRADY, HISTORIAN WITH A CAMERA. New York: Crown, 1955.

A sound, readable biography of the foremost early photographer. Largely based on Brady's pictures, some of which were not before available, the author does a good job in view of the paucity of documentary data.

4836. ———. TIMOTHY O'SULLIVAN, AMERICA'S FORGOTTEN PHOTOGRAPHER .... Garden City, New York: Doubleday, 1966.

A good biography of the man who is ranked generally next to Mathew Brady as the outstanding photographer of the Civil War.

4837. Hovey, Eugene B. "A Soldier's Sketchbook." CWTI, 8 [5] [1969]: 34-37.

Sergeant Hovey was from Massachusetts. This article describes the interesting sketchbook which he kept during the war and updated in 1914.

4838. Johnson, C. and M. McLaughlin. CIVIL WAR BATTLES. New York: Crown, 1977.

An oversized "coffee table" book, complete with text and over 140 photos. It covers 12 major battles, sketches of commanders, and their strategies and mistakes.

4839. Johnson, Rossiter. ... THE AMERICAN SOLDIER IN THE CIVIL WAR. New York, 1895.

A large, interesting picture book, "profusely illustrated with battle scenes, naval engagements and portraits" from the more celebrated artists of the war. Articles by Johnson, General Fitzhugh Lee, and others.

4840. ———. CAMPFIRE AND BATTLEFIELD: THE CLASSIC ILLUSTRATED HISTORY OF THE CIVIL WAR. New York, 1894.

Another of the author's large, pictorial histories, which includes sketches by Forbes, Taylor, and others.

4841. Joinville, Francois, Prince de. A CIVIL WAR ALBUM OF PAINTINGS BY THE PRINCE DE JOINVILLE. New York: Atheneum, 1964.

A reproduction of de Joinville's sketchbook of Civil War water colors, accompanied by an Andre Maurois essay [see number 4848], an introduction by the present Comte de Paris, a Joinville descendant, and an article by General James Gavin, discussing the French influence on the Civil War.

4842. Kaplan, Milton. "The Case of the Disappearing Photographers." US LIB CONG Q J, 24 [1967]: 40-45.

Discusses 25 original glass negatives marked "Haas and Peale." After extensive research, author concludes that one of the two may have been Lieutenant Philip Haas of the 1st New York Engineers. Peale's identity, however, remains unknown.

4843. Klemroth, Edgar H. "Shenandoah Sketchbook." CWTI, 14 [8] [1975]: 11-17.

Klemroth served with the 2nd U.S. Cavalry in 1864 and kept a notebook of sketches.

4844. Kurz, Louis. BATTLES OF THE CIVIL WAR, 1861-1865; A PICTORIAL PRESENTATION. Little Rock, Arkansas: Pioneer Press, 1960.

Excellent reproductions, in full color, of all 36 of the famous Kurz and Allison prints, covering the major battles. The text is written by present day Civil War historians.

4845. LESLIE'S WEEKLY. AT THE FRONT WITH THE ARMY AND NAVY. New York, 1912.

Although this book covers other wars, the emphasis is on the Civil War.

4846. Lossing, Benjamin J. PICTORIAL HISTORY OF THE CIVIL WAR IN THE UNITED STATES OF AMERICA. 3 v. Philadelphia, 1866-1868.

An excellent, detailed work by a famous artist-writer, who was both an eyewitness as well as an historian.

4847. Martin, Elizabeth R. "The Civil War Lithographs of Alfred Edward Mathews." OHIO HIS, 72 [1963]: 230-242.

Describes Mathews' work during the Civil War with particular emphasis on 35 of his lithographs.

4848. Maurois, André. "Princely Service: Excerpts From a Civil War Album of Paintings by Prince de Joinville." AM HER, 17 [3] [1966]: 52-64, 80-81.

A brief sketch of the service of Prince de Joinville, son of the exiled French King Louis Philippe, who spent a year as a civilian aide to McClellan and the Army of the Potomac. He was a distinguished naval officer as well as an accomplished artist. Joinville compiled a sketchbook of over 50 water colors [see number 4841], 13 of which are reproduced here.

4849. Meredith, Roy. MATHEW BRADY'S PORTRAIT OF AN ERA. New York: Norton, 1982.

A collection of nearly 150 daguerreotypes of politicians, businessmen, artists, and other celebrities by Brady.

4850. ———. MR. LINCOLN'S CAMERA MAN: MATHEW BRADY. New York: Scribners, 1946.

This volume contains many of Brady's photographs and a brief accompanying biography.

4851. ———. MR. LINCOLN'S CONTEMPORARIES: AN ALBUM OF PORTRAITS BY MATHEW B. BRADY. New York: Scribners, 1951.

Over 172 of Brady's prints are reproduced here. They cover his entire career of picture-taking. There is a brief connecting narrative which is not particularly well-done, but the illustrations stand on their own feet.

4852. ———. MR. LINCOLN'S GENERAL, U.S. GRANT.... New York: Dutton, 1959.

Because of the dearth of pictures of Grant's life, the text is taken from Grant's memoirs and the pictures are used to illustrate the text. Has some interesting photographs.

4853. Miers, Earl S. THE AMERICAN CIVIL WAR: A POPULAR ILLUSTRATED HISTORY OF THE YEARS 1861-1865 AS SEEN BY THE ARTIST-CORRESPONDENTS WHO WERE THERE. New York: Golden Press, 1961.

A pictorial history done in a most professional manner. Hundreds of drawings plus a well-written narrative.

4854. Milhollen, Hirst D. and James R. Johnson. BEST PHOTOS OF THE CIVIL WAR. New York: Fawcett, 1961.

A collection of approximately 300 photographs. The text covers the war and centers around the main battles. Paperback. Milhollen was for many years curator of the photographic collection of the Library of Congress.

4855. ———, James R. Johnson and Albert H. Bill. HORSEMEN BLUE AND GRAY: A PICTORIAL HISTORY. New York: Oxford University Press, 1960.

The cavalrymen, famous and infamous, have their moment in this well-done work. The illustrations are taken from the Library of Congress photographic collection. The written narrative clarifies any mysteries left from the pictorial matter. However, it is not easy to recapture the sweep of cavalry action in still shots.

4856. ——— and Bell I. Wiley. THEY WHO FOUGHT HERE. New York: Macmillan, 1959.

A volume of illustrations and text which nicely reveals Civil War army life from the vantage point of the common soldier. Wiley did the writing, while Milhollen was responsible for the pictures. Each did his job well. There are over 200 illustrations and many quotes from letters and diaries.

4857. Miller, Francis T. and Robert S. Lanier, editors. THE PHOTOGRAPHIC HISTORY OF THE CIVIL WAR. 10 v. New York, 1911. Reprint 1957.

The greatest photographic source for war pictures, these volumes consitute the largest collection of Brady pictures. It is sometimes referred to as the "Miller-Brady" book, although Gardner's and O'Sullivan's photographs are also included. Numerous errors appear in the text.

4858. Morgan, Matthew S. THE AMERICAN WAR. London, England: 1874.

A collection of cartoons by Matt Morgan and other English artists, which are very critical of Lincoln.

4859. Mottelay, Paul F. and T. Campbell-Copeland, editors. THE SOLDIER IN OUR CIVIL WAR. 2 v. New York, 1884-1885.

Effective illustrative material. Includes eyewitness accounts by generals and commanders both North and South as well as a chronological history of the war. Sketches by Forbes, Waud, Taylor, Hillen, Becker, Lovie, Schell, and Crane.

4860. Newhall, Beaumont and Nancy. T.H. O'SULLIVAN: PHOTOGRAPHER. Rochester, New York: Eastman House, 1966.

O'Sullivan's photographs rather than his career are the main focus of this work.

4861. O'Dea, Thomas. HISTORY OF O'DEA'S FAMOUS PICTURE OF ANDERSONVILLE PRISON.... Cohoes, New York: 1887.

This brief twenty page booklet gives a history of this well-known painting.

4862. Pratt: Fletcher. CIVIL WAR IN PICTURES. New York: Henry Holt, 1955.

An illustrated review of the war based on contemporary drawings from HARPERS WEEKLY and Frank Leslie's ILLUSTRATED NEWSPAPER. Over 300 sketches combined with many battlfield reports make this a good volume for the non-expert to study the Civil War

4863. Rawdon, Horace, Jr. "A Sketchbook Through the South." CWTI, 12 [7] [1973]: 22-27.

Rawdon, who served with the 105th Ohio, was a "primitive" artist. Article includes five pencil sketches and eleven water colors.

4864. Ray, Frederic. "Alfred R. Waud." CWTI, 2 [8] [1961]: 18-23.

Waud was an English artist who covered the Civil War.

4865. ———. ALFRED R. WAUD, CIVIL WAR ARTIST. New York: Viking, 1974

The author, a magazine art director himself, expertly analyzes the work of one of the most celebrated wartime artists, Alfred R. Waud. Included in this solid biography of the historian-reporter for HARPERS WEEKLY, are 108 plates illustrating the best of Waud's work.

4866. ———. "The Art of Gilbert Gaul - A Portfolio. CWTI, 2 [1] [1963]: 24-29.

Discusses Gaul's Civil War illustrations and includes 96 of them.

4867. ———. "The Civil War Artist as He Saw Himself." CWTI, 6 [5] [1967]: 22-25.

Self portraits by Alfred Waud, Theodore Davis, Fred B. Schell, Frank Vizetelly, and Winslow Homer are to be found here, in addition to a rare photograph of Waud.

4868. ———. "Pickett's Charge--Story Behind Painting." CWTI, 5 [2] [1966]: 25-27.

Recounts the history of the largest battle in North America, painted on a single sheet of canvas. The painter was Peter Frederick Rothermel.

4869. ———. "Rare Photographs of Troops Identified...." CWTI, 4 [1] [1965]: 22-24.

Presents the only known photograph showing Confederate troops on the march in a campaign.

4870. ———. "Sketches of Army Life." CWTI, 2 [2] [1963]: 34-37.

These sketches by Charles Reed, taken from John D. Billings' HARDTACK AND COFFEE, cover all phases of army life.

4871. Redway, Maurine W. and Dorothy K. Bracken. MARKS OF LINCOLN ON OUR LAND. New York: Hastings House, 1957.

A brief biography of Lincoln based on the many Lincoln statues and memorials throughout the country. Sketches the history of the memorials and describes them as well. A very interesting book.

4872. Robertson, James I. "The Concise Illustrated History of the Civil War." A HIS ILL, 6 [2] [1971]: 3-64.

A narrative of the Civil War which discusses secession and the comparative resources of each side.

4873. Russell, Andrew J. RUSSELL'S CIVIL WAR PHOTOGRAPHS.... New York: Dover, 1983.

Captain Russell was one of the few official Civil War photographers. The volume contains 116 of his photographs. This is a reprint of an earlier work.

4874. Schell, Frank H. "As An Artist Saw Antietam." CWTI, 8 [3] [1969]: 14-22.

Eyewitness account of the battle by Frank Schell, author-artist The article was "adapted from McCLURE'S MAGAZINE, February, 1904.

4875. Stedman, C.E. THE CIVIL WAR SKETCHBOOK OF CHARLES ELLERY STEDMAN.... J.D. Hill, editor. San Rafael, California: Presidio Press, 1976.

Reproduces drawings of Charles E. Stedman which were part of a Civil War album presented to the Massachusetts Military Order of the Loyal Legion. Includes biographical sketch and letters of Stedman.

4876. Stephans, Ann S.W. PICTORIAL HISTORY OF THE WAR FOR THE UNION. 2 v. New York, 1866.

Over two hundred illustrations, but the book is much too contemporary to be of great value.

4877. Stern, Philip Van Doren. THEY WERE THERE: THE CIVIL WAR IN ACTION.... New York: Crown, 1959.

Over 200 drawings and paintings, many in color, which appeared originally in LESLIE'S, HARPERS, and the ILLUSTRATED LONDON NEWS.

4878. Taylor, Joseph H. THE AMERICAN NEGRO SOLDIER IN THE CIVIL WAR: A PICTORIAL DOCUMENTARY. Durham, North Carolina: J.S.C. and A. Publishers, 1960.

4879. Thompson, W. Fletcher, Jr. "Illustrating the Civil War." WIS MAG HIS, 45 [1961/1962]: 10-20.

Author traces the evolution of the work of the sketch-artists during the war, noting how the early idealized illustrations gave way within a year to a more realistic image of war.

4880. U.S. Library of Congress. THE CIVIL WAR IN PICTURES, 1861-1961 .... Donald H. Mugridge, compiler. Washington, D.C.: Library of Congress, 1961.

A critical bibliography of selected pictorial works.

4881. ———. CIVIL WAR PHOTOGRAPHS, 1861-1865.... Hirst D. Milhollen and Donald H. Mugridge, compilers. Washington, D.C.: Reference Department, Library of Congress, 1961.

A catalogue of the Brady collection.

4882. U.S. National Gallery of Art. THE CIVIL WAR: A CENTENNIAL EXHIBITION OF EYEWITNESS DRAWINGS. Washington, D.C.: National

Gallery of Art, 1961.

Reproductions of the works of famous artists.

4883. Werstein, Irving. 1861-1865: THE ADVENTURE OF THE CIVIL WAR TOLD WITH PICTURES. New York: Pageant, 1960.

Reproductions from contemporary sources.

4884. Williams, George F. THE MEMORIAL WAR BOOK.... New York, 1894.

"Illustrated by two thousand ... engravings reproduced largely from photographs taken by the U.S. government photographers, M. B. Brady and Alexander Gardner...."

4885. Williams, Hermann W. THE CIVIL WAR: THE ARTISTS' RECORD. Washington, D.C.: Corcoran Gallery, 1961.

Contains reproductions of over 200 watercolors, drawings, paintings, and sketches which by themselves make it an outstanding volume. It also has a brief section on the artists of the era and an excellent narrative supplemented by quotations from soldiers' letters and diaries.

4886. Wilson, John L. THE PICTORIAL HISTORY OF THE GREAT CIVIL WAR: ITS CAUSES, ORIGINS, CONDUCT, AND RESULTS. Philadelphia, 1878.

A misnomer, but a beautifully printed, though non-scholarly, history written by a correspondent for the NEW YORK HERALD.

4887. Wright, Marcus J., editor. OFFICIAL PORTFOLIO OF WAR AND NATION .... Philadelphia, 1904-1905.

Narrative by a number of people including John Clark Ridpath, General Fitzhugh Lee, and General John T. Morgan. Illustrations are from LESLIE'S.

B. MUSIC

4888. Aldredge, James. "John Brown's 'Battle Hymn.'" MUSIC J, 24 [1966]: 30, 34, 38.

It will no doubt surprise most people to learn that the subject matter of the popular marching song, "John Brown's Body," was not Old Brown of Ossawatomie and Harper's Ferry, but young John Brown of the 12th Massachusetts. Words were put to an old camp meeting hymn, "Say, Brothers, Will You Meet Us?" by members of the regiment, words which poked wholesome fun at a good-natured young Scot, John Brown. Julia Ward Howe would compose more dignified words for the tune later on.

4889. Bernard, Kenneth A. "Lincoln and the Music of the Civil War." CWH, 4 [1958]: 209-284.

While not necessarily a student of the subject, Lincoln liked the music of the day. "Annie Laurie," "Rock of Ages," and "Blue-tailed Fly" were among his favorites.

4890. ———. LINCOLN AND THE MUSIC OF THE CIVIL WAR. Caldwell, Idaho: Caxton, 1966.

Although he could barely carry a tune, Lincoln's interest in music is evidenced by the number of White House activities--receptions, afternoon concerts, operatic and formal concerts--which were centered around music. This is not a book of wartime favorites.

4891. ———. "The Music at Gettysburg." LIN HER, 61 [1959]: 91-100.

A detailed look at the musical organizations which were present and the music which was played and sung at Gettysburg, both on the night before and the day of the dedication ceremonies. Five bands and two singing groups were featured.

4892. Blum, Fred. "Music During the Civil War: A Preliminary Survey." CWH, 4 [1958]: 325-337.

A look at all forms of music which were current during the war and some of the composers.

4893. Childs, Bert B. "Civil War Musicians." ANN IOWA, 25 [1943]: 122-128.

A brief sketch of the National Association of Civil War Musicians and Sons of Veterans, composed of soldiers who served as musicians in the war and their offspring.

4894. Crawford, Richard, editor. CIVIL WAR SONGBOOK.... Mineola, New York: Dover, 1977.

A compilation of 37 copies of original sheet music of the Civil War with introductory notes.

4895. Daniel, Elva S. "Music That Abe Heard." INSTRUCTOR, 76 [1967]: 23-25, 59.

Lincoln enjoyed listening to the folk ballads, square dance tunes, revival melodies, and the sad love songs, which were popular during the war. The words and music of 15 songs he must have heard and liked are included in this article.

4896. Emurian, Ernest K. STORIES OF CIVIL WAR SONGS. Natick, Massachusetts: Wilde, 1960.

An account of the stories behind the composing of many Civil War songs.

4897. Epstein, Dena J. "The Battle Cry of Freedom." CWH, 4 [1958]: 307-318.

A flood of music streamed from the presses at the outbreak of the war. Marching songs proved the most popular. This article traces the history of one of them, "The Battle Cry of Freedom."

4898. ———. "Lucy McKim Garrison, American Musician." NY PUB LIB BULL, 67 [1963]: 529-546.

The story of how slave songs reached print. Lucy McKim was one of the editors of the first collection of its kind, "Slave Songs of the United States" [1867].

4899. Fowke, Edith. "American Civil War Songs in Canada." MIDWEST FOLK, 13 [1963]: 33-42.

In this analysis of Civil War ballads in the United States and Canada, the author concludes that most of those which survived dealt with the human experience rather than the larger historical event.

4900. ———. "Canadian Variations of a Civil War Song." MIDWEST FOLK, 13 [1963]: 101-104.

"Tramp, Tramp, Tramp," written in 1863, proved popular with both North and South. In Canada five different versions of it were sung between 1865 and 1918. The song's popularity has diminished little over the years.

4901. Glass, Paul and Louis C. Singer. SINGING SOLDIERS: A HISTORY OF THE CIVIL WAR IN SONG. New York: Da Capo, 1975.

A good collection of Civil War songs, with descriptive notes accompanying each song. The prints on the covers are delightful and contribute to a feeling of the era. Published originally under the title SPIRIT OF THE SIXTIES.

4902. Gravele, Jean F. "The Civil War Songster of a Monroe County Farmer." NY FOLK Q, 27 [1971]: 163-230.

Reprints lyrics from an old manuscript.

4903. Heaps, Willard A. and Porter W. Heaps. THE SINGING SIXTIES: THE SPIRIT OF CIVIL WAR DAYS DRAWN FROM THE MUSIC OF THE TIMES. Norman: University of Oklahoma Press, 1960.

An attempt to collect under one cover the music of the Civil War and to portray the mood of the war years through this music. While there is much of interest in this handsome volume, it comes up a little short of its intended goal.

4904. Jones, Robert H. "Uncle Dan Emmett's 'Dixie.'" JISHS, 56 [1963]: 364-371.

Emmett's most famous song was written in 1859. The melody was preserved but the words were revised into a stirring southern fight song by General Albert Pike. It was Lincoln's hope that "Dixie" might prove to be a goodwill song of the re-united states. Although associated primarily with the Confederacy, many a Union soldier sang the melody.

4905. Lord, Francis A. and Arthur Wise. BANDS AND DRUMMER BOYS OF THE CIVIL WAR. New York: Yoseloff, 1966.

An illustrated history which portrays the lives of members of an unsung branch of the military forces. Musicians also performed other important duties when they were not making music.

4906. Moore, Frank, compiler. THE CIVIL WAR IN SONG AND STORY. New York, 1882. Reprint 1970.

A collection of songs, anecdotes, and incidents of the war.

4907. Olson, Kenneth E. MUSIC AND MUSKET: BANDS AND BANDSMEN OF THE AMERICAN CIVIL WAR. Westport, Connecticut: Greenwood, 1981.

A general reference guide to Union and Confederate Civil War bands. Includes an historical overview of American military bands.

4908. Semmes, Raphael. "Civil War Songsheets...." MD HIS MAG, 38 [1943]: 205-229.

A description of a collection of Civil War songsheets in the possession of the Maryland Historical Society.

4909. Silber, Irwin, compiler. SONGS OF THE CIVIL WAR. New York: Columbia University Press, 1960.

Author has collected over 125 songs and appended introductory notes to each. Lyrics and/or parodies are linked with events of the day.

4910. Stone, James. "War Music and War Psychology in the Civil War." J AB SOC PSYCH, 36 [1941]: 543-560.

Author seeks to test the long-accepted view that war music is always patriotic music by studying the kinds of music which were most popular in the Civil War. He finds no connection between war and music. Soldiers and civilians, North and South, sang the same kind of music they had always sung before the war.

4911. Stutler, Boyd B. "John Brown's Body." CWH, 4 [1958]: 251-260.

This mighty war song which was heard everywhere, was associated with the famous abolitionist, John Brown, only because of his fame and "propaganda."

4912. Tribble, Edwin. "'Marching Through Georgia.'" GA R, 21 [1967]: 423-429.

A sketch of the not very successful career of Henry Clay Work, composer of "Marching Through Georgia," the Civil War song which became popular throughout the world except in the American South.

4913. Ziff, Larzer. "Civil War Humor: Songs of the Civil War." CWH, 2 [1956]: 7-28.

Music ranked second only to reading as entertainment in the Union army. Author examines three types of war songs: sentimental, patriotic, and humorous. Emphasis of the article is on the latter.

C. AUDIO-VISUAL

The listings which follow are not intended to be comprehensive. They are, rather, a random sampling of the many items available in this ever-changing field. Because of their self-explanatory nature, no annotations were deemed necessary.

4914. American Heritage Media Collection. CENTURY COLLECTION OF CIVIL WAR ART. Stephen W. Sears, editor. Two filmstrips [150 pictures] and two cassettes. Also available in two 80-slide carousel trays with synchronized cassettes.

4915. American Heritage Media Collection. THE CIVIL WAR. Bruce Catton, narrator. Part 1: "A Nation Divided"; Part 2: "The Clash of Amateur Armies"; Part 3: "The Iron Vise is Forged"; Part 4: "Gettysburg"; and Part 5: "An Ending and A Beginning." Five color filmstrips with five synchronized cassettes. Also available in video casette.

4916. American Broadcasting System. ROAD TO GETTYSBURG. 16mm film. From "Saga of Western Man" series.

4917. Brunswick Productions. HIGH TIDE AT GETTYSBURG. 35mm filmstrip. "The Civil War in Prose and Poetry" series.

4918. Caedmon Records. THE RED BADGE OF COURAGE. Edmond O'Brian reader.

4919. ———. American History Cassette Library. RED BADGE OF COURAGE. Also available in 35mm filmstrips.

4920. ———. American History Cassette Library. EYEWITNESS TO THE CIVIL WAR. Ed Begley, narrator. Selections from Walt Whitman's poetry and journals.

4921. ———. A LINCOLN ALBUM. Carl Sandburg, reader. [Portrays Lincoln as an Illinois lawyer.]

4922. Centron Educational Films. GETTYSBURG: 1863. 16mm film.

4923. Coleman Film Enterprises. ORDEAL AT GETTYSBURG. 35mm filmstrip.

4924. COLUMBIA BROADCASTING SYSTEM. THE BATTLE OF GETTYSBURG ... AS REPORTED BY CBS CORRESPONDENTS.... 3 record set. From the CBS series "You Are There."

4925. Columbia Records. THE BATTLE OF GETTYSBURG: YOU ARE THERE. 1 record. An "eye-witness" account.

4926. ———. SONGS OF THE NORTH AND SOUTH: 1861-1865. Sung by the Mormon Tabernacle Choir; Richard P. Condie, Director.

4927. ———. THE UNION: BASED ON THE MUSIC OF THE NORTH DURING THE YEARS 1861-1865. National Gallery Orchestra, Richard Bales, Conductor. Includes essays by Bruce Catton, Clifford Dowdey, and Allan Nevins.

4928. Coral Records. THE TRUE STORY OF THE CIVIL WAR. Raymond Massey, narrator.

4929. Decca Records. THE BLUE AND THE GRAY. 2 records. Taken from a BBC television presentation. 21 songs.

4930. ———. SONGS OF THE NORTH AND SOUTH IN THE WAR BETWEEN THE STATES. Sung by Frank Luther and Zora Layman. 18 songs from the Union.

4931. Elektra Records. SONGS AND BALLADS OF AMERICA'S WARS. Frank Warner, singer. Contains some Civil War songs.

4932. Encyclopedia Britannica Films. THE CIVIL WAR. Eight 35mm filmstrips. Titles: "Causes of the Civil War," "From Bull Run to Antietam," "From Shiloh to Vicksburg," "The Civil War at Sea," "Gettysburg," "Sherman's March to the Sea," "The Road to Appomattox," and "The Reconstruction Period."

4933. ———. VICKSBURG AND GETTYSBURG: THE TURNING POINT. 35mm filmstrip. From "Civil War and Reconstruction Series."

4934. Enrichment Teaching Materials. LEE AND GRANT AT APPOMATTOX. 35mm filmstrip.

4935. ———. LINCOLN'S GETTYSBURG ADDRESS. Record.

4936. ———. THE MONITOR AND THE MERRIMAC and LEE AND GRANT AT APPOMATTOX. Record.

4937. Eye Gate House. BRADY'S WAR BETWEEN THE STATES. 35mm filmstrip.

4938. ———. A COUNTRY DIVIDED. 35mm filmstrip.

4939. ———. A NATION DIVIDED: SECESSION, WAR AND RECONSTRUCTION. Nine 35mm filmstrips. Titles: "King Cotton," "The Problem of Slavery," "The Abolitionists," "Abraham Lincoln," "Secession," "The War Between the States," "Rebuilding the South," "Other Problems of Slavery," and "Differences Between North and South.

4940. Film Associates of California. THE BACKGROUND OF THE CIVIL WAR. 16mm film.

4941. Films, Inc. THE BATTLE OF GETTYSBURG. 16mm film.

4942. Film Dallas. GETTYSBURG. 16mm film.

4943. Folkways Records. BALLADS OF THE CIVIL WAR. 2 records. Hermes Nye, soloist.

4944. ———. SONGS OF THE CIVIL WAR. 2 records. Sung by Pete Seeger and others. Based on Columbia University Press' SONGS OF THE CIVIL WAR.

4945. Friendly, Fred, producer. CARL SANDBURG AT GETTYSBURG. 16mm motion picture.

4946. Horizon Productions. GETTYSBURG. 35mm filmstrip. From "America" series.

4947. International Communication Film. CIVIL WAR SERIES. 16mm motion picture.

4948. Library of Congress. SONGS AND BALLADS OF AMERICAN HISTORY AND OF THE ASSASSINATION OF PRESIDENTS. From materials in the Archive of Folksong.

4949. McGraw Hill. TRUE STORY OF THE CIVIL WAR. 16mm film.

4950. ———. YOU ARE THERE. 16mm sound. Titles: "The Fall of Fort Sumter," "Battle of Antietam," "The Death of Stonewall Jackson," "The Emancipation Proclamation," "The Heroism of Clara Barton," "Grant and Lee at Appomattox," and "The Capture of John Wilkes Booth."

4951. Mercury Records. THE CIVIL WAR, ITS MUSIC AND ITS SOUNDS. Authentic music on authentic instruments. No re-arrangements. Explanatory comments on each song.

4952. Merit Audio-Visual. RED BADGE OF COURAGE. 35 mm filmstrip. From "American Literature Filmstrip Library."

4953. National Park Service. DOWN TO THE MONITOR. Video; 16mm film. 1980.

4954. ———. ANTIETAM VISIT. Video; 16mm film. 1982.

4955. ———. FREDERICKSBURG AND CHANCELLORSVILLE--THE BLOODY ROAD TO RICHMOND. Video. 1982.

4956. ———. FREDERICK DOUGLASS: AN AMERICAN LIFE. Video; 16mm film. 1985.

4957. ———. FROM THESE HONORED DEAD. [Gettysburg] Video; 16mm film. 1980.

4958. ———. IN MEMORY OF MEN. [Vicksburg] Video; 16mm film. 1970.

4959. ———. MANASSAS. [First and Second Bull Run] Video. 1983.

4960. ———. MR. LINCOLN'S SPRINGFIELD. Lincoln's Career in his home town. Video; 16mm film. 1977.

4961. ———. WILSON'S CREEK: A MEAN FOWT FIGHT. [Missouri]. Video; 16mm film. 1983.

[National Park Service videos and film are available in color through the National Audio Visual Center.]

4962. Net Film Service. HERITAGE, PART XI. 16mm sound. Four one-half hour interviews with Bruce Catton.

4963. RCA-Victor Bluebird Records. STORIES AND SONGS OF THE CIVIL WAR. Ralph Bellamy, narrator. Ed McCurdy, soloist.

4964. Roulette Records. CIVIL WAR ALMANAC. 2 records. Songs from both North and South, sung by the Cumberland Trio.

4965. Teaching Resources: AMERICA'S 19TH CENTURY WARS. "Civil War Parts 1 and 2." Filmstrip and cassettes.

4966. Tyrrell, William G. "Civil War History in Sight and Sound." NY HIS, 42 [1961]: 177-185.

This article describes approximately 40 16mm films, filmstrips, and recordings for educational use.

4967. U.S. Army College. ECHOES FROM CEMETERY RIDGE. F. Baldwin, director. Video. Joint production of the U.S. Army College, U.S. Military Academy, and the U.S.A. Military History Institute.

4968. Westinghouse Broadcasting Company. THE AMERICAN CIVIL WAR: A PICTORIAL HISTORY THROUGH THE PHOTOGRAPHS OF MATHEW B. BRADY. A series. 16mm motion picture.

4969. Westport Media. CELEBRATE AMERICA. Oscar Brand's "American Folksong Archive." 9 cassettes, one of which deals with the Civil War.

4970. WTTW Television Station. BATTLE FOR THE WORLD. 16mm motion picture. Adapted from Fletcher Pratt's ORDEAL BY FIRE.

4971. Yale University Press Film Service. DIXIE. 35mm filmstrip. From "Chronicles of America Filmstrips."

4972. ———. SLAVERY AND THE WAR BETWEEN THE STATES. 35mm filmstrip. From "The Chronicles of America Filmstrips."

4973. ———. UNION AND RECONSTRUCTION. 35mm filmstrips. From "The Pageant of America Filmstrips."

* * *

Educational Record Sales, Distributor.

4974. Copland, Aaron. A LINCOLN PORTRAIT. Carl Sandburg, narrator. Filmstrip with synchronized cassette.

4975. LINCOLN: THE KENTUCKY YEARS. Burgess Meredith, narrator. Video; 16mm filmstrip.

4976. MICRO COMPUTER PROGRAMS. "Simulation: Lincoln's Decisions." 1 disk.

4977. Spoken Arts Cassette Mini-Kits. "American Literature in Transition: Mini-Kit 19." Roy P. Basler, reader. Consists of 6 cassettes, which include Lincoln's speeches and letters.

4978. U.S. HISTORY: AN AUDIO CHRONOLOGY. Cassettes. Titles: "Prelude to the Civil War," "Fort Sumter to Gettysburg," The Monitor and the Merrimac," "Gettysburg to Appomattox," "Abraham Lincoln," and "Ulysses S. Grant."

X

MINORITIES

A. BLACKS AND EMANCIPATION

4979. Abbott, Martin, editor. "A New Englander in the South, 1865: A Letter." NEQ, 32 [1959]: 388-393.

Letter from a Union officer to General Howard of the Freedmen's Bureau, giving unfavorable impressions of the former slaves, now free.

4980. Abrahms, Ray. "The Copperhead Newspapers and the Negro." JNH, 20 [1935]: 131-152.

Discusses the free Negro in the North during the war as a "political issue."

4981. Adams, David W. "Illinois Soldiers and the Emancipation Proclamation." JISHS, 67 [1974]: 406-421.

While Illinois troops supported the Republicans and the Emancipation Proclamation, they were unable to vote in the 1862 midterm elections, which hurt the party.

4982. Adams, Neal M. "Northern Negrophobia During the Civil War: As Reported by the LONDON TIMES." NEG HIS BULL, 28 [1964]: 7-8.

The TIMES was hostile to blacks and their aspirations.

4983. Addeman, Joshua M. REMINISCENCES OF TWO YEARS WITH THE COLORED TROOPS. Providence, Rhode Island: 1880.

A brief but useful memoir of an officer of the 14th Rhode Island Heavy Artillery in the last two years of the war.

4984. Alexander, William T. HISTORY OF THE COLORED RACE IN AMERICA.... Kansas City, Missouri: 1887.

A rambling history, only one-fourth of which deals with the Civil War.

4985. Aptheker, Herbert. "Negro Casualties in the Civil War." JNH, 32 [1947]: 10-80.

Black people demonstrated that, in terms of the supreme sacrifice, they expended very much more than their proportionate share. They did this in spite of the long delay on the part of the government in allowing them to serve in the armed forces.

4986. ———. THE NEGRO IN THE CIVIL WAR. New York: International Publishers, 1938.

An early attack on the "Sambo" myth by the foremost Marxist student of American blacks.

4987. ———. "The Negro in the Union Navy." JNH, 32 [1947]: 169-200.

By examining muster rolls for several Union ships, Aptheker shows that an estimate of one-quarter does not overstate the percentage of crews made up by blacks during the Civil War. He also concludes that while discrimination existed, blacks in the navy were subjected to significantly less than that experienced in the army or in society, north or south. Compare to David Valuska's work.

4988. Armstrong, Warren B. "Union Chaplains and the Education of Freedmen." JNH, 52 [1967]: 104-115.

Discusses the contributions by Union army chaplains to the education of freedmen.

4989. ———. "The Freedmen's Movement and the Founding of the NATION." JAH, 53 [1967]: 708-726.

Substantial monetary backing from freedmen's groups, as well as abolitionists who favored the project, helped solve the financial problems involved with the founding of the NATION.

4990. Ayers, James T. THE DIARY OF JAMES T. AYERS, CIVIL WAR RECRUITER. John H. Franklin, editor. Springfield: State of Illinois, 1947.

Ayers was with the 129th Illinois and during the last year and a half of the war recruited for black units.

4991. Balch, John A. HISTORY OF THE 116TH UNITED STATES COLORED INFANTRY. Philadelphia, 1866.

Contains rosters of companies; regiment was formed in 1864.

4992. Basler, Roy P. "And For His Widow and His Orphan." US LIB CONG Q J, 27 [1970]: 291-294.

Text of letter from Lincoln to Sumner, May 19, 1864, in which it is urged that dependents of fallen black soldiers receive the same benefits as those of white soldiers.

4993. Beard, August F. A CRUSADE OF BROTHERHOOD, A HISTORY OF THE AMERICAN MISSIONARY ASSOCIATION. Boston, 1909.

The AMA worked conscientiously to assist the freedmen.

4994. Bell, Howard H. "Negro Emancipation in Historic Retrospect: The Nation, The Condition and Prospects of the Negro as

Reflected in the National Convention of 1864." J HU REL, 11 [1963]: 221-231.

The changing role and uncertain status of the blacks are discussed.

4995. Belz, Herman. "Law, Politics and Race in the Struggle for Equal Pay During the Civil War." CWH, 22 [1976]: 197-213.

An analysis of the debates leading to the passage of an 1864 law authorizing equal pay for both white and black Union troops.

4996. ———. "Origins of Negro Suffrage During the Civil War." SOUTH STUD, 17 [1978]: 115-130.

Free blacks in New Orleans demand the right to vote with the readmission of Louisiana to the Union in 1863.

4997. ———. "Protection of Personal Liberty in the Republican Emancipation Legislation of 1862." JSH, 42 [1976]: 385-400.

In looking at the motives behind the Emancipation Proclamation, it is asked whether the Republicans were concerned more about freedom for the blacks or the military advantage. Congressional Republicans and the Lincoln administration failed to deal with the problem of the "new birth of freedom" which the former slaves were supposed to enjoy.

4998. Bennett, Lerone, Jr. "The Day Slavery 'Died.'" EBONY, 31 [1976]: 72-82.

Deals with the passage of the Thirteenth Amendment outlawing slavery.

4999. ———. "Was Abe Lincoln a White Supremacist?" EBONY, 23 [1968]: 35-38.

Answer is "Yes." Author offers "hard" evidence to this effect in Lincoln's pre-presidential career. Lincoln changed some during the war but not much. He was a "white supremacist with good intentions."

5000. Bentley, George R. A HISTORY OF THE FREEDMEN'S BUREAU. Philadelphia: University of Pennsylvania Press, 1955.

The best volume on this important subject.

5001. Berlin, Ira, editor, with Joseph P. Reigy and Leslie S. Rowland. FREEDOM: A DOCUMENTARY HISTORY OF EMANCIPATION, 1861-1867. Series II. THE BLACK MILITARY EXPERIENCE. Cambridge, England: Cambridge University Press, 1982.

This work is an excellent collection of documents drawn from various Record Groups in the National Archives. The material is arranged into five major sections and covers topics such as black recruitment, life in the military, and some of the experiences of black soldiers in post-Civil War America. Many interesting letters from black soldiers are among the sources included in this volume.

5002. Berry, Mary F. "Negro Troops in Blue and Gray: The Louisiana Native Guards, 1861-1863." LA HIS, 8 [1967]: 165-190.

This study surveys the military service of Louisiana free blacks from colonial times through 1863. During the Civil War the Native Guards served both the North and South. Although the Confederacy limited them to non-combat duty, Union officials ultimately committed them to combat service where the Guards performed heroically in the assault on Port Hudson.

5003. Berwanger, Eugene H. THE FRONTIER AGAINST SLAVERY: WESTERN ANTI-NEGRO PREJUDICE AND THE SLAVERY EXTENSION CONTROVERSY. Urbana: University of Illinois Press, 1967.

In this study of popular attitudes in the midwestern, mountain, and far western states, the author is one of the first to demonstrate the strong racist sentiment outside of the South. Westerners, for example, may have opposed slavery extension but they did so not for humanitarian reasons but because they wanted the West to remain a white preserve.

5004. Bigelow, Martha M. "Freedmen of the Mississippi Valley, 1862-1865." CWH, 8 [1962]: 38-47.

The federal government had no fixed policy for dealing with blacks during the first year of the war. Problems arose, the primary one being that control of the blacks was split between the army and the treasury department.

5005. ———. "Vicksburg: Experiment in Freedom." J MISS HIS, 26 [1964]: 28-44.

A discussion of the various projects undertaken in dealing with freed blacks in the Vicksburg area.

5006. Binder, Frederick M. "Pennsylvania Negro Regiments in the Civil War." JNH, 37 [1952]: 383-417.

Negro volunteers and draftees became "United States Colored Troops" rather than state regiments because white units were not ready to receive them into their midst. Blacks were mustered in for three years' service and very few were ever commissioned as officers.

5007. Blackburn, George, editor. "The Negro as Viewed by a Michigan Civil War Soldier: Letters of John C. Buchanan." MICH HIS, 47 [1963]: 75-84.

Eight letters from an officer to his wife, in which he first opposed the use of blacks for combat duty, but later urged their enlistment.

5008. BLACK STUDIES: A SELECT CATALOG OF NATIONAL ARCHIVES MICROFILM PUBLICATIONS. Washington, D.C.: United States General Services Administration, 1984.

A 100-page large paperback catalog containing a detailed listing of microfilm holdings by Record Group in the National Archives dealing with black history. Record Group 94, "Records of the Adjutant General's Office," consisting of five rolls, is most applicable to the Civil War.

5009. Blassingame, John W. "Negro Chaplains in the Civil War." NEG HIS BULL, 27 [1963]: 23-24.

Describes the important role played by black chaplains in fostering morale and providing guidance for black troops.

5010. ———. "The Recruitment of Colored Troops in Kentucky, Maryland, and Missouri, 1863-1865." HISTORIAN, 29 [1967]: 533-545.

Almost a quarter of all black troops came from the three Border states of Kentucky, Maryland, and Missouri. The author provides an excellent survey of the efforts made to enlist and later conscript blacks. In addition to tactics employed such as impressment, he discusses the inducements that were offered to prospective recruits. Also, he reviews the problems that Lincoln encountered with this program, especially in Kentucky.

5011. ———. "The Recruitment of Negro Troops in Maryland." MD HIS MAG, 58 [1963]: 20-29.

While inequality in pay between blacks and whites discouraged many blacks from enlisting in the armed forces, more than 8,700 volunteered from Maryland and served in some of the most hard-fought battles of the war.

5012. ———. "The Recruitment of Negro Troops in Missouri During the Civil War." MO HIS R, 58 [1964]: 326-338.

Whereas slaves viewed military service as a step toward emancipation, this was not to be.

5013. ———. "The Selection of Officers and Non-Commissioned Officers of Negro Troops in the Union Army, 1863-1865." NEG HIS BULL, 30 [1967]: 8-11.

The careful selection of black and white commissioned and non-commissioned officers for the black regiments was a significant factor in contributing to the success of these troops in the field. Each candidate was scrutinized as to his ability and character, and some had attended the Free Military School of Philadelphia in an effort to prepare for their qualifying exams.

5014. ———. "The Union Army as an Educational Institution for Negroes, 1861-1865." J NEG ED, 34 [1965]: 152-159.

This study describes the efforts that Union officers made to provide some formal education for the black troops under their commands. As former slaves, many of them were illiterate and could not advance through the ranks. They nevertheless had a "burning desire for education," which was strengthened while in Union service and which had far-reaching social and political consequences in the postwar years.

5015. Blodgett, Geoffrey. "John Mercer Langston and the Case of Edmonia Lewis: Oberlin, 1862." JNH, 53 [1968]: 201-218.

In the winter of 1862 Mary Edmonia Lewis was accused of poisoning two of her friends with drugged wine. In the next few weeks she was beaten by vigilantes, arrested, brought to court, and tried on the charges. She was defended by John Mercer Langston, a celebrated black leader in Ohio, who won her acquittal.

5016. Boritt, G.S. "The Voyage to the Colony of Linconia: The Sixteenth President, Black Colonization, and the Defense Mechanism of Avoidance." HISTORIAN, 37 [1975]: 619-632.

Why did Lincoln continue to support colonization in 1860 when it had been shown to be a failure? By "avoidance," a psychological term suggesting he closed his eyes to reality and pressed forward with a dream.

5017. Botume, Elizabeth H. FIRST DAYS AMONGST THE CONTRABANDS. Boston, 1893.

This readable account of the Port Royal experiment was written by a northern teacher involved in the education phase of the endeavor. Secretary of the Treasury Salmon P. Chase had hoped the Port Royal experiment "would become a 'proving ground' for the reconstruction of the South." Full of interesting stories, lively dialogue, and accurate details.

5018. Boyd, Willis D. "The American Colonization Society and the Slave Recaptives of 1980-1861: an Early Example of United States-African Relations." JNH, 47 [1962]: 108-126.

Some 4,000 Africans from the Congo were aboard illegal slave ships which were captured by American patrol ships in 1860-1861. Called "recaptives," they were taken under the wing of the American Colonization Society and re-settled in Liberia.

5019. ———. "The Ile a Vache Colonization Venture, 1862-1864." THE AMERICAS, 16 [1959]: 45-62.

Describes the unsuccessful attempt to establish a colony for ex-slaves off the coast of Haiti.

5020. ———. "James Redpath and American Negro Colonization in Haiti, 1860-1862." THE AMERICAS, 12 [1955]: 169-182.

The story of the unsuccessful colonization of American blacks in Haiti early in the war. The organizer of the project, James

Redpath, was an outspoken Scottish immigrant, who had planned the matter carefully, but the obstacles to success were too numerous to overcome.

5021. Breiseth, Christopher N. "Lincoln and Frederick Douglass: Another Debate." JISHS, 68 [1975]: 9-26.

The relationship between Lincoln and Douglass reveals much about the race issue during the war. The president heard the conflicting arguments of a nation at war with itself and sought to blunt the differences, thereby establishing a common ground for preserving the Union. Douglass believed the war could be won and the Union preserved only if slavery was abolished.

5022. Briggs, Walter D. CIVIL WAR SURGEON IN A COLORED REGIMENT. Berkeley: University of California Press, 1960.

Keen observations of campaigning in the southeast. Author served with the 54th Massachusetts.

5023. Brown, William W. THE BLACK MAN, HIS ANTECEDENTS, HIS GENIUS, AND HIS ACHIEVEMENTS. Boston, 1865.

Disputing the theory of black inferiority, the author argues for the Emancipation Proclamation.

5024. ———. THE NEGRO IN THE AMERICAN REBELLION, HIS HEROISM AND HIS FIDELITY. Boston, 1887.

Relying on newspaper articles, Brown, an abolitionist lecturer, wrote a somewhat partisan, anecdotal, friendly survey of the efforts of black soldiers from the Revolution to the Civil War.

5025. Browne, Frederick W. MY SERVICE IN THE UNITED STATES COLORED CAVALRY. Cincinnati, Ohio: 1908.

A perceptive record of Negro cavalry service in both Virginia and along the Texas frontier.

5026. Buckmaster, Henrietta. "One Hundred Years Ago." NEW ENG GAL, 5 [1963]: 17-25.

Describes the actions of Boston abolitionists to insure the carrying out of the Emancipation Proclamation.

5027. Burchard, Peter. ONE GALLANT RUSH: ROBERT GOULD SHAW AND HIS BRAVE BLACK REGIMENT. New York: St. Martins, 1965.

An excellent regimental history of the famous black 54th Massachusetts and its commander. A very interesting volume, in some ways it is more a biography of Shaw than an in-depth study of the Negro's role in the Civil War. Twenty-five-year-old Shaw was offered the command of the Negro regiment in January of 1863.

5028. Cain, Marvin R. "Lincoln's View on Slavery and the Negro: A Suggestion." HISTORIAN, 26 [1964]: 502-520.

An analysis of various opinions concerning Lincoln's views on race, wherein the author suggests that we may find the sources of Lincoln's thinking more in the humanitarianism of Jefferson than in the pragmatism of Clay.

5029. Califf, Joseph M. RECORD OF THE SERVICES OF THE SEVENTH REGIMENT, U.S. COLORED TROOPS.... Providence, Rhode Island: 1878.

Author was an officer in the unit which performed with distinction in the last 18 months of the war.

5030. Castel, Albert. "Civil War Kansas and the Negro." JNH, 51 [1966]: 125-138.

Although this state enjoyed a reputation for being anti-slavery, many of its white residents were anti-Negro. Such a sentiment, however, did not prevent them from supporting the recruitment of black troops in the 1st Kansas Colored Volunteers.

5031. ———. "The Fort Pillow Massacre: A Fresh Examination of the Evidence." CWH, 4 [1958]: 37-50.

This is the best study of this tragic event that occurred on April 12, 1864, when Confederate troops slaughtered Union soldiers, especially blacks, after they had surrendered. See also 5032, 5036, 5089, 5100, and 5195.

5032. ———. "Fort Pillow: Victory or Massacre?" A HIS ILL, 9 [1] [1974]: 4-10, 46-48.

In 1864 a report of the Joint Committee on the Conduct of the War charged the Confederacy with violating a cease-fire, the slaughter of 231 Union soldiers, and committing various outrages. The Confederacy denied these charges. Author points out that the truth lies somewhere in between.

5033. Cheek, William F. "John Mercer Langston: Black Protest Leader and Abolitionist." CWH, 16 [1970]: 101-120.

Author laments lack of recognition of Langston's outstanding efforts in behalf of black rights before the Civil War.

5034. Chenery, William H. THE FOURTEENTH REGIMENT RHODE ISLAND HEAVY ARTILLERY [COLORED] IN THE WAR TO PRESERVE THE UNION, 1861-1865. Providence, Rhode Island: 1898.

Includes muster rolls and brief sketches of the members.

5035. Child, Lydia M. THE RIGHT WAY, THE SAFE WAY, PROVED BY EMANCIPATION IN THE BRITISH WEST INDIES.... New York, 1862.

Argues for emancipation.

5036. Cimprich, John and Robert C. Mainfort, Jr., editors. "Fort Pillow Revisited: New Evidence About An Old Controversy." CWH, 28 [1982]: 292-306.

Through the use of additional source material, the authors basically agree with Albert Castel's assessment that a massacre occurred. [See numbers 5031 and 5032]

5037. Cleven, N.A.N. "Some Plans for Colonizing Liberated Negro Slaves in Hispanic America." JNH, 11 [1926]: 35-49.

Europeans rejected Seward's idea of recolonizing slaves in European colonies due to the fear of legal entanglements of reclaiming fugitives. Central and South American countries did not want large waves of Negroes. Brazil, though a slave-holding country, was willing to take freed Negroes because of a labor shortage.

5038. Coffin, Levi. REMINISCENCES OF LEVI COFFIN.... Cincinnati, Ohio: 1880.

Outstanding memoirs of a famous abolitionist and acknowledged "President" of the Underground Railroad in Ohio and Indiana.

5039. Cornish, Dudley T. "Kansas Negro Regiments in the Civil War." KAN HIS Q, 20 [1953]: 417-429.

Describes the activities of the 1st and 2nd regiments in the campaigning on the western frontier.

5040. ———. THE SABLE ARM: NEGRO TROOPS IN THE UNION ARMY, 1861-1865. New York: Longmans, Green, 1956. Reprint 1966.

The classic study on the problems involved and the successes achieved in raising 178,895 black troops for Union service. Author thoroughly researched the subject and broke new ground with this work.

5041. Cowden, Robert. A BRIEF SKETCH OF THE ORGANIZATION AND SERVICES OF THE FIFTY-NINTH REGIMENT OF UNITED STATES COLORED INFANTRY.... Dayton, Ohio: 1883.

Not very well done, but still of some interest.

5042. Cox, LaWanda. LINCOLN AND BLACK FREEDOM: A STUDY IN PRESIDENTIAL LEADERSHIP. Columbia: University of South Carolina Press, 1981.

Examines Lincoln's policies on Reconstruction. Raises the question if Lincoln or anyone in a decision-making role could have guaranteed freedom and equality for freed slaves.

5043. ———. "The Promise of Land for the Freedmen." MVHR, 45 [1958]: 413-440.

Discusses the congressional intent behind the Freedmen's Bureau Act of March 3, 1865.

5044. Crawford, Samuel J. KANSAS IN THE SIXTIES. Chicago, 1911.

Author recalls the war years and his service in black regiments.

5045. Currie, James T. ENCLAVE VICKSBURG AND HER PLANTATIONS, 1863-1870. Jackson: University Press of Mississippi, 1980.

Examines Warren County, Mississippi, from a social as well as an economic standpoint. Under Union control, Vicksburg grew rapidly. The chapter dealing with Benjamin Montgomery, an ex-slave who formed a settlement and successful communal farm, is most interesting.

5046. Dennett, George M. HISTORY OF THE NINTH U.S.C. TROOPS, FROM ITS ORGANIZATION TILL MUSTER OUT.... Philadelphia, 1866.

The commander of the regiment describes its campaigns in the southeast.

5047. Donovan, Frank R. MR. LINCOLN'S PROCLAMATION: THE STORY OF THE EMANCIPATION PROCLAMATION. New York: Dodd, Mead, 1964.

Brief and undocumented; adds little that is new, like this annotation.

5048. Douglas, William O. MR. LINCOLN AND THE NEGROES: THE LONG ROAD TO EQUALITY. New York: Atheneum, 1963.

A not very successful attempt by the Supreme Court Justice to trace the evolution of black rights from Lincoln's time to the present. The text material is not extensive. Douglas recognizes Lincoln's growth on the issue of black equality, but his narrative becomes mired in the murky battleground of Reconstruction.

5049. Drago, Edmund L. "How Sherman's March Through Georgia Affected the Slaves." GA HIS Q, 57 [1973]: 361-375.

First the slaves were thrilled, then disillusioned, and then relieved by Field Order 15 forbidding their impressment and promising them land.

5050. DuBois, W.E.B. "The Negro and the Civil War." SCI SOC, 25 [1961]: 347-352.

A famous black historian of slavery and black history denounces the tendency he sees among historians at the outset of the Civil War Centennial, to distort the history of blacks, slavery, and abolition.

5051. Dumond, Dwight L. "Emancipation: History's Fantastic Reverie." JNH, 49 [1964]: 1-12.

The Emancipation Proclamation, asserts the author, is the basic charter of freedom for many Americans, a confession of previous error, and a simple act of justice issuing from the highest authority in the land. But, the promise inherent in it was not fulfilled.

5052. Durden, Robert F. "A. Lincoln: Honkie or Equalitarian?" S ATL Q, 71 [1972]: 281-291.

A discussion of Lincoln as a white supremacist. Author concludes Lincoln was exceedingly pragmatic in his outlook, realizing both North and South had to make adjustments.

5053. Dyer, Brainerd. "The Persistence of the Idea of Negro Colonization." PAC HIS R, 12 [1943]: 53-65.

The idea that the "Negro Problem" in the United States could be solved by removing blacks to faraway places still persists. The fundamental problem is still whether or not the two races can live side by side.

5054. ———. "The Treatment of Colored Union Troops by the Confederates, 1861-1865." JNH, 20 [1935]: 273-286.

The Confederate government announced early in the war that black Union soldiers who were captured would be returned to their masters or respective states for punishment. Although some captives were executed in places such as Fort Pillow, more often than not they were treated as other prisoners-of-war.

5055. Eaton, John. GRANT, LINCOLN AND THE FREEDOM: REMINISCENCES OF THE CIVIL WAR.... New York, 1907.

Intriguing memoirs of a Union chaplain who worked extensively with freed slaves in the western theater.

5056. Emilio, Luis F. A BRAVE BLACK REGIMENT: HISTORY OF THE FIFTY-FOURTH REGIMENT OF MASSACHUSETTS VOLUNTEER INFANTRY, 1861-1865. Boston, 1891. Reprint 1969.

Old, but still the best history of this famous black regiment. Contains many interesting photographs.

5057. Everett, Donald E. "Ben Butler and the Louisiana Native Guards, 1861-1862." JSH, 24 [1958]: 201-217.

When Butler assumed command in New Orleans in 1862 he decided to use the Louisiana Native Guards in the United States army. These men were free colored troops. While the government gave no official approval, it did not interfere. However, southern reaction to the plan proved a stumbling block.

5058. Farley, Ena L. "Methodists and Baptists on the Issue of Black Equality in New York, 1865-1868." JNH, 61 [1976]: 374-392.

Within three years after Appomattox, the two largest denominations in New York reaffirmed racial segregation as official church policy.

5059. Fehrenbacher, Don E. "Only His Stepchildren: Lincoln and the Negro." CWH, 20 [1974]: 292-310.

Author believes that too much "presentist" historical thinking has marred efforts to fairly evaluate Lincoln's opinions on the race question.

5060. Fen, Sing-Nan. "Notes on the Education of Negroes at Norfolk and Portsmouth, Virginia, During the Civil War." PHYLON, 28 [1967]: 197-207.

A discussion of the problems inherent in trying to establish a public school system for blacks in the Hampton Roads area during the war.

5061. ———. "Notes on the Education of Negroes in North Carolina During the Civil War." J NEG ED, 36 [1967]: 24-31.

Although a number of schools to educate blacks were founded in North Carolina during the war, numerous obstacles hampered the successful carrying out of an educational program for the freed slaves.

5062. Fishel, Leslie H., Jr. "Wisconsin and Negro Suffrage." WIS MAG HIS, 46 [1962/1963]: 180-196.

A survey of the campaign for black suffrage in Wisconsin, 1847-1866. While voters approved the idea in 1849, for many years it was held that the vote was not large enough to be legally valid. In 1866 a judge upheld the 1849 count. Through it all a spirit of apathetic opposition to black suffrage marked the majority of white opinion.

5063. Foner, Philip S. "The First Negro Meeting in Maryland." MD HIS MAG, 66 [1971]: 60-67.

The first meeting of blacks ever held in Maryland, the purpose of which was to encourage enlistments, took place on February 28, 1864. The forum was also used to bring about pressure for equal pay for black soldiers.

5064. Forten, Charlotte L. JOURNAL. Ray A. Billington, editor. New York: Dryden, 1953.

Charlotte Forten, the well-educated daughter of a reasonably prosperous black Philadelphia family, kept a revealing record of her active life among abolitionists. She spent two years at the Port Royal experiment during the war.

5065. Fosger, E.C. "The Battle of Milliken's Bend." CRISIS, 81 [1974]: 295-300.

Author discusses the importance of blacks in the Union army, beginning with this battle of early June 1863 above Vicksburg, in which new contraband units repulsed Confederate attacks on Union positions west of the river.

5066. Franklin, John H. "The Civil War and the Negro American." JNH, 48 [1962]: 77-107.

With the final announcement of the Emancipation Proclamation, January 1, 1863, blacks began to find acceptance in the army. Generally, there has been praise for the performance of black soldiers in the war.

5067. ———. THE EMANCIPATION PROCLAMATION. New York: Doubleday, 1983.

A fairly good though brief study of how the decision was made to emancipate the slaves. Author examines the background and consequences of the decision and notes its impact both at home and abroad.

5068. Fredrickson, George M. "A Man But Not A Brother: Abraham Lincoln and Racial Equality." JSH, 41 [1975]: 39-58.

Author attempts to go beyond the political rhetoric to learn Lincoln's true views on the subject. He reviews Lincoln's support for colonization.

5069. Fuke, Richard P. "A Reform Mentality: Federal Policy Toward Black Marylanders, 1864-1868." CWH, 22 [1976]: 214-235.

Author disputes revisionist thesis that federal officers in the South during the war and Reconstruction were opposed to bettering conditions for blacks.

5070. Gerteis, Louis S. FROM CONTRABAND TO FREEDMAN: FEDERAL POLICY TOWARD SOUTHERN BLACKS, 1861-1865. Westport, Connecticut: Greenwood, 1973.

An excellent account of the relatively harsh federal policy toward liberated slaves during the war. Author examines the Virginia-Carolina, Louisiana, and Mississippi theaters. It is clear that the government officials had no thoughts about giving full equality to the freedman.

5071. ———. "Salmon P. Chase: Radicalism and the Politics of Emancipation, 1863-1864." JAH, 60 [1973]: 42-62.

Radical Republicans may have been sincere in their desire to help southern blacks, but their efforts were unsuccessful.

5072. Gibbs, C.R. "Blacks in the Union Navy." NEG HIS BULL, 36 [1973]: 137-139.

This article traces the sea service of blacks prior to 1860. During the Civil War, black sailors performed admirably and were treated relatively well in the Union navy. The author provides, in addition, a sketch of the four black sailors who were awarded the Congressional Medal of Honor.

5073. Graham, Shirley. THERE WAS ONCE A SLAVE ... THE HEROIC STORY OF FREDERICK DOUGLASS. New York: Messner, 1947.

A novelized biography of Douglass intended for a popular audience.

5074. Greene, Larry A. "The Emancipation Proclamation in New Jersey and the Paranoid Style." NJ HIS, 91 [1973]: 108-124.

Gives background for New Jersey's opposition to the Emancipation Proclamation, even though Lincoln always carried the state.

5075. Gresham, Luveta W. "Colonization Proposals for Free Negroes and Contrabands During the War." J NEG ED, 16 [1947]: 28-33.

The article discusses the numerous proposals made during the war, both by foreign countries and Americans, for the colonization of freed blacks in the West Indies, South America, or Africa.

5076. Guthrie, James M. CAMP-FIRES OF THE AFRO-AMERICAN: OR, THE COLORED MAN AS A PATRIOT, SOLDIER, SAILOR, AND HERO.... Philadelphia, 1899.

A lengthy, sympathetic survey of black soldiers in all American wars, written by a white chaplain serving in a black regiment.

5077. Haller, John S. "Civil War Anthropometry: The Making of A Racial Ideology." CWH, 16 [1970]: 309-324.

An analysis of the impact of Civil War anthropometry--the study of one's physical dimensions--on postwar racial attitudes.

5078. Hallowell, Norwood P. SELECTED LETTERS AND PAPERS. Peterborough, New Hampshire: R.R. Smith, 1963.

Author writes on the black as a fighting man and urges that historians deal more fairly with the performance of black troops in the Civil War.

5079. Hansen, Chadwick. "The 54th Massachusetts Volunteer Black Infantry as a Subject for American Artists." MASS R, 16 [1975]: 745-759.

The 54th Massachusetts, the famous all-black unit led by Colonel Robert Shaw, has become the subject of many works of poetry, music, and sculpture.

5080. Harding, Leonard. "The Cincinnati Riots of 1862." CIN HIS SOC BULL, 25 [1967]: 229-239.

A week-long race riot in July 1862 was caused by labor unrest along the Cincinnati waterfront.

5081. Harris, Robert L., Jr. "H. Ford Douglas: Afro-American Anti-Slavery Emigrationist." JNH, 62 [1977]: 217-234.

Douglas, a free, black, anti-slavery activist, served in the Union army during the Civil War and became the only black captain to command combat troops.

5082. Haven, Gilbert. NATIONAL SERMONS. Boston, 1869.

Author, a Methodist clergyman from New England, spoke forcefully for racial equality and desegregation.

5083. Hawkins, Homer C. "Trends in Black Migration From 1863 to 1960." PHYLON, 34 [1973]: 140-152.

A survey of the black migration movements in the 100 years since emancipation with a look at the future of black migration.

5084. Heller, Charles E. "'Between Two Fires': The 54th Massachusetts." CWTI, 11 [1] [1972]: 32-41.

The first all-black regiment formed in the North faced both Confederate hostility and Union prejudice. They served for over a year without pay. Four of the men received the Medal of Honor.

5085. ———. "George Luther Stearns." CWTI, 13 [4] [1974]: 20-28.

Succinct account of Stearns' efforts and the frustrations he experienced in recruiting black troops in many northern states and occupied areas of the South.

5086. Hicken, Victor. "The Record of Illinois' Negro Soldiers in the Civil War." JISHS, 56 [1963]: 529-551.

Officially Illinois supplied 1,811 black soldiers during the war, but this is probably a conservative figure. The most important Negro organization credited to Illinois was the renowned 29th United States Colored Infantry. Its losses, mostly suffered around Petersburg, indicate it was truly a fighting unit.

5087. Higginson, Thomas Wentworth. ARMY LIFE IN A BLACK REGIMENT. Boston: Beacon, 1962. Reprint of 1869 edition.

The author commanded the first slave military unit that was mustered into Federal service, the 1st South Carolina Volunteers. This work, which is based on his notes and diaries, has become a classic for its description of life in a black Union regiment during the Civil War.

5088. ———. "The First Black Regiment." THE OUTLOOK, [July 2, 1898]: 521-531.

A short but candid review of the author's experiences in organizing and leading the first black regiment. It is a summary of Higginson's book published earlier. [See above]

5089. High, Ronald K. "Fort Pillow Massacre: The Aftermath of Paducah." JISHS, 66 [1973]: 62-70.

Confederate General Nathan B. Forrest's raid against Paducah was expected by the outnumbered Union forces. Three times the predominantly black Union artillery repulsed the enemy. This was remembered by the Confederates at Fort Pillow.

5090. Hill, Isaac J. A SKETCH OF THE 29TH REGIMENT OF CONNECTICUT COLORED TROOPS. Baltimore, 1867.

A brief but valuable account by a black soldier.

5091. Hinton, Richard J. REBEL INVASION OF MISSOURI AND KANSAS.... Chicago, 1865.

Written by an officer of a Kansas black unit, this is the story of the outstanding service of these soldiers in the army of the border against General Sterling Price and his raiders.

5092. Holliday, Joseph E. "Freedmen's Aid Societies in Cincinnati, 1862-1870." CINC HIS SOC BULL, 22 [1964]: 169-185.

An account of the work of two wartime Cincinnati organizations to provide help and counsel for freed slaves. The groups exercised an important influence in bringing about the creation of the Freedmen's Bureau in 1865.

5093. Horowitz, Murray M. "Ben Butler and the Negro: 'Miracles are Occurring.'" LA HIS, 17]1976]: 159-186.

An analysis of the almost overnight transformation of Ben Butler from a pro-slavery Democrat before the war to a radical abolitionist Republican during the war. The switch was motivated in part by politics, says the author, but also by a sincere change of heart.

5094. Howard, Victor B. BLACK LIBERATION IN KENTUCKY: EMANCIPATION AND FREEDOM, 1862-1884. Lexington: University of Kentucky Press, 1984.

A well-documented, well-written study of an aspect of Kentucky history which has generally been overlooked by historians.

5095. Hyman, Harold M. "Lincoln and Equal Rights for Negroes: The Irrelevancy of the 'Wadsworth Letter.'" CWH, 12 [1966]: 258-266.

Even though the "Wadsworth Letter" may have been spurious, Lincoln was still moving toward a full belief in Negro suffrage.

5096. James, Felix. "The Establishment of Freedmen's Village in Arlington, Virginia." NEG HIS BULL, 33 [1970]: 90-93.

A village for freed slaves and fugitive slaves who had fled to Washington was established in December, 1863.

5097. Johnson, Ludwell H. "Lincoln and Equal Rights: The Authenticity of the Wadsworth Letter." JSH, 32 [1966]: 83-87.

Author questions authenticity of this letter, allegedly written by Lincoln early in 1864 and frequently cited to prove that the president was a racial egalitarian.

5098. ———. "Lincoln and Equal Rights: A Reply." CWH, 13 [1967]: 66-73.

In reply to Harold Hyman, Johnson denies that Lincoln was moving toward equal rights for blacks.

5099. Jones, Howard J. "Letters in Protest of Race Prejudice in the Army During the American Civil War." JNH, 61 [1976]: 97-98.

A second lieutenant writes to his superior officer offering to resign because of the prejudice against black soldiers in the army.

5100. Jordan, John L. "Was There A Massacre at Fort Pillow?" TENN HIS Q, 6 [1947]: 99-133.

Author presents some new evidence on the Fort Pillow massacre and concludes General Forrest was done a grave injustice in being blamed for it.

5101. Kaplan, Sidney. "The Miscegenation Issue in the Election of 1864." JNH, 34 [1949]: 274-343.

A discussion of the race issue in northern politics.

5102. Keckley, Elizabeth. BEHIND THE SCENES: OR, THIRTY YEARS A SLAVE AND FOUR YEARS IN THE WHITE HOUSE. Buffalo: Stansil and Lee, 1931.

This book by Mrs. Lincoln's dressmaker provides revealing glimpses of life in the White House, and still may be read with profit. A reprint of the 1868 edition.

5103. Klement, Frank. "Midwestern Opposition to Lincoln's Emancipation Policy." JNH, 49 [1964]: 169-183.

Midwestern Democrats provided most of the opposition to the Emancipation Proclamation because it would discourage enlistments, breed discontent in the Border states and unite the South. Some Democrats continued to make the Emancipation Proclamation an issue in every election during the remainder of the war.

5104. Krug, Mark M. "The Republican Party and the Emancipation Proclamation." JNH, 48 [1963]: 98-114.

Determined to right a moral wrong and strengthen government's position, Lincoln was not influenced by Radical pressure in deciding to issue the proclamation.

5105. Langston, John M. FROM THIS VIRGINIA PLANTATION TO THE NATIONAL CAPITOL.... Hartford, Connecticut: 1894.

An articulate memoir by a black who became a member of Congress from Virginia.

5106. Levstik, Frank R. "The Fifth Regiment, United States Colored Troops, 1863-1865." NW OHIO Q, 42 [1970]: 86-98.

Detailed account of the organization and combat service of this unit. Other information includes an age analysis of the recruits and some general comments on their geographical origin.

5107. ———. "From Slavery to Freedom." CWTI, 11 [7] [1972]: 10-15.

Two rare wartime letters from a black Medal of Honor winner, Milton M. Holland.

5108. ———. "Robert A. Pinn: Courageous Black Soldier." NEG HIS BULL, 37 [1974]: 304-305.

Although overshadowed in history by the attention focused on the 54th and 55th Massachusetts [black regiments], the 5th United States Colored troops, formerly the 127th Ohio, performed very well during the war, rising "to the heights of martial glory." Four of the 16 Medals of Honor awarded to blacks in the Civil War went to members of the 127th Ohio.

5109. Litwack, Leon F. BEEN IN THE STORM SO LONG: THE AFTERMATH OF SLAVERY. New York: Borzoi, 1979.

An excellent glimpse of the slaves' hopes and aspirations as they approach freedom. The significance and harsh realities of freedom in the post-bellum South are also discussed.

5110. Lofton, Williston H. "Northern Labor and the Negro During the Civil War." JNH, 34 [1949]: 251-273.

The first of this two part study concerns disturbances in Buffalo, Chicago, Cincinnati, Boston, and Newark. The second portion focuses on the 1863 New York riots. The author concludes that the anti-Negro feeling that surfaced during these uprisings stemmed from prewar labor attitudes and fear of economic competition.

5111. Lovett, Bobby L. "The Negro's Civil War in Tennessee, 1861-1865." JNH, 61 [1976]: 36-50.

The "efficient utilization of that valuable source of manpower [blacks] made the difference between victory and defeat for the United States." The presence of black Tennesseans at the battle of Nashville was crucial to the northern victory.

5112. Main, Edwin M. THE STORY OF THE MARCHES, BATTLES, AND INCIDENTS OF THE THIRD UNITED STATES COLORED CAVALRY.... Louisville, 1908.

A solid history of a black regiment.

5113. May, J. Thomas. "Continuity and Change in the Labor Program of the Union Army and the Freedmen's Bureau." CWH, 17 [1971]: 245-254.

An examination of federal control of freed slaves in Louisiana from 1862-1866.

5114. Mays, Joe H. BLACK AMERICANS AND THEIR CONTRIBUTION TOWARD UNION VICTORY IN THE AMERICAN CIVIL WAR, 1861-1865. Lanham, Maryland: University Press of America, 1984.

A good account of the important roles played by blacks in aid of the Union cause. In addition to service as soldiers and sailors, they were laborers, spies, scouts, guides, and servants. Useful appendixes accompany the text.

5115. McConnell, Roland C., editor. "Concerning the Procurement of Negro Troops in the South During the Civil War." JNH, 35 [1950]: 315-319.

Of the nearly 200,000 black soldiers who served in the Union army, over half were recruited in the South. Procurement fell to the adjutant-general of the United States army.

5116. ———. "From the Preliminary to Final Emancipation: The First Hundred Days." JNH, 48 [1963]: 260-276.

Sampling northern opinion on the preliminary emancipation up until the final edict was issued on January 1, 1863.

5117. McCrary, Peyton. ABRAHAM LINCOLN AND RECONSTRUCTION: THE LOUISIANA EXPERIMENT. Princeton: Princeton University Press, 1948.

A good account of this preliminary effort at Reconstruction government. Louisiana was occupied by federal troops early in the war and was therefore a good place to make the experiment.

5118. McMurray, John. "A Union Officer's Recollections of the Negro as Soldier." Horace Montgomery, editor. PENN HIS, 28 [1961]: 156-186.

Recollections of John McMurray, an officer with the 6th U.S. Colored Infantry.

5119. McPherson, James M. "Abolitionist and Negro Opposition to Colonization During the Civil War." PHYLON, 26 [1965]: 391-399.

Numerous blacks and abolitionists opposed congressional action to colonize free blacks in the Caribbean.

5120. ———, editor. THE NEGRO'S CIVIL WAR: HOW AMERICAN NEGROES FELT AND ACTED DURING THE WAR FOR THE UNION. New York: Pantheon, 1965.

A collection of writings by both blacks and whites giving a valuable insight as to how blacks felt about the war which was being fought for their liberation. The book grew out of the author's earlier study THE STRUGGLE FOR EQUALITY, listed next.

5121. ———. THE STRUGGLE FOR EQUALITY: ABOLITIONISTS AND THE NEGRO IN THE CIVIL WAR AND RECONSTRUCTION. Princeton: Princeton University Press, 1964.

A comprehensive review of the activities of abolitionists from 1860 to the adoption of the Fifteenth Amendment in 1870. They were quite effective in pressing for government reforms in the direction of equality. Such complex issues as the relationship between the abolitionists and the Republican party are expertly handled.

5122. Messner, William F. "Black Education in Louisiana, 1863-1865." CWH, 22 [1976]: 41-59.

The politics behind the creation of a rudimentary educational system by General Nathaniel Banks.

5123. ———. FREEDMEN AND THE IDEOLOGY OF FREE LABOR: LOUISIANA, 1862-1865. Lafayette, Louisiana: University of Southwestern Louisiana, 1978.

During his period of control in Louisiana General Banks tried a system of free labor using blacks. It failed because owners of the slaves would not pay wages and the blacks themselves did not know what to do.

5124. ———. "The Vicksburg Campaign of 1862: A Case Study in the Federal Utilization of Black Labor." LAB HIS, 16 [1975]: 371-381.

The Vicksburg campaign of 1862 was the final instance where, after the fighting was finished, the Union army returned all escaping slaves to their owners.

5125. Miller, Randall M. "Freedom Time, 1865: An Ex-Slave Writes Home." NEG HIS BULL, 38 [1975]: 382-383.

James Smith, a slave liberated in southern Virginia near the close of the war, found himself near Philadelphia in July 1865. A letter written back to his adopted slave mother is printed here. It reflects deep affection for his family, friends, and former master.

5126. ———. "Letters From Nashville, 1862, II: 'Dear Master.'" TENN HIS Q, 33 [1974]: 85-92.

Letters written by a slave to her master, General William G. Harding, imprisoned in the North. The letters were dictated by Mrs. Harding's personal servant. The general was a planter and slaveholder of prominence in Tennessee.

5127. ——— and Jon W. Zaphy. "Unwelcome Allies: Billy Yank and the Black Soldier." PHYLON, 39 [1978]: 234-240.

Though fighting for the liberation of the blacks, the average Union soldier was racist.

5128. Mohr, Clarence L. "Before Sherman: Georgia Blacks and the Union War Effort." JSH, 45 [1979]: 331-352.

Whereas Sherman's march to the sea did not end slavery there, many slaves left their plantations to join his army.

5129. ———. "Southern Blacks in the Civil War: A Century of Historiography." JNH, 59 [1974]: 177-195.

Two stereotypes emerged after the war concerning black attitudes and behavior during the war. One idealized the Old South, the other glorified the moral stance of the abolitionists. Scholarly objectivity with respect to blacks was often tempered by racial bias.

5130. Montesano, Phillip M. "San Francisco's Black Churches in the Early 1860s: Political Pressure Groups." CAL HIS SOC Q, 52 [1973]: 145-151.

The black churches of San Francisco played an active part among northern sympathizers in California.

5131. Morgan, Thomas J. REMINISCENCES OF SERVICE WITH COLORED TROOPS IN THE ARMY OF THE CUMBERLAND, 1863-1865. Providence, 1885.

A short but valuable account of service with the 14th United States Colored Infantry.

5132. Moser, Harold D. "The Emancipation Proclamation." NC HIS R, 44 [1967]: 53-71.

A study of the reaction in North Carolina to the proclamation.

5133. Mothershead, Harmon. "Negro Rights in Colorado Territory [1859-1867]." COL MAG, 40 [1963]: 212-223.

Colorado was ready for statehood in 1864-1865, but admission was delayed a decade because of local opposition to granting voting rights to the tiny minority of 300 blacks.

5134. Nelson, Larry E. "Black Leaders and the Presidential Election of 1864." JNH, 63 [1978]: 42-58.

Leaders of the black community dwelt on the fate of blacks after the war.

5135. Newton, Alexander H. OUT OF THE BRIARS: AN AUTOBIOGRAPHY AND SKETCH OF THE TWENTY-NINTH REGIMENT, CONNECTICUT VOLUNTEERS. Philadelphia, 1910.

Few black soldiers wrote their memoirs, but this is one of the best.

5136. Noyes, Edward. "The Negro in Wisconsin's Civil War Effort." LIN HER, 69 [1967]: 70-82.

This article reveals the reluctance of state officials to accept the military services of their black residents. As the war dragged on the use of blacks came very much into favor. Wisconsin furnished only 353 black troops.

5137. ———. "White Opposition to Black Migration Into Civil War Wisconsin." LIN HER, 73 [1971]: 181-193.

As war enthusiasm waned, white opposition to black immigration into Wisconsin grew.

5138. Ofari, Earl. "LET YOUR MOTTO BE RESISTANCE": THE LIFE AND THOUGHT OF HENRY HIGHLAND GARNET. Boston: Beacon, 1972.

A biography, based on available sources, of a black man who was well-known for his efforts on behalf of black nationalism in the middle years of the 19th century. During the war he helped recruit black troops for the Union.

5139. Okron, Edet U. FROM SLAVERY TO PUBLIC SERVICE: ROBERT SMALLS, 1839-1915. New York: Oxford University Press, 1971.

The life story of Robert Smalls, a Beaufort, South Carolina black, who became a Union hero during the war and was active in South Carolina politics during Reconstruction. He also served several terms in the U.S. Congress.

5140. Owen, Robert D. THE WRONG OF SLAVERY, THE RIGHT OF EMANCIPATION, AND THE FUTURE OF THE AFRICAN RACE IN THE UNITED STATES. Philadelphia, 1864.

Revised report of a commission formed to advise policy on future of freedmen.

5141. ———. "Owen's Letter to Lincoln." IND HIS BULL, 43 [1966]: 50-54.

Robert Dale Owen wrote to the president on September 17, 1862, urging black emancipation.

5142. Parmet, Robert D. "Schools for the Freedmen." NEG HIS BULL, 34 [1971]: 128-132.

An account of the creation of educational institutions for freed slaves from 1861 on through Reconstruction and beyond. The Freedmen's Bureau was the principal, although not the only, agency to found such schools.

5143. Pease, William H. and Jane Pease. BLACK UTOPIA: NEGRO COMMUNAL EXPERIMENTS IN AMERICA. Madison: State Historical Society of Wisconsin, 1963.

A survey of the several black communes established in the

United States and Canada in the generation prior to the Civil War. Only 5,000 blacks at the most were involved in the experiments in black self-government, which apparently were not very successful.

5144. Perkins, Frances B. "Two Years With a Colored Regiment." NE MAG, 17 [1897/1898]: 533-543.

Service with the 33rd United States Colored Infantry regiment is recalled.

5145. Pettit, Arthur G. "Mark Twain's Attitude Toward the Negro in the West, 1861-1867." W HIS Q, 1 [1970]: 51-62.

The years Mark Twain spent in Nevada, California, and the Sandwich Islands, were connected with the war years and marked the peak of his racist feelings toward blacks.

5146. Philbrick, Edward S. LETTERS FROM PORT ROYAL WRITTEN AT THE TIME OF THE CIVIL WAR. Elizabeth W. Pearson, editor. Boston, 1906.

A detailed account of the Port Royal experiment from the letters of Edward S. Philbrick.

5147. Phillips, James R. "Phillips Brooks: Spokesman for Freedom." NEG HIS BULL, 27 [1963]: 10.

A brief note on Brooks who argued for full legal rights and social equality for blacks.

5148. Pierce, Edward L. ENFRANCHISEMENT AND CITIZENSHIP: ADDRESSES AND PAPERS. A.W. Stevens, editor. Boston, 1896.

A valuable study of a number of matters concerning black soldiers.

5149. Planck, Gary R. "Abraham Lincoln and Black Colonization: Theory and Practice." LIN HER, 71 [1970]: 61-77.

An examination of Lincoln's changing views on colonization of American blacks from 1845 onward. By the early 1860s he had concluded that the idea was impractical and he reconciled himself to the only other plan--racial adjustment within the United States.

5150. Qualls, Youra. "'Successors of Woolman and Benezet': The Beginnings of the Philadelphia Friends Freedmen's Association." FRIENDS HIS ASSN BULL, 45 [1956]: 82-104.

Details the first six month's activities of an organization formed to assist the freedmen.

5151. Quarles, Benjamin. BLACK ABOLITIONISTS. New York: Oxford University Press, 1969.

This is the most complete analysis to date of the efforts of blacks to bring about the ending of slavery. Their biggest success was in stirring the fires of the anti-slavery cause among northern whites.

5152. ———. LINCOLN AND THE NEGRO. New York: Oxford University Press, 1962.

A scholarly, well-written work which details Lincoln's developing attitude toward blacks.

5153. ———. THE NEGRO IN THE CIVIL WAR. Boston: Little, Brown, 1953.

In the first full-length examination of blacks during the Civil War, the author points out the numerous contributions they made to promote the war effort and their own emancipation. Best work on the subject to this time.

5154. Rampp, Lary C. "Incident at Baxter Springs on October 6, 1863." KAN HIS Q, 36 [1970]: 183-197.

A surprise attack on black troops by Quantrill's raiders.

5155. ———. "Negro Troop Activity in Indian Territory, 1863-1865." CH OK, 47 [1969]: 531-559.

Blacks campaigning in Indian Territory acquitted themselves well during the war.

5156. Rankin, David C. "The Impact of the Civil War on the Free Colored Community of New Orleans." PERS A HIS, 11 [1977/1978]: 377-416.

Before the war New Orleans' free blacks enjoyed a thriving, prosperous culture, but with Union occupation, their rights and social prestige were eroded.

5157. Reddick, L.D. "The Negro Policy of the United States Army." JNH, 34 [1949]: 9-29.

Four guidelines prevailed: [1] Blacks to be used only when and where manpower needs required it; [2] Blacks shall not be normally used in positions of authority and only then over other blacks; [3] Black troops shall be segregated; [4] There shall be no awards presented to black soldiers for heroic performance under fire against the foe.

5158. Richardson, Joe M. "The American Missionary Association and Black Education in Civil War Missouri." MO HIS R, 69 [1975]: 433-448.

One of the earliest sources of instruction for Missouri freedmen was the American Missionary Association. To the AMA emancipation meant more than freedom from slavery; it meant divesting freedmen of the shackles of ignorance, superstition, and sin.

5159. Rickard, James H. SERVICES WITH COLORED TROOPS IN BURNSIDE'S CORPS. Providence, Rhode Island: 1894.

Author was a captain with the 19th United States Colored Troops.

5160. Ripley, C. Peter. SLAVES AND FREEDMEN IN CIVIL WAR LOUISIANA. Baton Rouge: Louisiana State University Press, 1976.

The Louisiana Experiment, begun in 1862, failed because both politicians and military leaders joined in a "planters' mentality," and thus missed their great opportunity. The "racism, paternalism, and depriving blacks of land" caused the experiment to fail. An excellent book on "describing aspirations, abilities, and activities of blacks in Louisiana."

5161. Ritter, E. Joy. "Congressional Medal of Honor Winners." NEG HIS BULL, 26 [1963]: 135-136.

William H. Carney and Christian A. Fleetwood, both blacks, won the Medal of Honor.

5162. Robertson, James I., Jr. "Negro Soldiers in the Civil War." CWTI, 7 [6] [1968]: 21-31.

Blacks made up 12 per cent of the Union forces. Many were killed by fellow Union soldiers.

5163. Rollin, Frank A. LIFE AND PUBLIC SERVICES OF MARTIN R. DELANY .... Boston, 1868.

A useful examination of the life of a black man who served with the 104th United States Colored Troops and was an officer with the Freedmen's Bureau.

5164. Rose, Willie L. REHEARSAL FOR RECONSTRUCTION: THE PORT ROYAL EXPERIMENT. Indianapolis: Bobbs-Merrill, 1964.

A classic study of the wartime experiment with free black labor in the Sea Islands.

5165. Ross, Steven J. "Freed Soil, Freed Labor, Freed Men: John Eaton and the Davis Bend Experiment." JSH, 44 [1978]: 213-232.

At Davis Bend, Mississippi, 25 miles below Vicksburg, an experiment in free labor for the former slaves was instituted. It worked out well and seemed to suggest that, given modest grants of land, the freedmen could be successfully incorporated into a free labor economy.

5166. Ruchames, Louis. "William Lloyd Garrison and the Negro Franchise." JNH, 50 [1965]: 37-49.

Garrison believed that Lincoln's reelection in 1864 was essential for the cause of blacks' freedom.

5167. Scassellati, Robert R., Jr. "First Shots at Fort Barrancas." CWTI, 11 [9] [1973]: 38-43.

Relates an incident which occurred before the firing on the STAR OF THE WEST. Floridians attempted to sieze the powder stored at Fort Barrancas located southwest of Pensacola on January 8, 1861.

5168. Scheips, Paul J. "Lincoln and the Chiriqui Colonization Project." JNH, 37 [1952]: 418-453.

Lincoln believed that the coal mines at Chiriqui in Central America could give employment to colonized Free Negroes. A sufficient number applied and the experiment was begun. It was suspended shortly, however, because of the opposition of Costa Rica.

5169. Scroggs, Joseph J. and Sig Synnestvedt, editors. "'The Earth Shook and Quivered.'" CWTI, 11 [8]: [1972]: 30-37.

Diary observations of black troops during the siege of Petersburg.

5170. Sears, Cyrus. PAPER OF CYRUS SEARS.... Columbus, Ohio: 1909.

A short but good account of black troops in action by the commander of the 49th United States Colored Infantry.

5171. Seraile, William. "The Struggle to Raise Black Regiments in New York State, 1861-1864." NY HIS SOC Q, 58 [1974]: 215-233.

This study describes the resistance of Governor Horatio Seymour to the enlistment of black troops in New York State. His position angered many because resident blacks were enlisting in other states. The blacks were willing and eager to serve. The federal government had to intervene finally by authorizing the recruitment of some 4,125 New York blacks into the 20th, 26th, and 31st regiments of United States Colored Troops.

5172. Shannon, Fred A. "The Federal Government and the Negro Soldier, 1861-1865." JNH, 11 [1926]: 563-583.

The author examines the types of discrimination that black soldiers experienced. Those who were in a slave status when they entered the military fared worst of all.

5173. Shaw, James. OUR LAST CAMPAIGN AND SUBSEQUENT SERVICE IN TEXAS. Providence, Rhode Island: 1905.

Shaw commanded the 7th United States Colored Troops.

5174. Sherman, George R. THE NEGRO AS A SOLDIER. Providence, 1913.

A brief survey and an account of the formation of the 1st United States Colored Troops.

5175. Shewmaker, Kenneth R. and Andrew K. Prinz, editors. "A Yankee in Louisiana: Selections From the Diary and Correspondence of Henry R. Gardner, 1862-1866." LA HIS, 5 [1964]: 271-295.

Selections deal with army life, military operations, the black soldier, and cotton speculation.

5176. Simon, John Y. and Felix James. "Andrew Johnson and the Freedmen." LIN HER, 79 [1977]: 71-75.

Johnson favored emancipation, but opposed giving free blacks special protection or assistance from the national government.

5177. Slaughter, Linda W. THE FREEDMEN OF THE SOUTH. Cincinnati, Ohio: 1869.

A missionary teacher in the South reports on her experiences.

5178. Smith, John D. "The Recruitment of Negro Soldiers in Kentucky, 1863-1865." KY HIS SOC REG, 72 [1974]: 364-390.

Detailed account of the opposition in Kentucky to the enlistment of black troops. This discord reached a peak in March 1864 when Governor Thomas E. Bramlette allowed the enrollment of blacks to proceed after he had met with Lincoln.

5179. Sommers, Richard J. "The Dutch Gap Affair: Military Atrocities and Rights of Negro Soldiers." CWH, 21 [1975]: 51-64.

An analysis of an incident outside of Richmond in 1864, where the Confederates formed captured black Union soldiers into labor gangs.

5180. Spraggins, Tinsley L. "Mobilization of Negro Labor for the Department of Virginia and North Carolina, 1861-1865." NC HIS R, 24 [1947]: 160-197.

A discussion of the developing policy of the federal government to utilize Free Negroes and emancipated slaves as laborers. This would aid the North and would weaken the South.

5181. Staudenraus, P.J. THE AFRICAN COLONIZATION MOVEMENT, 1816-1865. New York: Columbia University Press, 1961.

A study of the futile efforts to colonize Free Negroes outside the United States from the founding of the American Colonization Society to the end of the Civil War.

5182. ———. "The Popular Origins of the Thirteenth Amendment." MID AM, 50 [1968]: 108-115.

Senator Lyman Trumbull of Illinois felt that all state and federal legislation was piecemeal so he introduced a bill to change the Constitution "to bring about nation-wide social reform."

5183. Stearns, Frank P., editor. THE LIFE AND PUBLIC SERVICES OF GEORGE LUTHER STEARNS. Philadelphia, 1907.

An important collection of material about a Boston abolitionist.

5184. Stein, A.H. HISTORY OF THE THIRTY-SEVENTH REGIMENT, U.S.C. INFANTRY.... Philadelphia, 1886.

Includes short histories of the companies and the regimental roster.

5185. Stotts, Gene. "The Negro Paul Revere of Quantrill's Raid." NEG HIS BULL, 26 [1963]: 169-170.

The story of a Negro servant's five-mile walk to warn settlers that a large Confederate raiding party was headed for Lawrence, Kansas.

5186. Swint, Henry L., editor. DEAR ONES AT HOME: LETTERS FROM CONTRABAND CAMPS. Nashville: Vanderbilt University Press, 1966.

A group of revealing and moving letters from two middle-aged Quaker sisters, Lucy and Sarah Chase, who describe their experiences while working as teachers in camps for freed slaves in Norfolk and the Sea Islands.

5187. ———. THE NORTHERN TEACHER IN THE SOUTH, 1861-1870. Nashville: Vanderbilt University Press, 1941.

An excellent study of northern teachers who worked diligently to assist former slaves adjust to freedom.

5188. Talbott, F. "Some Legislative and Legal Aspects of the Negro Question in West Virginia During the Civil War and Reconstruction." W VA HIS, 24 [1962/1963]: 1-31; 110-133; 211-247.

Discusses the developing rights of blacks in West Virginia, including basic civil rights, schools, suffrage, jury service, and office-holding.

5189. Taylor, Susie K. REMINISCENCES OF MY LIFE IN CAMP WITH THE 33rd UNITED STATES COLORED TROOPS. Boston, 1902.

An unusual narrative written by a black laundress and nurse attached to the 33rd United States Colored Troops. Useful not only for information on her personal situation with the 33rd, but also for the background she gives on troop activities.

5190. Thornbrough, Emma L. THE NEGRO IN INDIANA: A STUDY OF A MINORITY. Indianapolis: Indiana Historical Bureau, 1957.

A thorough examination of blacks in Indiana and how they were treated, 1830-1900. It is very apparent that they were not treated very well, even during the Civil War.

5191. ———. "The Race Issue in Indiana Politics During the Civil War." IND MAG HIS, 47 [1951]: 165-188.

The Indiana state legislature was hostile to Free Negroes in the state and took steps to prevent an increase in their numbers. Blacks and mulattoes were denied the right to vote, could not serve in the militia, and were prevented from testifying in a court case involving a white person.

5192. Toppin, Edgar A. "Emancipation Reconsidered." NEG HIS BULL, 26 [1963]: 233-236.

Discusses the Emancipation Proclamation in terms of various complex factors.

5193. ———. "Humbly They Served: The Black Brigade in the Defense of Cincinnati." JNH, 48 [1963]: 75-97.

After the Confederate invasion of Kentucky in the summer of 1862, the Black Brigade was organized and performed essentially as a civilian labor force. Despite this limited assignment, the Brigade was the first black military force to be raised in the North during the Civil War. This study describes the prejudice its members encountered and the contributions they made to Cincinnati's defenses.

5194. U.S. Army, Department of the Gulf. THE FREEDMEN OF LOUISIANA. New Orleans, 1865.

A detailed report on the affairs of the former slaves by the Union officer in charge of their welfare.

5195. U.S. Congress: Joint Committee on the Conduct of the War. FORT PILLOW MASSACRE. Washington, D.C.: 1864.

A report based on the investigation of the most celebrated "massacre" of black troops--the massacre at Fort Pillow, Tennessee, April 12, 1864.

5196. Vacha, John E. "The Case of Sara Lucy Bagby: A Late Gesture." OHIO HIS, 76 [1967]: 222-231.

The case occurred in Ohio's Western Reserve in 1861. Sara Lucy Bagby was possibly the last fugitive to be surrendered in the North under the Fugitive Slave Law.

5197. Valuska, David L. THE NEGRO IN THE UNION NAVY, 1861-1865. Ph.D. Dissertation, Lehigh University, 1973.

The author traces the various stages that characterized the recruitment of blacks into the Union navy including the manner in which the sensitive area of contrabands was handled. According to his analysis, blacks comprised only eight per cent of Union seamen and not 25 per cent as commonly believed. These sailors, however, were much more qualified than blacks who entered the Union army.

5198. Voegeli, V. Jacque. FREE BUT NOT EQUAL: THE MIDWEST AND THE NEGRO DURING THE CIVIL WAR. Chicago: University of Chicago Press, 1967.

Author discusses the unfriendly northern reaction to emancipation. While people in the Midwest wanted the slaves freed, they did not want them living in the Midwest.

5199. ———. "The Northwest and the Race Issue 1861-1862." MVHR, 50 [1963]: 235-251.

Although the Northwest opposed slavery, it continued to support anti-black laws.

5200. Wagandt, Charles L. "Election By Sword and Ballot: The Emancipationist Victory of 1863." MD HIS MAG, 59 [1964]: 143-164.

Efforts to free the slaves became a move to overthrow the old social, economic, and political order.

5201. ———. THE MIGHTY REVOLUTION: NEGRO EMANCIPATION IN MARYLAND, 1862-1864. Baltimore: Johns Hopkins Press, 1964.

An excellent study of the struggle between radicals--antislaveryites--and conservatives in an important state. Gradually the ground under the conservatives slips away. Author provides a vivid description of slavery in Maryland.

5202. Walker, Cam. "Corinth: The Story of a Contraband Camp." CWH, 20 [1974]: 5-22.

A record of the activities of a camp designed to handle the hordes of blacks fleeing to Union lines, 1861-1864.

5203. Weintraub, Andrew. "The Economics of Lincoln's Proposal for Compensated Emancipation." A J ECON SOC, 32 [1973]: 171-177.

How financially costly would Lincoln's plan of compensated emancipation have been at $400 per slave? From strictly a budgetary point of view, it was probably cheaper to fight the war than free the slaves at the $400 rate.

5204. Weisenburger, Francis P. "William Sanders Scarborough: Early Life and Years at Wilberforce." OHIO HIS, 71 [1962]: 203-226.

William Scarborough played an important part in the post-war contributions of blacks to American life. He served very ably as president of Wilberforce College.

5205. Wert, Jeffry D. "Camp William Penn and the Black Soldiers." PENN HIS, 46 [1979]: 335-346.

Black units trained at Camp William Penn, located outside of Philadelphia.

5206. Wesley, Charles H. "The Civil War and the Negro-American." JNH, 47 [1962]: 77-96.

Describes the isolation of Afro-Americans during the Centennial celebration. Suggests what Negro-Americans can do to make the Civil War Centennial more meaningful--that is, by interpreting the role of the Negro in the war.

5207. ———. "Great Man Theory of Emancipation." NEG HIS BULL, 28 [1965]: 101-102, 111-113, 115, 119.

While Lincoln did much to secure the freedom of the slaves, the achievement was not his alone but rather the work of thousands of anti-slavery people, black and white, who prepared the ground for the Emancipation Proclamation.

5208. ———. OHIO NEGROES IN THE CIVIL WAR. Columbus: Ohio State University Press, 1962.

Booklet provides an overview on the status of Ohio blacks in the pre-war years. The focus for the war years is on the recruitment and service of Ohio blacks. Although state officials were reluctant to enlist them at first, the attitude changed to one of active encouragement by 1863. Some 5,092 blacks were credited to Ohio.

5209. Westwood, Howard C. "Captive Black Union Soldiers in Charleston: What to Do?" CWH, 28 [1982]: 28-44.

The capture of black Union soldiers raised many questions for the Confederacy. It was Confederate policy to deny prisoner of war status to blacks. Those aiding in a slave insurrection were considered criminals. Thus the Confederacy had to wrestle with the question of white officers of black troops.

5210. Wiley, Bell I. "Billy Yank and the Black Folk." JNH, 36 [1951]: 35-52.

Strong hostility toward blacks is present in the letters white Union soldiers wrote home. This was owing to an innate prejudice, a feeling that the military was partial to Negroes, a belief that blacks were insolent or saucy, and the association of blacks with causing the war.

5211. ———. SOUTHERN NEGROES, 1861-1865. New York: Rinehart, 1938. Reprint 1953.

An important, scholarly work, one of the first to deal comprehensively with blacks both North and South.

5212. Will, Isaac J. A SKETCH OF THE 29th REGIMENT OF CONNECTICUT COLORED TROOPS. Balliman, Connecticut: 1867.

A short history of the regiment with unit rosters.

5213. Williams, G. Ward. A HISTORY OF THE NEGRO TROOPS IN THE WAR OF THE REBELLION 1861-1865.... New York, 1888. Reprint 1969.

Although old and somewhat flawed, this still remains a useful work.

5214. Williams, Lorraine A. "A Northern Intellectual Reaction to the Policy of Emancipation." JNH, 46 [1961]: 174-188.

Neither the confiscation acts nor the Emancipation Proclamation legally freed the slaves. Freedom had to come by constitutional amendment, which it did in 1865.

5215. Wilson, Henry. HISTORY OF THE ANTISLAVERY MEASURES OF THE THIRTY-SEVENTH AND THIRTY-EIGHTH UNITED STATES CONGRESSES, 1861-1864. Boston, 1864.

Still of use to any study of emancipation, the freedmen, and black troops in the war.

5216. Wilson, Joseph T. THE BLACK PHALANX: A HISTORY OF THE NEGRO SOLDIERS OF THE UNITED STATES IN THE WARS OF 1775-1812, 1861-1865. Hartford, Connecticut: 1892. Reprint 1968.

Written by a former black soldier, this book is of great interest but reading it is somewhat difficult. It does, however, contain "significant data on racial bias among the military."

5217. Wood, Forrest G. BLACK SCARE: THE RACIST RESPONSE TO EMANCIPATION AND RECONSTRUCTION. Berkeley: University of California Press, 1968.

The Civil War solved fewer problems than it created. The author analyzes the psychology of anti-black racism as it existed during the war and Reconstruction and seeks to show, using the knowledge and techniques of modern social scientists, how such attitudes were fallacious.

5218. Wright, John S. LINCOLN AND THE POLITICS OF SLAVERY. Reno: University of Nevada Press, 1970.

Lincoln's attitude toward slavery in the 1840s and 1850s is discussed. Author points out Lincoln's excellent sense of timing and how he kept anti-slavery "as the guiding principle through the crisis of 1860-1861."

B. WOMEN

By Linda DeLowry-Fryman

Ellen Coughlin. in "Women Studies: Changing the Landscape of the Traditional Academic Disciplines," [CHRONICLE OF HIGHER EDUCATION, August 1, 1984, p. 5], asserts, "The most visible achievement of the new scholarship in women's studies has been the deceptively simple act of 'putting women into the picture.'" The following selective bibliography of books and periodical articles on women's role in the Civil War is also an attempt to put women into the picture by focusing on northern women's volunteer activities, relief work, nursing, and simple moral and spiritual support given so freely to the Union soldier.

While historians have written volumes on troop movements, tactics, soldiers' life and the lives of military leaders, the role of women as volunteer nurses and Sanitary Commission workers has received only cursory treatment in most traditional histories. Most standard textbooks covering the Civil War period say virtually nothing about women's contributions and sacrifices for the war effort. This selective bibliography provides a survey of the most useful, informative, and readable sources on women during the Civil War, thus "putting women in the picture," which up to now has been predominantly a portrait of American males.

The types of materials included in the bibliography are books and journal articles, primary and secondary materials. First-person accounts and women's memoirs of the war years hold a central place in the bibliography since it is from these primary materials that the reader can derive the most profound sense of these women's dedication and self-sacrifice. The first person narratives are also the best source of specific detail about everyday activities and challenges, whether in hospitals or diet kitchens, on hospital boats or battlefields. The fullest appreciation of northern women's contributions to the war effort comes through cumulative exposure to many first person accounts.

Of the many first hand accounts, most deal with the volunteer nursing service. Some of the women were U.S. Sanitary Commission nurses; some were independents. Interestingly the two best known Civil War nurses, Clara Barton and Mother Bickerdyke, never worked for the Sanitary Commission and were not under the direction of Dorothea Dix, the Superintendent of Nurses. Most of the women whose narratives are represented are not well-known. In addition to the little known, the better known women are also represented in the bibiliography. Nursing activities among the soldiers are the more fully documented; but women's work with freed blacks and at home, in support of their sisters in the hospitals and on the battlefields, are also included in the bibliography.

Bolstering the numerous memoirs and reminiscences are selected secondary materials that provide syntheses of the women's materials and give helpful analyses of the historical background and the important persons of the time. A selection of official histories and documentary compilations related to the workings of the United States Sanitary Commission are included in this bibliography. These items were selected from among many titles because they provide the best overview of the Commission's work throughout the North. The books and journal articles that comprise this selective bibliography are all available either in larger library collections, through interlibrary loan or on microfilm. When an older title is available either in reprint or on microform, those options are noted.

Although many of the women who wrote their memoirs shrank from public recognition, they often felt that the story of their self-sacrificing sisters and friends deserved to be told. Elizabeth Cady Stanton, in her memoirs, EIGHTY YEARS AND MORE, wrote movingly of this need to make these women's contributions known to Americans everywhere:

> The story of the War will never be fully written if the achievements of women are left untold. They do not figure

> in the official records; they are not gazetted for gallant deeds; the names of thousands are unknown beyond the neighborhood where they lived, or the hospitals where they loved to labor; yet there is no feature in our War more creditable to us as a nation, none from its positive newness so well worthy of record. [p. 235]

5219. Austin, Anne L. THE WOOLSEY SISTERS OF NEW YORK: A FAMILY'S INVOLVEMENT IN THE CIVIL WAR AND A NEW PROFESSION [1860-1890]. Philadelphia: American Philosophical Society, volume 85, 1971.

Well-researched history of the three Woolsey sisters, Abby, Jane, and Georgeanna, who were energetic Sanitary Commission nurses during the Civil War. Georgeanna wrote a small book called THREE WEEKS AT GETTYSBURG which was disseminated to inspire the people at home to continue their donations to the Sanitary Commission.

5220. Alcott, Louisa May. HOSPITAL SKETCHES. Boston, 1863.

Even though Louisa Alcott apologizes for the roughness of these sketches, they are clearly the work of an accomplished writer. The clever, sometimes humorous, characterizations and her confident styling set this memoir apart from most of the other female memoirs of hospital service. Alcott writes of Hanna Ropes, another volunteer nurse whose letters and diary are also included in this bibliography.

5221. Baker, Nina B. CYCLONE IN CALICO.... Boston: Little, Brown, 1952.

The story of Mary Ann Bickerdyke, who devoted her time and efforts attempting to improve the hospital care for the boys in blue.

5222. Barton, George. ANGELS OF THE BATTLEFIELD.... Philadelphia, 1897.

"A history of the labors of the Catholic sisterhoods in the late Civil War." Tells of the hospital work and nursing done by the Sisters.

5223. Barton, William E. THE LIFE OF CLARA BARTON, FOUNDER OF THE AMERICAN RED CROSS. 2 v. Boston: Houghton Mifflin, 1922.

The author, a relative of Clara Barton, indicates in his "Introduction" that he had access to previously unavailable documents in the preparation of this book: "...more than forty closely packed boxes [of documents], is the chief source of the present volume...." More than half the first volume deals with the Civil War years. These books cannot be ignored as a source for the life of Barton, but they do not include any of the scholarly apparatus of footnotes and bibliography.

5224. Belden, Thomas G. and Marva R. Belden. SO FELL THE ANGELS. Boston: Little, Brown, 1956.

An excellent, readable biography of Kate Chase Sprague. She married to further her father's interests, but her "ambition was her undoing." Also offers insights on the lives of her father and husband.

5225. Blackburn, George M. "Letters to the Front: A Distaff View of the Civil War." MICH HIS, 49 [1965]: 53-67.

Perceptive and articulate letters written by Sophia Buchanan reveal "the anxieties and trials suffered by women left behind."

5226. Blackwell, Sara E. A MILITARY GENIUS: LIFE OF ANNA CARROLL OF MARYLAND. 2 v. Washington, D.C.: 1891-1895.

The author develops the theory of the central role of Anna Ella Carroll in both military and political decision making in the federal government.

5227. Brockett, Linus P. and Mary C. Vaughan. WOMAN'S WORK IN THE CIVIL WAR: A RECORD OF HEROISM, PATRIOTISM AND PATIENCE. Philadelphia, 1867.

A sincere, patriotic attempt to collect the biographies of many northern women. Includes over eighty separate biographical accounts of women in addition to several chapter-length histories of various Soldiers' Aid Societies, local Sanitary Commissions, and Voluntary Refreshment Saloons. Useful for its many engraved portraits [often difficult to find] of the women.

5228. Bucklin, Sophronia E. IN HOSPITAL AND CAMP: A WOMAN'S RECORD OF THRILLING INCIDENTS AMONG THE WOUNDED IN THE LATE WAR. Philadelphia, 1869. Also on microfilm, New Haven, Connecticut: Research Publications [History of Women, 2134].

An account of a government nurse who worked for nearly three years in military and field hospitals, including Camp Letterman General Hospital at Gettysburg. As a government nurse, she got "Pay and rations--twelve dollars a month and soldiers' fare."

5229. Burton, Margaret B.D. THE WOMAN WHO BATTLED FOR THE BOYS IN BLUE. MOTHER BICKERDYKE: HER LIFE AND LABORS FOR RELIEF OF OUR SOLDIERS.... San Francisco, 1886. Also on microfilm, New Haven, Connecticut: Research Publications [History of Women, 3161].

This book records the truly inspirational work of "Mother" Mary Bickerdyke, one of the best known women to minister to the wounded during the war, both in hospitals and on the field of battle. Contains details of hospital activities and tells of other women who served, but concentrates on Bickerdyke, "the Soldiers' Mother."

5230. Chase, Julia A. MARY A. BICKERDYKE, "MOTHER."…. Lawrence, Kansas: 1896. Also on microfilm, New Haven, Connecticut: Research Publications [History of Women, 3968].

This book describes the work of Mary Bickerdyke, one of the most well known female nurses of the Civil War. Accurately described as "possessing a strong constitution and a wonderful executive ability," she was a friend of many high-ranking officers, including General Sherman.

5231. Chittenden, Lucius E. AN UNKNOWN HEROINE, AN HISTORICAL EPISODE OF THE WAR BETWEEN THE STATES. New York, 1894.

The "unknown heroine" is Mrs. Van Metre of Clarke County, Virginia, who befriended Lieutenant Henry E. Bedell, 1st Vermont Heavy Artillery, wounded at the battle of Opequon in September 1864 and deserted by his comrades. On Bedell's return to the North, Mrs. Van Metre accompanied him and through the help of Secretary of War Stanton and others found her husband, a Confederate soldier confined in a northern prison under an assumed name, and secured his release.

5232. Collis, Septima M. A WOMAN'S WAR RECORD, 1861-1865. New York, 1889. Also on microfilm, New Haven, Connecticut: Research Publications [History of Women, 3175].

In this slim volume, Mrs. Collis describes her wartime experiences. Mrs. Collis' husband was General Charles Collis, who at the beginning of the war raised an independent company called the "Zouaves d'Afrique." Mrs. Collis tells of winter quarters in Frederick, Maryland, and life in Washington.

5233. Daly, Maria L. DIARY OF A UNION LADY, 1861-1865. Harold E. Hammond, editor. New York: Funk and Wagnalls, 1962.

This book has been compared to Mrs. Chesnut's diary for obvious reasons. Contains valuable glimpses of New York's political and social life during the war years. Maria Daly, born into a wealthy New York family, was the wife of a prominent judge and, as such, led an active social life even in the midst of war.

5234. Dannett, Sylvia G. NOBLE WOMEN OF THE NORTH. New York: Yoseloff, 1959.

This thoroughly researched book is a "must" for the study of women's role in the Civil War. Deals with many of the women whose memoirs are included in this bibliography.

5235. ———. "Rebecca Wright--Traitor or Patriot?" LIN HER, 65 [1963]: 103-112.

Relates how Wright provided Sheridan with information about the disposition of Confederate troops in the Shenandoah Valley, thus enabling Sheridan to capture Winchester, Virginia, in the "Valley" fighting of September 1864.

5236. ———. SHE RODE WITH THE GENERALS. New York: Thomas Nelson, 1960.

In this biography of Sarah Emma Edmonds, a woman who served almost two years as Frank Thompson of the 2nd Michigan, Dannett attempts to sift fact from fiction and comes up with an exciting, readable account of one of the most unusual women of the Civil War. She also follows Edmonds' life after her return to female garb, including her work with the Christian Commission, in army hospitals, and her civilian life after the war.

5237. ——— and Katherine M. Jones. OUR WOMEN OF THE SIXTIES. Washington, D.C. Civil War Centennial Commission, 1963.

This booklet consists of short essays which quickly cover the work of various women during the war.

5238. Deutrick, Bernice M. "Propriety and Pay." PROLOGUE, 3, [1971]: 67-72.

Details the first widespread government employment of women. They were needed to provide cheap labor to handle increasing demands on government. The few women who held the more important positions received lower salaries than did men who held similar jobs.

5239. Edmonds, Sarah E. NURSE AND SPY IN THE UNION ARMY.... Hartford, Connecticut: 1865.

This work was published under two other titles: THE FEMALE SPY OF THE UNION ARMY and UNSEXED: OR, THE FEMALE SOLDIER. It is a lively account of a young woman's two years with the 2nd Michigan as a male nurse and occasional spy. Emma Edmonds, alias Frank Thompson, wrote the book, an immediate "best seller," soon after whe returned to civilian life as a woman. The work provides first hand accounts of camp life, the hospital ward, and the battlefield.

5240. Epler, Percy H. LIFE OF CLARA BARTON. New York: Macmillan, 1915.

Epler was apparently not privy to the immense number of manuscripts, letters, etc., when he wrote his biography. The book was first published in 1915, about three years after Barton's death. It is a readable biography of Clara Barton, but it must be supplemented with other accounts of her life.

5241. Fischer, LeRoy H. "Cairo's Civil War Angel, Mary Jane Stafford." JISHS, 54 [1961]: 229-245.

Mary Jane Stafford was probably the first woman in the West to carry on military hospital relief work. As a civilian volunteer she was never paid.

5242. Fladeland, Betty. "New Light on Sarah Emma Edmonds Alias Franklin Thompson." MICH HIS, 47 [1963]: 357-362.

A corroboration of the story that Frank Thompson was actually Sarah Emma Edmonds.

5243. Gilbertson, Catherine P. HARRIET BEECHER STOWE. New York: Appleton-Century, 1937.

A good study of Harriet Beecher Stowe which gives an insight into her feelings regarding current events.

5244. Grant, Julia D. THE PERSONAL MEMOIRS OF JULIA DENT GRANT. John Y. Simon, editor. New York: Putnam, 1975.

These recollections written by Grant's widow complement the general's own memoirs. They reveal the private side of Grant as well as his thinking about important events in history. An excellent editing job.

5245. Greenbie, Marjorie B. LINCOLN'S DAUGHTERS OF MERCY. New York: Putnam, 1944.

This is an enthusiastic, well written history of the U.S. Sanitary Commission. Greenbie is a writer of strong opinions and little patience, especially when she describes the bumbling and short-sightedness of the military bureaucracy. Portraits of the women of the Sanitary Commission and evaluations of each woman's talents make this a useful study full of intelligent, sometimes ironic insights.

5246. ———. MY DEAR LADY: THE STORY OF ANNA ELLA CARROLL. New York: Whittlesey, 1940. Reprint 1974.

In this work of historical detection the author pieces together the story of Anna Carroll, a pro-Union southern woman, who was allegedly one of Lincoln's "kitchen cabinet."

5247. Greenbie, Sydney and Marjorie B. Greenbie. ANNA ELLA CARROLL AND ABRAHAM LINCOLN. Manchester, Maine: University of Tampa Press and Falmouth Publishing House, 1952.

Deals with the relationship between Carroll and Lincoln, but makes highly exaggerated claims for Carroll's role in the war and contains several errors.

5248. Hancock, Cornelia. SOUTH AFTER GETTYSBURG: LETTERS OF CORNELIA HANCOCK FROM THE ARMY OF THE POTOMAC, 1863-1865. Henrietta Jaquette, editor. Philadelphia: University of Pennsylvania Press, 1937. Reprint 1956.

The letters of Cornelia Hancock, a young Quaker girl from New Jersey, provide detailed information about hospital procedures and general wartime activities. One of her first letters reveals a girl thrown almost overnight into the midst of the dead and wounded at Gettysburg. The volume also contains letters which she wrote while working at the Contraband Hospital in the nation's capital in 1863 and 1864.

5249. Haviland, Laura S. A WOMAN'S LIFE WORK: LABORS AND EXPERIENCES OF LAURA S. HAVILAND. Cincinnati, 1881. Reprint 1969.

These popular memoirs went through several editions. Haviland was a truly pious abolitionist who wrote of the underground railway, safe houses, and the plight of the freed blacks. Work contains an honest appraisal of black-white relations at various levels, in and out of the military. The book itself is interestingly written, anecdotal, and valuable for its descriptions of human relations.

5250. Holland, Mary A.G., compiler. OUR ARMY NURSES. Boston, 1895.

Sketches and photographs of nearly 100 women who served as nurses in the Union army.

5251. Holstein, Anna M.E. THREE YEARS IN FIELD HOSPITALS OF THE ARMY OF THE POTOMAC. Philadelphia, 1867.

Holstein's memoirs of her three years' nursing experience in Virginia contain some grisly passages. A dedicated volunteer, she did not shrink from nursing the worst cases.

5252. Howe, Julia W. REMINISCENCES, 1819-1899. Boston, 1899.

As indicated in the prefatory note by the author's daughter, these reminiscences were "put together rather hastily, in my mother's eighty-first year, and were drawn almost entirely from memory." The Civil War period is not given much space.

5253. Hurn, Ethel A. WISCONSIN WOMEN IN THE WAR BETWEEN THE STATES. Madison, 1911.

This book concentrates on the women who stayed at home rather than those who saw service in faraway military hospitals. It provides valuable insight into the war work of those who labored in their home towns, knitting, packing boxes, preparing lint, pickling cucumbers, and making "rivers of blackberry juice."

5254. Jolly, Ellen R. NUNS OF THE BATTLEFIELD. Providence, Rhode Island: Visitor Press, 1927.

Material included in this survey of the "Soldier-Sister-Nurses" of the Civil War was originally gathered to convince government authorities that the Catholic nuns were worthy of a monument to their good works during the war. Includes accounts of many orders, complete with the names of the sisters who served. The monument was erected in 1924.

5255. Kellogg, Florence S. MOTHER BICKERDYKE AS I KNEW HER. Chicago, 1907.

A sensitive biography of a woman who was one of the Civil War's best known and most loved volunteer nurses. Includes a photograph of a monument to Mother Bickerdyke at Galesburg, Illinois.

5256. Lawrence, Catherine S. AUTOBIOGRAPHY: SKETCH OF LIFE AND LABORS OF MISS CATHERINE S. LAWRENCE.... Albany, New York: 1896. Also on microfilm, New Haven, Connecticut: Research Publications [History of Women, 4429].

Catherine Lawrence worked for temperance and abolition before she became involved in volunteer nursing. The autobiography contains too much preaching to be very readable or enjoyable. It is useful for some insight into hospital procedures.

5257. Livermore, Mary A.B. MY STORY OF THE WAR. Hartford, Connecticut: 1889. Also on microfilm, New Haven, Connecticut: Research Publications [History of Women, 3458].

Excellent account of women's work in hospitals and at home written by a woman who played a central role in the United States Sanitary Commission. This account, which runs to over 700 pages, is one of the best and most detailed on the subject, even though Livermore waited over 20 years to write it.

5258. Logan, Mary C. REMINISCENCES OF A SOLDIER'S WIFE: AN AUTOBIOGRAPHY. New York, 1913. Reprint 1970. Also on microfilm, New Haven, Connecticut: Research Publications [History of Women, 6733].

These memoirs of the wife of General John A. Logan include brief hospital scenes of "The Striped Hospital of the 31st Regiment" in Cairo, Illinois, named for the brightly colored striped blankets used to cover the sick and wounded. Author writes of life at home during the war and gives a history of her husband's activities.

5259. Long, E.B. "Anna Ella Carroll: Exaggerated Heroine?" CWTI, 14 [4] [1975]: 28-35.

A biographical sketch of Carroll, in which the author argues that her part in the Civil War was greatly exaggerated. Article also traces the controversy among historians about the facts of her career.

5260. Marshall, Helen. DOROTHEA DIX, FORGOTTEN SAMARITAN. Chapel Hill: University of North Carolina Press, 1937.

Author indicates in her preface that she wished to "clear up and explain certain misconceptions regarding Dorothea Dix's childhood, her relations with her Grandmother Dix and her Civil War work...." In dealing with Dix's tenure as Superintendent of Nurses, Marshall attempts to answer the charges by the medical establishment of the time that Dix kept young women out of her nursing corps because of a prejudice against youth. Author sees most of Dix's problems as coming from recalcitrant medical men.

5261. Massey, Mary E. BONNET BRIGADES. New York: Knopf, 1966.

This book deals with the impact of the war between the states on both northern and southern women. Using many diaries and letters, Massey has drawn important historical conclusions from a mass of individual experiences. She illustrates a commonalty of experiences, not only among northern women, but also between northern and southern women.

5262. Maxwell, William Q. LINCOLN'S FIFTH WHEEL: THE POLITICAL HISTORY OF THE U.S. SANITARY COMMISSION. New York: Longmans, Green, 1956.

Solid research on the history of the Sanitary Commission makes this book indispensable for the study of the women's role in the Civil War. Excellent bibliography, including relevant sources in many manuscript collections.

5263. McKay, Charlotte E.J. STORIES OF HOSPITAL AND CAMP. Philadelphia, 1876. Reprint 1971.

This work describes the author's 40 months in military hospitals [March 1862-July 1865]. A sympathetic but sensible account of the difficult circumstances the Union nurses encountered. Useful for details of hospital procedures and general military background.

5264. McKown, Bethia P. "The Civil War Letters of Bethia Pyatt McKown." James W. Goodrich, editor. MO HIS R, 67 [1973]: 227-252, 351-370.

The letters reflect a woman's grief and suffering occasioned by her sons fighting on opposite sides, relatives subjected to guerrilla activities, and other depredations. The letters also portray the repressive measures used by both civilian and military governments during the war.

5265. MICHIGAN WOMEN IN THE CIVIL WAR. Lansing: Michigan Civil War Centennial Observance Commission, 1963.

A pamphlet which deals rather lightly with the subject.

5266. Moore, Frank. WOMEN OF THE WAR: THEIR HEROISM AND SELF-SACRIFICE. Hartford, Connecticut: 1866. Also on microfilm, New Haven, Connecticut: Research Publications [History of Women, 2359].

Primarily a compilation of biographical sketches of numerous "loyal" women. Most of the chapters deal with volunteer nurses, although two chapters are entitled "Women as Soldiers" and "Loyal Southern Women." Contains a number of portraits of the women discussed and some sentimental engravings of the period.

5267. Newcomb, Mary A. FOUR YEARS OF PERSONAL REMINISCENCES OF THE WAR. Chicago, 1893.

Volume contains a sincere account of a volunteer Union nurse who lost her husband in the war but nevertheless continued to work with the wounded in a series of hospitals, in the field, and on hospital boats. "Mother Newcomb," usually the model of God-fearing gentleness, shows occasional moments of surprising spunkiness as, for example, when she threatened to pitch an abusive southern woman into the river for calling her names.

5268. O'Brien, Jean G. and Robert D. Hoffsommer. "Dorothea Dix." CWTI, 4 [5] [1965]: 39-44.

Outlines Dix's contributions to the Union war effort.

5269. Olnhausen, Mary P. von. ADVENTURES OF AN ARMY NURSE IN TWO WARS. James P. Munroe, editor. Boston, 1903. Also on microfilm, New Haven, Connecticut: Research Publications [History of Women, 5414].

The letters of Mary Phinney von Olnhausen are interspersed with commentary and biographical information by the editor. Work includes a first-hand account of interaction with Dorothea Dix and valuable background information on hospital conditions.

5270. Palmer, Sarah A. THE STORY OF AUNT BECKY'S ARMY-LIFE. New York, 1867. Also on microfilm, New Haven, Connecticut: Research Publications [History of Women, 2374].

Subtitled "The Story of the Ninth Corps Hospital Matron," this is an autobiography of Sarah Palmer, "Aunt Becky," a dedicated hospital nurse during the war. She describes hospital scenes and provides sketches of doctors and patients.

5271. Parsons, Emily E. MEMOIR OF EMILY ELIZABETH PARSONS. Boston, 1890. Also on microfilm, New Haven, Connecticut: Research Publications [History of Women, 3543].

An excellent source of information on military hospital procedures and small details of daily practices, written by a literate, dedicated woman who served in several of the largest military hospitals of the war from 1862-1864. Her nursing efforts were prodigious, interrupted only by periods of illness with malaria.

5272. Phelps, Mary K. KATE CHASE, DOMINANT DAUGHTER.... New York: Crowell, 1935.

A rather "uninspired" biography of this woman, the daughter of Salmon P. Chase, secretary of the treasury, who ruled social life in the nation's capital during the war years.

5273. Porter, Mary H. ELIZA CHAPPELL PORTER, A MEMOIR. Chicago, 1893. Also on microfilm, New Haven, Connecticut: Research Publications [History of Women, 4663].

Published as a memorial volume to her husband, book includes chapters on Mrs. Porter's hospital work in several western army hospitals. Particularly interesting because of her association with Mother Bickerdyke.

5274. Quynn, Dorothy L.M. and William R. Quynn. BARBARA FRIETCHIE. Baltimore: Maryland Historical Society, 1942.

A slim volume which deals with the Barbara Frietchie controversy, which has raged ever since she supposedly shouted, "Shoot if you must, this old gray head."

5275. Richards, Laura E. and Maud H. Elliott. JULIA WARD HOWE, 1819-1910. Boston: Houghton Mifflin, 1915.

Written by her daughters, this biography contains primary material from Julia Ward Howe's diaries and letters.

5276. Robbins, Peggy. "General Grant's Calico Colonel." A HIS ILL, 14 [1] [1979]: 4-7, 43-48.

Another article on "Mother" Bickerdyke, who ministered to the sick and wounded and set up field hospitals.

5277. Ropes, Hannah A. CIVIL WAR NURSE: THE DIARY AND LETTERS OF HANNAH ROPES. John R. Brumgardt, editor. Knoxville: University of Tennessee Press, 1980.

Book brings to light the neglected diary and letters of an "articulate New England reformer and abolitionist" who served as a Union hospital matron. Ropes was instrumental in correcting abuses at the hospital by going directly to the secretary of war.

5278. Ross, Ishbel. ANGEL OF THE BATTLEFIELD: THE LIFE OF CLARA BARTON. New York: Harper, 1956.

One of the many books about this famous humanitarian. Ross's account provides interesting reading based on solid research. Gives a well-rounded portrait of the woman called the "Angel of the Battlefield." Describes Barton's difficulties in working with Dorothea Dix's Sanitary Commission nurses.

5279. ———. THE GENERAL'S WIFE: THE LIFE OF MRS. ULYSSES S. GRANT. New York: Dodd, Mead, 1959.

This is a well-written biography of Grant's amiable, devoted wife Julia. Valuable for the carefully documented background information.

5280. ———. PROUD KATE: PORTRAIT OF AN AMBITIOUS WOMAN. New York: Harper, 1953.

Kate Chase was the colorful, opinionated daughter of Salmon P. Chase, a member of Lincoln's cabinet. While interesting for the illumination of the political and social scene of the times, portions of the work are fictional.

5281. Sarmiento, Ferdinand L. LIFE OF PAULINE CUSHMAN. Philadelphia, 1865.

"Prepared from Cushman's notes and memoranda," this account deals with her life as a Union scout and spy, her service with the Army of the Cumberland, and her life behind enemy lines. Factual, in part, it is also highly romanticized.

5282. Shattuck, George C. "Sarah Cabot Wheelwright's Account of the Widow Bixby." MASS HIS SOC PROC, 75 [1963]: 107-108.

Casts doubt on whether Widow Bixby really deserved the famous letter from Lincoln on the loss of five sons killed in action. Mrs. Wheelwright discovered that Bixby was "perfectly untrustworthy, operated a house of ill-fame, and had probably not more than two sons in the Union Army."

5283. Smaridge, Norah. HANDS OF MERCY.... New York: Benziger, 1960.

Work details the services performed by the various Catholic sisterhoods during the war.

5284. Snyder, Charles M. DR. MARY WALKER: THE LITTLE LADY IN PANTS. New York: Vantage, 1962. Reprint 1974.

A lively biography of Dr. Mary Walker, the only woman to serve as an assistant surgeon during the Civil War. It is a balanced assessment of Walker's activities both during the war and in later life. Walker served honorably in Virginia and Tennessee, where she performed duties that "more nearly paralleled those of a nurse or a hospital administrator, than a practicing physician or surgeon." She performed little if any surgery.

5285. Stanton, Elizabeth C. EIGHTY YEARS AND MORE [1815-1897] REMINESCENCES OF ELIZABETH CADY STANTON. London, England: 1898. Reprint 1970.

Chapter 15, "Women as Patriots," deals with women's many duties and contributions to the northern war effort. Stanton writes about the formation and work of the Women's Loyal League, an abolitionist organization begun by Stanton and Susan B. Anthony.

5286. Stearns, Amanda A. THE LADY NURSE OF WARD E. New York, 1909.

This interesting account of hospital service was written by a woman who served in Washington's Armory Square Hospital in 1863 and 1864. Presented through her letters and diary, it provides information on daily hospital routines in one of the "most complete and best conducted" hospitals of the Civil War.

5287. Stille, Charles J. HISTORY OF THE UNITED STATES SANITARY COMMISSION: BEING THE GENERAL REPORT OF ITS WORK DURING THE WAR OF THE REBELLION. Philadelphia, 1866.

Stille's one volume general history of the United States Sanitary Commission is a well-researched account of the "Commission's origin, purposes, and methods of operation." In preparing this official record, the author tried to strike a balance between comprehensiveness and readability for the general public. An indispensable history of the topic.

5288. Stowe, Charles E. and Lyman B. Stowe. HARRIET BEECHER STOWE: THE STORY OF HER LIFE. Boston, 1911.

Written by her son Charles and grandson Lyman, this biography is a pleasant treatment of her life.

5289. Stowe, Harriet B. LIFE OF HARRIET BEECHER STOWE, COMPILED FROM HER LETTERS AND JOURNALS. Charles E. Stowe, compiler. Boston, 1889.

A collection of Mrs. Stowe's letters and journal excerpts, compiled by her son.

5290. ———. LIFE AND LETTERS OF HARRIET BEECHER STOWE. Annie Fields, editor. Boston, 1897.

A eulogistic account based on Stowe's own letters.

5291. Swisshelm, Jane G.C. CRUSADER AND FEMINIST: LETTERS OF JANE GREY SWISSHELM, 1858-1865. Arthur J. Larsen, editor. St. Paul: Minnesota Historical Society, 1934.

This collection of the letters of Jane Grey Swisshelm chronicles the career of a progressive woman who was an editor of a western Pennsylvania newspaper and army nurse. Swisshelm was a small, almost frail woman with strong opinions.

5292. ———. HALF A CENTURY. Chicago, 1880. Also on microfilm. New Haven, Connecticut: Research Publications [History of Women, 3686].

In this autobiography Swisshelm describes in sensitive and graphic terms the often stupidly inept treatment inflicted on amputees. She tells of alleviating the pain by proper alignment of the limbs, a knowledge she garnered from a physician's lecture.

5293. Thompson, Harriet J. "Civil War Life: The Letters of Harriet Jane Thompson." Glenda Riley, editor. ANN IOWA, 44 [1978]: 214-231.

Letters written by Mrs. Thompson to her husband, Major William Thompson [see number 4482] of the 20th Iowa. She describes the feelings of a childless young wife left at home.

5294. Thompson, William Y. "The U.S. Sanitary Commission." CWH, 2 [1956]: 41-63.

Author points out that the Union victory was made easier by this little publicized but important commission. The organization and work of the Commission is examined.

5295. Tiffany, Francis. THE LIFE OF DOROTHEA LYNDE DIX. Boston, 1892.

This admiring biography of Dix deals only briefly with the Civil War years. It touches fleetingly on Dix's difficulties as Superintendent of Nurses and provides little useful insight into them.

5296. Towne, Laura M. LETTERS AND DIARY OF LAURA M. TOWNE; WRITTEN FROM THE SEA ISLANDS OF SOUTH CAROLINA, 1862-1864. Rupert S. Holland, editor. Cambridge, 1912. Reprint 1969. Also on microfilm. New Haven, Connecticut: Research Publications [History of Women, 7067].

The letters and diary chronicle 22 years in the career of a woman who established a school for the blacks of the Sea Islands, South Carolina, during the Civil War. Although a clearly dedicated abolitionist, Towne was not above an occasional complaint about the hardship and inconveniences of the early years. Contains perceptive insights into people and society.

5297. Turchin, Nadine. "'A Monotony Full of Sadness': The Diary of Nadine Turchin, May 1863-April 1864." Mary Ellen McElligott, editor. JISHS, 70 [1977]: 27-89.

Annotated diary of the wife of Union General John B. Turchin. The Turchins were strong abolitionists, but were disgusted with the temerity, inexperience, and lack of conviction of the Union army. Mrs. Turchin accompanied her husband into the field with the Army of the Cumberland; her reports reveal her own military expertise and private sentiments.

5298. U.S. Sanitary Commission. DOCUMENTS OF THE U.S. SANITARY COMMISSION. 3 v. New York: 1866-1871.

This three volume set contains a compilation of the official commission documents. Contents of the documents are given in Index-catalog of the Library of the Surgeon-General's Office, U.S. Army [Senate misdoc. 37-Report 2, Serial 1112]. Indispensible archival materials.

5299. Wagenknecht, Edward C. HARRIET BEECHER STOWE: THE KNOWN AND THE UNKNOWN. New York: Oxford University Press, 1965.

An early attempt at psycho-history of the celebrated abolitionist-writer. The author draws heavily on the Stowe papers to write a "sentimentalized" biography of Harriet Beecher Stowe, one which modern feminists might not greatly appreciate.

5300. Werlich, Robert. "Mary Walker: From Union Army Surgeon to Sideshow Freak." CWTI, 6 [3] [1967]: 46-49.

Mary Walker served the Union army as a contract surgeon. Although she failed in her efforts to be commissioned, she was awarded the Medal of Honor. The award was canceled in 1917 when the requirements for the medal were upgraded.

5301. Wheelock, Julia S. THE BOYS IN WHITE; THE EXPERIENCE OF A HOSPITAL AGENT IN AND AROUND WASHINGTON. New York, 1870.

The personal journal of a woman who served as a hospital nurse and agent with the Michigan Relief Association from 1862 to 1865. Useful for glimpses of day-to-day work of a typical woman nurse in voluntary hospital service. Describes the myriad little talks and kindnesses performed for the soldiers by the female volunteers.

5302. Whetten, Harriet D. "A Volunteer Nurse in the Civil War: The Letters of Harriet Douglas Whetten." Paul H. Hass, editor. WIS MAG HIS, 48 [1964]: 131-151.

Lively, literate letters written by a Sanitary Commission nurse attached to the hospital transport service. Although little is known about Harriet Whetten, her letters reveal a well-educated intelligent woman whose observations are valuable for their readability and accuracy.

5303. ———. "A Volunteer Nurse in the Civil War: The Diary of Harriet Douglas Whetten." Paul H. Hass, editor. WIS MAG HIS, 48 [1965]: 205-221.

Harriet Whetten was assigned to the hospital transport service during the final days of the Peninsular Campaign. Expertly edited, the entries reveal a sharply observant, intelligent woman who wrote unflinchingly of the hardships of the war.

5304. Wilson, Dorothy C. STRANGER AND TRAVELER: THE STORY OF DOROTHEA DIX, AMERICAN REFORMER. Boston: Little, Brown, 1975.

An excellent biography of the remarkable American reformer which includes a chapter on Dix's tenure as Superintendent of Nurses during the Civil War. Tells of her puritanical ideals in choosing her nurses, her immense dedication and energy which she directed toward the task of providing nursing care for the sick and wounded, and her stormy administration as Superintendent of Nurses.

5305. Wittenmyer, Annie T. UNDER THE GUNS; A WOMAN'S REMINISCENCES OF THE CIVIL WAR. Boston, 1895. Also on microfilm. New Haven, Connecticut: Research Publications [History of Women, 4951].

Annie Wittenmyer worked as a nurse and sanitary agent from 1861 until the end of the war. Provides accurate, first hand information on hospital procedures and abuses. Wittenmyer also discusses the special diet kitchens which she established in the United States hospital system. Very readable and not lacking in sympathy for the sick and wounded, the book also is spiced with interesting accounts of unusual and famous people she met.

5306. Wood, Ann Douglas. "The War Within A War: Women in the Union Army." CWH, 18 [1972]: 197-212.

Excellent article that discusses the contribution of women at home and in hospitals. Wood posits a direct influence between women's volunteer nursing experiences during the war and the subsequent emergence of accredited schools for nurses.

5307. Wormeley, Katherine P. THE OTHER SIDE OF THE WAR WITH THE ARMY OF THE POTOMAC. Boston, 1889.

These letters, by a leading woman in the United States Sanitary Commission, are valuable as a first-hand account of the operation of the Hospital Transport Service during the Peninsular Campaign in Virginia in 1862. Her letters, written primarily to her mother, tell the history of a Sanitary Commission service branch that "had no power, only the right of charity." Central collection of letters in the study of women's work in the Civil War.

5308. ———. THE UNITED STATES SANITARY COMMISSION. Boston, 1863.

"A sketch of its purposes and its work," this account only covers the commission's activities through 1863.

5309. Young, Agnes B. THE WOMEN AND THE CRISIS: WOMEN IN THE NORTH IN THE CIVIL WAR. New York: McDowell, Obolensky, 1959.

A readable, informative account of women's contributions to the war effort. Placing the women's activities in the context of the total war effort is the book's strongest feature. Young provides helpful chronologies throughout. The author also has a thorough grasp of the social history of the time which adds depth to the familiar stories of women like Mother Bickerdyke, Clara Barton, and others.

C. NATIVE AMERICANS

5310. Abel, Annie H. THE AMERICAN INDIAN AS PARTICIPANT IN THE CIVIL WAR. Cleveland, Ohio: Arthur H. Clark, 1919.

In conjunction with the second volume of this work, THE SLAVEHOLDING INDIANS, the author makes clear the amount of support for the Confederacy among the Indians.

5311. Armstrong, William H. WARRIOR IN TWO CAMPS: ELY S. PARKER, UNION GENERAL AND SENECA CHIEF. Syracuse: University of Syracuse Press, 1978.

A biography of the celebrated Seneca Indian who made the adjustment to white society and rose to be Grant's military secretary during the war. A pre-war graduate of Rensselaer, he became the first Commissioner of Indian Affairs after the war.

5312. Banks, Dean. "Civil War Refugees From Indian Territory, in the North, 1861-1864." CH OK, 41 [1963]: 286-298.

Describes the plight of the Upper Creek and Seminole Indians who fled because they were loyal to the Union. They were attacked, pursued, and often arrived at their destinations without supplies. Many of these braves enlisted and fought in the Union army.

5313. Britton, Wiley. THE UNION BRIGADE IN THE CIVIL WAR. Kansas City, Missouri: Franklin Hudson, 1922.

A readable account of the Indian soldiers in the Union army with emphasis on action in Missouri and Arkansas. Includes the story of the 6th Kansas Cavalry.

5314. Clifford, Roy A. "The Indian Regiments in the Battle of Pea Ridge." CH OK, 25 [1947]: 314-322.

Details the involvement of the Indians from the Five Civilized Tribes in the battle of Pea Ridge, March 6-8. 1962.

5315. Danziger, Edmund J. "The Crow Creek Experiment: An Aftermath of the Sioux War of 1862." ND HIS, 37 [1970]: 104-123.

Recounts the problems which arose when the Sioux were removed from Minnesota to Crow Creek in the southern Dakota Territory. The troubles typify the lack of response by Washington to the advancing frontier and the problems created by it.

5316. ———. "The Indian Office During the Civil War: Impotence in Indian Affairs." SD HIS, 5 [1974]: 52-72.

The Civil War years were crucial in Indian affairs. Indian lands in the Trans-Mississippi were violated. Lincoln deferred to the Office of Indian Affairs or congressional committees in dealing with Indian problems.

5317. ———. INDIANS AND BUREAUCRATS: ADMINISTERING THE RESERVATION POLICY DURING THE CIVIL WAR. Urbana: University of Illinois Press, 1974.

A most comprehensive, documented study of Indian affairs and administration during the war. In describing the events and policies of the period, the author makes clear the federal goverment's failure to safeguard the interests of the Indians. The errors, the bunglings, and the general inattention made any other outcome unlikely.

5318. ———. "The Office of Indian Affairs and the Problem of Civil War Indian Refugees in Kansas." KAN HIS Q, 35 [1969]: 257-275.

The vacuum caused by the withdrawal of federal troops from the West caused those tribes loyal to the Union to flee to Kansas. There "they wandered or were herded like their own cattle back and forth across the Kansas border."

5319. Davis, Jane S. "Two Sioux War Orders: A Mystery Unraveled." MINN HIS, 41 [1968]: 117-125.

A rather complicated story of the two copies of Lincoln's

order to execute some 38 Sioux after the uprising of 1862. It appears the "Hanging Order" was written by both Lincoln and his secretary, Nicolay.

5320. Ellis, Richard N. "Civilians, the Army and the Indian Problem on the Northern PLains, 1862-1866." ND HIS, 37 [1970]: 20-39.

Author considers the Indian campaigns of 1862 through 1866 from the viewpoint of military-civilian relations. The controversy between Newton Edmunds and General John Pope is scrutinized.

5321. ———. "Political Pressures and Army Policies on the Northern Plains, 1862-1865." MINN HIS, 42 [1970]: 43-53.

General John Pope, commander of the Department of the Northwest during the Sioux uprising of 1862 was caught between the clamor of the people on the frontier for more protection and the demands of the politicians that the soldiers be sent east.

5322. Gray, John S. "The Santee Sioux and the Lake Shetek Settlers: Capture and Rescue." MONT, 25 [1975]: 42-54.

The Santee Sioux had "had it" with government mismanagement and the exploitation of their people by ruthless traders. They attacked the settlement at Lake Shetek--fifteen people were killed and 11 were carried into captivity, to be held for ransom. In the Sioux uprising or "Minnesota Massacre" nearly 800 settlers were killed within a few weeks.

5323. Hofsommer, Donovan L. "William Palmer Dole, Commissioner of Indian Affairs, 1861-1865." LIN HER, 75 [1973]: 97-114.

Dole, a political patronage appointee, did his best. The article gives a good capsule history of Indian problems during the war.

5324. Hoig, Stan. THE SAND CREEK MASSACRE. Norman: University of Oklahoma Press, 1961.

An examination of the Indian massacre at Sand Creek, Colorado, in November 1864 by federal forces under Colonel John M. Chivington. Author concludes the ill-advised attack was a result of a wrong-headed decision based on ambiguous orders.

5325. Holman, Tom. "William G. Coffin, Lincoln's Superintendent of Indian Affairs for the Southern Superintendency." KAN HIS Q, 39 [1973]: 491-514.

With the advent of war, most of the personnel in the Southern Superintendency of the Bureau of Indian Affairs went with the Confederacy. William Dole moved quickly and appointed Coffin as superintendent. Article considers how Dole and Coffin responded to the problems which arose--pull-back of federal troops, Confederate attempts to get Indians to join the Confederacy, and the like.

5326. Kelsey, Harry. "Background to Sand Creek." COL MAG, 45 [1968]: 279-300.

Author argues that whether the peaceful Cheyenne Indians were massacred at Sand Creek, Colorado, November 29-30, 1864, by federal forces under Colonel John M. Chivington is the wrong question to ask. More important was the inept management of Indian matters by the federal government.

5327. ———. "William P. Dole and Mr. Lincoln's Indian Policy." JW, 10 [1971]: 484-492.

William P. Dole, Commissioner of Indian Affairs during Lincoln's presidency, did not have a very creditable tenure, although he was successful in attaining one administration goal, keeping most western tribes at peace.

5328. Lass, William E. "The Removal from Minnesota of the Sioux and Winnebago Indians. MINN HIS, 38 [1963]: 353-364.

Some 1,300 Sioux and 1,900 Winnebago Indians were moved from Minnesota to the Dakota Territory as a result of the Sioux uprising in 1862. Conditions proved so terrible that eventually the Winnebagoes settled in northeastern Nebraska and the Sioux in northern Nebraska.

5329. Moulton, Gary E. "Chief John Ross During the Civil War." CWH, 19 [1973]: 314-333.

Describes the efforts of John Ross, chief of the Cherokee Nation, to steer a neutral course during the Civil War.

5330. ———. "John Ross and W.P. Dole: A Case Study of Lincoln's Indian Policy." JW, 12 [1973]: 414-423.

An account of the difficult problems facing the Cherokee Nation with the outbreak of war and the efforts of their ancient chief to resolve them.

5331. Nichols, David A. LINCOLN AND THE INDIANS: CIVIL WAR POLICY AND POLITICS. Columbia: University Of Missouri Press, 1978.

Author emphasizes the unimportant position Indian affairs occupied among the Lincoln administration's priorities. While the president was more understanding of the Indians than most people, his policies proved to be harmful to them. This was particularly true with respect to the Five Civilized Tribes in Indian Territory and the Santee Sioux in Minnesota.

5332. ———. "The Other Civil War: Lincoln and the Indians." MINN HIS, 44 [1974]: 2-15.

Throughout the war Lincoln was plagued by the "Indian problem." After his "Hanging Order" the pressure increased. His plans for the West really meant doom for the Indians unless they could be integrated.

5333. Nicolay, John G. LINCOLN'S SECRETARY GOES WEST: TWO REPORTS BY JOHN G. NICOLAY ON FRONTIER INDIAN TROUBLES. Theodore G. Blegen, editor. LaCrosse, Wisconsin: Sumac Press, 1965.

Lincoln's secretary, Nicolay, was sent to Minnesota in July 1862, to negotiate a treaty with the Chippewa Indians. Just as he arrived the Sioux went on a rampage. Upon his return to Washington, he wrote two reports--one on the Chippewa and one on the Sioux, both of which were first published in 1863.

5334. Oehler, C.M. THE GREAT SIOUX UPRISING. New York: Oxford University Press, 1959.

A scholarly study of the Sioux revolt in Minnesota in 1862. Over 800 whites lost their lives before the uprising was quelled, compared to a small number of Sioux.

5335. Rampp, Lary C. "Civil War Battle of Barren Creek, 1863." CH OK, 48 [1970]: 74-82.

An account of a "running type of battle" between the 3rd Indian Home Guard and troops from Waite's command. The action took place on December 18, 1863.

5336. Roberts, Gary L. "Conditions of the Tribes - 1865: The McCook Report, A Military View." MON MAG W HIS, 24 [1974]: 14-25.

The havoc wrecked on Indians by the Civil War caused such a public outcry that a special joint committee was appointed in March 1865 to investigate "the condition of the Indian tribes and their treatment by ... the civil and military authorities of the United States." The report provides a "useful perspective on the committee, its work and the military viewpoint on the 'Indian question.'"

5337. Roddis, Louis H. THE INDIAN WARS OF MINNESOTA. Cedar Rapids, Iowa: Torch, 1956.

A review of Indian fighting in Minnesota from the 1850s to 1890s, which focuses special attention on the Sioux revolt of 1862 and its aftermath. This solid study was written by a retired naval captain, who, incidentally, edited the Second World War's medical history.

5338. Rowen, Richard D., editor. "The Second Nebraska's Campaign Against the Sioux." NEB HIS, 44 [1963]: 3-53.

Three accounts exist of this expedition--June 16, 1863-September 12, 1863--against the Sioux: a journal kept by Robert Furnas, a diary of Henry Pierce, and drawings by George Belden. The journal [the official account] gives a good picture of the difficulties of maintaining a cavalry regiment on the plains.

5339. Unrau, William E. "The Council Grove Merchants and Kansas Indians, 1855-1870." KAN HIS Q, 34 [1968]: 266-281.

Author uses the town of Council Grove on the upper Neosho river to illustrate the idea of the "urban frontier" in territorial Kansas.

5340. White, Lonnie J. "From Bloodless to Bloody: The Third Colorado Cavalry and the Sand Creek Massacre." JW, 6 [1967]: 535-581.

The 3rd Colorado saw its first action at Sand Creek, Colorado, November 29-30, 1864. It was indeed a bloody baptism.

D. JEWS

5341. Brav, Stanley R. "The Jewish Woman, 1861-1865." A JEW ARCH, 17 [1965]: 34-75.

Describes the home life, attitudes, and war activities of Jewish women, both North and South.

5342. Dubow, Sylvan M. "Identifying the Jewish Serviceman in the Civil War: A Re-appraisal of Simon Wolf's THE AMERICAN JEW AS A PATRIOT, SOLDIER AND CITIZEN." A JEW HIS Q, 59 [1970]: 357-369.

Author examines Simon Wolf's book which was, for the most part, a directory of Jewish servicemen. [See number 5360]

5343. Falk, Stanley L. "Alfred Mordecai, American Jew." A JEW ARCH, 10 [1958]: 125-132.

Surveys the career of this southern graduate of West Point. He served as a commander during the Mexican War, but refused to fight for either side during the Civil War.

5344. ———. "Divided Loyalties in 1861: The Decision of Major Alfred Mordecai." A JEW HIS SOC PUB, 48 [1959]: 147-169.

Another discussion of Moredecai's decision to resign his commission in the United States army and not accept a commission from the Confederacy. Author contends that concern for the feelings of his family provided the prime motivation for his actions.

5345. Fein, Isaac M. "Baltimore Jews During the Civil War." A JEW HIS Q, 51 [1961]: 67-96.

As a result of the war the Jewish community emerged stronger and more integrated. No longer a colony within the larger German colony, they became an independent Jewish community.

5346. Fried, Joseph P. "The Second Emancipation Proclamation." CWTI, 2 [9] [1964]: 23-25.

An important battle was won when Lincoln signed into law a bill recognizing Jewish chaplains in the Union army.

5347. Isaacs, Joakin. "Candidate Grant and the Jews." A JEW ARCH, 17 [1965]: 3-16.

Examines the issuance of Grant's Order No. 11 barring Jews from his Military Department and its significance during his presidential campaign.

5348. Isaacs, Myer S. "A Jewish Army Chaplain." A JEW HIS SOC PUB, 12 [1904]: 127-137.

Outlines Arnold Fischel's efforts as lobbyist for a law to legalize Jewish army chaplains and also his work as part-time chaplain.

5349. Katz, Irving I. THE JEWISH SOLDIER FROM MICHIGAN IN THE CIVIL WAR. Detroit: Wayne State University Press, 1962.

Contains biographical sketches and information on activities on the home front, as well as a list of Jewish servicemen.

5350. Korn, Bertram W. AMERICAN JEWRY AND THE CIVIL WAR. Philadelphia: Jewish Publication Society of American, 1951. Reprint 1962.

The author, in a well-done revision of his Ph.D. dissertation, has described the contribution of the Jewish community to the northern war effort, as well as its response to the bigotry it suffered. Jews hoped to be viewed as loyal supporters of the Union and not primarily as a religious group, but their way was not an easy one.

5351. ———. "Congressman Clement L. Vallandigham's Championship of the Jewish Chaplaincy in the Civil War." A JEW HIS Q, 53 [1963]: 188-191.

Vallandigham, better known for his activities as a Copperhead, was the first man to press for the appointment of Jewish chaplains in the Union army.

5352. ———, editor. "The Jews of the Union." A JEW ARCH, 13 [1961]: 131-230.

The entire issue is devoted to the role of Jews who sided with the Union in the Civil War. A number of documents are included.

5353. Marcus, Jacob R. "Southern Unionist: A Memoir." Phillip Phillips, editor. COMMENTARY, 21 [1] [1956]: 41-52.

Selections from Marcus' MEMOIRS OF AMERICAN JEWS. He was elected to the South Carolina Nullification Committee as an anti-secessionist.

5354. Rubinger, Haphtali J. ABRAHAM LINCOLN AND THE JEWS. New York: J. David, 1962.

A brief, interesting volume, which attempts to analyze Lincoln's policy toward the Jewish people.

5355. Shostek, Robert. "Leopold Karpeles: Civil War Hero." A JEW HIS Q 52 [1963]: 220-223.

Karpeles was typical of many who left Central Europe to seek greater freedom and opportunity. He served with the Union army and received the Medal of Honor in 1870 for his gallantry in the Wilderness.

5356. Simonhoff, Harry. JEWISH PARTICIPANTS IN THE CIVIL WAR. New York: Arco, 1963.

Biographical sketches of the more prominent Jewish servicemen.

5357. Spiegel, Marcus. YOUR TRUE MARCUS. Frank L. Byrne and Jean Soman, editors. Kent, Ohio: Kent State University Press, 1985.

Letters of a German Jewish immigrant who served with Ohio regiments and rose to the rank of colonel. "His letters are significant additions not only to eyewitness accounts of the Civil War but to the history of minority ethnic groups...." Of particular interest are letters written during the Vicksburg Campaign.

5358. Temkin, Sefton D. "Isaac Mayer Wise and the Civil War." A JEW ARCH, 15 [1963]: 120-142.

Traces the political views of this rabbi concerning secession, slavery, and peace. He toyed with the idea of running for the state senate but was forced by his congregation to withdraw from the race.

5359. Waxman, Jonathan. "Arnold Fischel: 'Unsung Hero' in American Israel." A JEW HIS Q, 60 [1971]: 325-343.

A brief biography of this native of Holland who moved to New York. A lecturer and writer, he fought for Jewish military chaplaincy.

5360. Wolf, Simon. THE AMERICAN JEW AS PATRIOT, SOLDIER AND CITIZEN. Louis E. Levy, editor. Philadelphia, 1895.

A list of Jewish staff officers in the Union army, the soldiers in both Union and Confederate armies, by state, and miscellaneous articles.

E. IMMIGRANTS

5361. Angle, Paul M. "George Merryweather's United States 1861-1862." CHI HIS, 7 [1965]: 245-263.

This English immigrant enlisted in the Union army. Article stresses his impressions of the United States.

5362. Aschmann, Rudolph. MEMOIR OF A SWISS OFFICER IN THE AMERICAN CIVIL WAR. Heinz K. Meier, editor. Bern, Switzerland: Herbert Lang, 1972.

These memoirs are based on the wartime diary of a 22-year-old Swiss resident of New York. He volunteered and served as a captain in the 1st United States Sharpshooters [Berdan's] from 1861 to 1864. He lost a leg three weeks before his enlistment expired. Aschmann is particularly good in describing the daily drudgery, boredom, and incidentals of camp life.

5363. Baxter, Maurice G. "Encouragement of Immigration to the Middle West During the Era of the Civil War." IND MAG HIS, 46 [1950]: 25-38.

A discussion of the efforts made by the federal and state governments and private agencies to encourage European immigration to the United States during the Civil War. Labor was needed to man the factories and railroads of the North.

5364. Bechler, Valentin. "A German Immigrant in the Union Army, Selected Letters of Valentin Bechler." Robert Goodell and P.A.M. Taylor, editors. J AM STUD, 4 [1971]: 145-162.

Bechler emigrated from Germany to Newark, New Jersey in 1856. He enlisted in the Union army and served until 1863.

5365. Conway, Alan. "Welshmen in the Union Armies." CWH, 4 [1958]: 143-174.

Although not numerous enough to form regiments, the Welshmen did form companies--Co. E, 97th New York and Co. G., 77th Pennsylvania, for example. They believed that every blow against Richmond was a "blow against Westminster and Anglican domination."

5366. Duszak, M.J. "Colonel Kriz of Washington." POL AM STUD, 23 [1966]: 108-110.

A brief sketch of General Vladimir Krzyzanowski citing his Polish background and his service during the war.

5367. Galwey, Thomas F. THE VALIANT HOURS; NARRATIVE OF "CAPTAIN BREVET," AN IRISH-AMERICAN IN THE ARMY OF THE POTOMAC. Wilbur S. Nye, editor. Harrisburg, Pennsylvania: Stackpole, 1961.

An account of Thomas Galwey who served with the 8th Ohio. It provides some insight into the daily routine of the soldier.

5368. Gottlieb, Amy Z. "Immigration of British Coal Miners in the Civil War Decade." INT R SOC HIS, 23 [1978]: 357-375.

The reasons for and the results of British coal miner immigration is discussed. Although many did work in the mines, a a number of others served with the Union forces.

5369. Hardt, Hanno R.E. "A German-American Editor Supports the Union 1860-1862." JOUR Q, 42 [1965]: 457-460.

Franz Grimm assisted in bringing about the nomination of Lincoln and in rallying support for the Union cause. War provided the German immigrants with a common goal.

5370. Heg, Hans C. THE CIVIL WAR LETTERS OF COLONEL HANS CHRISTIAN HEG. Theodore C. Blegen, editor. Northfield, Minnesota: Norwegian-American Historical Association, 1936.

A Norwegian-born Union officer writes about southern life as he viewed it. He served primarily in Mississippi, Tennessee, and Alabama.

5371. Hokanson, Nels M. SWEDISH IMMIGRANTS IN LINCOLN'S TIME. New York: Harper, 1942.

Contributions by Swedes to the war effort in both civilian life and in the military are described. Mention is also made of Swedish regiments which were raised in the North.

5372. Horowitz, Murray M. "Ethnicity and Command: The Civil War Experience." MIL AFF, 42 [1978]: 182-189.

Ethnic considerations in appointment to leadership was apparent in the North, especially in the case of Germans. It was also true to a lesser degree with the Irish and only negligibly with other ethnic groups.

5373. Kajencki, Francis C. STAR ON MANY A BATTLEFIELD: BREVET BRIGADIER GENERAL JOSEPH KARGE IN THE AMERICAN CIVIL WAR. Madison, New Jersey: Fairleigh Dickinson University Press, 1980.

Although material on the subject is not plentiful, the author has produced a balanced, scholarly biography of an immigrant Pole, who became an excellent cavalry officer in the Union army. Karge served with the 1st and 2nd New Jersey and later was a brigade commander.

5374. Keyser, Carl. "Leather Breeches at Chancellorsville." CWTI, 14 [5] [1975]: 24-34.

Captain Hubert Dilger was a native German who came to the United States to join the Union army. Article describes his actions at Fredericksburg and Chancellorsville.

5375. Kircher, Henry A. A GERMAN IN THE YANKEE FATHERLAND. THE CIVIL WAR LETTERS OF HENRY A. KIRCHER. Earl J. Hess, editor. Kent, Ohio: Kent State University Press, 1983.

For these "German-speaking soldiers in the Northern Army" the war was "among other things, a process of Americanization." The letters, originally in German, are "articulate, witty, and completely revealing."

5376. Kleppner, Paul L. "Lincoln and the Immigrant Vote: A Case of Religious Polarization." MID AM, 48 [1966]: 176-195.

A study to determine if German-Americans in Pittsburgh supported the Republican party in 1860. Author proves German- and Irish-Americans voted in terms of religion.

5377. Lonn, Ella. FOREIGNERS IN THE UNION ARMY AND NAVY. Baton Rouge: Louisiana State University Press, 1951.

The importance of immigrants in the Union forces is proved once again in this volume. One-fifth of the servicemen were foreigners. A good presentation of the problems involved. One chapter deals specifically with the Union navy.

5378. Marraro, Howard R. "Lincoln's Italian Volunteers From New York." NY HIS, 24 [1943]: 56-67.

The story of the "Garibaldi Guard," a regiment of New York City Italians, which served with distinction throughout the war in the eastern theater.

5379. ———. "Volunteers from Italy for Lincoln's Army." S ATL Q, 44 [1945]: 384-396.

This work describes the efforts of Italian soldiers to volunteer for service in the Union army throughout the war period. Due principally to diplomatic reasons, however, no real activity began to occur until 1864 when Governor John A. Andrew of Massachusetts became involved.

5380. Pula, James S. FOR LIBERTY AND JUSTICE: THE LIFE AND TIMES OF WLADIMIR KRYZANOWSKI. Chicago: Polish-American Congress Charitable Foundation, 1978.

A fairly good biography of a man who left Poland after taking part in an unsuccessful revolt there. Based largely on Kryzanowski's memoirs, the book relates the man's service as an officer with the XI Corps and later as a government official. A useful contribution to Civil War as well as immigrant history.

5381. Rosborough, Melanie R. "One Hundred Years Ago - The F L Soldier." S ATL BULL, 39 [2] [1965]: 8-11.

A brief glimpse at the various units, some Confederate but mostly Union, which were composed predominantly of foreign-born, foreign-language speaking soldiers.

5382. Rozanski, Edward C. "Civil War Poles of Illinois." POL AM STUD, 23 [1966]: 112-114.

Over 200 men of Polish extraction from the state of Illinois served in the Union army. Not deeply immersed in pro- or anti-slavery arguments, these men fought primarily for the country.

5383. Ruff, Joseph. "Civil War Experiences of a German Emigrant As Told By Joseph Ruff." MICH HIS MAG, 27 [1943]: 271-301, 442-462.

The reminiscences of Joseph Ruff of Albion, a member of the 12th Michigan. They deal primarily with the military actions of 1862, with emphasis on Shiloh.

5384. Thompson, Henry Y. AN ENGLISHMAN IN THE AMERICAN CIVIL WAR. THE DIARIES OF HENRY YATES THOMPSON, 1863. Christopher Chancellor, editor. New York: New York State University Press, 1971.

A 24-year-old Cambridge graduate, Thompson spent the last six months of 1863 in the United States and witnessed the battle of Chattanooga standing alongside Grant. A perceptive observer, Thompson was strongly supportive of the Union cause. The editor was his great-nephew.

5385. Vasvary, Edmund. LINCOLN'S HUNGARIAN HEROES; THE PARTICIPATION OF HUNGARIANS IN THE CIVIL WAR, 1861-1865. Washington, D.C.: The Hungarian Reformed Federation of America, 1939. Reprint 1961.

For the most part only outstanding Hungarians are covered in this book. It makes worthwhile reading, however, because no other book exists on this particular nationality's service in the war.

5386. Vogel, John. "Memoir of John Vogel Immigrant and Pioneer." B.G. Oosterbean, translator. H.S. Lucas, editor. MICH HIS MAG, 30 [1946]: 546-560.

Vogel served with the 2nd Michigan Cavalry.

5387. Walker, Mack. "The Mercenaries." NEQ, 39 [1966]: 390-398.

Early in August, 1864, 700 German immigrants who had been recruited by Massachusetts' agents for service in the 20th and 35th regiments arrived in Boston. These men provided exemption for a comparable number of Bostonians and were very unhappy about it.

5388. Wittke, Carl F. THE IRISH IN AMERICA. Baton Rouge: Louisiana State University Press, 1956.

An excellent work by one of the foremost historians of immigration.

XI

SPECIAL TOPICS

A. CONSTITUTIONAL

5389. Bestor, Arthur. "The American Civil War: A Constitutional Crisis." AHR, 69: [1964]: 327-352.

A lengthy analysis of conflicting views on the Constitution with respect to slavery, slavery extension, popular sovereignty, states rights, and more, on the eve of the Civil War.

5390. Binney, Horace. THE PRIVILEGE OF THE WRIT OF HABEAS CORPUS UNDER THE CONSTITUTION. 2 v. Philadelphia, 1862.

Several essays by a leader of the Pennsylvania bar who held strong views in support of Lincoln's suspension of the writ.

5391. Birkhimer, William E. MILITARY GOVERNMENT AND MARTIAL LAW. Washington, D.C.: 1892.

The author relied heavily on his own memory in writing this monograph on martial law, one which enjoyed considerable favor.

5392. Burgess, John W. THE CIVIL WAR AND THE CONSTITUTION, 1859-1865. 2 v. New York, 1901. Reprint 1971.

An older, detailed study of the Constitution during the war by one of the most celebrated political scientists in the United States at the turn of the century. As a teenager in the 1860s, Burgess served in the ranks. The books can still be read with benefit.

5393. Durkin, Joseph T. "The Thought That Caused a War: The Compact Theory in the North." MD HIS MAG, 56 [1961]: 1-14.

Author states that the "compact theory" of the nature of the Union was as strongly held in the North as in the South, and by people of all regions and stations.

5394. Fisher, Sidney G. THE TRIAL OF THE CONSTITUTION. Philadelphia, 1862.

Writing shortly after the war commenced, the author argues that in such a crisis as then faced the country, self-preservation justified expansion of federal power, sufficient to save the Union.

5395. Gambone, Joseph G. "Ex Parte Milligan: The Restoration of Judicial Prestige." CWH, 16 [1970]: 246-259.

Author reviews the Supreme Court's handling of habeas corpus and military commission cases which arose during the war and in the early years of Reconstruction.

5396. Halbert, Sherill. "The Suspension of the Writ of Habeas Corpus by President Lincoln." A J LEG HIS, 2 [1958]: 95-116.

A discussion of the conflicting views on the power of the president to suspend the writ during wartime.

5397. Hyman, Harold M. "Deceit in Dixie." CWH, 3 [1957]: 65-82.

A discussion of the dilemma facing southerners concerning the loyalty oath in Lincoln's "10 per cent plan" of Reconstruction. Some took the oath, some refused to take it, and the great middle group wavered.

5398. ———. "Law and the Impact of the Civil War: A Review Essay." CWH, 14 [1968]: 51-59.

It is pointed out that very little had as yet been written on the legal and constitutional aspects of the Civil War and Reconstruction.

5399. ———. "Mars and the Constitution." CWTI, 12 [2] [1973]: 36-42.

A look at the constitutional difficulties which emerged when there were clashes among the three "zones of law--civil, military and martial...." The real question was the place of the Union army in the Constitution.

5400. ———. A MORE PERFECT UNION: THE IMPACT OF THE CIVIL WAR AND RECONSTRUCTION ON THE CONSTITUTION. New York: Knopf, 1973.

This is the first comprehensive effort to bring J.G. Randall's CONSTITUTIONAL PROBLEMS UNDER LINCOLN up to date. While Hyman does not replace Randall, he makes greater use of contemporary materials and draws the picture on a larger canvas. The war evoked Lincoln's view of dynamic constitutional growth, whereas Reconstruction summoned forth a more active role for the federal court system.

5401. ———. "New Light on Cohen v. Wright: California's First Loyalty Oath Case." PAC HIS R, 28 [1954]: 131-140.

A well-researched study dealing with loyalty oaths in Civil War California.

5402. ——— and William M. Wiecek. EQUAL JUSTICE UNDER LAW: CONSTITUTIONAL DEVELOPMENT, 1835-1875. New York: Harper and Row, 1982.

A thoughtful, sound examination of American constitutional growth during the 19th century, by two noted authorities on the subject.

5403. Kelley, Darwin. "Lambdin P. Milligan's Appeal For States' Rights and Constitutional Liberty During the Civil War." IND MAG HIS, 66 [1970]: 263-283.

An account of the celebrated military commission case which took place in Indiana in 1864 and 1865.

5404. ———. MILLIGAN'S FIGHT AGAINST LINCOLN. New York: Exposition, 1973.

Extensive research went into this work and a considerable amount of new information came out of it. Author attempts to establish that Milligan's legalist opinions were designed to support principles of freedom of speech rather then southern disunion. He does not totally succeed. Book suffers from a number of editorial and structural shortcomings.

5405. Klaus, Samuel, editor. THE MILLIGAN CASE. New York: Knopf, 1929.

An elaborate study of the case, which while good in its day is now out of date.

5406. Long, Joseph C. "Ex Parte Merryman: The Showdown Between Two Great Antagonists: Lincoln and Taney." SD LAW R, 14 [1969]: 207-249.

A study of the first habeas corpus case of the war, in the spring of 1861 in Maryland, wherein Lincoln overruled the chief justice of the United States Supreme Court, Roger B. Taney.

5407. Marshall, John A. AMERICAN BASTILLE: A HISTORY OF THE ILLEGAL ARRESTS AND IMPRISONMENT OF AMERICAN CITIZENS DURING THE LATE CIVIL WAR. Philadelphia, 1869.

An angry attack on the alleged despotism of Lincoln and his administration. The big volume contains sketches of over 100 people who spent time in different prisons for criticizing the government.

5408. Paludan, Phillip S. COVENANT WITH DEATH: THE CONSTITUTION, LAW AND EQUALITY IN THE CIVIL WAR ERA. Urbana: University of Illinois Press, 1975.

By exploring the ideas of five mid-19th century constitutional authorities, the author seeks to demonstrate that a conservative view toward constitutional change prevailed throughout the Civil War and Reconstruction. Reconstruction failed, for example, because the necessary evolutionary attitudes about racial equality were not found acceptable.

5409. Randall, James G. THE CONFISCATION OF PROPERTY DURING THE CIVIL WAR.... Indianapolis, 1913.

Although over 70 years old, this refinement of the author's doctoral dissertation is an excellent work and still frequently cited.

5410. ———. CONSTITUTIONAL PROBLEMS UNDER LINCOLN. New York: Appleton, 1926. Reprint 1951.

In this seminal study, still the basic work on the subject, the author examines a host of complex issues raised by the abnormality of civil war. Among the major topics looked at in detail are the president's war powers, the legal nature of the war, the law of treason, habeas corpus, arbitrary arrests, military commissions, military government in occupied areas, the draft, confiscation, emancipation, freedom of the press, and state and federal relations.

5411. Riker, William H. "Sidney George Fisher and the Separation of Powers During the Civil War." J HIS IDEAS, 15 [1954]: 397-412.

A discussion of Fisher's challenge to the sanctity of the "separation of powers" principle.

5412. Shapiro, Henry D. CONFISCATION OF CONFEDERATE PROPERTY IN THE NORTH. Ithaca, New York: Cornell University Press, 1962.

A 58-page monograph on the confiscation of property owned by Confederates in northern states. A solid study, it is based on admiralty records, treasury records of confiscation suits, and reports of attorneys and marshals.

5413. Silver, David M. LINCOLN'S SUPREME COURT. Urbana: University of Illinois Press, 1956.

An excellent study of the subject. Work includes useful short biographies of all the members of the bench and discusses the presidential politics of court appointments. Basically, the determination of Lincoln to preserve the Union in spite of the obstructionist actions of the court is defended, although Chief Justice Taney's poor reputation is somewhat rehabilitated.

5414. Singley, Frederick J., Jr. "Denial of Habeas Corpus: A Contrast in Blue and Gray." A BAR ASSN J, 49 [1963]: 172-175.

Although the habeas corpus clause in the Confederate Constitution was taken directly from the federal Constitution, it was not applied in the same way in the North as in the South. The Lincoln government was much quicker to suspend the writ than was the Davis government.

5415. Spector, Robert M. "Lincoln and Taney: A Study in Constitutional Polarization." A J LEG HIS, 15 [1971]: 199-214.

An analysis of the opposing views on the Constitution held by Chief Justice Taney and President Lincoln. Lincoln, the broad constructionist, saw the Constitution as evolving and changing, while Taney, the strict constructionist, saw it as static.

5416. Surrency, Erwin C. "The Legal Effects of the Civil War." A J LEG HIS, 5 [1961]: 145-165.

A review of the many complex legal problems facing state and federal courts in the South after the war.

5417. Thornbrough, Emma L. "Judge Perkins, The Indiana Supreme Court and the Civil War." IND MAG HIS, 60 [1964]: 79-96.

Judge Samuel E. Perkins, a Democrat who was a member of the Indiana Supreme Court, became the spokesman for the anti-Lincoln administration cause both on and off the bench. He strongly denounced military arrests and some of Governor Oliver P. Morton's financial policies.

5418. Whiting, William. THE WAR POWERS OF THE PRESIDENT, MILITARY ARRESTS, AND RECONSTRUCTION OF THE UNION. Boston, 1864.

A valuable work which ran through many editions, explaining and justifying the expansion of federal power. The author was solicitor in the war department.

B. ECONOMIC

5419. Andreano, Ralph, editor. THE ECONOMIC IMPACT OF THE AMERICAN CIVIL WAR. Cambridge, Massachusetts: Schenkman, 1962.

A good readings book on the economic aspects of the war. The material is supported by useful, understandable statistical data.

5420. Barrett, Don C. THE GREENBACKS AND RESUMPTION OF SPECIE PAYMENTS 1862-1879. Cambridge: Harvard University Press, 1931.

"Greenbacks," unbacked paper money, were issued to help in the financing of the war in 1862. After the war, efforts by "hard money" interests to retire the greenbacks did not succeed. Eventually, in 1879, they were "brought to par."

5421. Bearss, Edwin C. "1862 Brings Hard Times to the Chesapeake and Ohio Canal." W VA HIS, 30 [1969]: 436-462.

It was not only the war which made 1862 the worst year in the canal's history, financially speaking. Poor management was also a factor.

5422. Belcher, Wyatt W. THE ECONOMIC RIVALRY BETWEEN ST. LOUIS AND CHICAGO, 1850-1880. New York: n.p., 1947.

Only a portion of the book deals with the war years.

5423. Belz, Herman. "Law, Politics and Race in the Struggle For Equal Pay During the Civil War." CWH, 22 [1976]: 197-213.

A review of the congressional debates which led to the passage of an 1864 law authorizing, but not granting, equal pay for both black and white Union troops. By the law Attorney General Edward Bates was given the power to determine the exact pay for blacks; he ruled for equal pay.

5424. Bogart, Ernest L. ... WAR COSTS AND THEIR FINANCING: A STUDY OF THE FINANCING OF THE WAR AND THE AFTER-WAR PROBLEMS OF DEBT AND TAXATION. New York: Appleton, 1921.

An old, but solid, study of the federal government's wartime financial policies.

5425. Boritt, Gabor. "Lincoln and Taxation During His Illinois Years." JISHS, 61 [1968]: 365-373.

Lincoln supported high taxation in Illinois after the state went insolvent over internal improvement projects in the late 1830s, but later he would resume his traditional low taxation position.

5426. Capron, John D. "Virginia Iron Furnaces of the Confederacy." VA CAV, 17 [1967]: 10-18.

It is argued that the Union forces could have shortened the war by many months if a concerted effort had been made to destroy the furnaces.

5427. Claussen, Martin P. "Peace Factors in Anglo-American Relations, 1861-1865." MVHR, 26 [1940]: 511-522.

Challenges and discredits Louis B. Schmidt's theory that the need for northern wheat was a major reason for Britain's neutral stance.

5428. Cochran, Thomas C. "Did the Civil War Retard Industrialization?" MVHR, 48 [1961]: 197-209.

A seminal study, in which the author demonstrates statistically that the Civil War did not stimulate industrial production, as had long been believed, but in many cases had actually slowed down production. The so-called "Cochran Thesis" was first presented at the 1960 convention of the Mississippi Valley Historical Association.

5429. Coulter, E. Merton. "Effects of Secession Upon the Commerce of the Mississippi Valley." MVHR, 3 [1916]: 275-300.

Secession disrupted the very significant North-South trade in the Mississippi Valley. This article provides an excellent discussion of the subject and lays an economic basis for Democratic dissent.

5430. Davis, Andrew M. THE ORIGIN OF THE NATIONAL BANKING SYSTEM. Washington, D.C.: 1910-1911.

A detailed discussion of the drafting of the legislation which created the National Bank during the war.

5431. Dean, Henry C. CRIMES OF THE CIVIL WAR, AND CURSE OF THE FUNDING SYSTEM. Baltimore: 1869.

A scathing critique of wartime monetary legislation by a leading and controversial Iowa Copperhead.

5432. De Canio, Stephen J. and Joel Mokyr. "Inflation and the Wage Lag During the American Civil War." EXPLO ECON HIS, 14 [1977]: 311-336.

Inflation played a significant role in financing the war in the North. Workers' wages fell and they bore a heavy burden of the overall cost.

5433. Dewey, Davis R. ... FINANCIAL HISTORY OF THE UNITED STATES. New York, 1903.

A classic in its day, but long since eroded by time.

5434. Deyrup, Felicia J. ARMS MAKERS OF THE CONNECTICUT VALLEY: A REGIONAL STUDY OF THE ECONOMIC DEVELOPMENT OF THE SMALL ARMS INDUSTRY, 1798-1870. Northampton, Massachusetts: n.p., 1948.

A solid study of a somewhat ignored subject.

5435. Dun, R.G. "A Northern Businessman Opposes the Civil War: Excerpts From the Letters of R.G. Dun." James D. Norris, editor. OHIO HIS, 71 [1962]: 138-147.

A selection of political materials from the letters of Dun to his family, 1861-1865.

5436. Ellis, L. Tuffly. "Maritime Commerce on the Far Western Gulf, 1861-1865." SW HIS Q, 77 [1973]: 167-226.

An extensive illegal maritime trade was carried on along the Texas coast in spite of the Union blockade, but because of poor organization, it was not as helpful to the Confederate war effort as it might have been.

5437. Ellison, Joseph. "The Currency Question of the Pacific Coast During the Civil War." MVHR, 16 [1929/1930]: 50-66.

A discussion of the impact of "greenback" currency, unbacked paper money issued by the federal government in 1862, on the Pacific Coast, where gold coins were the ordinary medium of exchange.

5438. Engelbourg, Saul. "The Economic Impact of the Civil War on Manufacturing Enterprise." BUS HIS GR BR, 21 [1979]: 148-162.

With minor exceptions, such as small arms and clothing, the Civil War did not accelerate the rate of growth in manufacturing enterprise. It did speed up the demand for specific products.

5439. Engerman, Stanley L. "The Economic Impact of the Civil War." EXPLO ENTRE HIS, 3 [1966]: 176-199.

Author examines the Charles Beard-Louis Hacker thesis that the Civil War marked a major turning point in the economic life of the country.

5440. Erickson, Charlotte. AMERICAN INDUSTRY AND THE EUROPEAN IMMIGRANT, 1860-1865. Cambridge: Harvard University Press, 1957.

An excellent study of labor legislation and the impact of immigration on the labor movement in the North during the war.

5441. Ernst, Dorothy H. "Wheat Speculation in the Civil War Era." WIS MAG HIS, 47 [1963]: 125-134.

A detailed account of speculation in Minnesota wheat by Daniel Wells of Milwaukee from 1860-1862.

5442. Fish, Carl R. "Social Relief in the Northwest During the Civil War." AHR, 22 [1917]: 309-324.

A pioneering study on the subject which is still of use today.

5443. Fishwick, Marshall. "Sheaves of Golden Grain." AM HER, 7 [6] [1956]: 80-85.

A discussion of the role of the reaper, invented by Cyrus McCormick, in the history of American agriculture. It is ironic that the invention of a Virginian should help the North win the Civil War.

5444. Fite, Emerson D. SOCIAL AND INDUSTRIAL CONDITIONS IN THE NORTH DURING THE CIVIL WAR. New York: P. Smith, 1930.

An older but still valuable study of economic conditions in the North. Useful interpretations enhance the mass of factual material.

5445. Foner, Philip S. BUSINESS AND SLAVERY: THE NEW YORK MERCHANTS AND THE IRREPRESSIBLE CONFLICT. Chapel Hill: University of North Carolina Press, 1941.

A scholarly examination of the impact of the war on the economy of New York City. The business men, with their economic links to the South, fought for years against anything which would disrupt the relations. In order to do this they had to enter the political arena and this book relates their activities in this area.

5446. Friedman, Milton. "Price, Income and Monetary Changes in Three Wartime Periods." A ECON R, 42 [1952]: 612-625.

Author concludes that "the quantity theory [of money] is and the income expenditure theory is not consistent with price and income behavior" in the Civil War, World War I, and World War II. This paper is to be found in AMERICAN ECONOMIC REVIEW: Papers and Proceedings [May 1951].

5447. Futrell, Robert. "Federal Trade With the Confederate States, 1861-1865." Ph.D. dissertation, Vanderbilt University, 1950.

An able study of an often overlooked aspect of the war.

5448. Gates, Paul W. AGRICULTURE AND THE CIVIL WAR. New York: Knopf, 1965.

An excellent account of all aspects of American agriculture, North and South, covering the ante-bellum period, the Civil War, and Reconstruction. Much new material is to be found in this work, written by an expert on agricultural history.

5449. ———. "The Homestead Law in an Incongruous Land System." AHR, 41 [1935/1936]: 652-681.

Author argues that the Homestead Act did not replace the former system of land disposition--sales and auctions--with the offer of free land. Rather, it tried to impose the new system on the old and it did not work.

5450. Gilchrist, David T. and W. David Lewis, editors. ECONOMIC CHANGES IN THE CIVIL WAR ERA. Greenville, Delaware: Eleutherian Mills-Hagley Foundation, 1965.

This volume includes the papers presented by 14 speakers at a conference designed to analyze the "Cochran Thesis" that the Civil War might have retarded industrialization. The participants dealt with a number of issues but concluded that Cochran was correct.

5451. Ginzberg, Eli. "The Economics of British Neutrality During the American Civil War." AGRIC HIS, 10 [1936]: 147-156.

Another challenge to the Schmidt thesis on the importance of northern wheat in British foreign policy.

5452. Gitelman, H.M. "The Labor Force at Waltham Watch During the Civil War Era." J ECON HIS, 25 [1965]: 214-243.

A detailed account of the Waltham Watch Company's employment problems during the Civil War. They attracted girls to their work force, imported skilled mechanics from abroad, paid good wages, and maintained a high moral tone in the factory. Statistical tables are included.

5453. Grossman, Jonathan P. WILLIAM SYLVIS, PIONEER OF AMERICAN LABOR: A STUDY OF THE LABOR MOVEMENT DURING THE ERA OF THE CIVIL WAR. New York: Columbia University Press, 1945.

This solid biography of an early giant in the field of organized labor provides a good glimpse of wartime labor activity.

5454. Hammond, Bray. "The North's Empty Purse, 1861-1862." AHR, 67 [1961]: 1-18.

Details the initial problems of the treasury department during the first year of the war.

5455. ———. SOVEREIGNTY AND AN EMPTY PURSE: BANKS AND POLITICS IN THE CIVIL WAR. Princeton, New Jersey: Princeton University Press, 1970.

Author demonstrates that the government's economic policies during the war accentuated the centralizing power of the nation at the expense of the states. He also notes that many problems suffered by the treasury department were avoidable.

5456. Hancock, Harold B. and Norman B. Wilkinson. "A Manufacturer in Wartime: DuPont, 1860-1865." BUS HIS R, 40 [1966]: 213-236.

During the war years the sales of E.I. DuPont de Nemours and Company, the nation's largest gunpowder manufacturer, more than doubled.

5457. Hepburn, Alonzo B. HISTORY OF COINAGE AND CURRENCY IN THE UNITED STATES AND THE PERENNIAL CONTEST FOR SOUND MONEY. New York, 1903.

A one-time comptroller of the currency analyzes money problems during the war.

5458. Hesseltine, William B. "The Civil War Industry." MICH HIS, 42 [1958]: 421-434.

A survey of various industries, businesses, and activities growing out of the Civil War, such as the manufacture of souvenirs, the construction of monuments, Civil War book clubs, museums, publications, the Civil War Roundtable and much else.

5459. Johnson, Ludwell H. "The Butler Expedition of 1861-1862: The Profitable Side of War." CWH, 11 [1965]: 229-236.

General Benjamin F. Butler loaded his command with cousins and cronies and countenanced various frauds connected with the supplying, feeding, and transporting of troops, as he outfitted his force for the move to New Orleans in the winter of 1861-1862.

5460. ———. "Commerce Between Northeastern Ports and the Confederacy, 1861-1865." JAH, 54 [1967]: 30-42.

Although elaborate efforts were made to suppress New York's

trade with the South, they were largely nullified by corrupt, ambitious politicians and military personnel.

5461. ———. "Contraband Trade During the Last Year of the Civil War." MVHR, 49 [1963]: 635-652.

An analysis of what proved to be a profitable business, but one which led to many difficulties.

5462. ———. "The Louis Welton Affair: A Confederate Attempt to Buy Supplies in the North." CWH, 15 [1969]: 30-38.

A bungled effort to secure northern supplies for the Trans-Mississippi Department of the Confederacy in 1864.

5463. ———. "Northern Profit and Profiteers: The Cotton Rings of 1864-1865." CWH, 12 [1966]: 101-115.

An account of the legal and illegal trade in cotton and other necessaries between North and South in the last year of the war.

5464. Jones, Robert H. "Long Live the King?" AGRIC HIS, 37 [1963]: 166-169.

A consideration of the federal hope that grain from the North would replace "King Cotton" as the most important export from the United States to Great Britain. Author concludes that it did.

5465. Klein, Maury. "The War and Economic Expansion." CWTI, 8 [9] [1970]: 35-43.

Though no new technological developments emerged from the war, the conflict did promote rapid industrial expansion, release the agricultural South's grip on the government, brought the Republican party to power, rendered the South ripe for industrialization, and speeded settlement of the West.

5466. Larson, Henrietta M. JAY COOKE, PRIVATE BANKER. Cambridge: Harvard University Press, 1936.

A thoroughgoing study of the financial giant whose banking house has traditionally been given credit for financing the northern cause in the war.

5467. Luthin, Reinhard H. "Abraham Lincoln and the Tariff." AHR, 49 [1943/1944]: 609-629.

Lincoln's support of the protective tariff was important to Pennsylvania Republicans, who played a central role in his winning both the nomination and the election. Yet while in office, Lincoln's chief interest in the tariff was for revenue not for protection.

5468. Michelman, Dorothea S. "Gold, Cotton, and Newsprint." LIN HER, 68 [1966]: 190-198.

General William Walton Murphy proved to be a very successful northern emissary. He countered efforts of Confederate agents to float loans in Frankfurt, solicited gifts of medical supplies for the Union army, and promoted a better understanding of Union war aims.

5469. Mitchell, Wesley C. A HISTORY OF THE GREENBACKS, WITH SPECIAL REFERENCE TO THE ECONOMIC CONSEQUENCES OF THEIR ISSUE, 1862-1865. Chicago, 1903. Reprint 1960.

An old, but excellent, scholarly account of a tricky subject.

5470. Montgomery, David. BEYOND EQUALITY: LABOR AND THE RADICAL REPUBLICANS, 1862-1872. New York: Knopf, 1967.

Author argues that many wartime Republican Radicals became identified with the rising labor movement after the war.

5471. Oberholtzer, Ellis P. JAY COOKE, FINANCIER OF THE CIVIL WAR. 2 v. Philadelphia, 1907.

A large and scholarly biography of the New York banker who financed the Civil War. Full treatment is given to the war years.

5472. Parks, Joseph H. "A Confederate Trade Center Under Federal Occupation: Memphis, 1862 to 1865." JSH, 7 [1941]: 289-314.

A discussion of the complicated task of regulating legal trade and suppressing illegal trade at the major river city of Memphis, from the time the federals occupied it in 1862 until the end of the war.

5473. Rasmussen, Wayne D. "The Civil War: A Catalyst of Agricultural Revolution." AGRIC HIS, 39 [1965]: 187-195.

The war served as a stimulus to agriculture, encouraging the adoption of horse-drawn machinery, newer implements, and the adoption of agricultural reform measures.

5474. Ratner, Sidney. AMERICAN TAXATION, ITS HISTORY AS A SOCIAL FORCE IN DEMOCRACY. New York: Norton, 1942.

A good discussion of Civil War taxation policies and their impact on society. This is the standard work on the subject.

5475. Reinfeld, Fred. THE STORY OF CIVIL WAR MONEY. New York: Sterling, 1959.

A 93-page monograph explaining the intricacies of paper money values during the war. A brief account of how the war was financed and how the hoarding of metal led to the use of paper currency.

5476. Rezneck, Samuel. "A Timely Pamphlet and the Making of a Fiscal Expert." NY HIS, 47 [1966]: 17-21.

In an August 1864 pamphlet, "Our Burden and Our Strength," David A. Wells demonstrated that the prospective increases of the national wealth and population would more than offset any future debt. Wells later became one of the country's leading authorities on financial and economic matters.

5477. Roberts, A. Sellew. "The Federal Government and Confederate Cotton." AHR, 33 [1926/1927]: 262-275.

Author argues that the illegal cotton trade between North and South, winked at by the federal government, was damaging to the northern cause and prolonged the war.

5478. Robinson, Marshall A. "Federal Debt Management: Civil War, World War I, and World War II." A ECON R, 45 [1955]: 388-401.

A provocative study, comparing the methods employed in the country's three big wars.

5479. Sabine, David B. "Resources Compared: North Versus South." CWTI, 6 [10] [1968]: 4-13.

The author compares the natural resources, industrial capacities, finances, transportation, and leadership potential of the two adversaries.

5480. Scheiber, Harry W. "Economic Change in the Civil War Era: An Analysis of Recent Studies." CWH, 11 [1965]: 396-411.

A perceptive analysis of all the literature to date on the impact of the Civil War on the American economy.

5481. Schmidt, Louis B. "The Influence of Wheat and Cotton on Anglo-American Relations During the Civil War." IOWA J HIS POL, 16 [1918]: 400-439.

This is the revolutionary and controversial theory that the need in Great Britain for northern wheat was the major reason that the British government maintained neutrality during the Civil War.

5482. Sears, Marian V. "Gold and the Local Stock Exchanges of the 1860's." EXPLO ENTRE HIS, 6 [1969]: 198-232.

Federal policy for financing the war and the boom in exploration and discovery of precious metals spawned a boom in local stock exchanges. Nearly 40 were established.

5483. Sharkey, Robert P. MONEY, CLASS, AND PARTY: AN ECONOMIC STUDY OF CIVIL WAR AND RECONSTRUCTION. Baltimore: Johns Hopkins Press, 1959.

It makes for heavy going in places, but if you can stand it, you will be rewarded in this outstanding examination of economic matters in the North during the war. Statistical data and tables help the reader understand the complexities of the subject.

5484. Smith, David C. "Middle Range Farming in the Civil War Era: Life on a Farm in Seneca County, 1862-1866." NY HIS, 48 [1967]: 352-369.

Drawn from the diaries of Henry K. Dey who farmed on the shores of Seneca Lake near Geneva, New York, article presents an interesting picture of farm life, prices, and crops raised during the years 1862-1866.

5485. Smith, George W. "Cotton From Savannah in 1865." JSH, 21 [1955]: 495-512.

Author traces the events surrounding the seizure of a cache of cotton when Sherman took Savannah in December 1864. These events foreshadowed many of the economic and social problems that attended the post-war years in the South.

5486. ———. HENRY C. CAREY AND AMERICAN SECTIONAL CONFLICT. Albuquerque: University of New Mexico Press, 1951.

A workmanlike account of the role of the celebrated economist in the Civil War.

5487. Trescott, Paul B. "Federal Government Receipts and Expenditures, 1861-1875." J ECON HIS, 26 [1966]: 206-222.

A technical study of federal income, expenses, and finances during the Civil War and Reconstruction.

5488. Vartanian, Pershing. "The Cochran Thesis: A Critique in Statistical Analysis." JAH, 51 [1964]: 77-89.

Author challenges Cochran's methodology in particular and the use of statistics in general as a tool for historical explanation. He finds the "Cochran Thesis" not very helpful to an understanding of the impact of the Civil War on industrialism.

5489. Wacht, Richard F. "A Note on the Cochran Thesis and the Small Arms Industry in the Civil War." EXPLO ENTRE HIS, 4 [1966]: 57-62.

Author supports the "Cochran Thesis" insofar as that thesis applies to the manufacture of small arms.

5490. Ware, Norman J. THE LABOR MOVEMENT IN THE UNITED STATES, 1860-1895: A STUDY IN DEMOCRACY. New York: Appleton, 1929.

An important work despite its age. Author holds that the Civil War stimulated labor unionization.

5491. Waters, William R. "The Economic Basis of the Civil War: A Reappraisal." TOPIC 2 [Fall 1961]: 30-39.

Author argues that the destruction of the Second Bank of the United States by Andrew Jackson precipitated an adverse balance of payments condition for the southern states, which in turn contributed importantly to secession and war.

5492. Weigley, Russell F. "The Civil War and Our Affluent Society." CWTI, 2 [1] [1963]: 38-46.

A general look at American economic development and the Civil War. Author speculates whether the war affected the American economy more than the economy affected the war.

5493. Weintraub, Andrew. "The Economics of Lincoln's Proposal For Compensated Emancipation." A J ECON SOC, 32 [1973]: 171-177.

A comparison of the costs of compensating southern slaveholders for buying their slaves' freedom with the costs of the war itself. Compensated emancipation would have been very expensive.

5494. Wells, David A. ... THE RECENT FINANCIAL, INDUSTRIAL AND COMMERCIAL EXPERIENCES OF THE UNITED STATES: A CURIOUS CHAPTER IN POLITICO-ECONOMIC HISTORY. New York, 1872.

A short, but classic, view of the subject matter, written by an expert.

5495. Williamson, Jeffrey G. "Watersheds and Turning Points: Conjectures on the Long-Term Impact of Civil War Financing." J ECON HIS, 34 [1974]: 636-661.

Tries to refute the idea that the Civil War did not have much impact on economics. Suggests the war may be a "watershed" in United States' economics, especially with regard to long term debt management and tariff policy.

C. HUMANITARIANISM, RELIGION, AND SOCIETY

5496. Abbott, Edith. "The Civil War and the Crime Wave of 1865-1870." SOC SCI R, 51 [1977]: 71-93.

A discussion of the bearing of the war on post-war crime.

5497. Albrecht, Robert C. "The Theological Response of the Transcendentalists to the Civil War." NEQ, 38 [1965]: 21-34.

Many of the American transcendentalist ministers remained in their pulpits during the war, interpreting the war in terms of redemption.

5498. Bacon, Georgeanna M. LETTERS OF A FAMILY DURING THE WAR FOR THE UNION. New Haven, Connecticut: 1899.

The author was a Woolsey, and this collection of Woolsey family letters provides a keen insight into the social issues of the day. Political matters are also given consideration. Interesting reading.

5499. Batcheler, Horatio P. JONATHAN AT HOME: OR, A STRAY SHOT AT THE YANKEES. London, England: 1864.

Reflections of an Englishman on wartime society in the North.

5500. Betts, John R. "Home Front, Battle Field, and Sport During the Civil War." RES Q, 42 [1971]: 113-132.

A pioneer in the field of "sport history" examines sport and recreation in wartime.

5501. Billingsley, Amos S. FROM THE FLAG TO THE CROSS, OR, SCENES AND INCIDENTS OF CHRISTIANITY IN THE WAR.... Philadelphia, 1872.

In addition to providing a glimpse of the religious experiences of soldiers in the field, this useful volume also tells of the work of northern clergymen at home and at the front.

5502. Blied, Benjamin J. CATHOLICS AND THE CIVIL WAR: ESSAYS. Milwaukee, Wisconsin: n.p., 1945.

An excellent group of articles dealing with varying Catholic opinion regarding the war and slavery.

5503. Bradley, George S. THE STAR CORPS: OR, NOTES OF AN ARMY CHAPLAIN DURING SHERMAN'S FAMOUS "MARCH TO THE SEA." Milwaukee, Wisconsin: 1865.

An account of the famous march by the chaplain of the 22nd Wisconsin, drawn from his own papers. Discusses the impact of the march on the people who fell in its path.

5504. Bremner, Robert H. "The Impact of the Civil War on Philanthropy and Social Welfare." CWH, 12 [1966]: 293-303.

The richer North engaged in more philanthropic effort than the South, but in both sections there was a substantial expansion in welfare activity.

5505. ———. "Prelude: Philanthropic Rivalries in the Civil War." SOC CASEWORK, 49: 77-81.

The United States Sanitary Commission and the United States Christian Commission both turned to relief work during the war. Gives a brief treatment of the evolution and rivalry of the two.

5506. ———. THE PUBLIC GOOD: PHILANTHROPY AND WELFARE IN THE CIVIL WAR ERA. New York: Knopf, 1980.

Views the Civil War as the real starting point of private relief work in this country. The war gave "an impetus to organized relief and reform" and even impacted on the organization of the philanthropic enterprises. People began giving generously to "deserving" poor, libraries, museums and colleges.

5507. Bristol, Frank M. THE LIFE OF CHAPLAIN McCABE, BISHOP OF THE METHODIST EPISCOPAL CHURCH. New York, 1908.

Bishop McCabe served with the 122nd Ohio and spent considerable time in Libby Prison.

5508. Brock, Peter. "The Problem of the Civil War." ADVENTIST HERITAGE, 1 [1964]: 23-27.

The Seventh-Day Adventist Church had to weigh its strong anti-slavery position against its equally strong objection to military service.

5509. Brown, Bruce T. "Grace Church, Galesburg, Illinois, 1864-1866: The supposed Neutrality of the Episcopal Church During the Years of the Civil War." HIS MAG PROT EPI CH, 46 [1977]: 187-208.

A sharp conflict arose over the authority of the bishops and the denomination's involvement in political issues. The dispute perhaps reflected the larger problems of the national church.

5510. CHRIST IN THE ARMY: A SELECTION OF SKETCHES OF THE WORK OF THE U.S. CHRISTIAN COMMISSION. Philadelphia, 1865.

Outlines the organization of the group and describes the work accomplished during the war. Two chapters deal specifically with women's activities.

5511. Coatsworth, Stella S. THE LOYAL PEOPLE OF THE NORTH-WEST.... Chicago, 1869.

"A record of prominent persons, places and events" of the area during the momentous years of the war.

5512. Cogshall, Israel. "The Journal of Israel Cogshall, 1862-1863." Cecil K. Byrd, editor. IND MAG HIS, 42 [1946]: 69-87.

The author kept a journal for about a year when chaplain of the 19th Michigan. He carried a spirit of evangelism with him into the war and concentrated on improving the spiritual well-being of the soldiers.

5513. Corby, William. MEMOIRS OF CHAPLAIN LIFE.... Notre Dame, Indiana: 1894.

A good book of recollections by a man who served for three years as a chaplain in the Irish Brigade.

5514. Curtis, Peter K. "A Quaker and the Civil War: The Life of James Parnell Jones." QUAKER HIS, 67 [1978]: 35-41.

Raised as a Quaker in Maine, Jones developed a passion for anti-slavery and temperance reforms. When he returned home after graduating from college and teaching, he joined the 7th Maine and was disowned.

5515. Danforth, Mildred E. A QUAKER PIONEER: LAURA HAVILAND, SUPERINTENDENT OF THE UNDERGROUND. New York: Exposition, 1961.

Haviland was a humanitarian reformer in Michigan before and during the war.

5516. Daniel, W. Harrison. "Protestant Clergy and Union Sentiment in the Confederacy." TENN HIS Q, 23 [1964]: 284-290.

Author discusses criticism of secession by the clergymen in the South.

5517. Davis, J. Treadwell. "The Presbyterians and the Sectional Conflict." SOUTH Q, 8 [1970]: 117-133.

The Civil War split the major Protestant churches into northern and southern factions. This is an account of the long struggle between the two Presbyterian forces until fraternal relations were finally restored in 1888.

5518. Dicey, Edward. SPECTATOR OF AMERICA. Herbert Mitgang, editor. Chicago: Quadrangle, 1971.

Dicey, a Cambridge graduate, was a young writer for THE SPECTATOR and visited America to report on the war. The book is filled with pungent observations and graphic descriptions. It is "alive with ... the sights, sounds and smells--of Civil War America."

5519. Duncan, Richard R. "Bishop Whittingham, the Maryland Diocese, and the Civil War." MD HIS MAG, 61 [1966]: 329-347.

Despite internal dissension over political and other matters, the Maryland Diocese of the Protestant Episcopal Church survived the war. While unable to exert strong leadership, Bishop William Robinson Whittingham played a role in keeping the organization intact.

5520. ———. "Maryland Methodists and the Civil War." MD HIS MAG, 59 [1964]: 350-368.

Maryland Methodism came out against slavery, but equivocal interpretations protected the slaveholder who might otherwise have left the church. An 1864 conference statement asserted support for the Union and emancipation.

5521. Dunham, Chester F. ... THE ATTITUDE OF THE NORTHERN CLERGY TOWARD THE SOUTH, 1860-1865. Toledo, Ohio: Gray, 1942.

An uncomplicated account of a complicated matter.

5522. Edwards, John. "An Account of My Escape From the South in 1861." CH OK, 43 [1965]: 58-89.

A Presbyterian missionary, Edwards was ordered to fight for the Confederacy. He and his family escaped to the North.

5523. Evans, Hugh D. "The 'Recollections' of Hugh Davey Evans." Edward N. Todd, editor. MAG PROT EPI CH, 34 [1965]: 297-332.

The reminiscences and political opinions of Evans, whose high church leanings and support of the Union cost him his elective post in the diocese.

5524. Ferguson, Robert. AMERICA DURING AND AFTER THE WAR. London, England: 1866.

An English clergyman who traveled through the North describes what he saw.

5525. Ferri-Pisani, Camille. PRINCE NAPOLEON IN AMERICA, 1861: LETTERS FROM HIS AIDE-DE-CAMP. George J. Joyaux, translator. Bloomington: Indiana University Press, 1959.

Perceptive letters written by an aide to the cousin of Louis Napoleon. The royal party toured the North and the descriptions of towns and the effects of the war on the people are well worth reading.

5526. Field, Henry M. BRIGHT SKIES AND DARK SHADOWS. New York, 1890.

A useful book of memoirs of a clergyman who traveled widely throughout the South during the war.

5527. Fielding, Lawrence W. "Gay and Happy Still: Holiday Sports in the Army of the Potomac." MD HIS, 7 [1976]: 19-32.

A deightful article on the diversions which the soldiers of the eastern army engaged in during the winter months.

5528. ———. "Sport as a Training Technique in the Union Army." PHYS ED, 34 [1977]: 145-152.

A discussion of the use of competitive activities--rifle shoots, sham battles--and such sports as foot races, wrestling, boxing, jumping, and football to relieve the boredom of drill and better prepare the men for combat situations.

5529. ———. "Sport: The Meter Stick of the Civil War Soldier." CAN J HIS SPORT PHYS ED, 9 [1978]: 1-18.

Sport was the measure of prowess among Civil War soldiers.

5530. ———. "War and Trifles: Sports in the Shadows of Civil War Army Life." J SPORT HIS, 4 [1977]: 151-168.

During the war soldiers frequently played sports to relieve the monotony, forget their problems, and display manliness.

5531. ——— and William T. Weinberg, Brenda G. Pitts, and Richard A. Fee. "The Demise of Officer Involvement in Soldiers' Sport During the American Civil War." CAN J HIS SPORT, 16 [1985]: 72-81.

Authors describe the difficulties which emerged when officers attempted to plan sport festivals for their troops. Their main error was in attempting to limit participation when practically all the men wanted to join in the fun.

5532. Fisher, Sidney G. "The Diary of Sidney George Fisher: 1861, 1862, 1863, 1864, 1865." PA MHB, 88 [1964]: 70-93, 199-226, 328-367, 456-484; 89 [1965]: 79-110, 207-227.

The perceptive diary of a member of a distinguished Philadelphia family. Fisher was a lawyer, who never practiced. He was a strong supporter of the Union cause and his diary reflects its ups and downs as the war progressed.

5533. Fiske, Samuel W. MR. DUNN BROWNE'S EXPERIENCES IN THE ARMY.... Boston, 1866.

Browne left the ministry to serve as an officer with the 14th Connecticut, but was killed in the fighting in the Wilderness. This volume is based on his journal.

5534. Fletcher, Calvin. THE DIARY OF CALVIN FLETCHER. VOLUME VII, 1861-1862: INCLUDING LETTERS TO AND FROM CALVIN FLETCHER. Gayle Thornbrough, Dorothy L. Riker, and Paula Corpuz editors. Indianapolis: Indiana Historical Society, 1980.

An excellent study of the career of banker-farmer Calvin Fletcher during the first two years of the war. He traveled to Canada to purchase arms, assisted in providing aid to the families of soldiers, and was influential in state politics. A good view of life on the home front.

5535. Fuller, Richard F. CHAPLAIN FULLER: BEING A SKETCH OF A NEW ENGLAND CLERGYMAN AND ARMY CHAPLAIN. Boston, 1863.

The last half of the book deals with the author's wartime experiences as a chaplain with the 16th Massachusetts.

5536. Gage, Moses D. FROM VICKSBURG TO RALEIGH. Chicago, 1865.

An engaging account of army camp life during Sherman's campaigns written by a chaplain.

5537. Greene, Nancy L. YE OLDE SHAKER BELLS. Lexington, Kentucky: Transylvania Printing, 1930.

An excellent diary reflecting the impact of war on the Shaker colony at Pleasanthill, Kentucky.

5538. Heathcote, Charles W. THE LUTHERAN CHURCH AND THE CIVIL WAR. New York: Fleming H. Revell, 1919.

A rather slim volume of somewhat dubious merit, which seeks to analyze the accomplishments of both the northern and southern synods during the war.

5539. Henry, James O. "The United States Christian Commission in the Civil War." CWH, 6 [1960]: 374-388.

A report of the excellent work performed by the United States Christian Commission in tending to the needs of Union soldiers at the front. The 5,000 "delegates" of the commission delivered packages and Bibles, preached sermons, held prayer meetings, and wrote letters for the soldiers.

5540. Hepworth, George H. THE WHIP, HOE, AND SWORD: OR, THE GULF DEPARTMENT IN 1863. Boston, 1864.

A description of the greed and corruption shown by the Union army in Occupied Louisiana, written by a federal chaplain.

5541. Hernon, Joseph M., Jr. "Irish Religious Opinion on the American Civil War." CATH HIS R, 49 [1964]: 508-523.

The Catholic, as well as most of the Protestant, churches in Ireland supported the Confederacy. Believing that slavery was doomed without war, they decried the bloodshed.

5542. Holliday, Joseph E. "Relief For Soldiers' Families in Ohio During the Civil War." OHIO HIS, 71 [1962]: 97-112.

Author describes tax levies and other relief programs designed to benefit the famlies of soldiers fighting at the front.

5543. Honeywell, Roy J. "Men of God in Uniform." CWTI, 6 [5] [1967]: 30-36.

Stories and anecdotes pertaining to the efforts of chaplains to bring spiritual comfort to and raise the morale of troops in combat.

5544. Hubbard, George U. "Abraham Lincoln as Seen By the Mormons." UTAH HIS Q, 31 [1963]: 91-108.

Lincoln has been honored and revered by Mormons since the Civil War because of his fair and generous treatment of them during the war.

5545. Hulbert, Eri B. "The Civil War Diary of a Christian Minister: The Observations of Eri Baker Hulbert, United States Christian Commission Delegate, While Assigned With the Army of the James February-March, 1865." Leo P. Kibby, editor. JW, 3 [1964]: 221-232.

Hulbert's diary records various events and impressions during the last two months of the war.

5546. Humphreys, Charles A. FIELD, CAMP, HOSPITAL AND PRISON IN THE CIVIL WAR, 1863-1865. Boston: George H. Ellis, 1918.

The author served as a chaplain with a Massachusetts cavalry unit.

5547. Huntington, [Mrs.] Henry. "Escape From Atlanta; The Huntington Memoir." Ben Kremenak, editor. CWH, 11 [1965]: 160-177.

The moving record of the escape to Union lines of a northern family which had moved to Georgia in 1851.

5548. Ingersoll, Charles W. "'Despotism of Traitors': The Rebellious South Through New York Eyes." NY HIS, 45 [1964]: 331-367.

These are a group of family letters from his home in Owego, New York, to Charles Ingersoll, member of the 50th New York Engineers, at the front.

5549. Jaquette, Henrietta S. "Friends' Association of Philadelphia For the Aid and Elevation of the Freedmen." FRIENDS HIS ASSN BULL, 46 [1957]: 67-83.

Author traces the origins of the organization and outlines its work with the government and with such governmental bodies as the Freedmen's Bureau.

5550. Jarvis, Mary C. THE SERVICES OF THE PROTESTANT EPISCOPAL CHURCH IN THE UNITED STATES OF AMERICA.... New York, 1864.

A slim volume containing the authorized version of the church's wartime role.

5551. Johnson, Thomas S. "Letters From A Civil War Chaplain." Mary E. Johnson, editor. J PRES HIS, 46 [1968]: 219-235.

A recent graduate from the Princeton Theological Seminary, the author sent these letters to his family in Wisconsin. He worked with the United States Commission and later became a chaplain in a black regiment.

5552. Jones, Edgar D. LINCOLN AND THE PREACHERS. New York: Harper, 1948.

Details Lincoln's relations with various northern clergyman, such as Peter Cartwright, Owen Lovejoy, and Bishop Matthew Simpson. Author does not prove that clergymen had any more influence on Lincoln than any other group of people.

5553. Kedro, Milan. "The Civil War's Effect Upon an Urban Church: The St. Louis Presbytery Under Martial Law." MO HIS SOC BULL, 27 [1971]: 173-193.

An analysis of the troublesome consequences resulting from the divided opinions within the St. Louis Presbytery during the war.

5554. Klingberg, Frank W. "The Reverend John T. Clark, Episcopal Unionist in Virginia." HIS MAG PROT EPI CH, 23 [1954]: 266-276.

Episcopalians formed a stalwart wing of the minority of Southern Unionists. Clark refused to contribute to the Confederate military effort and frequently found himself in trouble as a result. The narrative continues into the early years of Reconstruction.

5555. Lalli, Anthony B. and Thomas H. O'Connor. "Roman Views on the American Civil War." CATH HIS R, 57 [1971/1972]: 21-41.

Drawing heavily on two clerical newspapers, L'OSSERVATORE and CIVILTA CATTOLICA, the authors seek to show that the Vatican's attitude toward the North was far less sympathetic--actually it was quite critical--than has usually been supposed.

5556. Leftwich, William M. MARTYRDOM IN MISSOURI: A HISTORY OF RELIGIOUS PROSCRIPTION, THE SEIZURE OF CHURCHES, AND THE PERSECUTION OF MINISTERS OF THE GOSPEL.... St. Louis, 1870.

The author was a prominent Methodist clergyman and his work reflects his intense feelings on the subject.

5557. Macmillan, Margaret B. THE METHODIST EPISCOPAL CHURCH IN MICHIGAN DURING THE CIVIL WAR. Lansing: Michigan Civil War Centennial Observance Commission, 1965.

A short but valuable study of Michigan Methodism.

5558. ———. "Michigan Methodism in the Civil War." METH HIS, 3 [1965]: 26-38.

A discussion of the reactions to the fighting of three Michigan Methodists.

5559. Marks, James J. THE PENINSULAR CAMPAIGN IN VIRGINIA. Philadelphia, 1864.

A chaplain with the 63rd Pennsylvania, the author describes incidents and scenes pertaining to the fighting around Richmond in 1862.

5560. McDonald, Cornelia. A DIARY WITH REMINISCENCES OF THE WAR AND REFUGEE LIFE IN THE SHENANDOAH VALLEY 1860-1865. Nashville, Tennessee: Cullom and Ghertner, 1934.

Interesting glimpses of civilian life in the lower Shenandoah and the Eastern Panhandle of West Virginia during the war. The area saw constant troop movement and fighting for almost four years.

5561. Miller, James R. "Two Civil War Notebooks of James Russell Miller." Alvin D. Smith, editor. J PRES HIS SOC, 37 [1959]: 65-90.

A first-hand account of Miller's experiences in campaigns in Virginia and Tennessee. Includes observations of battles, his comments on life in camp, and his efforts to meet the spiritual needs of the soldiers.

5562. Moorhead, James H. AMERICAN APOCALYPSE: YANKEE PROTESTANTS AND THE CIVIL WAR. New Haven: Yale University Press, 1978.

An excellent volume of church history. Probes the relationship and attitudes of the churches to slavery, nationalism, dissent, suffrage, and postwar problems.

5563. Moss, Lemuel. ANNALS OF THE UNITED STATES CHRISTIAN COMMISSION. Philadelphia, 1868.

A mammoth work describing the work of the commission, prepared by the home secretary of the organization.

5564. Myers, Richmond E. "The Moravian Church and the Civil War." MOR HIS SOC TRAN, 20 [1965]: 226-248.

Drawing on primary sources, the author has painted a picture of the wartime Moravian Church in Pennsylvania, Maryland, and Salem, North Carolina.

5565. O'Hagan, Joseph B. "The Diary of Joseph B. O'Hagan, S.J., Chaplain of the Excelsior Brigade." William L. Lucey, editor. CWH, 6 [1960]: 402-409.

A short diary of a Jesuit priest who served as a chaplain in the Excelsior Brigade in the first 30 months of the war. Judging from the 18 entries [which cover only February 1863], Chaplain O'Hagan had little good to say about army life.

5566. Paterwick, Stephen. "The Effect of the Civil War on Shaker Societies." HIS J W MASS, 2 [1973]: 6-26.

The Civil War marked the beginning of the period of decline for Shakerism. Kentucky settlements suffered from plunder, arson, and the strain of attempting to feed, clothe, and nurse soldiers from both sides.

5567. Peters, Robert N. "Preachers in Politics: A Conflict Touching the Methodist Church in Oregon." PAC NW Q, 63 [1972]: 142-149.

The unsuccessful 1864 senatorial candidacy of Thomas H. Pearne, a Methodist minister in Oregon and a strong Unionist, generated an angry debate within the church whether preachers should get into politics.

5568. Pringle, Cyrus G. THE RECORD OF A QUAKER CONSCIENCE: CYRUS PRINGLE'S DIARY. New York: Macmillan, 1918.

An excellent case study of a Quaker "purist" who under no conditions would perform military service. He was drafted and assigned to the 4th Vermont.

5569. Quimby, Rollin W. "The Chaplains' Predicament." CWH, 8 [1962]: 25-37.

Recounts the role of Protestant chaplains in the Union army.

5570. ———. "Congress and the Civil War Chaplaincy." CWH, 10 [1964]: 246-259.

By virtue of wartime legislation, the chaplain ceased to be the "orphan of the army."

5571. RENDER UNTO CAESAR: A COLLECTION OF SERMON CLASSICS ON ALL PHASES OF RELIGION IN WARTIME. New York: Lewis Publishing, 1943.

A good collection of wartime sermons, which reflect certain continuing themes.

5572. Smith, Edward P. INCIDENTS AMONG SHOT AND SHELL.... Philadelphia, 1868.

An anecdotal record "giving many tragic and touching incidents" of the work of the Christian Commission. Written by a clergyman.

5573. Smith, George W. and Charles Judah. LIFE IN THE NORTH DURING THE CIVIL WAR: A SOURCE HISTORY. Albuquerque: University of New Mexico Press, 1966.

Authors have assembled a documentary history which reflects northern attitudes and opinions on nine different topics during the war and Reconstruction. While the work is of uneven quality it can still be of considerable usefulness.

5574. Spalding, Martin J. "Martin John Spalding's 'Dissertation on the American Civil War.'" David Spalding, editor. CATH HIS R, 52 [1966]: 66-85.

The Roman Catholic Bishop of Louisville sent a report to Rome to inform the Holy See on the constitutional issues and causes of the war. Principally, the war is blamed on the abolitionists, who transformed the purpose of the war from preservation of the Union to the emancipation of the slaves.

5575. Strange, Douglas C. "From Treason to Antislavery Patriotism: Unitarian Conservatives and the Fugitive Slave Law." HARV LIB BULL, 25 [1977]: 466-488.

An examination of the dilemma faced by conservative Boston Unitarians because of their opposition to slavery and support of the Fugitive Slave Law.

5576. Stanton, Robert L. THE CHURCH AND THE REBELLION.... New York, 1864.

A big, free-wheeling volume with some worthwhile observations.

5577. Stoltzfus, Grant M. "Virginia Mennonites in the Civil War." MENNON LIFE, 18 [1963]: 27-29.

Some experiences of conscientious objectors in the Shenandoah Valley are discussed. Caught between opposing armies their life was not easy.

5578. Strong, George T. DIARY OF THE CIVIL WAR, 1860-1865. Allan Nevins, editor. New York: Macmillan, 1962.

An excellent portrait of New York during the war by an articulate citizen and keen observer. This is Volume Three from the author's four volume diary.

5579. Sweet, William W. THE METHODIST EPISCOPAL CHURCH AND THE CIVIL WAR. Cincinnati, 1912.

A general survey of the Methodist Church in wartime, written by a leading church historian.

5580. Trollope, Anthony. NORTH AMERICA. Donald Smalley and Bradford A. Booth, editors. New York: Knopf, 1951.

A modern edition of an earlier book of memoirs by the famous English novelist, who traveled in the United States during the war.

5581. Trumbull, Henry C. WAR MEMORIES OF AN ARMY CHAPLAIN. New York, 1898.

Although written long after the war, this is still an important work for an understanding of the Civil War chaplain's role. The author was chaplain for the 10th Connecticut.

5582. Trussell, John B.B. "William A. Pile: The Union Army's Fighting Parson." CWTI, 17 [3] [1978]: 36-41.

Ordained a Methodist minister, Pile chose to participate fully in the fighting and ultimately rose to the rank of major general.

5583. UNITED STATES CHRISTIAN COMMISSION, FOR THE ARMY AND NAVY. WORK AND INCIDENTS. 4 v. Philadelphia, 1863-1866.

A detailed record of the work accomplished by the commission and all of its branches.

5584. Vander Velde, Lewis G. THE PRESBYTERIAN CHURCHES AND THE FEDERAL UNION, 1861-1869. Cambridge: Harvard University Press, 1932.

An excellent study of the church in war and peace.

5585. Vandiver, Frank E. "The Civil War as an Institutionalizing Force." ESSAYS ON THE AMERICAN CIVIL WAR. Austin: University of Texas Press, 1968.

An examination of the Civil War as the agent for major institutional changes in American life.

5586. Wiley, Bell I. "A Time of Greatness." JSH, 22 [1956]: 3-35.

Wiley proclaims that the "plain Americans" were the real heroes of the war. He uses letters and diaries to describe these "home folks" as poor, uneducated, sentimental, patriotic, dependable, and generous. The record of these people was more impressive than that of the privileged elite.

D. INTELLECTUAL

5587. Adams, Michael C.C. OUR MASTERS THE REBELS: A SPECULATION ON UNION MILITARY FAILURE IN THE EAST, 1861-1865. Cambridge: Harvard University Press, 1978.

Author contends that Union generals in the East were in awe of their Confederate counterparts, doubtful that they could defeat them. They saw the southern white males as virtuous, martial, experts in riding and shooting, and accustomed to hierarchy and violence, while living by a strict code of honor. In linking culture and combat, Adams seeks to show that the Civil War belongs at the center of any study of the intellectual, social, and psychological currents of the mid-19th century.

5588. Emerson, Ralph W. THE JOURNALS AND MISCELLANEOUS NOTEBOOKS OF RALPH WALDO EMERSON. Ralph H. Orth, editor. Volume 15. Cambridge, Massachusetts: Belknap Press, 1982.

Contained here are journal entries which express Emerson's belief that the Civil War was necessary to help strengthen moral convictions, assert civilization over barbarism, and cleanse the nation of slavery. An insight into the moderate militancy of northern liberal intellectuals. Includes accounts of meetings with major federal officials like Seward, Welles, Chase, and Lincoln.

5589. Forgie, George B. PATRICIDE IN THE HOUSE DIVIDED: A PSYCHOLOGICAL INTERPRETATION OF LINCOLN AND HIS AGE. New York: Norton, 1979.

A subtle and imaginative work, wherein Forgie suggests that young adults of the early 19th century considered themselves "sons" of the Founding Fathers. In keeping with this heritage they believed they must meet the challenges of their own time and achieve great things themselves. Author argues that the Civil War marked the failure of this hope and irrevocably separated the future from the past.

5590. Frederickson, George M. THE INNER CIVIL WAR: NORTHERN INTELLECTUALS AND THE CRISIS OF THE UNION. New York: Harper and Row, 1965.

The first important work to deal with the bearing of the Civil War on intellectual thought. Covering a number of important northern literary figures, the author examines the war's impact on ideological, philosophical, and aesthetic interests as well as how it shaped political attitudes and the national self-image.

5591. Hawthorne, Nathaniel. "Chiefly About War Matters." In THE WRITINGS OF NATHANIEL HAWTHORNE. Boston, 1903.

Originally published in the July 1862 ATLANTIC MONTHLY, this ironic article conveys an unfashionably dubious attitude toward the conduct and political objectives of the war as it describes Hawthorne's tour of Washington, D.C. and northern Virginia.

5592. Holmes, Oliver W. PAGES FROM AN OLD VOLUME OF LIFE, 1857-1881. In WRITINGS OF OLIVER WENDELL HOLMES. Volume 8. Boston, 1891.

Written originally for the ATLANTIC MONTHLY, these several essays suggest Holmes' olympian view of slavery, secession, and the war, but also provide eloquent descriptions of the Antietam battlefield.

5593. Hyman, Harold M. UNION AND CONFIDENCE: THE 1860'S. New York: Crowell, 1976.

A scholarly study of the business, political, and social history of the 1860s. A provocative work which was commissioned by Dun and Bradstreet.

5594. Martin, John S. "Henry Adams on War: The Transformation of History into Metaphor." ARIZ Q, 24 [1968]: 350-360.

Adams' personal and philosophical interpretation of the Civil War helped to shape his "dynamic theory of history" and clarified his understanding of the role of faith and leadership in the historical process.

5595. Miers, Earl S. THE GREAT REBELLION: THE EMERGENCE OF THE AMERICAN CONSCIENCE. Cleveland: World, 1958.

An impressionistic work, wherein the "American mind" is studied at three critical periods: Christmas week, 1860; the time of the firing on Fort Sumter; and Palm Sunday, 1865.

5596. Sharrow, Walter O. "Northern Catholic Intellectuals and the Coming of the Civil War." NY HIS SOC Q, 58 [1974]: 34-56.

Northern Catholic intellectuals viewed the war as an act of divine intervention, a punishment for the materialistic and weakening effects of Protestantism.

5597. Twombly, Robert C. "Not the Bond, Just the Coupon." R A HIS, 3 [1975]: 13-18.

A review article in which the Civil War becomes a turning point, directing American intellectual thought away from religious and toward secular interests.

5598. Williams, Lorraine A. "Northern Intellectual Attitudes Toward Lincoln: 1860-1865." JISHS, 57 [1964]: 270-283.

Northern intellectuals did not have a very high opinion of Lincoln when he was elected president. By the time of his death, however, they came to view him favorably, as a man of good judgment and profound faith in the democratic principle.

5599. ———. "Northern Intllectual Reaction to Military Rule During the Civil War." HISTORIAN, 27 [1965]: 334-349.

Author examines the reaction of northern intellectuals to the suspension of habeas corpus and the authorization of military rule during the war. Although such actions violated the basic freedoms, intellectuals supported the government in these matters, recognizing that the war demanded extreme measures.

ADDENDA

Through inadvertence, a few items were omitted from the text of the bibliography. Rather than not citing them, I have decided to group them together in one place and list them here. My apologies to all authors, living and dead, included herein.

5600. Acheson, Sam and Julia Ann O'Connell. GEORGE WASHINGTON DIAMOND'S ACCOUNT OF THE GREAT HANGING AT GAINESVILLE, 1862. Austin: Texas State Historical Association, 1963.

In 1861 the counties of north Texas voted overwhelmingly against secession. As the result of a "Peace Party Plot" about a year later, 42 Unionists were hung for treason and insurrection.

5601. Davis, William C., editor. THE IMAGE OF WAR: 1861-1865. Bell I. Wiley, consulting editor. 6 v. Garden City, New York: Doubleday, 1981-1984.

Basically a "coffee table" photographic history of the war. Excellent articles by noted historians give a continuous flow to the story. Pictures are by a multitude of photographers, including the best known--Brady, O'Sullivan, Gardner--and some not so well known.

5602. Davison, Kenneth E. CLEVELAND DURING THE CIVIL WAR. Columbus: Ohio State University Press, 1962.

Another in the series of booklets sponsored by the Ohio Civil War Centennial Commission, this excellent monograph describes all facets of the war's impact on Cleveland.

5603. Drum, Richard C., compiler. ORGANIZATION OF THE ARMY OF THE CUMBERLAND. Washington, D.C.: 1886.

Author was adjutant general of the army. The pamphlet provides the table of organization and a list of casualties.

5604. Hermance, W.L. "The Cavalry at Chancellorsville, May 1863." JUSCA, 4 [13] [1891]: 107-113.

Primarily, the story of the "Old Sixth" [6th New York Cavalry] which led the advance of the Twelfth Corps at Chancellorsville, and the 8th and 17th Pennsylvania cavalry. These three units were commended for distinguished service.

5605. Klement, Frank L. "Wisconsin and the Re-election of Lincoln in 1864: A Chapter of Civil War History." HISTORICAL MESSENGER [of the Milwaukee County Historical Society, now MILWAUKEE HISTORY], 22 [1966]: 20-42.

Describes and analyzes in details Lincoln's reelection in a state firmly controlled by the Republican party.

5606. Rittenhouse, Jack D., compiler. NEW MEXICO CIVIL WAR BIBLIOGRAPHY. Houston: Stagecoach Press, 1961.

A brief but good, annotated bibliography.

5607. Tucker, Louis L. CINCINNATI DURING THE CIVIL WAR. Columbus: Ohio State University Press, 1962.

A moving glimpse of wartime Cincinnati, perched on the edge of slavery, with a large black population, and menaced by the Confederates in September 1862 and Morgan in July 1863.

5608. Witham, George F. SHILOH, SHELLS, AND ARTILLERY UNITS. Memphis, Tennessee: Riverside, 1980.

A detailed examination of the organization, armaments, and battle performance of northern artillery units in the armies of the Tennessee, Ohio, and Mississippi at Shiloh. The work is well-illustrated with types of artillery ammunition.

AUTHOR INDEX

SUBJECT INDEX

CONTRIBUTORS

Compiler:

EUGENE C. MURDOCK. A graduate of Wooster College, he obtained his graduate degrees from Columbia University. He has been on the history faculty at Marietta College since 1956, serving as department chairman from 1972 until his retirement in May 1986. He is the author of a number of books and articles on the Civil War and baseball.

Contributors:

ERIC CARDINAL. 1860-1861. A graduate of Hiram College, he secured his Ph.D. in history from Kent State University. He is currently the Director of the Lake County [Ohio] Historical Society. He has published numerous articles in professional journals on the Civil War, Native American, and 19th century American history.

LINDA DeLOWRY-FRYMAN. WOMEN. She received her Master of Library Science and Ph.D. degrees from the University of Pittsburgh. At present she is English department bibliographer for the Hillman Library at the University of Pittsburgh. She has authored several reviews and articles and has a special interest in women's history.

JAMES W. GEARY. MANPOWER MOBILIZATION. A graduate of SUNY-Buffalo, he earned a Master of Library Science and history Ph.D. from Kent State University. He is professor of Library Administration at Kent State. His special interests are librarianship and the Civil War draft. He has published many articles in those areas.

LINDA L. GEARY. REFERENCE WORKS. A graduate of Benedictine College, she has her Master of Library Science and history M.A. from Kent State University. She is a reference librarian in the Medical Library at Akron City Hospital in Akron, Ohio. She has written several articles in the bibliographic field and is presently writing a biography of Betsey Mix Cowles, a 19th century women's rights activist.

JOHN KESLER. FOREIGN AFFAIRS AND OPINION. He has an M.A. in history from Bowling Green State University and a Ph.D. from Kent State University. A professor at Lakeland Community College, Mentor, Ohio, he specializes in American diplomacy. He has published in this field and is currently revising his dissertation on the "Good Neighbor Policy."

HARRY A. LUPOLD. GENERAL WORKS; PRISONS AND PRISONERS. A graduate of Marietta College, he has been a professor of history at Lakeland Community College since 1968. He has written two books, edited two others, and published over 80 articles, essays, and reviews. In addition to the Civil War, his special interests are Native American and Ohio history. He served as president of the Ohio Academy of History in 1985-1986.

FRASER G. MacHAFFIE. NAVY. He is member of the faculty at Marietta College, where he teaches finance and accounting. A graduate of the University of Glasgow, the University of Edinburgh, Princeton Seminary, and Cleveland State, he is a certified public accountant. Formerly associated with the Peninsular and Oriental Steam Navigation Company in Britain, his research and publishing activities concentrate on British coastal passenger shipping and blockade running in the Civil War.

CHARLES T. PRIDGEON. LITERATURE. A graduate of the College of William and Mary, he obtained his M.A. and Ph.D. degrees from Duke University. He has been teaching in the English Department at Marietta College since 1968. His fields of special interest include the relationship between literature and American society and "film and literature."